T0213425

Lecture Notes in Computer Science 10597

Commenced Publication in 1973
Founding and Former Series Editors:
Gerhard Goos, Juris Hartmanis, and Jan van Leeuwen

More information about this series at http://www.springer.com/series/7412

Editors
B. Uma Shankar (iD)
Indian Statistical Institute
Kolkata
India

Kuntal Ghosh (iD)
Indian Statistical Institute
Kolkata
India

Deba Prasad Mandal
Indian Statistical Institute
Kolkata
India

Shubhra Sankar Ray
Indian Statistical Institute
Kolkata
India

David Zhang (iD)
The Hong Kong Polytechnic University
Hong Kong
China

Sankar K. Pal
Indian Statistical Institute
Kolkata
India

ISSN 0302-9743   ISSN 1611-3349   (electronic)
Lecture Notes in Computer Science
ISBN 978-3-319-69899-1   ISBN 978-3-319-69900-4   (eBook)
https://doi.org/10.1007/978-3-319-69900-4

Library of Congress Control Number: 2017957548

LNCS Sublibrary: SL6 – Image Processing, Computer Vision, Pattern Recognition, and Graphics

Printed on acid-free paper

This Springer imprint is published by Springer Nature
The registered company is Springer International Publishing AG
The registered company address is: Gewerbestrasse 11, 6330 Cham, Switzerland

B. Uma Shankar · Kuntal Ghosh
Deba Prasad Mandal · Shubhra Sankar Ray
David Zhang · Sankar K. Pal (Eds.)

Pattern Recognition and Machine Intelligence

7th International Conference, PReMI 2017
Kolkata, India, December 5–8, 2017
Proceedings

 Springer

Preface

It is a great pleasure to introduce you all to the proceedings of the 7th International Conference on Pattern Recognition and Machine Intelligence (PReMI 2017), held at the Indian Statistical Institute (ISI), Kolkata, India, during December 5–8, 2017. The objective of the conference is to introduce to the community the most recent advancements in research in the domain of pattern recognition and machine intelligence. Our goal is to encourage academic and industrial collaboration in all related fields in machine learning involving scientists, engineers, professionals, researchers, and students from India and abroad. The conference is held biennially to make it an ideal platform for researcher all over the world to come and share their views and experiences. This was the seventh edition in this series, being held in the year marking the 125th birthday of late Prof. Prasanta Chandra Mahalanobis.

Professor Mahalanobis was the founder of the Indian Statistical Institute and the father of modern statistics in India. As researchers in pattern recognition and machine learning we are immensely indebted to him. He was instrumental in inspiring the design of the first analog computer in India in 1953. He brought to ISI the first digital computer to India in the year 1955. As a mark of our respect to this monumental personality, we organized a Special Session on "Celebration of 125th Birth Anniversary of Professor P.C. Mahalanobis" at PReMI 2017.

The conference comprised several keynote and invited lecturers delivered by eminent and distinguished researchers from around the world. Both the invited and the technical sessions featured interesting lectures in classic and contemporary aspects of machina intelligence. The topics range from deep learning and Internet of Things (IoT) to computer vision and big data analytics. There were two exclusive sessions on "Deep Learning" and "Spatial Data Science and Engineering" Like previous editions, PReMI 2017 had a very good response in terms of paper submissions. Altogether there were 293 submissions from about 15 countries spanning three continents. Each paper was critically reviewed by experts in the field, after which 85 papers (29% acceptance rate) were accepted for inclusion in these proceedings. The accepted papers are divided into ten groups, although there could be some overlap. Articles written by the keynote and invited speakers are also included in the proceedings (mostly abstracts).

We wish to express our appreciation to the Program Committee and Technical Review Committee members, who worked hard to ensure the quality of the contributions of this volume. We are thankful to the editors of the journals *Fundamenta Informaticae* and *Applied Soft Computing* for kindly agreeing to publish the extended versions of some of the selected papers in their esteemed journals. We also take this opportunity to thank Professors Vineet Bafna, Andrzej Skowron, Farzin Deravi, Upinder S. Bhalla, Uday B. Desai, Soumen Chakraborti, Ambarish Ghosh, Partha Pratim Majumder, Probal Chaudhuri, Subhasis Chaudhuri, David Zhang, and Shalabh Bhatnagar for accepting our invitation to deliver keynote, invited, and special lectures during the conference. We gratefully acknowledge Alfred Hofmann of Springer for his co-operation in the publication of the PReMI 2017 proceedings in the LNCS series, as done for the previous editions. We would like to thank all the organizations who either endorsed or sponsored this conference technically or financially. We are grateful to EasyChair for providing us with a wonderful platform for conducting the entire process of paper review. Last but not the least, we take this opportunity to thank all the contributors for their enthusiastic response, without which no conference can ever be successful.

While preparing the proceedings we mourned the sad demise of Professor Lotfi A. Zadeh, the founder of fuzzy mathematics, an imperative part of contemporary machine learning. He was on the advisory board of PReMI ever since its inception in 2005, including the present edition. Our institute honored him with a doctor honoris causa in 2006 during its annual convocation. We express our deep condolences to his family and all his friends and colleagues. It is a great loss to the pattern recognition and soft computing/computational intelligence community.

Our best wishes to all the participants of PReMI 2017 conference. May this volume, which contains the papers presented at PReMI 2017 prove to be a valuable source of reference for ongoing and future research work.

December 2017

B. Uma Shankar
Kuntal Ghosh
Deba Prasad Mandal
Shubhra Sankar Ray
David Zhang
Sankar K. Pal

Message from the General Chair

PReMI, the biennial International Conference on Pattern Recognition and Machine Intelligence, returned to Kolkata, the City of Joy, after its sixth edition in Warsaw, Poland, in June/July 2015! I am delighted that the seventh edition (PReMI 2017) was held in the year that marks the 125th birthday of late Prof. Prasanta Chandra Mahalanobis, the founder of our Indian Statistical Institute.

Like earlier versions, PReMI 2017 had a nice mixture of keynote and invited speeches, and quality research papers using both classic and modern computing paradigms, covering different facets of pattern recognition and machine intelligence with real-life applications. Apart from classic topics, special emphasis was given to contemporary research areas such as big data analytics, deep learning, Internet of Things, and computer vision through both regular and special sessions. Some post-conference special issues will be published as done in the past. All these make PReMI 2017 an ideal state-of-the-art platform for researchers and practitioners to exchange ideas and enrich their knowledge.

I thank all the participants, speakers, reviewers, and members of various committees for making this event a grand success. My thanks are also due to the sponsors for their support, and Springer for publishing the PReMI proceedings, since its first edition in 2005, in the prestigious LNCS series.

I trust, the participants had an academically fruitful and enjoyable stay in Kolkata.

December 2017   Sankar K. Pal

Organization

PReMI 2017 was organized by the Machine Intelligence Unit, Indian Statistical Institute (ISI) in Kolkata during December 5–8, 2017.

Conference Committee

Patron

Sanghamitra Bandyopadhyay	ISI, Kolkata, India

General Chair

Sankar K. Pal	ISI, Kolkata, India

Program Chairs

David Zhang	PolyU, Hong Kong, SAR China
Kuntal Ghosh	ISI, Kolkata, India
B. Uma Shankar	ISI, Kolkata, India

Organizing Chairs

Deba Prasad Mandal	ISI, Kolkata, India
Shubhra Sankar Ray	ISI, Kolkata, India

Special Session Chairs

Ashish Ghosh	ISI, Kolkata, India
Farid Melgani	University of Trento, Italy
Sambhunath Biswas	TIU, Kolkata, India
Alfredo Petrosino	University of Naples, Italy
Soumya K. Ghosh	IIT Kharagpur, India

Special Issue Chairs

Sushmita Mitra	ISI, Kolkata, India
P.N. Suganthan	NTU, Singapore

Industry Liaisons

Malay K. Kundu	ISI, Kolkata, India
C.A. Murthy	ISI, Kolkata, India
Santanu Chaudhury	CEERI, Pilani, India

International Liaisons

Sergei O. Kuznetsov   HSE, Moscow, Russia
Marzena Kryszkiewicz   WUT, Poland
Simon C.K. Shiu   PolyU, Hong Kong, SAR China

Advisory Committee

Lofti A. Zadeh, USA
C.R. Rao, USA
Anil K. Jain, USA
Josef Kittler, UK
Laveen N. Kanal, USA
B.L. Deekshatulu, India
Dwijesh Dutta Majumder, India
Andrzej Skowron, Poland
Rama Chellappa, USA
Witold Pedrycz, Canada
David W. Aha, USA
Gabriella Sanniti di Baja, Italy
B. Yegnanarayana, India
Shun-ichi Amari, Japan
Jayaram Udupa, USA
Jiming Liu, Hong Kong, SAR China
Ronald Yager, USA
Ning Zhong, Japan
Tharram Dillon, Australia
Henryk Rybinski, Poland

Program Committee

Jayadeva   Indian Institute of Technology Delhi, India
Tinku Acharya   Videonetics Technology Pvt. Ltd., India
Md. Atiqur Rahman Ahad   University of Dhaka, Bangladesh
Mohua Banerjee   Indian Institute of Technology Kanpur, India
Jayanta Basak   NetApp, India
Smarajit Bose   Indian Statistical Institute, India
Roberto M. Cesar   USP, Brazil
Goutam Chakraborty   Iwate Prefectural University, Japan
Bhabatosh Chanda   Indian Statistical Institute, India
Subhasis Chaudhuri   Indian Institute of Technology Bombay, India
Sung-Bae Cho   Yonsei University, South Korea
Partha Pratim Das   Indian Institute of Technology Kharagpur, India
Sukhendu Das   Indian Institute of Technology Madras, India
Dipankar Dasgupta   The University of Memphis, USA
Rajat K. De   Indian Statistical Institute, India

Farzin Deravi   University of Kent, UK
Shaikh A. Fattah   BUET, Bangladesh
Paolo Gamba   University of Pavia, Italy
Joydeep Ghosh   University of Texas, USA
Mark Girolami   University of Warwick, UK
Phalguni Gupta   NITTTR Kolkata, India
Larry Hall   University of South Florida, USA
Francisco Herrera   University of Granada, Spain
Qinghua Hu   Tianjin University, China
C.V. Jawahar   IIIT Hyderabad, India
John Kerekes   Rochester Institute of Technology, USA
Ravi Kothari   IBM Research, India
Pawan Lingras   Saint Mary's University, USA
Pradipta Maji   Indian Statistical Institute, India
Francesco Masulli   University of Genoa, Italy
Pabitra Mitra   Indian Institute of Technology Kharagpur, India
Jayanta Mukherjee   Indian Institute of Technology Kharagpur, India
M.N. Murty   Indian Institute of Science, India
Y. Narahari   Indian Institute of Science, India
B.L. Narayan   Yahoo! Labs, USA
Nasser Nasrabadi   West Virginia University, USA
Nikhil Rajan Pal   Indian Statistical Institute, India
Angel P. Del Pobil   Universitat Jaume I, Spain
Amit K. Roy-Chowdhury   University of California, USA
Punam Saha   University of Iowa, USA
P.S. Sastry   Indian Institute of Science, India
Faisal Shafait   National University of Sciences and Technology,
                              Pakistan
Sitabhra Sinha   The Institute of Mathematical Sciences, India
Dominik Slezak   University of Warsaw, Poland
Brijesh Verma   Central Queensland University, Australia
Dianhui Wang   La Trobe University, Australia

Technical Review Committee

Anand, Ashish   Bhandari, Dinabandhu   Chakraborty, Debasrita
Bagchi, Aditya   Bhattacharya, Bhargab   Chatterjee, Garga
Banerjee, Abhirup   Bhattacharya, Ujjwal   Chattopadhyay,
Banerjee, Minakshi   Bhattacharyya, Balaram   Tanushyam
Banerjee, Romi   Bhattacharyya, Dhruba K.   Chellu, Chandra Sekhar
Banerjee, Subhashis   Bhattacharyya, Malay   Chen, Bo
Banerjee, Swati   Bishnu, Partha Sarathi   Chowdhury, Ananda S.
Banka, Haider   Chaki, Nabendu   Chowdhury, Manish
Basu, Tanmay   Chakrabarty, Abhisek   Das, Apurba
Bhadra, Tapas   Chakraborty, Debarati   Das, Chandra

Das, Koel
Das, Monidipa
Das, Saurabh
Das, Sudeb
Dasgupta, Arindam
Datta, Aloke
Dehuri, Satchidananda
Dey, Bhaskar
Dutta, Paramartha
Ekbal, Asif
Garain, Utpal
Halder, Anindya
Kundu, Suman
Kuppili,
  Venkatanareshbabu
Law, Anwesha
Maitra, Sanjit
Majumdar, Debapriyo
Mandal, Ankita
Mazumdar, Debasis
Meher, Saroj K.
Mishra, Deepak
Misra, Sudip
Mitra, Mandar

Mitra, Suman
Mitra, Suman Kumar
Mittal, Namita
Mohanta, Partha Pratim
Mondal, Ajoy
Mukherjee, Dipti Prasad
Mukhopadhyay, Subhasis
Murthy, K. Ramachandra
Naik, Sarif
Nanda, Pradipta Kumar
Naresh, K.M.
Nayak, Losiana
Pal, Jayanta Kumar
Pal, Monalisa
Pal, Rajarshi
Pal, Rajat Kumar
Pal, Umapada
Parui, Swapan Kumar
Patil, Hemant
Patra, Swarnajyoti
Paul, Goutam
Paul, Sushmita
Phadikar, Amit
Prasad, M.V.N.K.

Prasanna, S.R.M.
Ray, Sumanta
Reddy, Damodar
Roy, Monideepa
Roy, Rahul
Roy, Shaswati
Sa, Pankaj K.
Saha, Sanjoy Kumar
Sanyal, Debarshi Kumar
Sen, Debashis
Senapati, Apurbalal
Shah, Ekta
Sharma, Anmol
Shrein, John M.
Sil, Jaya
Sinha, Debajyoti
Subrahmanyam, Gorthi
Subudhi, Badri Narayan
Trzcinski, Tomasz
Veerakumar, T.
Verma, Manisha
Zaveri, Mukesh
Zhang, Hao

Sponsoring Organizations

Endorsed by

International Association for Pattern Recognition (IAPR)

Technical Co-sponsor

IEEE Kolkata Section

Other Sponsors

Center for Soft Computing Research: A National Facility, ISI, Kolkata
Web Intelligence Consortium (WIC)
International Rough Set Society (IRSS)
INAE Kolkata Chapter
World Federation on Soft Computing (WFSC)
Springer International Publishing

Abstracts of Invited Talks

Interactive Granular Computing
in Data Science

Andrzej Skowron[1, 2]

[1] Faculty of Mathematics, Computer Science and Mechanics,
University of Warsaw, Poland
skowron@mimuw.edu.pl
[2] Systems Research Institute, Polish Academy of Sciences

We discuss Interactive Granular Computing (IGrC) as the basis of a Data Science computing model. IGrC binds together and brings a synchronous cooperation among the following four basic concepts of Artificial Intelligence: language, reasoning, perception, and action. This, together with information granulation, helps agents to deal with many complex tasks of perceiving or transforming compound abstract and physical objects (e.g., in the context of complex spatio-temporal space). One should consider that in Data Science agents collecting data have control over the data acquisition, i.e., they are deciding say which data, using which sources, at what time, and why should be collected.

Basic objects in IGrC are complex granules (c-granules or granules, for short). They are grounded in the physical reality and are, in particular, responsible for generation of the networks of information systems (data tables) through interactions with the configurations of physical objects. Development of a particular network of information systems is guided by the need to learn the relevant computational building blocks that are necessary for perception, using the formulation by Leslie Valiant. Among these blocks, often learned hierarchically, one can distinguish patterns, clusters or classifiers. The computational building blocks are used by agents, e.g., for approximation of conditions responsible for initiating actions or plans. Agents performing computations based on interaction with the physical environment learn new c-granules, in particular, in the form of interaction rules, representing knowledge not known a priori by agents. These new c-granules are used not only for construction of compound abstract objects but also of compound physical objects, e.g., sensors composed out of more primitive sensors. Learning of interaction rules also supports the control of agents, in particular the self-organized distributed control. Numerous tasks of agents may be classified as control tasks performed by agents aiming at achieving the high quality computational trajectories of configurations of c-granules relative to the considered quality measures over the trajectories.

Reasoning supporting agents in searching for solutions of their tasks is based on adaptive judgment, an important component of IGrC. Methods based on adaptive judgment allow agents to construct from given configurations of their c-granules new ones. These new configurations of c-granules should be constructed taking into account the needs of agents realized through interactions with the environment. Here, new challenges are related to developing strategies for predicting and controlling behaviors of agents. We propose to investigate these challenges using the IGrC framework with adaptive judgment used for controlling of computations performed on c-granules. For example, adaptive judgment is used in adaptive learning of rough set based approximations of complex vague concepts evolving with time. It is also used in the risk management of granular computations, carried out by agents, toward achieving the agent needs.

Identifying the Favored Allele
in a Selective Sweep

Vineet Bafna

Computer Science and Engineering University of California,
San Diego, USA
vbafna@eng.ucsd.edu

Abstract. Selection is a dominant force in evolution. Mutations arising at random might favor individuals in a specific environmental niche, and populations adapt by rapidly increasing the frequency of individuals carrying the favored mutations. The selection process results in distinct patterns (a signature) of allele frequencies and haplotype structures that can be exploited to identify the genes responding to selection pressure. A study of selection signals in humans has led to molecular insight into the evolution of many natural traits such as skin and eye color, as also adaptation to extreme environments.

Computational methods that scan population genomics data to identify signatures of selective sweep have been actively developed, but mostly do not identify the specific mutation favored by the selective sweep. In this talk, we describe an approach that uses population genetics and machine learning techniques to pin-point the favored mutation, even when the signature of selection extends to 5Mbp. Our method, iSAFE, was tested extensively on simulated data and 22 known sweeps in human populations using the 1000 genome project data with some evidence for the favored mutation. iSAFE ranked the candidate mutation among the top 15 (out of $\sim$ 21,000 candidates) in 14 of the 22 loci, and identified previously unreported mutations as favored the 5 regions.

Sequence Recognition as a Subcellular Computational Primitive in Neural Function

Upinder S. Bhalla

National Centre for Biological Sciences (NCBS), Bangalore, India
bhalla@ncbs.res.in

Abstract. Many sensory, motor, and cognitive processes involve sequences with complex hierarchical structures. In computational neuroscience these have typically been modeled as arising from network computation. We have analyzed how such computations may arise instead from subcellular reaction-diffusion processes on small (~ 30 micron) segments of neuronal dendrites. This formulation vastly increases the potential computational capacity of neuronal networks. We consider some possible mappings of subcellular sequence computation to the structure of deep learning networks. This is interesting because it provides for very compact and efficient biological implementations of LSTM-like networks. We speculate that there may be a parallel between some of the computational principles of engineered networks and the hippocampal-entorhinal cortex loop.

An Incremental Fast Policy Search
Using a Single Sample Path

Ajin George Joseph and Shalabh Bhatnagar

Indian Institute of Science, Bangalore, India
{ajin,shalabh}@iisc.ac.in

Abstract. In this paper, we consider the control problem in a reinforcement learning setting with large state and action spaces. The control problem most commonly addressed in the contemporary literature is to find an optimal policy which optimizes the long run γ -discounted transition costs, where $\gamma \in [0, 1)$. They also assume access to a generative model/simulator of the underlying MDP with the hidden premise that realization of the system dynamics of the MDP for arbitrary policies in the form of sample paths can be obtained with ease from the model. In this paper, we consider a cost function which is the expectation of a approximate value function w.r.t. the steady state distribution of the Markov chain induced by the policy, without having access to the generative model. We assume that a single sample path generated using a priori chosen behaviour policy is made available. In this information restricted setting, we solve the generalized control problem using the incremental cross entropy method. The proposed algorithm is shown to converge to the solution which is globally optimal relative to the behaviour policy.

Biometric Counter-Spoofing for Mobile Devices Using Gaze Information

Asad Ali⬤, Nawal Alsufyani⬤, Sanaul Hoque⬤,
and Farzin Deravi⬤

School of Engineering and Digital Arts,
University of Kent, Canterbury, Kent CT2 7NT, UK
F.Deravi@kent.ac.uk

Abstract. With the rise in the use of biometric authentication on mobile devices, it is important to address the security vulnerability of spoofing attacks where an attacker using an artefact representing the biometric features of a genuine user attempts to subvert the system. In this paper, techniques for presentation attack detection are presented using gaze information with a focus on their applicability for use on mobile devices. Novel features that rely on directing the gaze of the user and establishing its behaviour are explored for detecting spoofing attempts. The attack scenarios considered in this work include the use of projected photos, 2D and 3D masks. The proposed features and the systems based on them were extensively evaluated using data captured from volunteers performing genuine and spoofing attempts. The results of the evaluations indicate that gaze-based features have the potential for discriminating between genuine attempts and imposter attacks on mobile devices.

Contents

Signal and Image Processing

Computer Vision and Video Processing

Soft and Natural Computing

Speech and Natural Language Processing

Bioinformatics and Computational Biology

Spatial Data Science and Engineering

Applications of Pattern Recognition and Machine Intelligence

Invited Talks

An Incremental Fast Policy Search
Using a Single Sample Path

Ajin George Joseph and Shalabh Bhatnagar[(⊠)]

Indian Institute of Science, Bangalore, India
{ajin,shalabh}@iisc.ac.in

Abstract. In this paper, we consider the control problem in a reinforce-ment learning setting with large state and action spaces. The control problem most commonly addressed in the contemporary literature is to find an optimal policy which optimizes the long run γ-discounted tran-sition costs, where $\gamma \in [0, 1)$. They also assume access to a generative model/simulator of the underlying MDP with the hidden premise that realization of the system dynamics of the MDP for arbitrary policies in the form of sample paths can be obtained with ease from the model. In this paper, we consider a cost function which is the expectation of a approximate value function w.r.t. the steady state distribution of the Markov chain induced by the policy, without having access to the genera-tive model. We assume that a single sample path generated using a priori chosen behaviour policy is made available. In this information restricted setting, we solve the generalized control problem using the incremental cross entropy method. The proposed algorithm is shown to converge to the solution which is globally optimal relative to the behaviour policy.

1 Introduction

In this paper, we consider a reinforcement learning setting with the underlying Markov decision process (MDP) defined by the 4-tuple $(\mathbb{S}, \mathbb{A}, \mathrm{R}, \mathrm{P})$, where the finite sets $\mathbb{S}$ and $\mathbb{A}$ are referred to as the *state space* and *action space* respectively. Also, $\mathrm{R} : \mathbb{S} \times \mathbb{A} \times \mathbb{S} \to \mathbb{R}$ is the *reward function* which defines the state transition costs and $\mathrm{P} : \mathbb{S} \times \mathbb{A} \times \mathbb{A} \to [0, 1]$ is the *transition probability function*. A station-ary randomized policy (SRP) π is a probability mass function over the actions conditioned on the state space, *i.e.*, for $s \in \mathbb{S}$, we have $\pi(\cdot|s) \in [0, 1]^{|\mathbb{A}|}$ and $\sum_{a \in \mathbb{A}} \pi(a|s) = 1$. A policy determines the action to be taken at each discrete time step of an arbitrary realization of the MDP. In this paper, we employ a parametrized class of SRPs $\{\pi_w | w \in \mathbb{W} \subset \mathbb{R}^{k_2}\}$. We assume that $\mathbb{W}$ is compact.

By complying to a policy π_w, the behaviour of the MDP reduces to a Markov chain defined by the transition probabilities $\mathrm{P}_w(s, s') = \sum_{a \in \mathbb{A}} \pi_w(a|s)\mathrm{P}(s, a, s')$. The performance of a policy is usually quantified by a value function which is defined as the long-run γ-discounted transition costs ($\gamma \in [0, 1)$) incurred by the MDP while following the policy. The value function is formally defined as follows: $V^w(s) = \mathbb{E}_w \left[\sum_{t \in \mathbb{N}} \gamma^t \mathrm{R}(\mathbf{s}_t, \mathbf{a}_t, \mathbf{s}_{t+1}) | \mathbf{s}_0 = s \right], s \in \mathbb{S}$, where $\mathbb{E}_w[\cdot]$ is the expectation w.r.t. the probability distribution of the Markov chain induced by

© Springer International Publishing AG 2017
B.U. Shankar et al. (Eds.): PReMI 2017, LNCS 10597, pp. 3–10, 2017.
https://doi.org/10.1007/978-3-319-69900-4_1

the policy π_w. And the primary goal in an RL setting is to find the optimal policy which solves $\arg\max_{w\in\mathbb{W}} V^w$ without any knowledge of the model parameters P and R. However, observations in the form of sample paths which are realizations of the MDP under any arbitrary policy are made available.

Classical approaches have complexities which scale polynomial in the cardinality of the state space and hence are intractable. This is commonly referred to as the curse of dimensionality. Hence, one has to resort to approximation techniques in order to achieve tractability. In this paper, for value function estimation, we consider the linear function approximation. Here, for a given policy π_w, we approximate its value function V^w by projecting it on to the subspace $\{\Phi x | x \in \mathbb{R}^{k_1}\}$, where $\Phi = (\phi_1, \phi_2, \ldots, \phi_{k_1})^\top$, $k_1 \ll |\mathbb{S}|$ and $\phi_i \in \mathbb{R}^{|\mathbb{S}|}$, $1 \le i \le k_1$ called the *prediction features* are chosen a priori. In order for the projection to be well-defined, we require the following assumption:

(A1): *For each $w \in \mathbb{W}$, the Markov chain induced by the policy π_w is ergodic.*

Under this assumption, one can define the weighted norm $\|\cdot\|_\nu$ as follows: For $V \in \mathbb{R}^{|\mathbb{S}|}$, $\|V\|_\nu = (\sum_{s\in\mathbb{S}} V^2(s)\nu(s))^{\frac{1}{2}}$, where ν is the limiting distribution (steady state distribution) of the given sample path. If the sample path is generated using a policy π_{w_b}, $w_b \in \mathbb{W}$ (referred to as the *behaviour policy*), then the limiting distribution is the stationary distribution ν_{w_b} of the Markov chain induced by the behaviour policy π_{w_b}. Therefore, the linear function approximation of the value function V^w is defined as follows:

$$h_{w|w_b} \triangleq \arg\min_{x\in\mathbb{R}^{k_1}} \|\Phi x - V^w\|_{\nu_{w_b}} \tag{1}$$

In this paper, we solve the following problem: $w^* = \arg\max_{w\in\mathbb{W}} \mathbb{E}_{\nu_w}\left[h_{w|w}\right]$, $\quad$ (2)

where we assume that an infinitely long sample path $\{s_0, a_0, r_0, s_1, a_1, r_1, s_2, \ldots\}$ generated by the behaviour policy π_{w_b} ($w_b \in \mathbb{W} \subseteq \mathbb{R}^{k_2}$) is available.

(A2): *The behaviour policy π_{w_b}, where $w_b \in \mathbb{W}$, satisfies the following condition: $\pi_{w_b}(a|s) > 0$, $\forall s \in \mathbb{S}, \forall a \in \mathbb{A}$.*

2   Proposed Algorithm

Our proposed approach has two components:

1. A stochastic approximation (SA) version of the cross entropy (CE) method to solve the control problem (2). The SA version of the CE method is a zero-order, incremental, adaptive and stable global optimization method.
2. A variation of the off-policy LSTD (λ) to compute the objective function values (i.e., $\mathbb{E}_{\nu_w}\left[h_{w|w}\right]$).

We describe the above two components in detail here.

2.1 Stochastic Approximation Version of the Cross Entropy Method

Cross entropy method [4,9] solves global optimization problems where the objective function does not possess good structural properties, *i.e.*, those of the kind: Find $x^* = \arg\max_{x \in \mathbb{X} \subset \mathbb{R}^d} J(x)$, where $J : \mathbb{X} \to \mathbb{R}$ is a bounded Borel measurable function ($J_l < J(x) < J_u$, $\forall x$). CE is a zero-order method which implies that the algorithm does not require the gradient or higher-order derivatives of the objective function in order to seek the optimal solution. CE method has found successful application in diverse domains which include continuous multiextremal optimization [7], reinforcement learning [5,6] and several NP-hard problems [7,8].

CE method generates a sequence of model parameters $\{\theta_t\}_{t \in \mathbb{N}}$, $\theta_t \in \Theta$ (assumed to be compact) and a sequence of thresholds $\{\gamma_t \in \mathbb{R}\}_{t \in \mathbb{N}}$, $J_l \le \gamma_t \le J_u$ and the algorithm attempts to direct the sequence $\{\theta_t\}$ towards the degenerate distribution concentrated at the global optimum x^* and γ_t towards $J(x^*)$. The threshold γ_{t+1} is usually taken as the $(1 - \rho)$-quantile of J w.r.t the PDF f_{θ_t}. (For $\theta \in \Theta$, we denote by $\gamma_\rho(J, \theta)$ the $(1 - \rho)$-quantile of J w.r.t the PDF f_θ). Henceforth, $\gamma_{t+1} = \gamma_\rho(J, \theta_t)$. And the model parameter θ_{t+1} is generated by projecting (w.r.t. the Kullback-Leibler (KL) divergence) on to the family of distributions $\mathcal{F} \triangleq \{f_\theta | \theta \in \Theta\}$, the zero-variance distribution concentrated in the region $\{J(x) \ge \gamma_{t+1}\}$ with respect to the PDF f_{θ_t}. Thus,

$$\theta_{t+1} = \arg\min_{\theta \in \Theta} KL(f_\theta, g_t), \text{ where } g_t(x) = \frac{S(J(x)) f_{\theta_t}(x) \mathbb{I}_{\{J(x) \ge \gamma_{t+1}\}}}{\mathbb{E}_{\theta_t} \left[S(J(\mathsf{X})) \mathbb{I}_{\{J(\mathsf{X}) \ge \gamma_{t+1}\}} \right]} \quad (3)$$

with $S : \mathbb{R} \to \mathbb{R}_+$ is a positive, monotonically increasing function.

In this paper, we consider the Gaussian distribution as the family of distributions $\mathcal{F}$. In this case, the PDF is being parametrized as $\theta = (\mu, \Sigma)^\top$, where μ and Σ are the mean and the covariance of the Gaussian distribution respectively. Also, one can solve the optimization problem (3) analytically to obtain the following update rule:

$$\left. \begin{aligned} \mu_{t+1} &= \frac{\mathbb{E}_{\theta_t} \left[\mathbf{g}_1(J(\mathsf{X}), \mathsf{X}, \gamma_{t+1}) \right]}{\mathbb{E}_{\theta_t} \left[\mathbf{g}_0(J(\mathsf{X}), \gamma_{t+1}) \right]} \triangleq \Upsilon_1(\theta_t, \gamma_{t+1}), \\ \Sigma_{t+1} &= \frac{\mathbb{E}_{\theta_t} \left[\mathbf{g}_2(J(\mathsf{X}), \mathsf{X}, \gamma_{t+1}, \mu_{t+1}) \right]}{\mathbb{E}_{\theta_t} \left[\mathbf{g}_0(J(\mathsf{X}), \gamma_{t+1}) \right]} \triangleq \Upsilon_2(\theta_t, \gamma_{t+1}). \end{aligned} \right\} \quad (4)$$

$$\left. \begin{aligned} \text{where } \mathbf{g}_0(J(x), \gamma) &\triangleq S(J(x)) \mathbb{I}_{\{J(x) \ge \gamma\}}, \\ \mathbf{g}_1(J(x), x, \gamma) &\triangleq S(J(x)) \mathbb{I}_{\{J(x) \ge \gamma\}} x, \\ \mathbf{g}_2(J(x), x, \gamma, \mu) &\triangleq S(J(x)) \mathbb{I}_{\{J(x) \ge \gamma\}} (x - \mu)(x - \mu)^\top. \end{aligned} \right\} \quad (5)$$

Thus the CE algorithm can be expressed as $\theta_{t+1} = (\Upsilon_1(\theta_t, \gamma_{t+1}), \Upsilon_2(\theta_t, \gamma_{t+1}))^\top$. However, this is the ideal scenario which is intractable due to the inability to compute the quantities $\mathbb{E}_{\theta_t}[\cdot]$ and $\gamma_\rho(\cdot, \cdot)$. There are multiple ways one can track the ideal CE method. In this paper, we consider the efficient tracking of the ideal CE method using the stochastic approximation (SA) framework proposed in [1,2]. The SA version of the CE method consists of three stochastic recursions which are defined as follows:

$$\gamma_{t+1} = \gamma_t - \beta_t \Delta\gamma_t(J(X_{t+1})),$$
$$\text{where } \Delta\gamma_t(y) \triangleq -(1-\rho)\mathbb{I}_{\{y \geq \gamma_t\}} + \rho\mathbb{I}_{\{y \leq \gamma_t\}}. \tag{6}$$

$$\xi_{t+1}^{(0)} = \xi_t^{(0)} + \beta_t \Delta\xi_t^{(0)}(X_{t+1}, J(X_{t+1})),$$
$$\text{where } \Delta\xi_t^{(0)}(x, y) \triangleq g_1(y, x, \gamma_t) - \xi_t^{(0)} g_0(y, \gamma_t). \tag{7}$$

$$\xi_{t+1}^{(1)} = \xi_t^{(1)} + \beta_t \Delta\xi_t^{(1)}(X_{t+1}, J(X_{t+1})),$$
$$\text{where } \Delta\xi_{j+1}^{(1)}(x, y) \triangleq g_2(y, x, \gamma_t, \xi_t^{(0)}) - \xi_t^{(1)} g_0(y, \gamma_t). \tag{8}$$

Here, $\beta_t > 0$ and $X_{t+1} \sim \widehat{f}_{\theta_t}$, where the mixture PDF $\widehat{f}_{\theta_t}$ is defined as $\widehat{f}_{\theta_t} \triangleq (1 - \zeta)f_{\theta_t} + \zeta f_{\theta_0}$, $\zeta \in (0,1)$, f_{θ_0} is the initial PDF. The mixture approach facilitates extensive exploration of the solution space and prevents the model iterates from getting stranded in suboptimal solutions.

2.2 Computing the Objective Function $\mathbb{E}_{\nu_w}[h_{w|w}]$

In this paper, we employ the off-policy LSTD (λ) to approximate $h_{w|w}$ for a given policy parameter $w \in \mathbb{W}$. The procedure to estimate the objective function $\mathbb{E}_{\nu_w}[h_{w|w}]$ is formally defined in Algorithm 1. The *Predict* procedure in Algorithm 1 is almost the same as the off-policy LSTD algorithm. The recursion (step 9) attempts to estimate the objective function $\mathbb{E}_{\nu_w}[h_{w|w}]$ as follows:

$$\ell_{k+1}^w = \ell_k^w + \frac{1}{k}\left(\mathbf{x}_k^\top \phi(\mathbf{s}_{k+1}) - \ell_k^w\right), \tag{9}$$

Algorithm 1. Predict Function

---

1 **Input parameters:** $w \in \mathbb{W}$, $N \in \mathbb{N}$ ▶ *Input policy vector, Trajectory length;*
2 **Data:** *A priori chosen sample trajectory* $\{s_0, a_0, r_0, s_1, a_1, r_1, s_2, \dots\}$ *generated using the behaviour policy* π_{w_b};
3 $k = 0$;
4 **while** $k < N$ **do**
5 $\quad$ $\mathbf{e}_{k+1} = \gamma\lambda\rho_k \mathbf{e}_k + \phi(\mathbf{s}_k)$;   ▶ ρ_k *is the sampling ratio,* $\rho_k = \frac{\pi_w(\mathbf{a}_k|\mathbf{s}_k)}{\pi_{w_b}(\mathbf{a}_k|\mathbf{s}_k)}$;
6 $\quad$ $\mathbf{A}_{k+1} = \mathbf{A}_k + \frac{1}{k}\left(\mathbf{e}_k(\phi(\mathbf{s}_k) - \gamma\rho_k\phi(\mathbf{s}_{k+1}))^\top - \mathbf{A}_k\right)$;
7 $\quad$ $\mathbf{b}_{k+1} = \mathbf{b}_k + \frac{1}{k}(\rho_k \mathbf{r}_k \mathbf{e}_k - \mathbf{b}_k)$;
8 $\quad$ $\mathbf{x}_{k+1} = \mathbf{A}_{k+1}^{-1}\mathbf{b}_{k+1}$;   ▶ *Prediction vector;*
9 $\quad$ $\ell_{k+1}^w = \ell_k^w + \frac{1}{k}\left(\mathbf{x}_k^\top \phi(\mathbf{s}_{k+1}) - \ell_k^w\right)$;   ▶ *Objective function estimation;*
10 $\quad$ $k = k + 1$;
11 **return** ℓ_N^w;   ▶ *Outputs after N iterations;*

For a given $w \in \mathbb{W}$, ℓ_k^w attempts to find an approximate value of the objective function $J(w)$. The following lemma formally characterizes the limiting behaviour of the iterates ℓ_k^w.

Lemma 1. *For a given* $w \in \mathbb{W}$, $\ell_k^w \to \ell_*^w = \mathbb{E}_{\nu_{w_b}} \left[x_{w|w_b}^\top \phi(\mathbf{s}) \right]$ *as* $k \to \infty$ *w.p. 1, where*

$$
\begin{aligned}
x_{w|w_b} &= A_{w|w_b}^{-1} b_{w|w_b} \ with \ A_{w|w_b} = \Phi^\top D^{\nu_{w_b}} (\mathbb{I} - \gamma\lambda \mathrm{P}_w)^{-1} (\mathbb{I} - \gamma\mathrm{P}_w)\Phi \\
and \ b_{w|w_b} &= \Phi^\top D^{\nu_{w_b}} (\mathbb{I} - \gamma\lambda \mathrm{P}_w)^{-1} \mathrm{R}^w.
\end{aligned} \tag{10}
$$

Here $D^{\nu_{w_b}}$ *is the diagonal matrix with* $D_{ii}^{\nu_{w_b}} = \nu_{w_b}(i)$, $1 \le i \le |\mathbb{S}|$, *where* ν_{w_b} *is the stationary distribution of the Markov chain* P_{w_b} *induced by the behavior policy* π_{w_b} *and* $\mathrm{R}^w \in \mathbb{R}^{|\mathbb{S}|}$ *with* $\mathrm{R}^w(s) \triangleq \Sigma_{s' \in \mathbb{S}, a \in \mathbb{A}} \pi_w(a|s) \mathrm{P}(s, a, s') \mathrm{R}(s, a, s')$.

Remark 1. By the above lemma, for a given $w \in \mathbb{W}$, the quantity ℓ_k^w tracks $J_b(w) \triangleq \mathbb{E}_{\nu_{w_b}} \left[x_{w|w_b}^\top \phi(\mathbf{s}) \right]$. This is however different from the true objective function value $J(w) = \mathbb{E}_{\nu_w} \left[h_{w|w} \right]$, when $w \ne w_b$. This additional approximation error incurred is the extra cost one has to pay for the discrepancy in the policy which generated the sample path.

2.3 Proposed Algorithm

Our algorithm to solve the control problem (2) is illustrated in Algorithm 2. The following theorem shows that the model sequence $\{\theta_t\}$ and the averaged sequence $\{\bar{\theta}_t\}$ generated by Algorithm 2 converge to the degenerate distribution concentrated on the global maximum of the objective function J_b.

Theorem 1. *Let* $S(x) = exp(rx), r \in \mathbb{R}$. *Let* $\rho, \zeta \in (0,1)$ *and* $\theta_0 = (\mu_0, q\mathbb{I}_{k_2 \times k_2})^\top$, *where* $q \in \mathbb{R}_+$. *Also, let* $c_t \to 0$ *as* $t \to \infty$.. *Let the learning rates* $\bar{\beta}_t$ *and* β_t *satisfy* $\sum_t \beta_t = \sum_t \bar{\beta}_t = \infty$, $\sum_t \beta_t^2 + \bar{\beta}_t^2 < \infty$. *Let* $\{\theta_t = (\mu_t, \Sigma_t)\}_{t \in \mathbb{N}}$ *and* $\{\bar{\theta}_t = (\bar{\mu}_t, \bar{\Sigma}_t)\}_{t \in \mathbb{N}}$ *be the sequences generated by Algorithm 2 and also assume* $\theta_t \in \Theta$, $\forall t \in \mathbb{N}$. *Let* $\bar{\beta}_t = o(\beta_t)$. *Let* $w_b \in \mathbb{W}$ *be the chosen behaviour policy vector. Also, let the assumptions (A1–A2) hold. Then, there exists* $q^* \in \mathbb{R}_+$ *and* $r^* \in \mathbb{R}_+$ *s.t.* $\forall q > q^*$ *and* $\forall r > r^*$,

$$
\theta_t \to (w^{b*}, 0_{k_2 \times k_2})^\top, \bar{\theta}_t \to (w^{b*}, 0_{k_2 \times k_2})^\top \quad as \ t \to \infty, \quad w.p.1, \tag{13}
$$

where $w^{b*} \in \arg\max_{w \in \mathbb{W}} J_b(w)$ *with* $J_b(w) \triangleq \mathbb{E}_{\nu_{w_b}} \left[x_{w|w_b}^\top \phi(\mathbf{s}) \right]$.

3 Experimental Illustrations

The performance of our algorithm is evaluated on the chain walk MDP setting. This particular setting which is being proposed in [3] demonstrates the scenario where policy iteration is non-convergent when approximate value functions are

---

Algorithm 2. Proposed Algorithm

---

1 **Input parameters:** $\epsilon, \rho \in (0,1), \bar{\beta}_t, \beta_t, \zeta, c_t \in (0,1), c_t \to 0, \theta_0 = (\mu_0, \Sigma_0)^\top$, $\{N_t, t \in \mathbb{N}\}$ ▶ *Trajectory length rule chosen a priori;*

2 **Initialization:** $t = 0, \gamma_0 = 0, \xi_0^{(0)} = 0_{k_2 \times 1}, \xi_0^{(1)} = 0_{k_2 \times k_2}, T_0 = 0, \theta^p = NULL$, $\gamma_0^p = -\infty;$

3 **while** *stopping criteria not satisfied* **do**

4   **Sample generation** : $\mathsf{W}_{t+1} \sim \widehat{f}_{\theta_t}(\cdot)$, where $\widehat{f}_{\theta_t} = (1 - \zeta)f_{\theta_t} + \zeta f_{\theta_0};$

5   **Objective function estimation:** $\hat{J}(\mathsf{W}_{t+1}) = Predict(\mathsf{W}_{t+1}, N_{t+1});$

6   **Tracking** $\gamma_\rho(J_b, \widehat{\theta}_t)$**:** $\gamma_{t+1} = \gamma_t - \beta_t \Delta \gamma_t (\hat{J}(\mathsf{W}_{t+1}));$

7   **Tracking** $\Upsilon_1(\widehat{\theta}_t, \gamma_\rho(J_b, \widehat{\theta}_t))$**:** $\xi_{t+1}^{(0)} = \xi_t^{(0)} + \beta_t \Delta \xi_t^{(0)}(\mathsf{W}_{t+1}, \hat{J}(\mathsf{W}_{t+1}));$

8   **Tracking** $\Upsilon_2(\widehat{\theta}_t, \gamma_\rho(J_b, \widehat{\theta}_t))$**:** $\xi_{t+1}^{(1)} = \xi_t^{(1)} + \beta_t \Delta \xi_t^{(1)}(\mathsf{W}_{t+1}, \hat{J}(\mathsf{W}_{t+1}));$

9   **if** $\theta^p \neq NULL$ **then**

10       $\mathsf{W}_{t+1}^p \sim \widehat{f}_{\theta^p} = (1 - \zeta)f_{\theta^p} + \zeta f_{\theta_0};$

11       $\gamma_{t+1}^p = \gamma_t^p - \beta_t \Delta \gamma_t^p (\hat{J}(\mathsf{W}_{t+1}^p));$

12   **Threshold Comparison:** $T_{t+1} = T_t + c \left(\mathbb{I}_{\{\gamma_{t+1} \geq \gamma_t^p\}} - \mathbb{I}_{\{\gamma_{t+1} < \gamma_t^p\}} - T_t \right);$

13   **if** $T_{t+1} > \epsilon$ **then**

14   **Save previous model :** $\theta^p = \theta_t$; $\gamma_{t+1}^p = \gamma_t;$

15   **Update model:** $\theta_{t+1} = \theta_t + \beta_t \left((\xi_t^{(0)}, \xi_t^{(1)})^\top - \theta_t \right);$ (11)

16   **Polyak averaging:** $\bar{\theta}_{t+1} = \bar{\theta}_t + \bar{\beta}_t \left(\theta_{t+1} - \bar{\theta}_t \right);$ (12)

    else

17       $\gamma_{t+1}^p = \gamma_t^p$; $\theta_{t+1} = \theta_t;$

18     $t = t + 1;$

---

employed instead of true ones. Here $|\mathbb{S}| = 300$, $\mathbb{A} = \{L, R\}$, $k_1 = 5$, $k_2 = 10$ and the discount factor $\gamma = 0.99$. The reward function $R(\cdot, \cdot, 100) = R(\cdot, \cdot, 200) = 1.0$ and zero for all other transitions. The transition probability kernel is given by

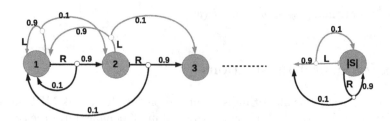

Fig. 1. Chain walk MDP

$P(s, L, s+1) = 0.1$, $P(s, L, s-1) = 0.9$, $P(s, R, s+1) = 0.9$ and $P(s, R, s-1) = 0.1$. We choose the behaviour policy vector $w_b = (0, 0, \ldots, 0)^\top$. We employ the Gibbs "soft-max" class of policies: $\pi_w(a|s) = \dfrac{e^{(w^\top \psi(s,a)/\tau)}}{\sum_{b \in \mathbb{A}} e^{(w^\top \psi(s,b)/\tau)}}$, where $\{\psi(s,a) \in \mathbb{R}^{k_2} | s \in \mathbb{S}, a \in \mathbb{A}\}$ is a given *policy feature set* and $\tau \in \mathbb{R}_+$ is fixed *a priori*. We employ radial basis functions (RBF) as both policy and prediction features, *i.e.*,

Policy features

$$\psi(s,a) = \begin{pmatrix} I_{\{a=L\}} e^{-\frac{(s-m_1)^2}{2.0v_1^2}} \\ \vdots \\ I_{\{a=L\}} e^{-\frac{(s-m_5)^2}{2.0v_5^2}} \\ I_{\{a=R\}} e^{-\frac{(s-m_1)^2}{2.0v_1^2}} \\ \vdots \\ I_{\{a=R\}} e^{-\frac{(s-m_5)^2}{2.0v_5^2}} \end{pmatrix}.$$

Prediction features

$$\phi_i(s) = e^{-\frac{(s-m_i)^2}{2.0v_i^2}},$$

where $m_i = 5 + 10(i-1)$, $v_i = 5$, $1 \le i \le 5$ (Fig. 1).
The results are shown in Fig. 2.

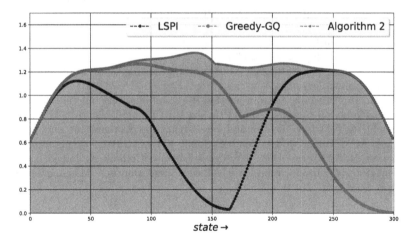

Fig. 2. The plot of the respective optimal value functions contrived by LSPI, Greedy-GQ and Algorithm 2 for the chain walk MDP setting. The optimal solutions of various algorithms are being developed by averaging over 10 independent trials. For Algorithm 2, we averaged the various optimal solutions obtained for different sample trajectories generated using the same behaviour policy, but with different initial states which are chosen randomly. Our approach (Algorithm 2) literally surpassed other algorithms in terms of its quality. The random choice of the initial state ineffectively favoured sufficient exploration of the state space which directly assisted in generating high quality solutions.

4   Conclusion

We propose an adaptation of the cross entropy method to solve the control problem in reinforcement learning under an information restricted setting, where only a single sample path generated using a priori chosen behaviour policy is available. The proposed algorithm is shown to converge to the solution which is globally optimal relative to the behaviour policy.

Acknowledgement. This work was supported in part by the Robert Bosch Centre for Cyber-Physical Systems, Indian Institute of Science, Bangalore.

References

1. Joseph, A.G., Bhatnagar, S.: A randomized algorithm for continuous optimization. In: Winter Simulation Conference, WSC 2016, Washington, DC, USA, 11–14 December 2016, pp. 907–918 (2016)
2. Joseph, A.G., Bhatnagar, S.: Revisiting the cross entropy method with applications in stochastic global optimization and reinforcement learning. In: Frontiers in Artificial Intelligence and Applications, (ECAI 2016), vol. 285, pp. 1026–1034 (2016)
3. Koller, D., Parr, R.: Policy iteration for factored MDPS. In: Proceedings of the Sixteenth Conference on Uncertainty in Artificial Intelligence, pp. 326–334. Morgan Kaufmann Publishers Inc. (2000)
4. Kroese, D.P., Porotsky, S., Rubinstein, R.Y.: The cross-entropy method for continuous multi-extremal optimization. Methodol. Comput. Appl. Probab. **8**(3), 383–407 (2006)
5. Mannor, S., Rubinstein, R.Y., Gat, Y.: The cross entropy method for fast policy search. In: ICML, pp. 512–519 (2003)
6. Menache, I., Mannor, S., Shimkin, N.: Basis function adaptation in temporal difference reinforcement learning. Ann. Oper. Res. **134**(1), 215–238 (2005)
7. Rubinstein, R.: The cross-entropy method for combinatorial and continuous optimization. Methodol. Comput. Appl. Probab. **1**(2), 127–190 (1999)
8. Rubinstein, R.Y.: Cross-entropy and rare events for maximal cut and partition problems. ACM Trans. Model. Comput. Simul. (TOMACS) **12**(1), 27–53 (2002)
9. Rubinstein, R.Y., Kroese, D.P.: The Cross-Entropy Method: A Unified Approach to Combinatorial Optimization, Monte-Carlo Simulation and Machine Learning. Springer, New York (2013)

Biometric Counter-Spoofing for Mobile Devices Using Gaze Information

Asad Ali⬭, Nawal Alsufyani⬭, Sanaul Hoque⬭, and Farzin Deravi(✉)⬭

School of Engineering and Digital Arts, University of Kent, Canterbury, Kent CT2 7NT, UK
F.Deravi@kent.ac.uk

Abstract. With the rise in the use of biometric authentication on mobile devices, it is important to address the security vulnerability of spoofing attacks where an attacker using an artefact representing the biometric features of a genuine user attempts to subvert the system. In this paper, techniques for presentation attack detection are presented using gaze information with a focus on their applicability for use on mobile devices. Novel features that rely on directing the gaze of the user and establishing its behaviour are explored for detecting spoofing attempts. The attack scenarios considered in this work include the use of projected photos, 2D and 3D masks. The proposed features and the systems based on them were extensively evaluated using data captured from volunteers performing genuine and spoofing attempts. The results of the evaluations indicate that gaze-based features have the potential for discriminating between genuine attempts and imposter attacks on mobile devices.

Keywords: Biometrics · Spoofing · Presentation attacks · Mobile security · Liveness detection

1 Introduction

Spoofing attacks on biometric systems are one of the major impediments to their use for secure unattended applications. With the growing use of biometric authentication on mobile devices, this problem may need special attention in the context of the limitations of such devices. This study will address the threat of spoofing attacks on mobile biometric systems using artefacts presented at the sensor (e.g. projected photograph, 2D mask or 3D mask of a genuine user). The focus will be on the development and evaluation of liveness detection and counter-spoofing technologies based on eye-gaze in operational mobile scenarios. Such technologies can enhance the trust and reliability of remote communications and transactions using the increasingly prevalent mobile devices.

Various approaches have been presented in the literature to establish "liveness" and to detect presentation attacks. Spoofing detection approaches can be grouped into two broad categories: active and passive. Passive approaches do not require user co-operation or even user awareness but exploit involuntary physical movements, such as spontaneous eye blinks, and 3D properties of the image source [1–13]. Active approaches require user engagement to enable the biometric system to establish the liveness of the

© Springer International Publishing AG 2017
B.U. Shankar et al. (Eds.): PReMI 2017, LNCS 10597, pp. 11–18, 2017.
https://doi.org/10.1007/978-3-319-69900-4_2

source through an evaluation of the sample captured at the sensor [14–23]. In this work, we present a novel active approach using gaze information for liveness detection for application on mobile devices. Section 2 presents the proposed system. Experimental results and a comparison with the state-of-the-art is presented in Sect. 3 while conclusions are provided in Sect. 4.

2   Liveness Detection Through Gaze Tracking

A block diagram of the proposed system is shown in Fig. 1. A visual stimulus (as part of the challenge) appears on the display which the participant is asked to follow and the camera (sensor) captures facial images at each position of the stimulus on the screen. A control mechanism is used to ensure that the placement of the target and the image acquisition are synchronized. The system extracts facial landmarks in the captured frames and computes various features from these landmarks which are then used to classify whether the presentation attempt is by a genuine user. The spoofing attack may be by means of an impostor attempting authentication by holding a projected photo, 2D or 3D mask of a genuine subject to the camera.

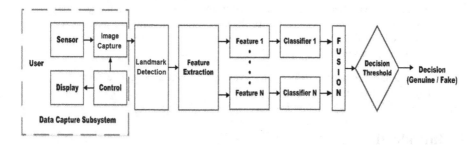

Fig. 1. Proposed system block diagram.

2.1   A Subsection Sample

The restricted geometry of a mobile phone display (6.45 × 11.30 cm) is simulated in the experiments that follow using a limited area of a desktop computer screen. A small shape ("x") is presented, at distinct locations on the screen as shown in Fig. 2. In this figure, the cross indicates the chosen locations in which the cross sign appears in 30 distinct locations (Points Challenge) (Fig. 2(a)) and along straight-line trajectories (Lines Challenge) (Fig. 2(b)). The order of points and lines is randomised for each presentation. During each presentation attempt images were acquired at every location of the challenge. The presentation of the challenge sequence lasted approximately 90 s, however, a small section of each session was used for spoofing detection.

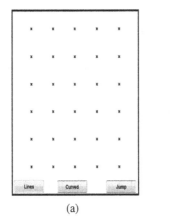   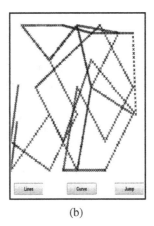

(a)   (b)

Fig. 2. Samples of challenge trajectory: (a) Points challenge, (b) Lines challenge.

Data was collected from 80 participants. This number of participants is sufficient to illustrate the potential of the proposed approach and is in line with current state-of-the-art. Participants were of both male and female gender aged over 18 years old. The volunteers were from Africa, Asia, Middle-East, and Europe. Three spoofing attempts (photo projection, 2D mask, 3D mask) and one genuine attempt for each challenge type (Points and Lines) were recorded for each participant.

2.2   Facial Landmark Detection and Feature Extraction

The images thus captured during the challenge-response operation were processed using Chehra Version 3.0 [24] in order to extract facial landmark points. Chehra returns 59 different landmarks on the face region. The coordinates of some of these landmarks were used for feature extraction in the proposed scheme. Features proposed here are based on eye movements during the challenge presentation.

2.3   Gaze-Based Collinearity and Colocation Features

A set of points lying on a straight line is referred to here as a collinear set and this property of collinearity is used for detecting presentation attacks. Collinearity features are, therefore, extracted from sets of images captured when the stimulus is on a given line. The novel gaze-based collinearity feature explored in this paper is designed to capture significant angular differences between the stimulus trajectory and the trajectory of the participant's pupil movement for each line segment.

Let (x_i, y_i) be points on the trajectory of the challenge, where the stimulus moves on a straight line, and (u_i, v_i) are the corresponding facial landmarks (e.g., pupil centres). Let θ_c be the angle of the challenge calculated using any two points along the line of the trajectory.

$$\theta_c = tan^{-1}\left(\frac{y_j - y_i}{x_j - x_i}\right) \tag{1}$$

Let θ_r be the angle of the response trajectory. The response angle is calculated using the Least Squares regression method as shown:

$$\theta_r = tan^{-1}\left(\frac{\sum (u_i - \bar{u})(v_i - \bar{v})}{\sum (u_i - \bar{u})^2}\right) \tag{2}$$

The feature vector is then defined as the absolute difference between these two angles $\Delta\theta (= |\theta_c - \theta_r|)$ for each of the line segments included in the challenge.

$$F_{collin} = [\Delta\theta_1, \Delta\theta_2, ...] \tag{3}$$

For the colocation feature, the Points stimulus is used, causing the user to fixate on a number of random locations on the screen. At each stimulus location, the facial image of the user is captured. The gaze colocation features are extracted from images where the stimulus is at the same locations at different times. It can, therefore, be assumed that the coordinates of the pupil centres in the corresponding frames should also be very similar. This should result in a very small variance, σ^2, in the observed coordinates of the pupil centres in genuine attempts. A feature vector is thus formed from the variances of pupil centre coordinates for all the frames where the stimulus is colocated. These variances are calculated for the horizontal and vertical directions independently,

$$\sigma_u^2 = \frac{1}{M}\sum_i (u_i - \bar{u})^2 \tag{4}$$

$$\sigma_v^2 = \frac{1}{M}\sum_i (v_i - \bar{v})^2 \tag{5}$$

where $\bar{u}$ and $\bar{v}$ are the mean of the observed landmark locations and M is cardinality of the corresponding subset of response points. These variances are concatenated together to form the feature vector as shown below:

$$F_{coloc} = [\sigma_u^2, \sigma_v^2, ...] \tag{6}$$

The features are passed to the classifier to detect attack attempts.

3   Experiments

The ROC curves using gaze-based colocation features are presented in Fig. 3 for photo attack (by displaying on an iPad Mini 2), 2D mask attack (using printed photos with holes at pupils) and 3D mask attack (using life-size 3D model made of hard resin with holes at pupils) detection. This experiment was conducted for the mobile Phone format using 10 sets of colocated points (amounting to a challenge duration of 30 s). At 10%

FPR, the TPR is 90% for photo attack. The performance is about 21 and 29% TPR for 2D mask and 3D mask respectively. Photo attack is easier to detect using this feature. 2D and 3D mask attacks are challenging and difficult to discriminate from genuine presentations using this feature.

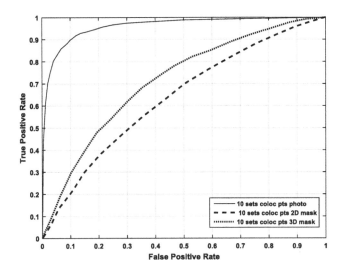

Fig. 3. ROC curves for photo, 2D mask and 3D mask for 10 sets of colocation points (approximately 30 s of challenge duration).

Table 1 summarizes the TPRs at FPR 0.10 for various sets of colocation points representing different challenge durations ranging from 9 s (3 colocated sets of points) to 45 s (15 colocated sets of points). The lowest performance is noticed for 2D and 3D mask attacks. Increasing the challenge duration did not significantly improve the results.

Table 1. TPR at FPR = 0.10 for various sets of colocation points

Attack type	Sets of collocated points		
	3	10	15
Photo	82%	90%	88%
2D mask	9%	21%	25%
3D mask	18%	29%	30%

In summary, it appears that the colocation feature does not work effectively when used with the smaller geometries of mobile devices in detecting 2D and 3D mask attacks. While it is effective in detecting photo attacks, the minimum challenge duration for the feature is around 9 s.

The ROC curves using collinearity features are presented in Fig. 4 for all attack scenarios for five line segments representing approximately 5 s of challenge duration. At 10% FPR, the TPR is 95%, 88% and 87% for photo, 2D and 3D mask attack detection respectively.

Although several lines are shown in the trajectory in Fig. 2b, only five consecutive line segments (picked at random) have been used for this analysis.

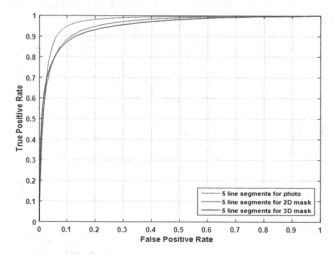

Fig. 4. ROC curves for photo, 2D mask, and 3D mask for 5 sets of line segments (approximately 5 s) for collinearity feature.

Changing the number of lines used has a significant effect not only on the execution time but also on accuracy.

Table 2 summarize the TPRs at FPR = 0.10 for various numbers of lines included in a challenge presentation. The proposed system was able to detect a majority of attacks when using a set of five line segments. When increased to 10 line segments, the performance is significantly improved, however, it drops to 83%, 62% and 62% for photo, 2D mask and 3D mask attack respectively when only three lines are used.

Table 2. TPR at FPR = 0.10 for various sets of lines of collinearity

Attack type	Number of line segments		
	3	5	10
Photo	83%	95%	99%
2D mask	62%	88%	97%
3D mask	62%	87%	99%

In summary, the collinearity feature appears to be more effective in detecting all the attack types compared with the colocation feature; even when the challenge duration is as low as 3 s.

Table 3 presents a comparison of the performance results obtained using the proposed novel collinearity feature with results reported in the literature. It is difficult to make a direct comparison between these results due to the different databases used for system evaluation and the novel and unique way that the challenge response mechanism is deployed in our proposed system. However, the results are very promising and indicate the potential of the proposed features and approach to substantially exceed current performance limits.

Table 3. FPR and FNR for various methods

	Method	FPR	FNR
	Kollreider et al. [22]	1.5%	19.0%
	Tan et al. cf. [7]	9.3%	17.6%
	Peixoto et al. [7]	6.9%	7.0%
Collinearity 10 s	Photo Detection	6.0%	2.2%
	2D Mask Detection	6.0%	7.8%
	3D Mask Detection	6.0%	2.4%

The choice of operating points on the ROC curve that determines the balance between FPR and FNR should be set according to the needs of particular applications. The proposed system allows for considerable flexibility in adjusting the system parameters to meet the needs of different applications.

4 Conclusion

This work reports on an investigation of novel gaze-based features for liveness detection on mobile devices. The research extends the authors' previous works on gaze-based presentation attack detection using enhanced features, mobile device geometry and additional attack artefacts. The work explored not only presentation of static photographs using another mobile device as the attack instrument but also the use of 2D and 3D masks representing different attack effort levels required by potential attackers. An important part of this work was evaluating the system with a large database (80 subjects) of genuine and attack presentations simulating mobile access scenarios.

The main conclusion of this investigation is to suggest that gaze information when captured in smaller device geometries such as those available on mobile phones has the potential to discriminate between genuine and subversive attempts.

References

1. Sun, L., Pan, G., Wu, Z., Lao, S.: Blinking-based live face detection using conditional random fields. In: Lee, S.-W., Li, S.Z. (eds.) ICB 2007. LNCS, vol. 4642, pp. 252–260. Springer, Heidelberg (2007). doi:10.1007/978-3-540-74549-5_27
2. Pan, G., Sun, L., Wu, Z., Lao, S.: Eyeblink-based anti-spoofing in face recognition from a generic webcamera. In: IEEE 11th International Conference on Computer Vision (ICCV), pp. 1–8 (2007)
3. Schwartz, W.R., Rocha, A., Pedrini, H.: Face spoofing detection through partial least squares and low-level descriptors. In: International Joint Conference on Biometrics (IJCB), pp. 1–8 (2011)
4. Chingovska, I., Anjos, A., Marcel, S.: On the effectiveness of local binary patterns in face anti-spoofing. In: Proceedings of IEEE BIOSIG, pp. 1–7 (2012)
5. Pinto, A., Schwartz, W.R., Pedrini, H., Rocha, A.: Using visual rhythms for detecting video-based facial spoof attacks. IEEE Trans. Inf. Forensics Secur. 10(5), 1025–1038 (2015)

6. Maatta, J., Hadid, A., Pietikainen, M.: Face spoofing detection from single images using texture and local shape analysis. IET Biometrics **1**(1), 3–10 (2012)
7. Peixoto, B., Michelassi, C., Rocha, A.: Face liveness detection under bad illumination conditions. In: 18th IEEE International Conference on Image Processing, pp. 3557–3560 (2011)
8. Wen, D., Han, H., Jain, A.K.: Face spoof detection with image distortion analysis. IEEE Trans. Inf. Forensics Secur. **10**(4), 746–761 (2015)
9. Georghiades, A.S., Belhumeur, P.N., Kriegman, D.J.: From few to many: illumination cone models for face recognition under variable lighting and pose. IEEE Trans. Pattern Anal. Mach. Intell. **23**(6), 643–660 (2001)
10. Anjos A., Marcel, S.: Counter-measures to photo attacks in face recognition: a public database and a baseline. In: 2011 International Joint Conference on Biometrics (IJCB), pp. 1–7 (2011)
11. Lagorio, A., Tistarelli, M., Cadoni, M., Fookes, C., Sridharan, S.: Liveness detection based on 3d face shape analysis. In: International Workshop on Biometrics and Forensics (IWBF), pp. 1–4 (2013)
12. Wang, T., Yang, J., Lei, Z., Liao, S., Li, S.Z.: Face liveness detection using 3d structure recovered from a single camera. In: 2013 International Conference on Biometrics (ICB), pp. 1–6 (2013)
13. De Marsico, M., Galdi, C., Nappi, M., Riccio, D.: Firme: face and iris recognition for mobile engagement. Image Vis. Comput. **32**(12), 1161–1172 (2014)
14. Frischholz R.W., Werner, A.: Avoiding replay-attacks in a face recognition system using head-pose estimation. In: IEEE International Workshop on Analysis and Modeling of Faces and Gestures (AMFG), pp. 234–235 (2003)
15. Ali, A., Deravi, F., Hoque, S.: Liveness detection using gaze collinearity. In: 2012 Third International Conference on Emerging Security Technologies (EST), pp. 62–65 (2012)
16. Ali, A., Deravi, F., Hoque, S.: Spoofing attempt detection using gaze colocation. In: 2013 International Conference of the Biometrics Special Interest Group (BIOSIG), pp. 1–12 (2013)
17. Ali, A., Deravi, F., Hoque, S.: Directional sensitivity of gaze-collinearity features in liveness detection. In: 4th International Conference on Emerging Security Technologies (EST), pp. 8–11 (2013)
18. Singh, A.K., Joshi, P., Nandi, G.C.: Face recognition with liveness detection using eye and mouth movement. In: 2014 International Conference on Signal Propagation and Computer Technology (IC- SPCT), pp. 592–597 (2014)
19. Smith, D.F., Wiliem, A., Lovell, C.: Face recognition on consumer devices: reflections on replay attacks. IEEE Trans. Inf. Forensics Secur. **10**(4), 736–745 (2015)
20. Boehm, A., Chen, D., Frank, M., Huang, L., Kuo, C., Lolic, T., Martinovic, I., Song, D.: Safe: secure authentication with face and eyes. In: 2013 International Conference on Privacy and Security in Mobile Systems (PRISMS), pp. 1–8 (2013)
21. Cai, L., Huang, L., Liu, C.: Person-specific face spoofing detection for replay attack based on gaze estimation. In: Yang, J., Yang, J., Sun, Z., Shan, S., Zheng, W., Feng, J. (eds.) Biometric Recognition. LNCS, vol. 9428, pp. 201–211. Springer, Cham (2015). doi: 10.1007/978-3-319-25417-3_25
22. Kollreider, K., Fronthaler, H., Bigun, J.: Evaluating liveness by face images and the structure tensor. In: 4th IEEE Workshop on Automatic Identification Advanced Technologies (AutoID 2005), pp. 75–80 (2005)
23. Ali, A., Hoque, S., Deravi, F.: Gaze stability for liveness detection. Pattern Anal. Applic. (2016). doi:10.1007/s10044-016-0587-2
24. Asthana, A., Zafeiriou, S., Cheng, S., Pantic, M.: Incremental face alignment in the wild. In: Proceedings of the IEEE Conference on Computer Vision and Pattern Recognition, pp. 1859–1866 (2014)

Pattern Recognition and Machine Learning

kNN Classification with an Outlier Informative Distance Measure

Gautam Bhattacharya[1] [iD], Koushik Ghosh[2] [iD],
and Ananda S. Chowdhury[3(✉)] [iD]

[1] Department of Physics, University Institute of Technology, University of Burdwan,
Bardhaman, India
gautamuit@gmail.com
[2] Department of Mathematics,
University Institute of Technology, University of Burdwan, Bardhaman, India
koushikg123@yahoo.co.uk
[3] Department of Electronics and Telecommunication Engineering,
Jadavpur University, Kolkata, India
aschowdhury@etce.jdvu.ac.in

Abstract. Classification accuracy of the kNN algorithm is found to be adversely affected by the presence of outliers in the experimental datasets. An outlier score based on rank difference can be assigned to the points in these datasets by taking into consideration the distance and density of their local neighborhood points. In the present work, we introduce a generalized outlier informative distance measure where a factor based on the above score is used to modulate any potential distance function. Properties of the new outlier informative distance measure are presented. Experiments on several numeric datasets in the UCI machine learning repository clearly reveal the effectiveness of the proposed formulation.

Keywords: Outliers · Distance measure · kNN classification accuracy

1 Introduction

Outliers can be considered as exceptional entities with respect to the remaining (large amount of) data [8]. Due to the unexpected behavior, detection of outliers became an important research problem for the data mining and the pattern recognition communities [7]. Finding outliers can be extremely useful for diverse applications like fraud detection, fault detection for safety in critical systems, and, military surveillance for enemy activities [1,6]. The problem of detecting outliers becomes quite challenging as they can create ambiguities within a dataset due to masking and swamping [2]. There exist many published works on detection of outliers [5,10,11]. In a recent work, the authors in [4] proposed a rank-difference and density based score as a measure of outlierness.

It is a well-known fact that the presence of outliers adversely affects the performance of a pattern classification algorithm like kNN. We choose the kNN

© Springer International Publishing AG 2017
B.U. Shankar et al. (Eds.): PReMI 2017, LNCS 10597, pp. 21–27, 2017.
https://doi.org/10.1007/978-3-319-69900-4_3

algorithm for our work as it still remains a popular choice due to its simplicity, ease of implementation and the fact that its classification accuracy is bounded by twice Bayes' error rate [9]. The main contribution of this paper is the formulation of a generalized outlier informative distance function based on the score in [4]. We state and prove various properties of the above distance function. Our proposed measure is extremely useful as it can improve the classification accuracy of the kNN algorithm and is generalized as it can be used with any potential distance function. With experiments carried out on fifteen numeric datasets in the UCI machine learning repository, we demonstrate the effectiveness of our approach for three different distance functions.

The rest of the paper is organized in the following manner: in Sect. 2, we briefly discuss the outlier score. In Sect. 3, we introduce the outlier informative distance measure and discuss its properties. In Sects. 4 and 5, we present the time-complexity analysis and experimental results respectively with detailed comparisons. The paper is concluded in Sect. 6 with an outline for directions of future research.

2   A Score for Outlierness

We briefly discuss here the Rank-difference and Density-based Outlier Score (RDOS) for ranking of the outliers following [4]. Let D denote the dataset for classification, k denotes the number of nearest neighbors $N_k(p)$ around some query point $p \in D$ and $d(p,q)$ denote the distance (e.g., Euclidean distance) between any two points $p, q \in D$. Further, let, R represent the reverse ranking of the point p with respect to the point $q \in N_k(p)$. If q is the kth neighbor of the point p at distance $d_k(p,q)$, then the forward density up to k^{th} neighbor is given by:

$$\Omega_k(p) = k/d_k(p,q) \qquad (1)$$

The positive value of the rank difference (R-k) signifies the higher concentration of the neighbors surrounding the training point q than that of the query point p. The negative and zero value respectively signify a lower or same concentration of the training points around q than that of p. The outlierness of the test point depends on the higher population of the neighborhood space of q with respect to the test point p, i.e., on the rank difference (R-k). The outlierness also varies inversely with its own forward density $\Omega_k(p)$. So, the Rank-difference and Density-based Outlier Score (RDOS) can be written as [4]:

$$RDOS_p = median\left(\frac{R-k}{\Omega_k(p)}\right) \qquad (2)$$

The median value has been used to have a more robust estimation of (RDOS).

3   Outlier Informative Distance Measure

In this section, we propose a novel distance measure based on RDOS score [4] and discuss its various properties. As the first step, we assign an RDOS to all the points in a given dataset using the Eq. (2). Note that RDOS for any point is determined based on the rank difference and density analysis within a local neighborhood. During classification using kNN, we capture the difference in the RDOS values of the test point and a point in the training set. Let $RDOS_{Train}$ and $RDOS_{Test}$ respectively denote the outlierness score for a training point and the test/query point. Let us define $|\Delta S(Train, Test)|$ as the absolute difference of the outlierness scores. So, we write:

$$|\Delta S(Train, Test)| = |RDOS_{Train} - RDOS_{Test}| \tag{3}$$

The higher the value of $|\Delta S|$, the higher will be the difference in their local densities. The physical distance between these two points in such a case cannot completely represent the extent of dissimilarity. In contrast, a small value of $|\Delta S|$ indicates that their local densities are somewhat similar. In this case, the physical distance should more appropriately capture their dissimilarity. We now introduce a generalized outlier informative distance measure by taking into consideration both these situations. The term $|\Delta S|$ is used as a scaling factor to slowly modulate any standard distance function. Let d_s be the outlier informative distance measure between the test point and the training point. Then, for any two points x and y, we propose:

$$d_s(x, y) = d(x, y)(1 + \ln(1 + |\Delta S(x, y)|)) \tag{4}$$

In the above equation, $d(x, y)$ represents any potential distance function between the points x and y. The use of logarithm function ensures a slow variation. It is clearly evident that if the factor $|\Delta S|$ becomes zero, then d_s in the Eq. (4) degenerates to d. In the present work, we have used three distance functions for d, namely, Euclidean, Cityblock and recently proposed affinity based local distance [3].

We now discuss various properties of the proposed distance measure. All the properties of a metric i.e., positive definiteness, symmetry and triangular inequality hold for both Euclidean and Cityblock distances. However, the distance used in [3] satisfies only the property of positive definiteness. Now, we denote the scaling factor as

$$\alpha_{xy} = (1 + \ln(1 + |\Delta S(x, y)|)) \tag{5}$$

Theorem 1: If $d(x, y)$ is positive definite, then $d_s(x, y)$ is also positive definite.

Proof: The term $|\Delta S(x, y)|$ is always ≥ 0. So, $ln(1 + |\Delta S(x, y)|)$ is always positive. Hence, α_{xy} is always ≥ 1. Thus, $d_s(x, y) \geq d(x, y)$. Hence the proof.

Theorem 2: If $d(x, y)$ is symmetric, then $d_s(x, y)$ is also symmetric.

Proof: The term $|\Delta S(x, y)|$ is symmetric. As a consequence $ln(1 + |\Delta S(x, y)|)$, α_{xy}, $d(x, y)$, $d_s(x, y)$ are all symmetric.

Theorem 3: If $d(x, y)$ satisfies distance triangle inequality, then under certain conditions $d_s(x, y)$ satisfies the triangle inequality.

Proof: Due to the introduction of nonlinear scaling factor α, the distances of different training points from the test point are scaled in different ratios. Based on Eqs. (4) and (5), we can write:

$$
\begin{aligned}
d_s(x,y) &= \alpha_{xy}d(x,y) \quad where, \alpha_{xy} \geq 1 \\
d_s(y,z) &= \alpha_{yz}d(y,z) \quad where, \alpha_{yz} \geq 1 \\
d_s(x,z) &= \alpha_{xz}d(x,z) \quad where, \alpha_{xz} \geq 1
\end{aligned}
\tag{6}
$$

In the above equation, α_{xy} equals α_{yx} and so on. Now, using the property 3 of $d(x,y)$ and Eq. (6), we have: $d_s(x,y) = \alpha_{xy}d(x,y) \leq \alpha_{xy}(d(x,z) + d(z,y)) = (\alpha_{xy}/\alpha_{xz})d_s(x,z)+(\alpha_{xy}/\alpha_{zy})d_s(z,y)$.

As affinity based local distance [3] is a directed distance, so triangle inequality is not applicable for this. On the other hand, for the inputs of Euclidean and Cityblock distance triangle inequality will always hold for the newly proposed scaled distance iff $(\alpha_{xy} \leq \alpha_{xz})$ and $(\alpha_{xy} \leq \alpha_{yz})$ which gives rise to the following mutually exclusive possibilities in view of (3) and (5):

1. $RDOS_y \leq RDOS_x \leq Min\left[(RDOS_y + RDOS_z)/2, RDOS_z\right]$
2. $Max\left[RDOS_z, (RDOS_y + RDOS_z)/2\right] \leq RDOS_x \leq RDOS_y$
3. $RDOS_x \leq RDOS_y \leq Min\left[(RDOS_x + RDOS_z)/2, RDOS_z\right]$
4. $Max\left[RDOS_z, (RDOS_x + RDOS_z)/2\right] \leq RDOS_y \leq RDOS_x$

In other cases the triangle inequality may not be satisfied for the newly proposed scaled distance even for the inputs of the Euclidean and Cityblock distance.

4 Time-Complexity

Out of n samples, let N and $(n - N)$ be the number of training and test samples respectively. Now, k and NC represents respectively the number of nearest neighborhood points and classes assigned for classification of patterns. Now, we present the detailed (worst-case) time-complexity analysis. As mentioned in [4] the total time complexity for assigning the $RDOS$ score to all n number of points is $O(n^2 \ln n)$. The total complexity for calculation of d_s, sorting, similarity and classification score calculation of each test sample: $O(N) + O(N \ln N) + O(k) + O(kNC)$ which turns to be approximately $O(nN \ln N)$ for $(n - N)$ number of test points as $k, NC, (n - N) << n, N$. Now, the overall time complexity for the $RDOS$ score calculation and classification using the modified kNN algorithm is: $O(n^2 \ln n) + O(nN \ln N)) \approx O(n^2 \ln n)$ as $N < n$.

5 Experimental Results

We compare the performances (Mean $\pm$ Standard deviation of the classification accuracy) of the kNN algorithm having outlier score weighted Euclidean, Cityblock, and the distance used in [3] (from Eq. (4)) with their baseline counterparts (i.e., the unweighted forms) in Table 1. In the first column, we provide the total count of instances (n), attributes (M) and classes (NC) within the braces. The classification accuracies of the kNN algorithm with Euclidean, Cityblock, and the distance used in [3] are (82.58 ± 5.77), (83.83 ± 5.71) and (84.91 ± 5.57) respectively. The corresponding classification accuracies of the kNN algorithm with the proposed outlier informative distance measure, are respectively given by (84.32 ± 5.68), (84.97 ± 5.57) and (85.22 ± 5.67). So, the quantitative values clearly indicate the supremacy of the proposed measure. We have also achieved wins in 10, 10 and 9 out of a total of 15 datasets with the new outlier score weighted distance measure over their unweighted counterparts for the Euclidean distance, the Cityblock distance, and the distance used in [3] respectively.

Table 1. Performance comparison of the new weighted distances with the original distances used in kNN

Datasets	Classification accuracy of the kNN algorithm without (Normal Distances) and with (Scaled Distances) the knowledge of outlier											
	Euclidean		Scaled Euclidean		Cityblock		Scaled Cityblock		Affinity distance in [3]		Scaled Affinity distance in [3]	
	Mean	S.D.	Mean	S.D.	Mean	S.D.	Mean	S.D.	Mean	S.D.	Mean	S.D.
Iris-Corrected(150, 4, 3)	96.17	5.11	96.10	5.10	94.63	5.71	**94.70**	5.75	95.43	5.26	95.03	5.48
Wine(178, 13, 3)	96.67	4.13	**97.81**	3.58	97.70	3.52	97.36	3.55	96.45	4.18	**97.47**	3.58
Glass(214, 9, 6)	67.96	8.25	**68.76**	9.19	71.90	8.20	**73.51**	8.14	73.35	8.48	**73.64**	8.89
Pima-Diabetes(768, 8, 2)	75.15	4.58	**75.55**	4.64	75.57	4.02	75.30	4.11	75.73	4.52	75.65	4.64
Breast(683, 10, 2)	96.87	2.01	96.15	2.30	96.34	2.15	95.89	2.33	96.89	1.97	**96.90**	1.94
Sonar(208, 60, 2)	74.46	7.92	**79.80**	8.09	79.88	7.45	**82.30**	7.76	80.04	7.84	**80.51**	7.83
Ionosphere(351, 33, 2)[a]	82.43	5.01	**94.14**	4.20	84.43	5.67	**93.46**	4.15	92.06	4.14	**94.37**	4.26
Vehicle(846, 18, 4)	69.21	4.04	69.11	4.27	70.14	3.84	**70.19**	3.91	70.20	3.69	70.15	3.75
Wdbc(569, 31, 2)	95.78	2.65	**96.03**	2.44	95.36	2.74	**95.66**	2.80	95.80	2.75	95.53	2.98
Spectf(267, 44, 2)	77.05	6.23	**79.03**	5.54	77.42	5.75	77.21	6.02	78.64	5.87	78.48	6.12
Musk1(476, 166, 2)	81.08	6.23	**85.48**	4.92	83.16	5.80	**85.65**	5.01	86.96	5.09	**88.32**	4.75
Breast-Tissue(106, 9, 6)[a]	65.30	11.51	**66.25**	11.52	66.73	11.59	**68.53**	11.35	68.78	11.32	**69.4**	11.50
Parkinson(195, 22, 2)[a]	89.18	6.49	**89.80**	6.94	91.04	6.79	**91.6**	6.41	91.08	6.40	**91.13**	6.69
Segmentation(210, 18, 7)	85.24	6.92	84.90	7.03	86.90	6.82	**87.76**	6.67	86.90	6.60	85.81	7.38
Ecoli(336, 7, 8)[a]	86.11	5.45	85.81	5.40	86.23	5.61	85.39	5.68	85.39	5.44	**85.90**	5.20
Average	**82.58**	**5.77**	**84.32**	**5.68**	**83.83**	**5.71**	**84.97**	**5.57**	**84.91**	**5.57**	**85.22**	**5.67**

[a] The 1st column of the dataset contain serial numbers which has not been considered as an attribute in present work.

We now show the goodness-of-fit of the new distances by the shepard plot for an example dataset (Iris) in Fig. 1. The narrow scattering shows the controlled deviation of the training instances at small distances with respect to the test point. For the large distances the scattering is also high. In Fig. 2 we have shown the boxplot comparison of the results of scaled distance with respect to their original form. Improvement in performances using metric distances like, Euclidean or Cityblock are significantly high or prominent than that of the nonmetric distance used in [3]. This is because the distance in [3] is based on local affinity and has already shown to perform better than many distance functions like Euclidean and Cityblock. The bottom line of the boxplot shows the baseline performance and the upper line indicates the level of improved accuracy due to the use of scaled distances in kNN.

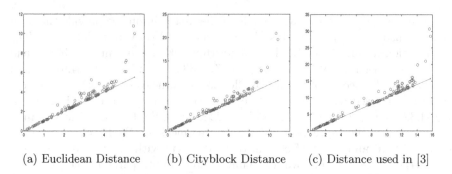

(a) Euclidean Distance   (b) Cityblock Distance   (c) Distance used in [3]

Fig. 1. Shepard plot (RDOS weighted vs. unweighted distance) using Iris dataset.

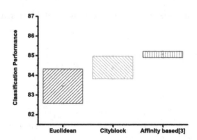

Fig. 2. Boxplot Comparison of improvements in classification performances on application of RDOS in Euclidean, Cityblock and Affinity based distance [3].

6   Conclusion

In this work, we proposed a generalized outlier informative distance function based on a measure of outlierness, introduced in [4]. Experimental results on fifteen datasets from the UCI machine learning repository with three different distance functions clearly reveal the effectiveness of our formulation. For future work, we plan to explore metric learning to have a more informative outlier based distance measure which in turn can further improve the performance of kNN classifiers and alike.

References

1. Aggarwal, C.C.: Outlier Analysis. Springer, New York (2013)
2. Ben-Gal, I.: Outlier detection. In: Maimon, O., Rokach, L. (eds.) Data Mining and Knowledge Discovery Handbook, pp. 131–146. Springer, Boston (2005)
3. Bhattacharya, G., Ghosh, K., Chowdhury, A.S.: An affinity-based new local distance function and similarity measure for kNN algorithm. Pattern Recogn. Lett. **33**(3), 356–363 (2012)
4. Bhattacharya, G., Ghosh, K., Chowdhury, A.S.: Outlier detection using neighborhood rank difference. Pattern Recogn. Lett. **60–61**, 24–31 (2015)

5. Breunig, M.M., Kriegel, H.P., Ng, R.T., Sander, J.: LOF: identifying density-based local outliers. In: Proceedings of the ACM International Conference on Management of Data (SIGMOD), Dallas, TX, pp. 93–104 (2000)

6. Chandola, V., Banerjee, A., Kumar, V.: Anomaly detection: A survey. ACM Comput. Surv. **41**(3), 15:1–15:58 (2009)

7. Chawla, S., Hand, D., Dhar, V.: Outlier detection special issue. Data Min. Knowl. Discov. **20**(2), 189–190 (2010)

8. Chen, Y., Miao, D., Zhang, H.: Neighborhood outlier detection. Expert Syst. Appl. **37**, 8745–8749 (2010)

9. Cover, T.M., Hart, P.E.: Nearest neighbor pattern classification. IEEE Trans. Inf. Theor. **13**, 21–27 (1967)

10. Huang, H., Mehrotra, K., Mohan, C.K.: Rank-based outlier detection. J. Stat. Comput. Simul. **83**(3), 518–531 (2013)

11. Tang, J., Chen, Z., Fu, A.W., Cheung, D.W.: Enhancing effectiveness of outlier detections for low density patterns. In: Chen, M.-S., Yu, P.S., Liu, B. (eds.) PAKDD 2002. LNCS (LNAI), vol. 2336, pp. 535–548. Springer, Heidelberg (2002). doi:10. 1007/3-540-47887-6_53

Tree-Based Structural Twin Support Tensor Clustering with Square Loss Function

Reshma Rastogi$^{(\boxtimes)}$ and Sweta Sharma

Department of Computer Science, Faculty of Mathematics and Computer Science,
South Asian University, New Delhi, India
reshma.khemchandani@sau.ac.in

Abstract. Most of the real-life applications involving images, videos etc. deals with matrix data (second order tensor space). Tensor based clustering models can be utilized for identifying patterns in matrix data as they take advantage of structural information in multi-dimensional framework and reduce computational overheads as well. Despite such numerous advantages, tensor clustering has still remained relatively unexplored research area. In this paper, we propose a novel clustering technique, termed as Treebased Structural Least Squares Twin Support Tensor Clustering (Tree-SLSTWSTC), that builds a cluster model as a binary tree, where each node comprises of proposed Structural Least Squares Twin Support Tensor Machine (S-LSTWSTM) classifier that considers the structural risk minimization of data alongside a symmetrical L2-norm loss function. The proposed approach results in time-efficient learning. Initialization framework based on tensor $k-$means has been proposed and implemented in order to overcome the instability disseminated by random initialization. To validate the efficacy of the proposed framework, computational experiments have been performed with relevant tensor based models on face recognition and optical digit recognition datasets.

Keywords: Twin Support Tensor Machine · Unsupervised learning · Tree-based clustering · Tensor space

1 Introduction

In machine learning applications, particularly image processing, computer vision and bioinformatics, data is often represented in matrix form (second order tensor space). For example- a gray scale image is a order-2 tensor and a video is a order-3 tensor. Here, one of the critical task is to identify the hidden patterns in training data [1]. Most commonly, such data are converted in vector form so as to facilitate the use of vector based clustering or classification models. This arrangements, however, suffers from the limitations of under-representation and high dimensionality (sometimes over-fitting) problem leading to high training time complexity [2,3].

© Springer International Publishing AG 2017
B.U. Shankar et al. (Eds.): PReMI 2017, LNCS 10597, pp. 28–34, 2017.
https://doi.org/10.1007/978-3-319-69900-4_4

Clustering is a powerful technique that aims to group together similar elements in same cluster while maximizing the segregation between dissimilar elements. Recently, in view of limitations of point-based clustering methods in dealing the data which is not distributed around several cluster points, plane based clustering methods such as Maximum Margin clustering (MMC) and Twin support vector Clustering (TWSVC) [4] have attracted considerable research interest. Taking motivation from TWSVC, we propose Treebased clustering framework for clustering second order tensor data. The main contributions of paper includes the following: First, we propose a modified tensor based LS-TWSTM named as Structural LSTWSTM (S-LSTWSTM) [5] classifier that formulates convex optimization problems as system of linear equations that takes care of structural risk associated with the data. Then, S-LSTWSTM has been extended to binary decision structure based clustering framework, termed as Tree-SLSTWSTC, which leads to fast and efficient cluster assignment in tensor framework. Finally, to make our Tree-SLSTWSTC more robust and stable, initialization technique based on Tensor k-means is proposed.

Experiments have been carried out on popular image datasets that establish the out-performance of our proposed algorithm over other vector and tensor based clustering techniques significantly.

The rest of the paper is organized as follows. Section 2 gives the background for our proposed approach. Section 3 discusses our proposed work. Experimental results have been shown in Sect. 4. Finally, Sect. 5 concludes our work and state possible future direction of work.

2   Related Work

Let $X = \{X_1, X_2, ..., X_m\}$ be a training set of m data samples in second order tensor space i.e. $X_i \in \mathbb{R}^{n_1} \times \mathbb{R}^{n_2}$. Let I_1 represent the set of indices with $y_i = 1$, and I_2 represent the set of indices with label $y_i = -1$.

2.1   Least Squares Twin Support Tensor Machine

Working on the tensor generalization of Twin Support Vector Machine [7], Zhao et al. [5] proposed Least Squares Twin Support Tensor Machine (LS-TWSTM) which aims to find a pair of non-parallel hyperplanes given by $f_1(X) = u_1^T X v_1 + b_1$ and $f_2(x) = u_2^T X v_2 + b_2$ where $u_1, u_2 \in \mathbb{R}^{n_1}$, $v_1, v_2 \in \mathbb{R}^{n_2}$ and $b_1, b_2 \in \mathbb{R}$. Following two QPPs are solved to find the corresponding non-parallel hyperplanes:

$$(\text{LS-TWSTM 1}) \quad \min_{u_1, v_1, b_1, \xi_2} \quad \frac{1}{2} \sum_{i \in I_1} (u_1 X_i v_1 + b_1)^2 + c_1 \sum_{j \in I_2} \xi_{2j}^2$$

$$\text{subject to} \quad -(u_1^T X_j v_1 + b_1) + \xi_{2j} = 1, \quad j \in I_2.$$

$$\text{(LS-TWSTM 2)}\quad \min_{u_2,v_2,b_2,\xi_1}\ \frac{1}{2}\sum_{j\in I_2}(u_2X_jv_2+b_2)^2 + c_2\sum_{i\in I_1}\xi_{1i}$$

$$\text{subject to } (u_2^T X_i v_2 + b_2) + \xi_{1i} = 1, \quad i \in I_1.$$

Since the hyperplane parameters are interdependent, the problems are solved using alternate projection method [6]. A test point is assigned a label depending upon its proximity from two hyperplanes. Please refer to [5] for details.

3   Proposed Work

In this work, we first propose a novel tensor classifier termed as Structural Least Squares Twin Support Tensor Machine (S-LSTWSTM), which we further use in an unsupervised framework to propose a binary treebased clustering approach termed as Tree-SLSTWSTC.

3.1   Structural Least Squares Twin Support Tensor Machine

In the spirit of Least Squares Twin Support Tensor Machine (LS-TWSTM) [5], the proposed S-LSTWSTM seeks two non-parallel hyperplanes by considering the following optimization problems:

$$\text{(S-LSTWSTM 1)}\quad \min_{u_1,v_1,b_1,\xi_2}\ \frac{1}{2}\sum_{i\in I_1}(u_1X_iv_1+e_1b_1)^2 + c_1\sum_{j\in I_2}\xi_{2j}^2 + c_2(u_1^T u_1 + v_1^T v_1 + b_1^2)$$

$$\text{subject to } (u_1^T X_j v_1 + b_1 e_2) = e_2 - \xi_{2j}, \quad j \in I_2, \tag{1}$$

$$\text{(S-LSTWSTM 2)}\quad \min_{u_2,v_2,b_2,\xi_1}\ \frac{1}{2}\sum_{j\in I_2}(u_2X_jv_2+e_2b_2)^2 + c_1\sum_{i\in I_1}\xi_{1i}^2 + c_2(u_2^T u_2 + v_2^T v_2 + b_2^2)$$

$$\text{subject to } (u_2^T X_i v_2 + b_2 e_1) = e_1 - \xi_{1i}, \quad i \in I_1, \tag{2}$$

where ξ_1 and ξ_2 are error variables; and e_1 and e_2 are appropriate dimensional matrices of ones. The first term of Eqs. (1) and (2) calculates the empirical risk of the data. Thus, minimizing this term tends to keep the hyperplane close to the data matrices and the constraints require the hyperplane to be at unit distance from the other class. Further, S-LSTWSTM takes care of structural risk minimization (SRM) by introducing the term $(u_i^T u_i + v_i^T v_i + b_i^2, i = 1, 2)$ in the objective function and thus improves the generalization ability. It also takes care of the possible ill-conditioning that might arise during matrix inversion.

Working on the lines on LS-TWSTM [5] for Eq. (1) and setting the gradient of objective function with respect to (u_1, v_1, b_1) to zero, indicates that u_1, v_1 and b_1 are inter-dependent and hence can not be solved independently. Therefore, we use alternating projection method [6].

For any given non-zero vector $u_k \in \mathbb{R}^{n_1}$, let $x_i^T = u_k^T X_i$ and $x_j^T = u_k^T X_j$, we then solve for the following modified optimization problem (obtained after substituting the value of ξ_{2j} in the objective function):

$$\min_{v_k, b_k} \tfrac{1}{2} \sum_{i \in I_1} (x_i v_k + b_k)^2 + c_1 \sum_{j \in I_2} \|e_2 - (x_j v_k + b_k e_2)\|^2 + c_2 (v_k^T v_k + b_k^2). \quad (3)$$

Differentiating Lagrangian corresponding to (3) with respect to v_k and b_k, leads to the following system of linear equations:

$$\begin{bmatrix} v_k \\ b_k \end{bmatrix} = - \left[\frac{1}{c_1} H_1^T H_1 + G_1^T G_1 + c_2 I \right]^{-1} G_1^T e_2, \quad (4)$$

where H_1 and G_1 are matrices of points x_i and x_j augmented with a column of ones; and I is an identity matrix of appropriate dimensions.

Once a non-zero vector $v_k \in \mathbb{R}^{n_2}$ is obtained, let $\hat{x}_i^T = X_i v_k$ and $\hat{x}_j^T = X_j v_k$, we solve for the following modified optimization problem:

$$\min_{u_k, b_k} \tfrac{1}{2} \sum (\hat{x}_i u_k + b_k)^2 + c_1 \|(\hat{x}_j u_k + b_k e_2) - e_2\| + c_2 (u_k^T u_k + b_k^2). \quad (5)$$

Working on the lines as above, we obtain (u_k, b_k) as follows

$$\begin{bmatrix} u_k \\ b_k \end{bmatrix} = - \left[\frac{1}{c_1} H_2^T H_2 + G_2^T G_2 + c_2 I \right]^{-1} G_2^T e_2, \quad (6)$$

where H_2 and G_2 are matrices of points $\hat{x}_i$ and $\hat{x}_j$ augmented with a column of ones. The Eqs. (4) and (6) are solved alternatively until u_k, v_k and b_k converges.

On the similar lines as above, the solution of (2) is obtained. A new test point is assigned a class label similar to LS-TWSTM [5] based on proximity criteria.

3.2 Tree-based Structural Least Squares Twin Support Vector Clustering

Tree-SLSTWSTC algorithm creates a binary tree of clusters which partitions the data at multiple levels of the tree until desired number of clusters are obtained. Unlike TWSVC [4], Tree SLSTWSTC uses symmetric squared loss function at each internal node that handles the issue of premature convergence of cluster framework. The proposed algorithm Tree-SLSTWSVC starts with initial labels $(+1, -1)$. By using the initial labels, the data X with m data matrices is divided into two clusters, A and B, of size $(n_1 \times n_2 \times m_1)$ and $(n_1 \times n_2 \times m_2)$ respectively (where $m = m_1 + m_2$). Each group is then individually partitioned further by considering inter-cluster relationship and is able to generate more stable results in lesser time. Tree-SLSTWSTC is summarized in Algorithm 1.

3.3 Initialization

In conventional plane-based clustering scenarios, the initial cluster labels for data are obtained by randomization which is highly unstable and inefficient

---

Algorithm 1. Tree-LSTWSTC

Input: X: Unlabeled data in order-2 tensor space i.e. $\mathbb{R}^{n_1 \times n_2}$; K: number of cluster; ϵ: tolerance level; $imax$: maximum number of iterations.
Output: Label Y_i corresponding to each datapoint in X_i, $i = 1, ..., m$.

1. Determine the initial labels Y_k, for each tensor data using approach discussed in Sect. 3.3 for K clusters.
2. Repeat
   (a) Create two clusters using tensor based k-means as A_{new} and B_{new}.
   (b) Select initial $[u_1^j, v_1^j, b_1^j]$ and $[u_2^j, v_2^j, b_2^j]$, where $j = 0$.
   (c) Update the hyperplane parameters to find $[u_1^{j+1}, v_1^{j+1}, b_1^{j+1}]$ and $[u_2^{j+1}, v_2^{j+1}, b_2^{j+1}]$.
   (d) Stop if $||[u_i^{j+1}; v_i^{j+1}; b_i^{j+1}] - [u_i^j; v_i^j; b_i^j]|| < \epsilon$, and then $u_i^{final} = u_i^{j+1}$, $v_i^{final} = v_i^{j+1}$ and $b_{final}^{j+1} = b_i^{j+1}$. Otherwise, go to step (c).
3. Use Y_k to determine if A_{new} and B_{new} can be further partitioned i.e. if there are labels from more than one clusters. If required, recursively partition A_{new} and B_{new} and goto Step 1.
4. End.

---

technique. Here, we propose a novel tensor-based initialization algorithms which uses frobenius norm to find the distance between two order-2 tensors (matrices). For example, the distance between two data points $x^\alpha = x(n_1, n_2, 1)$ and $x^\beta = x(n_1, n_2, 2)$ is calculated as

$$d_(x^\alpha, x^\beta) = \sqrt{\sum_{i=1}^{n_1} \sum_{j=1}^{n_2} (x_{ij}^\alpha - x_{ij}^\beta)^2}. \tag{7}$$

We have implemented Tensor k-means (Tk-means), which uses tensor data as input and return corresponding cluster labels in the spirit similar to vector based k-means algorithm. Similar to traditional k-means, iterative relocation algorithm is followed which minimize the mean squared error locally. Henceforth, the centroid of cluster is updated and the process is repeated until labels converges i.e. no more change in label is detected.

4   Experimental Results

To evaluate the performance of the proposed method, experiments were carried out on image dataset of face recognition and optical digit recognition systems. In order to prove competence of our proposed work, we used the Metric accuracy [4] and Learning time as the performance criteria.

For comparison of our proposed approach against other algorithms, we implemented conventional k-means and k−Nearest neighbour graph algorithm in tensor framework. Further, to minimize the effect of randomization (in k-means) and value of k (in NNG), the experiments were performed multiple times, and the best results are reported.

Table 1. Clustering results on face recognition and optical digit recognition application

Dataset	Size	Tensor k-means	Tensor NNG	Tree- SLSTWSTC$^+$	Other methods*
	($n_1 \times n_2 \times m$)	Metric accuracy (Learning time (in sec))			Accuracy
ORL[a]	($92 \times 112 \times 400$)	91.09 (20.04)	87.93 (38.22)	**92.09** (14.01)	78.81 [9]
Yale[b]	($32 \times 32 \times 165$)	88.23 (5.46)	85.02 (0.36)	**90.58** (2.52)	67.35 [9]
Optical digits[c]	($32 \times 32 \times 946$)	95.19 (33.34)	92.62 (34.86)	**96.19** (26.35)	69.12 [8]
MNIST[d]	($28 \times 28 \times 500$)	88.69 (9.46)	68.07 (6.25)	**89.99** (5.32)	82.04 [9]

*State-of-art vector based clustering results.
[a] http://www.cl.cam.ac.uk/research/dtg/attarchive/facedatabase.html
[b] http://archive.ics.uci.edu/ml
[c] http://www.cad.zju.edu.cn/home/dengcai/Data/FaceData.html
[d] http://www.cs.nyu.edu/~roweis/data.html

Table 1 summarizes the results of experiments on the above-mentioned datasets. It is clearly evident here that k-means initialization based Tree-SLSTWSTC outperforms other methods in terms of clustering performance as well as learning time. We have also discussed clustering results obtained from other approaches in Table 1. It can be observed that the prediction accuracy of Tree-SLSTWSTC is significantly better than these methods. Also, it should be noticed that these methods use vector-based representation for clustering.

5   Conclusions

Based on the recently proposed LS-TWSTM, in this paper, we have proposed a novel treebased tensor based clustering algorithm namely Treebased Structural Least Squares Twin Support Tensor Clustering (Tree-SLSTWSTC) which has the capability to directly deal with the real world matrix data (second order tensor space) resulting into improved generalization and reduced Computational complexity. Moreover, it also handles the premature convergence problem as it considers structural risk associated with data. For initializing cluster labels, we have proposed Tensor k-means algorithm which helps to overcome the instability incurred by random initialization. Experimental comparisons of proposed approach against other related approaches on face recognition and handwritten image dataset, establish the suitability of the proposed algorithms to deal with the tensor based data directly (as direct image input).

In future, the application of proposed approach in more challenging real-world applications with higher order tensor space like image segmentation and computer vision can be explored.

References

1. Khemchandani, R., Pal, A., Chandra, S.: Fuzzy least squares twin support vector clustering. Neural Comput. Appl. **1**, 1–11 (2016)
2. Cai, D., He, X., Wen, J.R., Han, J., Ma, W.Y.: Support tensor machines for text categorization (2006)
3. Zhang, X., Gao, X., Wang, Y.: Twin support tensor machines for MCs detection. J. Electron. (China) **26**(3), 318–325 (2009)

4. Wang, Z., Shao, Y.H., Bai, L., Deng, N.Y.: Twin support vector machine for clustering. IEEE Trans. Neural Netw. Learn. Syst. **26**(10), 2583–2588 (2015)
5. Zhao, X., Shi, H., Lv, M., Jing, L.: Least squares twin support tensor machine for classification. J. Inf. Comput. Sci. **11**(12), 4175–4189 (2014)
6. Tao, D., Li, X., Wu, X., Hu, W., Maybank, S.J.: Supervised tensor learning. Knowl. Inf. Syst. **13**(1), 142 (2007)
7. Jayadeva, Khemchandani, R., Chandra, S.: Twin support vector machines for pattern classification. IEEE Trans. Pattern Anal. Mach. Intell. **29**(5), 905–910 (2007)
8. Wang, X., Yang, C., Zhou, J.: Clustering aggregation by probability accumulation. Pattern Recogn. **42**(5), 668–675 (2009)
9. Peng, Y., Zheng, W.L., Lu, B.L.: An unsupervised discriminative extreme learning machine and its applications to data clustering. Neurocomputing **174**, 250–264 (2016)

Kernel Entropy Discriminant Analysis for Dimension Reduction

Aditya Mehta$^{(\boxtimes)}$ and C. Chandra Sekhar

Department of Computer Science and Engineering, Indian Institute of Technology
Madras, Chennai, India
aditya.mhta@gmail.com, chandra@cse.iitm.ac.in

Abstract. The unsupervised techniques for dimension reduction, such as principal component analysis (PCA), kernel PCA and kernel entropy component analysis, do not take the information about class labels into consideration. The reduced dimension representation obtained using the unsupervised techniques may not capture the discrimination information. The supervised techniques, such as multiple discriminant analysis and generalized discriminant analysis, can capture discriminatory information. However the reduced dimension is limited by number of classes. We propose a supervised technique, kernel entropy discriminant analysis (kernel EDA), that uses Euclidean divergence as criterion function. Parzen window method for density estimation is used to find an estimate of Euclidean divergence. Euclidean divergence estimate is expressed in terms of eigenvectors and eigenvalues of the kernel gram matrix. The eigenvalues and eigenvectors that contribute significantly to the Euclidean divergence estimate are used for determining the directions for projection. Effectiveness of the kernel EDA method is demonstrated through the improved classification accuracy for benchmark datasets.

Keywords: Euclidean divergence · Parzen windowing

1   Introduction

The goal of data transformation techniques is to transform a set of large number of features into a compact set of informative features. The data transformation techniques are unsupervised or supervised. In the unsupervised techniques, the aim is to preserve some significant characteristics of the data in the transformed space. The most commonly used unsupervised technique is the principal component analysis (PCA) [4]. It projects a given d-dimensional feature vector onto the eigenvectors of data covariance matrix corresponding to l most significant eigenvalues of the matrix. Kernel PCA [11] performs PCA in the kernel feature space of a Mercer kernel. The unsupervised techniques do not make use of class labels because of which the transformed representation may not be discriminative. In supervised data transformation techniques, the class label information is also used. The commonly used supervised techniques are Fisher discriminant analysis (FDA) [3], multiple discriminant analysis (MDA) [2] and their many

© Springer International Publishing AG 2017
B.U. Shankar et al. (Eds.): PReMI 2017, LNCS 10597, pp. 35–42, 2017.
https://doi.org/10.1007/978-3-319-69900-4_5

variants. The FDA finds a direction for projection along which the separability of projections of data belonging to two classes is maximum. The MDA is a multi-class extension of FDA. Kernel FDA [7] performs the FDA in the kernel feature space. Generalized discriminant analysis (GDA) [1] is extension of kernel FDA for multiple classes. A major limitation of these supervised techniques is that the dimension of transformed data is limited by the number of classes.

In the kernel entropy component analysis (kernel ECA) [5,6] technique, the eigenvectors of kernel gram matrix used for projection are determined based on their contribution to the Renyi quadratic entropy of the input data. The kernel ECA is an unsupervised technique.

In this paper, we develop a new discriminative transformation method that can be considered as an extension of kernel ECA modified for supervised dimension reduction. It chooses the directions for projection that maximally preserves the Euclidean divergence [10] between the probability density function of two classes. An estimator of Euclidean divergence is expressed in terms of eigenvectors and eigenvalues of kernel gram matrix of Gaussian kernel used in Parzen window [9] method for density estimation. The directions for projection are obtained using eigenvalues and eigenvectors that contribute significantly to the divergence estimate.

The paper is organized as follows. In Sect. 2, we present the kernel ECA method. We discuss the proposed kernel EDA method in Sect. 3. Experimental studies and results are presented in Sect. 4.

2   Kernel Entropy Component Analysis

Kernel entropy component analysis (Kernel ECA) focuses on entropy components instead of principal components that represent variance in kernel PCA. The Renyi's quadratic entropy of a distribution $p(\mathbf{x})$ is given by

$$H(p(\mathbf{x})) = -log \int p^2(\mathbf{x})\, dx \tag{1}$$

The information potential of a distribution $p(\mathbf{x})$ is defined as $V(p(\mathbf{x})) = \int p^2(\mathbf{x})\, dx$. The information potential can also be expressed as $V(p) = \mathcal{E}_p(p)$, where $\mathcal{E}_p(.)$ denotes expectation w.r.t. $p(\mathbf{x})$. Consider the data set $D = \{\mathbf{x}_1, \mathbf{x}_2, ...\mathbf{x}_N\}$. Let $k_\sigma(\mathbf{x}_m, \cdot)$ be the Gaussian kernel with σ as width of kernel used in the Parzen window method for estimation of density at $\mathbf{x}_m$. It may be noted that the Gaussian kernel is a Mercer kernel and, therefore, it is a positive semi-definite kernel. Then the estimate of density is given by

$$\hat{p}(\mathbf{x}_m) = \frac{1}{N} \sum_{\mathbf{x}_n \in D} k_\sigma(\mathbf{x}_m, \mathbf{x}_n) \tag{2}$$

Then the estimate of $V(p(\mathbf{x}))$ denoted by $\hat{V}(p)$ is given by

$$\hat{V}(p) = \frac{1}{N} \sum_{\mathbf{x}_m \in D} \hat{p}(\mathbf{x}_m) = \frac{1}{N} \sum_{\mathbf{x}_m \in D} \frac{1}{N} \sum_{\mathbf{x}_n \in D} k_\sigma(\mathbf{x}_m, \mathbf{x}_n) = \frac{1}{N^2} \bar{\mathbf{1}}^T \mathbf{K} \bar{\mathbf{1}} \tag{3}$$

where $\bar{1}$ is an $(N \times 1)$ vector consisting of all 1's and $\mathbf{K}$ is the kernel gram matrix of the kernel $k_\sigma(\cdot, \cdot)$ on the dataset D. Using the eigen decomposition of kernel gram matrix $\mathbf{K}$, Eq. (3) can be rewritten as

$$\hat{V}(p) = \frac{1}{N^2} \sum_{i=1}^{N} (\sqrt{\lambda_i} \mathbf{e}_i^T \bar{1})^2 \tag{4}$$

where λ_i and $\mathbf{e}_i$ are the eigenvalues and eigenvectors of $\mathbf{K}$ respectively. The eigenvectors of $\mathbf{K}$ used for projection are identified based on their extent of contribution to the information potential estimate. It is noted that the kernel ECA method does not make use of the information about the class labels of examples in D.

3   Kernel Entropy Discriminant Analysis

Let D be the data set that consists of data of two classes, $D_1 = \{\mathbf{x}_{11}, \mathbf{x}_{12}, .., \mathbf{x}_{1N_1}\}$ and $D_2 = \{\mathbf{x}_{21}, \mathbf{x}_{22}, .., \mathbf{x}_{2N_2}\}$ which we assume are generated from probability density functions (pdf) $p_1(\mathbf{x})$ and $p_2(\mathbf{x})$ of classes respectively. The Euclidean divergence between the pdfs of these two classes is given as

$$ED(p_1, p_2) = \int p_1^2(\mathbf{x})d\mathbf{x} - 2 \int p_1(\mathbf{x})p_2(\mathbf{x})d\mathbf{x} + \int p_2^2(\mathbf{x})d\mathbf{x} \tag{5}$$

Using the Parzen window technique for pdf estimation the estimate of $ED(p_1, p_2)$ denoted by $\hat{ED}(p_1, p_2)$ is given by

$$\hat{ED}(p_1, p_2) = \frac{1}{N_1^2} \sum_{\mathbf{x}_m, \mathbf{x}_n \in D_1} k_\sigma(\mathbf{x}_m, \mathbf{x}_n) - \frac{2}{N_1 N_2} \sum_{\substack{\mathbf{x}_m \in D_1, \\ \mathbf{x}_n \in D_2}} k_\sigma(\mathbf{x}_m, \mathbf{x}_n) + \frac{1}{N_2^2} \sum_{\mathbf{x}_m, \mathbf{x}_n \in D_2} k_\sigma(\mathbf{x}_m, \mathbf{x}_n)$$

$$\tag{6}$$

Let $\mathbf{z}_1 = [z_{11}, z_{12}, .., z_{1N}]^T$ and $\mathbf{z}_2 = [z_{21}, z_{22}, .., z_{2N}]^T$ be vectors with $z_{ij} = 1$ if $\mathbf{x}_j \in D_i$ and $z_{ij} = 0$ otherwise. Thus Eq. (6) can be written as

$$\hat{ED}(p_1, p_2) = \frac{1}{N_1^2} \mathbf{z}_1^T \mathbf{K} \mathbf{z}_1 - \frac{2}{N_1 N_2} \mathbf{z}_1^T \mathbf{K} \mathbf{z}_2 + \frac{1}{N_2^2} \mathbf{z}_2^T \mathbf{K} \mathbf{z}_2 \tag{7}$$

where $\mathbf{K}$ is the kernel gram matrix of the dataset D. Using the eigen decomposition of $\mathbf{K}$, Eq. (7) can be rewritten as

$$\hat{ED}(p_1, p_2) = \frac{1}{N_1^2} \sum_{i=1}^{N} (\sqrt{\lambda_i} \mathbf{e}_i^T \mathbf{z}_1)^2 - \frac{2}{N_1 N_2} \sum_{i=1}^{N} (\mathbf{e}_i^T \mathbf{z}_1) \lambda_i (\mathbf{e}_i^T \mathbf{z}_2) + \frac{1}{N_2^2} \sum_{i=1}^{N} (\sqrt{\lambda_i} \mathbf{e}_i^T \mathbf{z}_2)^2$$

$$\tag{8}$$

where λ_i are the eigenvalues and $\mathbf{e}_i$ are the eigenvectors of $\mathbf{K}$. We can write Eq. (8) as

$$\hat{ED}(p_1, p_2) = \sum_{i=1}^{N} \lambda_i \left(\frac{\mathbf{e}_i^T \mathbf{z}_1}{N_1} - \frac{\mathbf{e}_i^T \mathbf{z}_2}{N_2} \right)^2 \tag{9}$$

Let $\psi_i = \lambda_i \left(\frac{\mathbf{e}_i^T \mathbf{z}_1}{N_1} - \frac{\mathbf{e}_i^T \mathbf{z}_2}{N_2} \right)^2$. Then $\hat{ED}(p_1, p_2) = \sum_{i=1}^{N} \psi_i$

The term ψ_i is a measure of extent of contribution of λ_i and $\mathbf{e}_i$ to the Euclidean divergence. Certain eigenvalues and eigenvectors for which ψ_i is large contribute more to the Euclidean divergence than the others. By considering only those eigenvalue and eigenvector pairs that contribute significantly to the divergence, we identify the directions for projection that can capture discriminatory features for the data of two given classes.

As the Gaussian kernel is also a Mercer kernel, it is an inner product kernel. Therefore, $k_\sigma(\mathbf{x}_m, \mathbf{x}_n) = \langle \phi(\mathbf{x}_m), \phi(\mathbf{x}_n) \rangle$, where $\phi(\mathbf{x})$ is the kernel space representation of a data point $\mathbf{x}$. The mean vectors for two classes in $\phi(x)$-space are given by $\mathbf{m}_1^\phi = \frac{1}{N_1} \sum_{\mathbf{x}_m \in D_1} \phi(\mathbf{x}_m)$ and $\mathbf{m}_2^\phi = \frac{1}{N_2} \sum_{\mathbf{x}_m \in D_2} \phi(\mathbf{x}_m)$. Then each term in Eq. (6) can be expressed as follows:

$$\frac{1}{N_1^2} \sum_{\mathbf{x}_m, \mathbf{x}_n \in D_1} k_\sigma(\mathbf{x}_m, \mathbf{x}_n) = \frac{1}{N_1^2} \sum_{\mathbf{x}_m, \mathbf{x}_n \in D_1} \langle \phi(\mathbf{x}_m), \phi(\mathbf{x}_n) \rangle = \langle \mathbf{m}_1^\phi, \mathbf{m}_1^\phi \rangle \tag{10}$$

$$\frac{1}{N_2^2} \sum_{\mathbf{x}_m, \mathbf{x}_n \in D_2} k_\sigma(\mathbf{x}_m, \mathbf{x}_n) = \frac{1}{N_2^2} \sum_{\mathbf{x}_m, \mathbf{x}_n \in D_2} \langle \phi(\mathbf{x}_m), \phi(\mathbf{x}_n) \rangle = \langle \mathbf{m}_2^\phi, \mathbf{m}_2^\phi \rangle \tag{11}$$

$$\frac{1}{N_1 N_2} \sum_{\substack{\mathbf{x}_m \in D_1, \\ \mathbf{x}_n \in D_2}} k_\sigma(\mathbf{x}_m, \mathbf{x}_n) = \frac{1}{N_1 N_2} \sum_{\substack{\mathbf{x}_m \in D_1, \\ \mathbf{x}_n \in D_2}} \langle \phi(\mathbf{x}_m), \phi(\mathbf{x}_n) \rangle = \langle \mathbf{m}_1^\phi, \mathbf{m}_2^\phi \rangle \tag{12}$$

Therefore, the estimate of Euclidean divergence $\hat{ED}(p_1, p_2)$ can be expressed as

$$\hat{ED}(p_1, p_2) = \langle \mathbf{m}_1^\phi, \mathbf{m}_1^\phi \rangle - 2\langle \mathbf{m}_1^\phi, \mathbf{m}_2^\phi \rangle + \langle \mathbf{m}_2^\phi, \mathbf{m}_2^\phi \rangle = ||\mathbf{m}_1^\phi - \mathbf{m}_2^\phi||^2 \tag{13}$$

Thus the Euclidean divergence in $\mathbf{x}$ space corresponds to squared Euclidean distance between the means of the data of two classes in the kernel feature space. Let $\boldsymbol{\nu}_i$ be the direction for projections in the $\phi(\mathbf{x})$-space. As in kernel PCA, the vector $\boldsymbol{\nu}_i$ is expressed as follows:

$$\boldsymbol{\nu}_i = \frac{1}{\sqrt{\lambda_i}} \sum_{n=1}^{N} e_{in} \phi(\mathbf{x}_n) \tag{14}$$

where e_{in} is the nth element of $\mathbf{e}_i$. The projection of a given data point $\phi(\mathbf{x})$ in the kernel feature space is given by

$$a_i = \boldsymbol{\nu}_i^T \phi(\mathbf{x}) = \frac{1}{\sqrt{\lambda_i}} \sum_{n=1}^{N} e_{in} \phi(\mathbf{x}_n)^T \phi(\mathbf{x}) = \frac{1}{\sqrt{\lambda_i}} \sum_{n=1}^{N} e_{in} k(\mathbf{x}_n, \mathbf{x}), \tag{15}$$

For a given data point $\mathbf{x}$, the l-dimensional transformed representation using the kernel EDA method is obtained by computing a_i, $i = 1, 2, .., l$ where l is the number of directions for projection chosen.

4   Experiments

First, we analyze our proposed algorithm on a synthetic dataset. Then we evaluate the performance on two-class IDA benchmark datasets and multi-class datasets. We compare the performance of the proposed kernel EDA method with PCA, kernel PCA, kernel ECA, kernel FDA and GDA. We have used the Gaussian kernel for the data transformation techniques. The kernel width σ is chosen empirically for each dataset and in order to make a fair comparison, the same kernel width is used for all the techniques. Linear support vector machine is used for obtaining the classification accuracy on the transformed representation of data. The choice of using a linear classifier helps us identifying how effective is the transformed representation in performing the classification task. The data is split into 75%, 10% and 15% for training, validation and testing respectively.

4.1   Studies on Synthetic Dataset

The synthetic dataset contains 3424 data points randomly distributed on two spirals, shown in Fig. 1(a). The classification accuracies on the transformed data using linear SVM are plotted in Fig. 1(b). The accuracies are shown for kernel PCA, kernel ECA and kernel EDA methods and for different values of l. It is seen that kernel EDA performs better than the other two methods.

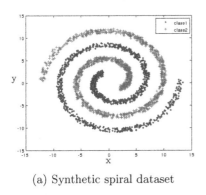

(a) Synthetic spiral dataset

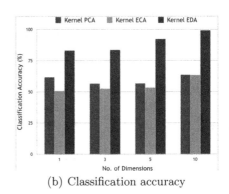

(b) Classification accuracy

Fig. 1. (a) Synthetic spiral dataset (b) Classification accuracies (in %) for different methods for data transformation and for different values of transformed dimensions.

Table 1. Details of the 2-class IDA benchmark datasets used.

Name	No. of Examples	Dimension
Breast Cancer	263	9
Diabetes	768	8
German	1000	20
Image	2086	18
Splice	2991	60
Waveform	5000	21

4.2 Studies on 2-Class Real World Datasets

Details of two-class IDA benchmark datasets [6] used in our study are listed in Table 1. The classification accuracies on transformed representation obtained using different methods are given in Table 2. The results show an improvement in performance for the proposed technique over the existing techniques on almost all of the datasets.

Table 2. Classification accuracies (in %) obtained on the 2-class IDA benchmark datasets for different methods of dimensionality reduction and for different values of reduced dimension.

Dataset	Reduced dimension (l)	PCA	Kernel PCA	Kernel ECA	Kernel FDA	Kernel EDA
Breast Cancer	1	**69.7**	68.2	68.2	68.1	68.2
	3	68.2	**69.7**	68.2	-	68.2
	5	69.7	69.7	69.7	-	**72.7**
	7	69.7	69.7	69.7	-	**72.7**
Diabetes	1	**69.8**	65.1	59.8	61.4	59.4
	3	**67.2**	66.1	66.1	-	**67.2**
	5	68.2	67.7	67.7	-	**71.4**
	7	72.9	75.5	75.5	-	**77.1**
German	1	**69.2**	**69.2**	**69.2**	**69.2**	**69.2**
	3	**69.2**	**69.2**	**69.2**	-	**69.2**
	5	71.6	73.2	74.0	-	**74.4**
	10	**76.0**	75.2	**76.0**	-	**76.0**
	15	75.2	74	74.4	-	**75.6**
Image	1	57.8	58.3	58.3	58.3	**69.9**
	3	71.0	70.8	69.7	-	**75.8**
	5	69.3	71.0	67.2	-	**80.2**
	10	72.2	82.7	82.7	-	**85.8**
	15	83.4	83.8	82.9	-	**87.7**
Splice	1	69.8	69.7	60.0	86.3	**75.0**
	3	67.2	80.6	69.1	-	**77.5**
	5	68.2	**82.1**	80.3	-	80.3
	10	66.1	81.3	81.1	-	**83.7**
	15	65.6	82.1	81.7	-	**84.8**
Waveform	1	57.8	74.3	66.9	**88.9**	73.3
	3	71.0	79.0	**86.7**	-	86.4
	5	69.3	85.6	**89.2**	-	**89.2**
	10	72.2	88.5	89.4	-	**89.6**
	15	83.5	89.0	**89.7**	-	89.4

4.3   Studies on Multi-class Datasets

The kernel EDA can be used in multiclass classification problem by converting the multiclass problem to multiple binary classification problems by using "One vs Rest" or "One vs One" scheme. The datasets of Vogel [12] and MIT [8] scene multi-class datasets used in our studies are given in Table 3. Local block features are used. Each image is divided into fixed size blocks. From each block, the color, edge direction histogram, and texture features are extracted. Thus, each block of image is represented by a 23-dimensional feature vector. The feature vectors from all the blocks in an image are concatenated to get the representation for an image.

The classification accuracies obtained on the transformed representation for the Vogel and MIT datasets using the linear SVM as classifier is given in Table 4. The kernel EDA technique gives a much higher accuracy as compared to the other techniques on MIT dataset. On Vogel dataset, all the techniques give a similar performance.

Table 3. Details of multi-class benchmark datasets used.

Name	No. of Examples	Dimension	No. of Classes
Vogel-6	700	2300	6
MIT-8	2688	828	8

Table 4. Classification Accuracies (in %) obtained on Vogel and MIT datasets for different methods for dimension reduction and for different values of reduced dimension. Performance is also compared for the one-versus-one (1-vs-1) and the one-vs-rest (1-vs-R) approach to multi class classification.

Dataset	Classification Approach	Reduced dimension (l)	PCA	Kernel PCA	Kernel ECA	Kernel FDA	GDA	Kernel EDA
MIT	1 vs 1	1	28.1	20.9	25.7	32.2	25.7	**38.9**
		5	42.9	37.2	41.3	-	46.3	**49.5**
		10	46.6	40.3	45.1	-	-	**50.9**
		20	47.8	45.6	47.2	-	-	**52.5**
		40	47.4	46.6	49.5	-	-	**53.4**
	1 vs R	1	19.4	9.6	**22.2**	16.5	16.5	21.8
		5	33.1	25.0	31.0	-	43.9	40.7
		10	39.3	35.7	39.9	-	-	**43.6**
		20	41.7	39.8	44.1	-	-	**46.3**
		40	46.5	42.1	45.6	-	-	**50.3**
Vogel	1 vs 1	1	30.3	29.6	32.9	25.0	24.3	**34.9**
		5	40.1	32.2	39.5	-	38.1	**42.8**
		10	**40.1**	39.5	38.8	-	-	**40.1**
		20	40.1	39.5	**43.2**	-	-	40.8
		40	40.1	**42.8**	**42.8**	-	-	40.8
	1 vs R	1	6.6	11.8	15.8	**16.4**	16.5	10.5
		5	30.9	29.6	37.5	-	**40.1**	35.5
		10	40.1	38.2	38.8	-	-	**45.4**
		20	**47.4**	39.5	40.1	-	-	42.1
		40	**49.3**	39.5	42.1	-	-	45.4

5   Conclusion

In this paper, we have proposed kernel entropy discriminant analysis as a data transformation method. It uses Euclidean divergence between the estimates of probability density functions of the two classes as the criterion function to decide the directions for projection. Though the kernel EDA is a supervised technique, it is not limited by the number of classes. Studies on various datasets show that proposed kernel EDA performs better or on-par as compared to PCA, kernel PCA, kernel ECA, kernel FDA and GDA.

References

1. Baudat, G., Anouar, F.: Generalized discriminant analysis using a kernel approach. Neural Comput. **12**(10), 2385–2404 (2000)
2. Duda, R.O., Hart, P.E., Stork, D.G.: Pattern Classification. Wiley-Interscience, Hoboken (2000)
3. Fisher, R.A.: The use of multiple measurements in taxonomic problems. Ann. Eugenics **7**(2), 179–188 (1936)
4. Hotelling, H.: Relations between two sets of variates. Biometrika **28**(3/4), 321–377 (1936)
5. Izquierdo-Verdiguier, E., Laparra, V., Jenssen, R., Gmez-Chova, L., Camps-Valls, G.: Optimized kernel entropy components. IEEE Trans. Neural Netw. Learn. Syst. **28**(6), 1466–1472 (2017)
6. Jenssen, R.: Kernel entropy component analysis. IEEE Trans. Pattern Anal. Mach. Intell. **32**(5), 847–860 (2010)
7. Mika, S., Ratsch, G., Weston, J., Scholkopf, B., Mullers, K.R.: Fisher discriminant analysis with kernels. In: Proceedings of the 1999 IEEE Signal Processing Society Workshop on Neural Networks for Signal Processing IX, pp. 41–48 (1999)
8. Oliva, A., Torralba, A.: Modeling the shape of the scene: a holistic representation of the spatial envelope. Int. J. Comput. Vision **42**(3), 145–175 (2001)
9. Parzen, E.: On estimation of a probability density function and mode. Ann. Math. Stat. **33**(3), 1065–1076 (1962)
10. Principe, J.: Information Theoretic Learning: Renyi's Entropy and Kernel Perspectives, 1st edn. Springer, New York (2010)
11. Schölkopf, B., Smola, A., Müller, K.-R.: Kernel principal component analysis. In: Gerstner, W., Germond, A., Hasler, M., Nicoud, J.-D. (eds.) ICANN 1997. LNCS, vol. 1327, pp. 583–588. Springer, Heidelberg (1997). doi:10.1007/BFb0020217
12. Vogel, J., Schiele, B.: Semantic modeling of natural scenes for content-based image retrieval. Int. J. Comput. Vision **72**(2), 133–157 (2007)

A New Method to Address Singularity Problem in Multimodal Data Analysis

Ankita Mandal[iD] and Pradipta Maji[(✉)][iD]

Biomedical Imaging and Bioinformatics Lab, Machine Intelligence Unit,
Indian Statistical Institute, Kolkata, India
{amandal,pmaji}@isical.ac.in

Abstract. In general, the 'small sample (n)-large feature (p)' problem of bioinformatics, image analysis, high throughput molecular screening, astronomy, and other high dimensional applications makes the features highly collinear. In this context, the paper presents a new feature extraction algorithm to address this 'large p small n' issue associated with multimodal data sets. The proposed algorithm judiciously integrates the concept of both regularization and shrinkage with canonical correlation analysis to extract important features. To deal with the singularity problem, the proposed method increases the diagonal elements of covariance matrices by using regularization parameters, while the off-diagonal elements are decreased by shrinkage coefficients. The concept of hypercuboid equivalence partition matrix of rough hypercuboid approach is used to compute both significance and relevance measures of a feature. The importance of the proposed algorithm over other existing methods is established extensively on real life multimodal omics data set.

1 Introduction

Unimodal based pattern recognition and analysis systems usually provide low level of performance due to the noisy nature and drastic variation of the acquired signals, which lead to inaccurate and insufficient pattern representation of the perception of interest. On the other hand, multimodal data contains more information, which is expected to provide potentially more discriminatory and complete description of the intrinsic characteristics of the pattern, which leads to improve system performance than single modality only [5].

Canonical correlation analysis (CCA) [4] finds the best linear transformation to achieve the maximum correlation between two multidimensional data sets. The modern technology has enabled more directions on data streams, which ensues in very high dimensional feature spaces (p), while the number of training samples (n) is usually limited. When the number of samples (n) is very less than the number of features (p), the features in both data sets tend to be highly collinear, which leads to ill-conditioned of the covariance matrices of the

This work is partially supported by the Department of Electronics and Information Technology, Government of India PhD-MLA/4(90)/2015-16).

B.U. Shankar et al. (Eds.): PReMI 2017, LNCS 10597, pp. 43–51, 2017.
https://doi.org/10.1007/978-3-319-69900-4_6

data sets. In effect, their inverses are no longer reliable, resulting in an invalid computation of CCA. There are two ways to overcome this problem. The first possible approach is regularized CCA (RCCA) [11], where the diagonal elements of covariance matrices are increased using a grid search optimization. However, the off-diagonal elements of these matrices remain constant. The another method of regularization algorithm is based on the optimal estimate of the correlation matrices and is known as fast RCCA (FRCCA) [1]. In FRCCA, shrinkage coefficients [10] are estimated to invert the covariance matrices. These shrinkage coefficients reduce the values of off-diagonal elements of covariance matrices, while the values of diagonal elements remain same. However, CCA, RCCA and FRCCA all are unsupervised in nature and fail to take complete advantage of available class label information [1,2]. To incorporate the class information, some supervised versions of RCCA have been proposed, termed as supervised RCCA (SRCCA) [2]. It includes available class label information to select maximally correlated features using grid search optimization.

One of the main problems in omics data analysis is uncertainty. Rough set theory [9] is an effective paradigm to deal with uncertainty, vagueness, and incompleteness. It provides a mathematical framework to capture uncertainties associated with the data [9]. In this context, a feature extraction algorithm, termed as CuRSaR [7], has been introduced. It judiciously integrates the merits of SRCCA and rough sets, to extract maximally correlated features from two multidimensional data sets. In [8], another method, named as FaRoC, has been proposed to generate canonical variables sequentially using rough hypercuboid based maximum relevance-maximum significance criterion. However, all these existing methods fail to produce the optimal set of features.

In general, RCCA increases the diagonal elements, whereas FRCCA decreases the off-diagonal elements to deal with the singularity issue of covariance matrices. So, it is expected to give better results if both can be done concurrently. In this regard, the paper presents a new feature extraction algorithm, which integrates the advantages of both RCCA and FRCCA to handle the ill-conditioned of the covariance matrices. The effectiveness of the proposed method, along with a comparison with other methods, is demonstrated on several real life data sets.

2   Basics of Canonical Correlation Analysis

Canonical correlation analysis (CCA) [4] obtains a linear relationship between two multidimensional variables. The objective of CCA is to extract latent features from two data sets $X \in \mathbb{R}^{p \times n}$ and $\mathcal{Y} \in \mathbb{R}^{q \times n}$. Here p and q are the number of features of X and $\mathcal{Y}$, respectively, whereas n is the number of samples. CCA obtains two directional basis vectors $w_x \in \mathbb{R}^p$ and $w_y \in \mathbb{R}^q$ such that, the correlation between $X^T w_x$ and $\mathcal{Y}^T w_y$ is maximum. The correlation coefficient ρ is given as

$$\rho = \max_{w_x, w_y} \frac{w_x{}^T C_{xy} w_y}{\sqrt{w_x{}^T C_{xx} w_x \, w_y{}^T C_{yy} w_y}} \tag{1}$$

where $C_{xx} \in \mathbb{R}^{p \times p}$ and $C_{yy} \in \mathbb{R}^{q \times q}$. are covariance matrices of X and $\mathcal{Y}$, respectively, while $C_{xy} \in \mathbb{R}^{p \times q}$ is the cross-covariance matrix of X and $\mathcal{Y}$. The basis vectors w_x and w_y are the eigenvectors of matrices $\mathcal{H}$ and $\tilde{\mathcal{H}}$, respectively, with eigenvalue ρ, where

$$\mathcal{H} = C_{xx}^{-1} C_{xy} C_{yy}^{-1} C_{yx}; \quad \text{and} \quad \tilde{\mathcal{H}} = C_{yy}^{-1} C_{yx} C_{xx}^{-1} C_{xy}. \tag{2}$$

If the number of features p and q of X and $\mathcal{Y}$, respectively, is larger than n, the covariance matrices C_{xx} and C_{yy} are ill-conditioned, which make the computation of CCA invalid. That means, the inverses of C_{xx} and C_{yy} do not make any sense [3]. To overcome this problem, RCCA [11] increases the diagonal elements of C_{xx} and C_{yy} by adding small positive quantities, $\mathfrak{r}_x$ and $\mathfrak{r}_y$, which are known as regularization parameters. The optimal parameter set of $\mathfrak{r}_x$ and $\mathfrak{r}_y$ is selected for which the Pearson's correlation is maximum. On the other hand, FRCCA [1] decreases the off-diagonal elements of C_{xx} and C_{yy} by subtracting the shrinkage parameters s_x and s_y. To find the minimum mean squared error estimator of cross-covariance matrix C_{xy}, the shrinkage parameter s_{xy} is used.

3   Proposed Method

This section presents a new feature extraction algorithm, integrating judiciously the advantages of both RCCA and FRCCA to take care of the singularity problem of covariance matrices. The proposed method also incorporates the available class label information to make it supervised. It extracts new features from two multidimensional data sets by maximizing their relevance with respect to class label and significance with respect to already-extracted features. Prior to describing the proposed method for multimodal data analysis, some important analytical formulations are reported next.

To deal with this singularity problem, the proposed method integrates the advantages of both RCCA and FRCCA. Here, regularization parameters $\mathfrak{r}_x$ and $\mathfrak{r}_y$ are varied within a range $[\mathfrak{r}_{min}, \mathfrak{r}_{max}]$, with common differences, d_x and d_y for $\mathfrak{r}_x$ and $\mathfrak{r}_y$, respectively. To address this singularity issue, the covariance and cross-covariance matrices can be formulated as

$$[\tilde{C}_{xx}]_{ij} = \begin{cases} (1 - s_x)[C_{xx}]_{ij}; & \text{where } i \neq j \\ [C_{xx}]_{ij} + (\mathfrak{r}_x + \mathit{l}d_x); & \text{where } i = j \end{cases}$$

$$\text{and} \quad [\tilde{C}_{xy}]_{ij} = (1 - s_{xy})[C_{xy}]_{ij}; \qquad \forall i, j \tag{3}$$

where $\forall k \in \{1, 2, \cdots, \mathfrak{t}_x\}$. Similarly, $[\tilde{C}_{yy}]_{ij}$ can be computed $\forall l \in \{1, 2, \cdots, \mathfrak{t}_y\}$. The parameters $\mathfrak{t}_x$ and $\mathfrak{t}_y$ denote the number of possible values of $\mathfrak{r}_x$ and $\mathfrak{r}_y$, respectively. The best estimator of the shrinkage parameters s_x, s_y and s_{xy}, which minimize the risk function of the mean squared error, can be calculated as [1]

$$s_x = \frac{\sum_{i \neq j} \hat{\mathcal{V}}([C_{xx}]_{ij})}{\sum_{i \neq j} [C_{xx}^2]_{ij}}; \quad s_y = \frac{\sum_{i \neq j} \hat{\mathcal{V}}([C_{yy}]_{ij})}{\sum_{i \neq j} [C_{yy}^2]_{ij}}; \quad \text{and} \quad s_{xy} = \frac{\sum_i \sum_j \hat{\mathcal{V}}([C_{xy}]_{ij})}{\sum_i \sum_j [C_{xy}^2]_{ij}}; \quad (4)$$

where $\hat{\mathcal{V}}([C_{xx}]_{ij})$, $\hat{\mathcal{V}}([C_{yy}]_{ij})$ and $\hat{\mathcal{V}}([C_{xy}]_{ij})$ are the unbiased empirical variance of $[C_{xx}]_{ij}$, $[C_{yy}]_{ij}$ and $[C_{xy}]_{ij}$, respectively. Let us assume that Λ_x and Λ_y be the diagonal matrices, where diagonal elements are the eigenvalues of $\tilde{C}_{xx}$ and $\tilde{C}_{yy}$, respectively and the corresponding orthonormal eigenvectors are in the columns of Ψ_x and Ψ_y, respectively. If $\mathfrak{r}_x$ and $\mathfrak{r}_y$ are varied within a range with arithmetic progression, then following two relations can be established, based on the theoretical analysis, reported in [8],

$$\mathcal{H}_{k\ell} = \Psi_x(\Lambda_x + (k-1)d_x I)^{-1}\Psi_x^T \tilde{C}_{xy}\Psi_y(\Lambda_y + (\ell-1)d_y I)^{-1}\Psi_y^T \tilde{C}_{yx};$$
$$\tilde{\mathcal{H}}_{k\ell} = \Psi_y(\Lambda_y + (\ell-1)d_y I)^{-1}\Psi_y^T \tilde{C}_{yx}\Psi_x(\Lambda_x + (k-1)d_x I)^{-1}\Psi_x^T \tilde{C}_{xy}. \quad (5)$$

As non-zero eigenvalues of $\mathcal{H}_{k\ell}$ are same as non-zero eigenvalues of $\tilde{\mathcal{H}}_{k\ell}$, one of the matrices is enough to compute the eigenvector of $\mathcal{H}_{k\ell}$ or $\tilde{\mathcal{H}}_{k\ell}$ [7], which are the basis vectors $w_{xt_{k\ell}}$ and $w_{yt_{k\ell}}$, respectively.

To compute both the relevance and significance of an extracted feature, the hypercuboid equivalence partition matrix of rough hypercuboid approach [6] is used. The regularization parameters are optimized through computing the relevance and significance measures [7]. Hence, the problem of extracting a relevant and significant feature set $\mathbb{S}$ from all possible combinations of regularization parameters $\mathfrak{r}_x$ and $\mathfrak{r}_y$ is equivalent to maximize the average relevance of all extracted features as well as to maximize the average significance among them. To solve this problem, the following greedy algorithm is used.

1. Compute two covariance matrices C_{xx} and C_{yy}, of X and $\mathcal{Y}$, respectively.
2. Compute the cross-covariance matrix C_{xy}, of X and $\mathcal{Y}$.
3. Determine the values of s_x, s_y and s_{xy} using (4).
4. Compute $\tilde{C}_{xx}$, $\tilde{C}_{yy}$ and $\tilde{C}_{xy}$ using (3).
5. Calculate eigenvalues $\Lambda_x \in \mathbb{R}^p$ and $\Lambda_y \in \mathbb{R}^q$ of $\tilde{C}_{xx}$ and $\tilde{C}_{yy}$, respectively, along with corresponding eigenvectors Ψ_x and Ψ_y.
6. Repeat the following six steps for all (k, ℓ)-th regularization parameters of $\mathfrak{r}_x$ and $\mathfrak{r}_y$, where $\forall k \in \{1, 2, \cdots, \mathfrak{t}_x\}$ and $\forall \ell \in \{1, 2, \cdots, \mathfrak{t}_y\}$.
   (i) Initialize $\mathbb{C}_{k\ell} \leftarrow \emptyset$.
   (ii) Compute $\mathcal{H}_{k\ell}$ or $\tilde{\mathcal{H}}_{k\ell}$ using (5).
   (iii) Calculate all $\mathcal{D}$ basis vectors $w_{x_{k\ell}}$ and $w_{y_{k\ell}}$, which are the eigenvectors of $\mathcal{H}_{k\ell}$ and $\tilde{\mathcal{H}}_{k\ell}$, respectively, where $\mathcal{D} = \min(p, q)$

$$\mathcal{H}_{k\ell} w_{x_{k\ell}} = \rho w_{x_{k\ell}}; \quad \text{and} \quad \tilde{\mathcal{H}}_{k\ell} w_{y_{k\ell}} = \rho w_{y_{k\ell}}. \quad (6)$$

   (iv) Calculate the $\mathcal{D}$ canonical variables $\mathcal{U}_{k\ell}$ and $\mathcal{V}_{k\ell}$,

$$\mathcal{U}_{k\ell} = w_{x_{k\ell}}^T X; \quad \text{and} \quad \mathcal{V}_{k\ell} = w_{y_{k\ell}}^T \mathcal{Y}. \quad (7)$$

(v) The extracted feature $\mathcal{A}_{k\ell}$ can be calculated using $\mathcal{A}_{k\ell} = \mathcal{U}_{k\ell} + \mathcal{V}_{k\ell}$.

vi) $\mathbb{C}_{k\ell} = \mathbb{C}_{k\ell} \bigcup \mathcal{A}_{k\ell}$.

7. Initialize $\mathbb{S} \leftarrow \emptyset$.

8. Repeat the following three steps until $t \leq \mathcal{D}$, where $\mathcal{D} = \min(p, q)$.

   (i) If $t = 1$, calculate the relevance $\gamma_{\mathcal{A}_{t_{k\ell}}}(\mathbb{D})$, otherwise calculate the sig-nificance $\sigma_{\{\mathcal{A}_{t_{k\ell}}, \mathcal{A}_i\}}(\mathbb{D}, \mathcal{A}_{t_{k\ell}})$ where $\mathcal{A}_i \in \mathbb{S}$, of all t-th extracted feature $\mathcal{A}_{t_{k\ell}} \in \mathbb{C}_{k\ell}, \forall k \in \{1, 2, \cdots, t_x\}$ and $\forall \ell \in \{1, 2, \cdots, t_y\}$. $\mathbb{D}$ denotes the decision attribute set. Discard that $\mathcal{A}_{t_{k\ell}}$, if it has zero significance with at least one of the selected features of $\mathbb{S}$.

   (ii) If $t = 1$, select a feature $\mathcal{A}_{t_{k\ell}}$ as t-th feature for which $\gamma_{\mathcal{A}_{t_{k\ell}}}(\mathbb{D})$ is maxi-mum. Otherwise, the feature $\mathcal{A}_{t_{k\ell}}$ has to be selected as optimal for which

   $$\gamma_{\mathcal{A}_{t_{k\ell}}}(\mathbb{D}) + \frac{1}{t-1} \sum_{\mathcal{A}_i \in \mathbb{S}} \sigma_{\{\mathcal{A}_{t_{k\ell}}, \mathcal{A}_i\}}(\mathbb{D}, \mathcal{A}_{t_{k\ell}}) \text{ is maximum.}$$

   (iii) $\mathbb{S} = \mathbb{S} \bigcup \mathcal{A}_{t_{k\ell}}$ and $t = t + 1$.

9. Stop.

4   Experimental Results and Discussion

In the current research work, the multimodal data set, named Ovarian Serous Cystadenocarcinoma (OV), is used with three different modalities, namely, gene expression, protein expression, and DNA methylation. The data set is down-loaded from TCGA. It has 379 samples with two categories: 51 samples of grade 2 and 328 samples of grade 3. This data set contains expressions of 17,814 genes and 222 proteins, and β values of 27,578 methylated DNAs. Total 2000 top-ranked features, based on their variances, are taken from both gene and methy-lation data in the current study. To evaluate the performance of different algo-rithms, both support vector machine (SVM) and nearest neighbor algorithm (NNA) are used. To compute the classification accuracy and F1 score of differ-ent approaches, 10-fold cross-validation is performed. A set of correlated features is first generated for each training set. Then, both SVM and NNA are trained with this feature set. The correlated features which are selected for the training set are used to generate test set. Finally, the class label of the test sample is predicted using the SVM and NNA. Twenty five top-ranked correlated features are selected for the analysis.

In the proposed method, both relevance and significance of an extracted fea-ture are computed using rough hypercuboid (RH) approach [6]. However, mutual information (MI) as well as rough sets (RS) with fuzzy discretization can also be used to compute these two measures. In order to establish the importance of rough hypercuboid (RH) approach over rough sets (RS) and mutual infor-mation (MI), extensive experimental results are reported in Table 1 for three pairs of modalities. All the results reported in Table 1 establish the fact that the rough hypercuboid equivalence partition matrix based approach performs better than other approaches, irrespective of the pair of modalities and classifier used. In 12 cases, out of total 24 cases, rough hypercuboid equivalence partition matrix based approach performs significantly better and in remaining 12 cases

Table 1. Classification accuracy and F1 score of the proposed algorithm

Measures	Classifier used	Different indices	Gene-Protein			Protein-DNA Methy.			Gene-DNA Methy.		
			Mean	StDv	p-value	Mean	StDv	p-value	Mean	StDv	p-value
Accuracy	SVM	MI	0.859	0.028	1.76E-02	0.864	0.030	1.85E-01	0.851	0.047	8.88E-02
		RS	0.854	0.036	3.31E-02	0.831	0.028	1.12E-02	0.844	0.025	7.65E-02
		RH	**0.908**	0.071		**0.879**	0.058		**0.879**	0.060	
	NNA	MI	0.838	0.068	4.50E-02	0.828	0.078	8.10E-02	0.756	0.084	5.55E-04
		RS	0.849	0.072	5.77E-02	0.838	0.077	1.61E-01	0.846	0.077	3.84E-02
		RH	**0.882**	0.069		**0.856**	0.054		**0.879**	0.066	
F1 Score	SVM	MI	0.923	0.014	1.79E-02	0.925	0.016	1.79E-01	0.917	0.027	8.94E-02
		RS	0.919	0.020	2.75E-02	0.907	0.017	1.11E-02	0.914	0.014	1.01E-01
		RH	**0.949**	0.038		**0.934**	0.031		**0.932**	0.034	
	NNA	MI	0.905	0.040	3.63E-02	0.897	0.047	5.48E-02	0.851	0.051	5.08E-04
		RS	0.913	0.041	5.24E-02	0.906	0.045	1.39E-01	0.910	0.046	3.59E-02
		RH	**0.933**	0.038		**0.918**	0.031		**0.931**	0.037	

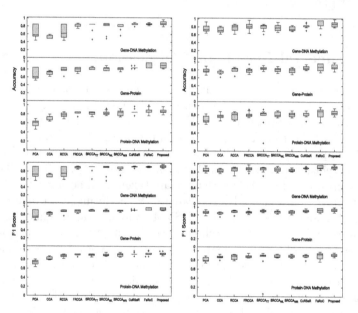

Fig. 1. Box and whisker plots for accuracy and F1 score (left: SVM; right: NNA)

it is better but not significant. This analysis establishes the importance of rough hypercuboid approach over other methods in proposed method.

The performance of the proposed feature extraction algorithm is compared in this section with that of some existing CCA based algorithms, namely, principal component analysis (PCA), CCA, RCCA, FRCCA, several variants of SRCCA using t-test (SRCCA$_{TT}$) [2], Wilcoxon rank sum test (SRCCA$_{WR}$) [2], and Wilks's lambda test (SRCCA$_{WL}$) [2], CuRSaR [7] and FaRoC [8]. The regularization parameters $\mathfrak{r}_x$ and $\mathfrak{r}_y$ are varied within $[0.0, 1.0]$ with 0.1 as common difference.

The box and whisker plots, tables of means, standard deviations, and p-value computed through paired-t (one-tailed) test are used to study the performance of different algorithms and the proposed algorithm. Fig. 1 shows the box and whisker plots for classification accuracy and F1 score. On the other hand, the means, standard deviations and p-values of accuracy and F1 score for all the methods are reported in Tables 2 and 3. The best mean values are marked in bold in these tables. The experimental results are presented on three pairs of modalities, namely, gene-protein, gene-DNA methylation, and protein-DNA methylation. All the results, presented in Fig. 1 and Tables 2 and 3, establish the fact that the proposed method attains the best mean classification accuracy and F1 score in all the cases, irrespective of the pairs of modalities, and classifiers used. The results, reported in Fig. 1 and Tables 2 and 3, demonstrate that the proposed algorithm performs significantly better than other algorithms in 83 cases out of total 108 cases, considering 0.05 as the level of significance. In remaining 25 cases, it is better but not significant.

Table 2. Classification accuracy of the proposed and other methods

Classifier used	Different algorithms	Gene-Protein			Protein-DNA Methy.			Gene-DNA Methy.		
		Mean	StDv	p-value	Mean	StDv	p-value	Mean	StDv	p-value
SVM	PCA	0.677	0.149	7.85E-04	0.595	0.080	7.32E-09	0.654	0.171	9.04E-04
	CCA	0.715	0.050	2.06E-05	0.695	0.055	2.50E-05	0.515	0.046	6.72E-09
	RCCA	0.787	0.068	6.00E-03	0.774	0.052	3.37E-04	0.667	0.164	6.39E-04
	FRCCA	0.792	0.059	2.32E-03	0.828	0.032	4.23E-03	0.823	0.044	2.31E-02
	SRCCA$_{TT}$	0.821	0.034	7.93E-04	0.813	0.042	3.73E-04	0.792	0.126	3.13E-02
	SRCCA$_{WL}$	0.823	0.046	4.36E-03	0.828	0.051	1.48E-02	0.787	0.146	4.56E-02
	SRCCA$_{WR}$	0.813	0.042	9.70E-04	0.828	0.062	1.37E-02	0.797	0.092	4.50E-02
	CuRSaR	0.851	0.026	2.10E-02	0.859	0.054	2.09E-01	0.851	0.026	1.35E-01
	FaRoC	0.897	0.066	2.31E-01	0.867	0.075	3.37E-01	0.859	0.028	1.76E-01
	Proposed	**0.908**	0.071		**0.879**	0.058		**0.879**	0.060	
NNA	PCA	0.677	0.149	9.99E-04	0.692	0.075	2.18E-05	0.759	0.090	5.62E-04
	CCA	0.726	0.050	5.48E-05	0.772	0.053	1.84E-04	0.726	0.072	5.21E-06
	RCCA	0.808	0.068	2.59E-02	0.782	0.083	2.72E-02	0.782	0.083	9.77E-03
	FRCCA	0.797	0.070	8.66E-05	0.805	0.061	1.08E-03	0.808	0.092	3.42E-04
	SRCCA$_{TT}$	0.841	0.050	3.16E-03	0.759	0.216	1.16E-01	0.797	0.082	2.18E-02
	SRCCA$_{WL}$	0.810	0.065	7.98E-04	0.813	0.051	9.60E-03	0.790	0.091	2.31E-04
	SRCCA$_{WR}$	0.797	0.060	4.36E-03	0.818	0.052	7.48E-03	0.762	0.057	2.06E-04
	CuRSaR	0.854	0.050	1.46E-01	0.821	0.065	6.88E-02	0.838	0.055	3.06E-02
	FaRoC	0.877	0.093	4.41E-01	0.849	0.113	4.12E-01	0.864	0.113	3.68E-01
	Proposed	**0.882**	0.069		**0.856**	0.054		**0.879**	0.066	

Table 3. F1 score of the proposed and other methods

Classifier used	Different algorithms	Gene-Protein			Protein-DNA Methy.			Gene-DNA Methy.		
		Mean	StDv	p-value	Mean	StDv	p-value	Mean	StDv	p-value
SVM	PCA	0.793	0.110	1.11E-03	0.731	0.057	1.64E-08	0.765	0.139	1.67E-03
	CCA	0.823	0.035	9.40E-06	0.814	0.034	1.02E-05	0.679	0.039	5.41E-09
	RCCA	0.878	0.045	6.01E-03	0.871	0.034	3.07E-04	0.776	0.130	1.24E-03
	FRCCA	0.882	0.038	2.19E-03	0.904	0.021	2.96E-03	0.901	0.026	2.58E-02
	SRCCA$_{TT}$	0.898	0.019	5.24E-04	0.895	0.027	2.08E-04	0.876	0.100	5.47E-02
	SRCCA$_{WL}$	0.899	0.025	2.62E-03	0.902	0.029	9.43E-03	0.860	0.131	6.21E-02
	SRCCA$_{WR}$	0.895	0.025	8.16E-04	0.901	0.037	8.63E-03	0.881	0.069	5.90E-02
	CuRSaR	0.918	0.014	2.01E-02	0.923	0.030	2.10E-01	0.918	0.016	1.71E-01
	FaRoC	0.944	0.035	2.39E-01	0.925	0.043	2.96E-01	0.922	0.015	2.01E-01
	Proposed	**0.949**	0.038		**0.934**	0.031		**0.932**	0.034	
NNA	PCA	0.793	0.110	9.35E-04	0.806	0.052	2.28E-05	0.853	0.057	5.00E-04
	CCA	0.838	0.035	5.23E-05	0.867	0.035	1.82E-04	0.837	0.046	7.90E-06
	RCCA	0.891	0.044	3.31E-02	0.870	0.056	2.71E-02	0.867	0.069	1.68E-02
	FRCCA	0.879	0.040	3.95E-05	0.885	0.035	1.35E-03	0.884	0.057	4.16E-04
	SRCCA$_{TT}$	0.908	0.027	1.43E-03	0.814	0.269	1.38E-01	0.878	0.070	3.66E-02
	SRCCA$_{WL}$	0.887	0.037	4.73E-04	0.889	0.028	5.67E-03	0.874	0.056	1.57E-04
	SRCCA$_{WR}$	0.881	0.036	3.54E-03	0.893	0.030	7.09E-03	0.856	0.037	2.08E-04
	CuRSaR	0.913	0.029	9.62E-02	0.892	0.040	5.58E-02	0.908	0.031	3.98E-02
	FaRoC	0.930	0.052	4.40E-01	0.904	0.077	2.79E-01	0.918	0.072	3.22E-01
	Proposed	**0.933**	0.038		**0.918**	0.031		**0.931**	0.037	

5   Conclusion

In present days, the 'large p small n' problem becomes a common issue in genetics research, medical studies, risk management, and other fields. If n is very small compared to p, the features become highly collinear, which leads to ill-conditioned of the covariance matrix. The current research work deals with this 'small n large p' problem to overcome the singularity issue of the covariance matrices. The effectiveness of the proposed algorithm, along with a comparison with other algorithms, has been demonstrated considering three different modalities, namely, gene expression, protein expression, and DNA methylation. The concept of hypercuboid equivalence partition matrix is found to be successful in extracting relevant and significant features from high dimensional multimodal real-life data sets.

References

1. Cruz-Cano, R., Lee, M.T.: Fast regularized canonical correlation analysis. Comput. Stat. Data Anal. **70**, 88–100 (2014)
2. Golugula, A., Lee, G., Master, S.R., Feldman, M.D., Tomaszewski, J.E., Speicher, D.W., Madabhushi, A.: Supervised regularized canonical correlation analysis: integrating histologic and proteomic measurements for predicting biochemical recurrence following prostate surgery. BMC Bioinform. **12**, 483 (2011)
3. Gou, Z., Fyfe, C.: A canonical correlation neural network for multicollinearity and functional data. Neural Netw. **17**(2), 285–293 (2004)

4. Hotelling, H.: Relations between two sets of variates. Biometrika **28**(3/4), 321–377 (1936)
5. Lanckriet, G.R.G., Bie, T.D., Cristianini, N., Jordan, M.I., Noble, W.S.: A statistical framework for genomic data fusion. Bioinformatics **20**(16), 2626–2635 (2004)
6. Maji, P.: A rough hypercuboid approach for feature selection in approximation spaces. IEEE Trans. Knowl. Data Eng. **26**(1), 16–29 (2014)
7. Maji, P., Mandal, A.: Multimodal omics data integration using max relevance-max significance criterion. IEEE Trans. Biomed. Eng. (2016). doi:10.1109/TBME.2016. 2624823
8. Mandal, A., Maji, P.: FaRoC: fast and robust supervised canonical correlation analysis for multimodal omics data. IEEE Trans. Cybern. (2017). doi:10.1109/ TCYB.2017.2685625
9. Pawlak, Z.: Rough Sets: Theoretical Aspects of Reasoning about Data. Kluwer Academic Publishers, Dordrecht, Boston and London (1991)
10. Schafer, J., Strimmer, K.: A shrinkage approach to large-scale covariance matrix estimation and implications for functional genomics. Stat. Appl. Genet. Mol. Biol. **4**(1), 1–32 (2005)
11. Vinod, H.D.: Canonical ridge and econometrics of joint production. J. Econometrics **4**(2), 147–166 (1976)

Label Correlation Propagation
for Semi-supervised Multi-label Learning

Aritra Ghosh$^{(\boxtimes)}$ⓘ and C. Chandra Sekharⓘ

Department of Computer Science and Engineering, Indian Institute of Technology
Madras, Chennai, India
aritrag94@gmail.com, chandra@cse.iitm.ac.in

Abstract. Many real world machine learning tasks suffer from the problem of scarce labeled data. In multi-label learning, each instance is associated with more than one label as in semantic scene understanding, text categorization and bio-informatics. Semi-supervised multi-label learning has attracted recent interest as gathering labeled data is both expensive and requires manual effort. Further, many of the labels have semantic correlation which manifests as co-occurrence and this information can be used to build effective classifiers in the multi-label scenario. In this paper, we propose two different graph based transductive methods, namely, the label correlation propagation and the k-nearest neighbors based label correlation propagation. Extensive experimentation on real-world datasets demonstrates the efficacy of the proposed methods and the importance of using the label correlation information in semi-supervised multi-label learning.

Keywords: Semi-supervised learning · Multi-label learning · Graph based learning

1 Introduction

In supervised learning based approaches to multi-class pattern classification, a training example represented by a corresponding feature vector is related to a distinct class (label) describing its semantics. However, for many real-world objects, the single label assumption may not be appropriate. In the task of image annotation, an image can have multiple labels, referred to as a relevant label set. Likewise, in the text categorization task, a news article can be associated with a number of topics like "military", "business" and "international". Multi-label learning has been used for a number of applications like automatic multimedia content annotation [1,2] and bioinformatics [3,4]. The multi-label learning task involves building models which can predict the relevant label set for a test example.

The existing techniques for multi-label learning are predominantly supervised learning based approaches. These techniques require huge amount of labeled data for building a classifier. As labeling the data is both time-consuming and costly,

© Springer International Publishing AG 2017
B.U. Shankar et al. (Eds.): PReMI 2017, LNCS 10597, pp. 52–60, 2017.
https://doi.org/10.1007/978-3-319-69900-4_7

it is undesirable to use only labeled data. However, unlabeled data is easily available and cheap, and the information from it can be used to build better classifiers. In the recent times, semi-supervised learning techniques have been found to be effective in building classifiers.

There have been a number of techniques for semi-supervised multi-label learning (SSMLL) [5–7]. Most of these methods are transductive in nature and they aim at predicting the label set for the existing unlabeled data. It is important to exploit the inherent label correlation present among the labels to boost the performance of the multi-label classifier. For example, it is common to have the natural scene images that contain both "hill" and "tree".

In [5], a graph-based learning framework that accounts for label consistency in the graph and the correlation among labels is presented. After optimising an objective function, a closed form solution for prediction of labels for the unlabeled data is obtained. In [6], the TRAnsductive Multi-label classification (TRAM) is formulated as an optimization problem of estimating label compositions and a closed-form solution is obtained. This method is extended for estimation of the cardinality of the predicted label set for the unlabeled examples based on the estimated label compositions. In [8], the non-negative matrix factorization algorithm is used to solve the problem where the basic hypothesis is that *"two examples which have high similarity in the input space should have similar label memberships"*. All the above methods build a graph with nodes representing the labeled and unlabeled examples, and a similarity measure used as weight of an edge between two nodes. Graph based methods form the majority of semi-supervised learning [9] because of their effectiveness and efficacy.

The rest of the paper is organized as follows. We present the graph based methods for semi-supervised learning from multi-label data in Sect. 2. In Sect. 3, we propose two methods to propagate the label correlation in multi-label learning. Studies on benchmark datasets that demonstrate the effectiveness of the proposed methods are presented in Sect. 4.

2   Graph Based Methods for Semi-supervised Learning with Multi-label Data

In semi-supervised multi-label learning, the training set $\mathcal{D} = \{(\mathbf{x}_1, Y_1), \ldots, (\mathbf{x}_i, Y_i), \ldots, (\mathbf{x}_L, Y_L), \mathbf{x}_{L+1}, \ldots, \mathbf{x}_{L+j} \ldots, \mathbf{x}_{L+U}\}$ consists of L labeled examples $\mathcal{D}_l = \{(\mathbf{x}_1, Y_1), \ldots, (\mathbf{x}_i, Y_i) \ldots, (\mathbf{x}_L, Y_L)\}$, and U unlabeled examples $\mathcal{D}_u = \{\mathbf{x}_{L+1}, \ldots, \mathbf{x}_{L+j} \ldots, \mathbf{x}_{L+U}\}$. The total number of examples is $N = L + U$. The task involves learning a family of K functions, $f_k : \mathcal{X} \times \mathcal{Y} \longrightarrow \mathbb{R}$. Here, $f_k(\mathbf{x}_i, y_k)$ is measure of the confidence of the kth label $y_k \in \mathcal{Y}$ being a label of $\mathbf{x}_i$. The label vector $\mathbf{y}_i = (y_{i1}, \ldots, y_{iK})^T$ is represented as a K-dimensional vector with $y_{ij} \in \{0, 1\}$, 0 indicating that the jth label is not associated with the example $\mathbf{x}_i$ and 1 indicating that the label y_j belongs to the label set of the example $\mathbf{x}_i$. Let $\mathbf{W}$ denote the $N \times N$ weight matrix where w_{ij} represents similarity between $\mathbf{x}_i$ and $\mathbf{x}_j$. The matrix $\mathbf{\Delta} = \mathbf{D} - \mathbf{W}$ is called the combinatorial graph Laplacian matrix where $\mathbf{D}$ is a $N \times N$ diagonal matrix with entries $d_{ii} = \sum_{j=1}^{N} w_{ij}$.

The normalized combinatorial Laplacian is $L = \mathbf{D}^{-1/2}\Delta\mathbf{D}^{-1/2}$. We define Λ, a $N \times N$ diagonal matrix with $\lambda_{ii} = \infty$ for $i \leq L$, and $\lambda_{ii} = 0$ otherwise. The vector $\mathbf{f} = [f_1 \ f_2 \cdots f_N]^T$ has the confidence scores for each of the N examples. This setting is for a binary setting that can be extended to multi-label setting.

In [9], the objective function in the Gaussian Random Field (GRF) method for graph based semi-supervised learning in the single label setting is formulated as follows:

$$E(\mathbf{f}) = E_l(\mathbf{f}) + \alpha E_s(\mathbf{f}) \text{ where} \tag{1}$$

$$E_l(\mathbf{f}) = \infty \sum_{i \in \mathcal{L}} (f_i - y_i)^2 = (\mathbf{f} - \mathbf{y})^T \Lambda (\mathbf{f} - \mathbf{y}) \tag{2}$$

$$E_s(\mathbf{f}) = \frac{1}{2} \sum_{i,j \in \mathcal{L} \cup \mathcal{U}} w_{ij}(f_i - f_j)^2 = \mathbf{f}^T \Delta \mathbf{f} \tag{3}$$

Here, $E_l(\mathbf{f})$ is the term that corresponds to deviation from the already assigned labels (labeled data) and $E_s(\mathbf{f})$ is the penalty term that corresponds to smoothness of labels over the graph. In the second term, if the two examples $\mathbf{x}_i$ and $\mathbf{x}_j$ are similar, the predictions f_i and f_j should be close as well.

In [10], the authors propose the Local and Global Consistency (LGC) method where the two terms are modified given below.

$$E_l(\mathbf{f}) = \sum_{i \in \mathcal{L} \cup \mathcal{U}} (f_i - y_i)^2 = (\mathbf{f} - \mathbf{y})^T (\mathbf{f} - \mathbf{y}) \tag{4}$$

$$E_s(\mathbf{f}) = \frac{1}{2} \sum_{i,j \in \mathcal{L} \cup \mathcal{U}} w_{ij}\left(\frac{f_i}{\sqrt{d_{ii}}} - \frac{f_j}{\sqrt{d_{jj}}}\right)^2 = \mathbf{f}^T L \mathbf{f} \tag{5}$$

In the multi-label setting, the matrix $\mathbf{Y}$ is an $N \times K$ matrix such that y_{ik} is equal to 1 if a labeled example $\mathbf{x}_i$ has label k associated with it, and 0 otherwise. This corresponds to the given ground truth. Similarly, the predicted matrix $\mathbf{F}$ is an $N \times K$ matrix where f_{ik} indicates the confidence of the example $\mathbf{x}_i$ in the label y_k.

The approach in [5] introduces a term $E_c(\mathbf{F})$ corresponding to regularizer for the label correlation. In the $K \times K$ label correlation matrix $\mathbf{C}$, the entry c_{kl} represents the correlation between label y_k and label y_l that can be estimated using the label based co-occurrence. The term $E_c(\mathbf{F})$ is defined as follows:

$$E_c(\mathbf{F}) = \sum_{i=1}^{N} \sum_{k,l=1}^{K} c_{kl}(f_{ik} - f_{il})^2 = -tr(\mathbf{F}\mathbf{C}'\mathbf{F}^T) \tag{6}$$

where $\mathbf{C}' = \mathbf{C} - \mathbf{D}_c$ and $\mathbf{D}_c$ is a diagonal matrix with diagonal entries $d_{c'_{ii}} = \sum_{j=1}^{K} c_{ij}$. Here, $tr(\mathbf{M})$ is the trace of the matrix $\mathbf{M}$. The term $E_c(\mathbf{F})$ quantifies the smoothness in the label space rather than in the input space. If the correlation between two labels y_k and y_l is high, the predictions f_{ik} and f_{il} should be similar.

In the multi-label case, the terms $E_l(\mathbf{F})$, $E_s(\mathbf{F})$, and $E_c(\mathbf{F})$ are computed as follows:

$$E_l(\mathbf{F}) = tr((\mathbf{F} - \mathbf{Y})^{\mathbf{T}}\mathbf{\Lambda}(\mathbf{F} - \mathbf{Y})) \tag{7}$$

$$E_s(\mathbf{F}) = tr(\mathbf{F}^{\mathbf{T}}\mathbf{\Delta}\mathbf{F}) \tag{8}$$

$$E_c(\mathbf{F}) = -tr(\mathbf{FC}'\mathbf{F}^{\mathbf{T}}) \tag{9}$$

$$E(\mathbf{F}) = tr((\mathbf{F} - \mathbf{Y})^{\mathbf{T}}\mathbf{\Lambda}(\mathbf{F} - \mathbf{Y})) + \alpha.tr(\mathbf{F}^{\mathbf{T}}\mathbf{\Delta}\mathbf{F}) - \beta.tr(\mathbf{FC}'\mathbf{F}^{\mathbf{T}}) \tag{10}$$

where α and β are the trade-off parameters. The formulation in (10) is referred to as Multi-Label Correlation Gaussian Random Field (MLC-GRF) and the solution turns out to be the Sylvester Equation [11].

Similarly, the objective function in the Multi-Label Correlation Local and Global Consistency (MLC-LGC) method is formulated in Eq. (11) where μ, ν are hyper-parameters. The solution to the optimization problem in (11) is given by Eq. (12)

$$E(\mathbf{F}) = tr((\mathbf{F} - \mathbf{Y})^{\mathbf{T}}(\mathbf{F} - \mathbf{Y})) + \mu.tr(\mathbf{F}^{\mathbf{T}}\mathbf{L}\mathbf{F}) - \nu.tr(\mathbf{FC}'\mathbf{F}^{\mathbf{T}}) \tag{11}$$

$$(\mu\mathbf{L} + \mathbf{I})\mathbf{F} - \nu\mathbf{FC}' = \mathbf{Y} \tag{12}$$

This equation also turns out to be a Sylvester equation similar to the solution of the MLC-GRF method.

3 Proposed Methods for Semi-supervised Multi-label Learning

3.1 Label Correlation Propagation-GRF (CP-GRF)

As discussed in previous sections, incorporating label correlation information can help improve the performance of the classifier. Our fundamental hypothesis here is that the predictions for a given example should be label correlation consistent i.e., if two labels are correlated and the prediction score for one of the labels is high, the score for the other label should also be high. Thus, the labels of one example are propagated to the correlated labels of that example as follows:

$$f_{ik}^{(t+1)} = f_{ik}^{initial} + \alpha \sum_{l=1}^{K} f_{il}^{t} c_{lk} \quad i = 1, 2...N \quad k = 1, 2...K \tag{13}$$

Here, f^t represents the prediction for a given example at iteration t. The prediction score of a label for a given example is obtained both from the initial prediction ($f^{initial}$) and the other labels based on the correlation between the labels. The parameter α balances the two terms and is chosen by cross-validation. This iterative update is repeated till convergence. The Eq. (13) in the matrix form is given below.

$$\mathbf{F}^{(t+1)} = \mathbf{F}^{inital} + \alpha\mathbf{F}^t\mathbf{C} \tag{14}$$

The CP-GRF method is similar to the page rank approach [12] where the page rank of a webpage is proportional to the page rank of its incoming neighbours. The CP-GRF method takes the higher order label correlations into consideration by iteratively propagating the second order correlations. This method involves the propagation on label correlation graph for each example. The CP-GRF method is expected to perform well when the number of labels is large and the labels have significant correlations. The initial predictions can in principle be obtained from any typical multi-label classifier. In order to validate our method, $\mathbf{F}^{initial}$ is obtained from the GRF method.

3.2   Weighted Label Correlation Propagation-GRF (WCP-GRF)

The WCP-GRF method is an extension of the CP-GRF method. In this method, the correlation is propagated not only from the other correlated labels but also based on the examples close to the particular example. The hypothesis here is that the label correlation is a local effect i.e., the predictions for a given label will be influenced by the predictions for correlated labels of neighbors. Let $kNN(\mathbf{x_i})$ represent the k-nearest neighbours of $\mathbf{x_i}$. The update equations in the proposed WCP-GRF method are given by:

$$f_{ik}^{t+1} = f_{ik}^{initial} + \alpha \sum_{\mathbf{x}_j \in kNN(\mathbf{x}_i)} w_{ij} f_{jl}^t c_{lk} \tag{15}$$

$$\mathbf{F}^{(t+1)} = \mathbf{F}^{inital} + \alpha \mathbf{W} \mathbf{F}^t \mathbf{C} \tag{16}$$

As seen in (15), in each iteration there is a contribution from the initial prediction (any multi-label classifier) as well as from the correlated labels of the k nearest neighbors in the feature space. Since the contribution is only from the nearest neighbors, the WCP-GRF method uses the k-NN based weight matrix $\mathbf{W}$ i.e., the weight entries are 0 if the two nodes are not in the k-nearest neighbors of each other. The matrix update in WCP-GRF method is given by Eq. (16). Here, the initial predictions $\mathbf{F}^{initial}$ are obtained from the GRF method and therefore this is called WCP-GRF method. We use the iterative method and terminate at convergence or after a sufficient number of iterations.

The rest of the proposed methods are the same as the previously discussed methods but use the normalized graph Laplacian instead of the usual graph Laplacian. The other two proposed methods use the LGC method for the initial predictions. The Label Correlation Propagation-LGC (CP-LGC) is the same as Section in 3.1 except for the fact the initial predictions come from the LGC method. Similarly, the Weighted Label Correlation Propagation (WCP-LGC) is the same as in Sect. 3.2 except for the fact that the initial predictions are taken from the LGC method.

4   Experiments and Results

Details of benchmark datasets used for comparison of the various methods are given in Table 1. The evaluation metrics used to compare the various methods are: One error, Coverage, Average precision, Hamming loss and Ranking loss [13]. The label correlation matrix C is calculated using the cosine similarity on the labeled data. For most of the datasets, the label correlation for several pairs of labels is low. However, there are a few pairs of labels with high correlation.

Table 1. Details of the datasets used for experimentation

Dataset	Domain	Examples	Attributes	Labels	Cardinality
Yeast	Biology	2417	103	14	4.237
Image	Image	2000	135	5	1.24
Scene	Image	2407	294	6	1.074
MSRC-v2	Image	591	630	21	2.394
Corel-5k	Image	5000	499	374	3.522

The dataset has been divided into 10% labeled data, 70% unlabeled data and the rest as test data. All hyper-parameters were selected by choosing the maximum average-precision on the validation data over 5 runs. All the results correspond to average of 5 runs and the standard deviation of each metric has also been recorded. The weight matrix used is k-nearest neighbours with a Gaussian function where the width parameter is chosen based on performance on the validation data. The number of nearest neighbours (k) is fixed to 15 as it does not affect the results much. For Hamming loss, the number of labels for a given example is chosen based on the average cardinality of the dataset. All the techniques have been implemented in MATLAB and run on 32 GB RAM 8-core machine. The parameters β, μ and ν were chosen based on cross-validation. The performance of different methods for multi-label classification on different datasets is presented in Table 2. In Fig. 1, the average precision for different sizes of the labeled dataset and for various datasets is plotted. The test ratio is fixed at 20% and the labeled data size is varied. In all the datasets, it is seen that the average precision increases with increase in size of labeled dataset.

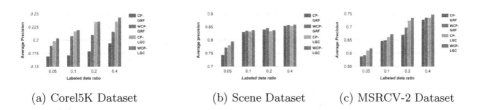

(a) Corel5K Dataset   (b) Scene Dataset   (c) MSRCV-2 Dataset

Fig. 1. Variation of average precision with size of the labeled data for different datasets

Table 2. Performance of the transductive methods for multi-label classification on different datasets

Dataset	Method	HLoss ↓	RLoss ↓	OneEr ↓	Cover ↓	AvePrec ↑
Corel-5k	GRF	0.0182	0.1705	0.8760	0.3571	0.1431
	MLC-GRF	0.0175	0.1699	0.8534	0.3592	0.1675
	CP-GRF	0.0179	0.1695	0.8423	0.3609	0.1715
	WCP-GRF	**0.0162**	0.1782	**0.7762**	0.3606	**0.2077**
	LGC	0.0161	0.1599	0.765	0.3498	0.2187
	MLC-LGC	0.0165	0.1594	0.7687	0.3521	0.2147
	CP-LGC	0.0162	0.1592	0.7697	0.3430	0.2168
	WCP-LGC	0.0163	**0.1554**	**0.7593**	0.3455	**0.2193**
Yeast	GRF	0.2217	0.1910	0.2526	0.4633	0.7304
	MLC-GRF	0.2148	0.1842	0.2601	0.4571	0.7389
	CP-GRF	0.2149	0.1819	0.2410	0.4605	0.7426
	WCP-GRF	**0.2082**	**0.1792**	**0.2373**	**0.4547**	**0.7467**
	LGC	0.2208	0.1933	0.2588	0.4639	0.7262
	MLC-LGC	0.2247	0.1949	0.3052	0.4662	0.7290
	CP-LGC	0.2096	0.1804	0.2422	0.4590	0.7421
	WCP-LGC	0.2133	0.1846	**0.2398**	0.4615	**0.7431**
Scene	GRF	0.1173	0.1066	0.3168	0.1017	0.8132
	MLC-GRF	0.1104	0.1002	0.2906	0.0988	0.8267
	CP-GRF	0.1078	0.0974	0.2865	0.0952	0.8310
	WCP-GRF	**0.1038**	**0.0958**	**0.2761**	**0.0932**	**0.8351**
	LGC	0.1107	0.1004	0.2919	0.0985	0.8274
	MLC-LGC	0.1066	0.0952	0.2869	0.092	0.8306
	CP-LGC	0.1058	0.0964	0.2798	0.0945	0.8326
	WCP-LGC	**0.1040**	**0.0916**	**0.2728**	**0.0910**	**0.8378**
Image	GRF	0.3336	0.2937	0.5275	0.2854	0.6628
	MLC-GRF	0.3355	0.2836	0.4920	0.2795	0.6783
	CP-GRF	0.3245	0.2664	0.4935	0.2656	0.6844
	WCP-GRF	**0.3215**	0.2695	**0.4795**	**0.2634**	**0.6898**
	LGC	0.3232	0.2699	0.4769	0.2678	0.6898
	MLC-LGC	0.3224	0.2687	0.4775	0.2662	0.6901
	CP-LGC	0.3188	0.2627	0.4761	0.2634	0.6945
	WCP-LGC	0.3235	**0.2626**	**0.4655**	**0.2622**	**0.6974**
MSRCv-2 DATASET	GRF	0.1085	0.1883	0.401	0.3227	0.6157
	MLC-GRF	0.1111	0.1917	0.4227	0.3178	0.6225
	CP-GRF	0.1090	0.1750	0.3672	0.3055	0.6468
	WCP-GRF	**0.1074**	**0.1585**	**0.3589**	**0.2810**	**0.6492**
	LGC	0.1316	0.1845	0.3728	0.3029	0.6464
	MLC-LGC	0.1246	0.1543	0.3985	0.2679	0.6525
	CP-LGC	0.1232	0.1609	0.3680	0.2786	0.6625
	WCP-LGC	0.1239	**0.1484**	**0.3611**	**0.2641**	**0.6732**

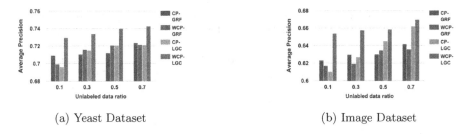

(a) Yeast Dataset   (b) Image Dataset

Fig. 2. Variation of average precision with the size of the unlabeled dataset for different datasets

In Fig. 2, the variation of average precision with size of unlabeled dataset for two of the datasets is plotted. We keep the labeled ratio fixed at 5% and test ratio at 20%. We vary the unlabeled dataset size and observe the effect on average precision. Again, we observe that the average precision increases with increase in the unlabeled data thus showing the importance of unlabeled data.

We observe the following for the transductive methods:

– In most of the cases, the weighted label correlation based method perform better than the other methods.
– In general, the LGC based methods perform better than the GRF based methods. This is expected as the normalized combinatorial Laplacian is a better representative than the conventional combinatorial graph Laplacian.
– Increase in labeled and unlabeled (to a certain extent) data results in an increase in performance

5   Summary and Conclusion

In this paper, we introduced the problem of semi-supervised multi-label learning and discussed some of the recent graph-based semi-supervised methods. We proposed the label correlation based propagation methods to improve the predictions. The proposed methods outperform the state-of-art methods. Extensive experiments validate our hypothesis of the importance of accounting for label correlation and also show the importance of using labeled data and unlabeled data. In our future work, we would like to incorporate higher order correlation directly.

References

1. Boutell, M.R., Luo, J., Shen, X., Brown, C.M.: Learning multi-label scene classification. Patt. Recogn. **37**(9), 1757–1771 (2004)
2. Qi, G.-J., Hua, X.-S., Rui, Y., Tang, J., Mei, T., Zhang, H.-J.: Correlative multi-label video annotation. In: Proceedings of the 15th ACM International Conference on Multimedia, MM 2007, pp. 17–26. ACM, New York (2007)

3. Clare, A., King, R.D.: Knowledge discovery in multi-label phenotype data. In: De Raedt, L., Siebes, A. (eds.) PKDD 2001. LNCS, vol. 2168, pp. 42–53. Springer, Heidelberg (2001). doi:10.1007/3-540-44794-6_4

4. Elisseeff, A., Weston, J.: A kernel method for multi-labeled classification. In: Advances in Neural Information Processing Systems, pp. 681–687 (2001)

5. Zha, Z.-J., Mei, T., Wang, J., Wang, Z., Hua, X.-S.: Graph-based semi-supervised learning with multiple labels. J. Vis. Commun. Image Representation **20**(2), 97–103 (2009)

6. Kong, X., Ng, M.K., Zhou, Z.-H.: Transductive multilabel learning via label set propagation. IEEE Trans. Knowl. Data Eng. **25**(3), 704–719 (2013)

7. Chen, G., Song, Y., Wang, F., Zhang, C.: Semi-supervised multi-label learning by solving a Sylvester equation. In: SDM, SIAM, pp. 410–419 (2008)

8. Liu, Y., Jin, R., Yang, L.: Semi-supervised multi-label learning by constrained non-negative matrix factorization. In: Proceedings of the National Conference on Artificial Intelligence, vol. 21(1), p. 42. AAAI Press, MIT Press, MenloPark, Cambridge, London (1999/2006)

9. Zhu, X., Ghahramani, Z., Lafferty, J.: Semi-supervised learning using Gaussian fields and harmonic functions. In: ICML, vol. 3, pp. 912–919 (2003)

10. Zhou, D., Bousquet, O., Lal, T.N., Weston, J., Scholkopf, B.: Learning with local and global consistency. Adv. Neural Inf. Process. Syst. **16**, 321–328 (2004)

11. Hu, Q., Cheng, D.: The polynomial solution to the Sylvester matrix equation. Appl. Math. Lett. **19**(9), 859–864 (2006)

12. Page, L., Brin, S., Motwani, R., Winograd, T.: The PageRank citation ranking: bringing order to the web. Stanford Info Lab, Technical Report 1999-66, November 1999, Previous number = SIDL-WP-1999-0120

13. Zhang, M.-L., Zhou, Z.-H.: A review on multi-label learning algorithms. IEEE Trans. Knowl. Data Eng. **26**(8), 1819–1837 (2014)

Formulation of Two Stage Multiple Kernel Learning Using Regression Framework

S.S. Shiju, Asif Salim, and S. Sumitra[✉]

Department of Mathematics, Indian Institute of Space Science and Technology, Thiruvananthapuram, India
{shijusnair.13,sumitra}@iist.ac.in, asifsalim.16@res.iist.ac.in

Abstract. Multiple kernel learning (MKL) is an approach to find the optimal kernel for kernel methods. We formulated MKL as a regression problem for analyzing the regression data and hence the data modeling problem involves the computation of two functions, namely, the optimal kernel function which is related with MKL and the optimal regression function which generates the data. As such a formulation demands more space requirements supervised pre-clustering technique has been used for selecting the vital data points. We used two stage optimization for finding the models, in which, the optimal kernel function is found in the first stage and the optimal regression function in the second stage. Using kernel ridge regression the proposed method had been applied on real world problems and the experimental results were found to be promising.

Keywords: Multiple kernel learning · Regression · Kernel ridge regression

1 Introduction

Kernel algorithms have been successfully applied to various machine learning applications. Compared to other machine learning approaches, kernel algorithms have a strong theoretical foundation and become a popular tool because of their guaranteed convergence and good generalization capacity. Support Vector Machine [3], Kernal Principal Component Analysis [16], Kernel Ridge Regression [14] etc. are examples of kernel algorithms.

Kernel methods represent the solution f of the learning problem in the form

$$f(x) = \sum_{i=1}^{N} \alpha_i k(x, x_i) \tag{1}$$

where $x_i \in \mathbb{R}^n, i = 1, \dots N$, are the given inputs, k is the reproducing kernel corresponding to the reproducing kernel Hilbert space in which f lies and $\alpha_i \in \mathbb{R}, i = 1, 2, \dots N$.

The performance of a kernel algorithm depends on the selection of reproducing kernel. The selection of suitable kernel can be automated using multiple

© Springer International Publishing AG 2017
B.U. Shankar et al. (Eds.): PReMI 2017, LNCS 10597, pp. 61–68, 2017.
https://doi.org/10.1007/978-3-319-69900-4_8

kernel learning (MKL) algorithms, that is, these algorithms select the most suitable reproducing kernel from a pool of kernels by itself. Many formulations of MKL are proposed for learning the kernels which are extensively surveyed in [12].

Generally, in multiple kernel learning algorithms, the reproducing kernel is defined as a linear combination of a set of kernels. Using this concept, (1) can be written as

$$f(x) = \sum_{i=1}^{N} \alpha_i \sum_{l=1}^{P} d_l k_l(x_i, x), d_l \geq 0 \tag{2}$$

where k_l are the reproducing kernels under consideration. The parameters in (2) can be optimized either by using two-step optimization [15] or one-step optimization [11]. In one-step method, all the parameters are updated in each iteration of optimization algorithm. In two step method, the learning parameters (α_i) are optimized in first step by fixing kernel weights and kernel weights (d_l) are updated in next step (fixing learning parameters) and this process continues until convergence. One step method mostly uses an alignment measure [5] which is defined between the kernels. [7,9,19] are extensions of one step optimization technique in which the objective is to minimize the alignment between ideal kernel and combination of kernels by applying techniques like semi-definite programming, advanced gradient based methods *etc*. The works, [6,18] use two stage optimization technique for solving the MKL. The faster optimization of parameters for adapting to large scale data set is detailed in [2,17]. The non linear combination of kernels have been used in [4].

[10] used binary classification approach for finding the optimal kernel associated with binary classification problems. That is in this approach the optimal kernel is a function $f^* : \mathcal{X}^* \subset \mathbb{R}^P \to \mathbb{R}$ such that

$$f^*(z) = d^T z \tag{3}$$

where $\mathcal{X}^* = Range(k_1(.,.)) \times Range(k_2(.,.)) \times ... \times Range(k_P(.,.))$ and $d = \{d_1, d_2, ... d_P\}^T \in \mathbb{R}^P$ is as given in (2). From (3) it is clear that f^* is a hyperplane defined on $\mathcal{X}^*$. Using this approach (2) is represented as

$$f(x) = \sum_{i=1}^{N} \alpha_i f^*(\tilde{K}(x, x_i)) \tag{4}$$

where $\tilde{K}(x, x_i) = [k_1(x, x_i) \ k_2(x, x_i) \ ... \ k_p(x, x_i)]^T$.

f^* is found out using the N^2 data points $\{(\tilde{K}(x_i, x_j), y_i y_j), i, j = 1, 2, ... N\}$. The output for f^* is generated using the ideal kernel, that is, $f^*(\tilde{K}(x_i, x_j)) = k(x_i, x_j) = y_i * y_j$ where x_i and x_j are input data points and y_i and y_j are corresponding labels.

The main contribution of this paper is the formulation of MKL as a regression problem for solving regression data sets. For that the methodology used by [10] is adopted. We proved that the ideal kernel for this formulation is same that of [10]. The main challenge in that approach is that, for training f^*, N^2 training points has to be stored in memory. [10] used a fast optimization algorithm using all N^2

points for training f^*. On the other hand we used data compression approach, namely, supervised pre-clustering approach for finding the vital points. Kernel Ridge regression was used for finding the models.

The rest of the paper can be summarized as follows. The details of the model we proposed is given in Sect. 2: we proved that ideal kernel concept used in classification MKL algorithms is valid for MKL Regression formulation also. Its description is given in Sect. 2.1; the concept of supervised pre-clustering is explained in Sect. 2.2, while the details of optimization we followed is discussed in Sect. 2.3. In Sect. 3 the experimental results and their analysis are given.

2   Regression Frame Work for MKL

We adopted the techniques used in [10] for developing the regression framework for MKL. This section explains the different components of the model we developed.

For developing f^* using regression, input and output data is needed. As the objective of MKL algorithms is to find the best possible kernel, it could be assumed that the output of f^* is the same as the output of the best available kernel (ideal kernel). We have proved that the ideal kernel for regression is $k(x_i, x_j) = y_i.y_j$ using kernel ridge regression framework. The description is given below.

2.1   Ideal Kernel Over Regression Data

The cost function corresponding to kernel ridge regression can be stated as

$$\min_{\alpha \in \mathbb{R}^n} \frac{1}{2}\|K\alpha - y\|^2 + \frac{\lambda}{2}\alpha^T K\alpha$$

where K is the kernel matrix, y is the training output vector, $\lambda > 0$ is the regularization parameter and α is the solution vector. The representation for optimal α is

$$\alpha = (K + \lambda I)^{-1}y \tag{5}$$

Let v be the actual output value for a data point x then its predicted output label v_{pred} can be written as

$$\tilde{k}^T \alpha = v_{pred} \tag{6}$$

where $\tilde{k} = [k(x_1, x)\ k(x_2, x)\ldots k(x_N, x)]^T$,

If the ij^{th} element of the kernel matrix is $k(x_i, x_j) = y_i * y_j$ then (5) can be written as below

$$\alpha = (yy^T + \lambda I)^{-1}y \tag{7}$$

where $y = [y_1, y_2, \ldots y_N]^T$

Now $\tilde{k} = yv$ and hence (6) becomes

$$v_{pred} = vy^T \alpha$$

Using Eq. (7)

$$v_{pred} = vy^T (yy^T + \lambda I)^{-1}y \tag{8}$$

Using Sherman-Morrison Theorem inverse associated with (8) can be found. If A is an invertible square matrix and u, v are column vectors, then Sherman-Morrison formula states that

$$(A + uv^T)^{-1} = A^{-1} - \frac{A^{-1}uv^T A^{-1}}{1 + v^T A^{-1}u} \tag{9}$$

If we consider $A = \lambda I$ and $u = v = y$ then

$$(\lambda I + yy^T)^{-1} = (\lambda I)^{-1} - \frac{(\lambda I)^{-1}yy^T(\lambda I)^{-1}}{1 + y^T(\lambda I)^{-1}y} = \frac{I}{\lambda} - \frac{\frac{yy^T}{\lambda^2}}{1 + \frac{y^T y}{\lambda}} \tag{10}$$

Now

$$y^T(yy^T + \lambda I)^{-1}y = y^T \left(\frac{I}{\lambda} - \frac{\frac{yy^T}{\lambda^2}}{1 + \frac{y^T y}{\lambda}} \right) y = \frac{y^T y}{\lambda} - \frac{\frac{y^T yy^T y}{\lambda^2}}{1 + \frac{y^T y}{\lambda}}$$

$$= \frac{\frac{y^T y}{\lambda}}{1 + \frac{y^T y}{\lambda}} \tag{11}$$

Therefore

$$y^T (yy^T + \lambda I)^{-1}y \to 1, \text{ when } \lambda \to 0 \tag{12}$$

Substituting Eq. (12) in Eq. (8) we get

$$v_{pred} = vy^T (yy^T + \lambda I)^{-1}y \sim v \times 1 \sim v \tag{13}$$

This means that $k(x_i, x_j) = y_i y_j$ is an ideal kernel for regression problems.

2.2   Data Compression

As discussed earlier the data points corresponding to f^* scales as $O(N^2)$. We used supervised pre-clustering approach for compressing the data in an efficient manner.

[13] developed a supervised pre-clustering approach for scaling kernel based regression by making use of the concepts of uniform continuity and compactness. In the pre-clustering approach developed by [13], the function f to be learned is uniformly continuous, by assuming that it lies in a continuous RKHS $\mathcal{F}$, having the domain of its members a compact set $\mathcal{X}$. i.e., for the function f, corresponding to similarity measure ϵ, there exists a radius, δ, independent of $x \in \mathcal{X}$, such that

$$\hat{d}(f(x), f(x')) < \epsilon \; \forall \; x' \in B(x, \delta) \tag{14}$$

The basic idea of pre-clustering is that any data points which satisfy (14) can be considered to be "similar" and therefore form pre-clusters. The centers of the clusters are then used as a sparse data set for the function estimation.

If $M << N$ are the data points after compression then f^* can be found using the $M^2 << N^2$ data points $\left\{ \left(\tilde{K}(x_i, x_j), y_i y_j \right), i, j = 1, 2, \dots M \right\}$.

2.3   Two Stage Approach

We used two stage optimization for finding f and f^*, that is f^* is first solved and then f is found out using the new f^*. Kernel ridge regression approach is used to find f and f^*.

M^2 data points find out using pre-clustering approach is used to train f^*, that is the input data is $\left\{ \left(\tilde{K}(x_i, x_j), y_i y_j \right), i, j = 1, 2, \ldots M \right\}$. The corresponding outputs are generated using the ideal kernel. As f^* is in the form of a hyperplane it is assumed that it lies in a RKHS whose reproducing kernel is the linear kernel.

Let $\tilde{K}$ be the kernel matrix associated with f. Then its ij^{th} element $\tilde{k}_{ij} = f^*(\hat{K}(x_i, x_j))$. The optimal α associated with f is found out by minimizing

$$\frac{1}{2}\|\tilde{K}\alpha - y\|^2 + \frac{\lambda}{2}\alpha^T \alpha$$

On solving this equation, we get α as

$$\alpha = (\tilde{K} + \lambda I)^{-1} y \tag{15}$$

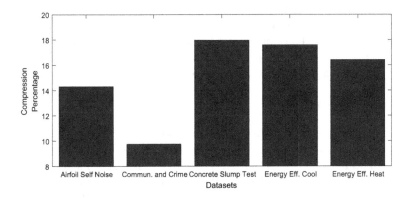

Fig. 1. Compression rate

3   Experiments

The algorithm we developed is named as Two stage Multiple kernel learning approach for regression (TSMKLR). The experimental results are given below.

3.1   Setup

We implemented the proposed algorithms in matlab. The performance of TSMKLR was compared with that of SimpleMKL [15] and SPG-MKL [8] (a modified version of GMKL [18]). The codes for SimpleMKL [15] and SPG-MKL [8] are

Table 1. TSMKL results table

Dataset	KRR	SimpleMKL	SPG-GMKL	TSMKL
Airfoil self noise	4.22529 ± 0.17282 (4)	3.83287 ± 0.20978 (3)	3.40593 ± 0.32411 (2)	3.13291 ± 0.29307 (1)
Commun. and crime	5.82782 ± 0.33076 (2)	5.79657 ± 0.29028 (2)	5.86840 ± 0.29237 (2)	5.00437 ± 0.31056 (1)
Concrete slump test	7.53245 ± 0.51391 (4)	6.48337 ± 0.45852 (3)	6.09983 ± 0.52536 (2)	5.46865 ± 0.38802 (1)
Energy eff. cool	1.85125 ± 0.12772 (3)	1.33792 ± 0.10755 (2)	1.23957 ± 0.10164 (2)	1.15763 ± 0.10176 (1)
Energy eff. heat	2.68947 ± 0.18045 (4)	2.40471 ± 0.21294 (3)	1.40673 ± 0.03337 (2)	1.04312 ± 0.14548 (1)
Average	3.4	2.6	2	1

taken from the author web pages. All the experiments were conducted on the same machine throughout under similar conditions.

Using different hyper parameters in reproducing kernel functions such as Laplacian Kernel, Gaussian Kernel and Polnomial Kernel, 42 base kernels were generated. The σ of both Laplace and Gaussian kernel are assigned with values from $[2^{-9}, 2^{-8}, ..., 2^9]$. The polynomial kernel of degree 1,2,3 and 4 were used. The performance for the proposed model were assessed using root mean square (RMSE). Datasets are collected from UCI repository [1].

3.2 Results and Analysis

Using pre-clustering approach data was compressed. The ratio of compression for the datasets are shown in Fig. 1. The compressed data are used to compute the training points for f^*. Using f^*, f was computed. The experimental results are shown in Table 1. It shows that TSMKLR produced superior results in comparison with other models. The difference between the results of TSMKLR and that of other models were statistically significant.

The t-test was performed over the 30 times hold out results for verifying the statistical significance of the results (significance level $\alpha = 0.1$). Based on the statistical significance measure, the models were ranked for their performance on each data. For example: let M_1 and M_2 are two models; let P_1 and P_2 are the values of a performance measure P for a given data set D. Then we say that M_1 is better than M_2 on the basis of P on D if $P_1 > P_2$ and their difference is statistically significant.

4   Conclusion

We have extended the two stage MKL algorithm binary classification framework to regression domain. For that we proved that the ideal kernel for regression is

$k(x_i, x_j) = y_i y_j$. The supervised pre-clustering approach was used to select the vital points. The experiment results clearly proved that the proposed framework is a suitable approach in finding the optimal kernel as far regression data is concerned.

References

1. Asuncion, A., Newman, D.: UCI machine learning repository (2007). http://www.ics.uci.edu/~mlearn/MLRepository.html
2. Bach, F.R., Lanckriet, G.R.G., Jordan, M.I.: Multiple kernel learning, conic duality, and the SMO algorithm. In: Proceedings of the Twenty-First International Conference on Machine Learning, ICML 2004, p. 6. ACM (2004)
3. Boser, B.E., Guyon, I.M., Vapnik, V.N.: A training algorithm for optimal margin classifiers. In: Proceedings of the Fifth Annual Workshop on Computational Learning Theory, COLT 1992, pp. 144–152. ACM, New York (1992). http://doi.acm.org/10.1145/130385.130401
4. Cortes, C., Mohri, M., Rostamizadeh, A.: Learning non-linear combinations of kernels. In: Bengio, Y., Schuurmans, D., Lafferty, J., Williams, C., Culotta, A. (eds.) Advances in Neural Information Processing Systems, vol. 22, pp. 396–404 (2009)
5. Cristianini, N., Kandola, J., Elisseeff, A., Shawe-Taylor, J.: On kernel-target alignment. In: Advances in Neural Information Processing Systems, vol. 14, pp. 367–373. MIT Press (2002)
6. Gonen, M., Alpaydn, E.: Localized algorithms for multiple kernel learning. Pattern Recogn. **46**(3), 795–807 (2013)
7. Igel, C., Glasmachers, T., Mersch, B., Pfeifer, N., Meinicke, P.: Gradient-based optimization of kernel-target alignment for sequence kernels applied to bacterial gene start detection. IEEE/ACM Trans. Comput. Biol. Bioinform. **4**(2), 216–226 (2007)
8. Jain, A., Vishwanathan, S.V.N., Varma, M.: SPG-GMKL: generalized multiple kernel learning with a million kernels. In: Proceedings of the ACM SIGKDD Conference on Knowledge Discovery and Data Mining, August 2012
9. Kandola, J., Shawe-Taylor, J., Cristianini, N.: Optimizing kernel alignment over combinations of kernels. Technical report 121, Department of Computer Science, Royal Holloway, University of London, UK (2002)
10. Kumar, A., Niculescu-Mizil, A., Kavukcuoglu, K., Daume III., H.: A Binary Classification Framework for Two-Stage Multiple Kernel Learning. ArXiv e-prints, June 2012
11. Lanckriet, G.R.G., Cristianini, N., Bartlett, P., Ghaoui, L.E., Jordan, M.I.: Learning the kernel matrix with semi-definite programming. J. Mach. Learn. Res. **5**, 27–72 (2004)
12. Mehmet, G., Ethem, A.: Multiple kernel learning algorithms. J. Mach. Learn. Res. **12**, 2211–2268 (2011)
13. Nair, S.S., Dodd, T.J.: Supervised pre-clustering for sparse regression. Int. J. Syst. Sci. **46**(7), 1161–1171 (2015)
14. Pozdnoukhov, A.: The analysis of kernel ridge regression learning algorithm. Idiap-RR Idiap-RR-54-2002, IDIAP, Martigny, Switzerland (2002)
15. Rakotomamonjy, A., Bach, F.R., Canu, S., Grandvalet, Y.: Simple MKL. J. Mach. Learn. Res. **9**, 2491–2521 (2008)
16. Schölkopf, B., Smola, A., Müller, K.R.: Nonlinear component analysis as a kernel eigenvalue problem. Neural Comput. **10**(5), 1299–1319 (1998). doi:10.1162/089976698300017467

17. Sonnenburg, S., Ratsch, G., Schafer, C., Scholkopf, B.: Large scale multiple kernel learning. J. Mach. Learn. Res. **7**, 1531–1565 (2006)
18. Varma, M., Babu, B.: More generality in efficient multiple kernel learning. In: Proceedings of the International Conference on Machine Learning, pp. 1065–1072, June 2009
19. Yu, S., Tranchevent, L.C., Moor, B.D., Moreau, Y.: Kernel-Based Data Fusion for Machine Learning, vol. 345. Springer, Heidelberg (2011)

A Two-Stage Conditional Random Field Model Based Framework for Multi-Label Classification

Abhiram Kumar Singh[✉] and C. Chandra Sekhar

Department of Computer Science and Engineering,
Indian Institute of Technology Madras, Chennai, India
{abhi,chandra}@cse.iitm.ac.in

Abstract. Multi-label classification (MLC) deals with the task of assigning an instance to all its relevant classes. This task becomes challenging in the presence of the label dependencies. The MLC methods that assume label independence do not use the dependencies among labels. We present a two-stage framework which improves the performance of MLC by using label dependencies. In the first stage, a standard MLC method is used to get the confidence scores for different labels. A conditional random field (CRF) is used in the second stage that improves the performance of the first-stage MLC by using the label dependencies among labels. An optimization-based framework is used to learn the structure and parameters of the CRF. Experiments show that the proposed model performs better than the state-of-the-art methods for MLC.

Keywords: Label dependence · Conditional Random Field · Multi-label Classification

1 Introduction

In the single-label classification (SLC) problem, each data instance is assigned to one class out of two or more classes. However, in real world tasks, an object can have multiple labels. For example, a news article may have multiple topics, an image may have multiple labels and a medical diagnosis may lead to multiple diseases. Multi-label classification (MLC) [1] deals with the task of assigning such instances to all its relevant classes.

Traditional methods for MLC either transform the MLC problem into several SLC problems (problem transformation methods) or adapt an SLC method for multi-label datasets (algorithm adaptation methods). These methods assume the label independence and may give inconsistent output. For example, an instance may be assigned to two mutually exclusive labels. A method that can correct these errors due to inconsistencies by exploiting the label dependencies is likely to give an improved performance.

We present a framework based on the conditional random field (CRF) that tries to correct the erroneous output from a multi-label classifier by using the dependencies among labels. Results of our studies show that capturing dependencies among the class labels significantly improves the performance of MLC.

© Springer International Publishing AG 2017
B.U. Shankar et al. (Eds.): PReMI 2017, LNCS 10597, pp. 69–76, 2017.
https://doi.org/10.1007/978-3-319-69900-4_9

The rest of the paper is organised as follows. In Sect. 2, we present a brief review of methods for using the label dependencies in MLC. Section 3 presents the proposed framework that uses the CRF to capture the label dependencies and then use the dependencies to correct the errors in the output of an MLC model. In Sect. 4, we present our experimental studies and results.

2   Approaches to Capture Label Correlations

Capturing label correlations and using them for multi-label learning is important for MLC. We review some of the methods for capturing the correlations among labels.

Classifier chain [2] is based on the chain rule decomposition of the joint probability distribution where each factor in the chain decomposition is realized using a binary classifier. The input to a classifier in the chain is augmented with the output from the previous binary classifiers in the chain. The limitation of this method is that the performance depends on the chain order. Ensemble of classifier chains [2] mitigate the problem of performance dependence on the chain order by taking the average over predictions obtained using different chain orders. A Bayesian network is used in [3] to learn the relationship among the labels. Then, it uses the classifier chain method where the topological ordering of labels in the Bayesian network is considered as the chain order and the feature vector is augmented with the output from the parent class classifier. In [4], a cyclic directed graphical model is used to capture the relationships among labels. The model is built by learning a binary classifier for a label given all other labels and input features. Then the Gibbs sampling is used for inference. In [5], a two stage binary relevance method is used. In this method, the input to the second stage of binary classifiers is augmented with the output from the binary classifiers in the first stage.

Methods for MLC using the undirected graphical model have been proposed in [6–9]. In [6], a pairwise Markov random field is used for joint prediction of labels. Similarly, in [7,8], a pairwise CRF is used where a tree-structured graph is constructed to identify the set of informative label pairs in [7]. In [8], a fully connected graph with the pairwise clique potentials is used.

3   Enhancing Multi-label Classification Using Label Dependencies

We propose a two-stage framework for multi-label classification. In the first stage, one of the MLC classifiers such as Binary Relevance (BR) [1], ML-kNN [10] or an ensemble of classifiers chains (ECC) is used. In the second stage, the output of MLC in the first stage is refined by using the dependencies among labels captured by a CRF model.

Let $\mathcal{D} = \{(\mathbf{x}_n, \mathbf{y}_n), 1 \leq n \leq N\}$ be the multi-label data where $\mathbf{x}_n \in \Re^d$ is the d-dimensional input instance and $\mathbf{y} = \{y_1, y_2, ..., y_m\}$ is the m-dimensional desired output vector. Here, m is the number of class labels and $y_j \in \{0,1\}$. MLC deals with learning the mapping $h : \Re^d \to \{0,1\}^m$.

In the BR method for MLC, the multi-label dataset is transformed into m binary classification datasets. In the jth dataset, the instances are considered as the positive instances if they belong to the jth class, otherwise they are considered as the negative instances. Any SLC method can be used to build each of the m classifiers. Prediction for a test instance is obtained from the outputs of the m classifiers. The ML-kNN method is an algorithm adaptation method based on the k-nearest neighbour (kNN) classification for SLC. For a given test instance, the ML-kNN first identifies its k-nearest neighbours. Then the prediction is obtained using the Bayes rule based on the statistical information obtained from the neighbours.

Let $\mathbf{s} = \{s_1, s_2, ..., s_m\}$ be the set of confidence scores obtained from the first stage where $s_j \in [0,1]$ is the output of the classifier corresponding to the jth class for a given instance $\mathbf{x}$.

3.1   Conditional Random Field

Conditional Random Field (CRF) [11] is a discriminative undirected probabilistic graphical model that directly models the conditional probability distribution $p(\mathbf{y}|\mathbf{s})$, where $\mathbf{y}$ is the set of output variables and $\mathbf{s}$ is the set of observed input variables as shown in Fig. 1. In the proposed method, the set of confidence scores $\mathbf{s}$ obtained from the first stage are used as the input to the CRF. The graph associated with the CRF encodes the dependencies among the output variables. An edge between two nodes in the graph indicates that the corresponding variables are dependent on each other. The conditional probability distribution $p(\mathbf{y}|\mathbf{s})$ is given by the normalized product of clique potentials.

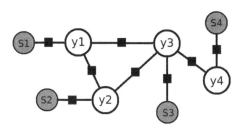

Fig. 1. A factor graph representation of the proposed CRF based model. The unshaded circles represent the class variables $\mathbf{y}$. The shaded circles represent the input variables $\mathbf{s}$. The edges amongst nodes represent the dependencies among class variables. The solid blocks represent the factors associated with those variables.

We use a CRF with the pairwise potentials to model the dependencies among the labels $\mathbf{y}$ using the output $\mathbf{s}$ from the first stage. Let $G = (V, E)$ be the graph associated with the CRF. The nodes V of the graph represents the class variables and the edges E represents the dependence relationships among class variables. The conditional distribution $p(\mathbf{y}|\mathbf{s})$ is given by

$$p(\mathbf{y}|\mathbf{s}) = \frac{1}{Z(\mathbf{s})} \prod_{i \in V} \Phi_i(y_i, \mathbf{s}) \prod_{(i,j) \in E} \psi_{ij}(y_i, y_j, \mathbf{s}) \tag{1}$$

where Φ_i is the node potential associated with i^{th} node and ψ_{ij} is the edge potential associated with the (i, j) edge. The normalization constant $Z(\mathbf{s})$, also known as the partition function is given by

$$Z(\mathbf{s}) = \sum_{\mathbf{y}} \left[\prod_{i \in V} \Phi_i(y_i, \mathbf{s}) \prod_{(i,j) \in E} \psi_{ij}(y_i, y_j, \mathbf{s}) \right] \tag{2}$$

For the binary variable $y_i \in \{0, 1\}$, the node potential Φ_i for different assignments of y_i is given by

$$\Phi_i(y_i, \mathbf{s}) = \left(e^{f_i(\mathbf{s})v_i^0}, e^{f_i(\mathbf{s})v_i^1} \right) \tag{3}$$

where v_i^0 and v_i^1 are the node parameters corresponding to the state $y_i = 0$ and $y_i = 1$ respectively, and $f_i(\mathbf{s}) = s_i$ is the node feature.

Similarly, the edge potential ψ_{ij} for different assignments of edge $(i, j) = \{00, 01, 10, 11\}$ is defined by

$$\psi_{ij}(y_i, y_j, \mathbf{s}) = \begin{pmatrix} e^{\mathbf{f}_{ij}(\mathbf{s})\mathbf{w}_{ij}^{0;0}} & e^{\mathbf{f}_{ij}(\mathbf{s})\mathbf{w}_{ij}^{0;1}} \\ e^{\mathbf{f}_{ij}(\mathbf{s})\mathbf{w}_{ij}^{1;0}} & e^{\mathbf{f}_{ij}(\mathbf{s})\mathbf{w}_{ij}^{1;1}} \end{pmatrix} \tag{4}$$

where $\mathbf{f}_{ij}(\mathbf{s}) = [s_i, s_j]^T$ are the edge features and $(\mathbf{w}_{ij}^{0,0}, \mathbf{w}_{ij}^{0,1}, \mathbf{w}_{ij}^{1,0}, \mathbf{w}_{ij}^{1,1})$ are the edge parameters.

Let $\boldsymbol{\theta} = [\mathbf{v}, \mathbf{w}]$ be the combined parametric vector and the respective feature functions be combined as $F(\mathbf{s}, \mathbf{y})$. The Eq. (1) can now be written succinctly as

$$p(\mathbf{y}|\mathbf{s}) = \frac{1}{Z(\boldsymbol{\theta}, \mathbf{s})} exp\left(\boldsymbol{\theta}^T F(\mathbf{s}, \mathbf{y}) \right) \tag{5}$$

3.2 Objective Function

The objective function for learning the CRF parameters, the negative log likelihood (nll) is given as

$$nll(\boldsymbol{\theta}) = -\sum_{n=1}^{N} log\, p(\mathbf{y}_n|\mathbf{s}_n) = -\sum_{n=1}^{N} \left[\boldsymbol{\theta}^T F(\mathbf{s}_n, \mathbf{y}_n) - log\, Z(\boldsymbol{\theta}, \mathbf{s}_n) \right] \tag{6}$$

The gradient for the negative log likelihood [12] is given by

$$\nabla nll(\boldsymbol{\theta}) = -\sum_{n=1}^{N} [F(\mathbf{s}_n, \mathbf{y}_n) - E_{\mathbf{y}'}[F(\mathbf{s}, \mathbf{y}')]] \tag{7}$$

where $E_{\mathbf{y}'}[F(\mathbf{s}, \mathbf{y}')] = \sum_{\mathbf{y}'} p(\mathbf{y}'|\mathbf{s}) F(\mathbf{s}, \mathbf{y}')$ are the expectations for the feature functions. To find these expectations, we have to run an inference algorithm to compute model distribution $p(\mathbf{y}'|\mathbf{s})$ for all values of $\mathbf{y}'$. This makes computing gradient very expensive. Two main solutions to address this issue are: (a) use an approximate inference algorithm such as loopy belief propagation and (b) use a surrogate objective function such as pseudo-likelihood. We consider the second method that uses the pseudo-likelihood. The negative log pseudo-likelihood (nlpl) for a CRF is given by

$$nlpl(\boldsymbol{\theta}) = -\sum_{n=1}^{N} log\ PL(\mathbf{y}_n|\mathbf{s}_n) = -\sum_{n=1}^{N}\sum_{i\in V} log\ p(y_{i,n}|\mathbf{y}_{\mathcal{N}_i,n}, \mathbf{s}_n; \boldsymbol{\theta}) \quad (8)$$

where $\mathbf{y}_{\mathcal{N}_i,n}$ is the set of neighbours $\mathcal{N}_i$ for the ith node and the nth instance. The negative log pseudo-likelihood is a convex function in parameters $\boldsymbol{\theta}$ and known to be a consistent estimator, i.e., it returns the same set of parameters as the maximum likelihood estimate for $\boldsymbol{\theta}$ when the number of instances goes to infinity [15].

Using the concise notation,

$$p(y_i|\mathbf{y}_{\mathcal{N}_i}, \mathbf{s}; \boldsymbol{\theta}) = \frac{1}{Z_i(\boldsymbol{\theta}_i, \mathbf{s})} exp\left(\boldsymbol{\theta}_i^T F_i(\mathbf{s}, \mathbf{y})\right) \quad (9)$$

where $\boldsymbol{\theta}_i = \left(\mathbf{v}_i, \{\mathbf{w}_{ij}\}_{j\in\mathcal{N}_i}\right)$ are the parameters corresponding to i^{th} node and its neighbours, Z_i is the local partition function, and F_i is the local feature vector. The local partition function Z_i can be computed by summing only over the values of y_i.

3.3   CRF Structure and Parameter Learning

The structure of a CRF can be learnt by minimizing the regularized negative log pseudo-likelihood function with L_1 regularization [13]. The L_1 norm based regularization is known to give a sparse solution. We impose L_1 regularization for each set of parameters associated with the edges in the graph [14]. This causes sparsity in the edge weight parameters where all parameters associated with a specific edge go to zero simultaneously. Using L_2 regularizer for the node parameters, the regularization term $R(\boldsymbol{\theta})$ can be written as

$$R(\boldsymbol{\theta}) = \lambda_1 \|\mathbf{v}\|_2^2 + \lambda_2 \sum_{b\in E} \|\mathbf{w}_b\|_2 \quad (10)$$

where $\mathbf{w}_b = (\mathbf{w}_{ij}^{0,0}, \mathbf{w}_{ij}^{0,1}, \mathbf{w}_{ij}^{1,0}, \mathbf{w}_{ij}^{1,1})$ is the set of weight parameters for different configuration of the edge $b = (i, j)$. Parameters of the CRF are found by minimizing the regularized loss function as given below

$$\boldsymbol{\theta}^* = argmin_{\boldsymbol{\theta}}(nlpl(\boldsymbol{\theta}) + R(\boldsymbol{\theta})) \quad (11)$$

We use the projected quasi-Newton [16] method to solve the above optimization problem. The structure of the CRF then corresponds to all edges in the graph that has non-zero weight parameters. After fixing the structure of the CRF, the L_2 norm regularization is used over the edge parameters. The limited-memory BFGS [17] method is used to further fine-tune the model's parameters for the given structure. After training the model, the loopy belief propagation method is used to obtain the final predictions.

4 Experiments

We performed the experiments on the following multi-label datasets; Emotion, Enron, Medical, Scene and Yeast from Mulan [18].

The evaluation metrics used to compare the various methods are: Accuracy, Subset-accuracy (exact match) and Hamming loss [1].

Table 1. Accuracy comparison of different single-stage MLC methods(BR, ML-kNN and ECC) with the proposed two-stage method using CRF.

Dataset	Method					
	BR	CRF_{BR}	ML-kNN	CRF_{ML-kNN}	ECC	CRF_{ECC}
Emotions	0.5360	0.5701	0.3366	0.4745	0.5850	0.6163
Enron	0.4059	0.4704	0.3321	0.3853	0.4620	0.4701
Medical	0.6450	0.6877	0.4428	0.5674	0.7410	0.7615
Scene	0.5836	0.7099	0.6353	0.7333	0.7030	0.7274
Yeast	0.5270	0.5416	0.5202	0.5435	0.5660	0.5692

We compared the performance of the proposed method with different existing methods for MLC. The BR, ML-kNN and ECC based MLC are used in the first stage. Logistic regression with L_2 regularization is used as the base classifier for BR method. SVMs were used as base classifiers for ECC. For ML-kNN, we used the code released on the internet by the author. We used the UGM-toolbox [19] for CRF implementation. Other MLC methods were implemented using *MEKA*[1]. All hyper-parameters are tuned using the cross-validation method.

The performance of proposed two-stage method using different MLCs in the first stage is presented in Table 1. For all the three MLC methods, the CRF based two-stage method is able to enhance the performance. The improvement is more significant in datasets that have a high correlation among class labels. Table 2 presents the comparison of the proposed method against the other existing methods. The proposed method performs better than all other methods. This shows the effectiveness of capturing label dependencies for MLC.

---

[1] http://meka.sourceforge.net/.

Table 2. Performance comparison of our proposed method (CRF_{ECC}) with other state-of-the-art-methods: Collective Multi-Label classification (CML) [8], Meta Binary Relevance (MBR) [5] and Conditional Dependency Network (CDN) [4]

Dataset	Method	Accuracy	Exact-match	Hamming loss
Emotions	CML	0.5664	0.3465	0.2244
	MBR	0.5850	0.3470	0.1910
	CDN	0.5840	0.3230	**0.1820**
	CRF_{ECC}	**0.6163**	**0.3861**	0.1914
Enron	CML	0.4319	0.1399	0.0575
	MBR	0.4370	0.1490	**0.0490**
	CDN	0.4670	0.1360	0.0540
	CRF_{ECC}	**0.4701**	**0.1606**	0.0508
Medical	CML	0.7209	0.6450	0.0113
	MBR	0.6990	0.6140	0.0120
	CDN	0.6460	0.5190	0.0150
	CRF_{ECC}	**0.7615**	**0.6698**	**0.0109**
Scene	CML	0.6198	0.5493	0.1282
	MBR	0.6090	0.5730	0.0860
	CDN	0.6580	0.5680	0.1020
	CRF_{ECC}	**0.7274**	**0.6706**	**0.0842**
Yeast	CML	0.4662	0.1897	0.2565
	MBR	0.5300	0.2070	**0.1900**
	CDN	0.5170	0.1620	0.2170
	CRF_{ECC}	**0.5692**	**0.2225**	0.1967

5   Conclusion

In this paper, we proposed a two-stage framework for multi-label classification using the conditional random field. It captures the dependencies among labels to improve the MLC performance. An optimization-based framework is used for learning the structure of the CRF. Experimental results shows the effectiveness of the proposed method for benchmark multi-label datasets.

References

1. Zhang, M.-L., Zhou, Z.-H.: A review on multi-label learning algorithms. IEEE Trans. Knowl. Data Eng. **26**(8), 1819–1837 (2014)
2. Read, J., Bernhard, F.P., Holmes, G., Frank, E.: Classifier chains for multi-label classification. Mach. Learn. **85**(3), 333–359 (2011)
3. Zhang, M.-L., Zhang, K.: Multi-label learning by exploiting label dependency. In: Proceedings of the 16th ACM SIGKDD International Conference on Knowledge Discovery and Data mining, pp. 999–1008. ACM (2010)

4. Guo, Y., Gu, S.: Multi-label classification using conditional dependency networks. In: IJCAI Proceedings-International Joint Conference on Artificial Intelligence, vol. 22, p. 1300 (2011)

5. Godbole, S., Sarawagi, S.: Discriminative methods for multi-labeled classification. In: Dai, H., Srikant, R., Zhang, C. (eds.) PAKDD 2004. LNCS, vol. 3056, pp. 22–30. Springer, Heidelberg (2004). doi:10.1007/978-3-540-24775-3_5

6. Arias, J., Gamez, J.A., Nielsen, T.D., Puerta, J.M.: A scalable pairwise class interaction framework for multidimensional classification. Int. J. Approximate Reasoning 68, 194–210 (2016)

7. Li, X., Zhao, F., Guo, Y.: Multi-label image classification with a probabilistic label enhancement model. In: Proceedings of Uncertainty in Artificial Intelligence (2014)

8. Ghamrawi, N., McCallum, A.: Collective multi-label classification. In: Proceedings of the 14th ACM International Conference on Information and Knowledge Management, pp. 195–200. ACM (2005)

9. Naeini, M.P., Batal, I., Liu, Z., Hong, C., Hauskrecht, M.: An optimization-based framework to learn conditional random fields for multi-label classification. In: Proceedings of the 2014 SIAM International Conference on Data Mining, pp. 992–1000. Society for Industrial and Applied Mathematics (2014)

10. Zhang, M.-L., Zhou, Z.-H.: ML-KNN: a lazy learning approach to multi-label learning. Pattern Recogn. 40(7), 2038–2048 (2007)

11. Lafferty, J., McCallum, A., Pereira, F.: Conditional random fields: probabilistic models for segmenting and labeling sequence data. In: Proceedings of the Eighteenth International Conference on Machine Learning, ICML, vol. 1, pp. 282–289 (2001)

12. Murphy, K.P.: Machine Learning: A Probabilistic Perspective. MIT press, Cambridge (2012)

13. Schmidt, M.W., et al.: Structure learning in random fields for heart motion abnormality detection. In: CVPR, vol. 1(1) (2008)

14. Yuan, M., Lin, Y.: Model selection and estimation in regression with grouped variables. J. R. Stat. Soc. Ser. B (Stat. Methodol.) 68(1), 49–67 (2006)

15. Besag, J.: Efficiency of pseudolikelihood estimation for simple Gaussian fields. Biometrika 64(3), 616–618 (1977)

16. Schmidt, M.W., Van Den Berg, E., Friedlander, M.P., Murphy, K.P.: Optimizing costly functions with simple constraints: a limited-memory projected quasi-Newton Algorithm. In: AISTATS, vol. 5 (2009)

17. Liu, D.C., Nocedal, J.: On the limited memory BFGS method for large scale optimization. Math. Prog. 45(1), 503–528 (1989)

18. Tsoumakas, G., Spyromitros-Xioufis, E., Vilcek, J., Mulan, I.V.: A Java library for multi-label learning. J. Mach. Learn. Res. 12, 2411–2414 (2011)

19. Schmidt, M.: UGM: a Matlab toolbox for probabilistic undirected graphical models (2007). http://www.cs.ubc.ca/~schmidtm/Software/UGM.html

A Matrix Factorization & Clustering Based Approach for Transfer Learning

V. Sowmini Devi⊙, Vineet Padmanabhan$^{(\boxtimes)}$⊙, and Arun K. Pujari⊙

School of Computer and Information Sciences, Univeristy of Hyderabad,
Hyderabad, India
sowmiveeramachaneni@gmail.com, {vineetcs,akpcs}@uohyd.ernet.in

Abstract. Recommender systems that make use of *collaborative filtering* tend to suffer from data sparsity as the number of items rated by the users are very small as compared to the very large item space. In order to alleviate it, recently *transfer learning* (TL) methods have seen a growing interest wherein data is considered from multiple domains so that ratings from the first (source) domain can be used to improve the prediction accuracy in the second (target) domain. In this paper, we propose a model for transfer learning in collaborative filtering wherein the latent factor model for the source domain is obtained through Matrix Factorization (MF). User and Item matrices are combined in a novel way to generate cluster level rating pattern and a Code Book Transfer (CBT) is used for transfer of information from source to the target domain. Results from experiments using benchmark datasets show that our model approximates the target matrix well.

1 Introduction

Recommender systems provide recommendations on products or services so that users get to know about items that match their interests. In order to learn user profiles, predict users' intensions and recommend items of interest, recommender systems usually employ techniques like Collaborative Filtering (CF) where recommendation for a user (target user) is done by utilizing the observed preferences of other users with similar tastes as that of the target user. Popular methods include MMMF [1,2] and PMF [3]. However, these methods can only utilize the data from a single domain and cannot take into account user-item interaction from other domains. Moreover, most CF-based recommender systems perform poorly when there are very few ratings. To address this data sparsity, transfer learning methods have emerged.

The idea behind transfer learning [4] is to extract and transfer common knowledge across the source and the target domain so as to built a predictive model across different domains. In the case of recommender systems, for successful knowledge transfer, TL has to address two critical problems (1) Knowledge transfer when two domains have aligned users or items and (2) Knowledge transfer when the domains have no aligned users or items. The second problem is very difficult and in this paper we use a representative method to solve this issue using

© Springer International Publishing AG 2017
B.U. Shankar et al. (Eds.): PReMI 2017, LNCS 10597, pp. 77–83, 2017.
https://doi.org/10.1007/978-3-319-69900-4_10

CBT (CodeBook Transfer) [5]. We propose a model for transfer learning in collaborative filtering in which the latent factor model for the source domain is obtained through matrix factorization techniques like MMMF (Maximum Margin Matrix Factorization) and PMF (Probabilistic Matrix factorization) and the cluster level patterns are generated via clustering techniques like *Spectral Clustering* and *k-means Clustering*. Thereafter, we use a tri-factorization method with the help of CBT that exploits matrix tri-factorization for transfer of information from the source to the target domain.

One work that comes close to ours is that of [6] where matrix approximation is combined with cluster-level factor vectors. However, their approach is limited to a single domain only. In [7] a coordinate system transfer method is proposed in which the latent features of users and items of source domain are learnt and adapted to a target domain. However, they require either common users or items between the two domains. In [5], co-clustering is applied on a separate *auxiliary* rating matrix to directly get cluster level rating pattern(*B*), which is then used in matrix tri-factorization. Our approach differs from theirs as we do not use a separate dense *auxiliary* rating matrix. The rest of the paper is organized as follows: Sect. 2 gives a brief description about Matrix Factorization. The proposed approach is given in Sect. 3. Finally experimental results are shown in Sect. 4, and we conclude our work in Sect. 5.

2 Matrix Factorization

Matrix factorization (MF) [2,8,9] techniques are a family of algorithms in collaborative filtering which try to approximate a low dimensional representation of the data. The users and items are projected to a lower dimensional embedding which are modelled as latent variables or hidden factors. The idea is that inference on these hidden factors lead to accurate predicton for ratings.

Formally, given a user-item rating matrix $Y \in \mathbb{R}^{m \times n}$ where m is the number of users and n is the number of items. Assuming that k is the number of latent factors, we need to find two matrices, $U \in \mathbb{R}^{m \times k}$ and $V \in \mathbb{R}^{n \times k}$ such that their product is approximately equal to Y, i.e., $U \times V^T = \hat{Y} \approx Y$. Since we need to use only the observed ratings $\mathcal{O}$, the objective then reduces to find $\hat{Y} = UV^T$ by minimizing

$$J = \sum_{(i,j) \in \mathcal{O}} (y_{ij} - u_i v_j)^2 \tag{1}$$

Of the different matrix factorization techniques proposed we have chosen MMMF and PMF to be used in this paper.

Maximum Margin MF (MMMF)- When predicting discrete values such as ratings in recommender systems, a loss function other than the sum-squared error is more appropriate. In MMMF [1,10] sum-squared error is replaced with hinge loss. MMMF constrains the norms of U and V (trace norm) instead of their dimensionality and the predicted matrix contains only discrete values in $\{1, 2, ...r\}$. In order to output only the discrete values in MMMF we have to learn $r - 1$ thresholds θ_{ia} ($1 \leq a \leq r - 1$) for every user i in addition to the latent feature matrices U and V. For that, we need to minimize the following objective function:

$$J(U, V, \theta) = \sum_{(i,j) \in \mathcal{O}} \sum_{a=1}^{r-1} h(T_{ij}^a(\theta_{ia} - u_i v_j^T)) + \lambda(||U||_F^2 + ||V||_F^2) \tag{2}$$

where $T_{ij}^a = \begin{cases} +1 & \text{if } a \geq y_{ij} \\ -1 & \text{if } a < y_{ij} \end{cases}$ $h(.)$ is a smoothed hinge loss function defined as $h(z) = (1 - z)$, if $z < 1$ and $= 0$, otherwise, $\lambda > 0$ is regularization parameter.

Probabilstic MF- Probabilstic MF (PMF) is a generative model which presupposes a Gaussian distribution for the data. In this, ratings (Y) are modeled as draws from a Gaussian distribution with mean for Y_{ij} as $U_i V_j^T$. Zero-mean spherical gaussian priors are placed on U and V. i.e., Each row of U and V are drawn from a multi variate gaussian distribution with mean as 0 and precision is multiple of identity matrix I, as shown in equations below (3) and (4).

$$P(U|\sigma_U^2) = \prod_{i=1}^{m} \mathcal{N}(U_i|0, \sigma_U^2 I) \tag{3}$$

$$P(V|\sigma_V^2) = \prod_{j=1}^{n} \mathcal{N}(V_j|0, \sigma_V^2 I) \tag{4}$$

Given the user feature vectors and movie feature vectors, the distribution for the corresponding rating is given by Eq. (5),

$$P(Y|U, V, \sigma^2) = \prod_{i=1}^{m} \prod_{j=1}^{n} [\mathcal{N}(Y_{ij}|U_i V_j^T, \sigma^2)]^{I_{ij}} \tag{5}$$

Goal of PMF is to maximize the log-posterior of (5) over U and V. Maximizing the log posterior of (5) is equivalent to minimizing (6).

$$J = \frac{1}{2}(\sum_{i=1}^{m} \sum_{j=1}^{n} I_{ij}(Y_{ij} - U_i V_j^T)^2 + \lambda_U \sum_{i}^{m} ||U||_F^2 + \lambda_V \sum_{j}^{n} ||V||_F^2) \tag{6}$$

where, I_{ij} is the indicator matrix which equals 1 if item j is rated by user i otherwise 0, $\lambda_U = \frac{\sigma^2}{\sigma_U^2}$ and $\lambda_V = \frac{\sigma^2}{\sigma_V^2}$. One can solve the optimization functions given in Eqs. (2) and (6) using gradient descent.

3 Proposed Approach

For a target matrix (Y') of size $m' \times n'$ denoting users rating of items, our goal is to recommend the items in target domain using the source domain data. Initially, we apply MMMF (2) and PMF (6) individually on source domain to get latent feature vectors U_s, V_s. Then we apply k-means clustering [11] or Spectral Clustering [12] on row vectors of U_s and V_s to get user-cluster latent matrix and item-cluster latent matrix. Following that we multiply them to get cluster level rating pattern (C). Once the rating pattern is formed, we try to minimize the objective function (7) which is a tri-factorization method so as to get the user and item membership matrices U_t, V_t of the target domain. After which predicted matrix can be obtained using Eq. (8) as outlined in Algorithm 1.

$$\min_{U_t \in \{0,1\}^{m' \times p}, V_t \in \{0,1\}^{n' \times q}} ||[Y' - U_t C V_t^T] \circ W||_F^2 \quad s.t., U_t 1 = 1, V_t 1 = 1. \quad (7)$$

$$\tilde{Y}' = W \circ Y' + [1 - W] \circ [U_t C V_t^T], \quad (8)$$

where W is the indicator matrix of size $m' \times n'$ in which the value is 1 if the rating exists in original rating matrix, 0 otherwise. W ensures that the error is calculated only for the predicted ratings and, $\circ$ denotes element wise product. U_t and V_t are binary matrices, in which the value 1 (best cluster indicator) indicates whether a user or item belongs to a particular cluster and $U_t 1 = 1$, $V_t 1 = 1$ ensures that each user or item belongs to only one cluster. The solution to the optimization problem (Eq.-7) relates the source and target tasks and is NP-hard. Smaller value of Eq. (7) indicates that a better rating pattern between source and target while larger values indicate weak correspondence, which may result in negative transfer [13]. To get the minimum local solution, Alternating Least Squares (ALS) technique is used. ALS monotonically decreases Eq. (7), by updating U_t and V_t alternatively. This has been demonstrated in algorithm 2 of [5], where updating U_t is given in lines 7-10, and updating V_t is given in lines 11-14. Once we get U_t, V_t by solving the optimization function (7), we construct the predicted target matrix using Eq. (8), which is illustrated in Fig. 2. Consider Fig. 1, where source rating matrix (presented at level-1) is factorized into user latent factor matrix (U_s) and item latent factor matrix (V_s) as shown in level-2. Clustering technique is applied on U_s and V_s to get user and item cluster matrices (P, Q) which are at level-3. Finally, level-4 shows that these cluster matrices are multiplied to get cluster-level rating pattern (C) which is to be used in the target domain.

Algorithm 1. MF combined with clustering

1: **Input:**   Source domain ratings
2: **Output:** Predicted target domain ratings
3: Find U_s, V_s by minimizing the optimization function of MMMF (2) or PMF (6).
4: Apply k-means clustering or spectral clustering on U_s, V_s to get user-cluster latent matrix(P) and item-cluster latent matrix(Q).
5: Calculate $C = P * Q'$ as cluster level rating pattern, which is assumed to be shared between two domains.
6: Use C, and find U_t, V_t of target domain by minimizing Eq. (7).
7: Using these U_t and V_t, find the predicted matrix using (8).

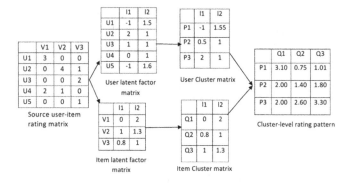

Fig. 1. Construction of cluster-level rating pattern using source rating data

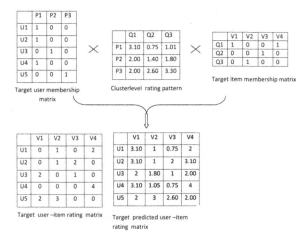

Fig. 2. Approximation of target rating matrix using cluster-level rating pattern.

4   Experimental Setup

The two datasets used in our experiments are MovieLens (https://grouplens.
org//datasets/movielens/) as *source* dataset (6040 users and 3952 movies) and
Books (https://grouplens.org/datasets/book-crossing/) as *target* dataset (2095
users and 4544 books). In movielens each user has ratings range of 1-5, whereas
in books the range is 1-10, and we have scaled it to 1-5. In all experiments 80% of
the total rating data is taken for training, and the rest 20% is used for testing.
We evaluated our algorithm using Root Mean Squared Error (RMSE) Eq. (9)
and Mean Absolute Error (MAE) Eq. (10), where smaller the values of these,
better the performance. If we observe Table 1, we can see that MMMF or PMF,
when combined with spectral clustering is giving better result (i.e., lesser RMSE
and MAE) when compared with MMMF or PMF combined with k-means, which
says that spectral clustering is more general and powerful compared to k-means

clustering technique. In some cases, even if the number of clusters is known, k-means clustering may fail to effectively cluster, because k-means is ideal to discover globular clusters, in which the members are in compact form but not connected.

$$RMSE = \sqrt{\sum_{(i,j)\epsilon\mathcal{O}} \frac{(y_{ij} - \hat{y}_{ij})^2}{|\mathcal{O}|}} \tag{9}$$

$$MAE = \sum_{(i,j)\epsilon\mathcal{O}} \frac{|(y_{ij} - \hat{y}_{ij})|}{|\mathcal{O}|} \tag{10}$$

where y_{ij} is the original rating and $\hat{y}_{ij}$ is the predicted rating.

Table 1. RMSE and MAE comparison of MMMF, PMF combined with k-means clustering and spectral clustering

	Number of clusters	RMSE		MAE	
		K-means	Spectral	K-means	Spectral
MMMF	40	0.9702	**0.9372**	0.6963	**0.6029**
PMF	40	0.8205	**0.8001**	0.6674	**0.6476**
MMMF	140	0.9690	**0.9171**	0.6986	**0.5864**
PMF	140	0.8282	**0.799**	0.799	**0.6867**
MMMF	200	1.0603	**0.9277**	0.777	**0.6044**
PMF	200	0.8535	**0.8362**	0.6778	**0.6473**
MMMF	300	1.0180	**0.9089**	0.7187	**0.5925**
PMF	300	0.8337	**0.8138**	0.6578	**0.6208**
MMMF	500	1.0927	**0.9247**	0.7813	**0.6105**
PMF	500	0.8452	**0.8123**	0.6508	**0.6222**

5   Conclusion and Future Work

We have proposed a novel model for cross-domain recommendation when multiple domains do not share a latent common rating pattern. We made use of Matrix Factorization techniques to get the initial latent hidden factor models and apply clustering techniques to find cluster-level rating pattern which is then used in a tri-factorization approximation. Experimental results using benchmark datasets shows that our model approximates the target matrix well. In the future we would like to vary the number of items in different domains which requires a special treatment and aslo investigate different techniques of tensor-based knowledge transfer learning.

References

1. Srebro, N., Rennie, J.D.M., Jaakkola, T.S.: Maximum-margin matrix factorization. In: NIPS, vol. 17, pp. 1329–1336 (2004)
2. Sowmini, V., Venkateswara Rao, K., Pujari, A.K., Padmanabhan, V.: Collaborative filtering by pso-based MMMF. In: Systems, Man and Cybernetics (SMC), pp. 569–574. IEEE (2014)
3. Ruslan, S., Mnih, A.: Probabilistic matrix factorization. In: NIPS, vol. 1 (2007)
4. Pan, S.J., Yang, Q.: A survey on transfer learning. IEEE Trans. Knowl. Data Eng. **22**(10), 1345–1359 (2010)
5. Li, B., Yang, Q., Xue, X.: Can movies and books collaborate? cross-domain collaborative filtering for sparsity reduction. IJCAI **9**, 2052–2057 (2009)
6. Ji, K., Sun, R., Li, X., Shu, W.: Improving matrix approximation for recommendation via a clustering-based reconstructive method. Neurocomputing **173**, 912–920 (2016)
7. Pan, W., Xiang, E.W., Nan Liu, N., Yang, Q.: Transfer learning in collaborative filtering for sparsity reduction. In: AAAI, vol. 10, pp. 230–235 (2010)
8. Koren, Y., Bell, R., Volinsky, C.: Matrix factorization techniques for recommender systems. Computer **42**(8) (2009)
9. Wu, M.: Collaborative filtering via ensembles of matrix factorizations. In: Proceedings of KDD Cup and Workshop, vol. 2007 (2007)
10. Rennie, J.D.M., Srebro, N.: Fast maximum margin matrix factorization for collaborative prediction. In: ICML, pp. 713–719 (2005)
11. Anil, K.J., Dubes, R.C.: Algorithms for clustering data. Prentice-Hall Inc. (1988)
12. Ng, A.Y., Jordan, M.I., Weiss, Y., et al.: On spectral clustering: analysis and an algorithm. In: NIPS, vol. 14, pp. 849–856 (2001)
13. Rosenstein, M.T., Marx, Z., Kaelbling, L.P., Dietterich, T.G.: To transfer or not to transfer. In: NIPS 2005 Workshop on Transfer Learning, vol. 898 (2005)

Signal and Image Processing

Feature Selection and Fuzzy Rule Mining for Epileptic Patients from Clinical EEG Data

Abhijit Dasgupta[1], Losiana Nayak[1], Ritankar Das[2], Debasis Basu[3],
Preetam Chandra[3], and Rajat K. De[1(✉)]

[1] Machine Intelligence Unit, Indian Statistical Institute, Kolkata, India
`rajat@isical.ac.in`
[2] Department of Bioinformatics, West Bengal University of Technology,
Kolkata, India
[3] Department of Neuro-Medicine, Medical College and Hospital, Kolkata, India

Abstract. In this paper, we create EEG data derived signatures for differentiating epileptic patients from normal individuals. Epilepsy is a neurological condition of human beings, mostly treated based on a patient's seizure symptoms. Clinicians face immense difficulty in detecting epileptic patients. Here we define brain region-connection based signatures from EEG data with help of various machine learning techniques. These signatures will help the clinicians in detecting epileptic patients in general. Moreover, we define separate signatures by taking into account a few demographic features like gender and age. Such signatures may aid the clinicians along with the generalized epileptic signature in case of complex decisions.

Keywords: Epileptic signature · Brain connectivity network · Fuzzy rule mining · EEGLAB · MATLAB

1 Introduction

Epilepsy is one of the most serious and frequently occurring neuropathological condition affecting around fifty million people globally[1]. Epileptic seizures can be lethal [1]. Epileptogenesis is a long term dynamic progressing process of hyperexcitability and abnormal synchronization of brain neurons until the manifestation of seizure. Available drugs treat epileptogenesis indirectly by suppressing ictogenesis (the expression of seizures) [2]. Treatment of epileptic patients is mostly symptomatic based on clinical features.

The "epileptic network", can be defined as a distributed network of distinct and distant brain regions causing hyperexcitability and hypersynchrony in a case of epilepsy [3]. Here we discuss the EEG data based computationally derived epileptic networks. Analysis of the epileptic networks may help in localization of a brain-region based signature in epileptic patients [4]. Till date, we have a

---

[1] http://www.who.int/mediacentre/factsheets/fs999/en/ visited on 21st March 2017 10:48 AM Indian Standard Time.

© Springer International Publishing AG 2017
B.U. Shankar et al. (Eds.): PReMI 2017, LNCS 10597, pp. 87–95, 2017.
https://doi.org/10.1007/978-3-319-69900-4_11

limited idea of epileptogenesis. Epilepsy does not have a cure yet. Moreover, there does not exist any signature pattern of brain region based connections that can successfully categorize epileptic patients from normal human beings. The case becomes more complex when we try to incorporate demographic features like gender or age to EEG data of epileptic patients.

In this article, we differentiate epileptic patients from normal individuals based on brain-region connection based signatures derived from EEG data. Moreover, we try to answer a few questions like how different is male epilepsy from female epilepsy? Do they over-represent different connections among various brain regions? How child epilepsy differs from teenage and adult epilepsy? Do we find different patterns of over/under-representation of connections among various brain regions for different demographic categories? Can they be used as signature patterns clinically? In addition, we have aided our results with findings by a fuzzy rule mining based approach. Each discovered rule is a different combination of presence/absence of brain region based connections.

2   Data

The dataset consists of electroencephalography (EEG) data collected from 60 healthy individuals and 80 patients suffering from epilepsy. The data has also been grouped and studied according to gender and age. We have data of 31 normal males and 29 normal females in our dataset. Likewise, we have data of 43 epileptic males and 37 epileptic females in our dataset. Patients with less than 13 years of age have been defined as children. We have data of 23 normal and 41 epileptic children in our dataset. Teenagers have an age range of 13–19. We have found 14 such normal and 22 epileptic cases in our data. Patients with more than 19 years of age have been defined as adult epileptic patients. We have 23 normal and 17 epilepsy adult patients.

3   Data Acquisition and Filtering

Data collection has been done with a computerized EEG machine (16 channels Recorders & Medicare Systems Pvt. Ltd. (RMS)). It has been used to record the EEG for an interval of 20–30 min. The data of each epileptic patient has been split into epochs of 10 seconds interval. The internationally accepted Modified Combinatorial Nomenclature (MCN) system accepted scheme for the location of electrodes has been followed. According to this scheme, each location is denoted by a combination of letter(s) and number. The letter(s) are used to identify the position of the electrodes on the brain lobes, whereas the numbers denote the hemispherical regions on the brain. The frontal polar, frontal, temporal, parietal and occipital lobes are represented by the letters 'FP', 'F', 'T', 'P', and 'O' respectively, whereas odd and even numbers stand for electrode position on the left and right hemisphere respectively. The letter 'C' is used for identification only. During the collection of data, it has been asked to all participants to stay awake and motionless with wide open eyes. Subsequently, they have been requested to attain a no-thinking state as far as possible. Each data has been recorded using a series of activation procedures, *i.e.*, eye blinking, photic stimulation, and hyperventilation among others.

After the recording of EEG data, firstly, the noise has been removed manually by experienced neurotechnologists. Then we have used EEGLAB toolbox version 13 [5], implemented in MATLAB R2015a for further data filtering purpose. The EEGLAB plugin, called CleanLine, has been used to remove sinusoidal noise from raw EEG data. The resultant data have been filtered again using Finite Impulse Response (FIR) filter, within the range of 4–60 Hz to remove sleep waves and noise due to electrical circuits. Here, we have used Independent Component Analysis (ICA) by applying the Runica algorithm [6]. Thus, a multivariate signal is decomposed into its additive independent non-Gaussian components. We have separated the maximum likely components from a number of noisy components using neural networks. Lastly, a final manual check has been done to assure that artifacts from the data have been removed.

4 Methodology

We have divided the methodology into four different steps. The steps have helped in selecting significant features and in finding important rules for epileptic patients in general and for different demographic categories. Figure 1 depicts the flowchart of our methodology pipeline.

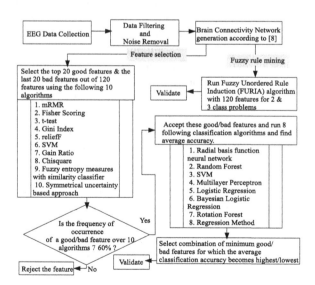

Fig. 1. Flow chart of the methodology.

1. **Brain connectivity network generation:** We have calculated the correlation between two certain electrode positions using Pearson's correlation coefficient [7]. We have considered the 16 electrode positions as vertices. If two vertices are found to be correlated (positively or negatively), we have created an edge between them. Thus, we have developed the brain connectivity network of normal individuals and epileptic patients. The detailed explanation of this step can be found in one of our previous research work [8].
2. **Determination of maximum features:** We have developed a 16×16 adjacency matrix for each brain connectivity network representing either a healthy volunteer or an epileptic patient. This adjacency matrix is symmetric with '0's in its diagonal elements. Thus, maximum ($\frac{16 \times 15}{2}$) = 120 unique undirected connections are possible from such a matrix. These 120 connections have been considered as features.
3. **Feature selection and classification:** We have identified the key features discriminating normal individuals from epileptic patients (a two class problem), male epileptic patients from female epileptic patients (another two class problem) and child epileptic patients from teenage as well as adult epileptic patients (a three class problem). We have used ten well-established feature selection algorithms, *i.e.*, mRMR [9], Fisher scoring [10], t-test, Gini index, reliefF, Support Vector Machine (SVM) [11], gain Ratio, Chisquare, fuzzy entropy measures with similarity classifier [12], and symmetrical uncertainty based approaches [13–15] among others to identify top twenty most significant features and last twenty least significant features for the above mentioned classification problems. We have selected those most/least significant features whose frequency of occurrence over the ten algorithms is more than 60%. We have used eight well-known classification algorithms, *i.e.*, radial basis function neural network [16], random forest [17], SVM [11], multilayer perceptron, logistic regression, Bayesian logistic regression, rotation forest [18], and regression method among others to classify the combination of the minimum number of most and least significant features. It has been done to maximize the average classification accuracy of the most significant features and minimize the same for the least significant features. Thus, a combination of minimum features has been selected for each of the classification problems mentioned earlier.
4. **Fuzzy rule mining:** We have used Fuzzy Unordered Rule Induction Algorithm (FURIA) [19] to identify a few rules for differentiation of the aforementioned classes. Here, we have considered all 120 features as input to FURIA. Besides, we have calculated the Certainty Factor (CF) for each rule. CF lies in a range of [-1, 1]. If the antecedent and consequent are related, the value of CF becomes positive. A higher value of CF represents more significant rule.

5   Results and Discussion

We have found certain brain-region based connections (features) over represented and a few under represented while comparing epileptic patients with normal volunteers. C3-F3, F7-O1, F7-O2, T7-F7, F8-FP1, P8-P4 and P8-P7 features have been found to be over represented in epilepsy. On the other hand, P7-P4 and T8-F3 features have been found to be under represented. The combination of these nine significant features (Table 1) has shown 82.59% average classification accuracy with 20 fold cross validation to separate normal individuals from epileptic patients in general. The representation pattern of these features constitutes a generalized epileptic signature.

In a similar way, we have found a few over represented and under represented features while comparing male and female epileptic patients. P4-F4 and P8-C4 features have been found to be over represented along with under representation of O2-C3, O2-P3, P7-O2 and F8-F7 features in case of female epileptic patients. Here, we have found 70.94% average classification accuracy with 20 fold cross validation for a combination of these six significant features (Table 1) for identifying male and female epileptic patients separately. Over or under representation pattern of these features constitute the gender-specific epileptic signatures.

On the other hand, the combination of eight promising good features (Table 1) has shown 62.14% average classification accuracy to discriminate child epileptic patients from teenage along with adult epileptic patients. The F8-F3 feature has been found to be over represented along with two under represented P8-FP1 and P8-T8 features in case of child epilepsy. In the cases of teenage epilepsy we have found an over represented O2-F3 feature and under represented F7-P4 feature. P8-T8 and O2-F4 features have been found to be over represented in the case of adult epilepsy. The representation pattern of these features constitutes the age-specific epileptic signatures. The rest of the features seem inconclusive at this point according to their frequency of occurrence. However, the average classification accuracy value may increase with a larger sample size.

In support of the aforementioned results, a fuzzy rule based association mining study has been done with the all possible 120 features (connections among different nodes) as given in Table 2 to find unique rules. We have performed this study to generate support for our earlier findings. Moreover, this study has provided additional associated features. The additional features helped in defining a proper rule for the general, age-wise and gender-wise epileptic signatures. Some features, i.e., T7-F7 and P8-P7 has been found to be associated with epilepsy as described earlier in Table 1. The presence of the feature T7-F7 has been found coupled with the presence of two additional features P7-F3 and P3-FP1. The rule indicates epilepsy with a certainty factor of 0.95. The presence of P8-P7 feature has been found with the presence of a new feature C4-FP1 with a certainty factor of 0.93.

Moreover, multiple rules have been found for the P7-P4 feature. The absence of the feature along with the absence of two additional features P8-F7 and O2-C4 have been found to be associated with epilepsy with a certainty factor of 0.97. On contrary, the presence of the P7-P4 feature along with the absence of three additional P4-FP2, T7-F7, and F8-P3 features has been found in normal individuals with a certainty factor of 0.96. Also, the presence of the same factor along with the absence of three additional O2-FP2, T7-F7, and P3-C3 features

Table 1. List of significant features differentiating epilepsy from normal individuals; male from female epilepsy; and child from teenage and adult epilepsy. Odd numbers succeeding node names indicate left hemisphere of the brain and similarly, even numbers indicate right hemisphere of the brain. The frequency of occurrence is given in percentage.

Normal Individuals vs Epileptic Patients

Connection between lobes (Features)	Nodes	Epileptic	Normal	In epilepsy
Left identification point & frontal lobe	C3-F3	40	16.66	More
Left frontal lobe & occipital lobe	F7-O1	57.50	23.33	More
Left frontal lobe & right occipital lobe	F7-O2	52.50	0.10	More
Left temporal lobe & frontal lobe	T7-F7	35	0.12	More
Left parietal lobe & right parietal lobe	P7-P4	45	88.33	Less
Right frontal lobe & left frontal polar lobe	F8-FP1	42.50	0.13	More
Right temporal lobe & left frontal lobe	T8-F3	0.15	38.33	Less
Right parietal lobe & parietal lobe	P8-P4	33.75	0.10	More
Right parietal lobe & left parietal lobe	P8-P7	35	0.07	More

Male vs Female Epileptic Patients

Connection between lobes (Features)	Nodes	Male	Female	In female
Right parietal lobe & frontal lobe	P4-F4	0.06	35.13	More
Right occipital lobe & left identification point	O2-C3	44.18	27.02	Less
Right parietal lobe & identification point	P8-C4	60.46	83.78	More
Right occipital lobe & left parietal lobe	O2-P3	32.55	18.91	Less
Left parietal lobe & right occipital lobe	P7-O2	48.83	29.72	Less
Right frontal lobe & left frontal lobe	F8-F7	48.83	29.72	Less

Child vs Teenage & Adult Epileptic Patients

Connection between lobes (Features)	Nodes	Child	Teenage	Adult
Right frontal lobe & left frontal lobe	F8-F3	49	13.63	11.76
Right parietal lobe & left frontal polar lobe	P8-FP1	0.07	40.90	35.29
Right parietal lobe & temporal lobe	P8-T8	29.26	40.90	64.70
Right occipital lobe & frontal lobe	O2-F4	12	9.09	35.29
Right occipital lobe & left occipital lobe	O2-O1	68	86.36	47.05
Left occipital lobe & frontal polar lobe	O1-FP1	34.14	18.18	11.76
Right occipital lobe & left frontal lobe	O2-F3	48.78	54.54	23.52
Left frontal lobe & right parietal lobe	F7-P4	19.51	9.09	17.64

has been found in normal individuals with a certainty factor of 0.96. In both the cases, the feature T7-F7 and its absence is a common factor. Such findings reflect the variable states of brain regions even for a very specific disease state.

Table 2. Fuzzy rules with its certainty factor (CF) for differentiating epilepsy from normal individuals; male from female epilepsy; and child from teenage and adult epilepsy. Range of CF is [-1,1].

Normal Individuals vs Epileptic Patients

IF condition	Then	CF
(P7-P4) absent & (P8-F7) absent & (O2-C4) absent	Epilepsy	0.97
(P4-FP2) present & (O2-FP2) present & (C3-FP1) absent	Epilepsy	0.96
(F7-O2) present & (O2-FP2) absent & (O2-F4) absent	Epilepsy	0.96
(T7-F7) present & (P7-F3) present & (P3-FP1) absent	Epilepsy	0.95
(P8-P7) present & (C4-FP1) present	Epilepsy	0.93
(P3-C3) present & (F8-FP2) absent & (O2-FP1) absent	Epilepsy	0.92
(P7-P4) present & (P4-FP2) absent & (T7-F7) absent & (F8-P3) absent	Normal	0.96
(F7-O2) absent & (T7-P3) absent & (P7-F7) absent	Normal	0.92
(P7-C3) absent & (P4-FP2) absent & (F7-C4) present & (P3-F3) absent	Normal	0.94
(P8-O1) present & (F8-O1) present & (O1-C3) absent	Normal	0.84
(P7-P4) present & (O2-FP2) absent & (T7-F7) absent & (P3-C3) absent	Normal	0.96

Male vs Female Epileptic Patients

IF condition	Then	CF
(F8-T7) present & (O1-FP1) present	Male epilepsy	0.92
(O2-P3) present & (O1-FP1) absent	Male epilepsy	0.91
(P7-O2) present & (F7-F3) absent & (T8-F8) absent	Male epilepsy	0.93
(P4-F4) present & (P8-P3) present	Female epilepsy	0.89
(C3-FP1) present & (T7-C4) absent & (F8-T7) absent	Female epilepsy	0.91
(P8-F7) present & (F8-F7) absent & (P3-C3) present	Female epilepsy	0.88
(F8-O1) present & (F4-P3) absent & (C3-FP1) absent	Female epilepsy	0.86

Child vs Teenage & Adult Epileptic Patients

IF condition	Then	CF
(F8-F3) present & (T7-FP2) absent	Child epilepsy	0.94
(O1-C3) present & (C4-C3) present	Child epilepsy	0.89
(F8-P4) present & (P8-FP1) absent & (C4-F3) present	Child epilepsy	0.92
(P8-F4) present & (T7-C4) absent & (FP2-O1) absent	Child epilepsy	0.89
(P7-P4) absent & (P8-FP1) present & (F7-P4) absent	Teenage epilepsy	0.86
(P7-P3) present & (C3-FP1) absent & (O1-C3) absent	Teenage epilepsy	0.82
(P8-T8) present & (F8-P4) absent & (T8-FP1) absent	Adult epilepsy	0.8
(F4-C3) absent & (T7-F7) present & (F7-O1) present	Adult epilepsy	0.74
(T8-FP2) present & (P8-P4) present & (F3-FP1) absent	Adult epilepsy	0.74

The feature F7-O2 has been found to be associated with both epileptic patients and normal individuals. The presence of the feature along with the absence of two additional O2-FP2 and O2-F4 features has been associated with epilepsy with a certainty factor of 0.96. On contrary, the absence of the feature along with the absence of two additional T7-P3 and P7-F7 features has been seen in normal individuals with a certainty factor of 0.92. These rules altogether contribute to the generalized epileptic signature.

In the case of male versus female epileptic patients, the presence of O2-P3 feature along with the absence of an additional feature O1-FP1 has been found to be associated with male epilepsy with a certainty factor of 0.91. Similarly, the presence of the feature F8-T7 along with the presence of another additional feature O1-FP1 has been found to be associated with male epilepsy with a certainty factor of 0.92. In contrast, the presence of P4-F4 feature along with the presence of an additional feature P8-P3 has been found to be associated with female epilepsy with a certainty factor of 0.89. The absence of the feature F8-F7 along with the presence of two additional features P8-F7 and P3-C3 have been found to be associated with female epilepsy. Such results support our earlier finding of features in male and female epilepsy as given in Table 1. These rules contribute to the gender-specific epileptic signatures.

We have also done an age-specific fuzzy rule mining study as given in Table 2. Here the presence of F8-F3 and the absence of P8-FP1 features have been found in two separate rules. They have been found to be associated with child epilepsy with certainty factors 0.94 and 0.92 respectively. The absence of P8-FP1 feature along with the presence of two additional features P7-P4 and F7-P4 with a certainty factor of 0.86 has been found to be associated with teenage epilepsy. In the case of adult epilepsy, the presence of the feature P8-T8 along with the absence of two additional features F8-P4 and T8-FP1 has been found to be associated with a certainty factor of 0.8. These results provide support to our earlier findings as given in Table 1 as well as contribute to the age-specific epileptic signatures.

Moreover, the fuzzy rule mining study has discovered some new rules which we have not spotted in our earlier findings. We have found 2 new rules each for epileptic patients and normal individuals. One male and two female epilepsy related new rules have also been found by this study as given in Table 2. In addition, two child, one teenage and two adult epilepsy associated new rules have been found. These new rules along with our earlier findings (Table 1) helped in creating well-defined signatures for future machine learning based detection of epilepsy in general and complicated cases.

6   Conclusions

In this paper, we have found a generalized epileptic signature from EEG data of patients along with gender and age specific signatures. It is not always easy for medical practitioners to rightly identify an epileptic patient, the reason being similar kind of EEG spikes found in other neurobiological disorders. The created epileptic signatures may help them in overcoming these hurdles in epilepsy patient detection. Moreover, these kinds of predictions can come in handy with minimal human intervention in peripheral areas where the proper medical facility is not available yet. They can quickly be employed to detect probable epilepsy. Then the patient can be referred for proper medical care. In this paper, we were also able to distinguish between patients from different age groups and gender but it has not yet been clinically tested. According to clinicians, identifying the gender-specific epileptic signatures is an interesting concept and may be helpful in the future.

Acknowledgment. Abhijit Dasgupta acknowledges Visvesvaraya Ph.D. scheme for Electronics and IT empowered by Ministry of Electronics and Information Technology, Government of India, for a research fellowship. Losiana Nayak acknowledges University Grants Commission, India for a UGC Post-Doctoral Fellowship (No. F.15-1/2013-14/PDFWM-2013-14-GE-ORI-19068(SA-II)).

References

1. Devinsky, O.: N. Engl. J. Med. **365**(19), 1801–11 (2011)
2. Giourou, E., et al.: Cyberphysical Systems for Epilepsy and Related Brain Disorders, pp. 11–38. Springer, Cham (2015)
3. Wendling, F., et al.: Front Syst. Neurosci. **4**, 154 (2010)
4. Dixit, A.B., et al.: Neurol. India **63**(5), 743 (2015)
5. Delorme, A., et al.: J. Neurosci. Methods **134**(1), 9–21 (2004)
6. Naik, G.R., et al.: 8th IEEE International Conference on Computer and Information Technology (2008)
7. Sedgwick, P.: BMJ **345**, 7 (2012)
8. Dasgupta, A., et al.: IEEE International Conference Bioinformatics Biomedical, pp. 815–821. IEEE (2015)
9. Peng, H., et al.: IEEE Trans. Pattern Anal. Mach. **27**(8), 1226–38 (2005)
10. Mika, S., et al.: 9th IEEE Workshop on Neural Networks for Signal Processing. IEEE (1999)
11. Wang, L. (ed.): Support Vector Machines: Theory and Applications, vol. 177. Springer, Heidelberg (2005)
12. Luukka, P.: Expert Syst. Appl. **38**(4), 4600–7 (2011)
13. Saeys, Y., et al.: Bioinformatics **23**(19), 2507–17 (2007)
14. Shang, W., et al.: Expert Syst. Appl. **33**(1), 1–5 (2007)
15. Liu, H., et al. (eds.): Computational methods of feature selection. CRC Press, Boca Raton (2007)
16. Yingwei, L., et al.: IEEE Trans. Neural Netw. **9**(2), 308–18 (1998)
17. Liaw, A., et al.: R News **2**(3), 18–22 (2002)
18. Rodriguez, J., et al.: IEEE Trans. Pattern Anal. Mach. **28**(10), 1619–30 (2006)
19. Huhn, J., et al.: Data Min. Knowl. Discov. **19**(3), 293–319 (2009)

Selection of Relevant Electrodes Based on Temporal Similarity for Classification of Motor Imagery Tasks

Jyoti Singh Kirar[✉][iD], Ayesha Choudhary[iD], and R.K. Agrawal[iD]

Jawaharlal Nehru University, New Delhi, India
kirarjyoti@gmail.com, ayesha978@gmail.com, rkajnu@gmail.com

Abstract. Selection of relevant electrodes is of prime importance for developing efficient motor imagery Brain Computer Interface devices. In this paper, we propose a novel spectral clustering based on temporal similarity of electrodes to select a reduced set of relevant electrodes for classification of motor imagery tasks. Further, Stationary common spatial pattern method in conjunction with Composite kernel Support Vector Machine is utilized to develop a decision model. Experimental results demonstrate improvement in classification accuracy in comparison to variants of the common spatial pattern method on publicly available datasets. Friedman statistical test shows that the proposed method significantly outperformed the variants of the common spatial pattern method.

Keywords: Motor imagery · Brain computer interface · Common spatial pattern · Spectral clustering

1 Introduction

Brain computer interfaces (BCI) enable people with neurological disorders to establish communication and repair lost motor functions by transforming the brain signals into device commands. Non-invasive nature, low measurement cost and high resolution of EEG based BCI has favored its wide use for analysis of brain signals as compared to other modalities. EEG based BCI systems associated with motor imagery has received particular attention that involve visualizing movement of a specific motor part of the body [2]. Motor imagery BCIs use brain dynamics originating in primary sensorimotor area called sensorimotor rhythms (*mu* and *beta* rhythms), induced by execution or imagination of hand or leg movement, to translate EEG signals into device commands [2]. During motor imagination or execution, the amplitude of sensorimotor rhythms reduces, which is known as Event-Related Desynchronization (ERD). Increment in the amplitude of sensory-motor rhythms just after the motor imagination or execution is called as Event-Related Synchronization (ERS) [8].

© Springer International Publishing AG 2017
B.U. Shankar et al. (Eds.): PReMI 2017, LNCS 10597, pp. 96–102, 2017.
https://doi.org/10.1007/978-3-319-69900-4_12

Common spatial pattern (CSP) [2] is a well known spatial filtering method that finds subject specific data dependent spatial filters which maximizes variance of one class and minimizes variance of the other class simultaneously [2]. Extraction of information using the CSP is challenging as this method suffers from the small sample size (SSS) problem [4], i.e. the quantity of electrodes is high and the number of task specific EEG samples is less. In such circumstances, Eigen decomposition of the covariance matrix, whose dimension is number of electrodes x number of electrodes, is highly computational and may lead to imprecision.

To reduce the number of electrodes, the research work [3] has utilized neurological information to segregate the electrodes placed on the brain on the basis of various anatomical areas of brain cortex and select all electrodes of relevant brain areas. However, this method utilizes topographical information based stationary division of electrodes. Further, this approach either uses all electrodes of a chosen cluster or removes all electrodes of a minimum significant cluster. There is a possibility that few of the chosen electrodes may not be pertinent or might be repetitive and few of the removed electrodes of the not chosen brain region might be applicable for recognizing two motor imagery tasks. Hence, in this work, the electrodes are partitioned into many clusters such that each cluster contains a set of similar electrodes to reduce the number of electrodes. For this we use the spectral graph clustering method [7], where the optimal number of clusters is decided using the Davies Bouldin (DB) index criterion [5]. Features are extracted from each cluster using stationary CSP (SCSP) method [6]and composite kernel based support vector machine (CKSVM) is utilised to build a decision model.

The major contributions of this paper include: (i) To select a subject specific reduced subset of relevant electrodes; (ii) To evaluate and compare the performance of the proposed method and variants of CSP on the publicly available datasets; (iii) Friedman test is used to demonstrate that the proposed method significantly outperforms variants of the CSP method. Rest of the article is organized as follows. Section 2 discusses the proposed work. Experimental results are discussed in Sect. 3 and finally, Sect. 4 concludes the article and provides future directions.

2 Proposed Method: Temporal Similarity Based Clustering in Conjunction with CKCSP (TSC-CKCSP)

The flow diagram of the proposed model is shown in Fig. 1. A brief description of each step is described as follows:

2.1 Spectral Graph Clustering Based Division of Electrodes

Spectral clustering is a graph theoretic approach to obtain clusters using spectral decomposition of a similarity matrix $\mathbf{S}$. To measure similarity between two

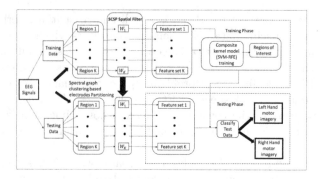

Fig. 1. Flow diagram of proposed model

samples, x_i and x_j, we have used Gaussian kernel which is defined as:

$$S(i,j) = \exp\left(-\frac{\parallel x_i - x_j \parallel^2}{2\sigma^2}\right) \qquad (1)$$

where σ is a tuning parameter. Let $\mathbf{d}$ denotes the vector $d = [d_1, d_2, \cdots, .d_N]$ where $d_i = \sum_{j=1}^{N} S(i,j)$ measures similarity of ith sample with all other samples. The larger value of d_i signifies more similarity of sample x_i with rest of the samples. Thus, the degree matrix $\mathbf{D}$ is given by:

$$\mathbf{D}(i,j) = \begin{cases} d_i & if\,i = j \\ 0 & otherwise \end{cases} \qquad (2)$$

The Laplacian matrix $\mathbf{L}$ and normalized Laplacian matrix $\tilde{\mathbf{L}}$ are defined as:

$$\mathbf{L} = \mathbf{D} - \mathbf{S} \ and \ \tilde{\mathbf{L}} = \mathbf{D}^{-\frac{1}{2}} \mathbf{L} \mathbf{D}^{-\frac{1}{2}} \qquad (3)$$

Eigenvalues and eigenvectors of the normalized Laplacian matrix $\tilde{\mathbf{L}}$ is solved as:

$$\tilde{\mathbf{L}}\gamma = \delta\gamma \qquad (4)$$

Let the Eigenvector γ_2 correspond to the second smallest Eigenvalue δ_2. Binary partitioning of electrodes using Eigenvector γ_2 is done as follows:

$$Electrode_i = \begin{cases} Cluster\ 1 & if\ \gamma_{i,l} < 0 \\ Cluster\ 2 & otherwise \end{cases} \qquad (5)$$

A given cluster is further recursively partitioned using spectral clustering method. To obtain an optimal number of clusters, a well-known Davies Bouldin (DB) criterion is used, which minimizes the ratio of within-cluster dispersion to between-cluster separation. The within-cluster dispersion for i^{th} cluster, Sw_i and between-cluster separation for cluster i and cluster j, $db_{i,j}$ are computed as:

$$Sw_i = \frac{1}{\mid C \mid} \sum_{x \epsilon C_i} \{\|x - z_i\|\} \ and \ db_{i,j} = \|z_i - z_j\| \qquad (6)$$

where z_i is the centroid of the ith cluster. The similarity measure between cluster i and cluster j and the corresponding DB index are given as:

$$M_{i,j} = \frac{Sw_i + Sw_j}{db_{i,j}} \ and \ DB = \frac{1}{k}\Sigma_{i=1}^k M_i \tag{7}$$

where $M_i = \max_{ij} M_{i,j}$ and k is the number of clusters. The number of clusters that provides minimal DB index value is considered optimal. The division of electrodes on both datasets is shown in Fig. 2.

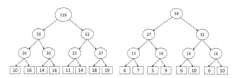

Fig. 2. Temporal Similarity based division of electrodes for Dataset 1 and Dataset 2

2.2 Stationary Common Spatial Patterns (SCSP)

Relevant features from each cluster of electrodes are computed using SCSP, which is evolved by introducing variations in the Rayleigh criterion function of the traditional CSP technique. Let $\mathbf{\Sigma_1}$ and $\mathbf{\Sigma_2}$ be the average covariance matrices of motor imagery left and right hand movement (class 1 and class 2), respectively and $\mathbf{W}$ is a spatial filter matrix for a given cluster. The Rayleigh criterion maximization function using SCSP is given as:

$$R(\mathbf{w}) = \frac{\mathbf{w^T\Sigma_1 w}}{\mathbf{w^T(\Sigma_1 + \Sigma_2)w + \beta P(w)}} \tag{8}$$

where $\mathbf{P(W)}$ is the introduced penalty term and β is a constant obtained after cross validation method. Further, the features computed from each cluster are transformed to a high dimensional Hilbert kernel space using a Gaussian kernel function to capture the non-linear relations of the extracted features as:

$$k_l(f_{i,l}, f_{j,l}) = \exp\left(-\frac{\| f_{i,l} - f_{i,l} \|}{2\sigma^2}\right) \tag{9}$$

where $f_{i,l}$ represents features from cluster l for trial i, obtained using SCSP method.

2.3 Feature Selection and Classification

In the proposed method, we have used CKSVM method for classification of motor imagery tasks. CKSVM considers the relevancy of an electrode cluster for recognition of motor imagery tasks.

$$\begin{cases} \max_{\alpha} -\frac{1}{2}\Sigma_{i,j}\alpha_i\alpha_j\gamma_i\gamma_j\Sigma_{l=1}^L k_l(f_{i,l}, f_{j,l}) + \Sigma_i\alpha_i \\ s.t \ \Sigma_i\alpha_i\gamma_i = 0, \ 0 \leqslant \alpha_i \leqslant C, \ 1 \leqslant l \leqslant R, \ 1 \leqslant i \leqslant N \end{cases} \tag{10}$$

where α_i is the classifier parameter, C is a classifier regularization parameter, N is the number of samples and R is the number of clusters. Recursive Feature Elimination (RFE) is used to order the electrode cluster of a specific brain region by calculating the quadratic norm of each cluster of electrodes. Higher is the estimation of the quadratic norm, more important is that cluster to a motor imagery task. The cluster with lowest value of quadratic normal form is removed in each iteration till maximum classification accuracy is achieved.

3   Experimental Setup and Results

The experimental evaluation of the proposed work is performed on publicly available BCI Competition III dataset 4a (Dataset 1) and BCI competition IV dataset Ia (Dataset 2) [3]. Dataset 1 and Dataset 2 consist of motor imagery data acquired from five and seven healthy subjects respectively. The data captured for each trial belongs to the time window of 0.5–2.5 s after the onset of stimulus. Thus, from each electrode, 200 time units are utilized. Whole data is filtered using a [7–30 Hz] bandpass filter. SCSP penalty parameter $\beta = 0.1$ was used for all the experiments on both datasets, which is determined using cross-validation. Number of spatial patterns was fixed to r = 1. The average classification accuracy of the proposed method is reported in terms of 10 fold cross-validation run 10 times and is compared to CSP, SCSP and CKSCSP methods as shown in Tables 1 and 2 for subjects of Dataset 1 and Dataset 2, respectively.

Table 1. Comparison of TSC-CKCSP with existing methods in terms of average classification accuracy for Dataset 1.

Subject	CSP	SCSP	CKSCSP	TSC-CKCSP
aa	75.37	80.45	81.14	**82.8052**
al	97.73	94.38	**98.34**	96.91304
av	69.14	69.82	77.56	**78.1667**
aw	82.27	82.43	86.64	**88.5667**
ay	82.17	89.33	88.17	**90.13**
MEAN	81.34	83.28	86.37	**87.3163**

We can observe the following from Table 1: (i) The proposed method TSC-CKCSP achieves highest average classification accuracy for Dataset 1; (ii) An overall increment of 7.35%, 4.85%, and 1.1% in classification accuracy as compared to CSP, SCSP and CKSCSP is achieved with our proposed method TSC-CKCSP for Dataset 1. Similarly, the following can be observed from Table 2: (i) The proposed method TSC-CKCSP achieves highest average classification accuracy for Dataset 2 (ii) An overall increment of 12.08%, 3.54%, and 3.17% in classification accuracy as compared to CSP, SCSP and CKSCSP is achieved with our proposed method TSC-CKCSP. The spectral graph clustering is a data

Table 2. Comparison of TSC-CKCSP with existing methods in terms of average classification accuracy for Dataset 2.

Subject	CSP	SCSP	CKSCSP	TSC-CKCSP
ds1a	73.1	81.75	67.05	**82.65**
ds1b	65.4	59.95	71.45	**71.89**
ds1c	70.5	75.1	75.35	**77.55**
ds1d	76.8	89.2	90.3	**90.55**
ds1e	83.3	**90.35**	89.55	90.15
ds1f	82.8	86.9	88.3	**87.35**
ds1g	79	91.45	94.75	**94.89**
MEAN	75.84	82.1	82.39	**85.0043**

centric approach, hence provide relevant and subject specific clusters. Thus, the proposed method performs better than existing methods.

Table 3. The Friedman ranking obtained for each method.

Algorithm	Ranking
TSC-CKCSP	1.333
CKSCSP	2.166
SCSP	2.833
CSP	3.66

A non-parametric Friedman statistical test [1], is carried out to find the statistical difference between the proposed method and existing methods at significance value of $\alpha = 0.5$. Table 3 shows the Friedman ranking obtained for each method. P-value computed by Friedman Test is 1.5642 E-6, which signifies that the all methods under comparison are statistical significantly different from each other. Smaller value of Friedman ranking suggests proposed method outperforms variants of CSP.

4   Conclusion

An immense interest has been garnered by Motor imagery BCI due its wide applicability for communication. CSP is a widely used feature extraction technique for motor imagery BCI. However, it suffers from SSS problem due to numerous electrodes and smaller quantity of samples. The proposed method determines a reduced set of relevant electrodes using spectral clustering and CKSVM.

However, the proposed method uses only temporal information of data for division of electrodes and does not consider frequency information for clustering of electrodes. Thus, in future, we will incorporate both spatial, temporal and frequency information for obtaining a reduced and relevant subset of electrodes. Further, RFE in conjunction with SVM utilized in this work is computationally intensive, which requires improvement for real time-applications.

References

1. Iman, R.L., Davenport, J.M.: Approximations of the critical region of the fbietkan statistic. Commun. Stat.-Theor. Methods **9**(6), 571–595 (1980)
2. Kirar, J.S., Agrawal, R.: Optimal spatio-spectral variable size subbands filter for motor imagery brain computer interface. Proc. Comput. Sci. **84**, 14–21 (2016)
3. Kirar, J.S., Agrawal, R.: Composite kernel support vector machine based performance enhancement of brain computer interface in conjunction with spatial filter. Biomed. Sig. Process. Control **33**, 151–160 (2017)
4. Lu, H., Eng, H.L., Guan, C., Plataniotis, K.N., Venetsanopoulos, A.N.: Regularized common spatial pattern with aggregation for EEG classification in small-sample setting. IEEE Trans. Biomed. Eng. **57**(12), 2936–2946 (2010)
5. Maulik, U., Bandyopadhyay, S.: Performance evaluation of some clustering algorithms and validity indices. IEEE Trans. Patt. Anal. Mach. Intell. **24**(12), 1650–1654 (2002)
6. Samek, W., Vidaurre, C., Müller, K.R., Kawanabe, M.: Stationary common spatial patterns for brain-computer interfacing. J. Neural Eng. **9**(2), 026013 (2012)
7. Von Luxburg, U.: A tutorial on spectral clustering. Stat. Comput. **17**(4), 395–416 (2007)
8. Wolpaw, J., Wolpaw, E.W.: Brain-Computer Interfaces: Principles and Practice. OUP, USA (2012)

Automated Measurement of Translational Margins and Rotational Shifts in Pelvic Structures Using CBCT Images of Rectal Cancer Patients

Sai Phani Kumar Malladi[1(✉)], Bijju Kranthi Veduruparthi[2], Jayanta Mukherjee[2], Partha Pratim Das[2], Saswat Chakrabarti[3], and Indranil Mallick[4]

[1] Advanced Technology Development Centre, Indian Institute of Technology, Kharagpur, India
saiphani.malladi@gmail.com

[2] Department of Computer Science and Engineering, Indian Institute of Technology, Kharagpur, India
{bijjukranthi,jay,ppd}@cse.iitkgp.ernet.in

[3] G S Sanyal School of Telecommunications, Indian Institute of Technology, Kharagpur, India
saswat@ece.iitkgp.ernet.in

[4] Department of Radiation Oncology, Tata Medical Centre, Kolkata, India
indranil.mallick@tmckolkata.com

Abstract. Clinical radiotherapy procedures target to achieve high accuracy which is inhibited by various error sources. As a result, a safety margin is needed to ensure that the planned dosage is delivered to the target. In this work, 3D image coordinates of Pubic Symphysis (pb) and *Coccyx* are evaluated from Cone Beam CT images of colo-rectal cancer patients. Using those coordinates, we propose an automated method to obtain systematic and random error components. The standard deviations of systematic and random errors are used to evaluate the 3D PTV margin. We have also measured rotational variations in the positioning of patients using those locations. We have validated and found that the automated measurements show a very good match with those measured by oncologists manually.

Keywords: Coccyx · Pb · PTV · Rotational shifts · Random · Systematic errors

1 Introduction

The procedures of clinical radiotherapy target to achieve high accuracy [1]. As treatment preparation involves various errors, a safety margin is required to ensure that the planned dose is actually delivered to the target. The margin calculations require reference bony structures because bones are good surrogates to detect internal motion of organs like rectum [1]. In [2], the authors evaluate the

© Springer International Publishing AG 2017
B.U. Shankar et al. (Eds.): PReMI 2017, LNCS 10597, pp. 103–109, 2017.
https://doi.org/10.1007/978-3-319-69900-4_13

3D locations of Pubic Symphysis (pb) and *Coccyx*. These are then used as reference structures in the pelvic region from Cone Beam Computed Tomography (CBCT) image volumes of colo-rectal cancer patients. On a day to day basis, there are considerable variations in the locations of pb and *coccyx*. The CBCT image volumes are, therefore, registered using Mean Shift assisted Mutual Information based 3D Registration (MSMIR) technique to reduce these uncertainties. In the report given by International Commission on Radiation Units and Measurements (ICRU) [3], it is mentioned that the volume that should receive the prescribed dose, is Clinical Target Volume (CTV), comprising of demonstrable tumor and/or areas of suspected subclinical disease. To account for the geometrical uncertainties, CTV must be expanded with a 3D margin thereby yielding Planning Target Volume (PTV).

In our study, the acquisition of CBCT images of a rectal cancer patients is carried out for a series of 27 days to obtain 27 CBCT image volumes. Only on the first day of the diagnosis, along with CBCT, a planning CT scan is also carried out with reference to which the shifts in the positions of pb and *coccyx* are evaluated. Usually, radiation treatment (RT) is given in multiple fractions of radiation to the evaluated PTV. When the total dose of radiation is divided into several, smaller doses over a period of several days, there are fewer toxic effects on healthy cells.

During a treatment regime, any deviation from planned irradiation geometry may be systematic or random. Systematic errors occur if the mean irradiation geometry in the fractionated treatment differs from the geometry in the treatment plan. The mean deviations of coordinates are then called systematic errors. Day-to-day differences around the mean deviation are called random errors [4]. Van Herk [1] proposed a model for deriving the PTV margin which is given as Margin $= 2.5 \, \Sigma + 0.7 \, \sigma$. The criterion for this was that on an average, more than 99% of the CTV should get at least 95% of the dose. Mainly, our contributions in this work are as follows:

1. Automated computation of translational and rotational shifts, 3D PTV margins for colo-rectal cancer patients,
2. Higher accuracy in the computation of error margins, and
3. Use of conventional imaging procedure only, requiring no additional imaging or investigation procedure on the patients.

Conformal radiotherapy treatment on patients suffering from prostate cancer is done using infrared (IR) marker based positioning system over 553 treatment fractions [5]. Standard deviation of anteroposterior (AP) and lateral set up errors was considerably reduced to 4.8 mm compared to conventional technique. The main drawback is that IR system could not correctly locate markers which lead to execution failure in 21% of 553 fractions.

Using kilovoltage CBCT in combination with a diet and mild laxatives, work in [6] evaluated clinical results of adaptive radiotherapy protocol for prostate cancer. Compared to historical data which was without diet and laxatives, systematic and random errors for organ motion were reduced by a factor of 2.

The laxatives, that were used, improved image quality, and thereby helped in detecting prostate reducing high dose region by 29%.

The work in [7] gives the effect of random and systematic deviations on target dose in the form of an analytical description. Higher random variations imply underdosage to CTV for a large number of patients, while the equal systematic error implies much larger underdosage for some of the patients. During the preparation stage of radiotherapy for prostate cancer, it reduces the uncertainty in the position of prostate and the shape of rectum. The motion of prostate relative to pelvic bone is quantified by matching CT scan with planning CT. The systematic error was 5.1°, and the random error was 3.6°.

2   Computation of Translational and Rotational Error Margins

In this work, we consider the first day 3D image coordinates of pb and $coccyx$ as reference, to find out the shift in their positions for next 26 consecutive days. These shifts are considered to evaluate the systematic and random errors. The shifts in the positions are represented by a vector $\boldsymbol{E}_{B_{ij}}$ for the ith patient on the jth day, where $B \in [pb, coccyx]$. In this work, a vector is represented by a bold and italicized alphabet like $\boldsymbol{E}$.

$$\boldsymbol{E}_{B_{ij}} = [(X_{ij} - X_{i1}), (Y_{ij} - Y_{i1}), (Z_{ij} - Z_{i1})], \forall i \in [1, P] \text{ and } \forall j \in [1, N]$$

where P is the number of patients under study, and N is the number of days of diagnosis. In our study, the values of P and N are 25 and 27, respectively. The vector $\boldsymbol{E}$ is averaged for pb and $coccyx$ to find shift in entire patient volume which is represented as $\boldsymbol{E}_{a_{ij}}$, where subscript $\boldsymbol{a}$ denotes the averaging operation.

The 3D mean of the shifts for N days is represented by $\boldsymbol{M}_{a_i}$ for a particular (the ith) patient.

$$\boldsymbol{M}_{a_i} = \left(\frac{\sum_{j=1}^{N}(X_{ij} - X_{i1})}{N}, \frac{\sum_{j=1}^{N}(Y_{ij} - Y_{i1})}{N}, \frac{\sum_{j=1}^{N}(Z_{ij} - Z_{i1})}{N}\right), \forall i \in [1, P]$$

The 3D standard deviations of the shifts for daily measurements are represented by $\boldsymbol{S}_{a_i}$ for a particular (the ith) patient. We represent unit vectors in the directions of X, Y and Z by $\hat{x}$, $\hat{y}$ and $\hat{z}$ respectively. Dot product of any vector with $\hat{x}$, $\hat{y}$ and $\hat{z}$ gives out only the x, y and z components, respectively.

$$\boldsymbol{S}_{a_i} = \left(\sqrt{\frac{\sum_{j=1}^{N}(\boldsymbol{E}_{a_{ij}} \cdot \hat{x} - \boldsymbol{M}_{a_i} \cdot \hat{x})^2}{N}}, \sqrt{\frac{\sum_{j=1}^{N}(\boldsymbol{E}_{a_{ij}} \cdot \hat{y} - \boldsymbol{M}_{a_i} \cdot \hat{y})^2}{N}}, \sqrt{\frac{\sum_{j=1}^{N}(\boldsymbol{E}_{a_{ij}} \cdot \hat{z} - \boldsymbol{M}_{a_i} \cdot \hat{z})^2}{N}}\right), \forall i \in [1, P]$$

Then the Group Systematic Error (GSE), which is the mean evaluated over the entire group of patients is represented by a vector $\boldsymbol{G}_a$.

$$\boldsymbol{G}_a = \left(\frac{\sum_{i=1}^{P}\boldsymbol{M}_{a_i} \cdot \hat{x}}{P}, \frac{\sum_{i=1}^{P}\boldsymbol{M}_{a_i} \cdot \hat{y}}{P}, \frac{\sum_{i=1}^{P}\boldsymbol{M}_{a_i} \cdot \hat{z}}{P}\right)$$

The standard deviations of the systematic errors is represented by a vector Σ_a.

$$\Sigma_a = (\sqrt{\frac{\sum_{i=1}^{P}(M_{a_i}.\hat{x} - G_{a_i}.\hat{x})^2}{P}}, \sqrt{\frac{\sum_{i=1}^{P}(M_{a_i}.\hat{y} - G_{a_i}.\hat{y})^2}{P}}, \sqrt{\frac{\sum_{i=1}^{P}(M_{a_i}.\hat{z} - G_{a_i}.\hat{z})^2}{P}})$$

And the standard deviations of the random errors are the root mean square of all the standard deviations of all the patients represented by a vector σ_a.

$$\sigma_a = (\sqrt{\frac{\sum_{i=1}^{P}(S_{a_i}.\hat{x})^2}{P}}, \sqrt{\frac{\sum_{i=1}^{P}(S_{a_i}.\hat{y})^2}{P}}, \sqrt{\frac{\sum_{i=1}^{P}(S_{a_i}.\hat{z})^2}{P}})$$

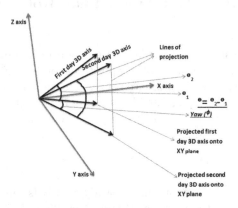

Fig. 1. Demonstration of the calculations of Pitch and Yaw.

On a day-to-day basis, along with translational variations, there occur rotational variations in the position of patients. Before RT, to prepare treatment planning, the positioning of the patient has to be corrected in terms of rotations made in all the three axes. In this work, we have considered the first day 3D axis joining pb and $coccyx$ as the reference to find rotational variations for the next 26 consecutive days. The sequence of steps to do this are:

1. We translate 3D coccyx coordinates of second day to that of the first day.
2. Then we project the 3D axes (defined by pb and $coccyx$) of two days onto the XY plane.
3. The angles made by the 3D axes with their projected 2D axes are denoted by $\theta1$ and $\theta2$, respectively, whose difference is referred to $Pitch$ (θ) in Fig. 1.
4. The angle between the projected 2D axes is referred to Yaw (ϕ) in Fig. 1.

3   Results

The box plots showing variation of different measurements are shown in Fig. 2. The Euclidean norm of vectors M and S provide average shifts in locations of *pb* and *coccyx*. We observe that the means (horizontal line) in first two boxes (*automated and manual-translational*) of a patient are close to each other validating the computational process. The two ends or whiskers of those two boxes show that their distributions are also similar. The third box of each patient gives the Euclidean norm of rotational variations which are relatively constant for all the patients. We observe that smaller rotational values indicate the better adherence to the fractionated RT for a patient [8]. The observations done till now in prior works were all about tracking the motion of a particular organ. But, in this work, we provided a more generalised way of detecting shifts in the position of patients. As rectum stays relatively more stable with respect to pelvic bony structures (i.e. *pb* and *coccyx* in this case), the most suitable way of detecting the motion of rectum is to detect the motion of bones. Lesser the difference between Σ and σ, lesser the underdosage to the target [7], as shown in Table 1. We observe that the difference between Σ and σ is small. As a result, it is expected that the underdosage to the PTV would be less probable during RT.

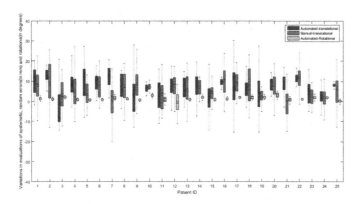

Fig. 2. Variations in translational and rotational shifts for all the patients.

It can be observed that the vector G in Table 1 deviating a little from zero which is expected because of imprecision in the equipment. It is found that the vectors G and Σ in z-direction are slightly higher which indicates a slight higher internal organ motion in that direction [8]. We also observe that the vectors G, Σ, σ and 3D PTV margin calculated automatically are highly matching with those values evaluated manually. It shows that this automated system can be a very good replacement for manual efforts which aids oncologists in treatment planning before RT.

4   Conclusion

In this work, the 3D image coordinates of *pb* and *coccyx* are used to calculate the translational and rotational shifts. The average of shifts in the positions of *pb*

Table 1. PTV margins evaluated considering the standard deviations of random and systematic errors.

Evaluations considering the shifts given by Oncologists											
G			Σ			σ			3D PTV		
x	y	z	x	y	z	x	y	z	x	y	z
0.53	−0.36	0.30	3.71	3.77	4.15	5.46	3.17	4.55	13.11	12.66	13.56
Automatic evaluations averaging the shifts of pb and coccyx											
G			Σ			σ			3D PTV		
x	y	z	x	y	z	x	y	z	x	y	z
0.62	−0.54	−0.42	3.80	3.48	5.38	5.33	3.49	4.64	13.24	11.16	16.68

and *coccyx* are considered to find variations in the position of the whole patient volume on day-to-day basis. These variations are used to obtain the 3D PTV margin using Van Herk [1] recipe for focusing prescribed radiation dose to the target. The first day 3D axis joining *pb* and *coccyx* is taken as reference to align 3D axes of remaining days with it. The 3D locations of *pb* and *coccyx* found in this work are more accurate than those found in [9]. We have validated our results with the measurements provided by an oncologist for the same set of patients as shown in Table 1. From Fig. 2, we observe that the rotational variations are quite small compared to those evaluated in [8]. This automated process of estimating the systematic, random errors, 3D PTV margin and rotations requires only the CBCT image volumes of the patients and does not need any other supportive data or expensive imaging technology. The proposed technique is fast, it involves no manual intervention, and reduces the occurrence of human errors.

Acknowledgment. This work is carried out under the MHRD sponsored project entitled as "Predicting Cancer Treatment outcomes of lung and colo-rectal cancer by modeling and analysis of anatomic and metabolic images" (Grant No. IIT/SRIC/CSE/ILA/2013-14/214 dt. 16/04/2014).

References

1. Van Herk, M.: Errors and margins in radiotherapy. Semin. Radiat. Oncol. **14**, 52–64 (2004). Elsevier
2. Malladi, S.P.K., Veduruparthi, B.K., Mukherjee, J., Das, P.P., Chakrabarti, S., Mallick, I.: Reduction of variance of observations on pelvic structures in CBCT images using novel mean-shift and mutual information based image registration? In: Proceedings of the Tenth Indian Conference on Computer Vision, Graphics and Image Processing, ICVGIP 2016, pp. 84:1–84:8. ACM, New York (2016)
3. Wambersie, A., Landberg, T., Chavaudra, J., Dobbs, J., Hanks, G., Johansson, K., Moller, T., Purdy, J., Akanuma, A., Gerard, J., et al.: Prescribing, recording, and reporting photon beam therapy presentation of the ICRU report# 50. J. Med. Phys. **17**(4), 5 (1992)

4. de Boer, H.C., van Sörnsen de Koste, J.R., Senan, S., Visser, A.G., Heijmen, B.J.: Analysis and reduction of 3d systematic and random setup errors during the simulation and treatment of lung cancer patients with ct-based external beam radiotherapy dose planning. Int. J. Radiat. Oncol.* Biol.* Phys. **49**(3), 857–868 (2001)
5. Soete, G., Van de Steene, J., Verellen, D., Vinh-Hung, V., Van den Berge, D., Michielsen, D., Keuppens, F., De Roover, P., Storme, G.: Initial clinical experience with infrared-reflecting skin markers in the positioning of patients treated by conformal radiotherapy for prostate cancer. Int. J. Radiat. Oncol.* Biol.* Phys. **52**(3), 694–698 (2002)
6. Nijkamp, J., Pos, F.J., Nuver, T.T., De Jong, R., Remeijer, P., Sonke, J.-J., Lebesque, J.V.: Adaptive radiotherapy for prostate cancer using kilovoltage cone-beam computed tomography: first clinical results. Int. J. Radiat. Oncol.* Biol.* Phys. **70**(1), 75–82 (2008)
7. van Herk, M., Remeijer, P., Rasch, C., Lebesque, J.V.: The probability of correct target dosage: dose-population histograms for deriving treatment margins in radiotherapy. Int. J. Radiat. Oncol.* Biol.* Phys. **47**(4), 1121–1135 (2000)
8. Owen, R., Kron, T., Foroudi, F., Milner, A., Cox, J., Duchesne, G.: Interfraction prostate rotation determined from in-room computerized tomography images. Med. Dosim. **36**(2), 188–194 (2011)
9. Mandal, S., Veduruparthi, B.K., Mukherjee, J., Das, P.P., Mallick, I.: Study of variation of pelvis positioning for patients suffering from rectal cancer using daily kilo-voltage cone beam CT images. In: 2015 Fifth National Conference on Computer Vision, Pattern Recognition, Image Processing and Graphics (NCVPRIPG), pp. 1–4. IEEE (2015)

Exploring the Scope of HSV Color Channels Towards Simple Shadow Contour Detection

Jayeeta Saha and Arpitam Chatterjee[(✉)] [iD]

Department of Printing Engineering, Jadavpur University, Kolkata, India
jayeetasaha03@gmail.com, arpitamchatterjee@gmail.com

Abstract. This paper presents a comparatively simple approach towards shadow contour detection in image. The methods of shadow detection during the last decade is based on chromacity, physical, geometry and texture of the image but most of the reported techniques are time consuming and computationally expensive. The presented method is based on color space and color channel selection on terms of co-occurrence matrix (GLCM) feature. The original images are converted to HSV color space from its native RGB color space for examining the separation of shadow and non-shadow regions in different color channels. The study reveals that value (V) and saturation (S) component is visibly influenced by the shadow and the same is reflected in their GLCM feature values. Thus further segmentation and morphological operations on those channels can result into a comparatively easier detection of shadow for simple and well as complex cases. The pictorial presentations of the results show the considerable potential of the presented technique.

Keywords: Shadow detection · Shadow contour detection · Color space · GLCM features

1 Introduction

When the illumination or the light is blocked by an object a natural phenomenon called shadow is occurred. In computer vision and computer graphics applications, shadow detection and manipulation have an important role to study the object shape [1, 2], size, movement [3], number of light sources and illumination condition [4]. But when shadows are merged with the background image it causes degradation of image quality. Shadow free images can help to improve the performance of the task such as object recognition, object tracking and information enhancement.

According to earlier work on shadow detection, the algorithm mainly depends on spectral, spatial and temporal feature of image. Intensity, chromacity, physical, geometrical and textural features of pixel play important role to find out the shadow in image. However, all those feature based techniques [5] have strict assumptions as they are not compatible for different environment as well as some features are robust and take longer time to implement. A successive thresholding technique (STS) [6] is applied to detect shadow more accurately. Moreover shadow can be detected by dividing the cast shadow region into sub region- umbra, shallow umbra and penumbra shadow region [7]. Multiple

© Springer International Publishing AG 2017
B.U. Shankar et al. (Eds.): PReMI 2017, LNCS 10597, pp. 110–115, 2017.
https://doi.org/10.1007/978-3-319-69900-4_14

convolution neural networks are used to understand the feature of shadow pixels and Bayesian formulation is modeled to extract the shadow region [8]. For high spatial resolution detection of shadow is very critical and difficult to find the contour of the shadow region in degraded image. To get high quality shadow free image the first problem is to detect the area boundary of the shadow region and for the image with complex shadow it is really a difficult and challenging task.

In this paper, we present a comparatively simpler shadow contour detection approach which is based on the color space and the gray level co-occurrence matrix (GLCM) [9, 10] feature of the individual color channel. For this purpose we choose at first the HSV color space since HSV color space contains better information than RGB color space and it is not a device dependent color space representing a closer approximation of human perception to color. Generally hue component are almost same in shadow and non-shadow region in HSV whereas saturation and value component have different characteristics between the two regions.

2   Presented Method

2.1   Color Space Conversion

The purpose of color space is to specify each color by a single point of a coordinate and a subspace within a system. Most commonly used color model or color space is RGB for color monitors and video cameras. As human being is strongly perceptive to the red, green, blue primaries this color space is suitable for hardware implementations. But for describing a color of an object we rather use the terms hue, saturation and its intensity values where hue is a color attribute which describes a pure color like pure red or blue. Saturation is defined as the colorfulness of an area with respect to its brightness. The intensity values describe the color sensation and it can be easily measured by the gray level of the image pixel [11]. So this model carries better information than RGB and frequently used for image processing algorithms like image segmentation, image smoothing and sharpening.

In HSV model hue can be described in terms of an angle in the circular coordinate. Although a circle contains 360 degrees of rotation, the hue value is normalized to a range from 0 to 255, with 0 being red. Saturation value ranges from 0 to 255. The lower the saturation value, the more gray is present in the color, causing it to appear faded. Value represents the brightness of the color. It ranges from 0 to 255, with 0 being completely dark and 255 being fully bright. The hue and saturation level do not make a difference when value is at max or min intensity level. RGB to HSV space conversion can be done using standard equations.

The example of an image in RGB and HSV including the individual channel information is presented in Fig. 1. The interesting observation in Fig. 1 is that the shadow information and background information is not almost same in all channels like RGB channels. Particularly in the S and V channel the shadow and non-shadow difference is well visible. But it is not always that a particular channel or combination of channels will be good for contour extraction for all the cases. This can be addressed by GLCM feature based channel(s) selection mechanism as described in following section.

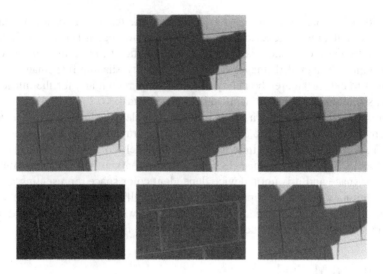

Fig. 1. Example of original image and its different channels. The top row: original RGB image; middle row from left to right R, G and B channel; bottom row from left to right H, S and V channel.

2.2   Channel Selection for Contour Extraction

In HSV color space hue component is almost same for shadow and non-shadow region but the saturation and value component shows the different characteristic for this two regions. GLCM may be a possible choice for channel selection towards shadow contour detection.

GLCM is a method of extracting the second order statistical texture feature. From the GLCM matrices [9] many features can be extracted [10]. Among those features inertia and inverse difference moment (IDM) of the image pixels in each channel have been used in this work. Inertia is mainly used as a measure of intensity contrast between a pixel and its neighbor pixel over the entire image. Inertia can be expressed as Eq. (1) where i, j are row and column index, respectively, G is the dimension of GLCM matrices and $P(i, j)$ denotes the probability matrix calculated from the co-occurrence matrices.

$$Inertia = \sum_{i=0}^{G-1} \sum_{j=0}^{G-1} \{i - j\}^2 \times P(i, j) \tag{1}$$

Inverse difference moment (IDM) is also known as homogeneity and can be expressed as Eq. (2). It measures image homogeneity as it assumes larger values for smaller gray tone differences in pair elements. It is more sensitive to the presence of near diagonal elements in the GLCM. It has maximum value when all elements in the image are same. GLCM contrast and homogeneity are strongly, but inversely, correlated in terms of equivalent distribution in the pixel pairs population. It means homogeneity decreases if contrast increases while energy is kept constant.

$$IDM = \sum_{i=0}^{G-1} \sum_{j=0}^{G-1} \frac{1}{1 + \{i - j\}^2} \times P(i,j) \qquad (2)$$

Further from GLCM features the standard deviation in each channel were also calculated. The feature set of each channel was constructed using inertia, IDM and standard deviation.

From the statistical data analysis of the feature sets it was observed that a channel with lower inertia and IDM values with a higher standard deviation is more suitable for shadow contour detection. But some of images do not follow this criterion particularly for complex images where the background and shadow are mixed in a higher degree that means the contrast between the background and shadow is comparatively low. For those images singular value decomposition (SVD) was calculated. The channel having lower value of SVD is considered suitable for shadow detection. It was also found that for complex images a single channel is not sufficient for shadow contour detection, therefore a logical operation between two channels with lower most SVD values was performed. The final contour was extracted by adaptive thresholding of Otsu's method [12] followed by suitable morphological operations. In this case erosion and dilation morphological operation with standard structuring elements was performed.

3   Results and Discussions

The results found with the database [13] are presented here. The databases also contain shadows under a variety of illumination conditions such as sunny, cloudy and dark environments. Most of the images shadow contour is detected in value channel but in some image shadow can also be detected in saturation channel which we named as complex image. The contour extractions for simple and complex images are shown in Figs. 2 and 3, respectively.

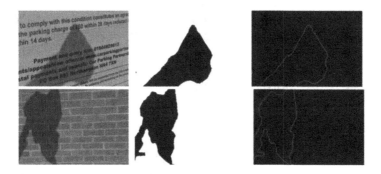

Fig. 2. Example of extracted shadow contour with single color channel (V channel).

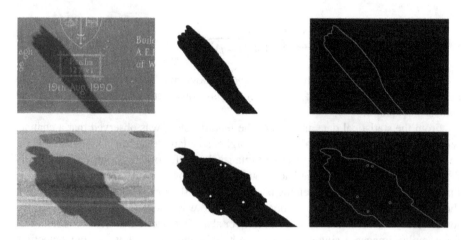

Fig. 3. Example of extracted shadow contour with two channel logical operation (S and V channel).

Figures 2 and 3 both show that in all the presented test cases the shadow contour is well detected. Figure 2 comprises two test images that are comparatively simple since the background and the shadow is not well mixed. These cases can be handled by the V channel alone which is showing the lower inertia and IDM values and higher standard deviation values as shown in Table 1. But, in case of images in Fig. 3 which are comparatively complex cases two channels information are used based on the SVD values as shown in Table 1 right side.

Table 1. Feature values for test image in Figs. 2 and 3

Test image (Fig. 2)	Color channel	Inertia	IDM	Standard deviation	Test image (Fig. 3)	SVD
Test image 1	H	0.4749	1.4749	2.8336	Test image 1	3.7517
	S	0.9908	1.9908	2.6703		**3.2084**
	V	**0.2219**	**1.2219**	**3.2152**		**3.2467**
Test image 2	H	0.7339	1.7339	2.1366	Test image 2	5.0721
	S	0.0555	1.0555	2.6648		**3.0118**
	V	**0.0378**	**1.0378**	**2.6757**		**2.7381**

4   Conclusion

A simple approach of shadow contour detection based on the HSV color space and the GLCM texture feature of the image pixels is presented in this paper. The method took both simple and complex test cases under consideration. The simple images can be processed by single color channel information while for the complex images two channels information were used for logical operation prior the thresholding and morphological operations to obtain the shadow contour. The results show the possible potential of the technique. The process is less time consuming as well. A major limitation of the process may be appearance of some unwanted bubble which may be outside the contour of interest or within. This can be handled using appropriate post-processing operations. The study can be further extended to the different perception based color spaces, application of adaptive structuring element for morphological operations, channel interaction of different color spaces, etc. This study is focused to the contour detection only while the reconstruction of the image without shadow is probably the most important follow up work in future.

References

1. Matsushita, Y., Nishino, K., Ikeuchi, K., Sakauchi, M.: Illumination normalization with time-dependent intrinsic images for video surveillance. IEEE Trans. Pattern Anal. Mach. Intell. **26**(10), 1336–1347 (2004)
2. Okabe, T., Sato, I., Sato, Y.: Attached shadow coding: estimating surface normals from shadows under unknown reflectance and lighting conditions. In: IEEE 12th International Conference on Computer Vision (2009)
3. Kersten, D., Knill, D., Mamassian, P., Bülthoff, I.: Illusory motion from shadows. Nature **379**(6560), 31 (1996)
4. Sato, I., Sato, Y., Ikeuchi, K.: Illumination from shadows. IEEE Trans. Pattern Anal. Mach. Intell. **25**(3), 290–300 (2003)
5. Sanin, A., Sanderson, C.D., Lovell, B.C.: Shadow detection: a survey and comparative evaluation of recent methods, journal homepage. www.elsevier.com
6. Chung, K.L., Lin, Y.R., Huang, Y.H.: Efficient shadow detection of color Aerial images based on successive thresholding scheme. IEEE Trans. Geosci. Remote Sensing **47**(2), 671–682 (2009)
7. Wang, Y., Tang, M., Zhu, G.: An improved cast shadow detection method with edge refinement. In: Proceedings of the Sixth International Conference on Intelligent Systems Design and Applications, (ISDA 2006) (2006)
8. Khan, S.H., Bennamoun, M., Sohel, F., Togneri, R.: Automatic shadow detection and removal from a single image. IEEE Trans. Pattern Anal. Mach. Intell. **38**(3), 431–446 (2016)
9. Albregsten, F.: Statistical Texture Measures Computed from Gray Level Coocurrence Matrices (2008)
10. Pathak, B., Barooah, D.: Texture analysis based on the gray-level co-occurrence matrix considering possible orientations. Int. J. Adv. Res. Electr. Electron. Instrumentation Eng. **2**(9), 4206–4212 (2013)
11. Gonzalez, R.C., Woods, R.E.: Digital Image Processing. Pearson Education India, New Delhi (2009)
12. Sezgin, M., Sankur, B.: Survey over image thresholding techniques and quantitative performance evaluation. J. Electron. Imaging **13**(1), 146–165 (2004). doi:10.1117/1.1631315
13. Stony Brook University Shadow Dataset (SBU-Shadow5k). http://ww3.cs.stonybrook.edu/~cvl/dataset.html

Linear Curve Fitting-Based Headline Estimation in Handwritten Words for Indian Scripts

Rahul Pramanik$^{(\boxtimes)}$ (ID) and Soumen Bag (ID)

Department of Computer Science and Engineering, Indian Institute of Technology
(ISM) Dhanbad, Dhanbad, India
rahul.wbsu@gmail.com, bagsoumen@gmail.com

Abstract. Most segmentation algorithms for Indian scripts require some prior knowledge about the structure of a handwritten word to efficiently fragment the word into constituent characters. Zone detection is a considerably used strategy for this purpose. Headline estimation is a salient part of zone detection. In the present work, we propose a method that uses simple linear regression for estimating headlines present in handwritten words. This method efficiently detects headline in three Indian scripts, namely Bangla, Devanagari, and Gurmukhi. The proposed method is able to detect headlines in skewed word images and provides accurate result even when the headline is discontinuous or mostly absent. We have compared our method with a recent work to show the efficacy of our proposed methodology.

Keywords: Handwritten words · Headline estimation · Indian scripts · Linear regression

1 Introduction

Segmentation is one of the most consequential phase in optical character recognition. Presence of cursiveness in Indian scripts makes the segmentation task much more harder [1]. Most segmentation algorithms for Indian scripts require some prior knowledge about the structure of a handwritten word to efficiently fragment the word into constituent characters. Zone detection is a considerably-used strategy for this purpose. Zone detection separates a word into three segments, namely upper, middle, and lower zone. The upper zone is detected by exploiting the headline, a special feature present in most Indian scripts. Sarkar *et al.* [2] have computed the headline in Bangla words by extracting horizontalness and verticalness features from the words. Roy *et al.* [3] have estimated headline in Bangla words using the height of the word, horizontal projection analysis and certain heuristics. Bag and Krishna [4] have used horizontal density row and local maximum row for detecting headlines in handwritten Hindi words. But, these methods suffer when the words are skewed or when the headline is discontinuous or mostly absent. Furthermore, there is an inadequacy of methodologies that are capable of handling multi-script in a document.

© Springer International Publishing AG 2017
B.U. Shankar et al. (Eds.): PReMI 2017, LNCS 10597, pp. 116–123, 2017.
https://doi.org/10.1007/978-3-319-69900-4_15

Fig. 1. Horizontal line called *mātrā* in Bangla, *shirorekhā* in Devanagari script, and headline in Gurmukhi script.

In the present work, we propose a method that uses simple linear regression for estimating headlines present in handwritten words. This method efficiently detects headline in three Indian scripts, namely Bangla, Devanagari, and Gurmukhi. It can be effectively used in word images extracted from a document comprising of multi headline-based script without any prior knowledge about the scripts. The proposed method is able to detect headlines in skewed word images and provides accurate result even when the headline is discontinuous or mostly absent.

The rest of the paper is organized as follows. The proposed methodology is delineated in Sect. 2. In Sect. 3, the experimental results and analysis are discussed, followed by conclusion in Sect. 4.

2   Proposed Method

Most Indian scripts have a distinctive feature called headline (also known as *mātrā* in Bangla and *shirorekhā* in Devanagari script) (Fig. 1) present in words. All the characters are connected by the headline at the upper portion of a word. This headline is sometimes discontinuous depending on the individuality of a person's handwriting. We propose a strategy that utilises this distinctive feature to estimate headline present in word images. The method employed is very simple and effective.

2.1   Preprocessing

Initially we binarize all gray level word image (τ_k) (Fig. 2a). We denote the binarized image as $\nu(\tau_k)$. We use Rosenfeld and Kak component labelling algorithm to label all the connected components and calculate the size (w.r.t. total number of pixels) of each connected component in $\nu(\tau_k)$. Next, we remove each connected component that appears on the top three-fourth of $\nu(\tau_k)$ and constitutes pixels below a certain threshold, $\rho(=30)$ as a noise normalization procedure. We have used 150 word images for the validation of the optimal value of ρ.

2.2   Headline Estimation

We take $\nu(\tau_k)$ with dimension m × n as input (Fig. 2b) and select q of the n columns in $\nu(\tau_k)$ based on a predefined distance. These q selected columns are denoted as $\mathcal{Q} = < c_1, c_2, \cdots, c_q >$. The columns are selected at a distance

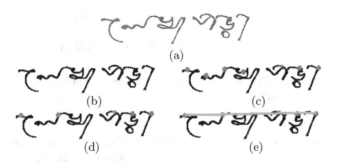

Fig. 2. Stepwise illustration of headline estimation. (a) Input grayscale image; (b) After binarization and noise normalization; (c) First encountered foreground pixels on equidistant columns marked with magenta colour; (d) After removal of ineligible pixels; (e) Estimated headline marked with cyan colour.

of 12% of the width of $\nu(\tau_k)$. We used a subset of 350 images to validate this optimal percentage. We detect and store the first encountered foreground pixel on each column in Q while traversing $\nu(\tau_k)$ from top to bottom. The stored foreground pixels are denoted as $P = <p_1, p_2, \cdots, p_q>$ (Fig. 2c). Each stored pixel p_i is associated with a row and a column number denoted as $p_i(r)$ and $p_i(c)$ respectively. We use three sets namely, $\mathcal{E}$, $\mathcal{E}'$, and $\mathcal{I}$ to represent the pixels in P as eligible, ineligible, and intermediate respectively. $\mathcal{E}$ represents pixels that are eligible for further headline estimation. $\mathcal{E}'$ represents pixels that will be deleted from P and will not be considered for further computation. $\mathcal{I}$ represents pairs of pixels that are temporarily put here before checking their belongingness in $\mathcal{E}$ or $\mathcal{E}'$. For every three consecutive pixels p_i, p_{i+1}, and p_{i+2} in P, we evaluate the angle $\angle p_i p_{i+1} p_{i+2}$ (denoted as θ_q). If $\theta_q <= 165°$, we conclude that any one of the three pixels is not a headline pixel. To determine which pixel among the three is not a headline pixel, we compute $|p_i(r) - p_{i+1}(r)|$ and $|p_{i+1}(r) - p_{i+2}(r)|$. The difference of column values of the pixels in P will mostly be zero, as the columns are equi-distant from each other. So, we only take row values of pixels in P into consideration for distance computation. We have used a subset of 150 word images to validate 165 as the optimal angle. If $|p_i(r) - p_{i+1}(r)| > |p_{i+1}(r) - p_{i+2}(r)|$, then we conclude that either p_i or p_{i+1} is not a headline pixel and as a result we consider $\{p_i, p_{i+1}\}$ as intermediate pixel pair and store the pair in $\mathcal{I}$. Otherwise, we conclude that either p_{i+1} or p_{i+2} is not a headline pixel and consider $\{p_{i+1}, p_{i+2}\}$ as intermediate pixel pair and store the pair in $\mathcal{I}$ instead. If a pixel p_i in P is considered twice as intermediate in a single iteration, then we conclude that p_i is not a headline pixel and transfer p_i from the set $\mathcal{I}$ to $\mathcal{E}'$, while the pixel paired with p_i in $\mathcal{I}$ is removed from $\mathcal{I}$. Once all the intermediate pixels are marked in a single iteration, we compute the eligible pixels in $\mathcal{E}$ as $\mathcal{E} = P - (\mathcal{I} \cup \mathcal{E}')$.

For every pixel pair $\{p_i, p_{i+1}\}$ in $\mathcal{I}$, we compute the row-wise difference, df_{p_i} and $df_{p_{i+1}}$ of p_i and p_{i+1} with every pixel in $\mathcal{E}$. We compute the maximum of the two differences df_{p_i} and $df_{p_{i+1}}$ as max_{df}. A non-headline pixel will always

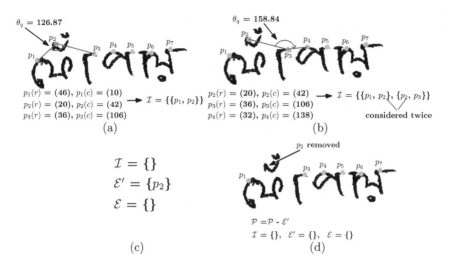

$p_1(r) = (46), p_1(c) = (10)$
$p_2(r) = (20), p_2(c) = (42)$ $\longrightarrow I = \{\{p_1, p_2\}\}$
$p_3(r) = (36), p_3(c) = (106)$

(a)

$p_2(r) = (20), p_2(c) = (42)$ $\longrightarrow I = \{\{p_1, p_2\}, \{p_2, p_3\}\}$
$p_3(r) = (36), p_3(c) = (106)$
$p_4(r) = (32), p_4(c) = (138)$ considered twice

(b)

$I = \{\}$
$\mathcal{E}' = \{p_2\}$
$\mathcal{E} = \{\}$

(c)

p_2 removed

$\mathcal{P} = \mathcal{P} - \mathcal{E}'$
$I = \{\}, \ \mathcal{E}' = \{\}, \ \mathcal{E} = \{\}$

(d)

Fig. 3. Stepwise illustration of ineligible pixel removal. (a) Angle $\angle p_1 p_2 p_3 \leq 165°$ and $|p_1(r) - p_2(r)| > |p_2(r) - p_3(r)|$, so, $\{p_1, p_2\}$ is stored in I; (b) For the next three pixels, angle $\angle p_2 p_3 p_4 \leq 165°$ and $|p_2(r) - p_3(r)| > |p_3(r) - p_4(r)|$, so, $\{p_2, p_3\}$ is stored in I, but two consecutive pixel pairs contain the same pixel, i.e., p_2; (c) As p_2 consecutively appears twice in I, so p_2 is transferred to $\mathcal{E}'$, while the two pixels associated with it, i.e., p_1 and p_3, are removed; (d) Pixels in $\mathcal{E}'$ are removed from $\mathcal{P}$.

have a greater row difference with headline pixels than the difference between a headline pixel with other headline pixels. So, the pixel in the pixel pair $\{p_i, p_{i+1}\}$ that is associated with most number of max_{df} is transferred from I to $\mathcal{E}'$ while the other is transferred to $\mathcal{E}$. Once all the pixel pairs in I are checked, the pixels belonging to $\mathcal{E}'$ are removed from $\mathcal{P}$ (Fig. 2d). $\mathcal{E}$, I, and $\mathcal{E}'$ are all emptied. This procedure is carried out until no three consecutive pixel in $\mathcal{P}$ creates an angle less than or equal to 165°. We remove ineligible pixels from $\mathcal{P}$ to ensure that the headline estimation does not get affected due to the presence of upper modifiers and certain consonants that appear above the headline in a word. ৗ, ৗ, ি,ৈ and ৺ are some examples of upper modifier and consonant that appear above the headline in Bangla script. Example of headline estimation of words with such modifiers appearing in Indian scripts are shown in the next section.

We use the word কৈলাস as a working example to demonstrate the proposed methodology. Due to the presence of the consonant ৺ , the second pixel p_2 in $\mathcal{P}$ is marked much higher compared to the position of headline (Fig. 3a). As a result, for the first three pixels in $\mathcal{P}$, angle $\angle p_1 p_2 p_3$ is $\leq 165°$ and $|p_1(r) - p_2(r)| > |p_2(r) - p_3(r)|$. We conclude that either p_1 or p_2 is a non-headline pixel and store $\{p_1, p_2\}$ in I as a pixel pair (Fig. 3a). Again, when we shift one pixel right and consider the next three pixels, angle $\angle p_2 p_3 p_4$ becomes $\leq 165°$ and $|p_2(r) - p_3(r)| > |p_3(r) - p_4(r)|$. So, we conclude that either p_2 or p_3 is a non-headline pixel and we store $\{p_2, p_3\}$ in I (Fig. 3b). As, p_2 repeats in two consecutive pixel pairs in $\mathcal{I}$, we infer that p_2 is a non-headline pixel. As a result, we transfer p_2 from $\mathcal{I}$ to $\mathcal{E}'$ and remove the pixels associated with p_2, i.e., p_1 and p_3, from $\mathcal{I}$ (Fig. 3c). We check all the remaining consecutive pixels in $\mathcal{P}$. Once checking completes, we remove the ineligible pixels in $\mathcal{E}'$ from $\mathcal{P}$ (Fig. 3d).

Now, we predict the row values $\hat{\mathcal{P}}(r)$ based on the row and column values of pixels in $\mathcal{P}$ using the following equation:

$$\hat{\mathcal{P}}(r) = b_0 + b_1 \times \mathcal{P}(c) \tag{1}$$

where,

$$b_1 = \sum_{i=1}^{|\mathcal{P}|} \frac{(p_i(c) - \overline{p(c)})(p_i(r) - \overline{p(r)})}{(p_i(c) - \overline{p(c)})^2},$$

$$b_0 = \overline{p(r)} - b_1 \times \overline{p(c)},$$

$$\overline{p(c)} = \frac{\sum_{i=1}^{|\mathcal{P}|} p_i(c)}{|\mathcal{P}|} \text{ and } \overline{p(r)} = \frac{\sum_{i=1}^{|\mathcal{P}|} p_i(r)}{|\mathcal{P}|}.$$

We use the polyfit function in Matlab to employ these equations. Based on the $\hat{\mathcal{P}}(r)$ and $\mathcal{P}(c)$ values, we draw a regression line which gives the final estimated headline of each word (Fig. 2e).

3   Experimental Results and Analysis

3.1   Dataset

For experimentation, we have used four datasets for three different scripts, namely Bangla, Devanagari, and Gurmukhi. For Bangla script, we have used Cmaterdb dataset version 1.1.1 [5] and ICDAR 2013 Segmentation Dataset [6]. For Devanagari and Gurmukhi script, we have used Cmaterdb dataset version 1.5.1 [7] and PHDIndic_11 [8] dataset respectively. A total of 4050 words are used for our current experimentation. We have used Matlab for the entire implementation part.

3.2   Test Results and Comparative Analysis

We have delineated the experimental results and analysis of our proposed work in this section. Few outputs of our proposed technique are shown in Fig. 4. Last two rows of each script in Fig. 4 delineates the removal of ineligible pixels due to the presence of upper modifiers as discussed in previous section. A detailed analysis of the headline estimation performance achieved in each script is provided in Table 1. As per the tabulated results, Devanagari and Gurmukhi script provides the most and least precise result with an accuracy of 96.15% and 89.41% respectively. We achieved an overall accuracy of 92.59% when accuracy of all the 3 scripts are considered.

The efficiency of our proposed method is compared with Sarkar *et al.* [2]. This method utilises sum of length of horizontal runs, maximum horizontalness,

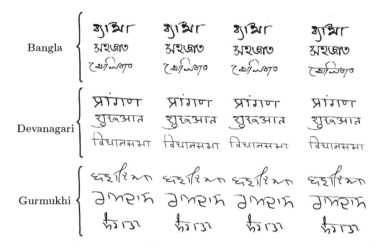

Fig. 4. Test results on different Indian scripts. **First column:** Word images; **Second column:** First encountered foreground pixels on equi-distant columns marked with cyan colour; **Third column:** Eligible pixels are kept while ineligible pixels are discarded; **Fourth column:** Estimated headline marked with magenta colour.

Table 1. Headline estimation accuracy achieved in different Indian scripts.

Script	Total # words	# Words with correct headline estimation	Accuracy (%)
Bangla	1350	1245	92.22
Devanagari	1350	1298	96.15
Gurmukhi	1350	1207	89.41
Overall	4050	3750	92.59

Table 2. Comparison of our proposed method with Sarkar *et al.* [2].

Method	Script	Total # words	# Words with correct headline estimation	Accuracy (%)
Sarkar *et al.* [2]	Bangla	500	397	79.40
Proposed method			467	93.40

horizontalness, and verticalness feature to identify the headline in handwritten Bangla words before segmentation is performed. This method is limited to handle non-skew words and also provides inaccurate result when the headline is mostly absent. Our proposed method is able to provide accurate result even when the headline is mostly absent and can handle skewed word images as well. A comparison of our proposed method with [2] has been provided in Table 2. We have also provided a visual comparison of few word images with [2] in Table 3

Table 3. Headline estimation comparison of few word images of our proposed method with Sarkar *et al.* [2]. Input for the last row is a synthetically oriented word image at 30°.

Original Image	Headline Estimated by [2]	Headline Estimated by our proposed method

demonstrating that our proposed method provides more accurate headline estimation than [2].

4   Conclusion

Most segmentation algorithms require some prior knowledge about the location of the headline to swiftly and efficiently fragment a handwritten word into constituent characters in majority of Indian scripts. In the present work, we have proposed a method that uses simple linear regression for estimating headline present in handwritten words. This method efficiently detects headline in three Indian scripts, namely Bangla, Devanagari, and Gurmukhi. The proposed method is able to detect headlines in skewed word images and provides accurate result even when the headline is discontinuous or mostly absent.

References

1. Bag, S., Harit, G.: A survey on optical character recognition for Bangla and Devanagari scripts. Sadhana **38**(1), 133–168 (2013)
2. Sarkar, R., Das, N., Basu, S., Kundu, M., Nasipuri, M., Basu, D.K.: A two-stage approach for Segmentation of Handwritten Bangla word Images. In: Proceedings of ICFHR, pp. 403–408 (2008)
3. Roy, P.P., Dey, P., Roy, S., Pal, U., Kimura, F.: A novel approach of Bangla handwritten text recognition using HMM. In: Proceedings of ICFHR, pp. 661–666 (2014)
4. Bag, S., Krishna, A.: Character segmentation of hindi unconstrained handwritten words. In: Barneva, R.P., Bhattacharya, B.B., Brimkov, V.E. (eds.) IWCIA 2015. LNCS, vol. 9448, pp. 247–260. Springer, Cham (2015). doi:10.1007/978-3-319-26145-4_18
5. Sarkar, R., Das, N., Basu, S., Kundu, M., Nasipuri, M., Basu, D.K.: CMATERdb1: a database of unconstrained handwritten Bangla and BanglaEnglish mixed script document image. IJDAR **15**(1), 71–83 (2012). Accessed 8 Feb 2017
6. Stamatopoulos, N., Gatos, B., Louloudis, G., Pal, U., Alaei, A.: ICDAR 2013 handwriting segmentation contest. In: Proceedings of ICDAR, pp. 1402–1406 (2013). Accessed 12 Mar 2017

7. CMATERdb 1.5.1: http://archive.is/xDqG6#selection-621.0-623.41. Accessed 2 Jan 2017
8. Das, N., Halder, C., Obaidullah, S.M., Roy, K., Santosh, K.C.: PHDIndic_11: page-level handwritten document image dataset of 11 official Indic scripts for script identification. In: Multimedia Tools and Applications, pp. 1–36 (2017)

Object Segmentation in Texture Images Using Texture Gradient Based Active Contours

Priyambada Subudhi$^{(\boxtimes)}$ and Susanta Mukhopadhyay

Indian Institute of Technology (Indian School of Mines), Dhanbad, India
priyambadasubudhi@gmail.com

Abstract. Active contour models are one of the most popular and effective models for object segmentation. These models are usually dependant on the intensity gradient of the image. However, using such a model it is not possible to segment texture objects due to local convergence problem. So, we have used texture gradient instead of the intensity gradient in our proposed active contour model for texture segmentation, which is found out using non-decimated complex wavelet transform. Experimental results show that the proposed active contour model can effectively segment texture objects from their complex backgrounds in case of synthetic as well as natural texture images.

1 Introduction

Segmenting a textured object from its complex background is one of the most important and challenging task in the field of computer vision and image processing as most of the natural textures do not follow any specific pattern [1]. Nevertheless, many algorithms have been proposed for segmenting texture images. Among them deformable models like Active Contours (AC) are one of the most popular choices because of their flexibility, capability of achieving sub-pixel accuracy and providing smooth and close contour as segmentation result [2].

In Active Contour Model (ACM), an initial close contour is made to move in the image domain minimizing an energy functional containing two types of energy terms, internal energy and external energy [3]. In most of the traditional ACMs [4,5], the external energy which is used to drive the active contour towards the object boundary, is based on the intensity gradient of the image and usually the contour converges when this intensity gradient maximizes. However, in case of texture images, intensity gradient will give many such local maxima and the contour may converge inaccurately. To overcome this problem, many different external energies have been proposed for AC which incorporate texture features of the image [6,7]. The main idea of this paper is to use texture gradient instead of intensity gradient which highlights step changes instead intensity changes in the image and we find out the texture gradient of the image using non-decimated complex wavelet transform that is subsequently used to determine the external energy of the proposed ACM. We compare the results of our proposed approach with two other ACMs designed for texture object segmentation which are based

B.U. Shankar et al. (Eds.): PReMI 2017, LNCS 10597, pp. 124–131, 2017.
https://doi.org/10.1007/978-3-319-69900-4_16

on the Gabor transform [8] and statistical moments [9] of the image. The main advantages of our method over other state of the art parametric ACM for texture segmentation are as follows.

- The proposed method only requires initial contour selection, but no object point selection like other state of the art approaches.
- It is faster than others as it does not require any transform calculation for the active contour convergence.

The remaining of this article is organized as follows. Next section introduces the preliminaries involved in our method, Sect. 3 gives details of our proposed approach, experimental results are provided in Sect. 4 and concluding remarks are drawn in Sect. 5.

2   Preliminaries

2.1   Mathematical Model of Active Contour Model

A parametric active contour is a parametrized curve represented by a set of control points $X(s) = [x(s), y(s)]^T$. It moves in the image domain to minimize the energy functional given by

$$E = \int_0^1 \underbrace{\frac{1}{2}[\alpha|x'(s)|^2 + \beta|x''(s)|^2]}_{Internal\ energy} + \underbrace{E_{ext}(x(s))}_{External\ energy}\ ds \tag{1}$$

The internal energy of the ACM controls the stretching and bending of the contour and external energy which is generally derived from the image properties is given by the following expressions in traditional ACM.

$$E_{ext}(x,y) = -|\bigtriangledown I(x,y)|^2 \tag{2}$$

Or

$$E_{ext}(x,y) = -|\bigtriangledown (G_\sigma(x,y) * I(x,y))|^2 \tag{3}$$

Here G_σ is a two-dimensional Gaussian kernel with σ being the standard deviation and $\bigtriangledown$ is the gradient operator. The energy functional in Eq. (1) will be minimized when the following force balance equation will get satisfied.

$$\alpha x''(s) - \beta x''''(s) - \bigtriangledown E_{ext} = 0 \tag{4}$$

2.2   Non-decimated Complex Wavelet Transform (NDCWT)

Complex Wavelet Transforms (CWT) are the complex valued extensions of the standard DWT, which provide both amplitude and phase information and were first given by Magarey et al. [10]. These original CWT were based on two complex valued FIR filters that approximate two Gabor filters. These are

$$h_0(n) \approx a_0 e^{(n+0.5)^2} / 2\sigma_0^2 e^{jw_0(n+0.5)} \tag{5}$$

$$h_1(n) \approx a_1 e^{(n+0.5)^2} / 2\sigma_1^2 e^{jw_1(n+0.5)} \tag{6}$$

for $n = -D......D$

These low pass (h_0) and high pass (h_1) filters are used in standard DWT structure to give the CWT. With $D = 2, w_0 = \pi/6, w_1 = 0.76\pi, \sigma_0 = 0.97, \sigma_1 = 1.07, a_0 = 0.47, a_1 = 0.43j$, Eqs. (5) and (6) will produce two even length complex filters (length=4). The non-decimated form of the CWT can be found out by using the same DWT structure excluding the sub-sampling part. This will produce sub-bands which have the same size as that of the original image. The non-decimated form achieves the advantages of complete shift invariance and one-one mapping with the original image pixel. However, the even length complex filters obtained using Eqs. (5) and (6), will place the subband coefficients half way between the original signal samples [11]. As a consequence, there will be no direct one-one mapping between the sub-band and original image pixel. This problem can be overcome by using odd length filters which can be obtained by dropping 0.5 from Eqs. (5) and (6). So the filters obtained by using the parameter values $D = 2, w_0 = \pi/6, w_1 = 0.82\pi, \sigma_0 = 0.97, \sigma_1 = 1.07, a_0 = 0.47, a_1 = 0.43j$ are

$$h_0 = \frac{1 - 4j, 19 - 11j, 36, 19 + 11j, 1 + 4j}{76} \tag{7}$$

$$h_1 = \frac{-4 + 1j, 9 - 14j, 26j, -9 - 14j, 4 + 1j}{60} \tag{8}$$

The NDCWT using these complex valued filters are used in our proposed approach to find the texture gradient.

3   Proposed Method

3.1   Texture Gradient Using NDCWT

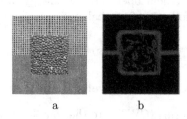

a   b

Fig. 1. (a) A synthetic texture image (b) its corresponding texture gradient

The subbands of the NDCWT of an image highlight the texture contents at different scales and orientations. Let I be such a texture image and being decomposed using NDCWT into n subbands and let these subbands be represented as S_i *where $i = 1$ to n.*

The texture gradient of the image can be obtained by finding the gradient of each of the subbands and then adding them. However, the gradient of each subband will give double edge at the intensity boundaries in non-textured regions. So in order to detect steps rather than edges, octave scale separable median filtering is performed on the subband images followed by gradient extraction. Let the median filtered subbands be MS_i and obtained like as follows.

$$MS_i(x, y) = MedianFilter(S_i(x, y)) \qquad for\ 1 \leq i \leq n \qquad (9)$$

Following this, the gaussian derivative gradient of each median filtered subband image is performed and let us denote them as ∇MS_i. Now, the texture gradient of the image can be obtained as follows and an example is also given in Fig. 1

$$TG(x, y) = \sum_{i=1}^{n} \nabla MS_i(x, y) \qquad (10)$$

3.2   Texture Gradient Based ACM

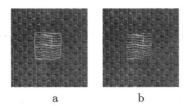

a   b

Fig. 2. Segmentation result using (a)texture gradient based external energy (b) intensity gradient based external energy

We can find from Fig. 1 that, the texture gradient obtained in the previous section highlights the boundary of two different texture regions. However, along with the major texture boundaries (with high magnitude), it will also give some spurious boundaries (with low magnitude) for smaller texture variations as can be seen inside the square box in the figure. Additionally, we can see the edges of the gradient image are spread as an effect of multilevel wavelet decomposition. Thus, before utilizing this texture gradient in our proposed ACM, we have eroded it using a suitable structuring element which will thin the edges along with removing some of the spurious edges. Let the texture gradient after erosion using a structuring element B be TG_e and is obtained like as follows.

$$TG_e = TG \ominus B \tag{11}$$

The shape and size of the structuring element is decided based upon the structure of the texture patterns present in the image. Now, in order to segment the texture object from the background perfectly, we have used the magnitude of eroded texture gradient above as the external energy of our proposed ACM i.e.

$$E_{ext} = k.|TG_e(x, y)| \tag{12}$$

Here, k is the weighting factor and TG_e is the eroded texture gradient as obtained in Eq. (11). By putting this defined external energy in the force balance equation of ACM in Eq. (4), the force balance equation for texture gradient based ACM is obtained as follows.

$$\alpha x''(s) - \beta x''''(s) - k|TG_e(x(s))| = 0 \tag{13}$$

So, when $TG_e(x(s))$ maximizes i.e. at the boundary of the texture object, then Eq. (13) minimizes and gets stabilized providing the desired solution as the converged contour. A comparison of segmentation results of a texture object using intensity gradient based ACM (GVF) and texture gradient based ACM is shown in Fig. 2 and we can find that in case GVF the contour converges locally based on the magnitude of the intensity gradient resulting in inaccurate segmentation of the object of interest which is not the case in our proposed approach.

4   Experimental Results and Performance Evaluation

To analyse the validity of our method, experiments are conducted on a number of synthetic and natural texture images. In this section, the results obtained in our proposed texture gradient based ACM is presented along with the results of parametric ACM for texture segmentation using moment based method [9] and Gabor balloon energy based method [8] for the purpose of comparison. All the experiments are conducted on Intel Core 2 platform with 3 GHz processor, 4 GB RAM and CentOS operating system. Figure 3 shows four texture images with the first row showing the contour initialization, corresponding texture gradient images are shown in second row and the object segmentation results using the proposed ACM is shown in third row of the figure. The value of parameters set for all our experiments are $\alpha = 0.2, \beta = 0$ and $k = 0.02$ which are decided by trial and error. In the same context, Fig. 4 shows the results of using ACM based on statistical moment and Gabor balloon energy in the first and second row respectively with the same initial contour. However, these methods require some initial object point selection along with contour, which is not a requirement in our case making our method more automatic. Now, we can find from the above mentioned figures, for the synthetic texture image, all the three methods achieve same good results. However, for all the three natural texture images, our

Fig. 3. Segmentation results using proposed ACM. The first row:initialization. Second row: Eroded texture gradients. Third row: segmentation results.

Fig. 4. Segmentation results using other approaches. The first row: Results of moment based approach [9]. Second row: results of Gabor Balloon energy based method [8].

proposed method segments the object of interest more accurately as compared to the other two methods.

To evaluate the performance of a method it is very important to quantify how good or bad it is, through some quantitative parameters. We have used two such quantitative parameters namely Maximum Distance of Active contour from Desired contour (MDAD) [12] and execution time in second. Table 1 shows MDAD value for the above images in all the three approaches. It is clear from the table that consistently low value of MDAD is obtained in our proposed approach which means active contour is close to the actual object contour implying

Table 1. Comparison of MDAD (in pixels) among our method and its variants for various test images

Images	Moment based	Gabor based	Proposed
Texture1	8.0000	7.0000	**4.0000**
Tiger	17.4642	14.5602	**9.2195**
Leopard	39.6242	32.0384	**13.9283**
Zebra	11.1803	8.0622	**7.6023**

Table 2. Comparison of Time (in sec.) among our method and its variants for various test images

Images	Moment based	Gabor based	Proposed
Texture1	26.3730	14.2260	**8.1038**
Tiger	27.4642	24.5602	**10.8040**
Leopard	55.3898	47.6811	**15.0041**
Zebra	34.2351	26.3486	**11.0849**

better segmentation. Next is the time for execution which is significantly less as compared to the other two approaches as can be seen in Table 2.

5   Conclusion

This paper presents a novel and fast active contour model driven by a new external energy based on the texture gradient of the image. This texture gradient is derived from the non-decimated complex wavelet transform of the image and has a high magnitude at the boundary of two different texture regions. Experimental results evident that the proposed method succeed to segment a texture object against its complex background in a comparatively lesser amount of time with better segmentation accuracy as compared to its other variants.

References

1. Tatu, A., Bansal, S.: A novel active contour model for texture segmentation. In: International Workshop on Energy Minimization Methods in Computer Vision and Pattern Recognition, pp. 223–236 (2015)
2. Wu, B., Yang, Y.: Local-and global-statistics-based active contour model for image segmentation. Math. Probl. Eng. **2012**, 16 (2012)
3. Kass, M.: Andrew Witkin, et al.: Snakes: Active contour models. Int. J. Comput. Vision **1**(4), 321–331 (1988)
4. Cohen, L.D.: On active contour models and balloons. CVGIP Image understanding **532**, 211–218 (1991)
5. Xu, C., Prince, J.L.: Snakes, shapes, and gradient vector flow. IEEE Trans. Image Process. **7**(3), 359–369 (1998)

6. Houhou, N., Thiran, J.-P., Bresson, X.: Fast texture segmentation model based on the shape operator and active contour. In: IEEE Conference on Computer Vision and Pattern Recognition, CVPR (2008)
7. Sagiv, C., Sochen, N.A., Zeevi, Y.Y.: Integrated active contours for texture segmentation. IEEE Trans. Image Process. **15**(6), 1633–1646 (2006)
8. Moallem, P., Tahvilian, H., et al.: Parametric active contour model using Gabor balloon energy for texture segmentation. SIViP **10**(2), 351–358 (2016)
9. Vard, A.R.: Moallem, Payman et al.: Texturebased parametric active contour for target detection and tracking. Int. J. Imaging Syst. Technol. **19**(3), 187–198 (2009)
10. Magarey, J., Kingsbury, N.: Motion estimation using a complex-valued wavelet transform. IEEE Trans. Signal Process. **46**(4), 1069–1084 (1998)
11. Hill, P.R., Canagarajah, C.N., Bull, D.R.: Image segmentation using a texture gradient based watershed transform. IEEE Trans. Image Process. **12**(12), 1618–1633 (2003)
12. Subudhi, P., Mukhopadhyay, S.: A pyramidal approach to active contours implementation for 2D gray scale image segmentation. In: Wireless Communications, Signal Processing and Networking (WiSPNET) (2016)

A Variance Based Image Binarization Scheme and Its Application in Text Segmentation

Ranjit Ghoshal[(✉)] [iD], Aditya Saha[iD], and Sayan Das[iD]

St. Thomas' College of Engineering and Technology, Kolkata, India
ranjit.ghoshal.stcet@gmail.com , adi96saha@gmail.com, sayandas896@gmail.com

Abstract. This paper presents a novel variance based image binarization scheme for automatic segmentation of text from low resolution images. First, the variance based binarization scheme is separately carried out on the three color planes of the image. Then, we merge these planes to obtain final binarized image. This creates several connected components (CCs). Now, these CCs are studied in order to segment possible text CCs. Now, a number of features that classify between text and non-text components, are considered. Further, KNN and SVM classifiers are applied for the present two class classification problem. For the training of KNN and SVM, ground-truth information of text CCs and our laboratory made non-text CCs are considered. We conduct extensive experiments on publicly available ICDAR 2011 Born Digital Data set. Concerning comparison, we consider a number of previously reported methods. Our binarization scheme significantly outperforms the existing methods and segmentation results are also satisfactory.

1 Introduction

Text in scene images includes important information and is exploited in many content-based video and image applications [1]. Text segmentation is a challenging problem due to variations of font, color, size and orientation etc. Binarization is also a great challenge, especially in the process of text based scene images where binarization result can directly influence the OCR rate. Several methods exist for binarization in document images but they cannot be directly applied on low resolution images. Conventional binarization techniques are either *global* [2] or *local* ([3,4]) thresholding. Existing techniques for scene text segmentation can generally be classified into two sets: sliding window [5] and CC [6] based schemes. Sliding window based schemes use a sliding window to find for possible texts in the scene image and then use machine learning methodologies to identify text. CC based methods separate out character candidates from scene images by CC analysis. Due to their relatively simple implementation, CC-based methods are widely used. Here, we take an interest into color images embedding text. In the following sections, our methods are presented.

© Springer International Publishing AG 2017
B.U. Shankar et al. (Eds.): PReMI 2017, LNCS 10597, pp. 132–138, 2017.
https://doi.org/10.1007/978-3-319-69900-4_17

2 Variance Based Image Binarization Scheme

Consider a color image which consists of red (R), green (G) and blue (B) planes. Now, it is required to retrieve the information from each plane. Further, the image contains highly varying gray pixel values which make binarization a difficult task. This can be overcome to a great extent using variance to perform binarization.

Each plane is separately passed through the binarization process. First, the variance matrix is calculated from the gray scale image, which marks the change in pixel intensities in the image. Binarizing the variance matrix, we separate the image into two regions, one having high variance values and other having low variance values. Now, using each region, two gray scale images (one from the white and other from the black region of the binarized image) are formed. Binarizing these two images separately will produce more even binarization as they don't contain any fluctuating pixel intensities. These gray scale images are binarized by a window based Otsu binarization method, as illustrated in the algorithm. Finally, binarized image from each plane is merged together to form the final binarized image. The details have been presented in Algorithm 1.

Algorithm 1. Algo. of Binarization

Input: Gray Scale Image **G**

Output: Binarized Image

Step1: Find the variance matrix **M** of **G** by sliding a 5×5 window throughout **G** and replace the variance of the window at the centre pixel of the window in **M**.

Step2: Apply Otsu's method on variance matrix to obtain a binerized images (**MBW**).

Step3: Obtain two gray scale images from **MBW** by considering pixel intensities of **G**. Let these are **GW** and **GB** respectively.

Step4: Apply Canny's method On **GW** to obtain an edge image say **GWE**. Further, apply Otsu's method on **GW** and let it be **GWBW**. Let complement of **GWBW** is $\sim$ **GWBW**.

Step5: Run two windows (**WBW** and **WBC**) of size 21×21 over the images **GWBW** and $\sim$ **GWBW** respectively.

Step6: Now construct two matrices **M1** and **M2** and are defined as follows:
$\mathbf{M1}(i,j) = \mathbf{M1}(i,j) + \mathbf{WBW}(i,j)$, where $1 \leq i \leq m$ and $1 \leq j \leq n$
$\mathbf{M2}(i,j) = \mathbf{M2}(i,j) + \mathbf{WBC}(i,j)$, where $1 \leq i \leq m$ and $1 \leq j \leq n$

Step7: From **M1** and **M2** final binerized image of **GW** is calculated as follows:
$\mathbf{GWBWF}(i,j) = 1$, where $\mathbf{M1}(i,j) > \mathbf{M1}(i,j)$ and $1 \leq i \leq m$ and $1 \leq j \leq n$

Step8: Similiarly final binerized images of **GB** is calculates, say **GBBWF**.

Step9: Merge **GWBWF** and **GBBWF** to obtain the final resultant Binerized Image.

Consider the RGB image(Fig. 1(a)) as an input. The image has separated into three different planes(Figs. 1(b), (c) and (d)). Consider the R plane, which is passed into the proposed binarization algorithm. Figure 2(a) represents the binarized image of variance matrix, which is calculated by moving a 5×5 window throughout the image. For white pixels and black pixels, separate gray scale images are again formed and a window based Otsu algorithm is performed.

(a)   (b)   (c)   (d)

Fig. 1. (a) Input color image. (b) R plane. (c) G plane. (d) B plane. (Color figure online)

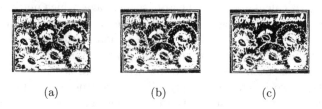

(a)   (b)   (c)

Fig. 2. Binarization for variance matrices on (a) R plane, (b) G plane and (c) B plane.

(a)   (b)   (c)   (d)   (e)

Fig. 3. Binerized image of gray scale corresponding to (a) White pixel in 2(a). (b) Black pixel in 2(a). (c) White pixel in 2(b). (d) Black pixel in 2(b). (e) Merged image of 3(a) and 3(b).

Results are presented in Figs. 3(a) and (b). These are merged to obtain binarized image for R plane(Fig. 3(e)). Similarly, binarized images for G and B planes are presented in Figs. 4(c) and (d). Binarized images from each planes are merged to obtain the final binarized image(Fig. 4(e)).

3   Shape Based Feature Extraction

Image binarization creates a number of CCs. In order to segment text, we have considered a number of features from each CC.

AL: Axial ratio (AL) of a CC is the ratio of the length of the two axes to each other - the longer axis divided by the shorter.
LO: Number of lobes in a CC [7].
 A: Aspect ratio of a CC [7].
 E: Elongation ratio of a CC [7].
 O: Object to background pixels ratio of a CC [7].

(a)   (b)   (c)   (d)   (e)

Fig. 4. Binerized image of gray scale corresponding to (a) White pixel in 2(c) and (b) Black pixel in 2(c). Merged images (c) (3(c) and 3(d)), (d) (4(a) and 4(b)) and (e) (3(e), 4(c), and 4(d)).

AR: Area ratio of a CC. It is the ratio of (area of the CC and area of input image).

L: Length ratio (L) of a CC. It is the ratio of (max (height of CC, width of CC), max (height of the I, width of the I)), where I is the input image.

Now, we construct the feature vector $Y = \{AL, LO, A, E, O, AR, L\}$ for a CC.

4   KNN and SVM Based Text Segmentation

To segment the text components, K-NN and SVM classifiers are applied. The feature vector Y for text and non-text CCs are calculated. The dataset contains 420 train images and 102 test images. Ground truth information of train images are used to create the feature file for 21700 text components. Next, the input images are binarized with our binarization method. Then the components present in the ground truth images are eliminated. Thus we create 78800 non-text CCs. These are used to prepare the feature file for non-text components. Based on these feature files, K-NN and SVM classifiers are trained separately. To segment the text components from test images, an input image is binarized using our binarization method and the feature vector Y is obtained. Now, each CC is fed to both the trained K-NN and SVM classifiers to decide whether the component is text or non-text. Thus, two output images from K-NN and SVM classifiers are obtained. Finally, these two images are merged using *logical OR* operation to get the final image consisting only text components.

5   Results and Discussion

The experimental results are obtained on ICDAR 2011 Born Digital Dataset [8]. These images are inherently low-resolution. So, automatic segmentation of text is therefore an important project. Our experiments are divided into two parts based on our aim of the paper.

5.1   Results of Binarization Scheme

Let us first pictorially observe some binarization results. A few example results are presented in Table 2. First column represents the sample input images and second column presents the corresponding binarized images. Evaluation of our binarization scheme is done in terms of the precision, recall and F-measure [7]. Also the performance of our binarization scheme has been compared with a few known methods in terms of recall, precision and FM on ICDAR 2011 Born Digital data set. It can be seen from the results (Table 1) that our binarization method has significantly outperformed.

Table 1. Recall, Precision and FM for different binarization technique.

	Proposed	Otsu [2]	Niblack [4]	Sauvola [3]	Bhatt et al. [9]	Kumar et al. [10]
Recall	**91.15**	88.98	87	91	91.14	85.56
Precision	**71.36**	65.36	36	14	47.85	47.09
FM	**73.78**	65.05	38.17	20.4	53.81	46.81

5.2   Text Identification Results

We present the text segmentation results obtained by our KNN and SVM classifiers. A few images and their corresponding segmented text using KNN, SVM and merged KNN and SVM classifier are presented in Table 2. Visually, it is clear that our approach good towards text segmentation. A robust comparison analysis has been performed by means of Recall, Precision and FM values of our different classification methods obtained on the basis of ICDAR 2011 Born Digital data set images are presented in the Table 3. Final evaluation of our scheme is

Table 2. Input images, binarized images and segmented text (using KNN, SVM and merged of KNN and SVM) are presented respectively 1st, 2nd, 3rd, 4th and 5th columns.

RGB	BW	KNN	SVM	Merged

Table 3. Recall, Precision and FM for different text segmentation methods.

	Merged KNN and SVM	SVM	KNN	TexStar	SASA
Recall	**77.72**	60.80	63.49	65.23	71.28
Precision	45.53	50.89	52.53	63.63	55.54
FM	53.63	51.07	52.85	64.64	62.52

presented by comparing with other known techniques. The ICDAR 2011 Robust Reading Competition presented evaluation results of a number of methods from different participants. In Table 3, a few of these techniques are compared with our scheme. Our scheme has achieved highest recall (77.72).

6   Summary and Future Scope

This paper provides a new variance based image binarization scheme and its application in text segmentation. A number of shape based features are defined towards segmentation of text. Then, SVM and KNN classifiers are trained for classification of text and non-text. Finally, the results obtain from SVM and KNN are merged to get the final segmented text. The proposed method is very effective for low resolution images. Future study may aim towards combining machine learning tools to improve the binarization scheme.

References

1. Yin, X.C., Hao, H.W., Sun, J., Naoi, S.: Robust vanishing point detection for mobile cam-based documents. In: Proceedings of ICDAR, pp. 136–140 (2011)
2. Otsu, N.: A threshold selection method from gray-level histograms. IEEE Trans. Syst. Man Cybern. **9**(1), 377–393 (1979)
3. Sauvola, J., Pietikinen, M.: Adaptive document image binarization. Pattern Recogn. **2**, 225–236 (2000)
4. Niblack, W.: An Introduction to Digital Image Processing. Prentice Hall, Englewood Cliffs (1986)
5. Lee, J.J., Lee, P.H., Lee, S.W., Yuille, A., Koch, C.: Adaboost for text detection in natural scene. In: ICDAR, pp. 429–434 (2011)
6. Yi, C., Tian, Y.: Localizing text in scene images by boundary clustering, stroke segmentation, and string fragment classification. IEEE Trans. Image Process. **21**(9), 4256–4268 (2012)
7. Ghoshal, R., Roy, A., Parui, S.K.: A copula based statistical model for text extraction from scene images. In: Maji, P., Ghosh, A., Murty, M.N., Ghosh, K., Pal, S.K. (eds.) PReMI 2013. LNCS, vol. 8251, pp. 489–494. Springer, Heidelberg (2013). doi:10.1007/978-3-642-45062-4_67
8. Karatzas, D., Robles Mestre, S., Mas, J., Nourbakhsh, F., Roy, P.P.: Icdar 2011 robust reading competition-challenge 1: Reading text in born-digital images (web and email). In: ICDAR, pp. 1485–1490 (2011)

9. Bhattacharya, U., Parui, S.K., Mondal, S.: Devanagari and bangla text extraction from natural scene images. In: Proceedings of the International Conference on Document Analysis and Recognition (ICDAR), pp. 171–175 (2009)
10. Kumar, D., Ramakrishnan, A.G.: Octymist: otsu-canny minimal spanning tree for born-digital images. In: DAR, DAS 2012, pp. 389–393 (2012)

Computer Vision and Video Processing

Variants of Locality Preserving Projection for Modular Face and Facial Expression Recognition

Gitam Shikkenawis$^{(\boxtimes)}$ⓘ and Suman K. Mitraⓘ

Dhirubhai Ambani Institute of Information and Communication Technology,
Gandhianagar, India
{201221004,suman_mitra}@daiict.ac.in

Abstract. Locality Preserving Projection (LPP) is one of the widely used approaches for finding intrinsic dimensionality of high dimensional data by preserving the local structure. Data points which are neighbors but belong to different classes are thereby projected as neighbors in the projection space, causing problem of discrimination. Various extensions of LPP have been proposed to enhance the discrimination power achieve better between class separation. In case of face recognition using full face images, if any portion of the face image is distorted, it may reflect on the recognition performance. Humans have the capability to recognize faces even by looking at some parts of the face. This article is an attempt to replicate the same on machines by only considering some of the informative regions of the face. Instead of the entire image, variants of LPP are applied on parts of face images and recognition is performed by combining the results of their reduced dimensional representations. Face and facial expression recognition experiments have been performed on some of the benchmark face databases.

1 Introduction

Recognizing human faces and expressions comes naturally to humans even under adverse viewing conditions such as various lighting conditions, viewing angles, poses, expression and appearance changes, occlusions etc. Though, significant advances have been achieved in last few decades in the area of face recognition especially in constrained environment, a face recognition system as good as the Human Visual System (HSV) is yet to be achieved. Feature based techniques mark prominent features from faces such as eyes, nose, mouth and compare the test images based on selected group of features [3,5,6]. On the other hand, appearance based techniques work on the idea that high dimensional face images often belong to intrinsically lower dimensional manifold and can be represented using very few coefficients. Such approaches, generally known as dimensionality reduction (DR) approaches, Principle Component Analysis (PCA) [13], Linear Discriminant Analysis (LDA) [1], Locality Preserving Projections (LPP) [4] etc. transform high dimensional face data into significantly lower dimensions and perform recognition task have become very popular.

© Springer International Publishing AG 2017
B.U. Shankar et al. (Eds.): PReMI 2017, LNCS 10597, pp. 141–147, 2017.
https://doi.org/10.1007/978-3-319-69900-4_18

The property of preserving local information make LPP one of the most popular DR techniques to be used for face recognition lately. Various extensions of LPP to make it more robust and suitable to face recognition have been proposed [2,10,11,14]. So far, these DR approaches have been applied on full face images. In such cases, if any portion of face image is distorted, it may reflect on the recognition performance. Also, it has been observed that even after looking at some of the informative regions of the face such as eyes, nose and lips, humans can easily recognize the person. Hence, a more robust face recognition system can be developed by combining the feature based and appearance based techniques. Instead of whole face images, some of the specific informative regions of a face can be extracted and DR techniques can be applied only on the extracted parts from the face.

In one such approach, PCA is performed on the nose and eyes of the face images [8]. A modular PCA based approach [9] divides the face image in smaller parts and then PCA is applied on these portions separately. As face regions are considered for recognition, variations in expressions or pose or illumination in the image will affect only some part of the image, hence a better recognition rate can be expected. Modular Locality Preserving Projection (MLPP) is proposed in this article, which takes the local regions such as eye, nose and lips of a face as input of the DR approach separately and produces final result by fusing the outcome of these regions. In particular, utilization of Extended Locality Preserving projection (ELPP) [10] and Locality Preserving Discriminant Projection (LPDP) [11] for the proposed modular face and expression recognition is explored in this article. Suitability of the proposal is tested on databases having expression variation.

Organization of the paper is as follows: Sect. 2 discusses variants of LPP. Modular Locality Preserving Projection (MLPP) that works on some prominent regions of face images is explained in Sect. 3 along with face and expression recognition experiments.

2   Variants of Locality Preserving Projection

As discussed in Sect. 1, in this article, variants of LPP i.e. Extended Locality Preserving Projection (ELPP) [10] and Locality Preserving Discriminant Projection (LPDP) [11] have been used for modular face recognition.

Extended Locality Preserving Projection
Extended LPP [10] is an extension of LPP [4] towards making it more robust and enhance the DR capability. LPP [4] emphasizes on the local structure of the data to preserve the neighborhood information. Due to the property of LPP to depend only on a few nearest neighbors, ambiguity may arise as a result of adjacency of data points from different classes. ELPP not only extends the neighborhood to a moderate distance from the point of interest, it also tries to explore natural grouping of the data with the use of k-means clustering.

The goal of ELPP is, data points that are neighbors in the high dimensional space should continue to remain neighbors in the lower dimensional space as well. Transformation matrix $\mathbf{w}$ to represent data in the lower dimensional space is obtained by solving the generalized eigenvalue problem: $\mathbf{XLX^Tw} = \lambda\mathbf{XMX^Tw}$; here, $\mathbf{X}$ is the data matrix, $\mathbf{L}$ is the Laplacian matrix i.e. $\mathbf{L} = \mathbf{M} - \mathbf{S}$. $\mathbf{S}$ is similarity matrix that takes care of neighborhood information and $M_{ii} = \sum_i S_{ij}$. Data points clustered in one class using k means clustering are considered neighbors and assigned weight in $\mathbf{S}$. Weighing is performed using a monotonically decreasing function that weighs the neighboring data points depending on the distance between them [10]. This choice of weight makes sure that neighboring data points remain neighbors in the newly obtained ELPP subspace as well.

Locality Preserving Discriminant Projection
Though ELPP tries to resolve the ambiguity arising due to closeness of data points belonging to different classes, no emphasis is given by LPP and ELPP to enhance the between class discriminating power. LPDP [11], in addition to inheriting the properties of ELPP of preserving the similarity information, tries to discriminate data points from different classes by taking into consideration the dissimilarity information as well. The aim is to achieve better class separation by using weighing functions for both similarity and dissimilarity of the data points. The generalized eigen value problem thus turns out to be: $(\mathbf{XL_SX^T} - \mathbf{XL_DX^T})\mathbf{w} = \lambda\mathbf{XX^Tw}$; as in case of ELPP, here, $\mathbf{X}$ is the data matrix, $\mathbf{L_S}$ is the Laplacian matrix obtained from the similarity matrix i.e. $\mathbf{L_S} = \mathbf{M_S} - \mathbf{S}$. Similarity matrix $\mathbf{S}$ is computed in the same manner as that of ELPP and $MS_{ii} = \sum_i S_{ij}$. Data points that belong to different classes are considered dissimilar and weights in $\mathbf{D}$ are assigned to ensure maximum class discrimination [11] in a monotonically increasing fashion. $\mathbf{L_D} = \mathbf{M_D} - \mathbf{D}$ and $MD_{ii} = \sum_i D_{ij}$. Thus, in addition to preserving the local information, LPDP also takes into account the dissimilarity between data points to achieve enhanced class discrimination.

In this article, ELPP and LDPD have been used to reduce the dimensionality of data. The main contribution of this article is use of DR technique only on some of the informative regions of the face image instead of full face as discussed in next section.

3   Modular Locality Preserving Projection

Dimensionality reduction methods, when applied for full face images, may not work as expected, if any portion of the face image is distorted. Any obstacles, changes in the facial expressions or pose may also degrade the performance. Lower dimensional representations of the regions which are not affected by changes will match with that of the same individual's face regions in normal conditions. Hence, it is expected that the recognition results can be improved by applying the DR techniques on local face regions separately. It seems that eyes, nose and lips are more informative for identifying a person. By having a look only at one of these face parts the person can be identified. Suitability of ELPP and LPDP for identifying faces and facial expressions is tested by applying it locally on the faces. In particular, dimensionality reduction is applied on significant regions such as eyes, nose and lips. Here, these parts have been cut manually from the face regions. The process of extracting the regions from face can be also automated by first detecting the eyes [5] and then using the golden ratio to cut other informative regions.

Intrinsic dissimilarity between pair of eyes of two different persons is hard to be identified by machine as there will be a lot of overlap between eye regions of different persons. ELPP is expected to find out this dissimilarity in a little better way than LPP as it performs much better in the overlapping regions. However, as LPDP takes into consideration both similarity and dissimilarity information while obtaining the basis, it should be able enhance the discrimination ability and result in improved recognition performances. As we are moving towards more local areas of the face and then applying LPP, ELPP and LPDP on these local regions, this method is called Modular Locality Preserving Projection (MLPP). Two different modular approaches are analyzed here.

Modular Approach #1

In the first approach, eyes, nose and lip regions are considered separately; LPP, ELPP and LPDP are applied on these regions and classification using different parts is carried out. Clustering experiments are performed on Video database [12] containing face images of 11 persons having four different expressions and the Japanese Female Facial Expression JAFFE database [7] are used. All the face images are cut as shown in Fig. 1. Only the eyes, nose and lip regions are extracted from the whole image. The results of clustering the projected data using LPP, ELPP and LPDP using different number of dimensions are shown in Table 1.

Fig. 1. Examples of the selected face regions used from Video database for modular approach #1 (Left) modular approach #2 (right)

From the results, it can be concluded that eyes are the most informative and discriminative portions of the human face. All three approaches are able to discriminate between different person's eyes. On the Video database, with LPP, almost all the dimensions are required for discrimination, whereas the other two approaches are doing it using much less dimensions, thus enhancing the reducibility capacity. For JAFEE database also, more than 96% accuracy is achieved using the all three approaches. For only nose portion, the accuracies are higher than 80% for both the databases. In Video database, results on lip regions are not that encouraging because of a lot of lip variation in the database with LPP and ELPP but LPDP is performing very well, achieving almost 100%

Table 1. Results (%) of clustering eyes, nose and lip regions separately from the Video and JAFFE database using nearest neighbor approach.

DA-IICT	# Dimensions														
	2			10			50			500			MAX		
	LPP	ELPP	LPDP	LPP	ELPP	LPDP	LPP	ELPP	LPDP	LPP	ELPP	LPDP	LPP	ELPP	LPDP
Eyes	11.3	74.8	99.52	20.5	99.45	**100**	18	100	100	21.46	100	100	97.82	100	100
Nose	16.91	84.55	99.16	18.55	91.64	**100**	14.91	91.64	100	15	91.82	100	88.55	92	100
Lips	20.19	18.55	98.40	20	17.10	**100**	19.82	19.20	100	19.20	21.82	100	19.82	22.55	100
JAFFE	# Dimensions														
	2			10			50			150			MAX		
	LPP	ELPP	LPDP	LPP	ELPP	LPDP	LPP	ELPP	LPDP	LPP	ELPP	LPDP	LPP	ELPP	LPDP
Eyes	13.16	41.53	73.68	23.16	89.48	91.58	25.27	94.22	93.68	59.43	95.79	**96.84**	96.32	96.32	96.84
Nose	6.85	43.11	63.68	13.79	81.58	75.26	13.16	87.37	83.16	47.37	85.79	85.26	86.32	**87.8**	85.26
Lips	14.22	27.9	60.50	14.22	69.43	84.00	10	82.11	85.00	47.9	84.74	85.00	82.11	85.27	**85.50**

accuracy. In case of JAFFE database, where there is a lot of expression variation, much better results are obtained for all the three DR approaches using only lip region.

The experimental results show that in this manner, the faces could even be recognized easily from eyes only. However, joining the decisions of face recognition separately from these regions is yet to be explored. In cases such as video database where there is a lot of lip variation because of expressions, if full face images are considered, variation in expressions can cause problems for recognition tasks. On the other hand, as suggested here, if the regions are considered separately, faces could easily be recognized using only the eyes and nose regions. Hence, by combining the decisions of these face regions; a robust face recognition system can be designed.

Modular Approach #2

During the task of expression analysis, we observed that apart from eyes, nose and lips/mouth, forehead also plays very important role as far as expressions are concerned. Hence, in the second approach, these four portions from the face image are used for recognition purpose. The regions cut from the face image are shown in Fig. 1.

Unlike the first approach discussed earlier, here, all portions are combined together in vector format to form a data point. The data points generated this way undergo dimensionality reduction and are classified using nearest neighbor approach. This approach is tested on the video database for both face and expression recognition. It is also to be noted that for expression recognition, expression labels of the data points are considered to be known, hence the neighbors are decided based on the class labels. These can be considered as the supervised variants of LPP and ELPP. Face recognition results with varying dimensions using LPP, ELPP and LPDP are reported in Table 2. It can be observed that LPP, ELPP and LPDP perform extremely well achieving almost 100% recognition accuracy using only 10 dimensions. With 2 most significant dimensions, LPDP surpasses both LPP and ELPP.

The Video database mainly contains four facial expressions for each subject namely normal, happy (laughing), angry and shock. Expression recognition

Table 2. Face recognition accuracy (in %) on Video database using LPP, ELPP and LPDP

# Dimensions	2	10	20	30	40	50
LPP	87.65	**100**	100	100	100	100
ELPP	93.85	99.85	100	100	100	100
LPDP	97.15	**100**	100	100	100	100

experiments have been performed in two different ways: (1) Randomly selecting training and testing samples from the same set of persons, (2) Randomly selecting training and testing samples from different persons i.e. testing set contains face images of the persons that have not been included for training. This liberty can be taken as we are recognizing the expressions and training set contains similar expressions for other persons. This exercise makes expression recognition more challenging.

When the training and testing samples are randomly selected from the same set of persons for LPP, ELPP and LPDP, more than 98% expression recognition accuracy is attained using ELPP and LPDP with only 40 strongest dimensions as opposed to 12000 dimensions of the raw data points in the original space as shown in Table 3.

Table 3. Expression recognition accuracy (in %) on Video database using LPP, ELPP and LPDP

# Dimensions	Same persons for training, testing						Different persons for training, testing					
	2	10	20	30	40	50	2	10	20	30	40	50
LPP	79.25	94.9	96.3	97.25	97.65	97.8	66	76.50	82.25	80.50	77.75	79.00
ELPP	79.40	97.45	98.05	98.60	**98.65**	98.65	71.25	81.00	83.00	83.25	85.25	88.00
LPDP	93.10	95.85	96.75	97.45	98.2	98.45	85.00	93.75	94.00	94.00	94.00	**94.25**

In practical scenarios, it is not possible to have training data for all the test samples whose expressions are being recognized. A similar experiment, where the person whose expressions are to be recognized has not been included in the training set, is performed. Though the recognition rate has reduced, 88% accuracy has been achieved using ELPP with only 50 dimensions. On the other hand, LPDP is able to produce 94% recognition rate with only 20 most significant dimensions. Though ELPP performs better than LPP with less number of dimensions, in most of the scenarios, LPDP surpasses both LPP and ELPP in terms of both recognition accuracy and reducibility capacity.

The initial set of experiments reported in this article suggest that the modular approaches using only some prominent portions of face images can be useful for face and expression recognition. The idea needs to be further explored for other databases having distortions and occlusions in the face image.

4   Conclusion

Capability of ELPP and LPDP to recognize a person using partial information from the whole face image is explored in this work. Dimensionality reduction is applied on most informative regions of the face i.e. eyes, nose and lips. It is observed that only eyes are significant enough to distinguish faces of different persons in most of the cases, however, by fusing the results of different face parts, a more robust face recognition system can be deployed. In addition to face recognition, expression recognition results also support the argument of using only informative regions from face images for recognition tasks. Thus, the modular approach suggested in this article can further be applied for face and expression recognition task to attain more robust results specially for challenging databases having distorted or occluded face images.

References

1. Belhumeur, P., Hespanha, J., Kriengman, D.: Eigenfaces vs. fisherfaces: Recognition using class specific linear projection. IEEE Trans. Patt. Anal. Mach. Intell. **19**(13), 711–720 (1997)
2. Dornaika, F., Assoum, A.: Enhanced and parameterless locality preserving projections for face recognition. Neurocomputing **99**, 448–457 (2013)
3. Govindaraju, V., Srihari, S.N., Sher, D.B.: A computational model for face location. In: International Conference on Computer Vision, pp. 718–721 (1990)
4. He, X., Niyogi, P.: Locality preserving projections. In: NIPS (2003)
5. Lam, K., Yan, H.: Locating and extracting the eye in human face images. Patt. Recogn. **29**(5), 771–779 (1996)
6. Li, S., Jain, A.: Hand Book of Face Recognition. Springer, New York (2011)
7. Lyons, M.J., Akamatsu, S., Kamachi, M., Gyoba, J.: Coding facial expressions with gabor wavelets. In: Automatic Face and Gesture Recognition, pp. 200–205. IEEE Computer Society (1998)
8. Pentland, A., Moghaddam, B., Starner, T.: View-based and modular eigenspaces for face recognition. In: IEEE Conference on Computer Vision and Pattern Recognition, pp. 84–91 (1994)
9. Gottumukkal, V.K.A.R.: An improved face recognition technique based on modular PCA approach. Patt. Recogn. **25**, 429–436 (2004)
10. Shikkenawis, G., Mitra, S.K.: Improving locality preserving projection for dimensionality reduction. In: Emerging Applications of Information Technology, pp. 161–164. IEEE Computer Society (2012)
11. Shikkenawis, G., Mitra, S.K.: Locality preserving discriminant projections. In: IEEE International Conference on Identity, Security and Behavior Analysis (ISBA) (2015)
12. Shikkenawis, G., Mitra, S.K.: On some variants of locality preserving projection. Neurocomputing **173**(2), 196–211 (2016)
13. Turk, M., Pentland, A.: Eigenfaces for face recognition. Cogn. Neurosci. **3**(1), 71–86 (1991)
14. Xu, Y., Zhong, A., Yang, J., Zhang, D.: LPP solution schemes for use with face recognition. Patt. Recogn. **43**(12), 4165–4176 (2010)

A Robust Color Video Watermarking Technique Using DWT, SVD and Frame Difference

Sai Shyam Sharma$^{(\boxtimes)}$ ⓘ, Sanik Thapa ⓘ, and Chaitanya Pavan Tanay

Sri Sathya Sai Institute of Higher Learning, Puttaparthi, Andhra Pradesh, India
saishyam@sssihl.edu.in, sanik918@gmail.com, chaitanyapavantanay@gmail.com

Abstract. In the last decade there has been a steep rise in the amount of digital media. This has made entertainment comfortable for the consumer but insecure for the producer. With affordable broadband and innumerable methods, protecting proprierty digital media assets is difficult. Digital watermarking is one way to protect these assets. In this paper, we propose an efficient watermarking method for a colour video sequence. This method improves the execution time than existing techniques due to choosing lesser number of frames to embed the watermark, while still maintaing the robustness against various attacks. The robustness is measured using PSNR values and the correlation coefficient.

Keywords: Frame difference video watermarking · Singular value decomposition · Discrete wavelet transform

1 Introduction

In digital watermarking, there is a host signal (cover signal) and a watermark signal. The vulnerability of easily available multimedia assets is due to many factors, like high speed internet, piracy etc. Copyright protection, authentication, traitor tracing are some of major issues in the industry [1]. Digital watermarking is considered to be a tool for verifying the owner and the unauthorized user of a document [2,3]. Watermarking of an image is usually performed in two domains, viz. Spatial domain and Transform domain. In the spatial domain, the pixels of the host image are directly modified [4]. In the transform domain, the host image is first transformed using transforms like DCT, DWT, DFT, etc., and the watermark is then embedded into the host image [5]. We propose a hybrid method that combines the benefits of transforms like DWT and SVD along with making use of frame differences, a term familiar in video encoding. Instead of adding a watermark into all the frames of an input, a random frame is selected to add the watermark [2,6], the frame differences are then added to this frame to generate a sequence of watermarked frames. In Sect. 2, the proposed algorithm is explained. In Sect. 3 the experimental setup and results are provided, explaining the improvement of the proposed technique over existing ones. In the end, we conclude that this is a robust as well as efficient algorithm.

© Springer International Publishing AG 2017
B.U. Shankar et al. (Eds.): PReMI 2017, LNCS 10597, pp. 148–154, 2017.
https://doi.org/10.1007/978-3-319-69900-4_19

2   Proposed Method

Like every other watermarking algorithm, the proposed method too consists of an embedding and an extraction/detection algorithm. In this method, the stability of the singular values of an image is combined with the adaptive nature of DWT. To increase the efficiency of the algorithm, a basis frame is identified to be watermarked. As will be shown later, the novelty in this algorithm is reducing the watermark embedding time and improving the robustness of the embedded watermark too.

2.1   Embedding Algorithm

A frame is chosen randomly from the video sequence. In order to obtain the motion parts, this frame is subtracted from all frames over all channels. DWT is applied to the basis frame, the LL band is chosen and transformed further using DWT. Then the HH subband in this double transformed image is chosen and further processed using SVD. Simultaneously, the watermark image is also transformed using DWT, unlike the basis frame, DWT is applied only once on the watermark image. SVD is applied on the HH sub band. The frame's modified singular values are obtained by adding the watermark's singular values. Using this newly obtained singular values, the high frequency sub-band is reconstructed. The low frequency sub-band is reconstructed using IDWT. Using this low frequency sub-band, the watermarked frame is constructed. All the respective frame differences are added to this watermarked frame to obtain all the video frames. The video frames are then used for obtaining the watermarked video (Fig. 1).

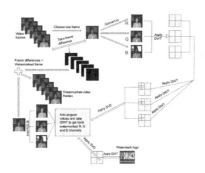

Fig. 1. Diagrammatic representation of the embedding process

2.2   Extracting Algorithm

The watermarked/attacked video frames are divided into RGB channels. DWT is applied to these frames to get the four sub-bands as in the step 3 of the embedding algorithm. DWT is applied to the low frequency sub-bands obtained in the above step as in the step 4 of the embedding algorithm. SVD is applied to second level high-frequency sub-bands (HH). The singular values obtained are then subtracted from the original singular values. These resultant singular values are then used for extracting the watermark from the watermarked or the attacked video.

3   Experimental Results

In our study, we consider two colour videos, one is a standard video called *Akiyo video* and the other one is a video made locally called *Sangsay sports video*. These videos consist of 233 and 173 frames respectively and are of dimension 1024×1024. Figure 2 shows a frame each, of the Akiyo video and the Sangsay sports video. In the Akiyo video, there is no change of background whereas in the Sangsay video, there is scene change with lot of motion. It is observed that the algorithm works well for both the cases. The watermark is a gray scale image, logo of our department in college as shown in Fig. 2 and is of size 512×512.

Akiyo video frame Sangsay video frame Watermark

Fig. 2. Sample frames of the videos and the watermark

PSNR measures the visual quality of the modified image and is expressed in decibel (dB) scale. There exists a direct proportionality between the quality of the image and the PSNR value of the image. The imperceptibility factor which plays a crucial role in watermarking is measured by PSNR [5,7]. The PSNR of 40 dB is regarded to have high frame quality. Here in this paper, we have obtained the PSNR values to be above 65 dB.

We compare the PSNR of the proposed technique with the existing methods, Pejman Rasti et al. [1], Lai and Tsai [8] and Agoyi et al. [9] in Figs. 3 and 4. The proposed method shows better results. Correlation coefficient is another metric used frequently in measuring the robustness of the watermark. It finds the similarity of the watermark that is extracted and the original embedded watermark.

In order to measure the proposed technique's robustness, the watermarked video was tested against attacks like frame averaging, cropping, compression, rotation and many more as mentioned in [10].

Figure 5 shows some of the various attacks that have been performed on the watermarked Sangsay sports video. Figure 6 shows the watermark images extracted after various attacks. Table 1 shows the correlation coefficient values of the watermarked Akiyo video frame and its comparison with the existing methods [1,8,9]. Table 2 shows the correlation coefficient values of the watermarked Sangsay sports video frame against the same methods.

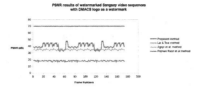

Fig. 3. PSNR values of watermarked Sangsay video frames with DMACS logo as a watermark

Fig. 4. PSNR values of watermarked Akiyo video frames with DMACS logo as a watermark

Frame Averaging   Cropping   Rotation   Flipped

Fig. 5. Manipulated/attacked frames

Fig. 6. Extracted watermark images

3.1 Robustness and Efficiency Improvement

To show the robustness of the scheme, we performed multiple attacks on the same frame. It is observed that the correlation coefficient values are very good. Some of the combinations are (i) Gaussian, Poisson and Salt & pepper noise attacks, (ii) Blurring, Rotation and Gaussian noise attacks, (iii) Gaussian noise, Gamma correction and rotation, (iv) Poisson noise, sharpening and flipping, (v) Frame averaging, salt & pepper noise and flipping attacks. Figure 7 shows the frames that have been introduced to multiple attacks and their respective extracted watermarks. Table 3 shows the correlation coefficient results of the frames that have been exposed to multiple attacks. This shows that the proposed technique

Table 1. Correlation coefficient values of watermarked Akiyo video.

Attacks	Proposed method	Pejman Rasti et al.	Lai and Tsai	Agoyi et al.
Contrast enhancement	**0.9997**	0.9671	0.9149	0.1394
Gaussian noise	**0.97**	0.9454	0.7777	0.5199
Poisson noise	**0.9963**	0.9945	0.8245	0.5263
Salt & pepper noise	**0.9987**	0.9979	0.9103	0.5300
Blurring	**0.9999**	0.9336	0.1880	0.7051
Frame averaging	**0.9998**	0.9231	0.2543	0.3352
Frame rotation	1	0.9562	0.8652	0.5682
Flipping	1	1	0.9641	0.0422
Compression	1	0.9396	0.9194	0.0612
Gamma correction	1	0.9854	0.9476	0.0998
Cropping	1	0.9854	0.8552	0.2961
Sharpening	**0.9982**	0.9979	0.7570	0.8561

Table 2. Correlation coefficient values of watermarked Sangsay video.

Attacks	Proposed method	Pejman Rasti et al.	Lai and Tsai	Agoyi et al.
Contrast enhancement	**0.9899**	0.9671	0.9149	0.1394
Gaussian noise	**0.9961**	0.9454	0.7777	0.5199
Poisson noise	**0.9997**	0.9945	0.8245	0.5263
Salt & pepper noise	0.9869	**0.9979**	0.9103	0.5300
Blurring	**0.9861**	0.9336	0.1880	0.7051
Frame averaging	**0.9851**	0.9231	0.2543	0.3352
Frame rotation	**0.9999**	0.9562	0.8652	0.5682
Flipping	1	1	0.9641	0.0422
Compression	**0.9999**	0.9396	0.9194	0.0612
Gamma correction	**0.9864**	0.9854	0.9476	0.0998
Cropping	**0.9988**	0.9854	0.8552	0.2961
Sharpening	0.9481	**0.9979**	0.7570	0.8561

even survives the multiple attacks as it can extract the watermarks with high visual quality.

This technique includes the watermark being embedded only in the basis frame, much in contrary to other techniques where all the frames are watermarked by repeating the same embedding steps for each frame. Because of this, the execution time of the proposed embedding algorithm is very less in comparison to the other techniques. The proposed algorithm takes **3.975 s** to embed a watermark in a video whereas the other technique takes **95.020 s**. The time taken for embedding the watermark decreases by **24x**.

Fig. 7. Video frames introduced to multiple attacks and its respective extracted watermarks

Table 3. Correlation coefficient values of exposed to multiple attacks

Attacks	Correlation coefficient
Gaussian + Poisson + Salt & pepper	0.9164
Blurred + rotate + Gaussian	0.985
Gaussian noise+Gamma correction +rotation	0.9912
Poisson noise+Sharpening+Flipping	0.9597
Frame averaging+Salt & pepper noise+flipping	0.9415

4 Conclusion

The proposed technique of adding a watermark to all the frames by actually adding it to only a single frame, which is selected randomly, is the novelty of this algorithm. Since this scheme embeds watermark in all the color channels of all the frames, it survives temporal attacks like FDAS (frame dropping, averaging and swapping). The watermark is found even if multiple frames are dropped. If on a lower bandwidth, the watermarked video can be transferred as a pair of, watermarked frame and the frame differences. The recipient can reconstruct the watermarked video using this single frame and the differences. The watermark can be extracted from any of the frames to prove the authenticity of the media being transmitted. This method is robust against various attacks and even combinations of them. It outperforms the existing video watermarking schemes on the correlation coefficient and PSNR values.

References

1. Rasti, P., Samiei, S., Agoyi, M., Escalera, S., Anbarjafari, G.: Robust non-blind color video watermarking using QR decomposition and entropy analysis. J. Vis. Commun. Image Represent. **38**, 838–847 (2016)
2. Shaik, A.F., Anjaneyulu, S.: A hybrid DWT-SVD method for digital video watermarking using random frame selection. Int. J. Eng. Sci. **6**(6), 43–48 (2016)
3. Dorr, G.J., Dugelay, J.-L.: Video watermarking, overview and challenges. Multimedia Communications, Image Group (2003)

4. Zhang, L., Li, A.: A novel watermark algorithm for non-compressed digital video. In: 2010 Second International Workshop on Education Technology and Computer Science (ETCS), vol. 1, pp. 268–271. IEEE (2010)
5. Agilandeeswari, L., Muralibabu, K.: A robust video watermarking algorithm for content authentication using discrete wavelet transform (DWT) and singular value decomposition (SVD). Int. J. Secur. Appl. **7**(4), 145–158 (2013)
6. Rathod Jigisha, D., Modi, R.V.: A hybrid DWT-SVD method for digital video watermarking. Int. J. Adv. Res. Comput. Commun. Eng. **2**(7), 2771–2775 (2013)
7. Thind, D.K., Jindal, S.: A semi blind DWT-SVD video watermarking. Procedia Comput. Sci. **46**, 1661–1667 (2015)
8. Lai, C.-C., Tsai, C.-C.: Digital image watermarking using discrete wavelet transform and singular value decomposition. IEEE Trans. Instrum. Measur. **59**(11), 3060–3063 (2010)
9. Agoyi, M., Çelebi, E., Anbarjafari, G.: A watermarking algorithm based on chirp z-transform, discrete wavelet transform, and singular value decomposition. Signal Image Video Process. **9**(3), 735–745 (2015)
10. Sharma, H., Kumar, A., Mandoria, H.L.: Study and comparison analysis of a video watermarking scheme for different attacks. Int. J. Res. Manag. Technol. **4**, 51–56 (2015)

Aggregated Channel Features with Optimum Parameters for Pedestrian Detection

Blossom Treesa Bastian$^{(\boxtimes)}$ and C. Victor Jiji

College of Engineering Trivandrum, Thiruvananthapuram, Kerala, India
{blossombastian,jijicv}@cet.ac.in

Abstract. Aggregated Channel Features (ACF) proposed by Dollar [3] provide strong framework for pedestrian detection. In this paper we show that, fine tuning the parameters of the baseline ACF detector can achieve competitive performance without additional channels and filtering actions. We experimentally determined the optimized values of four parameters of ACF detector: (1) size of training dataset, (2) sliding window stride, (3) sliding window size and (4) number of bootstrapping stages. Accordingly, our optimized detector using pre learned eigen filters achieved state of the art performance compared with other variants of ACF detector on Caltech pedestrian dataset.

Keywords: Pedestrian detection · ACF detector · Boosting algorithm

1 Introduction

Detection of pedestrians from images has got special interest due to its wide spread applications in vision based systems. Aggregated Channel Features (ACF) proposed by Dollar [3], have a simple framework, used HOG [2] based channel features and produced the best result on Caltech-pedestrian dataset till that date. Vision researchers keep on increasing the performance of ACF detector either by adding more and more channels [6,8] or by applying some filters on the existing channels on ACF [5,9], such that they have achieved a miss rate almost less than 15% than that of original ACF detector. At this point, adding more channels or some more filtering actions on channels itself is not able to improve the performance further and so, researchers are now coupling the best performing ACF variant with deep networks [9].

In order to increase the performance of a detector, fine tuning of parameters like sliding window size, sliding window stride, training dataset size, number of bootstrapping stages *etc.* is also important. In this paper we study the effect of these parameters on the performance of the detector in terms of miss rate and propose an optimized set of parameters. In fact our ACF detector with the optimized parameter set outperformed many variants of ACF detector which either uses extra channels or additional filters on the existing channels. We further used decorrelated channel features (by convolution of the channels with decorrelated filters) along with our optimized parameter set and obtained the second best result on Caltech pedestrian dataset.

© Springer International Publishing AG 2017
B.U. Shankar et al. (Eds.): PReMI 2017, LNCS 10597, pp. 155–161, 2017.
https://doi.org/10.1007/978-3-319-69900-4_20

2 Related Work

In this section we briefly describe the variants of ACF detector. Detectors based on ACF can be basically classified into two; methods which add more channels to basic ACF detector and methods which apply appropriate filters on the existing channels of ACF detector. Paisitkriangkrai et al. [6] used spatially pooled covariance descriptors and local binary patterns as additional channels (total 259 channels), where as [8] Yang et al. [6] proposed Convolutional Channel Features (CCF) by adding channels extracted from images using a pre trained convolutional neural network (CNN). Squares Channel Features introduced by Benenson et al. [1] applied square sized averaging filters on the channels. Locally Decorrelated Channel Features (LDCF) proposed by Nam et al. [5] used decorrelated channel features for the training of the classifier. CheckerBoards [9] also uses a set of filters which consists of averaging filters, horizontal and vertical gradient filters and all possible checker board pattern filters in the given model window. CheckerBorads and its more faster version RotatedFilters [9] currently have the state of the art miss rate in Caltech pedestrian dataset. Even though detectors based on deep networks also provided state of the art result on Caltech pedestrian dataset [7], it comes at the cost of expensive hardware supports like GPUs and complex computations. Nevertheless, variants of ACF detector achieved comparable results with respect to methods based on deep networks in spite of lesser computations and hardware support.

Table 1. Parameters under study and their values for ACF baseline detector

Parameter	Sliding window size	Training dataset size	Sliding stride	Number of bootstrapping stages
Values	64 × 32	4250	4	4

3 Optimized ACF Detector

In this section we learn the best parameter values for ACF detector. In the baseline ACF detector we used, a given input image is represented as 10 lower resolution channels (LUV channels + gradient magnitude + six HOG channels). Table 1 shows the parameters used for fine tuning of ACF detector and their values used in the baseline detector. All the experiments are done on Caltech pedestrian dataset. Also, we used the new annotations provided by Benenson et al. [9] for training and testing. Figure 4 shows the number of pedestrian instances for two different heights (between 50–80 pixels and greater than 80 pixels) which are missed by the baseline detector and detected by the four variants of ACF detector (obtained by changing the above mentioned parameters).

3.1   Sliding Window Size

Sliding window size determines the number of features available for learning. Higher the number of features, better will be the performance of the detector and can be achieved by increasing the window size. But our experiments showed that changing the window size to 120×60 increases the miss rate to 73.14% (Fig. 1). This result is reasonable since the number of pedestrian instances in Caltech test set with height less than 120 pixels is very large. In order to get a reduced miss rate for bigger window size, sliding window scanning has to be done at upsampled scales along with down sampled scales for the input image. When we attempted this for the window size 120×60, miss rate reduced by $\sim 5\%$. Figure 1 shows the miss rate value for three different model sizes, with and without upsampling of the image. When upsampling is done for window size 64×32, the miss rate is increased by 5%, due to over fitting. From Fig. 4, when the window size is changed to 120×60 with upsampling, large number of small pedestrian instances ($\sim$60) are detected, which means pedestrian of very small resolutions correctly fit into the new window size, when the images are upsampled. Figure 2 shows the learned classifier representation for the two window sizes 120×60 and 64×32. It can be observed that, bigger window size classifier representation have more similarity to human silhouette when compared with that of smaller window size. Hence window size of 120×60 (with upsampling) is taken as the most effective sliding window size of the ACF detector for Caltech dataset.

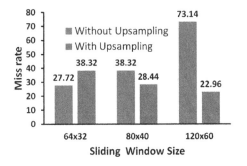  

Fig. 1. Miss rate for baseline ACF detector with different window size

Fig. 2. Learned classifier representation: 64×32 Window size (left), 120×60 Window size (right)

3.2   Training Dataset Size

Six set of videos are available for training in the Caltech pedestrian dataset. Number of images available for training can be varied by changing the number of frames taken from the videos. From Fig. 3 it can be observed that miss rate decreases with increase in training dataset size upto a certain extent and then it is either increases or remains almost constant. The training dataset obtained by taking every third frame provided the best result and after that the classifier was getting over fitted, hence increase in miss rate. This indicates that further change in dataset size beyond that of 42782 images is needless and hence it is taken as the best dataset size. From Fig. 4 it is evident that the baseline detector is able to detect more instances of both low resolution and high resolution using the dataset obtained by taking every third frame from training video set.

3.3   Sliding Window Stride

Sliding window stride value defines the number of pixels skipped in between adjacent sliding window scans. Increasing the stride value will reduce computations, but detector will also miss out small instances of pedestrians. Decreasing the stride value has two advantages, while training it will enrich the detector with more false positives and while testing, the detector will not miss out small instances of pedestrians. Table 2 shows the miss rate for changing the stride value for four different cases. Decreasing the stride value for the both training and testing decreases the miss rate, but when we changed the stride value for training only miss rate increases, which indicates that baseline detector is over fitted when more false positives are added in training stage. For the third case (stride value change for testing stage only) miss rate attained the least value since there is no over fitting of classifier and detector is able to detect more small pedestrian instances in comparison with that of baseline detector and this

Table 2. Miss rate for different stride value

Stride		Miss rate
Training	Testing	
4	4	27.72
2	2	23.37
2	4	30.69
4	2	21.36

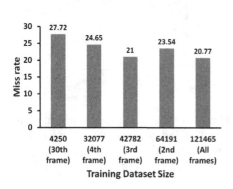

Fig. 3. Miss rate for baseline ACF detector with varying training dataset size

Table 3. Miss rate for different number of bootstrapping stages and training dataset size

No. of Bootstrapping stages	Training dataset size	Miss rate
4	4250	27.72
5	4250	25.71
5	42782	19.59

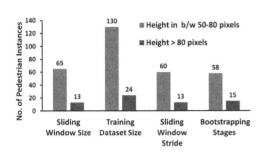

Fig. 4. Number of pedestrian instances detected correctly while each parameter value is changed.

Table 4. Step by step reduction in the miss rate of baseline ACF detector by changing each parameter

Specifications	Miss rate
Baseline ACF detector	27.72%
+ Sliding window size	22.96%
+ Training dataset size	17.45%
+ No. of bootstrapping stages	16.14%
+ Sliding window stride	15.73%
+ Filtering using [5]	12.72%

is also depicted in Fig. 4. The optimum value of sliding window stride is taken as two.

3.4 Number of Bootstrapping Stages

Bootstrapping stages feed the detector with hard examples and hence increase the discriminative power of the detector. In our experiments, we modified the number of bootstrapping stages from four to five. Table 3 shows the miss rate of the baseline detector with respect to change in number of bootstrapping stages. The table shows that miss rate is reduced with increased number of bootstrapping rounds. Also, increasing the number of bootstrapping stages should always supplemented with larger training dataset. Hence we performed training with the optimum training dataset size as obtained in Sect. 3.2 and the result is provided in Table 3. We can see that miss rate is reduced by 8% from the baseline detector.

3.5 Final Detector

Combining all these best performing parameters together, we achieved state of the art performance for the ACF detector. Table 4 shows the step by step reduction in miss rate achieved by ACF detector by adding each optimized parameters we obtained from the above experiments. We have also further enhanced our optimized ACF detector by filtering the channels with top four pre learned eigenvectors which produces locally decorrelated channels [5]. This optimized ACF detector + eigen filters has provided the best result for Caltech database among the other variants of ACF detector. Table 5 shows the miss rate of our enhanced ACF detector and enhanced ACF detector + eigen filters along with other state of the art detectors for Caltech dataset. Rows in grey shade represents

Table 5. Miss rate of state if the art methods on Caltech pedestrian dataset

Detector	Miss rate
ACF [3]	27.72
LDCF [5]	23.72
AlexNet [4]	21.59
SpatialPooling [6]	21.56
TACNN [7]	18.75
Rotated Filters [9]	16.69
CheckerBoards[9]	15.81
Optimized ACF Detector	15.73
Optimized ACF Detector + eigen filters	12.72
Rotated Filters + VGG [9]	10.00

Table 6. Comparison of parameter values of our proposed detector and CheckerBoards

Parameter	CheckerBoards	Our method
Channels	10	10
Filters	61	4 (LDCF)
Training dataset size	42782	42782
Stride	6	2
Window size	120×60	120×60
Bootstrapping stages	5	5
Detection speed for an image of size 480×640	50.23 s	2.3 s

detectors using deep networks and all other methods are variants of ACF detector including our two proposed methods. The table depicts that our proposed method Optimized ACF + eigen filters detector has reduced miss rate than that of CheckerBoards [9] (the best method among the variants of ACF detector). Table 6 shows the comparison between different parameters of CheckerBoards and our proposed optimized ACF detector. From table we can see that Checker-Boards has a stride value of 6, which means reduced computations, but they have 61 filters, while we use only 4 filters, so the detection speed of our method is much faster (nearly 25x) than CheckerBoards (Table 6). Hence our method is completely efficient in comparison to CheckerBoards.

4   Conclusion

In this work, we fine tuned the four different parameters of ACF detector and found the optimized parameter set. Our ACF detector with improved parameter set achieved superior performance compared to other variants of ACF detector on Caltech pedestrian dataset. Also when we used decorrelated channels obtained by filtering with top four eigen filters on our optimized ACF detector we have achieved state of the art result on Caltech dataset. Our future work includes the use of the optimized parameters for deep network based detection.

Acknowledgements. We gratefully acknowledge for the research fellowship (3501/(NET-DEC.2014)) provided by the University Grants Commission (UGC) Govt. of India.

References

1. Benenson, R., Mathias, M., Tuytelaars, T., Van Gool, L.: Seeking the strongest rigid detector. In: CVPR (2013)
2. Dalal, N., Triggs, B.: Histograms of oriented gradients for human detection. In: 2005 IEEE Computer Society Conference on Computer Vision and Pattern Recognition (CVPR 2005), vol. 1, pp. 886–893. IEEE (2005)
3. Dollár, P., Appel, R., Belongie, S., Perona, P.: Fast feature pyramids for object detection. IEEE Trans. Pattern Anal. Mach. Intell. **36**(8), 1532–1545 (2014)
4. Hosang, J., Omran, M., Benenson, R., Schiele, B.: Taking a deeper look at pedestrians. In: Proceedings of the IEEE Conference on Computer Vision and Pattern Recognition, pp. 4073–4082 (2015)
5. Nam, W., Dollár, P., Han, J.H.: Local decorrelation for improved pedestrian detection. In: Advances in Neural Information Processing Systems, pp. 424–432 (2014)
6. Paisitkriangkrai, S., Shen, C., van den Hengel, A.: Strengthening the effectiveness of pedestrian detection with spatially pooled features. In: Fleet, D., Pajdla, T., Schiele, B., Tuytelaars, T. (eds.) ECCV 2014. LNCS, vol. 8692, pp. 546–561. Springer, Cham (2014). doi:10.1007/978-3-319-10593-2_36
7. Tian, Y., Luo, P., Wang, X., Tang, X.: Pedestrian detection aided by deep learning semantic tasks. In: Proceedings of the IEEE Conference on Computer Vision and Pattern Recognition, pp. 5079–5087 (2015)
8. Yang, B., Yan, J., Lei, Z., Li, S.Z.: Convolutional channel features. In: Proceedings of the IEEE International Conference on Computer Vision, pp. 82–90 (2015)
9. Zhang, S., Benenson, R., Omran, M., Hosang, J., Schiele, B.: How far are we from solving pedestrian detection? In: CVPR (2016)

Object Tracking with Classification Score Weighted Histogram of Sparse Codes

Mathew Francis$^{(\boxtimes)}$ and Prithwijit Guha

Indian Institute of Technology Guwahati, Guwahati 781039, Assam, India
{m.francis,pguha}@iitg.ernet.in

Abstract. Object tracking involves target localization in dynamic scenes using either generative models, discriminative classifiers or their combination. We propose a combined approach consisting of generative models (learned in sparse representation framework) and discriminative classifiers (SVM). Sparse codes are initially computed from two different dictionaries constructed from foreground and background patches using K-SVD. SVM learned on these sparse codes provides classifier scores for patches. These scores for sparse codes of patches drawn from a region are used to form a weighted histogram. This weighted histogram of sparse codes form the object and candidate models. The learned dictionaries provide distinct representations for object and background patches. This discrimination is further enhanced by classifier scores. The object is localized by maximizing Bhattacharyya coefficient between target and candidate models in a particle filter framework. Performance of the proposed tracker is benchmarked on videos from VOT2014 dataset against existing generative and discriminative approaches. Our proposal was able to handle different challenging situations involving background clutter, in-plane rotations, scale and illumination changes.

Keywords: Dictionary learning · Histogram of sparse codes · Generative model · Support vector machine · Particle filter · Bhattacharyya coefficient

1 Introduction

Object tracking algorithms can be broadly categorized into generative, discriminative and hybrid approaches. A generative approach models the target appearance and localizes it by optimizing a (dis)similarity measure between target and candidate(s) [1–4]. A discriminative approach learns classifiers from target and background appearance features in a supervised framework [5–7]. A hybrid methodology combines both by modeling target appearance in a generative framework while discriminating the same against background [8].

In generative approach, the first notable work which makes uses of a sparse representation based target model was proposed by Mei et al. [4]. Tracking was formulated as a $L1$ minimization problem where the candidate model is represented as a sparse linear combination of object and trivial templates. Thereafter,

© Springer International Publishing AG 2017
B.U. Shankar et al. (Eds.): PReMI 2017, LNCS 10597, pp. 162–169, 2017.
https://doi.org/10.1007/978-3-319-69900-4_21

a number of variants of this basic formulation has been successfully applied in object tracking [9–13]. Successful use of classifier in tracking has been demonstrated in [6,7].

We propose a hybrid approach that employs sparse representation based target modeling and uses classifiers for better discrimination of target model from that of background. We propose to extract patches from both background and foreground and learn dictionaries on these patches using K-SVD [14] and spherical clustering. We learn a SVM classifier to discriminate the sparse codes of object from that of background. Sparse codes extracted from (multiple overlapping) patches of non-overlapping cells are weighed by their classification scores to compute cell histogram. These cell histograms together form the object model. The average of cell histogram similarities between target and candidate models are maximized in a particle filter framework [15]. The main contributions of this work are as follows.

- Proposal of a target model in a hybrid generative-discriminative approach.
- Object representation by histogram of sparse codes (HSC) obtained from foreground-background dictionaries (generative model).
- Enhancing discrimination of object models by weighing HSC with patch classification (by SVM) scores (discriminative approach).

The rest of the paper is organized as follows. The proposed approach is elaborated in Sect. 2. Experimental results are presented in Sect. 3. Finally, Sect. 4 summarizes the present work and sketches the future extensions.

2   Proposed Work

The object rectangle is divided into non-overlapping regions called cells. Proposed target model is learned in two stages. The first stage involves generative modeling. Here, object and background patches are used to learn two different dictionaries using K-SVD [16]. It learns the dictionary by solving the following sparse constrained optimization problem

$$\min_{\boldsymbol{\Gamma},\mathbf{D}} \|\mathbf{X} - \mathbf{D}\boldsymbol{\Gamma}\|_F^2 \text{ subject to } \forall i \; \|\gamma_i\|_0 \leq T \tag{1}$$

where, γ is the sparse code vector, $\mathbf{D}$ is the dictionary, $\mathbf{X}$ is the set of signals, $\boldsymbol{\Gamma}$ has the sparse codes of all the signals and T is the sparsity threshold. The two learned dictionaries are then used to from a combined foreground-background dictionary. In the second stage, sparse codes of background and foreground patches are used to train a SVM classifier in a discriminative framework. Patch classification obtained from this SVM provides further discrimination in the object model. Sparse codes and the classification scores of patches are used to compute the weighted sparse code histogram of the cells, which form the object model. The candidate models are constructed from object state (position, rotation and scaling) proposals obtained through particle filtering. Next, we discuss dictionary learning in detail.

2.1 Learning Foreground-Background Dictionaries

A single dictionary learned from only object patches might provide good reconstruction but poor recognition against background clutter. Rectangular patches are extracted from minimum bounding box of the object ($\mathbf{bb}^{obj}$) and a background region ($\mathbf{bb}^{bg}$) around $\mathbf{bb}^{obj}$. The extracted patches are first vectorized and magnitude normalized (using $l2$-norm). Next, they are arranged to construct the input data matrices $\mathbf{X}^{obj} \in \mathcal{R}^{n \times np}$ and $\mathbf{X}^{bg} \in \mathcal{R}^{n \times nn}$ of respective object (positive) and background (negative) classes. Here, np and nn are the total number of object and background patches respectively and n is the dimension of patch vector. Magnitude normalization helps to make the object model robust to the illumination changes. Spherical k-means clustering is performed on the object patch vectors $\mathbf{X}^{obj}$ and background patch vectors $\mathbf{X}^{bg}$ separately. The dominant clusters are selected and K-SVD algorithm is performed on each of them to obtain m representative atoms from each cluster. These are stacked together to form the foreground-background dictionary. Common patches of foreground and background may to lead drift in tracking. In order to reduce the effect of such patches, we introduce discriminability through a binary classifier. The dictionary learning procedure is shown in Fig. 1.

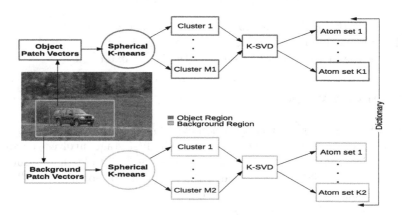

Fig. 1. Patches extracted from foreground and background regions are vectorized and magnitude normalized. These are further grouped using spherical clustering. K-SVD performed on cluster members provides us with different atom sets. These atom sets obtained from background and object clusters are combined to form a single dictionary.

2.2 Classifier Learning

A binary classifier is learned on the sparse codes generated using K-SVD algorithm with foreground-background dictionary for the object and background patches. The learned classifier provides confidence scores for object patches. These scores are used in constructing the proposed object model. Let, $\mathbf{\Gamma}^{obj}$ and $\mathbf{\Gamma}^{bg}$ be the respective sparse codes corresponding to patch vectors coming from positive set $\mathbf{X}^{obj}$ and negative set $\mathbf{X}^{bg}$. A SVM classifier is learned on the sparse code representations of patch vectors. The sparse vector corresponding to an ambiguous patch will lie closer to the classification boundary and will have a lower classification score compared to the object patches. This will improve the discriminative power of the object model against background and ambiguous patches. The proposed object model is explained next.

2.3   Object Model

The object bounding box is first divided into non-overlapping cells $\mathbf{C} = \{\mathbf{c}_i : \mathbf{c}_i \in \mathcal{R}^{cw \times ch}\}$, where cw and ch are the width and height of the cell respectively. The sparse codes corresponding to the rectangular patches from a cell computed using OMP is used to compute the histogram of sparse codes. The set of all cell histograms define the object model i.e. $\mathbf{H} = \{\mathbf{h}^i\}$ and $\mathbf{h}^i, i = 1, \ldots |C|$. The sparse codes required for computing the object model are computed as

$$\min_{\Gamma} \|\mathbf{X}^{obj} - \mathbf{D}\Gamma\|_F^2 \ \text{ s.t. } \|\Gamma\|_0 \leq \gamma_s \tag{2}$$

where Γ is the sparse code matrix, $\mathbf{D}$ is the foreground-background dictionary and $\gamma_s \leq m$ is the sparsity constraint. The sparse code histogram of the cell is created from the sparse codes Γ of its component patches as

$$\mathbf{h}^c(j) = L \sum_{i=1}^{nc} |\gamma_{ij}| \ \omega_i, \ \mathbf{x}_i \in \mathbf{X}^{obj} \tag{3}$$

where $\mathbf{x}_i$ is the ith object patch belonging to cell c, ω_i is the normalized classification score of the ith patch as given by the classifier, nc is the total number of patches in the cell and L is the normalization constant for the histogram. The cell-wise histograms are stacked together to form the object model $\mathbf{H}$ which is a collection of classifier weighted histogram of sparse codes given by $\mathbf{H} = [\ \mathbf{h}^{c_1} \ \mathbf{h}^{c_2} \ \ldots \ \mathbf{h}^{c_P}\ ]$, where P is the total number of cells. The entire object model creation is depicted in Fig. 2. The particle filter framework for target tracking is explained next.

2.4   Particle Filter

Particle Filter otherwise also known as sequential Monte Carlo sampling is used for object localization in tracking. It predicts the posterior distribution of the state of a dynamic system. The particle with the maximum a posteriori is selected as the best particle and is taken as the state of the object in the current frame. Here, we define the object state as $\mathbf{s} \in \mathcal{R}^5$ and is given by $\mathbf{s} = [x^c \ y^c \ w \ h \ \theta]^T$ where (x^c, y^c) are the image plane co-ordinates of the object bounding box centroid, w, h, θ are the respective width, height and orientation of the object. The motion model defines the temporal evolution of state. We consider simple random walk as our motion model. The current state is assumed to be sampled from a Gaussian distribution centered at the previous state as, $\mathbf{s}_t \sim$

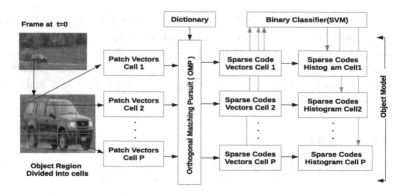

Fig. 2. Object model as set of weighed sparse code histogram computed from non-overlapping cells of the object bounding box $\mathbf{bb}^{obj}$. Sparse codes for the patches are computed using OMP (Orthogonal Matching Pursuit) with the learned dictionary. Sparse code vectors of the object patches and background patches are used for training the classifier. Classification score weighted sparse codes are then used to compute the histogram of each cell.

$\mathcal{N}(\mathbf{s}_{t-1}, \mathbf{\Sigma})$ where Σ is a diagonal covariance matrix of state variables given by $diag(\sigma_x^2, \sigma_y^2, \sigma_w^2, \sigma_h^2, \sigma_\theta^2)$. The observation probability is defined as the similarity measure between the target model and the candidate model of the particle. The average of Bhattacharyya Coefficients (ρ) of cell histograms is used as the observation probability given by $p(\mathbf{y}|\mathbf{s}) = \frac{1}{|C|} \sum_{i=1}^{|C|} \rho^{c_i} = \frac{1}{|C|} \sum_{j=1}^{k} \sqrt{\mathbf{h}_q^{c_i}(j) \times \mathbf{h}_p^{c_i}(j)}$. The c_i^{th} cell histograms of the target and candidate respectively given by $\mathbf{h}_q^{c_i}$ and $\mathbf{h}_p^{c_i}$ and, k is the dimension of the sparse code vector. The state with highest average Bhattacharyya coefficient is selected as the state of the object in t^{th} frame. Experimental verification of our proposal and its performance analysis are presented next.

3   Experimental Results

The performance of the algorithm is evaluated on dataset VOT2014[1][17] and the tracker performance is compared with other trackers in the literature like Mean-Shift tracker (MST) [1], Track Learn and Detect (TLD) [6] and CMT [3] tracker. The trackers were executed with their default parameter settings. The experimental results show that our proposal fares sufficiently well compared to the state of art trackers (Table 1). The results of the proposed tracker on different challenging sequences from VOT2014 are shown in Fig. 3.

3.1   Quantitative Evaluation

The performance of the proposed tracker is evaluated using one pass evaluation (OPE) [18] scheme where the tracker is initialized with ground truth value

---

[1] http://www.votchallenge.net/vot2014/dataset.html.

in first frame and allowed to track over entire sequence. The results obtained on different sequences are reported in Table 1. The performance measures used are average overlap (AO) and success rate (SR). The overlap measure of a sequence is given by $\phi_t(\Lambda_G, \Lambda_P) = \frac{\Lambda_t^G \cap \Lambda_t^P}{\Lambda_t^G \cup \Lambda_t^P}$ where, Λ^G is the area of the bounding box described by the ground truth, Λ^P is the area of the bounding box predicted by the tracker. The average overlap is given by $\Phi_{avg} = \frac{1}{N_s} \sum_{t=1}^{N_s} \phi_t$ where, N_s is the total number of successfully tracked frames in the sequence. Tracking is assumed to be successful if ϕ_t exceeds the threshold value $\phi_{th} = 0.33$. The other parameters of the proposed algorithm are number of clusters ($K = 100$), number of atoms per cluster ($m = 3$), the sparsity constraint ($T = 3$) and number of particles ($p = 75$). Patches of dimension 5×5 (i.e. patch vector size is $n = 25$) were extracted from cells of size 10×10.

The computational complexity depends on number of particles (p), dictionary size ($n \times l$), number of OMP iterations (T), number of candidate region patches (u) and the computations (t_d) required for evaluating the orthogonal projection for OMP. The total computational time per frame can be computed as $p \times u \times t_{OMP}$, where t_{OMP} is the computational load for OMP algorithm [14] given by $t_{OMP} = t_d T + 2nT + 2T(l + n) + T^3$.

Table 1. Performance comparison of the proposed tracker with the trackers MST [1], TLD [6], CMT [3]

Sequence	Challenge	Proposed tracker		MST		TLD		CMT	
		AO(%)	SR(%)	AO(%)	SR(%)	AO(%)	SR(%)	AO(%)	SR(%)
ball	sc, ro	78.43	98.50	66.00	99.50	66.50	69.26	56.00	99.83
car	sc, po	67.73	93.65	48.90	55.18	81.80	84.52	72.90	91.51
bicycle	sc, po	55.78	86.72	50.30	30.99	64.80	97.41	65.80	94.04
surfing	sc	64.79	97.87	59.10	94.68	67.90	100.00	63.70	99.29
polar bear	sc	76.43	100.00	63.90	99.73	64.30	22.10	64.70	89.75
sphere	il, sc	70.67	87.06	59.40	99.50	80.10	52.23	52.70	92.53
sunshade	il	66.28	76.16	59.00	88.95	72.40	96.51	59.70	81.39
jogging	po	66.28	97.07	56.80	85.99	73.20	98.0	69.00	85.99

3.2   Qualitative Evaluation

The results of the proposed tracker on different sequences are shown in Fig. 3. There are continuous changes of appearance and orientation in "ball" and "polar bear" sequences. The target undergoes partial occlusions (frames: $156 - 177$) as well as scale changes in "car" sequence. The cell histogram based object model (constructed using patches) and particle filter based localization helps in handling these challenges. Illumination change is significant in "tunnel" sequence as target moves through differently illuminated regions. Here, patch normalization and sparse coding helps in achieving illumination invariant tracking.

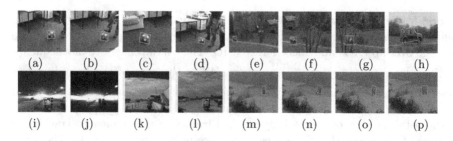

Fig. 3. Results of single object tracking for proposed Tracker on (a)-(d) "ball" (frames: 7, 217, 440, 586); (e)-(h) "car" (frames: 35, 141, 168, 235); (i)-(l) "tunnel" (frames: 6, 252, 483, 694) and (m)-(p) "polar bear" (frames: 77, 171, 251, 326) sequences from VOT2014 dataset covering different challenges like illumination change (il), scale change (sc), in-plane rotation (ro) and partial occlusions (po)

4   Conclusion

We have proposed a novel target model in a hybrid generative-discriminative framework. The object patches are represented using foreground and background dictionaries (generative model). These representations are further weighed by SVM based classification scores (discriminability). The object is localized in a particle filter framework. The proposed tracker was able to handle different challenging scenarios like background clutter, partial occlusions, in-plane rotations, scale and illumination changes. Performance of the proposed tracker is benchmarked with state of art trackers on sequences from VOT2014 dataset.

The present work did not incorporate continuous dictionary and classifier update schemes in the object model. This extension will enable the tracker to trail targets for longer durations, under sever appearance changes and occlusions. Also, the present approach is somewhat slower due to repeated application of OMP at the particle filtering stage. We propose to extend the present formulation through discriminative dictionary learning and fast OMP solvers.

References

1. Comaniciu, D., Ramesh, V., Meer, P.: Kernel-based object tracking. IEEE Trans. Pattern Anal. Mach. Intell. **25**, 564–577 (2003)
2. Isard, M., Blake, A.: Condensationconditional density propagation for visual tracking. Int. J. Comput. Vision **29**, 5–28 (1998)
3. Nebehay, G., Pflugfelder, R.: Clustering of static-adaptive correspondences for deformable object tracking. In: Proceedings of the IEEE Conference on Computer Vision and Pattern Recognition, pp. 2784–2791 (2015)
4. Mei, X., Ling, H.: Robust visual tracking using l1 1 minimization. In: 2009 IEEE 12th International Conference on Computer Vision, pp. 1436–1443. IEEE (2009)
5. Babenko, B., Yang, M.H., Belongie, S.: Visual tracking with online multiple instance learning. In: IEEE Conference on Computer Vision and Pattern Recognition, CVPR 2009, pp. 983–990. IEEE (2009)

6. Kalal, Z., Mikolajczyk, K., Matas, J.: Tracking-learning-detection. IEEE Trans. Pattern Anal. Mach. Intell. **34**, 1409–1422 (2012)
7. Avidan, S.: Ensemble tracking. IEEE Trans. Pattern Anal. Mach. Intell. **29**, 261–271 (2007)
8. Lei, Y., Ding, X., Wang, S.: Visual tracker using sequential bayesian learning: discriminative, generative, and hybrid. IEEE Trans. Syst. Man Cybern. B Cybern. **38**, 1578–1591 (2008)
9. Wang, D., Lu, H., Yang, M.H.: Online object tracking with sparse prototypes. IEEE Trans. Image Process. **22**, 314–325 (2013)
10. Bai, T., Li, Y.F.: Robust visual tracking with structured sparse representation appearance model. Pattern Recogn. **45**, 2390–2404 (2012)
11. Zhang, S., Yao, H., Sun, X., Lu, X.: Sparse coding based visual tracking: Review and experimental comparison. Pattern Recogn. **46**, 1772–1788 (2013)
12. Yang, X., Wang, M., Zhang, L., Sun, F., Hong, R., Qi, M.: An efficient tracking system by orthogonalized templates. IEEE Trans. Industr. Electron. **63**, 3187–3197 (2016)
13. Liu, B., Huang, J., Kulikowski, C., Yang, L.: Robust visual tracking using local sparse appearance model and k-selection. IEEE Trans. Pattern Anal. Mach. Intell. **35**, 2968–2981 (2013)
14. Rubinstein, R., Zibulevsky, M., Elad, M.: Efficient implementation of the k-svd algorithm using batch orthogonal matching pursuit. CS Technion **40**, 1–15 (2008)
15. Arulampalam, M.S., Maskell, S., Gordon, N., Clapp, T.: A tutorial on particle filters for online nonlinear/non-gaussian bayesian tracking. IEEE Trans. Signal Process. **50**, 174–188 (2002)
16. Aharon, M., Elad, M., Bruckstein, A.: k-svd: an algorithm for designing overcomplete dictionaries for sparse representation. IEEE Trans. Signal Process. **54**, 4311–4322 (2006)
17. Kristan, M., Matas, J., Leonardis, A., Vojíř, T., Pflugfelder, R., Fernandez, G., Nebehay, G., Porikli, F., Čehovin, L.: A novel performance evaluation methodology for single-target trackers. IEEE Trans. Pattern Anal. Mach. Intell. **38**, 2137–2155 (2016)
18. Wu, Y., Lim, J., Yang, M.H.: Online object tracking: a benchmark. In: Proceedings of the IEEE Conference on Computer Vision and Pattern Recognition, pp. 2411–2418 (2013)

A Machine Learning Inspired Approach for Detection, Recognition and Tracking of Moving Objects from Real-Time Video

Anit Chakrabory[1,2(✉)] and Sayandip Dutta[1,2]

[1] RCC Institute of Information Technology, Kolkata, India
ianitchakraborty@gmail.com, sayandip199309@gmail.com
[2] MCKV Institute of Engineering, Howrah, India

Abstract. In this paper, we address the problem of recognizing moving objects in video im-ages using Visual Vocabulary model and Bag of Words. Initially, the shadow free images are obtained by background modelling followed by object segmentation from the video frame to extract the blobs of our object of interest. Subsequently, we train a Visual Vocabulary model with human body datasets in accordance with our domain of interest for recognition. In training, we use the principle of Bag of Words to extract necessary features to certain domains and objects for classification, similarly, matching them with extracted object blobs that are obtained by subtracting the shadow free background from the foreground. We track the detected objects via Kalman Filter. We evaluate our algorithm on benchmark datasets. A comparative analysis of our algorithm against the existing state-of-the-art methods shows very satisfactory results to go forward.

Keywords: Background modelling · Bag of words · Object detection · Object recognition · Visual vocabulary

1 Introduction

Effective recognition of objects for tracking in video stream and processing of data involve integration of background modelling, shadow removal, analysis of segmented objects from the video frames and proper detection of objects. Subsequently, recognition of the detected objects is done by extracting the features adopting the machine learning inspired principle, bag of words.

In our paper, we use the Visual Vocabulary Model using Bag of Words to extract the necessary features of certain instances of objects through rigorous high-level training. Subsequently, we apply the extracted feature sets to the test domain to recognize and locate our objects of interest in the video scenes. Using visual instance occurrence and their probabilistic presence to imply a certain domain, we obtain optimum accuracy in domain recognition as well.

The contributions of this paper are:

- Background modelling and extraction of astute shadow free images using color invariant approach.

© Springer International Publishing AG 2017
B.U. Shankar et al. (Eds.): PReMI 2017, LNCS 10597, pp. 170–178, 2017.
https://doi.org/10.1007/978-3-319-69900-4_22

- Extraction of the features of the objects captured in the blobs via the principle of Bag of Words.
- Classification of the objects in a certain domain of interest using probabilistic word occurrence for domain recognition.

The organization of the paper constitutes: Sect. 2 briefly explains the related works in the respective domain, Sect. 3 explains the proposed method for detection and recognition, specifically, Sect. 3.3 describes the concept of Visual Vocabulary Model for object recognition. Experimental results on several datasets and the comparative analysis with some state-of-the-art algorithms are presented in Sect. 4. Section 5 concludes the paper and discusses future possibilities for further improvements.

2 Brief Review of Related Works

Numerous color histograms based object detection algorithms have been proposed in recent years. He et al. [4] developed a locality sensitive histogram at each pixel for finer distribution of the visual feature points for object tracking in video scenes. Haar-like features have been proposed for appearance based tracking of objects [5–7, 9]. Spatiotemporal representation combined with genetic algorithm has also been used for feature extraction [1]. Recently pixel based segmentations have been applied [2] to handle tracking.

In recent years, the classifiers that have been extensively used for object tracking are: ranking SVM [7], semi-boosting [14], support vector machine (SVM) [12], boosting [13], structured output SVM [8], and online multi-instance boosting [6]. Various detection and tracking codes are available for evaluation with significant effort of the authors, e.g., MIL, IVT, TLD, FCT, VTD and likes.

3 Proposed Method

Initially, we model the segmented objects from the video frames and subtract the background model without shadow to obtain the blob of an object. Before recognizing the object inside the blob, we train a machine learning inspired Visual Vocabulary Model with a set of objects which can represent our domain of interest for recognition and tracking. We extract the features of the objects of both the training data and test data by principle of Bag of Words, in the training and testing phases respectively.

3.1 Background Modeling

In [10], Li et al. proposed an idea for background modelling. In our work, we introduce some modification over the same work and proceed as follows: At each time step an image I_m^t is obtained by subtracting two successive video frames and F_m^t can be obtained by subtracting the current video frame with the background model. To deal with sudden illumination variation an AND-OR operation is performed over I_m^t and F_m^t. The extracted frame I^t is compared with its previous frame I^{t-1} in order to obtain I_m^t by predicting the similarity between the two consecutive pixel values of frames I_t (x, y) and I_{t-1}(x, y). Pixel centers are compared between the succeeding images (I^t (x, y), I^{t-1} (x, y)). Temporal binary image of the moving object (I_m) has a radiometric similarity value, formally expressed as:

$$I_m(x,y) = \begin{cases} 1, & if\ R(x,y) > T_b \\ 0, & otherwise \end{cases}.$$ (1)

Similarly, F_m^t is formulated on a hypothesis based on the difference threshold (T_b), between background frame and the current frame, formally:

$$F_m^t = \begin{cases} 1, & if\ |I^t(x,y) - B^t(x,y)| > T_b \\ 0, & otherwise \end{cases}.$$ (2)

The pixels (x,y) of moving objects are formulated by operating on $I_m(x,y)$ and $F^t(x,y)$:

$$M^t(x,y) = \begin{cases} 1, & if\ (I_m(x,y) \cap F^t(x,y)) = 1) \\ 0, & otherwise \end{cases}.$$ (3)

The moving pixels in video frames are identified by $M^t(x,y)$.

In our implementation, a vector history V, with the six last values updated cumulatively, is considered as:

$$V = [E(t), E(t-1), E(t-2), E(t-3), E(t-4), E(t-5)].$$ (4)

At time t, the mean value of pixel intensities in the frame is E(t). For each frame, we calculate proper learning rate α, based on this vector:

$$\alpha = a + b\frac{|E(t) - E(t-5)|}{\max(E(t), E(t-5))},$$ (5)

Let d be a pixel of the image, the gray histogram of the pixel is $h(d)$, and background pixels and foreground pixels are denoted by I_B and I_F respectively. Probability of a background pixel misidentified as foreground pixel and vice versa are as follows:

$$P_{F|B} = \sum_{d \in I_F} p(d|B) \text{ and } P_{B|F} = \sum_{d \in I_B} p(d|F),$$ (6)

where $P_{d|B}$ is the probability of background pixel and $P_{d|F}$ is the probability of foreground pixel.

Our goal is to minimize $P_{d|B}$ and $P_{d|F}$ as much as possible.

The Min $P_{F|B}$ is significant, as after morphological operation in the post-process, $P_{B|F}$ will be smaller.

$p(B)$ is the priori probability of the background as calculated from gray histogram of the image I_m^t.

$$p(B) = \sum_{d=-T}^{T} h(d) \quad \mu = 0. \tag{7}$$

3.2 Shadow Removal

As mentioned in [11] by Xu et al., by formally normalizing the pixels to r, g, b color space the shadow-free color invariant image can be constructed:

$$r' = \frac{r}{\sqrt{r^2 + g^2 + b^2}}, g' = \frac{g}{\sqrt{r^2 + g^2 + b^2}}, b' = \frac{b}{\sqrt{r^2 + g^2 + b^2}}. \tag{8}$$

where r, g, b are input image color channels, r', b', g'.

Application of Gaussian smooth filter suppresses the high frequency textures in both invariant and original images, formally:

$$E_{ori} = ||edge(I_{ori})||, E_{inv(i)} = ||edge(I_{inv(i)})||, \tag{9}$$

where E_{ori} is the edge of the original image after applying smooth filter and I_{ori} is the original image. $E_{inv(i)}$ is the edge of the color invariant image after applying smooth filter and $I_{inv(i)}$ is the color invariant image. The hard shadow edge mask is constructed by choosing the strong edges of original images that are absent in the invariant images. Thus, we get:

$$HS(x,y) = \begin{cases} 1, & E_{ori}(x,y) > t1, \& \\ & \min_i(E_{inv(i)}(x,y) < t2), \\ 0, & otherwise \end{cases} \tag{10}$$

where $t1$, $t2$ are thresholds, set manually, based on the empirical analysis of datasets and assessed hard shadow edge mask is $HS(x,y)$. In (10), $t1$ maps the selected shadow edges to the strong edges of the subsequent hard shadows in images. $t2$ selects edges belonging only to shadows, as shown in Fig. 1.

3.3 Visual Vocabulary Model for Object Recognition

Visual Vocabulary Model is a machine learning based image classification model, specifically, handling images as documents, by labelling specific features as words by observing presence of such feature key words in an image.

First, we localize the key words by extracting the features of the object of interest such that they are distinct and invariant under different scale and illumination based conditions even with the presence of noise. We have used Nonlinear (cubic) Support Vector Machine (SVM) as the feature classifier. Polynomial kernel for cubic SVM is:

$$K(x,y) = (x^T y + c)^3. \tag{11}$$

Here x and y are input vector features, calculated from the training samples. A free parameter, $c \geq 0$, is indicating how far the equation is from homogeneity.

The following equation expresses the contribution of a feature f, at location l, at position x in the object class o_n with matching visual keyword index (C_i) indicating its potentiality of belonging to the class o_n. Thus, we get:

$$p(o_n, x | f, l) = \sum_i p(o_n, x | C_i, l) p(C_i | f), \tag{12}$$

Mean-shift mode estimation with a kernel K, along with scale-adaptive kernel, is used to obtain the maxima in this space:

$$\hat{p}(o_n, x) = \frac{1}{V_b(x_s)} \sum_k \sum_j p\left(o_n, x_j | f_k, l_k\right) K\left(\frac{x - x_j}{b(x_s)}\right). \tag{13}$$

Kernel bandwidth is denoted by b, and volume is denoted by V_b, which are varied over the radius of the kernel. In order to fix the hypothesized interest object, size and scale coordinate x_s is updated in parallel. This strategy makes it easier to deal with partial occlusions and also typically requires fewer training examples.

The pictorial structure model represents any object of interest as collection of parts, connected in pairs, and defined by a graph $G = (V, E)$, where the nodes $V = \{v_1, \ldots, v_n\}$ defines the parts and the edges $(v_i, v_j) \in E$ describes the corresponding connections.

$L = \{l_1, \ldots, l_n\}$ be a certain arrangement of part frame locations. Then the matching of the model to a video frame is formulated using an energy minimization function:

$$l_1^* = \arg\min_{l_1}\left(m_1(l_1) + \sum_{i=2}^n \min_{l_i} m_i(l_i) + ||l_i - T_{1i}(l_1)||_{M_{ij}}^2\right). \tag{14}$$

where M_{ij} is the diagonal covariance between transformed locations $T_{ij}(l_i)$ and $T_{ji}(l_j)$.

For further improvement of our validation score by approximating the similarity measures, we discriminatively model a linear time matching function, represented by the Pyramid Match Kernel (PMK) model to bridge the feature sets to the variable cardinalities. Let the input of a histogram pyramid be $X \in S$ where $\Psi(X) = [H_0(X), \ldots, H_{L-1}(X)]$, number of pyramid levels expressed as L. The histogram vector of point X is defined by $H_i(X)$.

Similarity between two input set of features Y and Z is expressed as:

$$\kappa_{PMK}(\Psi(Y), \Psi(Z)) = \sum_{i=0}^{L-1} \omega_i(I(H_i(Y), H_i(Z)) - I(H_{i-1}(Y), H_{i-1}(Z))), \tag{15}$$

where $I(H_i(Y), H_i(Z))$ signifies the histogram intersection of two input set of features Y and Z at i^{th} level of the pyramid.

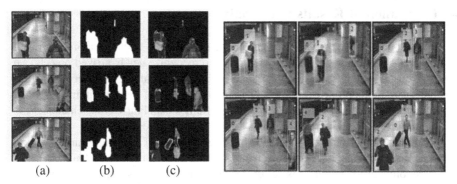

Fig. 1. (a) Video Frame, (b) Segmented Object Model, (c) Foreground Model.

Fig. 2. Tracking results on INRIEA.

Finally, the features of the recognized objects are tracked via the classical Kalman Filter, which can also efficiently handle the tracking under partial occlusions as shown in Fig. 2. The performance measure of the proposed algorithm is done with respect to available benchmark datasets and we obtain very satisfactory and competitive results.

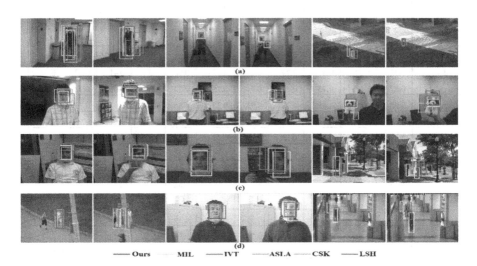

Fig. 3. Sample tracking results of the eight top performed trackers on challenging sequences. (a) Result samples on BlurBody, Boy and Crossing sequences. Challenging factors: background clutter and deformation. (b) Result samples on David, David2 and Dog1 sequences. Challenging factors: scale variation, motion blur, and occlusion. (c) Result samples on Dudek, FaceOcc1 and Human9 sequences. Challenging factors: deformation and occlusion. (d) Result samples on Jogging, Mhyang and Walking2 sequences. Challenging factors: fast motion, scale variation, and occlusion.

4 Experimental Results and Analysis

We test our algorithm on various benchmark datasets [3] with the aforementioned settings. Using the trained model as a reference to recognize newly arrived objects, we compare our algorithm with the other state-of-the-art algorithms, in other datasets as well for the validation our experiment. The tracking result of our algorithm on INRIA Person dataset and on other datasets in multiple frames handling various challenges, is shown in Figs. 2 and 3 respectively.

The overlap rate of tracking methods indicates stability of each algorithm by taking the pose and size of the target object into consideration in Table 1. Our algorithm achieves competitive, rather satisfactory results compared to the other state-of-the-art tracking algorithms [3]. Figure 4 represents a comparative analysis of the overlap rate in video frames against the other state-of-the-art methods showing competitive as well as satisfactory outcomes.

Table 1. Average overlap rate of tracking methods. The red, yellow and orange colors indicate the results ranked at the first, second and third places, respectively.

Sequences	Ours	CSK	FCT	HT	IVT	ASLA	MIL	PT	SPT	TLD	VTD
Blurbody	**0.59**	0.43	0.31	0.35	0.25	0.35	0.22	0.51	0.46	**0.56**	**0.72**
Boy	**0.74**	0.69	**0.77**	**0.78**	0.65	0.51	**0.72**	0.46	0.34	**0.78**	0.29
Crossing	0.39	0.58	0.69	0.36	0.68	0.75	0.29	0.49	**0.76**	**0.80**	**0.79**
David	**0.74**	0.57	**0.71**	0.31	**0.73**	0.65	0.38	0.28	0.52	0.47	0.34
David2	**0.67**	0.41	0.53	0.61	**0.75**	0.44	0.21	**0.71**	0.21	0.21	**0.67**
Dog1	0.70	0.34	**0.74**	0.25	0.58	0.39	**0.67**	0.27	0.33	**0.80**	0.24
Dudek	**0.73**	0.23	0.56	**0.79**	0.26	0.37	0.68	0.56	0.41	0.57	**0.72**
FaceOcc1	0.57	0.58	**0.73**	0.24	0.22	**0.75**	**0.73**	0.54	0.61	**0.73**	**0.71**
Gym	**0.50**	0.48	0.45	0.22	0.33	0.20	0.52	**0.66**	0.47	0.39	**0.77**
Jogging2	0.70	0.23	0.44	**0.77**	0.34	0.24	0.74	0.55	0.61	**0.75**	0.40
Mhyang	**0.51**	**0.65**	0.38	0.25	**0.73**	0.43	0.54	0.32	0.37	0.35	0.37
Walking2	**0.76**	**0.80**	0.51	0.37	0.23	0.45	**0.75**	0.31	0.40	0.58	0.33
BlurFace	**0.72**	0.43	0.31	0.26	0.40	**0.63**	0.37	0.21	**0.61**	0.22	0.33
Deer	0.55	0.63	0.51	0.36	0.65	0.40	**0.80**	0.28	0.60	**0.73**	**0.78**
Dog	**0.74**	0.45	0.56	0.44	0.34	0.30	**0.73**	0.52	**0.67**	0.49	0.38
Football	**0.67**	0.21	0.24	**0.80**	0.35	0.54	0.39	0.65	0.66	**0.77**	**0.67**
Jump	0.48	**0.64**	0.63	0.56	**0.75**	0.55	0.56	0.26	**0.75**	0.48	**0.79**
Dancer	**0.69**	0.30	**0.46**	0.26	0.32	0.41	0.31	0.33	**0.46**	0.37	**0.66**
Couple	0.63	**0.76**	**0.76**	0.72	**0.80**	**0.79**	0.24	0.43	0.73	0.68	0.32
Trellis	0.50	0.27	0.51	0.41	**0.61**	0.48	0.30	**0.68**	**0.64**	0.35	0.47
Woman	**0.62**	0.40	0.49	0.61	0.22	**0.68**	0.34	**0.62**	0.50	**0.69**	**0.68**
Girl2	0.52	0.43	0.31	0.35	0.25	0.35	0.22	**0.51**	0.46	**0.56**	**0.72**
Average	**0.62**	0.48	0.53	0.46	0.47	0.48	0.49	0.46	0.53	**0.56**	**0.55**

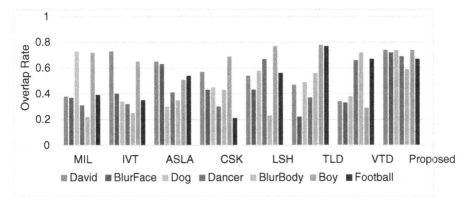

Fig. 4. Comparative analysis of overlap rate against the state-of-the-art methods on various benchmark datasets and challenges.

5   Conclusion

This paper presents object detection and recognition of the detected objects based on Visual Vocabulary Model. We train different objects separately in several images with multiple aspects and camera viewpoints to find the best key word points for recognition. Subsequently, we verify the extracted features of the training images after classification of the feature sets. These key word points are applied to the regions based on visual feature point analysis. The performance measure of the proposed algorithm is analyzed with respect to available benchmark data and we obtain very satisfactory and competitive results. This has great potentials in the field of problem solving integrating vision and pattern recognition with more robustness and variability, with exciting opportunities to explore in near future.

References

1. Learning spatio-temporal representations for action recognition: a genetic programming approach, IEEE Trans. Cybern. **46**(1), November 2016
2. Xiao, F., Lee, Y.J.: Track and segment: an iterative unsupervised approach for video object proposals (2016)
3. Wu, Y., Lim, J., Yang, M.: Object tracking benchmark. IEEE Trans. Pattern Anal. Mach. Intell. **37**(9), 1837–1838 (2015)
4. He, S., Yang, Q., Lau, R.W.H., Wang, J., Yang, M.-H.: Visual tracking via locality sensitive histograms. In: Proceedings of IEEE Conference Computer Vision Pattern Recognition, pp. 2427–2434 (2013)
5. Zhang, K., Zhang, L., Yang, M.-H.: Real-time compressive tracking. In: Fitzgibbon, A., Lazebnik, S., Perona, P., Sato, Y., Schmid, C. (eds.) ECCV 2012. LNCS, vol. 7574, pp. 864–877. Springer, Heidelberg (2012). doi:10.1007/978-3-642-33712-3_62
6. Babenko, B., Yang, M.-H., Belongie, S.: Robust object tracking with online multiple instance learning. IEEE Trans. Pattern Anal. Mach. Intell. **33**(7), 1619–1632 (2011)

7. Li, H., Shen, C., Shi, Q.: Real-time visual tracking using compressive sensing. In: CVPR, pp. 1305–1312 (2011)
8. Hare, S., Saffari, A., Torr, P.H.S.: Struck: structured output tracking with kernels. In: Proceedings IEEE International Conference Computer Vision, pp. 263–270 (2011)
9. Kalal, Z., Matas, J., Mikolajczyk, K.: P-N learning: bootstrapping binary classifiers by structural constraints. In: Proceedings of IEEE Conference Computer Vision Pattern Recognition, pp. 49–56 (2010)
10. Li, G., Wang, Y., Shu, W.: Real-time moving object detection for video monitoring systems. In: International Symposium on Intelligent Information Technology Application (2008)
11. Xu, L., Qi, F., Jiang, R.: Shadow removal from a single image. In: Proceedings of IEEE International Conference on Intelligent Systems Design and Applications, pp. 1049–1054 (2006)
12. Avidan, S.: Support vector tracking. IEEE Trans. Pattern Anal. Mach. Intell. **26**(8), 1064–1072 (2004)
13. Grabner, H., Grabner, M., Bischof, H.: Real-time tracking via on-line boosting. In: Proceedings of British Machine Vision Conference, pp. 6.1– 6.10 (2006)
14. Sevilla-Lara, L., Learned-Miller, E.: Distribution fields for tracking. In: Proceedings of IEEE Conference Computer Vision Pattern Recognition, pp. 1910–1917 (2012)

Does Rotation Influence the Estimated Contour Length of a Digital Object?

Sabyasachi Mukherjee[1], Oishila Bandyopadhyay[2](✉), Arindam Biswas[1], and Bhargab B. Bhattacharya[2]

[1] Department of Information Technology, Indian Institute of Engineering Science and Technology, Shibpur, Howrah 711103, India
[2] Center for Soft Computing Research, Indian Statistical Institute, Kolkata 700108, India
oishila@gmail.com

Abstract. In this work, we study the variation of estimated contour length of a digital object when it is rotated with respect to its centroid. This analysis also helps to ascertain the unknown angle of rotation of an object relative to a reference position. Additionally, we propose a new technique for estimating the length of a digital contour based on stitched digital cover. The proposed study on rotational variation of contour length finds applications to various image-registration problems such as the detection of positioning-errors that are often encountered during X-ray imaging of patients. Experimental results are presented for some regular curves, natural objects, and X-ray images.

Keywords: Length estimator · Chain code · X-ray image analysis · Digital object · Rotation · Perimeter estimation

1 Introduction

Accurate estimation of the length of a digital contour of an object is needed for various image-processing applications. The length estimated from a digital contour is often found to differ significantly from the actual geometric length of the contour corresponding to the real object. Additionally, the rotation of a digital object with respect to coordinate-axes impacts the length of its contour. In other words, because of the discreteness of the underlying pixel-grid, the estimated length varies with the orientation on the object. To the best of our knowledge, the variation of contour-length with respect to rotation has not yet been studied in the literature. In this paper, we propose a new length-estimator based on the concept of stitched digital cover for digital curves and digital objects. We also study the change in contour-length caused by rotation of the object and analyze their correlation for the purpose of identifying the angle of its rotation with respect to a reference position.

Digitization of the continuous contour of a real object leads to a sequence of discrete points that are sampled from the contour based on the chosen pixel-grid

© Springer International Publishing AG 2017
B.U. Shankar et al. (Eds.): PReMI 2017, LNCS 10597, pp. 179–186, 2017.
https://doi.org/10.1007/978-3-319-69900-4_23

geometry. For the purpose of length estimation [5] for a digital contour, previous researchers used different measures such as chain code [8] digital straight line segment (DSS) [10], or minimum-length polygonal approximation (MLP) [13]. The DSS-method is based on the partition of a digital curve into digital straight segments, whereas the MLP-method relies on the construction of the minimum-length polygon in an open boundary of a digital region [10]. Klette et al. reported a comparative study on the performance and accuracy of such length-estimators [10]. Further studies on length-estimators for binary images were reported by Kulpa [12]. Proffit and Rosen [15] derived various properties of a digital contour. Kenmochi et al. [9] had proposed had proposed a boundary-extraction method using combinatorial topology.

The effect of rotation on digital contours has been studied by several research groups. Bennett et al. [2] defined quantization noise and analyzed the curvature of a digital object in a quantized environment. Contour length and area estimation through volume measurement was reported by Verbeek et al. [16]. The change in object-contour and shape due to rotation is observed to satisfy certain characteristics for rotation and scaling-invariant systems [6,14]. Wang et al. designed a rotation and scaling-invariant shape descriptor by introducing a hierarchical string-cut method to partition a shape into multi-level curve segments [17]. Farooque et al. proposed a scale-invariant feature-transformation system for object recognition [7]. In this work, we propose a new method for length-estimation and study the effect of rotation on the contour-length of a digital object We show that this technique can be effectively used to detect positioning error (rotation) [4] in an X-ray imaging system.

2   Definitions

Digital plane - The digital plane, $\mathbb{Z}^2$, is the set of all points having integer coordinates in the real plane $\mathbb{R}^2$. A point in the digital plane is called a digital point, or a pixel in the case of a digital image.

k-connectedness - The set of k adjacent points of a point $p(x, y) \in \mathbb{Z}^2$ is represented as $N_k(p) := \{(x', y') : (x', y') \in \mathbb{Z}^2 \wedge max(|x - x'|, |y - y'|) = 1\}$. Each point in $N_k(p)$ is said to be a k-neighbor ($k = 4$ or 8) of p. Two points p and q are k-connected in a digital set $S \subset \mathbb{Z}^2$ if and only if there exists a sequence $h_p := p_0; p_1; \ldots; p_n := q_i \subseteq S$ such that $p_i \subset N_k(pi - 1)$ for $1 \leq i \leq n$. For any point $p \in S$, the set of points that are k-connected to $p \in S$ is called a k-connected component of S. In this work, we have used 8-connectedness to define the inner and outer digital cover of an object.

Digital object - A digital object is a finite subset of $\mathbb{Z}^2$, which consists of one or more k-connected components.

Digital grid - A digital grid $G := (H; V)$ consists of a set H of horizontal (digital) grid lines and a set V of vertical (digital) grid lines. The intersection of vertical and horizontal grid line at the point $(i; j) \in \mathbb{Z}^2$, is called a grid point.

Object Cover - The contour points of a real life object may not exactly fall on the pixel grid points after digitization (as shown in Fig. 1(a) shows the outer cover of the object). For a given digital object S, the outer Jordan digitization $J^+(S)$ is defined as the union of all such 2-cells (grid squares) that have non-empty intersections with S, and the inner Jordan digitization $J^-(S)$ is the union of all 2-cells that are completely contained within S [11]. Jordan digitization (inner or outer) gives the union of cells but does not specify the (inner/outer) covers as a sequence of vertices.

To define the digital contour of a real object, we propose single-pixel thin inner and outer cover using 8-connectedness. We consider $\mathfrak{J}$ to be a finite rectangular subset of $\mathbb{Z}^2$, which contains the entire object S. Let the height h and the width w of $\mathfrak{J}$ be such that the grid size, g, divides both $h-1$ and $w-1$, and the boundary unit grid blocks (UGBs) of $\mathfrak{J}$ do not contain any part of S [3].

Outer digital cover- The outer digital cover of an object is defined as the set of pixels (C_o's) that belong to the 8-neighbour of any contour point (cp_i) of the object outside the object region. Thus, from any point outside the object boundary, if we move towards a point on the object contour, the respective outer digital cover point will be the last pixel point (outside the object region) before reaching the object contour. Figure 1(b) shows the outer digital cover of the object with yellow points mark the selected pixel grids for outer cover.

Inner digital cover- The inner digital cover of an object is defined as the set of pixels (C_i's) that belong to the 8-neighbour of any contour point (cp_i) of the object inside the object region. Thus, from any point inside the object, if we move towards a contour point, the respective inner digital cover point will be the last pixel point before reaching the object boundary. Figure 1(b) shows the inner digital cover of the object with red points mark the selected pixel grids for inner cover.

Stitched digital cover- In the proposed length estimator, we have used a novel stitched digital cover. The stitched digital cover of an object is defined as the set of points (C_s's), where each C_s denotes the middle point between every pixel (C_o) on the outer-cover and its nearest pixel (C_i) lying on the inner-cover.

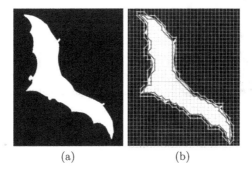

(a)   (b)

Fig. 1. (a) Object without pixel grid, (b) Object on pixel grid with outer (yellow) and inner (red) cover (Color figure online)

3   Proposed Approach

Accurate computation of the perimeter of a real life object in digital domain is a challenging task. We have proposed an approach based on stitched digital cover to compute the perimeter of the object. In this approach, the object (S) is placed on a digital grid (g) and the inner and outer digital covers are generated based on the occupancy of the object contour in each grid cell [3]. The stitched cover is then computed by using the pixels from both inner and outer cover. The proposed algorithm ($getstitchlength(S,g)$) is shown in Fig. 2. Here the grid is considered as unit grid ($g = 1$) for generation of the tightest cover. For each pixel p_i in the outer cover of S, the nearest inner cover pixel q_i is identified from 8-neighbouring pixels of p_i (clock-wise direction). The arithmetic mean (m_i) of the coordinate positions of each (p_i,q_i) pair is computed from the pixel positions of p_i and q_i (as shown in Fig. 3).

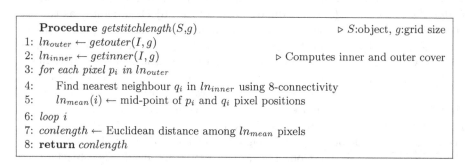

> **Procedure** $getstitchlength(S,g)$ ▷ S:object, g:grid size
> 1: $ln_{outer} \leftarrow getouter(I,g)$
> 2: $ln_{inner} \leftarrow getinner(I,g)$ ▷ Computes inner and outer cover
> 3: *for each pixel p_i in ln_{outer}*
> 4:   Find nearest neighbour q_i in ln_{inner} using 8-connectivity
> 5: $ln_{mean}(i) \leftarrow$ mid-point of p_i and q_i pixel positions
> 6: *loop i*
> 7: *conlength* $\leftarrow$ Euclidean distance among ln_{mean} pixels
> 8: **return** *conlength*

Fig. 2. Stitched cover generation and length estimation algorithm

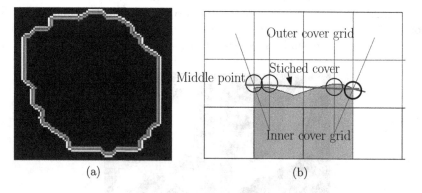

(a)   (b)

Fig. 3. (a) Proposed stitched cover (in red), (b) Magnified view of region 'A' (Color figure online)

3.1   Effect of Rotation on Object Contour

On rotation of the object, the position of 8-nearest neighbour grid pixels change for inner and outer digital contour. This results in the change in digital contour length under rotation. Chain code representation of object contour [8] shows that the direction of contour pixel traversal can have three possible values - vertical (top and bottom), horizontal (left and right), and diagonal (corners positions) (Fig. 4(a)). Thus the length of each move in contour traversal is unity (for vertical and horizontal move) and $\sqrt{2}$ (for diagonal move). Figure 4(b) shows the chain code direction of pixels in a digital curve contour. The contour length of the curve is computed from the number of diagonal pixels (5 pixels, each contributing $\sqrt{2}$) and number of horizontal or vertical pixels (3 pixels, each contributing unit length). As a result of object rotation, few horizontal or vertical pixels are re-positioned as diagonal pixels, and few diagonal pixels are re-positioned as vertical pixels. This results in change in contour length of the object. We have studied this change in digital contour length with each 10° of object rotation with respect to its centroid. Figure 4(c) shows the variation in contour length of a rectangular object with angle of rotation varies from 0° to 90°. It can be noticed that the contour length is minimum at 0° and it changes with increase in angle of rotation. The contour length becomes minimum again at 90°.

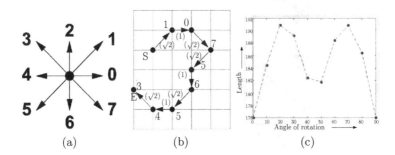

(a)   (b)   (c)

Fig. 4. (a) Chain code directions, (b) Digital curve of length $(3 + 5\sqrt{2})$, (c) Length variation of rectangle with angle of rotation

4   Applications to Positioning-Error Detection

Studies on object rotation may find several applications in image registration, hand-writing analysis, contour-length estimation, and in other areas [2,7,17]. We have studied the application of object rotation in the domain of medical image processing. A common error in X-ray imaging is positioning error. In many situations, portable X-ray machines are used to take X-ray of bedridden patients. In such scenarios, the chest, femur, knee X-ray images appear with position error due to angular posture of the patient [4]. The study on change in image contour length with rotation can be applied to detect the wrong posture of the patient automatically and help technician to correct the position before capturing the final image. Figure 5(a) and (b) show the chest X-ray taken at correct position and the segmented contour of the left chest. Entropy based segmentation [1] is applied to segment the chest contour from the X-ray image. If positioning error occurs, the chest appear in rotated posture (shown in Fig. 5(e) and (f)). We have performed the analysis of normal and rotated chest contour. These contour images are rotated from 0° to 90° and the histogram of vertical and horizontal pixels and diagonal pixels at every 10° change in rotation are generated. Figure 5(d) shows that number of diagonal pixels is minimum at 0° and it changes with rotation for normal chest contour (Fig. 5(b)). For rotated chest contour (Fig. 5(f)), the minimum number of diagonal pixel doesn't appear at 0° (as shown in Fig. 5(h)). This analysis indicates that the positioning error (rotation) in X-ray can be detected by analysing the erroneous X-ray image.

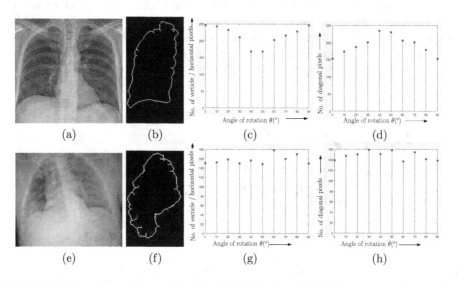

(a)   (b)   (c)   (d)

(e)   (f)   (g)   (h)

Fig. 5. (a) Chest X-ray (normal position), (b) Segmented left chest contour (normal), (c) Horizontal and vertical pixel count of (b), (d) Diagonal pixel count of (b), (e) Chest X-ray (positioning error-rotation), (f) Segmented left chest contour (positioning error), (g) Horizontal and vertical pixel count of (f), (h) Diagonal pixel count of (f)

5   Experimental Results

To quantify the effect of rotation on object contours, several binary test images are taken. The expected or actual perimeter length is calculated using chain code. After that, the objects are placed on digital grid of size 1×1 to calculate the inner and outer digital cover and compute the stitched cover length. For each pixel on the outer cover, the nearest inner cover pixel is identified and the stitched cover point is computed as the mid-point of the inner and outer cover pixels. We calculate the Euclidean distance (e_i) between each pair of stitched cover points (p_i, p_{i+1}) and the stitched cover length is computed as $\sum e_i$. For an arbitrary curve with concave or convex curvatures, the number of pixels in the outer-cover (inner-cover) may be larger (smaller) than that on the actual contour. In such scenarios, multiple outer-cover pixels may map to the same inner-cover pixel while generating the stitched-cover; the number of pixels on the stitched-cover points may be less than that on the actual contour of the object. Since the chain-code is constructed on the basis of the connected contour-pixels of the object, the length computed based on stitched-cover is observed to be slightly less than or equal to that computed from the chain code length. For some convex polygonal shapes such as rectangle and square, the two method yields the same value of the estimated length. Figure 6(a) shows the variation of estimated length from chain code length of different images. We have also predicted the length of an object at any unknown angle from the length at known angles. Figure 6(b) shows that the length of heel X-ray image at any unknown angle is predicted from the length of the same object at known angles. Here the contour length of heel X-ray is computed by proposed approach after each 10° of rotation about its centroid. The contour length at any unknown angle is predicted by computing the mean length between two known angles. This prediction performs better for symmetric objects.

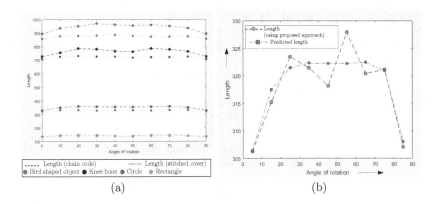

Fig. 6. (a) Comparison of contour length estimation of different object, (b) Length estimation at different angles for heel X-ray image

6   Conclusion

In this paper we study the effect of rotation on the length of a digital contour and propose a new contour-length estimator. This study can be extended to develop an automated system for the detection of X-ray positioning-error. It can also be applied for efficient image registration.

References

1. Bandyopadhyay, O., Chanda, B., Bhattacharya, B.B.: Automatic segmentation of bones in X-ray images based on entropy measure. Int. J. Image Graph. **16**(1), 1650001–32 (2016)
2. Bennett, J.R., Mac Donald, J.S.: On the measurement of curvature in a quantized environment. IEEE Trans. Comput. **24**(8), 803–820 (1975)
3. Biswas, A., Bhowmick, P., Bhattacharya, B.B.: Construction of isothetic covers of a digital object: a combinatorial approach. J. Vis. Commun. Image Represent. **21**, 295–310 (2010)
4. Bontrager, K., Lampignano, J.: Textbook of Radiographic Positioning and Related Anatomy. Elsevier, St. Louis (2013)
5. Coeurjolly, D., Klette, R.: A comparative evaluation of length estimators of digital curves. IEEE Trans. Pattern Anal. Mach. Intell. **26**(2), 252–257 (2004)
6. Costa, L.d.F.D., Cesar Jr, R.M.: Shape Analysis and Classification: Theory and Practice. CRC Press Inc., Boca Raton (2000)
7. Farooque, G., Sargano, A.B., Shafi, I., Ali, W.: Coin recognition with reduced feature set sift algorithm using neural network. In: Proceedings International Conference on Frontiers of Information Technology (FIT), pp. 93–98 (2016)
8. Freeman, H.: On the encoding of arbitrary geometric configurations. IRE Trans. Electron. Comput. **EC–10**(2), 260–268 (1961)
9. Kenmochi, Y., Imiya, A., Ichikawa, A.: Boundary extraction of discrete objects. Comput. Vis. Image Underst. **71**(3), 281–293 (1998)
10. Klette, R., Kovalevsky, V., Yip, B.: On the length estimation of digital curves. In: SPIE's International Symposium on Optical Science, Engineering, and Instrumentation, pp. 117–128 (1999)
11. Klette, R., Rosenfeld, A.: Digital Geometry: Geometric Methods for Digital Picture Analysis. Elsevier, Boston (2004)
12. Kulpa, Z.: Area and perimeter measurement of blobs in discrete binary pictures. Comput. Graph. Image Process. **6**, 434–454 (1977)
13. Lachaud, J.O., Provençal, X.: Dynamic minimum length polygon. In: Proceedings of International Workshop on Combinatorial Image Analysis, pp. 208–221 (2011)
14. Loncaric, S.: A survey of shape analysis techniques. Pattern Recogn. **31**(8), 983–1001 (1998)
15. Proffit, D., Rosen, D.: Metrication errors and coding efficiency of chain-encoding schemes for the representation of lines and edges. Comput. Graph. Image Process. **10**(4), 318–332 (1979)
16. Verbeek, P.W., Van Vliet, L.J.: An estimator of edge length and surface area in digitized 2d and 3d images. In: Proceedings 11th IAPR International Conference on Pattern Recognition, 1992, Conference C: Image, Speech and Signal Analysis, vol. 3, pp. 1–5. IEEE (1992)
17. Wang, B., Gao, Y.: Hierarchical string cuts: A translation, rotation, scale, and mirror invariant descriptor for fast shape retrieval. IEEE Trans. Image Process. **23**(9), 4101–4111 (2014)

Abnormal Crowd Behavior Detection Based on Combined Approach of Energy Model and Threshold

Madhura Halbe, Vibha Vyas, and Yogita M. Vaidya[✉]

College of Engineering, Pune, India
{halbems15.extc,vsv.extc,ymv.extc}@coep.ac.in

Abstract. The world population continues to grow. The size of gatherings at various venues under different circumstances is tremendously increasing. Any mass assembly has potential risk of the lethal crowd disaster. The various algorithms in computer vision techniques are being developed as a part of proactive system for crowd management. This paper presents novel approach to identify abnormal crowd behavior. The algorithm employedoptical flow method to estimate displacement vectors of moving crowd and computation of crowd motion energy. The crowd motion energy was further modified by crowd motion intensity (CMI). The peaks in the CMI characteristics were the indicators of abnormal activity and were detected more accurately by applying threshold. The algorithm has been tested on standard UMN dataset with an average accuracy of 91.66 percentages. The accuracy has been improved with application of threshold. Adaptive threshold may aid to further improve the performance of algorithm.

Keywords: Crowd motion analysis · Mixture of Gaussian · Motion estimation · Crowd motion intensity · Farneback method

1 Introduction

It has been observed that, the public security has become important and necessary issue [1]. With increase in population as well as increase in urbanization, human activities are becoming more and more frequent. Traditional video surveillance systems require security personnel to monitor the screen for long time and that causes fatigue [2]. Also monitoring multiple screens at the same time is a tedious job. In order to monitor the human activity from multiple screens, it is necessary to interpret abnormal events automatically.

1.1 Previous Work

Crowd behavior analysis from surveillance systems has become popular in the field of computer vision. The methods for crowd analysis can be either machine learning or threshold based. When the crowd activities aremodeled perfectly to differentiate between normal and abnormal activity, machine learning methods are used. But such modeling is difficult. While threshold based methods are used to extract indicators for recognition. T. Cao et al. [1] has used histograms of direction of optical flow vectors for

© Springer International Publishing AG 2017
B.U. Shankar et al. (Eds.): PReMI 2017, LNCS 10597, pp. 187–195, 2017.
https://doi.org/10.1007/978-3-319-69900-4_24

crowd behavior analysis. G. Wang et al. [2] have used Harris corner as feature and detected motion state by adjacent flow estimation. Z. Zhang et al. [3] have analyzed crowd behavior based on motion intensity variation and wavelet analysis. Yang Liu et al. [4] have detected abnormal behavior in crowd using dynamic threshold on crowd motion intensity.

1.2   Overview

The crowd behavior is modeled by the crowd motion energy. The proposed method combines motion estimation and crowd motion energy for abnormality detection. Farneback method is applied on preprocessed video frames to find optical flow vectors of nonstationary objects i.e. moving crowd. Estimated vectors are used for calculating crowd motion intensity (CMI) of a frame. The thresholding of estimated CMI values further improves the performance of the system. The paper discusses the method in sections. Section 2 discuss the methodology, Sect. 3 proposes the method of abnormal event detection, Sect. 4analyses experimental results, Sect. 5 concludes the method and Sect. 6 proposes some future work.

2   Methodology

The Fig. 1 shows the algorithm of method. The subsections describe each step in detail.

2.1   Preprocessing of Video Frames

The background subtraction is one of the preprocessing steps in vision based application. The Mixture of Gaussian (MoG) model is used for background subtraction [5]. MoG requires less computations and memory. It is adaptable to illumination changes in the scenes. The main equation of MoG is

$$\sum_{i=1}^{K} \omega_{i,t}.\eta\left(u;u_{i,t}, \sigma_{i,t}\right) \tag{1}$$

It is modeled by Gaussian components. Here K are components of weight 'ω', intensity mean 'u' and deviation of 'σ' for each frame, 't' [5]. These Gaussian components are used to model background pixels [5]. Gaussian components are updated by comparing learning factor of new pixel and previous pixel. If both are same then that pixel is considered as foreground. Figure 2 shows sample frame of the dataset [6] and its background extracted frame.

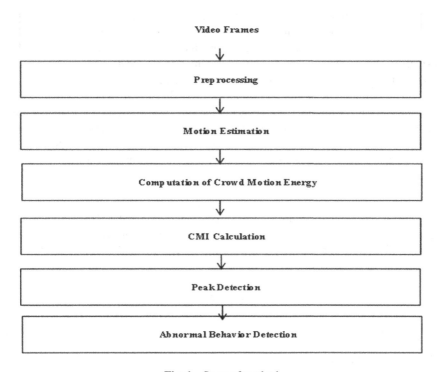

Fig. 1. Steps of method

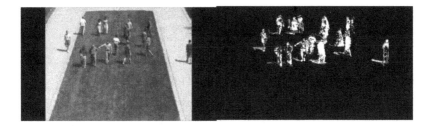

Fig. 2. Sample frame(left), background extracted frame (right)

2.2 Motion Estimation

The preprocessed image is used to find out the motion of the crowd. To estimate motion from the scene, gradient based optical flow method is popular [7]. Following paragraph describes advantages and disadvantages of optical flow methods. Lucas and Kanade [7] method can work even in noise and can detect several actions but is not practical for overlapping objects. While Censos [7] method can handle large displacement and can work in real time even in variable illumination. But it cannot work with edges; it does not consider low contrast information. Black and anandan [7] method provides smooth optical flow even at boundaries but cannot work in real time. Brox method can work in variable illumination and also with large displacement but cannot consider complex crowd scenes. Farneback [8] method is fast and linear and does not assume spatio-temporal consistency but it cannot handle large displacement. For the application like crowd analysis Farneback method of motion estimation is used as it serves the purpose of finding displacement. In Farneback method, two successive frame are considered for finding displacement vector and it considers spatial change [8]. When compared with various methods in the literature, Farnebackis fast and linear and does not assume spatio-temporal consistency. While applying Farneback method video frames are approximted by polynomials and then motion for each pixel is estimated. Only the quadratic poly-nomialis considered as it gives local change. Each pixel is approximated as

$$f(x) \sim x^T A x + b^T x + c \tag{2}$$

Where 'A' is symmetric matrix, 'b' is a vector and 'c' is scalar. The weighted least square fit to signal values of neighborhood is used to find out the coefficients. Now consider polynomial for the first frame pixels as Eq. (3) and for next frame with displacement 'd' as Eq. (4)

$$f_1(x) \sim x^T A_1 x + b_1^T x + c_1 \tag{3}$$

$$f_2(x) = f_1(x - d) = (x - d)^T A_1 (x - d) + b_1^T (x - d) + c_1 = x^T A_2 x + b_2^T x + c_2 \tag{4}$$

Equating coefficients of Eqs. (3) and (4),

$$A_2 = A_1 \tag{5}$$

$$b_2 = b_1 - 2A_1 d \tag{6}$$

$$c_2 = d^T A_1 d - b_1^T d + c_1 \tag{7}$$

If $A_1$is non-singular then Eq. (6) can be solved to find 'd' as

$$d = -\frac{1}{2} A_1^{-1} (b_2 - b_1) \tag{8}$$

This displacementvector, 'd' will give motion vector corresponding to displacement. Figure 3 shows optical flow of consecutive frames and color codes to interpret it. For each angle the color is different.

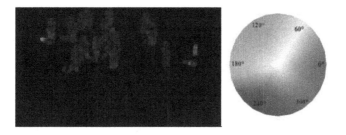

Fig. 3. Optical flow of consecutive frames (left),color code (right)

2.3 Computation of Crowd Motion Energy and CMI

Every moving object has motion energy which is kinetic energy that is proportional to magnitude of displacement vector [3].

$$E_i = \sum_{j=1}^{n} m_j d_j^2 \tag{9}$$

E_i is the kinetic energy of crowd of ith, frame, d_j is the magnitude of motion vector of jth frame, n is the total number of frames and m_j is the weight of motion vector. For similar objects, $m_j = 1$ but for global scene it is modified by multiplying kinetic energy by ρ_i, which is foreground to background ratio and this modified equation is known as CMI given by Eq. (10), further the CMI is normalized to plot.

$$CMI_i = \rho_i \sum_{j=1}^{n} d_j^2 \tag{10}$$

3   Detection of Abnormal Behavior

CMI values are quite steady when the crowd is walking with normal speed. CMI values are changing drastically when the speed of the crowd changes. The variation in CMI values are indicated by the plot in Fig. 4. The peak values are the maximum values of CMI. These peak values are detected using first order difference as shown in Fig. 5 by using Eq. (11).

$$Diff(i) = CMI(i + 1) - CMI(i) \tag{11}$$

As CMI values are collected in an array the first order difference is same as difference of consecutive values. From Fig. 5, it is clear that the abnormal activity has been definitely started at frame number indicated by first detected pointand safety measures can be taken further after detecting such activity to evacuate crowd from dangerous or panic situations.

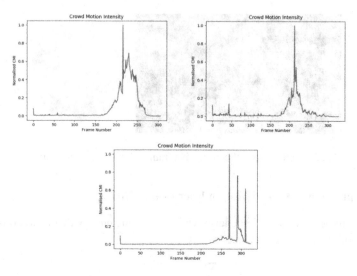

Fig. 4. CMI plots of datasets

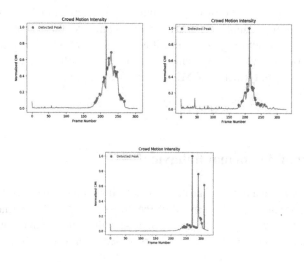

Fig. 5. Abnormal crowd behavior detection

4 Experimental Results

The proposed method is tested successfully on standard UMN dataset [6] which is publicly available. The analysis is done by using OpenCV-Python. The dataset is divided into set of videos. Each video has sequences of normal walking of people as well as running people. The event where they start to run is detected. The resolution of the video dataset is 1280×720. Some set of videos in dataset has same type of background while some has different. Table 1 shows experimental results on dataset. It show peak values of CMI from graphs as well as observed change in behavior of crowd. The accuracy of algorithm can be found out by Eq. (12).

$$\%Accuracy = 100 - \frac{ExperimentalValue - ActualValue(Manuallyobserved)}{ActualValue(Manuallyobserved)} * 100 \qquad (12)$$

Table 1. Experimental results on datasets

Dataset	Total number of Frames	Applied threshold	Observed change in behavior of crowd at frame number (Actual value)	Observed first peak at frame number (Experimental value)	Accuracy (in %)
Dataset1	307	0.05	179	183	97.77
Dataset2	330	0.05	179	179	100
Dataset3	325	0.05	220	239	91.36
Dataset4	328	0.05	253	282	88.54
		0.04		278	90.12
Dataset5	330	0.05	160	186	83.75
		0.02		175	90.62
		0.01		167	95.62
Dataset6	271	0.05	170	195	85.30
		0.02		177	95.82
		0.01		174	97.65
Dataset7	302	0.05	164	200	78.05
		0.02		165	99.39
Dataset8	313	0.05	220	239	91.36
		0.01		231	95.00
Dataset9	310	0.05	174	204	82.76
		0.02		190	90.80
		0.01		179	97.13
Dataset10	291	0.05	180	199	89.44
		0.02		193	92.78

From Table 1, it is observed that the peaks of CMI are detected accurately by varying threshold values to CMI. It is observed that if the threshold value is less than 0.05, some dataset shows false detection, while some shows more accurate detection. For some datasets it is observed that if threshold is decreased accuracy is increased. The proposed algorithm is tested successfully on dataset with average accuracy of 91.66%.

5   Conclusion

The proposed system presents novel method of detection of abnormal events in crowd by finding crowd motion energy and applying variable threshold. The advantages of this system are:

1. The threshold based crowd energy method does not require any supervision hence this method is novel in its approach as compared to existing methods.
2. The method is independent of background of the scene.

3. Since from experimental results, it effectively detects abnormal event at the beginning it can be used for management of crowd.
4. The system can be used in crowd surveillance applications such as stampede detection and prevention in places where people gather together in large number.

The proposed method effectively detects the abnormal events from video scenes with accuracy of 91.66 percentages. The adaptive threshold technique will further improve the accuracy.

6 Future Work

The proposed system can be made more robust by including method which will work even in bad illumination and more crowd characteristics. It will also cover tracking methods for complex situations. The system accuracy can be further improved by using algorithm for adaptive threshold which will be adaptable as per the crowd motion intensity values. Further the algorithm can be enhanced to work in real time using hardware platform.

References

1. Cao, T., Wu, X., Guo, J., Yu, S., Xu, Y.: Abnormal crowd motion analysis. In: 2009 IEEE International Conference on Robotics and Biomimetics (ROBIO), Guilin, pp. 1709–1714 (2009). doi:10.1109/ROBIO.2009.5420408
2. Wang, G., Fu, H., Liu, Y.: Real time abnormal crowd behavior detection based on adjacent flow location estimation. In: 2016 4th International Conference on Cloud Computing and Intelligence Systems (CCIS), Beijing, pp. 476–479 (2016). doi:10.1109/CCIS.2016.7790305
3. Zhong, Z., Yang, M., Wang, S., Ye, W., Xu, Y.: Energy methods for crowd surveillance. In: 2007 International Conference on Information Acquisition, Seogwipo-si, pp. 504–510 (2007). doi:10.1109/ICIA.2007.4295785
4. Liu, Y., Li, X., Jia, L.: Abnormal crowd behavior detection based on optical flow and dynamic threshold. In: Proceedings of the 11th World Congress on Intelligent Control and Automation, Shenyang, pp. 2902–2906 (2014). doi:10.1109/WCICA.2014.7053189
5. Tabkhi, H., Bushey, R., Schirner, G.: Algorithm and architecture co-design of Mixture of Gaussian (MoG) background subtraction for embedded vision. In: 2013 Asilomar Conference on Signals, Systems and Computers, Pacific Grove, CA, pp. 1815–1820 (2013). doi:10.1109/ACSSC.2013.6810615
6. Unusual crowd activity dataset of University of Minnesota http://mha.cs.umn.edu
7. Kajo, I., Malik, A.S., Kamel, N.: Motion estimation of crowd flow using optical flow techniques: A review. In: 2015 9th International Conference on Signal Processing and Communication Systems (ICSPCS), Cairns, QLD, pp. 1–9 (2015). doi:10.1109/ICSPCS.2015.7391778
8. Farnebäck, G.: Two-Frame Motion Estimation Based on Polynomial Expansion. In: Bigun, J., Gustavsson, T. (eds.) SCIA 2003. LNCS, vol. 2749, pp. 363–370. Springer, Heidelberg (2003). doi:10.1007/3-540-45103-X_50

9. Zhong, Z., Ye, W., Wang, S., Yang, M., Xu, Y.: Crowd Energy and Feature Analysis. In: 2007 IEEE International Conference on Integration Technology, Shenzhen, pp. 144–150 (2007). doi:10.1109/ICITECHNOLOGY.2007.4290448
10. Wang, S., Miao, Z.: Anomaly detection in crowd scene. In: IEEE 10th International Conference on Signal Processing Proceedings, Beijing pp. 1220–1223 (2010). doi:10.1109/ICOSP.2010.5655356

Unsupervised Feature Descriptors Based Facial Tracking over Distributed Geospatial Subspaces

Shubham Dokania, Ayush Chopra$^{(\boxtimes)}$, Feroz Ahmad, S. Indu,
and Santanu Chaudhury

Central Electronics Engineering Research Institute, Delhi Technological University,
Pilani, India
shubham.k.dokania@gmail.com,
{ayushchopra_2k14,ferozahmad_2k14,}@dtu.ac.in, s.indu@dce.ac.in,
schaudhury@gmail.com

Abstract. Object Tracking has primarily been characterized as the study of object motion trajectory over constraint subspaces under attempts to mimic human efficiency. However, the trend of monotonically increasing applicability and integrated relevance over distributed commercial frontiers necessitates that scalability be addressed. The present work proposes a system for fast large scale facial tracking over distributed systems beyond individual human capabilities leveraging the computational prowess of large scale processing engines such as Apache Spark. The system is pivoted on an interval based approach for receiving the input feed streams, which is followed by a deep encoder-decoder network for generation of robust environment invariant feature encoding. The system performance is analyzed while functionally varying various pipeline components, to highlight the robustness of the vector representations and near real-time processing performance.

Keywords: Distributed facial tracking · Auto-encoders · Spark streaming

1 Introduction

Recently, visual representation and tracking has been subject to motivated research owing to increased relevance and interoperability with innumerable application domains such as criminal tracking, object tagging [3] etc. Efficient tracking requires learning of good feature representations that exhibit discriminative ability as well as robustness to data variance. Consequently, voluminous literatures have been produced and feature extraction methodologies have evolved significantly. These have largely been holistic or patch based [8]. Advancements in localized vectorization for generation of feature maps forms the basis of recent progress.

Auto-encoders [1] produce a non-linear representation which, unlike that of PCA or ICA, can be stacked to yield deeper levels of representation. More

© Springer International Publishing AG 2017
B.U. Shankar et al. (Eds.): PReMI 2017, LNCS 10597, pp. 196–202, 2017.
https://doi.org/10.1007/978-3-319-69900-4_25

abstract features [5] can be perceived at deeper levels, enhancing the discriminative power of the feature descriptor. Facial features are subject to variance due to pose problems, background clutter, illumination variations. Using an implicit algorithm for capturing geometric information encoded into the descriptors, the issue of pose problem and misalignment can be tackled [2]. Simple elastic and partial metric proposed by Gang can also handle pose change and clutter backgrounds [4].

Object tracking has largely been characterised and defined as the problem of estimating the trajectory of a moving object [9] over constrained subspace. Several near real-time systems such as A Real-time face tracker [11], Pfinder [10], patch flow based [9] have been researched and reported with attempts to achieve human like accuracy in effortlessly tracking objects of interest. Eigenfaces, obtained by performing PCA on a set of faces are commonly used [11] to identify faces. However, increasing demands of real life applications such as vehicle navigation, traffic monitoring and surveillance, search and rescue operations to name a few imply that flexibility be exercised to include tracking that may require optimally fast and efficient search over large geographical subspaces that is beyond individual human capabilities involving the use of large scale distributed datasets.

2   Problem Formulation

In the present work, we propose a near real-time system employing an interval based programming approach for nodal tracking over distributed live streams or databases using a non-parametric supervised classification technique. The present work simulates the proposed approach with facial tracking over unconstrained geo-spatial subspaces owing to enhanced relative generality and reliability, while stating that similar work shall be extended to other vision based applications with relative ease. The system we propose seeks to leverage the particular computational prowess of large scale processing engines in applications involving reuse of working set across parallel operations [12] while assuring fault tolerance, consistency and seamless integration with batch processing, all which are critical considerables for scalable and reliable execution.

3   Proposed System

The proposed system is used to achieve near real-time, efficient tracking of individuals over large geographical subspaces. The system constituents can be largely characterised as A Master Node, Worker Nodes, Camera Nodes and Request Tracking Node. A high level overview of the system architecture has been depicted in Fig. 1. The stages in the pipeline are

- Feature Generation
- Facial Identification

We utilize spark streaming, from the Apache Spark stack, as a core component for streaming computation tasks. The system defines multiple input streams obtained by receiving records feed directly from client or by interval defined loading from external data storage file systems, where it may be placed by a log collection system [13]. The feature generation stage is represented in Fig. 2. Facial Extraction and Component Definition is done using a region based Single Shot Detector [6]. The fast processing speed, 30–35 fps, and efficiency at various aspect scales enabled segregation of the components. The feature vectors are generated by passing the concatenated component vectors through the CAE. The feature vectors generated as a result of the computation associated with the previous phase are stored in the spark database distributed optimally over the worker nodes by the master. The database is characterised by 2 major tables T_1 and T_2. T_1 contains tuples of unique human faces identified or obtained from organizational records with attributes: *human id, feature vector*. T_2 characterises the occurrences of the human faces at different nodes as unique tuples, having attributes as: *auto id, human id, node id, timestamp*. This facilitates querying over the table using a nearest neighbor approach to identify the individual.

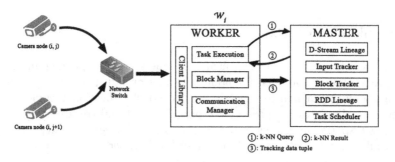

Fig. 1. Overall System Architecture - The jth camera node with unique IP on the local network, of ith block transmits the live feed to the block worker via network switch for the block. Apache Worker kept at control room of ith block receives live feeds from all cameras are fed to Apache Spark Worker. For every face detected in the frame, the computation flow takes place as discussed in Fig. 2.

4   Experiments and Results

In the following section, the proposed system performance is analyzed as a function of various deterministic parameters, by simulating under approximate settings. For the simulation, we hand-picked images from standard facial benchmarks - Labeled Faces in the Wild-a (LFW-a) & IARPA Janus Benchmark A (IJB-A). The images were fed into the client library following an interval based

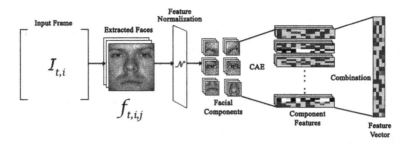

Fig. 2. Generation of Feature Vector - A representation of the generation of feature vectors for the jth extracted face $f(t, i, j)$ from the ith time variant input frame $I(t, i)$ at the time t. The output of normalization procedure $N(f(t, i, j))$ is operated upon to extract components for generation of robust descriptors using CAE.

approach to facilitate micro-batch generation for processing on the cluster workers. We used a multi-node Apache Spark cluster, with nodal configuration 2.6 GHz Intel i7 second generation processors and 8 GB RAM. Near real-time tracking was achieved employing k-Nearest Neighbours (k-NN) algorithm over the distributed database generated over the multi-node by integrating with MLlib [7]: the machine learning library supported by Apache Spark in simulated video feed environments while varying the parameters to obtain appropriate results as explained next.

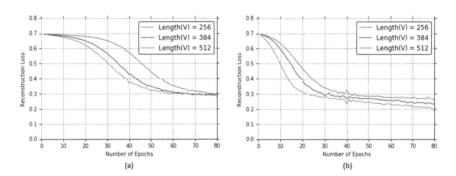

Fig. 3. The reconstruction loss is plotted against the number of training epochs for varying lengths of feature vectors for the auto-encoder trained with (a) adadelta (b) adam optimizer.

4.1 Reconstruction Loss Analyzed on the Variation of Feature Length

From Fig. 3(a) and (b) we see that applying Adam optimizer produces better results in the present problem setting. Adam, if compared to Adadelta, is seen to perform better because, in addition to saving a functional average of past squared gradients, it also stores the functional average of past gradients. Decreasing reconstruction loss depicts the increasing descriptive efficiency and invariance of the feature descriptors by a contractive auto-encoder.

4.2 Query Processing Time Analyzed as a Measure of the Facial Components

As evident from Fig. 4, an increase in number of facial components extracted is associated with a marked increase in the processing time for 300 queries in case of a single worker node scenario. Graphical representation for 2 and 3 node scenario exhibit a slightly leaner growth rate of the processing time as a functional measure of the number of components, but these may have significant considerations in practical settings.

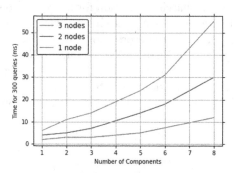

Fig. 4. Processing time for 300 queries, measured in ms, is plotted against differing number of components for 1, 2 and 3 worker nodes.

4.3 Query Processing Time with Varying Worker Nodes

Increasing range to greater geographical subspaces implies the need for enhanced computational processing power, which can be achieved by more worker nodes. The master ensures locality of computation on worker nodes, however in specific scenarios it may shift records between the worker nodes to ensure more equitable load balancing. Keeping the total record penetration of the database constant, a decrease in query processing time is observed on increasing the number of slave worker nodes in Fig. 5. Further this rate of growth is witnessed to depict flattening tendencies as number of worker nodes are further added to the cluster.

4.4 Performance of Proposed System

The number of facial components impacts the dimensional complexity of the feature descriptors and correspondingly their descriptive power. The performance

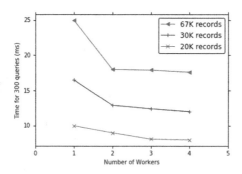

Fig. 5. The processing time for 300 queries on the database generated by the system is plotted against the number of workers for varying number of records. The system exhibits near real-time performance taking time less than 20 ms for 300 queries.

of the system in terms of True Acceptance Rate at False Acceptance Rate = 0.01 and Recognition Rate at Rank-10 is presented in Table 1. Query processing is analyzed for different number of facial components (hence, varying feature length) under consideration.

Table 1. Performance of the proposed system. TAR is reported at FAR = 0.01 for verification, Recognition Rate at Rank-10 is reported for identification.

Feature length	TAR	Rank-10
256 bits (4 components)	0.587	0.608
384 bits (6 components)	0.651	0.694
512 bits (8 components)	0.718	0.732

5   Conclusions

Recent attempts in tracking have sought to implement paradigm like human vision for analysing motion trajectory. No work to our knowledge has performed tracking at similar scale in real-time, rather major works have focussed on subspaces small as frames of single camera feed. The present work tries to provide a solution into the particularly untapped and critical task involving large subspaces that is beyond individual human capabilities. The work aimed to provide a baseline to propel further penetration in the domain. The proposed system is a multilevel hierarchical model based on Spark streaming to feed input streams that uses a deep contractive encoder-decoder model to generate robust vector encoding and a penultimate classifier for searching over the distributed database prior to final path determination. The processing and path retrieval depicted near real-time performance that provides encouragement for applicability into varied commercial settings.

References

1. Bengio, Y., Lamblin, P., Popovici, D., Larochelle, H., et al.: Greedy layer-wise training of deep networks. Adv. Neural Inf. Process. Syst. **19**, 153 (2007)
2. Cao, Z., Yin, Q., Tang, X., Sun, J.: Face recognition with learning-based descriptor. In: 2010 IEEE Conference on CVPR, pp. 2707–2714. IEEE (2010)
3. Cui, J., Wen, F., Xiao, R., Tian, Y., Tang, X.: EasyAlbum: an interactive photo annotation system based on face clustering and re-ranking. In: Proceedings of the SIGCHI Conference on Human Factors in Computing Systems, pp. 367–376. ACM (2007)
4. Hua, G., Akbarzadeh, A.: A robust elastic and partial matching metric for face recognition. In: 2009 IEEE 12th ICCV, pp. 2082–2089. IEEE (2009)
5. Lee, H., Grosse, R., Ranganath, R., Ng, A.Y.: Convolutional deep belief networks for scalable unsupervised learning of hierarchical representations. In: Proceedings of the 26th Annual ICML, pp. 609–616. ACM (2009)
6. Liu, W., Anguelov, D., Erhan, D., Szegedy, C., Reed, S., Fu, C.-Y., Berg, A.C.: SSD: single shot MultiBox detector. In: Leibe, B., Matas, J., Sebe, N., Welling, M. (eds.) ECCV 2016. LNCS, vol. 9905, pp. 21–37. Springer, Cham (2016). doi:10.1007/978-3-319-46448-0_2
7. Meng, X., Bradley, J.K., Yavuz, B., Sparks, E.R., Venkataraman, S., Liu, D., Freeman, J., Tsai, D.B., Amde, M., Owen, S., Xin, D., Xin, R., Franklin, M.J., Zadeh, R., Zaharia, M., Talwalkar, A.: Mllib: machine learning in apache spark. CoRR abs/1505.06807 (2015). http://arxiv.org/abs/1505.06807
8. Mishra, R., Kumar, P., Chaudhury, S., Indu, S.: Monitoring a large surveillance space through distributed face matching. In: 2013 Fourth National Conference on Computer Vision, Pattern Recognition, Image Processing and Graphics (NCVPRIPG), pp. 1–5. IEEE (2013)
9. Prabhu, N., Ramakanth, S.A., Babu, R.V.: Patch flow based visual object tracking. In: Proceedings of the 2014 ICVGIP, p. 86. ACM (2014)
10. Wren, C.R., Azarbayejani, A.J., Darrell, T.J., Pentland, A.P.: Pfinder: real-time tracking of the human body. In: Photonics East 1995, pp. 89–98. International Society for Optics and Photonics (1996)
11. Yang, J., Waibel, A.: A real-time face tracker. In: 1996 Proceedings of 3rd IEEE Workshop on Applications of Computer Vision, WACV 1996, pp. 142–147. IEEE (1996)
12. Zaharia, M., Chowdhury, M., Franklin, M.J., Shenker, S., Stoica, I.: Spark: cluster computing with working sets. In: Proceedings of the 2nd USENIX Conference on Hot Topics in Cloud Computing, HotCloud 2010, pp. 10–10. USENIX Association, Berkeley (2010). http://dl.acm.org/citation.cfm?id=1863103.1863113
13. Zaharia, M., Das, T., Li, H., Hunter, T., Shenker, S., Stoica, I.: Discretized streams: fault-tolerant streaming computation at scale. In: Proceedings of the Twenty-Fourth ACM Symposium on Operating Systems Principles, pp. 423–438. ACM (2013)

Face Detection Based on Frequency Domain Features

B.H. Shekar$^{(\boxtimes)}$⓪ and D.S. Rajesh⓪

Department of Computer Science, Mangalore University, Mangalagangothri,
Mangalore 574199, Karnataka, India
bhshekar@gmail.com, rajeshds1972@gmail.com

Abstract. In this paper we have developed a novel face detection method using the Stockwell and the log dyadic wavelet transform features, following the cascaded face detectors framework. Stockwell transform (ST) time frequency distribution of an image region is known for its excellent feature representational capabilities (due to the high resolution of the distribution). Log dyadic wavelet transform (LDWT) is capable of representing image patches with high accuracy. We have used the Stockwell transform and the log dyadic wavelet transform for representing the facial features effectively. Our face detection method consists of two stages. The first stage consists of a cascade of 4 face detectors constructed using discriminative facial ST features selected by the ADABOOST feature selection method. The second stage consists of a cascade of 4 more face detectors, each of them is a SVM classifier trained with face/nonfacial LDWT features. We have conducted our face detection experiments on the well known CMU-MIT and FDDB face detection datasets to verify the efficacy of our method.

1 Introduction

Face detection system involves location of human face regions and their size in a given digital image. A face recognition system relies heavily on a good face detection system. A face recognition system can recognize faces in an image only after a face detection system has identified regions of face in it. Recently Jun et al. [5] also developed a face detection system based on cascaded face detector framework. They used the ADABOOST algorithm [3] to select the best LBP features and their location on the face images. For each detector of the cascade, multiple LBP features were selected and incorporated in the detector until nearly 100% detection rate and around 50% false alarm rate was achieved on the test face/nonface images. They then repeated their work by replacing the LBP features by the LGP features which showed an improvement over their LBP based face detector. Further they repeated the same experiment using a hybrid of LBP, LGP and BHOG descriptors. In each stage of the ADABOOST feature selection based face detector system, they selected highly discriminative mixture of LBP, LGP and BHOG features on the face images. While LBP was global illumination invariant, LGP was local illumination invariant and BHOG

© Springer International Publishing AG 2017
B.U. Shankar et al. (Eds.): PReMI 2017, LNCS 10597, pp. 203–211, 2017.
https://doi.org/10.1007/978-3-319-69900-4_26

captured bigger facial parts like nose, eyes, etc. Because of all these features they could develop a more better face detection system than their previous one.

2   The Stockwell Transform and the Log Dyadic Wavelet Transform

Stockwell transform [1] based time frequency distribution (TFD) of a signal is found to be more accurate (Fig. 1 shows the results of our experiments conducted to demonstrate this fact) than the time frequency distribution obtained through other traditional transforms like the short time Fourier transform (STFT) and the Gabor transform. The log dyadic wavelet transform based representation of image signals [4] is more accurate than the representations obtained through the traditional discrete wavelet transform (Fig. 2 shows the results of our experiments conducted to demonstrate this fact). Hence we have used the ST and the LDWT in our face detection system for representation of image features.

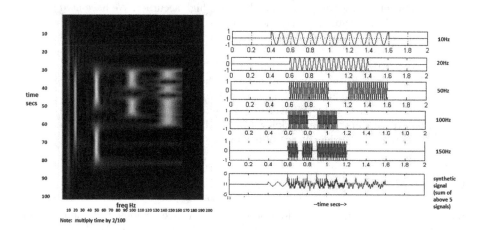

Fig. 1. (right) The last row is a synthetic signal obtained as a sum of the other 5 sinusoids above. (left) The Stockwell transform based time frequency distribution characterizing the synthetic signal accurately both in time and frequency axes.

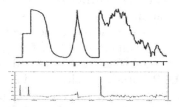

Fig. 2. (plot at the top) 1D Signal with sharp edges. (plot at the bottom) Edges detected accurately by convolving the signal with the 1D LDWT kernel.

3   Proposed Method

Our face detection system consists of two stages. The first stage is made up of a cascade of 4 face detectors each being constructed using highly discriminative Stockwell transform based feature classifiers and the second stage is made up of a cascade of 4 more face detectors each being a SVM classifier trained using LDWT coefficients of face/non face training images. Each face detector is constructed in such a way that they have 99.5% face detection rate and 50% false alarm rate. Given a sample image at the input of the face detection system, each detector rejects non face regions in it and forwards the probable face image regions to the next face detector in the cascade. At the output, our system is supposed to localize the face regions in the input image.

3.1   Construction of Stage 1 Face Detectors

Highly discriminative Stockwell transform based features (Stockwell transform of 3×3 and 5×5 size regions on face/non face training image samples) are selected as classifiers using the ADABOOST feature selection method, in constructing the face detectors of stage 1. We have set the parameters of the Stockwell transform in such a way that for a 3×3 size image signal, we obtain a 3×9 size TFD plot and for a 5×5 size image signal we obtain a 7×25 size TFD plot. Following are our Stockwell transform based features from which highly discriminative ones are selected as feature classifiers of the face detector.

1. Stockwell transform TFD of a 3×3 size image region, $ST3_{Fi}(x, y)$, around every pixel (x,y) of a face image sample is computed (at x = 2,3,4,......21, y = 2,3,4......23) for all face image samples i = 1,2,3.....16000. Figure 3 shows some of the 3×3 size image regions (at locations (2,2), (2,7), (2,21), (23,2) and (23,21) of an imaginary face image Fi), whose Stockwell transform TFDs $ST3_{Fi}(2, 2)$, $ST3_{Fi}(2, 7)$, $ST3_{Fi}(2, 21)$, $ST3_{Fi}(23, 2)$ and $ST3_{Fi}(23, 21)$ are computed.
2. Similarly Stockwell transform of a 5×5 size image region, $ST5_{Fi}(x, y)$, around every pixel (x,y) of a face image sample is computed (at x = 3,4,......20, y = 3,4......22) for all face image samples i = 1,2,3.....16000.
3. Stockwell transform of a 3×3 size image region, $ST3_{NFi}(x, y)$, around every pixel (x,y) of a non face image sample is computed at x = 2,3,4,......21, y = 2,3,4......23, for non face image samples i = 1,2,3.....16000.
4. Stockwell transform of a 5×5 size image region, $ST5_{NFi}(x, y)$, around every pixel (x,y) of a non face image sample is computed at x = 3,4,......20, y = 3,4......22, for non face image samples i = 1,2,3.....16000. Note that $ST3_{Fi}(x, y)$, $ST5_{Fi}(x, y)$, $ST3_{NFi}(x, y)$ and $ST5_{NFi}(x, y)$ are all vectors of either size 3×3 or 5×5.

Apart from these our method uses the following features during the face detector construction.

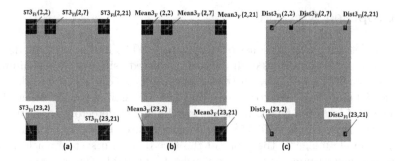

Fig. 3. The 3×3 size image regions used in computing ST based features.

1. Mean Stockwell transform feature $mean3_F(x, y)$, of 3×3 size image regions of face image samples at location (x,y) is computed as $\sum ST3_{Fi}(x, y)/16000$, where the summation is over i = 1,2,3.....16000. This mean is computed at all locations x = 2,3,4,......21, y = 2,3,4......23, using face image samples. Figure 3 shows some of the mean features computed at locations (2,2), (2,7), (2,21), (23,2), (23,21) i.e. $mean3_F(2, 2)$, $mean3_F(2, 7)$, $mean3_F(2, 21)$, $mean3_F(23, 21)$ and $mean3_F(23, 2)$

2. Mean Stockwell transform feature $mean3_{NF}$(x,y), of 3×3 size image regions of non face image samples is computed at location (x,y) as $\sum ST3_{Nfi}(x, y)/16000$ where i = 1,2,3.....16000. This mean is computed at all locations x = 2,3,4,......21, y = 2,3,4......23, using non face image samples.

3. Similarly $mean5_F$(x,y) and $mean5_{NF}$(x,y) are computed using $ST5_{Fi}$(x,y) and $ST5_{NFi}$(x,y) features respectively (at x = 3,4,......20, y = 3,4......22). Note that $mean3_F(x, y)$, $mean5_F(x, y)$, $mean3_{NF}(x, y)$ and $mean5_{NF}(x, y)$ are all vectors.

4. $Dist3_{Fi}(x, y) = \frac{chi\ square\ distance\ of\ ST3_{Fi}(x,y)\ from\ mean3_F(x,y)}{chi\ square\ distance\ of\ ST3_{Fi}(x,y)\ from\ mean3_{NF}(x,y)}$ is the chi square distance between the Stockwell transform feature of face image Fi, $ST3_{Fi}$(x,y) and mean facial Stockwell transform feature $mean3_F$(x,y) over the mean non facial Stockwell transform feature $mean3_{NF}$(x,y).

5. $Dist3_{NFi}(x, y) = \frac{chi\ square\ distance\ of\ ST3_{NFi}(x,y)\ from\ mean3_F(x,y)}{chi\ square\ distance\ of\ ST3_{NFi}(x,y)\ from\ mean3_{NF}(x,y)}$ is the chi square distance between the Stockwell transform feature of non face image NFi, $ST3_{NFi}$(x,y) and mean facial Stockwell transform feature $mean3_F$(x,y) over the mean non facial Stockwell transform feature $mean3_{NF}$(x,y). Also $Dist5_{Fi}$(x,y) and $Dist5_{NFi}$(x,y) correspond to 5×5 features. Note that $Dist3_{Fi}$(x,y), $Dist3_{NFi}$(x,y), $Dist5_{Fi}$(x,y) and $Dist5_{NFi}$(x,y) are all scalars.

A low value of $Dist3Fi(x, y)$ indicates that this Stockwell transform feature at (x,y) is a dominant feature of face images and also a recessive feature of non face images. A large value of $Dist3NFi(x, y)$ indicates that this Stockwell transform feature at (x,y) is a dominant feature of non face images and also a recessive feature of face images. Locations (x,y) which have a small $Dist3Fi(x, y)$ and a large $Dist3NFi(x, y)$ (over all i = 1,2,3...16000) are the best candidates to be a feature classifier (and hence are capable of distinguishing face image regions from non face image regions). This is what our ADABOOST feature selection method does during face detector construction

Construction of First Face Detector of Stage 1: The cascade of face detectors framework based on ADABOOST feature selection method (followed by Viola and Jones [2]) is used in our method. Each of the face detectors in the cascade is capable of performing face detection with around 99.5% detection rate and 50% false alarm rate. Here we explain the procedure followed in constructing the first face detector (out of the cascade of face detectors) of our face detection system. Algorithm 1 along with Algorithms 2 and 3 is used in constructing the face detector. Algorithm 1 goes through several iterations (calling Algorithms 2 and 3 in each iteration) selecting the next most discriminative Stockwell transform feature classifier in each iteration and constructs the face detector using these classifiers. The number of feature classifiers thus selected must be capable of performing face detection with a 99.5% face detection rate and 50% false alarm rate. Using the Stockwell transform features explained above, Algorithms 1, 2 and 3 construct face detector as follows.

Algorithm 1

1. Assign weights to face training samples as $Wf(i)=1/(2*$number of face training samples) and and non face training samples $Wnf(i)=1/(2*$number of non face training samples) for all i $= 1,2,3....16000$.
2. Using Algorithm 2 select the next most discriminative Stockwell transform feature classifier
3. Construct a face detector using the feature classifiers selected so far and evaluate its classification performance (the detection and false alarm rate) using the classification method given by Algorithm 3.
4. If the classification performance of 99.5% detection rate and 50% false alarm rate is achieved, the face detector construction is complete. Otherwise go to step 2 to include the next most discriminative feature classifier into the face detector under construction, after the following procedure:
   - update (reduce) the weights of training samples which were correctly classified in this round (in Algorithm 2 during step 2) as follows, $Wf(i)= Wf(i)*Feat(iter).beta$ where i $=$ index of correctly classified face samples, $Wnf(i)=Wnf(i)*Feat(iter).beta$ where i $=$ index of correctly classified non face samples. By doing so the algorithm will not reselect a feature classifier already selected in the previous rounds.
   - Find $weight\_sum$, sum of weights of all samples. Normalize the weights as follows: $Wf(i) = \frac{Wf(i)}{weight\_sum}$ where i $= 1,2,3,...fnum$ and $Wnf(i) = \frac{Wnf(i)}{weight\_sum}$ where i $= 1,2,3,....nfnum$ such that the sum of sample weights is again 1. Proceed to step 2 to incorporate a new feature classifier.

Algorithm 2

1. The minimum possible classification error corresponding to location (x,y) (assuming the Stockwell transform feature at location (x,y) as the classifier) and scale 3 (i.e. 3×3 size features) is computed. For this computation classification is done over all training samples (face/non face images). Minimum possible classification error at location (x,y) and scale 3 is computed as follows:

- Sort the array $Dist3_{Fi}(x,y)$ where $i = 1,2,3.....16000$, in ascending order and store it in Dist_3xy. Also sort $Dist3_{NFi}(x,y)$ where $i = 1,2,3.....16000$ and concatenate it to Dist_3xy.
- **for i =1:16000**
  set **thresh**=Dist_3xy(i);
  Classify the training samples whose values in Dist_3xy are less than **thresh** as faces and the rest as non faces. Comparing the classification result with the ground truth compute the classification error. The sum of weights of the misclassified samples is the classification error of iteration i, err3[i].
  endfor

- min3(x,y)=minimum(err3) is the minimum possible classification error at position (x,y) and scale 3.

2. Similarly we can find the min3(x,y) at all positions $x = 2,3,4,......21$, $y = 2,3,4......23$. Similarly, using $Dist5_{Fi}(x,y)$ and $Dist5_{NFi}(x,y)$ we can find min5(x,y) at all positions $x = 3,4,......20$, $y = 3,4......22$. The minimum among all min3(x,y) (i.e. at positions $x = 2,3,4,......21$, $y = 2,3,4......23$) and min5(x,y) (at all positions $x = 3,4,......20$, $y = 3,4......22$) gives us the position (X,Y) and scale (which is 3 if minimum is from min3(x,y) or else 5 if minimum is from min5(x,y)) of the most discriminative feature classifier of this round.

3. Now the best classifier of the current iteration is at location (X, Y). Record classifier as $Feat.loc$=[X, Y]; $Feat.scale$=3 if minimum was obtained in err3 and $Feat.scale$=5 if minimum was obtained in $err5$; Let $\beta = \frac{min\_err}{1-min\_err}$ and $Feat.beta$=β, $Feat.thresh$=**thresh** value at (X, Y) corresponding to the minimum classification error, $Feat.confidence$=$log(\frac{1}{\beta})$.
return $Feat$

Algorithm 3: Tries to build a classifier of 99.5% detection and 50% false alarm rate
    val=0; **conf_sum**=0
for i = 1:no of feature classifiers selected so far.
    conf_sum=**conf_sum** + $Feat(i).confidence$
end

Repeat

> **for** each given test sample

1. **for** i=1:no of feature classifiers selected so far
   - The ratio of sample-to-mean_face by sample-to-mean_nonface distance at $(x, y) = Feat(i).Loc$ i.e.

$$Dist_{sample}(x, y) = \frac{chi\_square\_dist(ST3_{sample}(x, y), Mean3_F(x, y))}{chi\_square\_dist(ST3_{sample}(x, y), Mean3_{nF}(x, y))} \tag{1}$$

   computed. Use scale 5 features if the classifier belongs to scale 5.
   - If this ratio is less than $Feat(i).threshold$ it implies that the ith feature classifier of current iteration has decided the sample to be a face and the classifier confidence is accumulated as **val=val+** $Feat(i).confidence$.
   end
2. **val** contains the confidence values of all the feature classifiers that decided the sample as face. if **val > par*conf_sum** the sample is decided as face else as non face.

   end
Compute the detection and false alarm rate using the decisions in step 2.

Until the best possible detection and false alarm rate is obtained by varying the "par" value

After the construction of the first face detector, the non face training samples are classified (**Algorithm 3** is used for classification) and unclassified samples are collected. For the construction of the second face detector of the cascade of stage 1, we use the full set of face training samples and these misclassified non face training samples. Like this 4 detectors of first stage are constructed.

3.2   Stage 2

Log dyadic wavelet transform (LDWT) features of the training samples are used in constructing the 4 face detectors of stage 2. A SVM classifier is trained using the LDWT features until the classifier shows a performance 99.5% detection and 50% false alarm rate on the training samples. During the estimation of this performance, the misclassified training non face samples are collected and along with the full set of the training face samples the construction of the second face detector of this stage continues. This method is followed until the 4 face detectors of the stage is constructed.

4   Experiments and Data Set Preparation

Using face recognition dataset samples of ORL, LFW, FERET, ABERDEEN, PIE and MIT datasets we have formed our training and testing face samples (the cropped face images include variations like scaling, rotation, poor illumination, poor resolution in them). 16000 each of training and testing face samples were obtained. 32000 non face samples were collected from the MIT dataset, of which 16000 were reserved for training and the rest for testing. We have conducted face detection experiments on the CMU-MIT dataset (both rotated and normal version) and the FDDB dataset, the qualitative and quantitative experimental results can be seen in Figs. 4 and 5. Given a test face sample, the first four face detectors of stage 1 removed the easier non face regions from the sample and forwarded the remaining regions to the next face detector of the cascade.

Fig. 4. The detection performance on the (a). FDDB (top two rows) and (b). CMU-MIT dataset (middle row). (c). shows the output of each of the 8 face detectors of the cascade of the face detection system, on a rotated CMU-MIT image. Also it shows the detected image regions.

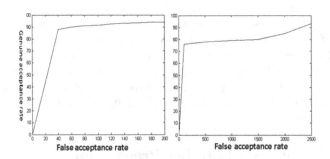

Fig. 5. The ROC curves of the performance of the proposed method on CMU-MIT (left) and FDDB (right) datasets

The tougher image regions (that contained nearly face-like-looking non-face regions) were removed from the test sample by the next 4 face detectors of stage 2. Each face detector of the cascade has checked the presence of face regions at a given location on the test sample at 8 different scales.

5   Conclusion

We have developed a face detection system following the cascade of detectors model. We have used Stockwell transform and log dyadic wavelet transform feature representation of images. Using these features we have built the face detection system to classify face and non face samples. Our experiments on the FDDB and CMU-MIT face detection datasets have shown comparable performance with the state of the art methods.

References

1. Todorov, T.I., Margrave, G.F.: Variable factor S-transform seismic data analysis. CREWES research report, vol. 21 (2009)
2. Viola, P., Jones, M.: Robust real-time face detection. In: Proceedings of the Eighth IEEE International Conference on Computer Vision, ICCV 2001, vol. 2, p. 747 (2001)
3. Freund, Y., Shapire, R.E.: A short introduction to boosting. J. Jpn. Soc. Artif. Intell. **14**(5), 771–780 (1999)
4. Tu, G.J., Karstoft, H.: Logarithmic dyadic wavelet transform with its applications in edge detection and reconstruction. Appl. Soft Comput. **26**, 193–201 (2015)
5. Jun, B., Choi, I., Kim, D.: Local transform features and hybridization for accurate face and human detection. IEEE Trans. Pattern Anal. Mach. Intell. **35**(6), 1423–1436 (2013)

A Study on the Properties of 3D Digital Straight Line Segments

Mousumi Dutt[1]([✉])(iD), Somrita Saha[2](iD), and Arindam Biswas[2](iD)

[1] Department of Computer Science and Engineering,
St. Thomas' College of Engineering and Technology, Kolkata, India
duttmousumi@gmail.com
[2] Department of Information Technology,
Indian Institute of Engineering Science and Technology, Shibpur, India
somrita.besu@gmail.com, barindam@gmail.com

Abstract. Digital representation of three-dimensional straight line segments is considered here. A 3D straight line, given its direction vector, when projected on any two planes gives two 2D straight lines. The chain codes of these two 2D straight lines combined together give the chain code representation of the corresponding 3D straight line. The properties of 3D digital straight lines are studied and analyzed.

Keywords: Digital straight line segment · Chain code · Digital arc

1 Introduction

The computer representation of lines and curves have been an active subject of research for nearly half a century and produced some well-established facts regarding digital straightness. Digitization of a real coordinate value to an integer value is called quantization. There exist many quantization schemes for 2D and 3D curves— *Square Quantization* [7,8,10], *Convex Quantization* [13], *3D Convex Quantization* [13], etc.

One of the applications of digital quantization occurred in digital straight line. The digital arc, S, is the digitization of a straight line segment which is stated in [12,17]. The representation of digital straight line and its various properties are discussed in [3–6,14,16,19]. The 2D and 3D representations of digital curve are proposed in [9]. The representation of 3D curves using chain codes are stated in [1]. A quantitative approach to represent, generate, and classify 3D discrete closed curves are discussed in [2]. In [18], a new chain code to represent 3D discrete curves is discussed which is based on a search for relative changes in the 3D Euclidean space. A set of 3D curve-skeletons is also studied. The 3D extension of Bresenham's algorithm is proposed in [15]. The main contribution of the paper is the study of the chord property in 3D and the properties of 3D digital straight lines, which have not yet been done as far as our knowledge goes.

© Springer International Publishing AG 2017
B.U. Shankar et al. (Eds.): PReMI 2017, LNCS 10597, pp. 212–218, 2017.
https://doi.org/10.1007/978-3-319-69900-4_27

2   Preliminaries

There are three neighborhoods in $\mathbb{Z}^3$. Those are *6-neighborhood* (face neighbors), *18-neighborhood* (face-edge neighbors), and *26-neighborhood* (face-edge-vertex neighbors). Let $r = (x_r, y_r, z_r) \in \mathbb{Z}^3$ and $s_i = (x_{s_i}, y_{s_i}, z_{s_i}) \in \mathbb{Z}^3$ be all points satisfying $max(|x_r - x_{s_i}|, |y_r - y_{s_i}|, |z_r - z_{s_i}|) \leqslant 1$.
$N_6(r) = \{s_i : |x_r - x_{s_i}| + |y_r - y_{s_i}| + |z_r - z_{s_i}| \leqslant 1\}$
$N_{18}(r) = \{s_i : |x_r - x_{s_i}| + |y_r - y_{s_i}| + |z_r - z_{s_i}| \leqslant 2\}$
$N_{26}(r) = \{s_i : |x_r - x_{s_i}| + |y_r - y_{s_i}| + |z_r - z_{s_i}| \leqslant 3\}$
These are shown in Fig. 1. The voxels at distance '1', '2', and '3' are shown in red, magenta, and yellow colors respectively.

The 3D digital curve can move in any of the 26 directions. These directions are denoted by 26 English alphabets (Fig. 2). The sequence of these letters gives a 3D arc and the sequence is termed as *chain codes* in 3D. For example, a denotes movement along X-axis, b denotes movement along XZ plane, i denotes movement along XY plane, j denotes movement along three directions at a time (i.e., X-, Y-, and Z-directions), etc. A 3DSS can be represented by chain codes using these directions in alphabetical notations.

3   Chord Property in 3D

Let p and q be points of the subset of a 3D digital object S, and let pq denote the (real) line segment between p and q. We can define the chord property as follows.

6-neighborhood 18-neighborhood 26-neighborhood

Fig. 1. The three neighborhoods. (Color figure online)

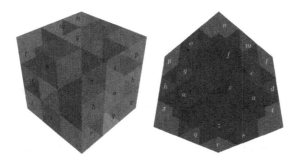

Fig. 2. The 26 directions of 3DSS.

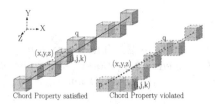

Fig. 3. The chord property of a 3D digital straight line.

pq lies near S if, for any (real) point (x, y, z) of pq, there exists a (lattice) point (i, j, k) of S such that $max(|i - x|, |j - y|, |k - z|) < 1$. In Fig. 3(left), pq lies near S as, for any (real) point (x, y, z) on pq, there exists a (lattice) point (i, j, k) on S such that $max(|i - x|, |j - y|, |k - z|) < 1$. So, the chord property is satisfied. In Fig. 3(right), there are (real) points (x, y, z) on pq, for which there does not exist a (lattice) point (i, j, k) on S such that the above mentioned inequality satisfy. Thus, the chord property is violated.

A digital arc in 3D is the digitization of a straight line segment if and only if it has the chord property. Whenever a 3D straight line is projected on any plane (XY-, ZX-, or YZ-plane), then it becomes a 2D digital straight line on that plane. A 3D digital straight line can be represented using a chain code.

Let us consider the direction vectors be $\triangle x$, $\triangle y$, and $\triangle z$ which may be in $\mathbb{Z}^+$ or $\mathbb{Z}^-$. When $\triangle x$ is positive, there are four possible combinations for positive or negative values of $\triangle y$ and $\triangle z$. Each combination corresponds to each outer face of the octant (Fig. 2). Each of $\triangle x$, $\triangle y$, and $\triangle z$ may be positive or negative and can have six possibilities in total. Thus, in total there are 24 (4×6) possible direction sets where each set has four directions. In other words, in a 2D plane there are eight possible direction sets considering three planes (XY-, YZ-, and ZX-planes). So, there are in total 24 (8×3) possible direction sets.

Lemma 1. *The digitization of a 3D straight line segment can have at most four directions in its chain code.*

Proof. The possible directions where the straight line can move when $\triangle x, \triangle y,$ $\triangle z > 0$ and $\triangle x \geqslant \triangle y, \triangle z$ is shown in Fig. 4(a) in blue color. There are four faces (directions) through which the continuous straight line may pass. At each step when the straight line proceeds, there are four possible faces (directions) through which the continuous straight line may pass (Fig. 4(b)). Thus, there are four directions in the chain code of 3D straight line.

Theorem 1. *The combination of any two chain codes of two 2D digital straight lines in any two 2D planes, gives the chain code of 3D digital straight line segment.*

Proof. The projection of 3D digital straight line on XY-, YZ-, and ZX-plane are 2D digital straight lines [11]. Let two 2D digital straight line segment in XY- and ZX-plane be combined (chain codes having two types of values). There

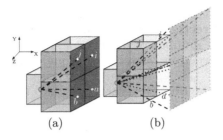

Fig. 4. (a) One face of 3DSS and four directions are there in one face, (b) Possible faces for the next step of the 3DSS. (Color figure online)

must be four possibilities while combining the two above mentioned 2D digital straight line segment as each one contains two types of values (considering all possible combinations for it). Four possible directions give a 3D digital straight line (Lemma 1).

Table 1. The conditions for a direction to have runs of multiple lengths for the direction vectors having $\triangle x \geqslant \triangle y, \triangle z$.

Conditions	Directions having multiple lengths	Direction vectors	Example
$\frac{1}{2}\| \triangle x\| > \| \triangle y\|$ and $\frac{1}{2}\| \triangle x\| > \| \triangle z\|$	'a'	$(10,3,1)$	aia^2ja^3ia
$\frac{1}{2}\| \triangle x\| < \| \triangle y\|$ and $\frac{1}{2}\| \triangle x\| > \| \triangle z\|$	'i'	$(10,9,2)$	$i^2ji^2aiji^2$
$\frac{1}{2}\| \triangle x\| > \| \triangle y\|$ and $\frac{1}{2}\| \triangle x\| < \| \triangle z\|$	'b'	$(10,2,9)$	$b^2jb^2abjb^2$
$\frac{1}{2}\| \triangle x\| < \| \triangle y\|$ and $\frac{1}{2}\| \triangle x\| < \| \triangle z\|$	'j'	$(13,11,12)$	$j^3bj^2ij^2bj^3$

4 Properties of 3D Digital Straight Line Segment

The properties of 3DSS represented by chain codes are explained as follows.

Property 1: A chain code has at most four directions and one of the runs of a 3DSS may have multiple lengths and others will have length one.

The first part of the property 1 follows directly from Lemma 1. Here, we are considering the direction vectors where $\triangle x \geqslant \triangle y, \triangle z$. The conditions for a direction to have runs of multiple length are stated in Table 1 with examples.

Property 2: The number of directions in 3DSS chain code is one

– **when the three direction vectors are equal and non-zero**

- when any two direction vectors are zero
- when any two direction vectors are non-zero and equal but the other is zero. The number of directions in 3DSS chain code is two
- when any two direction vectors are equal and non-zero but the other is non-zero
- when any one of the direction vectors is zero but the other two are not equal and non-zero

Table 2. The direction vectors and the corresponding chain codes.

Conditions	Direction vectors	Chain codes
$\triangle x = \triangle y \neq 0$	$(18, 18, 0)$	i^{18}
$\triangle y = \triangle z = 0$	$(18, 0, 0)$	a^{18}
$\triangle x = \triangle y = \triangle z$	$(18, 18, 18)$	j^{18}
$\triangle z = 0, \triangle x \neq \triangle y$	$(13, 10, 0)$	$i^2 a i^3 a i^3 a i^2$
$\triangle y = 0, \triangle x \neq \triangle z$	$(13, 0, 8)$	$babab^2 ab^2 abab$
$\triangle y = \triangle z \neq \triangle x$	$(13, 5, 5)$	$ajaja^2 ja^2 jaja$

Table 3. The middle direction in 3DSS chain code when $\triangle x$ is odd.

$\triangle y$	$\triangle z$	Middle direction	Direction vectors	Chain code
Even	Even	'a'	$(13, 10, 12)$	$j^2 bj^3 \, a \, j^3 bj^2$
Even	Odd	'b'	$(13, 10, 3)$	$i^2 bi^3 \, b \, i^3 bi^2$
Odd	Even	'i'	$(13, 9, 4)$	$ibi^2 bi \, i \, ibi^2 bi$
Odd	Odd	'j'	$(13, 9, 7)$	$jajibi \, j \, ibijaj$

See examples in Table 2. The 3DSS will move in same direction when three direction vectors are equal and non-zero (i.e., movement in all three directions in each step). When the two direction vectors are equal, non-zero and the other is zero, the 3DSS will move in one direction only. If the two direction vectors are equal and all three direction vectors are non-zero, then the number of directions in the chain code is two. When the two direction vectors are equal to zero and the other is non-zero, the movement will be in one direction only. When the three direction vectors are not equal and any one of them is zero, the number of directions in the chain code is two.

Property 3: For the direction vectors $\triangle x \geqslant \triangle y, \triangle z$, if $\triangle x$ is odd, then the direction in the chain code of 3DSS at position $\lceil \frac{\triangle x}{2} \rceil$ can be determined as stated in Table 3. If $\triangle x$ is even, then the directions in the chain code of 3DSS at positions $\frac{\triangle x}{2}$ and $\frac{\triangle x}{2} + 1$ can be determined (i.e., direction at the middle positions) as per the conditions stated in Table 4.

Table 4. The middle direction in 3DSS chain code when $\triangle x$ is even.

$\triangle y$	$\triangle z$	Middle Direction	Direction Vectors	Chain Code
Even	Odd	'ji' if $\triangle y > \frac{\triangle x}{2}$	$(10, 6, 5)$	$jaja\,ji\,bibi$
		'ba' if $\triangle y \leqslant \frac{\triangle x}{2}$	$(10, 4, 5)$	$bibi\,ba\,jaja$
		'bi' if $\frac{\triangle y}{2}$ is even and $\triangle y = \frac{\triangle x}{2}$	$(8, 4, 5)$	$jaj\,bi\,bib$
Odd	Even	'ia' if $\triangle z < \frac{\triangle x}{2}$	$(10, 5, 2)$	$iaja\,ia\,ibia$
		'jb' if $\triangle z \geqslant \frac{\triangle x}{2}$	$(10, 5, 8)$	$jbib\,jb\,jajb$
		'ib' if $\frac{\triangle z}{2}$ is even and $\triangle z = \frac{\triangle x}{2}$	$(16, 5, 8)$	$bibajab\,ib\,abibaja$
Odd	Odd	'ja'	$(16, 9, 5)$	$ibiaibi\,ja\,ibiaibi$

Here, we are considering only one case where $\triangle x \geqslant \triangle y, \triangle z$. If all the three direction vectors are even, then direction vectors can be reduced by dividing with their GCD. When any one of the direction vectors is odd, then some conditions are applied to determine the directions at middle positions (see Table 4).

Property 4: For the direction vector $\triangle x \geqslant \triangle y, \triangle z$, if $\triangle x$ is odd, the directions in the chain code of 3DSS are mirror w.r.t. the middle position (i.e., at the position $\lceil \frac{\triangle x}{2} \rceil$) in the chain code and the first and the last directions are equal to multiple occurring directions (stated in Table 1).

See the examples in Table 3. No such relation can be derived when $\triangle x$ is even. For the direction vectors $(13, 2, 5)$ the chain code is $abajaa\,b\,aajaba$, where $abajaa$ and $aajaba$ are mirror to each other. Here, the multiple occurring direction a appears at first and last positions in the chain code.

5   Conclusion

The chord property in 3D and 3D digital arcs are defined here, from which several properties of 3DSS in 26-neighborhood are analysed. The 3DSS will be different for other neighborhoods. This work has a theoretical importance in the field of combinatorics and digital geometry. In connection to this work, the properties of 3D digital plane can be determined as related future work.

References

1. Bribiesca, E.: 3D-curve representation by means of a binary chain code. Math. Comput. Model. **40**(3–4), 285–295 (2004)
2. Bribiesca, E.: Classification and generation of 3D discrete curves. Appl. Math. Sci. **1**(57), 2805–2825 (2007)

3. Bruckstein, A.M.: The self-similarity of digital straight lines. In: Proceedings of 10th International Conference on Pattern Recognition, vol. 1, pp. 485–490 (1990)
4. Dorst, L., Duin, R.P.W.: Spirograph theory: a framework for calculations on digitized straight lines. IEEE Trans. Pattern Anal. Mach. Intell. 6(5), 632–639 (1984)
5. Dorst, L., Smeulders, A.W.: Discrete representation of straight lines. IEEE Trans. Pattern Anal. Mach. Intell. 6(4), 450–463 (1984)
6. Dorst, L., Smeulders, A.W.: Discrete straight line segments: parameters, primitives and properties. In: Vision Geometry, series Contemporary Mathematics, pp. 45–62. American Mathematical Society (1991)
7. Freeman, H.: Boundary encoding and processing. Picture Processing and Psychopictorics, pp. 241–266 (1970)
8. Freeman, H.: Computer processing of line-drawing images. ACM Comput. Surv. (CSUR) 6(1), 57–97 (1974)
9. Jonas, A., Kiryati, N.: Digital representation schemes for 3D curves. Pattern Recogn. 30(11), 1803–1816 (1997)
10. Kim, C.E.: On cellular straight line segments. Comput. Graph. Image Process. 18(4), 369–381 (1982)
11. Kim, C.E.: Three-dimensional digital line segments. IEEE Trans. Pattern Anal. Mach. Intell. 5(2), 231–234 (1983)
12. Klette, R., Rosenfeld, A.: Digital straightness: a review. Discrete Appl. Math. 139(1–3), 197–230 (2004)
13. Koplowitz, J.: On the performance of chain codes for quantization of line drawings. IEEE Trans. Pattern Anal. Mach. Intell. 3(2), 180 (1981)
14. Lindenbaum, M., Koplowitz, J.: A new parameterization of digital straight lines. IEEE Trans. Pattern Anal. Mach. Intell. 13(8), 847–852 (1991)
15. Liu, X.W., Cheng, K.: Three-dimensional extension of Bresenham's algorithm and its application in straight-line interpolation. J. Eng. Manufact. 216(3), 459–463 (2002)
16. Mcllroy, M.D.: A note on discrete representation of lines. AT&T Tech. J. 64(2), 481–490 (1984)
17. Rosenfeld, A.: Digital straight line segments. IEEE Trans. Comput. 12, 1264–1269 (1974)
18. Sánchez-Cruz, H., López-Valdez, H.H., Cuevas, F.J.: A new relative chain code in 3D. Pattern Recogn. 47(2), 769–788 (2014)
19. Wu, L.D.: On the chain code of a line. IEEE Trans. Pattern Anal. Mach. Intell. 4(3), 347–353 (1982)

Unlocking the Mechanism of Devanagari Letter Identification Using Eye Tracking

Chetan Ralekar[1]($\boxtimes$) (iD), Tapan K. Gandhi[1], and Santanu Chaudhury[1,2]

[1] Department of Electrical Engineering, IIT Delhi, New Delhi, 110016, India
chetan.ralekar@ee.iitd.ac.in, {tgandhi,santanu}@iitd.ac.in
[2] CSIR-Central Electronics Engineering Research Institute (CEERI), Pilani, India

Abstract. The present day computers can outperform the human in many complicated tasks very precisely and efficiently. However, in many scenarios like pattern recognition and more importantly, character recognition; a school going child can outperform the sophisticated machines available today. The modern machines present today find handwritten, calligraphic text difficult to recognize because such texts hardly contain rationalized straight lines or perfect loops or circles. Therefore, most of the optical character recognition systems fail to recognize the characters beyond certain levels of distortions and noise. On the other hand, the human brain has achieved a remarkable ability to recognize visual patterns or characters in various distortion conditions with high speed. The present work tries to understand how human perceive, process and recognize the Devanagari characters under various distortion levels. In order to achieve this objective, eye tracking experiment was performed on 20 graduate participants by presenting stimuli in decreasing level of distortions (from highly distorted to more normal one). The eye fixation patterns along with the time course of recognition gave us the moment-to-moment processing involved in letter identification. Upon understanding the level of distortion acceptable for correct letter recognition and the processes involved in the identification of the letters, the OCR can be made more robust and the gap between human reading and machine reading can be narrowed down.

Keywords: Eye tracking · Perception · Character recognition · OCR

1 Introduction

Optical character recognition is highly researched domain in the area of image processing and computer vision. The commercial OCR systems can be divided into four generations, depending on the robustness and efficiency [1]. The first generation OCR can be characterized by the constrained letter shapes readable to the OCR, whereas the second generation is characterized by the recognition capabilities of the set of regular machine printed characters. The third generation OCR is focused on the poorly printed characters and handwritten characters. OCR dealing with complex documents intermixing with the text, graphics, table and mathematical symbols, unconstrained handwritten characters, low quality noisy documents comes under the fourth generation OCR [1]. However, there are

© Springer International Publishing AG 2017
B.U. Shankar et al. (Eds.): PReMI 2017, LNCS 10597, pp. 219–226, 2017.
https://doi.org/10.1007/978-3-319-69900-4_28

several instances where, if the characters are a bit distorted the OCR systems fail. In most of the situations, a school going kid can outperform the highly sophisticated OCR systems. Therefore, there is a need to understand how a person can recognize the letter irrespective of different variations.

There are some roots in the domain of psychology, cognitive science and neuroscience, which may help us to address the posed question. It has been rightly said that letter recognition is the foundation of human reading [2]. However, the attempts being made to understand the letter perception are very rare. In order to understand the nature of letter representation, two broad theories of visual recognition have been proposed viz. template matching and feature based approach. In the template matching, letter recognition is achieved by matching the letter stimulus to an internal template [3] and in feature based approach, visual features of the letters are extracted in the early stage of processing and then comparing those features with the list of features stored in memory, a letter is recognized [4]. It is hard to believe that we have stored all the features and templates of all the characters to be recognized. Therefore, we are trying to understand how the processing of the letter takes place under various distortion levels of letters and understand what features one considers while recognizing the letter.

There is a cognitive link between eye movement and brain. Therefore, eye tracking seems to be a promising technology to shed more light on visual letter processing. Rayner stated [5] that eye movement data reflects moment-to-moment cognitive processes in the various tasks. In the literature, we find various researchers had used eye tracking technology to understand language expertise [6], number of words read [7], type of document read [8] etc. However, no one has talked about a letter recognition or letter processing. Along with this there is hardly any attempt being made to understand the Devanagari script using eye tracking technology. Therefore, the proposed paper aims to identify the visual features and understand the visual processing of the Devanagari letters by human using eye tracking metrics.

This paper has been divided into four sections. Section 1 talks about the introduction; experimental setup has been discussed in Sect. 2. Section 3 highlights the results and discussions over the results. Concluding remarks with possible future extensions are presented in the last section.

2   Experimental Setup and Details

We had performed the eye tracking experiment on 20 healthy, graduate participants (7 females and 13 males) with normal or corrected to normal vision and with age ranging in between 20–30 years. These participants were frequent readers of the Devanagari script. In order to capture the eye movement, the Tobii T120 eye tracker was used which was a camera based, remote eye tracker with a sampling frequency of 120 Hz.

2.1   Stimulus Design

Initially, we grouped the characters based on the common elements as shown in Fig. 1. After that, we selected some characters showing high variations in their structure and the characters which are frequently used, for our experiment. Mangal font with point size 72 was used for designing the stimuli which were reduced to a single pixel contour through morphological operations. We were trying to incorporate the handwritten variations in the character and trying to understand how readers process the letter. Based on the variations which were commonly observed in the different parts of the handwritten letters, we divided the letter in different parts as shown in Fig. 2. Then each letter part was scaled in the range from 0.2 to 5. The stimuli were thus formed by combing the scaled letter parts with unchanged/unscaled part of the same letter. Thus, the letter formed was termed as distorted letter and was presented in black color against a white background. The prototype of the stimuli is shown in the Table 1.

Letters	Common element	Letters	Common element	Letters	Common element
ग म भ न	̃ and/or ̽	प ष फ ण	ण	अ आ ओ औ अं अः	अ
र स (ग ख)	र (़)	ट ठ ढ द (क्ष)	ट	ए ए	ए
त ल लृ	̥	ङ ड इ ई म ह ड	ड	म़ म़	ऩ
व ब क ख	व	य थ	य	उ ऊ	३
च (ज) घ घ छ	व or ध	श ळ म ब	—		

Fig. 1. Bhagwat's group based on graphical similarity [9]

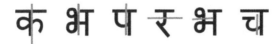

Fig. 2. Dividing the letter in different parts

2.2 Experimental Procedure

All the equipment required for the experiment had been set properly in the experimental room. Before starting the experiment, participants were given all the instructions about the experiment and explained their exact role in the study. When the participants agreed to participate, they were asked to sign the consent form and the necessary details such as name, age, eyesight, first language etc. were recorded. Each participant was seated in front of the eye tracker keeping the distance of 60–70 cm. The experiment started with the welcome message on the screen, followed by instructions and trial. The experiment was conducted in three phases. In each phase, participants were presented 6–7 letters with 25 variations each. The experiment started with the calibration of the eye tracker, according to the participant's eyes. In order to maintain good quality of eye tracking data, calibration was done in all phases separately and participants were allowed to take a break of 2 min after each phase if they wished to do so.

After successful calibration, actual experiment started. The stimuli were presented as different variations of the different letters chosen randomly, however the decreasing order of distortion was maintained i.e. high distortion of letter1, high distortion for letter2, lesser distortion of letter1 and so on. The participants were asked to press the

Table 1. Prototype of the stimuli

Part of the letter to be distorted (scaled)	Complete Letter with distorted (scaled) parts			
	Scale- 5	Scale- 3	Scale- 2	Scale- 1
ट	टㄱ	टㄱ	टㄱ	च
ㄷ	ㄷ	ㄷ	ㄷ	त
?	?क	?क	क	क
L	ㄴ	ㄴ	ㄴ	प

arrow key on the keyboard as well as spell the letter if they recognized the letter. If they were not able to recognize the letter, they could skip the letter by pressing the space bar key. This procedure continued till the end of the phase. The total time spent on the letter for recognition lets us know where the participants had faced difficulty in recognition. The pressing of a key allowed us to get to know the level of distortion participants were able to tolerate and recognize the letter.

The eye tracking data was collected throughout all the phases. In order to get fixations and saccades from the raw eye tracking data as shown in Fig. 3. Velocity based

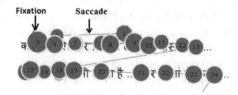

Fig. 3. Gaze plot generated during reading. The circle shows fixations where readers gaze at particular location for certain time duration and line joining two fixations is a saccade which indicates fast and rapid movement of eyes.

classification algorithm called as Velocity-Threshold Identification (I-VT) fixation classification algorithm was used. The algorithm classified the eye movements into fixation and saccades based on the velocity of the directional shift of the eye [10].

3 Results and Discussions

The analysis of the eye tracking data was carried out based on the fixation duration and fixation count. The participants were allowed to spend certain time to recognize the letter and allowed to proceed further by skipping the letter if they were unable to recognize the letters. The key pressed and letter pronounced loudly corresponding to correct letter recognition enabled us to know the level of distortion each one was able to tolerate. The correct recognition response is plotted for each letter as shown in Figs. 4, 5 and 6.

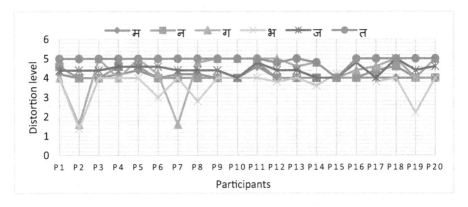

Fig. 4. Recognition of Devanagari letters in phase I

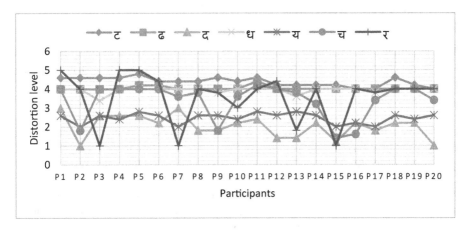

Fig. 5. Recognition of Devanagari letters in phase II

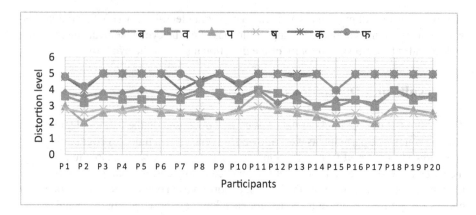

Fig. 6. Recognition of Devanagari letters in phase III

From these responses, it could be observed that almost all the participants had successfully recognized the letters क, त, म, ट, ढ, फ, ध, ग, न, ज in less time i.e. with higher levels of distortion. On the other hand, the letters भ, द, र, य, व, ब, प, ष, च were recognized a bit late by most of the participants. The recognition of the letters sharing same structural features such as प and ष, व and ब, क and फ had occurred almost at the same time. There was a similarity in the eye tracking patterns of the participants and particular eye fixation pattern that had been observed among the participants as well. Maximum eye fixation duration on the character region implies the difficulty in understanding or encoding the information. Participants have to spend much more time to encode what exactly it represents. As there was a change in distortion level, there was an interesting change in response as well.

3.1 Delayed Letter Recognition

There had been many incorrect responses reported in the recognition of the letters sharing similar visual features. Therefore, the correct recognition of these letters got delayed and had occurred when the letter has lesser distortion level. This can be observed from Figs. 4, 5 and 6. This was due to the different way of processing the letters. Most of the participants reported द as ट, च as प, भ as म, र as ए etc. at a higher level of distortion. As the letter was getting normal, the participants fixated on different locations and then recognized the letter correctly. We have created the heat map using number of fixations and fixation duration as shown in Fig. 7. The variation in the fixation duration and number of fixations has enabled us to understand how the letter was processed and how the fixation pattern changed which had enabled the participant to recognize the letter correctly. The particular observations are tabulated in Table 2. The pronouncing the letter had given us the exact idea about what the participant had recognized and it had provided us the cross check whether the recognition was correct or not.

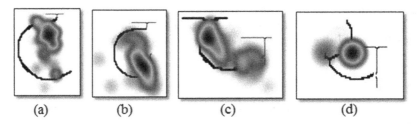

(a)   (b)   (c)   (d)

Fig. 7. The heat map based on the fixation count (number of fixations) for (a), (b) and fixation duration for (c), (d)

Table 2. Understanding the processing of the Devanagari letters through eye fixations

The letters	Analysis of eye fixations
म,न,ग,भ	Initially more number of fixations were observed on the middle knot or loop of the letter. The later fixations were on the contact joining either headline or vertical bar attached to the letter
ट,ड,द	The number of fixations observed on the curvilinear terminal increased as the distortion level of the letter got decreased. (Figure 7(a) and (b))
प,ष,य,र	In case of most of the participants, the initial fixations, were found to be on the curve joining the headline followed by the middle portion of the letter. (Figure 7(d))
व, ब, क, फ	Initial fixations were on the curvilinear part followed by middle portion
त, ज	The fixation duration was more on the contact joining horizontal line with vertical bar. Most of the participants found these letters easy to recognize
ध	The fixation duration was more on the loop with the curve of the character which enable most of the participants recognize the letter
च	The fixation duration was more on the contact between the horizontal line and the curved part of the letter. The separation between header line and horizontal bar/line of the letter enable participants to recognize the letter correctly. (Figure 7(c))

4   Conclusions

The proposed research unfolds insights about how Devanagari letters are processed by the readers. The eye tracking seems to be the promising technique to understand the moment-to-moment processing of the letter. In this work, we have incorporated the maximum variations that are generally seen in the handwritten characters and subsequently recorded readers' behavior using eye tracking for these characters. The results demonstrate that the maximum attention of the reader is along the curves, knots, loops and contacts with the headline. There is also a change in fixation patterns along with various distortion levels. This peculiar eye movement behavior might have provided some crucial visual cues to the participant for efficient recognition. In our future work, all these demonstrated visual cues would be used to build the smart OCR model for robust character recognition.

Acknowledgements. We would like to thank all the participants participated in our study. We would also like to thank the Ministry of Electronics and Information Technology Government of India and the Media Lab Asia for financial assistance to carry out research.

References

1. Pal, U., Chaudhuri, B.B.: Indian script character recognition: a survey. Patt. Recogn. **37**(9), 1887–1899 (2004)
2. Chang, Y.N., Furber, S., Welbourne, S.: Modelling normal and impaired letter recognition: implications for understanding pure alexic reading. Neuropsychologia **50**(12), 2773–2788 (2012)
3. Neisser, U.: Cognitive Psychology. Appleton-Century-Crofts, New York (1967)
4. Gibson, E.L.: Principles of Perceptual Learning and Development. Appleton-Century-Crofts, New York (1969)
5. Rayner, K.: Eye movements in reading and information processing: 20 years of research. Psychol. Bull. **124**(3), 372 (1998)
6. Yoshimura, K., Kise, K., Kunze, K.: The eye as the window of the language ability: estimation of English skills by analyzing eye movement while reading documents. In: 2015 13th International Conference on Document Analysis and Recognition (ICDAR), pp. 251–255. IEEE (2015)
7. Kunze, K., Kawaichi, H., Yoshimura, K., Kise, K.: The Wordometer–Estimating the number of words read using document image retrieval and mobile eye tracking. In: 2013 12th International Conference on Document Analysis and Recognition (ICDAR), pp. 25–29. IEEE (2013)
8. Kunze, K., Utsumi, Y., Shiga, Y., Kise, K., Bulling, A.: I know what you are reading: recognition of document types using mobile eye tracking. In: Proceedings of the 2013 International Symposium on Wearable Computers, pp. 113–116. ACM (2013)
9. Bhagwat, S.V.: Phoniemic Frequencies in Marathi and Their Relation to Devising a Speed-script, vol. 1. Deccan College Post-graduate and Research Institute (1961)
10. Salvucci, D.D., Goldberg, J.H.: Identifying fixations and saccades in eye-tracking protocols. In: Proceedings of the 2000 Symposium on Eye Tracking Research and Applications, pp. 71–78. ACM (2000)

Video Stabilization Using Sliding Frame Window

Keerthan S. Shagrithaya[ID], Eeshwar Gurushankar[ID], Deepak Srikanth[ID],
Pravin Bhaskar Ramteke[✉][ID], and Shashidhar G. Koolagudi[ID]

National Institute of Technology Karnataka, Surathkal, Karnataka, India
keerthanss9@gmail.com, eeshwarg13@gmail.com, deepakks96@gmail.com,
ramteke0001@gmail.com, koolagudi@nitk.ac.in

Abstract. Shaky videos are visually unappealing to viewers. Digital
video stabilization is a technique to compensate for unwanted camera
motion and produce a video that looks relatively stable. In this paper,
an approach for video stabilization is proposed which works by estimating a trajectory built by calculating motion between continuous frames
using the Shi-Tomasi Corner Detection and Optical Flow algorithms for
the entire length of the video. The trajectory is then smoothed using a
moving average to give a stabilized output. A *smoothing radius* is defined,
which determines the smoothness of the resulting video. Automatically
deciding this parameter's value is also discussed. The results of stabilization of the proposed approach are observed to be comparable with the
state of the art YouTube stabilization.

Keywords: Video stabilisation · Feature trajectories · Smoothing
radius

1 Introduction

With advances in smart-phone technology and the ubiquity of these hand-held
devices, every important moment of our lives is captured on video. But these
videos are of often poor quality: lacking stabilizing equipment such as tripods,
steady-cams, gimbals, etc. They are often shaky and unstable, especially when
the videographer, the subject, or both are in motion. To deal with this, affordable techniques that do not require hardware to stabilize such videos are of the
essence. Post-processing techniques that need no additional hardware are effective in removing the effects of jerky camera motion, and are independent of the
device capturing the video and the subject of the video. The proposed approach
is a five step sequential process that covers the different stages of video stabilization from feature extraction and tracking to camera motion estimation and
compensation. This method is run on a set of videos and is compared to the
state of the art YouTube video stabilizers.

Section 2 discusses the relevant work done in the field of video stabilization. The proposed video stabilization technique is discussed in detail in
Sect. 3. Section 4 describes the experiments performed and results obtained. The
paper concludes with Sect. 5 which gives the inferences made along with future
directions.

© Springer International Publishing AG 2017
B.U. Shankar et al. (Eds.): PReMI 2017, LNCS 10597, pp. 227–232, 2017.
https://doi.org/10.1007/978-3-319-69900-4_29

2   Literature Survey

2D video stabilization methods perform three tasks - motion estimation, motion compensation, and image correction. Feature matching is done using Scale Invariant Feature Transform (SIFT) [1] or Oriented FAST and Rotated BRIEF (ORB) operators [12]. Robust feature trajectories [5] involve using features matched along with neighboring features information. It use SIFT or ORB descriptors to match features between frames to calculate feature trajectories, and then pruning and separating them into local and global motion. The motion inpainting algorithm, which fills frame's unpainted regions by observing motion history [5], serves well for image correction. Another approach modified the optical flow algorithm [3,8], where pixels were tracked to find which feature trajectories cross it [7]. The approach worked well with videos possessing large depth change, but failed in cases with dominant large foreground objects. Videos having large parallax or rolling shutter effects are challenging to stabilize. To tackle this, a bundle of trajectories were calculated for different subareas of the image and these were all processed together [6]. Applying L1-norm optimization [2] can generate camera paths that consist of only constant, linear and parabolic motions, which do follow cinematography rules. YouTube has since adopted this algorithm into their system.

Most of the approaches discussed here witness a significant difference in performance on videos with an object of interest and ones without, with the latter facing a dip. In this paper, an approach based on [10] is investigated whose performance does not change for videos with objects of interest or ones without.

3   Methodology

The proposed approach uses two structures - *transform parameter* and *trajectory*. The first holds the frame-to-frame transformation- dx, dy, da. Each represents changes in the x-coordinate, y-coordinate and rotational change respectively. The latter structure stores the positions and angle of the feature points, which together form the trajectory. Algorithm 1 shows the working of the proposed approach, given a smoothing radius.

Features points are found for each frame by using Shi-Tomasi Corner detection algorithm [4]. These feature points are used to obtain the corresponding matching features in the next consecutive frames using optical flow algorithm [3,8]. Transformation matrix $T^{(k)}_{original}$ is estimated from the feature points of frame k and frame $k + 1$, that encompasses the change between the two frames [11]. $T^{(k)}_{original}$ provides the *transform parameter* values as:

$$[dx^{(k)}, dy^{(k)}, da^{(k)}] = \left[T^{(k)}_{original}[0, 2], T^{(k)}_{original}[1, 2], \tan^{-1} \left(\frac{T^{(k)}_{original}[1, 0]}{T^{(k)}_{original}[0, 0]} \right) \right]$$

$$(1)$$

Algorithm 1: Stabilisation using sliding window

Input: Shaky camera footage
Parameter : Smoothing radius, r
Output: Stabilized video
1 Process each frame to obtain frame-to-frame transform $\Delta_{original}$
2 Using $\Delta_{original}$, compute trajectories $I_{original}$
3 **while** $k <$ *Number of frames - r* **do**
4 $\quad Sum = \sum_{i=k-r}^{i=k+r} I_{original}^{i}$
5 $\quad WindowSize = 2 * r$
6 $\quad I_{smooth}^{k} = Sum/WindowSize$
7 **end**
8 Compute Δ_{smooth} to raise each point from its position in $I_{original}$ to I_{smooth}
9 Using Δ_{smooth}, obtain and apply transformation matrices Γ on the sequence of frames
10 Resultant sequence of frames is the stabilized output

These values are stored as a list,

$$\Delta_{original} = \{tp^{(k)} | tp^{(k)} = (dx^{(k)}, dy^{(k)}, da^{(k)})\} \qquad (2)$$

where, $\Delta_{original}$ is then used to generate a single image trajectory, $I_{original}$. First, trajectory point is initialized to $x=0$, $y=0$, $a=0$. Each point thereafter is updated by adding to it a *transform parameter*. The final list contains the image trajectory, $I_{original} = \{p^{(k)}\}$. Camera shake is removed in the third step. For this, a new smooth trajectory, I_{smooth} is computed using a sliding average window algorithm. This requires a parameter, namely the constant smoothing radius r. The value of r is the number of frames on either side of the current frame used for the sliding window.

Figure 1 depicts that, as smoothing radius increases, stability tends to increase. But having arbitrarily high values of smoothing radius can be detrimental. As smoothing radius increases, the absolute values of the transformations applied to the frames increases leading to more data being lost as shown in Fig. 2. Data loss can be quantitatively defined as the ratio of black data-void areas in the stabilized frame to the original frame area. An optimal smoothing radius is thus desired.

Let $S_V(r)$ and $D_V(r)$ represent the stability and data loss respectively in the video obtained by smoothing video V with a smoothing radius of r. Let $s_V(r)$ and $d_V(r)$ be the corresponding min-max normalized functions. As a high value of $s_V(r)$ and a low value of $d_V(r)$ is desirable, the *goodness* of a video is:

$$G(s_V(r), d_V(r)) = \sqrt{s_V(r) * (1 - d_V(r))} \qquad (3)$$

and the optimal smoothing radius is then given by

$$r^* = argmax_r(G(s_V(r), d_V(r))) \qquad (4)$$

To reduce the time taken for calculation, following constraints are introduced.

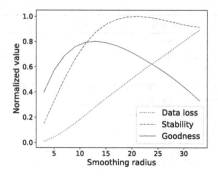

Fig. 1. Effect of smoothing radii on goodness of a video, stability and data loss

1. $0 < r \leq R_{max}$: High radius causes high data loss and can be disregarded. The exact value of R_{max} is chosen empirically to be 40.
2. $D_V(r) < 0.1$: Fixing a range on just r is insufficient as the data loss function can ascend very quickly even within that range. Thus, to preclude that, a constraint on data loss is also introduced.

Having obtained the desired smooth trajectory, *transform parameter* values are required to transform every frame such that their old trajectory points are shifted to the ones in line with the smooth trajectory. For a particular frame, the distance between its $I_{original}^{(k)}$ and $I_{smooth}^{(k)}$ is calculated and added to the corresponding $\Delta_{original}^{(k)}$, to obtain a new *transform parameter* $\delta_{smooth}^{(k)}$. In effect, a point from a previous frame is translated to the current point of current frame and then translated from there to the smooth point of the current frame. These calculated values are brought together into a sequence by $\Delta_{smooth} = \{\delta_{smooth}^{(k)}\}$. Subsequently, the transformation matrix for the new smoothened trajectory and *transform parameter* values are computed using Δ_{smooth}, and applied to produce a stable video output. Suppose smooth transform for the kth frame is $st^{(k)}$, then the transformation matrix is given as,

$$T_{smooth}^{(k)} = \begin{bmatrix} \cos(da^{(k)}) & -\sin(da^{(k)}) & dx^{(k)} \\ \sin(da^{(k)}) & \cos(da^{(k)}) & dy^{(k)} \end{bmatrix} \tag{5}$$

This affine transformation matrix is calculated for every frame to obtain the required sequence of transformations by $\Gamma = \{T_{smooth}^{(k)}\}$. Each transformation $T_{smooth}^{(k)}$ is then applied on the corresponding frame k. The resultant sequence of frames is the stabilized video.

4   Results and Comparison

The proposed approach is tested on videos with and without objects of interest. To assess the performance of the proposed method, two performance criteria - stability and distortion - suggested by [6] are used to compare the proposed

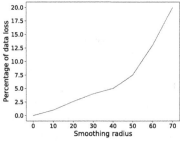
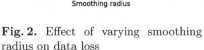

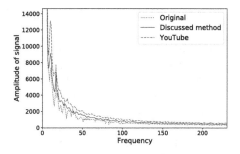

Fig. 2. Effect of varying smoothing radius on data loss

Fig. 3. Frequency domain representation of the X coordinate signal

method with the YouTube stabilizer [2], and non-stabilized videos. Distortion between two continuous frames is the sum of pixel-by-pixel difference in intensity. Overall distortion of a video is the average of the pairwise distortion between continuous frames over the length of the video. A lower average implies a less distorted video. Table 1 compares the result of the proposed method with the original video and YouTube stabilized video. In most cases distortion is relatively higher than YouTube using the proposed method.

Table 1. Results of Distortion measure and Stability measure

Video	Distortion			Stability		
	Non-stabilized	Proposed method	YouTube	Non-stabilized	Proposed method	YouTube
1	0.4219	0.4179	0.4182	95.32	95.61	95.93
2	0.4003	0.3988	0.3729	95.57	95.57	95.68
3	0.4322	0.4206	0.3890	91.76	93.74	93.59

Stability approximates how stable the video appears to a viewer. Quantitatively, a higher fraction of energy present in the low frequency region of the Fourier transform of the estimated motion implies higher stability. Figure 3 shows the frequency domain representation of the X-coordinate motion. Over a dataset of 11 videos, it is observed that the proposed method shows an average of 3.92% improvement in stability over the original video, while the YouTube stabilizer shows a 4.28% improvement. The proposed method outperforms the YouTube stabilizer in three out of eleven videos. The results of this metric on three videos are shown in Table 1. The stability of the proposed method is usually comparable with that of YouTube, and in a few cases outperforms it. The proposed method does not handle sudden jerks well. Its performance is however unaffected by the presence or absence of an object in focus, thus making it applicable to a large class of videos.

5   Conclusions and Future Work

In this paper an algorithm for video stabilization has been proposed. This was accomplished by obtaining a global 2-D motion estimate for the optical flow of the video in both the X and Y directions. The algorithm is simpler than most current implementations, and provides comparable accuracy with YouTube's stabilizer. It also takes into account the image degradation to maintain optimal video quality. Taking into consideration multiple paths to estimate the motion [6] and motion inpainting [9] for image correction can improve the performance of this implementation. Future work can also include adaptively varying the smoothing radius over the video.

References

1. Battiato, S., Gallo, G., Puglisi, G., Scellato, S.: Sift features tracking for video stabilization. In: 14th International Conference on Image Analysis and Processing, ICIAP 2007, pp. 825–830. IEEE (2007)
2. Grundmann, M., Kwatra, V., Essa, I.: Auto-directed video stabilization with robust l1 optimal camera paths. In: 2011 IEEE Conference on Computer Vision and Pattern Recognition (CVPR), pp. 225–232. IEEE (2011)
3. Horn, B.K., Schunck, B.G.: Determining optical flow. Artif. Intell. **17**(1–3), 185–203 (1981)
4. Jianbo, S., Carlo, T.: Good features to track. In: Proceedings of 1994 IEEE Computer Society Conference on Computer Vision and Pattern Recognition, CVPR 1994, pp. 593–600. IEEE (1994)
5. Lee, K.Y., Chuang, Y.Y., Chen, B.Y., Ouhyoung, M.: Video stabilization using robust feature trajectories. In: 2009 IEEE 12th International Conference on Computer Vision, pp. 1397–1404. IEEE (2009)
6. Liu, S., Yuan, L., Tan, P., Sun, J.: Bundled camera paths for video stabilization. ACM Trans. Graph. (TOG) **32**(4), 78 (2013)
7. Liu, S., Yuan, L., Tan, P., Sun, J.: Steadyflow: spatially smooth optical flow for video stabilization. In: Proceedings of the IEEE Conference on Computer Vision and Pattern Recognition, pp. 4209–4216 (2014)
8. Lucas, B.D., Kanade, T., et al.: An iterative image registration technique with an application to stereo vision. In: Proceedings DARPA Image Understanding Workshop, pp. 121–130 (1981)
9. Matsushita, Y., Ofek, E., Ge, W., Tang, X., Shum, H.Y.: Full-frame video stabilization with motion inpainting. IEEE Trans. Pattern Anal. Mach. Intell. **28**(7), 1150–1163 (2006)
10. Nghia, H.: Simple video stabilisation using opencv (2014), http://nghiaho.com/?p=2093. Accessed 17 Mar 2017
11. Nghia, H.: Understanding opencv cv::estimaterigidtransform (2015), http://nghiaho.com/?p=2208. Accessed 15 Aug 2017
12. Rublee, E., Rabaud, V., Konolige, K., Bradski, G.: Orb: an efficient alternative to sift or surf. In: 2011 IEEE International Conference on Computer Vision (ICCV), pp. 2564–2571. IEEE (2011)

Palmprint and Finger Knuckle Based Person Authentication with Random Forest via Kernel-2DPCA

Gaurav Jaswal$^{(\boxtimes)}$ ⓘ, Amit Kaul ⓘ, and Ravinder Nath ⓘ

Signal Processing and Biomedical Instrumentation Laboratory,
Department of Electrical Engineering, National Institute of Technology,
Hamirpur, India
{gauravjaswal,amitkaul,r.nath}@nith.ac.in
http://www.nith.ac.in

Abstract. This paper presents a hand biometric system by fusing information of palmprint and finger knuckle to check the loopholes that are present in transfer of payments through various levels of bureaucratic financial inclusion projects. Initially, a novel, fixed size ROIs of palm and finger knuckle has been extracted. The poor contrast ROI images are enhanced using modified CLAHE algorithm. To minimize the pose and illumination effects, Line Ordinal Pattern (LOP) based transformation scheme has been applied. The generation of dense feature representation by using dual tree complex wavelet transform can increase the discrimination power of independent local features. Then, the original feature space is mapped into high dimensional sub feature set, where K2DPCA is performed on each subset to extract high order statistics. Addressing to the matching problem, a high-performance Random Forest method has been employed. Finally, the two modalities are combined at weighted sum score level fusion rule which has shown the increased performance (CRR (100%), EER (0.68%), and (computation time (2130 ms)) of combined approach. The proposed method is evaluated using a virtual combination of publicly available PolyU palm print and PolyU FKP databases.

Keywords: Line Ordinal Pattern · DTCWT · K2DPCA · Random forest

1 Introduction

A biometric system based on hand characteristics has been playing a substantial role in instituting human identity in most access control applications [1,9]. The unimodal hand biometric systems such as palm print, and FKP traits are not completely perfect to be used exclusively in large security applications like forensic, defense etc. Their performance is often affected by varying environment situations, sensor accuracy, poor quality images, spoof attacks etc. Grouping of a palm print, and FKP traits take the advantage to improve the performance of

© Springer International Publishing AG 2017
B.U. Shankar et al. (Eds.): PReMI 2017, LNCS 10597, pp. 233–240, 2017.
https://doi.org/10.1007/978-3-319-69900-4_30

single modality based hand recognition systems. Biometric fusion is the key to multimodal biometrics that consolidate the different information given by more than one biometric trait. In [3], authors suggested to incorporate an Iterative Closest Point (ICP) alignment to improve line detection schemes. In addition to this, Palmcode [2], Compcode [4] are well defined in literature. Authors [6] presented another significant method called as monogenic code which reflected the phase and orientation information of knuckle images. Authors [7] used a weighted sum rule to fuse local and global information for FKP recognition. Authors [8] applied SIFT over Gabor filter based enhanced FKP images.

Contribution: It is aimed to compute important edge information over gradient images and then capture non-linear information from them. In this article, the input hand image is segmented and novel region of interest (ROI) of palm and knuckle images are obtained. Then novel image transformation scheme named as Line Ordinal Pattern (LOP) is presented to obtain the illumination invariance and robust edge information along vertical and horizontal directions. To obtain better texture information against pose variation, the images are processed in wavelet domain. To preserve spatial information and to select the most expressive features by removing redundant data, the K-2DPCA is implemented on wavelet images. The robust features between two images are compared using Random Forest Classifier. Finally, the scores of both palm print and FKP are fused using weighted SUM rule. The publicly available databases i.e. PolyU Palmprint [10], and PolyU FKP [11] are considered to evaluate the performance of proposed system.

2   Proposed Biometric System:

The main objective is to enumerate the performance improvement of Hand based personal recognition system by integrating palm and knuckle features.

Palmprint ROI Extraction: First, re-size the input image to 176×176 and contrast adjust the input image as shown in Fig. 1(a). Smooth the image using Gaussian low pass filter (size= 15×15 and standard deviation=4). Obtain gradient image for the gaussian filtered image as shown in Fig. 1(b, c). Then, multiply gradient image by 2 and add the result to the Gaussian filtered image in order to brighten the gaussian filtered image at the boundary of the foreground as shown in Fig. 1(d). Find otsu threshold for the image obtained in last step. Obtain the Otsu thresholded (bw) image and erode remove small objects and dilate the Otsu thresholded image to get fingers separated from each other in case of noise in the image. Fill holes in the image and remove all white connected regions other than the largest one as shown in Fig. 1(e, f, g). This removes any other small objects in the back ground and removes background portions that appear white in image. Obtain cropped palm region. Following this, find 2 points at the bottom of the ring and middle fingers in the image. For this, obtain cetroid and boundary of palm region as shown in Fig. 1(h, i). Remove boundary on top right and bottom portion of image and retain the boundary on the left side of the image where fingers are present. Find distance from the left end of image to the finger boundary. Take only 3 prominent peaks. The peaks will occur at the bottom point of index, middle and ring finger. Take the first and third points. Find out the angle between the horizontal line and the line joining the 2 points. Now, rotate the image to make the line joining the 2 point horizontal as shown in Fig. 1(j, k). Find out the largest square inside the palm region by removing 35 pixels from all 4 borders of the ROI image obtained in previous step. Finally, re-size the final ROI obtained in previous step to 176 × 176 as shown in Fig. 1(l).

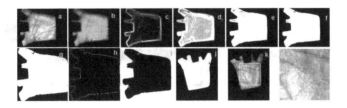

Fig. 1. Palmprint ROI extraction

FKP ROI Extraction: Firstly, remove the top border in the background. Next, remove small imperfections in the image by performing reconstruction based opening and closing operation as shown in as shown in Fig. 2(b, c). Then, obtain foreground markers from regional maxima of the image as shown in Fig. 2(d). the edges of the marker blobs and shrink them by performing closing followed by erosion as shown in Fig. 2(e). Apply otsu thresholding to find the approximate finger region as shown in Fig. 2(f). Obtain a rectangular box surrounding the finger region by dilating the otsu thresholded image. In order to find gradient image, filter the image in the horizontal and vertical direction as shown in Fig. 2(f). If I_x is the horizontal filter output and I_y is the vertical filter output, the total magnitude is obtained as:

$$A = \sqrt{I_x^2 + I_y^2} \tag{1}$$

Finally, watershed segmentation is performed on the gradient image using foreground and background markers to obtain the finger segmented image as shown in Fig. 2(g, h). In the next step, filter the full original finger image in the horizontal direction with a filter that gives high magnitude along the edge of the knuckle region. The filter used is a basic derivative filter of the first order derivative type that obtain highest magnitude at thick edges as shown in Fig. 2(i). Now, obtain the finger knuckle region as the brightest region in the finger that is close to the brightest region identified in the filtered image. In actual image the brightest region will be either on the left side or right side of the knuckle joint in the filtered image. Therefore, we try to identify the edges that separate this bright region. The filtered image is now thresholded such that only about 5% of the image is white to obtain the approximate finger knuckle region as shown in

Fig. 2(j). Obtain the x-axis midpoint of the bounding box of the largest white region in the black and white image as the knuckle mid-point which is just the approximate value as shown in Fig. 2(j). Now, obtain the finger knuckle region as the brightest region in the original image that is close to the brightest region around mid-point of filtered image. The reflected or accurate center of the segmented image is shown in Fig. 2(l). Finally, the finger knuckle ROI is segmented at specified distances from the mid-point and normalized to fixed size (220×110) as shown in Fig. 2(m).

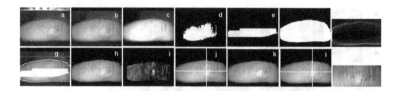

Fig. 2. Finger kiuckle print ROI extraction

Image Enhancement: To enhance the raw ROI samples so that a well distributed texture image can be obtained, we assume that noise is multiplicative in nature and its effects can be seen in Fig. 3(a)(a4, b4) as it adds brightness. Now, the uniform brightened ROI sample is enhanced using Contrast Limited Adaptive Histogram Equalization (CLAHE) that improves the contrast as shown in Fig. 3(a)(a5, b5). Finally, Weiner filtering is performed to smooth the boundaries, and minimizes the additive noise.

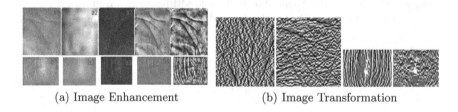

(a) Image Enhancement   (b) Image Transformation

Fig. 3. Pre-processing

Image Transformation: To get a robust texture representation under the effects of varying light conditions, pose, and scale, a Line Ordinal Pattern (LOP) based encoding scheme is presented which provides a transverse and longitudinal representations as shown in Fig. 3(b). The proposed encoding mechanism utilized sobel longitudinal and transverse kernels to assign a 8-bit code (l_{LOP} and t_{LOP}) for every pixel by taking derivatives of eight neighbors. It has been noted that the neighborhood is in a straight-line shape with length N pixels.

Therefore, to obtain practicable LOPcode response, every pixel is encoded as a 8 bit binary sequence whose k_{th} bit is expressed as:

$$LOP_{Code}(u, v)[k] = (L_K > L_{k+1}) ? 1 : 0 \qquad (2)$$

where, $I_{u,v}$ defines the spatial location of each pixel, L_K, k=1,2,3....8 describes the gradients of eight adjoining pixels positioned along $I_{u,v}$ with the use of longitudinal and transverse kernels.

Dual Tree Complex Wavelet Transform based Feature Extraction: A classic DWT suffers from shift variance, scale variance, limited directionality in 2 dimensions, and aliasing. In order to report such issues, the use of complex form of wavelets (DT-CWT) is crucial which primarily consist of two real wavelets with a 90-degree phase difference. A 2D dual-tree complex wavelet can be defined as:

$$\psi(x, y) = \psi(x)\psi(y) \qquad (3)$$

where, $\psi(x)$ and $\psi(y)$ are two complex wavelets. In 2D-DCWT, a quadtree architecture decomposes each palm/knuckle LOP image into desired decomposition levels by performing sum/difference of two separable wavelet filter banks with 4:1 redundancy. Thus, we obtain six directional sub-bands (real and imaginary with orientation ±15, ±45, ±75 degrees) for each scale (s) at any decomposition level. Specifically, a set of statistical features such as variance (v), energy (E), entropy (e), and homogeneity (h) are computed from the wavelet coefficients at various sub-bands. Therefore, the feature vector (f) correspond to four set of statistical features extracted from complex wavelet coefficients at six directional selective sub-bands.

Kernel-2DPCA: Here, a 2-D nonlinear version of the classical 2DPCA approach termed as kernel 2DPCA, has been applied directly over palm/ knuckle wavelet image matrices. However, classic PCA and 2DPCA could not effectively represent the non-linear distribution of input data. Thus, we are projecting the image into M dimensional non-linear space so that multiple classes should be linearly separable in non-linear space. Since, kernel is a nonlinear function by which coefficients of wavelet palm/ knuckle (D dimensional space) are transformed into non-linear feature space M, where $M \gg D$. In this work, we have used sigmoid kernel function for non-linear mapping.

3 Classification and Fusion

The score is considered genuine match if both the images belong to same class, otherwise imposter. Random forests are inherently multi-class and advantage of such classifier is the ease of training and testing. Random forest combines individual decision tree classifiers $k_{1x}, k_{2x}, ..., k_{nx}$ based on boosting and bagging mechanisms. Each classifier votes for one of the classes and a sample being classified is categorized with the winning class. The best used attribute splitting rules are: Information Gain, Gain Ratio, and Gini index. Among them, Gini

Index is the most successful splitting rule that consider a binary split for each attribute.

$$Gini = 1 - \sum_{i=1}^{m} P_i^2 \tag{4}$$

where P_i is the probability that a training vector belong to class C_i and m is total number of classes. The choice of suitable fusion rule is very important for better performance. In this work, a weighted sum rule is employed to integrate the normalized scores.

4   Experimental Results

The palm print and finger knuckle image databases are obtained from The Hong Kong Polytechnic University (PolyU) [10,11] respectively for the validity of proposed work. All the experiments are performed using inter session based testing protocol.

Experiment 1: In the first test, each category of PolyU Palmprint database (RP-193, LP-193) and PolyU FKP database (LI-165, LM-165, RI-165, RM-165) are assumed separately and the proposed palmprint (P1, P2) and finger knuckle (P3, P4, P5, P6) algorithms are tested. The respective ROC and CRR curves are plotted in Fig. 4. The conclusions from the first test illustrate that: (a) Among individual performance, the longitudinal (l_{LOP}) based Random Forest matching signifies the superior results, because palm and knuckle naturally consist of dark vertical lines. (b) In case of performance of palmprint recognition, the combined ($l_{LOP}+t_{LOP}$) accuracy (CRR- 99.58%; EER-1.45%; speed-1454 ms) over Right Palm dataset are somewhat better than Left Palm dataset. (c) The use of K2DPCA enhances recognition accuracy as well as improve computation speed of these methods. (d) Among four categories of Finger knuckles, Right Middle (P6) achieves higher performance (CRR-99.18%; EER-2.52%; speed-1108 ms).

Experiment 2: In this test, the whole 386 (LP+RP) subjects from PolyU palm dataset and their corresponding poses ($386 \times 10 = 3860$) are included for performance evaluation of proposed palmprint (P7) recognition. Thus, 14861000 number of impostor and 38600 genuine matchings are computed. Likewise, all

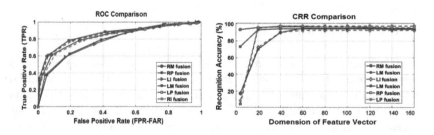

Fig. 4. Unimodal recognition performance: (a) ROC Analysis, (b) CRR Analysis

the subjects from finger knuckle dataset 660 (LI+LM+RI+RM) and their corresponding poses (660 × 12 = 7920) are included for performance evaluation (P8) which count 16681600 impostor and 23760 genuine. Further, in the next case the fusion (P9) of full Palmprint and full FKP datasets is performed. Thus, a common of 386 subjects from both the datasets are considered to create a multimodal virtual dataset. This experiment results into 5349960 number of impostor and 13896 genuine matchings. The results over complete data sets are described in Table 1. Also, the ROC and CMC curves are shown in Fig. 5. It is clear that the optimum results (CRR-100%; EER-0.68%; speed-2130 ms) are achieved with proposed multimodal scheme (P9) over full palm and knuckle datasets which is significantly higher than the individual modality based schemes. It largely depends upon the easiness in allocating score weights to individual methods and combination of longitudinal and transverse information. Table 1 presents comparison of three state-of art methods with our proposed work on the basis of CRR, and EER parameters.

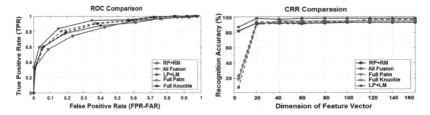

Fig. 5. Multimodal recognition performance: (a) ROC Analysis, (b) CRR Analysis

Table 1. Comparative performance analysis

Method	CRR(%)	EER(%)
CompCode [4]	-	GAR-98.4
MoriCode and MtexCode [12]	-	1.048
Log Gabor Filter (multimodal) [13]	99.85	-
P1-Left Palm($l_{LOP} + t_{LOP}$)	98.44	2.38
P2-Right Palm($l_{LOP} + t_{LOP}$)	99.58	1.45
P3-Left Index FKP($l_{LOP} + t_{LOP}$)	98.05	3.45
P4-Left Middle FKP($l_{LOP} + t_{LOP}$)	98.55	3.02
P5-Right Index FKP($l_{LOP} + t_{LOP}$)	98.76	2.66
P6-Right Middle FKP($l_{LOP} + t_{LOP}$)	99.18	2.52
P7-Full Palm($l_{LOP} + t_{LOP}$)	99.34	1.35
P8-Full Finger Knuckle($l_{LOP} + t_{LOP}$)	99.12	2.65
P9-All Fusion($l_{LOP} + t_{LOP}$)	100	0.68

5   Conclusion and Important Findings

This paper presents a novel multimodal biometric authentication system using multiple features of finger knuckle and palmprint. The proposed multimodal algorithm is also compared with some well-known existing systems which reveal the significance of our multi-feature fusion strategy. Moreover, it has been observed that longitudinal features of both palm and knuckle are much useful and robust than transverse features.

References

1. Jaswal, G., Kaul, A., Nath, R.: Knuckle print biometrics and fusion schemes-overview, challenges, and solutions. ACM Comput. Surv. (CSUR) **49**(2), 34 (2016)
2. Zhang, D., Kong, W.K., You, J., Wong, M.: Online palmprint identification. IEEE Trans. Pattern Anal. Mach. Intell. **25**(9), 1041–1050 (2003)
3. Li, W., Zhang, B., Zhang, L., Yan, J.: Principal line-based alignment refinement for palmprint recognition. IEEE Trans. Syst. Man Cybern. **42**(6), 1491–1499 (2012)
4. Kong, A. K., and Zhang, D.: Competitive coding scheme for palmprint verification. In: 17th IEEE International Conference on Pattern Recognition, pp. 520–523 (2004)
5. Kumar, A.: Importance of being unique from finger dorsal patterns: exploring minor finger knuckle patterns in verifying human identities. IEEE Trans. Inf. Forensics Secur. **9**(8), 1288–1298 (2014)
6. Zhang, L., Zhang, L., Zhang, D.: Monogeniccode: a novel fast feature coding algorithm with applications to finger-knuckle-print recognition. In: IEEE International Workshop on Emerging Techniques and Challenges for Hand-Based, Biometrics, pp. 1–4 (2010)
7. Zhang, L., Zhang, L., Zhang, D., Zhu, H.: Ensemble of local and global information for finger-knuckle-print recognition. Pattern Recognit. **44**(9), 1990–1998 (2011)
8. Morales, A., Travieso, C.M., Ferrer, M.A., Alonso, J.B.: Improved finger-knuckle-print authentication based on orientation enhancement. Electron. Lett. **47**(6), 380–381 (2011)
9. Jaswal, G., Nigam, A., Nath, R.: DeepKnuckle: revealing the human identity. Multimedia Tools and Appl. **76**(18), 1–30 (2017)
10. The Hong Kong Polytechnic University palmprint Database. http://www4.comp.polyu.edu.hk/~biometrics/
11. The Hong Kong Polytechnic University Finger-Knuckle-Print Database. http://www4.comp.polyu.edu.hk/biometrics/FKP.htm
12. Gao, G., Yang, J., Qian, J., Zhang, L.: Integration of multiple orientation and texture information for finger-knuckle-print verification. Neurocomputing **135**, 180–191 (2014)
13. Meraoumia, A., Chitroub, S., Bouridane, A.: Palmprint and finger-knuckle-print for efficient person recognition based on log-gabor filter response. Analog Integr. Circ. Sig. Process. **69**(1), 17–27 (2017)

Soft and Natural Computing

A Fuzzy-LP Approach in Time Series Forecasting

Pritpal Singh[1]([✉])(iD) and Gaurav Dhiman[2](iD)

[1] Smt. Chandaben Mohanbhai Patel Institute of Computer Applications,
CHARUSAT Campus, Anand 388421, Gujarat, India
drpritpalsingh82@gmail.com
[2] Department of Computer Science and Engineering, Thapar University,
Patiala 147004, Punjab, India
gdhiman0001@gmail.com

Abstract. In this study, a novel model is presented to forecast the time series data set based on the *fuzzy time series (FTS)* concept. To remove various drawbacks associated with the FTS modeling approach, this study incorporates significant changes in the existing FTS models. These changes are: (a) to apply the linear programming (LP) model in the FTS modeling approach for the selection of appropriate length of intervals, (b) to fuzzify the historical time series value (TSV) based on its involvement in the universe of discourse, (c) to use the high-order fuzzy logical relations (FLRs) in the decision making, and (d) to use the degree of membership (DM) along with the corresponding mid-value of the interval in the defuzzification operation. All these implications signify the effective results in time series forecasting, which are verified and validated with real-world time series data set.

1 Introduction

In time series data analysis and forecasting, it includes the problems associated with prediction of daily temperature, short-range as well as long-range rainfall amount, daily stock index price, economic growth of a country, etc. The fuzzy logic has the capability to deal with uncertainties involved in time series events. Using the concept of fuzzy logic, Song and Chissom [1] introduced the first model in 1991 to deal with the uncertainty and imprecise knowledge contained in time series data. In their modeling approach, each of the TSVs is represented by the fuzzy linguistic variables, and modeled and simulated them together to obtain the predicted value. They referred their model as "fuzzy time series (FTS)". Recently, various modifications are suggested by the researchers [2–5] to improve the predictive skill of one-factor time series data set.

In the FTS modeling approach, there are four significant factors, which predominantly impact on the performance of the FTS model [5], as: (a) selection of the effective length of intervals, (b) determination of the DM of each historical TSV, (c) inclusion of the high-order FLRs, and (d) defuzzification operation. Hence, the contribution of this work is fourfold, as: (a) **First**, for the selection of

© Springer International Publishing AG 2017
B.U. Shankar et al. (Eds.): PReMI 2017, LNCS 10597, pp. 243–253, 2017.
https://doi.org/10.1007/978-3-319-69900-4_31

the effective length of intervals, an LP model has been formulated and integrated with the FTS model. Its main objective is to minimize the proximities between lower and upper bounds of the corresponding interval; (b) **Second**, the DM of each historical TSV is determined based on its involvement in the universe of discourse; (c) **Third**, this study employs the high-order FLRs (see Eq. (2)) to improve the performance of the model, because high-order FLRs consider more linguistic values in comparison to first-order FLRs [5]; and (d) **Fourth**, for the defuzzification operation, this study uses the corresponding DM of each TSV along with the mid-value of each corresponding interval.

Based on these improvements, this study presents two models. The first model is exclusively based on the concept of FTS. The second model is based on the integration of an LP model with the FTS model (i.e., first model). The main intent of this LP model is to optimize the proximities between intervals. To validate the proposed models, experiments are conducted with the TAIEX index data set [6].

Organization of the article is presented as follows. Various theories of the FTS modeling approach are discussed in Sect. 2. Basics of the LP and model formulation are also discussed in this section. Two proposed models are presented in Sect. 3. In Sect. 4, various empirical analyzes are discussed followed by conclusion in Sect. 5.

2   Preliminaries

In this section, basic concepts of the FTS and LP are briefly discussed.

2.1   FTS: Basic Definitions

Here, a few important definitions of the FTS are presented. In the FTS, each TSV is represented by the fuzzy linguistic variable.

Definition 1 (Fuzzy time series (FTS)) [1]. Let $M(t)(t = \ldots, 0, 1, 2, \ldots) \subseteq R$, and can be considered as the universe of discourse on which fuzzy sets $\mu_i(t)(i = 1, 2, \ldots)$ be defined. Let $G(t)$ be a collection of $\mu_i(t)(i = 1, 2, \ldots)$. Then, $G(t)$ is called a FTS on $M(t)(t = \ldots, 0, 1, 2, \ldots)$.

Definition 2 (Fuzzy logical relationship (FLR)) [1]. Consider that $G(t-1) = A_i$ and $G(t) = A_j$, where $G(t)$ is assumed to be caused by $G(t-1)$. The relationship between $G(t)$ and $G(t-1)$ is termed as a FLR between A_i and A_j, which is defined, as:

$$A_i \to A_j, \tag{1}$$

where A_i and A_j are termed as left-hand side (LHS) and right-hand side (RHS) of the FLR "$A_i \to A_j$", respectively.

Definition 3 (High-order FLR) [5]. In any FLR, if a $G(t)$ is influenced by more than one events $G(t-1), G(t-2), \ldots$, and $G(t-n)$ $(n > 0)$, then such relationship is referred as high-order FLR. This can be represented, as:

$$G(t-n), \ldots, G(t-2), G(t-1) \to G(t) \tag{2}$$

2.2   Formulation of LP Model for the Proximity Problem

Let $U = [L_B, U_B]$ be the universe of discourse, where L_B and U_B be its lower and upper bounds. The U is discretized into n-intervals of equal lengths, as: $I_1 = [l_1, u_1]$, $I_2 = [l_2, u_2]$, ..., $I_n = [l_n, u_n]$. Let $M_1, M_2, \ldots, M_n$ be the centroids or mid-values of the corresponding intervals. A process of intervals optimization is depicted in Fig. 1. In this study, it is assumed that this process initiates from the initial lower bound (i.e., l_1), then goes to the initial upper bound (i.e., u_1), then moves to the second upper bound, third upper bound, and so on until the last upper bound is covered (i.e., $u_2, u_3, \ldots, u_n$). Based on this assumption, the objective function (OF) and constraints are defined [7], which is presented next.

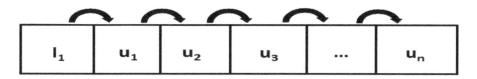

Fig. 1. Process of interval optimization.

The LP model formulation. Let x_i = effective length of interval which is required to maintain the proximity $(i = 1, 2, \ldots, n)$.

The LP model. The OF is defined, as:

$$\text{Min (total lengths) } Z = l_1 x_1 + u_1 x_2 + u_2 x_3 + u_3 x_4 + \cdots + u_n x_{n+1} \qquad (3)$$

subject to the constraints

$$l_1 x_1 + u_1 x_2 \geq M_1$$
$$l_2 x_2 + u_2 x_3 \geq M_2$$
$$l_3 x_3 + u_3 x_4 \geq M_3$$
$$\vdots$$
$$l_n x_{n-1} + u_n x_n \geq M_n \qquad (4)$$

and $\qquad\qquad x_1, x_2, \cdots, x_n \geq 0.$

In Eq. (3), the set of $b_i = \{l_1, u_1, u_2, u_3, \ldots, u_n\}$ are coefficients representing the per unit change of the decision variable $x_i = \{x_1, x_2, x_3, \ldots, x_n\}$, which is associated with the value of the OF. In Eq. (4), the set of $a_{ij} = \{(l_1, u_1), (l_2, u_2), (l_3, u_3), \ldots, (l_n, u_n)\}$ are referred as the input-output coefficients. These represent the boundaries of the intervals associated with the variable x_i. These coefficients can be positive, negative or zero. The set of $m_i = \{M_1, M_2, M_3, \ldots, M_n\}$ are the total availability of the ith resource. Forecasting accuracy of the FTS modeling approach mainly depends on the selection of appropriate interval lengths. Therefore, to resolve this problem, an LP model is formulated using Eq. (3) to select the appropriate length of intervals. For this LP model, constraints are defined in Eq. (4).

To solve this LP model using the simplex method [7], it is required to convert the problem into its standard form. Therefore, for the minimization type of the OF (see Eq. (3)), it is required to convert it into maximization type, by using the relation presented, as follows:

$$\text{Min (total lengths) Z} = -\text{Max } Z^* \tag{5}$$

where $Z^* = -Z$.

Again, all the constraints in Eq. (4) are of type "$\geq$", so we should add m surplus variables (S_i) and subtract m artificial variables (A_i) in each constraint. Hence, the resulting constraints becomes:

$$\sum_{i=1}^{n} l_i x_i + \sum_{i=2}^{n} l_i x_{i+1} - S_i + A_i = M_n \tag{6}$$

where $x_i, S_i, A_i \geq 0, i = 1, 2, \ldots, m$.

Each slack variable (A_i) represents an unused resource, therefore, such variables are added to the OF with zero coefficients. Each surplus variable (S_i) is considered as the amount exceed values *w.r.t.* a particular resource. These variables are also termed as *negative slack variables*. Both surplus and slack variables carry a zero coefficient in the OF.

Now, the OF (see Eq. (3)) and the constraints (see Eq. (4)) can be converted into the standard form based on the Eqs. (5) and (6), as:

$$\text{Min (total lengths) Z} = -l_1 x_1 - u_1 x_2 - u_2 x_3 - u_3 x_4 - \cdots - u_n x_n \tag{7}$$

subject to the constraints

$$l_1 x_1 + u_1 x_2 - S_1 + A_1 = M_1$$
$$l_2 x_2 + u_2 x_3 - S_2 + A_2 = M_2$$
$$l_3 x_3 + u_3 x_4 - S_3 + A_3 = M_3$$
$$\vdots$$
$$l_n x_{n-1} + u_n x_n - S_n + A_n = M_n \tag{8}$$

and $x_1, x_2, \cdots, x_n \geq 0$; $S_1, S_2, \cdots, S_n \geq 0$; $A_1, A_2, \cdots, A_n \geq 0$.

Detail descriptions to solve this LP model using simplex method can be found in [7].

3   Proposed Models

This section introduces two different models. In the first phase, the existing Chen's model [8] is modified, and try to obtain the predictive values. This initial model is termed as *High-Order FTS Model (HOFTSM)*. In the second phase, an LP model is formulated, and integrated with the *HOFTSM* to obtain the optimal interval lengths. This model is referred as *High-Order FTS-LP Model (HOFTS-LPM)*.

Table 1. TAIEX index data set.

Date (dd/mm/yyyy)	Actual TAIEX index
1/12/1992	3646.80
2/12/1992	3635.70
3/12/1992	3614.10
4/12/1992	3651.40
...	...
22/12/1992	3578.00
23/12/1992	3448.20
24/12/1992	3456.00
28/12/1992	3327.70
29/12/1992	3377.10

Table 2. Intervals along with their corresponding mid-values for the TAIEX index data set.

Interval	Mid-Value	Corresponding data
$a_1 = [3325.70, 3363.69]$	3344.70	3327.70
$a_2 = [3363.69, 3401.68]$	3382.69	3377.10
$a_3 = [3401.68, 3439.68]$	3420.68	Nil
...	...	...
$a_{12} = [3743.61, 3781.60]$	3762.60	3755.80, 3761.00, 3776.60, 3746.80

3.1 High-Order FTS Model (HOFTSM)

The HOFTSM is simulated using the historical time series data set of the TAIEX index [6] (see Table 1). The functionality of each phase of the model is presented next.

Step 1. *Provide the boundary of the historical time series data set by defining the universe of discourse U, as:* $U = [A_{min} - M_1, A_{max} + M_2]$, *where A_{min} and A_{max} be the minimum and maximum values of the historical time series data set. Here, M_1 and M_2 are two positive numbers. In Table 1, it is observed that $A_{min} = 3327.70$ and $A_{max} = 3776.60$. Therefore, initially, it is considered that $M_1 = 2$ and $M_2 = 5$. Hence, in this study, the universe of discourse is, as:* $U = [3325.70, 3781.60]$.

Step 2. *Descretize the universe of discourse U into n-intervals of equal lengths based on Eq. (9), as:*

$$a_i = [L_B + (i-1)\frac{U_B - L_B}{j}, L_B + i\frac{U_B - L_B}{j}] \qquad (9)$$

Table 3. Fuzzified TAIEX index data set and their corresponding DMs.

Date (dd/mm/yyyy)	Actual TAIEX index	Fuzzified TAIEX index	Degree of membership	Mid-Value
1/12/1992	3646.80	A_9	0.70	3648.63
2/12/1992	3635.70	A_9	0.68	3648.63
3/12/1992	3614.10	A_8	0.63	3610.64
4/12/1992	3651.40	A_9	0.71	3648.63
5/12/1992	3727.90	A_{11}	0.88	3724.61
...	...	...	...	...
22/12/1992	3578.00	A_7	0.55	3572.65
23/12/1992	3448.20	A_4	0.27	3458.67
24/12/1992	3456.00	A_4	0.29	3458.67
28/12/1992	3327.70	A_1	0.004	3344.70
29/12/1992	3377.10	A_2	0.11	3382.69

Table 4. Fourth-order FLRs for the TAIEX index data set.

Fourth-order FLR
$A_9, A_9, A_8, A_9 \rightarrow ?\langle 5/12/1992 \rangle$
$A_9, A_8, A_9, A_{11} \rightarrow ?\langle 7/12/1992 \rangle$
$A_8, A_9, A_{11}, A_{12} \rightarrow ?\langle 8/12/1992 \rangle$
$A_9, A_{11}, A_{12}, A_{12} \rightarrow ?\langle 9/12/1992 \rangle$
...

for $i = 1, 2, \ldots, n$, and j represents the number of intervals which are considered during the simulation. Here, $L_B = 3325.70$, $U_B = 3781.60$, and $j = 12$. In this study, simulation is initiated with maximum 12 intervals, because more than 12 intervals can convert the whole sample into the crisp value, which would be the violation of the FTS modeling approach. All these intervals, their corresponding data, and mid-values are listed in Table 2.

Step 3. *Define fuzzy linguistic variable* A_i, *for each of the defined intervals.* For this purpose, 12 fuzzy linguistic variables are defined, as: A_1 (very low), A_2 (not very low), ..., A_{12} (very very high), on the U, for the historical time series data set of the TAIEX index, because total 12 intervals are defined.

Step 4. *Obtain the DM for each historical TSV on the* U, *based on the triangular membership function.* In this step, the DM of each historical TSV is determined using the triangular membership function. This function can be defined by the following equation, as [9]:

$$f(X_i; L_B, U_B) = \frac{X_i - L_B}{U_B - L_B}, \quad L_B \leq X_i \leq U_B \tag{10}$$

Here, each input vector X_i is represented by the historical TSV corresponding to each day.

Step 5. *Fuzzify each of the historical TSVs.* The fuzzified TSVs, their corresponding DMs and mid-values are listed in Table 3.

Step 6. *Obtain the high-order FLRs (based on Eq. (2)).* Based on Eq. (2), the fourth-order FLRs are established between the fuzzified TSVs. For example, in Table 3, the fuzzified TSVs for days 1/12/1992, 2/12/1992, 3/12/1992, 4/12/1992, and 5/12/1992 are A_9, A_9, A_8, A_9, and A_{11}, respectively. Here, to establish the fourth-order FLR among these fuzzified TSVs, it is considered that A_{11} is caused by the previous four fuzzified TSVs A_9, A_9, A_8, and A_9. Hence, the fourth-order FLR is represented in the following form:

$$A_9, A_9, A_8, A_9 \rightarrow A_{11} \tag{11}$$

Remaining fourth-order FLRs are obtained in the manner, and depicted in Table 4. In this table, each symbol "?" represents the *desired output* for corresponding day "t" in the symbol "$\langle \rangle$", which would be determined by the proposed model.

Step 7. *Defuzzify the historical TSVs, and obtain the forecasted values, as:*
- Initially, obtain the nth-order FLR for forecasting the $G(t)$, as:

$$A_{tn}, A_{t(n-1)}, \ldots, A_{t1} \rightarrow ?\langle t \rangle, \tag{12}$$

where "t" represents a day, which we want to obtain the forecasted value, and "n" is the order of FLR ($n \geq 4$). Here, $A_{tn}, A_{t(n-1)}, \ldots$, and A_{t1} are the previous state's fuzzified TSVs from days, $G(t-n), \ldots, G(t-2)$ to $G(t-1)$.

- Find the intervals that are associated with fuzzy linguistic variables $A_{tn}, A_{t(n-1)}, \ldots$, and A_{t1}, and let these intervals be $a_n, a_{n-1}, \ldots, a_1$, respectively. Consider that these intervals have the corresponding midpoints, as: $P_n, P_{n-1}, \ldots, P_1$.

- Replace each of the previous state's fuzzified TSVs of Eq. (12) with their corresponding mid-points, as:

$$P_n, P_{n-1}, \ldots, P_1 \rightarrow ?\langle t \rangle, n \geq 4 \tag{13}$$

- Get the DM of historical TSV corresponding to each fuzzy linguistic variable involved in Eq. (12), as:

$$D_n, D_{n-1}, \ldots, D_1 \rightarrow ?\langle t \rangle, n \geq 4 \tag{14}$$

- Use the following formula to compute the desired output "?" for the corresponding day "t", as:

$$Forecast(t) = \frac{\sum_{i=1}^{N} P_i D_i}{\sum D_i} \tag{15}$$

Here, N is the total number of mid-points (P_i) to be used, and each D_i represents the DM of the TSV corresponding to each fuzzy linguistic variable.

3.2   High-Order FTS-LP Model (HOFTS-LPM)

To make the proposed HOFTSM more efficient, an LP model is formulated, and integrated with it. The main intent of this LP model is to select the appropriate interval lengths by minimizing the proximities between lower and upper bounds of the intervals (Tables 5 and 6).

Step 1. *Repeat Steps 1–7 of the HOFTSM (presented in Subsect. 3.1).*

Step 2. *Define the OF and constraints based on Eqs. (3) and (4), respectively. In the HOFTSM, the universe of discourse, $U = [3325.70, 3781.60]$, is partitioned into 12 equal length of intervals, as: $a_1 = [3325.70, 3363.69]$, $a_2 = [3363.69, 3401.68]$, ..., $a_{12} = [3743.61, 3781.60]$. Here, each a_i can be represented, as: $a_i = [l_i, u_i]$, where each l_i and u_i represent the lower and upper bounds of an interval. Now, based on these lower and upper bounds, an LP model can be represented, as:*
The LP model formulation. *Let x_i = effective length of interval which is required to maintain the proximity $(i = 1, 2, \ldots, n)$.*
The LP model. *The OF is defined, as:*

$$\text{Min (total lengths) } Z = 3325.70x_1 + 3363.69x_2 + 3401.68x_3 + \cdots + 3781.60x_{13} \tag{16}$$

subject to the constraints

$$3325.70x_1 + 3363.69x_2 \geq 3344.70$$
$$3363.69x_2 + 3401.68x_3 \geq 3382.69$$
$$3401.68x_3 + 3439.68x_4 \geq 3420.68$$

$$\vdots$$

$$3743.61x_{12} + 3781.60x_{13} \geq 3762.60 \tag{17}$$

and $$x_1, x_2, \cdots, x_{13} \geq 0$$

Step 3. *Obtain the solution of the LP model in terms of x_i, as defined in Step 2, based on the simplex method.*

Step 4. *Compute the proximities for each of the intervals, as:*

$$x_i(new) = x_i(old) + Rand(-c_v, c_v) \tag{18}$$

Here, *Rand* is a random function that gives the random value in the range of $[-c_v, c_v]$, where c_v is a user's defined constant value.

Step 5. *Update the set of intervals, as:*

$$a_1(new) = [l_1(old) + x_1(new), u_1(old) + x_2(new)]$$
$$a_2(new) = [l_2(old), u_2(old) + x_3(new)]$$
$$\vdots$$
$$a_n(new) = [l_n(old), u_n(old) + x_n(new)] \tag{19}$$

Step 6. *Repeat Steps 1–5 until the optimal solution is found.*

Table 5. A sample of intervals produced by the HOFTS-LPM for the TAIEX index data set.

Iteration No	Value of $x_i(i = 1, 2, \ldots, 13)$	Value of Z	Produced intervals
1	$x_1 = 0.0$, $x_2 = 2.0$, $x_3 = -15.0$, ..., $x_{13} = 0.0$	0.0	$a_1 = [3325.70, 3365.69]$, $a_2 = [3363.69, 3386.68]$, $a_3 = [3401.68, 3423.68]$, ..., $a_{12} = [3743.61, 3781.60]$
2	$x_1 = 0.0$, $x_2 = -7.0$, $x_3 = -2.995$, ..., $x_{13} = 0.0$	21435.88	$a_1 = [3325.70, 3365.69]$, $a_2 = [3363.69, 3398.69]$, $a_3 = [3401.68, 3440.68]$, ..., $a_{12} = [3743.61, 3781.60]$
3	$x_1 = 0.0$, $x_2 = -34.0$, $x_3 = -29.99$, ..., $x_{13} = 0.0$	21483.88	$a_1 = [3325.70, 3329.69]$, $a_2 = [3363.69, 3371.69]$, $a_3 = [3401.68, 3471.68]$, ..., $a_{12} = [3743.61, 3781.60]$
4	$x_1 = 0.0$, $x_2 = -31.0$, $x_3 = -13.99$, ..., $x_{13} = 0.0$	21455.88	$a_1 = [3325.70, 3332.69]$, $a_2 = [3363.69, 3387.70]$, $a_3 = [3401.68, 3434.68]$, ..., $a_{12} = [3743.61, 3781.60]$
5	$x_1 = 0.0$, $x_2 = -26.0$, $x_3 = -52.99$, ..., $x_{13} = 0.0$	21409.82	$a_1 = [3325.70, 3337.69]$, $a_2 = [3363.69, 3348.70]$, $a_3 = [3401.68, 3433.69]$, ..., $a_{12} = [3743.61, 3781.60]$

Table 6. Forecasting results of TAIEX index data set for 5 different iterations using HOFTS-LPM (based on 4th-order FLRs).

Evaluation parameter	1st iteration	2nd iteration	3rd iteration	4th iteration	5th iteration
RMSE	85.48	84.57	109.16	48.12	47.11

4   Empirical Analyzes

The performance of the two proposed models is evaluated using two parameters, namely root mean square error (RMSE) and average forecasting error rate (AFER) [10]. Performance of the two proposed models are compared together based on the forecasting results, obtained for the TAIEX index data set. During the simulation process, 12 intervals are used. Experimental results are obtained with 4th-order to 7th-order of FLRs. Comparison results are presented in Table 7, in terms of the average of RMSEs. From Table 7, it is obvious that the proposed HOFTS-LPM outperforms the HOFTSM.

Table 7. Performance analysis of the proposed models (in terms of Average RMSE) for different orders of FLRs (with number of intervals = 12).

Order (Data set)	HOFTSM	HOFTS-LPM
4th (TAIEX index)	93.21	47.11
5th (TAIEX index)	105.85	65.12
6th (TAIEX index)	118.40	88.57
7th (TAIEX index)	129.78	94.74
Average RMSE	349.91	73.89

Table 8. Comparison of the proposed HOFTS-LPM with existing FTS models.

Evaluation parameter	Model [8]	Model [11]	Model [12]	Model [13]	Model [6]	Proposed HOFTS-LPM
RMSE	134.4	114.2	107.2	85.7	74.7	47.11
AFER	3.50	2.37	2.47	1.65	1.71	1.04

Forecasting accuracy of the proposed HOFTS-LPM is compared with the existing FTS models [6,8,11–13]. In this comparison, the forecasted values for the TAIEX index data set are obtained with 12 intervals. During this simulation process, the forecasted values for the proposed HOFTS-LPM are obtained using the 4th-order FLRs. Comparison results are presented in Table 8. The smaller values of RMSE and AFER for the proposed HOFTS-LPM show that its forecasting accuracy is far better than considered competing models.

5   Conclusion

In this study, two models are proposed to improve the predictive skill of one-factor time series data set. The initial model is termed as the HOFTSM. This model is the modification of the Chen's model [8]. In this model, initially equal-sized of intervals are used to fuzzify the historical time series data set. Simulation of this model is performed using the high-order FLRs. However, in the searching for more optimal results, this study further suggests the integration of the LP model with the HOFTSM. This model is referred as the HOFTS-LPM. In the HOFTS-LPM, solutions of the integrated LP model is obtained using the simplex method. The proposed two models are verified and validated with the historical time series data set of the TAIEX index. The empirical analyzes show that the predictive skill of the HOFTS-LPM is more robust than the HOFTSM.

Acknowledgment. This research is supported by the Department of Science and Technology (DST)-SERB, Government of India, under Grant EEQ/2016/000021.

References

1. Song, Q., Chissom, B.S.: Forecasting enrollments with fuzzy time series: Part I. The Annual Meeting of the Mid-South Educational Research Association, Lexington, KY (1991)
2. Chen, T.L., Cheng, C.H., Teoh, H.J.: Fuzzy time-series based on fibonacci sequence for stock price forecasting. Phys. A Stat. Mech. Appl. **380**, 377–390 (2007)
3. Wong, H.L., Tu, Y.H., Wang, C.C.: Application of fuzzy time series models for forecasting the amount of Taiwan export. Expert Syst. Appl. **37**(2), 1465–1470 (2010)
4. Singh, P.: Rainfall and financial forecasting using fuzzy time series and neural networks based model. Int. J. Mach. Learn. Cybern. 1–16 (2016). doi:10.1007/s13042-016-0548-5
5. Singh, P.: High-order fuzzy-neuro-entropy integration-based expert system for time series forecasting. Neural Comput. Appl. **28**(12), 3851–3868 (2016)
6. Lu, W., Chen, X., Pedrycz, W., Liu, X., Yang, J.: Using interval information granules to improve forecasting in fuzzy time series. Int. J. Approximate Reasoning **57**, 1–18 (2015)
7. Sharma, J.K.: Operation Reserach, 4th edn. Macmillan Publishers India Ltd., New Delhi (2009)
8. Chen, S.M.: Forecasting enrollments based on fuzzy time series. Fuzzy Sets Syst. **81**, 311–319 (1996)
9. Ross, T.J.: Fuzzy Logic with Engineering Applications, 3rd edn. Wiley India Pvt Ltd., New Delhi (2013)
10. Singh, P., Borah, B.: An efficient time series forecasting model based on fuzzy time series. Eng. Appl. Artif. Intell. **26**(10), 2443–2457 (2013)
11. Wang, L., Liu, X., Pedrycz, W.: Effective intervals determined by information granules to improve forecasting in fuzzy time series. Expert Syst. Appl. **40**(14), 5673–5679 (2013)
12. Wang, L., Liu, X., Pedrycz, W., Shao, Y.: Determination of temporal information granules to improve forecasting in fuzzy time series. Expert Syst. Appl. **41**(6), 3134–3142 (2014)
13. Chen, S.M., Kao, P.Y.: TAIEX forecasting based on fuzzy time series, particle swarm optimization techniques and support vector machines. Inf. Sci. **247**, 62–71 (2013)

Third Order Backward Elimination Approach for Fuzzy-Rough Set Based Feature Selection

Soumen Ghosh⬤, P.S.V.S. Sai Prasad$^{(\boxtimes)}$⬤, and C. Raghavendra Rao⬤

School of Computer and Information Sciences,
University of Hyderabad, Hyderabad, India
hitkmca@yahoo.in, {saics,crrcs}@uohyd.ernet.in

Abstract. Two important control strategies for Rough Set based reduct computation are Sequential Forward Selection (SFS), and Sequential Backward Elimination (SBE). SBE methods have an inherent advantage of resulting in reduct whereas SFS approaches usually result in superset of reduct. The fuzzy rough sets is an extension of rough sets used for reduct computation in Hybrid Decision Systems. The SBE based fuzzy rough reduct computation has not attempted till date by researchers due to the fuzzy similarity relation of a set of attributes will not typically lead to fuzzy similarity relation of the subset of attributes. This paper proposes a novel SBE approach based on Gaussian Kernel-based fuzzy rough set reduct computation. The complexity of the proposed approach is the order of three while existing are fourth order. Empirical experiment conducted on standard benchmark datasets established the relevance of the proposed approach.

Keywords: Rough sets · Fuzzy-rough sets · Feature selection · Reduct computation · Gaussian Kernel · Backward elimination

1 Introduction

Feature selection is an important technique for dimensionality reduction which is widely used in the field of Data mining and Machine Learning. It is a crucial preprocessing stage in Knowledge Discovery in Databases (KDD). The feature selection or feature subset selection is the process of selecting a subset of features by removing redundant features without resulting in information loss. Pawlak [13] developed Rough Set Theory (RST), which got established as a popular soft computing methodology for knowledge discovery amidst uncertainty. Reduct denotes the subset of the features selected using RST.

Classical RST is used for reduct computation in complete symbolic decision systems. But it is inappropriate for reduct computation in real-valued or hybrid decision systems (HDS). Fuzzy rough set model was introduced by Dubois and Prade [3] in 1990 for dealing with hybrid decision systems. Several extensions to Dubois and Prade Fuzzy-Rough Set model were introduced in literature such as

© Springer International Publishing AG 2017
B.U. Shankar et al. (Eds.): PReMI 2017, LNCS 10597, pp. 254–262, 2017.
https://doi.org/10.1007/978-3-319-69900-4_32

Radzikowska and Kerre's model [14], Hu model [5] and Gaussian Kernel-based Fuzzy Rough Set model [6] etc. Parallely reduct computation approaches are developed in these models which are primarily Sequential Forward Selection (SFS) based algorithms [4, 6, 7, 9, 16–20].

Computing all the possible reducts of a given decision system or computing minimum length optimal reduct is proved to be an NP-Hard problem [14]. Hence researchers are developing the heuristic approach for near optimal reduct computation algorithms. Two important aspects of reduct computing algorithm are the dependency measure (heuristic), used for assessing the quality of the reduct, and the control strategy used for attribute selection. Two important control strategies for reduct computation in literature are SFS and SBE approaches. In SFS, reduct is initialized to empty set and in every iteration the attribute with the optimal heuristic measure is included into the reduct till the end condition is reached. In SBE, reduct is initialized to all the attributes, and with every attribute, a test is conducted to check whether the omission of the attribute doesn't lead to information loss. If an attribute is found to be redundant then it is removed from the reduct. The SBE approaches will always result in a reduct without redundancy, and the SFS approaches can not guaranty the redundancy less reduct computation.

The complexity of the reduct computation algorithm is much higher in fuzzy rough sets compared to classical rough sets. It is observed that while many SFS and SBE approaches are available for the classical rough sets, in our literature exploration, we have not come across any SBE approach for fuzzy rough sets.

This paper presents an efficient and effective SBE based reduct computation algorithm for Gaussian Kernel-based fuzzy rough sets (GK-FRS). The proposed methodology acquires significance as the theoretical time complexity is of third order $(O(|C||U|^2))$ which is significantly better in comparison to existing fuzzy rough set reduct algorithm having fourth order complexity $(O(|C|^2|U|^2))$. Cardinality of conditional attributes and universe of objects is denoted by $|C|$ and $|U|$ respectively.

The organization of this paper is given here. Section 2 discusses the basic concepts of rough sets and fuzzy rough sets. Section 3 describes the fundamentals of GK-FRS. Section 4 details the proposed approach for SBE reduct computation in GK-FRS. Experiments and results are provided in Sect. 5 followed by conclusion.

2   Theoretical Background

2.1   Rough Sets and Fuzzy-Rough Sets

The Rough Set Theory is a useful tool to discover data dependency and reduce the dimensionality of the data using data alone. Fuzzy-rough sets is a hybrid model of rough sets and fuzzy sets with ability to deal with quantitative data. Basic rough set theory and fuzzy-rough set theory are described in [4, 18]. The concepts of GK-FRS are described below using the Hybrid Decision Systems (HDS):

HDS is represented by $(U, C \cup \{d\}, V, f)$ where in U is the set of objects and C is the collection of heterogeneous attributes such as quantitative, qualitative, logical, set valued, interval based etc., and 'd' is the qualitative decision attribute.

2.2   Gaussian Kernel Function

The Gaussian function is a very popular kernel which is extensively used in SVM and RBF neural networks. The similarity between two objects $u_i, u_j \in U$ is computed using Gaussian kernel function $k(u_i, u_j)$ given in Eq. (1)

$$k(u_i, u_j) = exp\left(-\frac{||u_i - u_j||^2}{2\delta^2}\right) \qquad (1)$$

The distance of object u_i to object u_j is given by $||u_i - u_j||$ and a user controlled parameter δ influences the resulting quality of approximation. $||u_i - u_j||$ is computed as [20]:

$$||u_i - u_j|| = \frac{|a(u_i) - a(u_j)|}{4\delta_a} \qquad (2)$$

where $a \in C$ is a quantitative conditional attribute and δ_a represents the standard deviation of a.

3   Gaussian Kernel Based Fuzzy Rough Sets

The kernel method and rough set theory are the two imperative aspects of pattern recognition. The kernel function maps the data into a high dimensional space whereas rough set approximate the space. Qinghua Hu et al. [6] introduced Gaussian kernel function with fuzzy rough sets (GK-FRS) by incorporating Gaussian Kernel function with fuzzy-rough sets. The Gaussian kernel based fuzzy lower and upper approximations [6,20] of a decision system is calculated as:

$$\underline{R_G}d_i(x) = inf_{y \notin d_i}\sqrt{1 - R_G^2(x, y)} \qquad (3)$$

$$\overline{R_G}d_i(x) = sup_{y \in d_i}R_G(x, y) \qquad (4)$$

where $d_i \in U/\{d\}$ and $x \in U$. For a given $B \subseteq C$, R_G^B denotes Gaussian Kernel-based fuzzy similarity relation expressed as a matrix of order $|U| \times |U|$. For any $x, y \in U$, $R_G^B(x, y)$ represents the fuzzy similarity between the object x and object y based on B attributes. Based on Proposition 3 in [20], $R_G^{\{a\} \cup \{b\}}$ can be calculated using $R_G^{\{a\}}$ and $R_G^{\{b\}}$ by element-wise matrix multiplication as given in Eq. (5)

$$R_G^{\{a\} \cup \{b\}}(x, y) = R_G^{\{a\}}(x, y) \times R_G^{\{b\}}(x, y) \qquad \forall x, y \in U \qquad (5)$$

Indiscernible classes based on decision attribute is $U/\{d\} = \{d_1, d_2, ...d_l\}$, a partition of U. The fuzzy positive region is computed as:

$$POS_B(\{d\}) = \bigcup_{i=1}^{l} \underline{R_G^B} d_i. \tag{6}$$

The measure of dependency of 'd' on $B \subseteq C$ is given by

$$\gamma_B(\{d\}) = \frac{|POS_B(\{d\})|}{|U|} = \frac{|\bigcup_{i=1}^{l} \underline{R_G^B} d_i|}{|U|} \tag{7}$$

where $\bigcup_{i=1}^{l} \underline{R_G^B} d_i = \sum_i \sum_{x \in d_i} \underline{R_G^B} d_i(x)$.

In 2010 Qinghua Hu et al. [6], proposed a feature selection algorithm FS-GKA which is based on computing Dependency with Gaussian kernel approximation (DGKA). Later Zeng et al. [20] used this DGKA algorithm and proposed FRSA-NFS-HIS [20] algorithm for feature selection of the HDS. In 2016, Ghosh et al. [4] proposed an Improved Gaussian kernel approximation (IDGKA) algorithm for dependency computation and developed the algorithm MFRFS-NFS-HIS using IDGKA algorithm.

4   Proposed Backward Elimination Approach for Feature Selection

The nature of SBE based reduct computation requires $|C|$ iterations irrespectively of size of the reduct Red. The SFS based reduct computation benefit from the fact that the number of iterations is limited by the size of the reduct $|Red|$. In addition to this observation, the primary reason for the computational complexity of SBE stems from the fact that the relational representation (indiscernibility for classical RST, fuzzy similarity relation in fuzzy rough sets) of $C - \{a\}$ ($\forall a \in C$) can not be obtained from the relational representation of C. For example in fuzzy rough sets, fuzzy similarity matrix $R^{C-\{a\}}$ is usually not derivable directly from the R^C. This results in the requirement for recomputation of $R^{C-\{a\}}$ from similarity matrices of attributes of $C - \{a\}$.

The proposed SBE reduct computation algorithm BEA-GK-FRFS using GK-FRS emerged from the identification of possibility for deriving $R_G^{C-\{a\}}$ directly from R_G^C and $R_G^{\{a\}}$ as described bellow:

The Eq. (5) originally from literature [20] can be casted as Eq. (8)

$$R_G^C = R_G^{C-\{a\}} * R_G^{\{a\}} \tag{8}$$

where operator * represents the element wise matrix multiplication. Hence from Eq. (8) the required $R_G^{C-\{a\}}$ is obtained by

$$R_G^{C-\{a\}} = R_G^C / R_G^{\{a\}} \tag{9}$$

Equation (9) is well defined only when the atomic component $R_G^{\{a\}}$ does not contain zeros. The $R_G^{\{a\}}$ is free from zeros due to the Gaussian Kernel adaptation. However, the possible occurrence of zeros due to the system limitation is addressed by thresholding to ϵ (infinitesimal number). It is found by experimental verification that reduct computation is insensitive for this infinitesimal modification.

The composite component R_G^C, resulting from the multiplication of matrices is expected to have very very small value (> 0) and more so when $|C|$ is becoming larger. This infinitesimally small value will be represented by exact zero due to the system limitation in representation of numerical precision. These zeros are detrimental for carrying out the computation in Eq. (9). A logarithmic transformation aptly engineered to overcome this ill-conditioning scenario as shown in Eqs. (10–13).

$$R_G^C = e^{log_e(R_G^C)} \tag{10}$$

$$where \quad log_e(R_G^C) = \sum_{b \in C} log_e(R_G^{\{b\}}) \tag{11}$$

Here operations of log, exp and $\sum$ are defined as element-wise matrix operations. The required $R_G^{C-\{a\}}$ is computed as:

$$R_G^{C-\{a\}} = e^{log_e(R_G^{C-\{a\}})} \tag{12}$$

$$where \quad log_e(R_G^{C-\{a\}}) = log_e(R_G^C) - log_e(R_G^{\{a\}}) \tag{13}$$

The Eq. (13) follows from the Eq. (11).

Algorithm 1. Backward Elimination Approach for Gaussian Kernel based Fuzzy Rough Feature Selection (BEA-GK-FRFS)

Input: $DS = (U, C \cup \{d\})$
Output: Reduced attribute set *Red*
1: $Red = C$
2: Compute $R_G^{\{a\}}, \forall a \in C$ // Using Eq. (1)
3: Compute R_G^C and $\gamma_C(\{d\})$ // Using Eq. (10) and Eq. (7)
4: Order the attributes in assending order with respect to their $\gamma_{\{a\}}(\{d\}), \forall a \in C$
5: **for each** $a \in C$ **do**
6:      Compute $R_G^{Red-\{a\}}$ // Using Eq. (12)
7:      **if** $\gamma_{Red-\{a\}}(\{d\}) == \gamma_C(\{d\})$ **then**
8:          $Red = Red - \{a\}$
9:          $R_G^{Red} = R_G^{Red-\{a\}}$
10:      **end if**
11: **end for**
12: **return** *Red*

The proposed algorithm BEA-GK-FRFS is given in Algorithm 1. The order of checking the redundancy in SBE reduct algorithms has an influence on the resulting reduct [8]. BEA-GK-FRFS (line: 4) uses attributes in the ascending order by gamma measure. The time complexity of sequential forward selection based reduct computation algorithms is $O(|C|^2|U|^2)$ [20]. The order of time complexity of SBE based algorithms also is $O(|C|^2|U|^2)$ where in an iteration $R_G^{Red-\{a\}}$ requires $O(|C|)$ matrix operations. In BEA-GK-FRFS using Eqs. (12 and 13), $R_G^{Red-\{a\}}$ requires only two matrix operations. Hence, the time complexity of algorithm BEA-GK-FRFS is $O(|C||U|^2)$.

5   Experiments, Results and Analysis

The configuration of the system used for experiments is: CPU:Intel(R) Core i5, Clock Speed: 2.66 GHz, RAM:4 GB, OS:Ubuntu 16.04 LTS 64 bit, and Software:R Studio Version 1.0.136. Nine benchmark quantitative decision systems from UCI Machine Learning Repository [10] were used in the experiments. Out of these datasets, four(6–9 in Table 1) datasets were of large magnitude that memory for representing the fuzzy similarity matrices exceed the system limit. Hence, for these datasets, a stratified random sampling based sub-dataset are used in our experiment. The original size of the dataset is indicated in the bracket.

5.1   Comparative Experiments with MFRSA-NFS-HIS and FRSA-SBE Algorithms

The proposed BEA-GK-FRFS is implemented in R environment. Its performance is compared with the R implementation of MFRSA-NFS-HIS by Ghosh et al. [4] which was established to be an efficient fuzzy-rough set based reduct computation algorithm using SFS strategy. To aptly illustrate the relevance of proposed SBE algorithm FRSA-SBE is implemented in R environment following traditional SBE approach. FRSA-SBE is exactly same as BEA-GK-FRFS except for 6th step in Algorithm 1 wherein $R_G^{Red-\{a\}}$ is computed from the atomic component $R_G^b, \forall b \in (Red - a)$. These results are summarized in Table 1 reporting reduct length, computation time in seconds. Table 1 also reports computation gain percentage obtain by BEA-GK-FRFS over MFRSA-NFS-HIS and FRSA-SBE.

Analysis of Results

Based on the results in Table 1, BEA-GK-FRFS in general computationally efficient in comparison to other algorithms. MFRSA-NFS-HIS has performed better than FRSA-SBE establishing the reason for the precedence given to SFS approaches in comparison to SBE approaches till date. It is observed that on all decision systems especially large scale datasets such as Web, DNA, batch1cifar, Spambase, BEA-GK-FRFS has obtained significant computational gained (greater than 34%) over MFRSA-NFS-HIS validating empirically the betterment observed in theoretical time complexity of BEA-GK-FRFS.

Table 1. Comparison of BEA-GK-FRFS, MFRSA-NFS-HIS and FRSA-SBE algorithms

No	Name	Objects	Features	Reduct	Time(s)	Reduct	Time(s)	Reduct	Time(s)	MFRSA-NFS-HIS	FRSA-SBE
	Datasets			BEA-GK-FRFS		MFRSA-NFS-HIS		FRSA-SBE		Computation Gain	
1	German	1000	21	14	4.3639	10	6.5429	14	4.6329	33.30%	5.80%
2	Web	149	2557	34	18.6663	21	77.2455	34	243.9479	75.83%	92.34%
3	Movement libras	360	91	16	3.4101	14	9.8869	16	4.1788	65.50%	18.39%
4	Sonar Mines Rocks	208	61	9	0.6475	7	0.8072	9	0.6541	19.78%	1.01%
5	Image Segmentation	2310	19	14	29.1026	14	61.5604	14	28.1081	52.72%	-3.53%
6	Semeion	750(1593)	266	9	35.4708	10	47.2925	9	105.7689	24.99%	66.46%
7	Spambase	2000(4601)	58	40	66.2703	31	151.0811	40	279.2641	56.13%	76.26%
8	batch1cifar	200(10000)	3073	11	46.3598	7	70.7362	11	6236.6101	34.46%	99.25%
9	DNA	1000(2000)	181	22	63.8159	17	178.2636	22	106.8351	64.20%	40.26%

On small scale dataset such as German, Image Segmentation (small scale due to less $|C|$) Sona_Mines_Rocks no significant gain are obtained with respect to FRSA-SBE. This is due to the observation that when $|C|$ is less, direct matrix multiplication is performing similar to exponential and logarithmic operation.

5.2   Comparative Experiments with L-FRFS and B-FRFS Algorithms

R package "Rough Set" [15] is a collaborative effort by several researchers in bringing together established algorithm of rough sets and fuzzy rough sets into a unified framework. L-FRFS and B-FRFS are SFS based fuzzy rough reduct algorithm [9] were made available in Rough Set package. The experiment of reduct computation is performed with B-FRFS and L-FRFS using package implementation, in the same system used for proposed algorithm. It is observed from Table 2 that BEA-GK-FRFS has achieved highly significant computational gained (greater than 95%) compared to L-FRFS and B-FRFS.

Table 2. Comparison of algorithm L-FRFS and B-FRFS available in R package with BEA-GK-FRFS algorithm

No	Name	Objects	Features	Reduct	Time(s)	Reduct	Time(s)	Reduct	Time(s)	L-FRFS	B-FRFS
	Datasets			BEA-GK-FRFS		L-FRFS		B-FRFS		Computation Gain	
1	German	1000	21	14	4.3639	11	232.3581	11	230.9857	98.12%	98.11%
2	Web	149	2557	34	18.6663	20	2039.8099	19	1999.0284	99.08%	99.06%
3	Movement libras	360	91	16	3.4101	8	322.3365	8	323.5018	98.94%	98.95%
4	Sonar Mines Rocks	208	61	9	0.6475	5	24.7539	5	24.5041	97.38%	97.36%
5	Image Segmentation	2310	19	14	29.1026	16	2167.3889	16	2057.0676	98.65%	98.58%
6	Semeion	750(1593)	266	9	35.4708	10	2173.5678	10	2398.7749	98.36%	98.52%
7	Spambase	2000(4601)	58	40	66.2703	38	8730.7236	40	7893.0504	99.24%	99.16%
8	batch1cifar	200(10000)	3073	11	46.3598	2	1630.7886	2	1570.8852	97.15%	97.04%
9	DNA	1000(2000)	181	22	63.8159	1	1495.3266	18	4190.3028	95.73%	98.47%

We have also analysed performance of reduct in construction of classifier model[1], using 10 fold cross validation. No significant differences were observed in the classifier analysis between BEA-GK-FRFS and MFRSA-NFS-HIS.

---

[1] The details of classification experiment are not reported due to the space constraint.

6   Conclusion

Researchers of fuzzy rough sets have preferred SFS based reduct computation over SBE based owing to increased computation requirements in SBE. This work presented a novel SBE based reduct computation algorithm BEA-GK-FRFS in GK-FRS. The time complexity of BEA-GK-FRFS is third order $(O(|C||U|^2))$ in comparison to existing fuzzy rough set reduct algorithms having fourth order time complexity $(O(|C|^2|U|^2))$. Experiments conducted on benchmark datasets have validated the computation efficiency of BEA-GK-FRFS in comparison to existing fuzzy rough set reduct algorithms.

Acknowledgments. This work was supported by the Universities with Potential for Excellence (UPE) Phase-II, University of Hyderabad, Hyderabad, India.

References

1. Chouchoulas, A., Shen, Q.: Rough set-aided keyword reduction for text categorization. Appl. Artif. Intell. **15**(9), 843–873 (2001)
2. Cornelis, C., Jensen, R., Hurtado, G., Śle, D.: Attribute selection with fuzzy decision reducts. Inf. Sci. **180**(2), 209–224 (2010)
3. Dubois, D., Prade, H.: Rough fuzzy sets and fuzzy rough sets. Int. J. Gen. Syst. **17**(2–3), 191–209 (1990)
4. Ghosh, S., Sai Prasad, P.S.V.S., Raghavendra Rao, C.: An efficient Gaussian kernel based fuzzy-rough set approach for feature selection. In: Sombattheera, C., Stolzenburg, F., Lin, F., Nayak, A. (eds.) MIWAI 2016. LNCS (LNAI), vol. 10053, pp. 38–49. Springer, Cham (2016). doi:10.1007/978-3-319-49397-8_4
5. Hu, Q., Xie, Z., Yu, D.: Hybrid attribute reduction based on a novel fuzzy-rough model and information granulation. Pattern Recogn. **40**(12), 3509–3521 (2007)
6. Hu, Q., Zhang, L., Chen, D., Pedrycz, W., Yu, D.: Gaussian kernel based fuzzy rough sets: model, uncertainty measures and applications. Int. J. Approximate Reasoning **51**(4), 453–471 (2010)
7. Jensen, R., Shen, Q.: Fuzzy-rough attribute reduction with application to web categorization. Fuzzy Sets Syst. **141**(3), 469–485 (2004)
8. Jensen, R., Shen, Q.: Rough set based feature selection: a review. In: Rough Computing: Theories, Technologies and Applications, pp. 70–107 (2007)
9. Jensen, R., Shen, Q.: New approaches to fuzzy-rough feature selection. IEEE Trans. Fuzzy Syst. **17**(4), 824–838 (2009)
10. Lichman, M.: UCI machine learning repository (2013)
11. Mi, J.-S., Zhang, W.-X.: An axiomatic characterization of a fuzzy generalization of rough sets. Inf. Sci. **160**(1), 235–249 (2004)
12. Moser, B.: On representing and generating kernels by fuzzy equivalence relations. J. Mach. Learn. Res. **7**, 2603–2620 (2006)
13. Pawlak, Z.: Rough sets. Int. J. Comput. Inf. Sci. **11**(5), 341–356 (1982)
14. Radzikowska, A.M., Kerre, E.E.: A comparative study of fuzzy rough sets. Fuzzy Sets Syst. **126**(2), 137–155 (2002)
15. Riza, L.S., Janusz, A., Slezak, D., Cornelis, C., Herrera, F., Benitez, J.M., Bergmeir, C., Stawicki, S.: Package roughsets, 5 September 2015

16. Sai Prasad, P.S.V.S., Raghavendra Rao, C.: IQuickReduct: an improvement to quick reduct algorithm. In: Sakai, H., Chakraborty, M.K., Hassanien, A.E., Ślęzak, D., Zhu, W. (eds.) RSFDGrC 2009. LNCS (LNAI), vol. 5908, pp. 152–159. Springer, Heidelberg (2009). doi:10.1007/978-3-642-10646-0_18

17. Sai Prasad, P.S.V.S., Raghavendra Rao, C.: Extensions to IQuickReduct. In: Sombattheera, C., Agarwal, A., Udgata, S.K., Lavangnananda, K. (eds.) MIWAI 2011. LNCS (LNAI), vol. 7080, pp. 351–362. Springer, Heidelberg (2011). doi:10.1007/978-3-642-25725-4_31

18. Sai Prasad, P.S.V.S., Raghavendra Rao, C.: An efficient approach for fuzzy decision reduct computation. In: Peters, J.F., Skowron, A. (eds.) Transactions on Rough Sets XVII. LNCS, vol. 8375, pp. 82–108. Springer, Heidelberg (2014). doi:10.1007/978-3-642-54756-0_5

19. Wei, W., Liang, J., Qian, Y.: A comparative study of rough sets for hybrid data. Inf. Sci. **190**, 1–16 (2012)

20. Zeng, A., Li, T., Liu, D., Zhang, J., Chen, H.: A fuzzy rough set approach for incremental feature selection on hybrid information systems. Fuzzy Sets Syst. **258**, 39–60 (2015)

A Novel OCR System Based on Rough Set Semi-reduct

Ushasi Chaudhuri$^{(\boxtimes)}$, Partha Bhowmick, and Jayanta Mukherjee

Indian Institute of Technology Kharagpur, Kharagpur, India
ushasi.cdry@gmail.com, {pb,jay}@cse.iitkgp.ernet.in

Abstract. Most of the well-known OCR engines, such as Google Tesseract, resort to a supervised classification, causing the system drooping in speed with increasing diversity in font style. Hence, with an aim to resolve the tediousness and pitfalls of training an OCR system, but without compromising with its efficiency, we introduce here a novel rough-set-theoretic model. It is designed to effectuate an unsupervised classification of optical characters with a suboptimal attribute set, called the semi-reduct. The semi-reduct attributes are mostly geometric and topological in nature, each having a small range of discrete values estimated from different combinatorial characteristics of rough-set approximations. This eventually leads to quick and easy discernibility of almost all the characters irrespective of their font style. For a few indiscernible characters, Tesseract features are used, but very sparingly, in the final stages of the OCR pipeline so as to ensure an attractive run time of the overall process. Preliminary experimental results demonstrate its further scope and promise.

Keywords: OCR · Geometric features · Combinatorial features · Approximate reasoning · Rough set · Semi-reduct

1 Introduction

Optical character recognition (OCR) continues to remain a demanding subject in the field of document digitization [12]. It has a multitude of connections with many text- and image-related applications, and to name a few, these are editing, searching, and formatting of text for a better recognition model [7–9].

With growing demand of OCR, designing of an efficient OCR system is gradually becoming more challenging and cumbersome. The challenge, in fact, shoots up to an inordinate level when the optical characters are scripted using atypical and complex font styles, thus making the datasets huge in volume and diversity. Training the OCR system becomes a natural way out to meet this challenge, but this has several pitfalls. One is the immense time and tenacity required to selectively prepare the training set. Another is the slowdown of the OCR engine owing to too much dependence on the training-set prototypes for getting a reasonable solution.

© Springer International Publishing AG 2017
B.U. Shankar et al. (Eds.): PReMI 2017, LNCS 10597, pp. 263–269, 2017.
https://doi.org/10.1007/978-3-319-69900-4_33

Fig. 1. Different instances of 'B' where (approximate) Euler number remains invariant as a semi-reduct attribute (red = outer polygon, green = hole polygons). (Color figure online)

Clearly, with increasing volume and diversity of datasets, it is required that we perform the recognition of characters in the least computational time possible. There exist several algorithms implemented and tested for performing this task. We refer to [5,6] and the bibliographies therein for their comparative study.

The Google Tesseract, an open-sourced OCR [13], is recognized as a powerful model since a long time. It uses various geometric features for its OCR engine. However, it requires a tedious training process to improve the efficiency of the character recognition. The training set, when large in size, also reduces the speed of the OCR engine quite drastically. Hence, to strike a balance, up to 32 trained data samples can be provided to the Tesseract after which its performance starts deteriorating.

In order to circumvent the pitfalls of training and supervised classification in case of large datasets with rich and diverse scripting styles, we address the OCR problem with a new perspective of rough set. Each optical character is treated as a digital object, laid on a cellular grid, and approximated by its tightest cover called *rough-set cover* [14]. In order to define the reduct, a small set of attributes is considered, which are mostly geometric and topological in nature and defined in a combinatorial way in the discrete domain of rough set. As an introductory example, we have shown in Fig. 1 how different complex instances of the English optical character 'B' get associated with the same value of (approximate) Euler number (discussed in Sect. 2) when its rough-set cover is considered. Notice that this is not feasible by a usual image analysis, wherein lies the importance of rough set.

We aim to create a rough-set semi-reduct for an alphanumeric character set so as to design an efficient OCR pipeline. As the dataset we have taken up is quite complex and challenging, the reduct attributes are sometimes not enough in discriminating two characters with a high confusion. Hence, as a reinforcement, we use Tesseract features, although very occasionally and only towards the final stages of the pipeline. This not only improves the overall performance of the system but also significantly gains in the average runtime, as shown in Sect. 3.

2   Rough Set Reduct

We use the concepts of rough set mostly from [10,11]. We use them in two stages—first for construction of upper and lower approximations of a 2D digital object and next for defining the approximations of their attributes comprising the reduct.

Let S be a 2D digital object and $\mathbb{G}$ a cellular grid. We denote by $\overline{\mathcal{P}}_{\mathbb{G}}(S)$ and $\underline{\mathcal{P}}_{\mathbb{G}}(S)$ the respective *tight upper approximation* and *tight lower approximation* of S induced by $\mathbb{G}$. Each of them essentially consists of one or more polygons with axis-parallel edges induced by $\mathbb{G}$.

Each polygon has two types of vertices, one of 90^0 and another of 270^0 interior angle, which we denote by '+' and '−', respectively. Depending on the grid resolution, the *accuracy* of the rough-set representation of S is given by $\alpha_{\mathbb{G}}(S) =$ $\frac{\text{area}(\underline{\mathcal{P}}_{\mathbb{G}}S)}{\text{area}(\overline{\mathcal{P}}_{\mathbb{G}}S)}$. In the inset figure, there are two such approximations for cell size 6×6 and 12×12; the upper approximation is shown in red and the lower one in yellow.

Since each digital object S corresponds to a specific optical character, we first apply an isotropic scaling on S so that S fits inside a box of predefined height (128 in our experimental setup), and then set the grid by cell-size 4×4. We use the algorithm in [1] for construction of $\overline{\mathcal{P}}_{\mathbb{G}}(S)$. From the vertex sequence of the polygon(s) in $\overline{\mathcal{P}}_{\mathbb{G}}(S)$, we compute the values of the semi-reduct attributes (i.e., features), as discussed next.

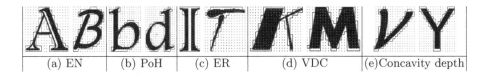

| (a) EN | (b) PoH | (c) ER | (d) VDC | (e)Concavity depth |

Fig. 2. Some typical examples on the discriminating power of rough-set attributes.

1. Euler number. The upper approximation $\overline{\mathcal{P}}_{\mathbb{G}}(S)$ consists of one or more polygons. The largest among them is the *outer polygon*, and it tightly circumscribes S. Each other polygon tightly inscribes a hole or cavity of S, and is treated as a *hole polygon*. To capture this information, we consider approximate Euler number (EN) as an important attribute, and define it as $2 - n$, where n is the total number of polygons in $\overline{\mathcal{P}}_{\mathbb{G}}(S)$. In Fig. 2a, the character images 'A' and 'B' have $n = 2$ and $n = 3$, whereby EN $= 0$ and 1, respectively, thus discriminating them. Notice that without rough-set interpretation, the instance of 'B' would have EN $= 1$ by conventional image processing, which would produce erroneous result in subsequent analysis.

2. Hole positions. The relative position (PoH) of each hole polygon is determined by comparing its center c with the top-left vertex v_0 of the outer polygon in $\overline{\mathcal{P}}_{\mathbb{G}}(S)$. In Fig. 2b, we see how the characters 'b' and 'd' are differentiated by this attribute: c lies right of v_0 for 'b', and left in case of 'd'. We assign '−' and '+' to denote left and right lateral halves, and '1' and '2' for respective upper and lower halves; hence, the hole polygon in 'b' has PoH $= +2$ and that in 'd' has PoH $= -2$.

3. Edge ratio. For each polygon in $\overline{\mathcal{P}}_{\mathbb{G}}(S)$, we define horizontal perimeter component (HPC) as the sum of lengths of its horizontal edges and vertical perimeter component (VPC) as that corresponding to its vertical edges. The ratio VPC:HPC, discretized to the nearest value in $\{\frac{1}{2}, 1, 2\}$, is called edge ratio (ER). As clear from Fig. 2c, this attribute really comes handy for discriminating characters like 'I' and 'T'.

4. U-turns. While traversing along the boundary of the outer polygon, the number of 'U-turns' along the vertical direction is defined as vertical direction change (VDC). Each U-turn is defined by a vertex sequence where two consecutive vertices are of type $\langle +, + \rangle$; and for each such U-turn, we also consider their relative positions similar to PoH. Figure 2d shows how two characters are discriminated by VDC; here, VDC('K') $= 6$ and VDC('M') $= 8$. A similar measure along the horizontal direction gives horizontal direction change (HDC), which, however, is not found to be a strong discriminating attribute as VDC. It is hence omit-able from the reduct, while keeping the classification preserved, as inferred from our experimentation and hence not included in the semi-reduct.

5. Concavities. As shown in [2], concavity serves as an important characteristic of any shape. Hence, we use concavity as an attribute and define it as two consecutive vertices of type $\langle -, - \rangle$. We classify a concavity depending on its orientation: left (L), right (R), upward (U), and downward (D). Further, as a rough-theoretic measure, we discretize the relative depth of each concavity to the nearest value in $\{1, 2, 3\}$. It is represented by a 3-tuple of the form $\langle$concavity direction, region, depth$\rangle$. In Fig. 2e, the characters 'V' and 'Y' have similar concavities (i.e., U) but have respective depths 2 and 1, and hence get discriminated.

In Table 1, we have shown the composition of reduct attributes for a subset of the English alphanumeric set. Notice that the attribute tuples are well-discernible, which justifies their merit in playing a decisive role in our OCR system. Figure 3 shows the pipeline in stages where each stage is based on a particular semi-reduct attribute. Observe that in the initial stages of the pipeline, the average number of objects per equivalence class is more, and the equivalence classes gradually get smaller in size down the pipeline until each character gets uniquely recognized. The characters in red-colored nodes are discernible using the semi-reduct attributes only, while those in yellow nodes are discriminated using Tesseract features on top of the semi-reduct towards the final stage of the pipeline.

3   Experimental Results

For testing, we have checked several datasets and finally have picked up `Chars74k` [3,4] to report here the test result. We select this dataset for its challenging scripting styles to OCR design. It contains images of 26 capital letters, 26 small

Table 1. Sample information table (shown partial) containing the object properties against the semi-reduct.

Characters	EN	PoH	VDC	Concavity	ER
B	-1	$+1, +2$	2	$(L, +1, -)$	2
E	$+1$	$-$	2	$(L, +1, -), (L, +2, -)$	$\frac{1}{2}$
I	$+1$	$-$	2	$-$	2
M	$+1$	$-$	8	$(D, -2, -), (D, +2, -), (U, +1, -)$	1
T	$+1$	$-$	2	$-$	1
V	$+1$	$-$	8	$(U, +1, 2)$	2
Y	$+1$	$-$	8	$(U, +1, 1)$	2
b	0	$+2$	8	$-$	2
d	0	-2	8	$-$	2
3	$+1$	$-$	8	$(R, +1, -), (R, +2, -)$	1

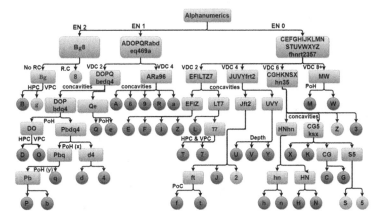

Fig. 3. Semi-reduct attributes working down the pipeline leads to decomposition of equivalence classes. (Color figure online)

letters, and ten numeric digits in English, written with 1016 different font styles. Each image has a resolution of 128×128 pixels.

We get an average CPU time of 0.051 s for the recognition of a character using our OCR engine. This is computationally attractive w.r.t. Google Tesseract engine that takes 0.203 s per character. This CPU time is achieved on a 64-bit Intel® 2-Core™ i5 processor, with 4 GB RAM, DELL machine. As shown in Table 2, we get a result of 88.98% accuracy using our model, while Google Tesseract, version 3.02.02, gives 64.79% with `eng.traineddata` training set.

Since the characters are isolated objects, the classification is context-free; as a result, some character images are not mutually discernible. Hence, we categorize them in the same class: (0/o/O), (i/l/I/1), (C/c), (J/j), (K/k), (M/m),

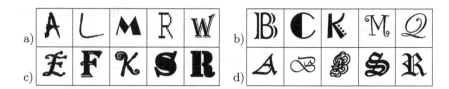

Fig. 4. Some typical instances of test cases to adjudge the quality of the proposed rough-set approach. (a) Semi-reduct and Tesseract are independently successful. (b) Semi-reduct is successful, Tesseract is not. (c) Semi-reduct combined with Tesseract is successful. (d) None is successful.

Table 2. Comparison by accuracy

Rough set	Letters	Tesseract
Above 90%	CEIJKLMSVXYZf83	75.49–90.84%
80–90%	ABDFHNOPQRTUW	4.90–87.00%
70–80%	Gbdem247	5.01–80.70%
60–70%	anqrt56	0.78–52.85%
50–60%	gh9	1.08–60.33%
Average 88.98%	–	64.79%

(P/p), (S/s), (U/u), (V/v), (W/w), (X/x), (Y/y), (Z/z). Also, other than these, there are a few characters which bear very close resemblance with each other over a varied font style, e.g., (z/2), (s/5), and (g/8/9). When the font style is complex, such as the ones used in scripting the letters shown in Fig. 4, there might be erroneous result owing to erratic mapping of the attribute values in the discretized space defined for the rough set. With larger dataset and more minute observation of their differences, discernibility of these characters can be targeted.

4   Conclusions

We have shown how a rough-set model with a small-cardinality semi-reduct can indeed be useful for quick and efficient discernibility of optical characters over varying font style. It has a significant operational difference with the existing techniques and can be designed to an efficient OCR with less runtime. The semi-reduct attributes used in our model are found to have strong discriminating power and can extend the concept further for OCR design in scripts other than English. Additional attributes can be explored and tested in different combination with these attributes to downsize a suboptimal semi-reduct to an optimal reduct, especially when a script has a large alphabet size.

References

1. Biswas, A., Bhowmick, P., Bhattacharya, B.: Construction of isothetic covers of a digital object: a combinatorial approach. JVCIR **21**(4), 295–31 (2010)
2. Bag, S., Bhowmick, P., Harit, G.: Detection of structural concavities in character images–a writer-independent approach. In: Kundu, M.K., Mitra, S., Mazumdar, D., Pal, S.K. (eds.) Perception and Machine Intelligence. LNCS, vol. 7143, pp. 260–268. Springer, Heidelberg (2012). doi:10.1007/978-3-642-27387-2_33
3. The Chars74K dataset: EnglishFnt (2009). http://www.ee.surrey.ac.uk/CVSSP/demos/chars74k/. Accessed 27 Mar 2017
4. de Campos, T.E., Babu, B.R., Varma, M.: Character recognition in natural images. In: Proceedings of the International Conference on Computer Vision Theory & Applications, Portugal (2009)
5. Fujisawa, H.: Forty years of research in character and document recognition—an industrial perspective. Pattern Recogn. **41**(8), 2435–2446 (2008)
6. Govindan, V.K., Shivaprasad, A.P.: Character recognition—a review. Pattern Recogn. **23**(7), 671–683 (1990)
7. Kumar, A., Jawahar, C.V., Manmatha, R.: Efficient search in document image collections. In: Yagi, Y., Kang, S.B., Kweon, I.S., Zha, H. (eds.) ACCV 2007. LNCS, vol. 4843, pp. 586–595. Springer, Heidelberg (2007). doi:10.1007/978-3-540-76386-4_55
8. Laroum, S., Béchet, N., Hamza, H., Roche, M.: Hybred: an OCR document representation for classification tasks. Int. J. Comput. Sci. Issues **8**(3), 1–8 (2011)
9. Pati, P.B., Ramakrishnan, A.G.: Word level multi-script identification. Pattern Recogn. Lett. **29**(9), 1218–1229 (2008)
10. Pawlak, Z.: Rough sets. Int. J. Comput. Inf. Sci. **11**, 341–356 (1982)
11. Pawlak, Z.: Rough Sets: Theoretical Aspects of Reasoning About Data. Kluwer Academic Publishing, Boston (1991)
12. Sarkar, P.: Document image analysis for digital libraries. In: Proceedings of the IWRIDL 2006, pp. 12:1–12:9 (2007)
13. Smith, R.: An overview of the Tesseract OCR engine. In: Proceedings of the ICDAR 2007, pp. 629–633 (2007)
14. Yao, Y.: Probabilistic rough set approximations. Int. J. Approx. Reason. **49**, 255–271 (2008)

Rough Set Rules Determine Disease Progressions in Different Groups of Parkinson's Patients

Andrzej W. Przybyszewski[1,3($\boxtimes$)] ⓘ, Stanislaw Szlufik[2] ⓘ,
Piotr Habela[1] ⓘ, and Dariusz M. Koziorowski[2] ⓘ

[1] Polish-Japanese Academy of Information Technology,
02-008 Warsaw, Poland
{przy,piotr.habela}@pja.edu.pl
[2] Department of Neurology, Faculty of Health Science,
Medical University Warsaw, Warsaw, Poland
stanislaw.szlufik@gmail.com, dkoziorowski@esculap.pl
[3] Department of Neurology, University of Massachusetts Medical School,
Worcester, MA 01655, USA

Abstract. Parkinson's disease (PD) is the second after Alzheimer most popular neurodegenerative disease (ND). We do not have cure for both NDs. Therefore the purpose of our study was to predict results of different PD patients' treatments in order to find an optimal one.

We have used rough sets (RS) and machine learning (ML) rules to describe and predict disease progression (UPDRS - Unified Parkinson's Disease Rating Scale) in three groups of Parkinson's patients: 23 BMT patients on medication; 24 DBS patients on medication and on DBS therapy (deep brain stimulation) after surgery performed during our study; and 15 POP patients that have surgery earlier (before beginning of our study). Every PD patient had three visits approximately every 6 months. The first visit for DBS patients was before surgery.

On the basis of the following condition attributes: disease duration, saccadic eye movement parameters, and neuropsychological tests: PDQ39, and Epworth tests we have estimated UPDRS changes (as the decision attribute).

By means of ML and RS rules obtained for the first visit of BMT/DBS/POP patients we have predicted UPDRS values in next year (two visits) with the global accuracy of 70% for both BMT visits; 56% for DBS, and 67, 79% for POP second and third visits.

We have used rules obtained in BMT patients to predict UPDRS of DBS patients; for first session DBSW1: global accuracy was 64%, for second DBSW2: 85% and the third DBSW3: 74% but only for DBS patients during stimulation-ON. These rules could not predict UPDRS in DBS patients during stimulation-OFF visits and in all conditions of POP patients.

Keywords: Neurodegenerative disease · Rough set · Decision rules · Granularity

B.U. Shankar et al. (Eds.): PReMI 2017, LNCS 10597, pp. 270–275, 2017.
https://doi.org/10.1007/978-3-319-69900-4_34

1 Introduction

Only very experience PD neurologists are successful in implementing individually adjusted therapy. In general doctors have very limited time for each patient and different approaches to patients that may lead to confusions and ineffective therapy. We propose to improve doctor's approach by additional more automatic measurements and intelligence symptom classification [1] that is similar to that found in the visual system for the complex objects recognition [2].

It is important to estimate the disease stage because it determines different sets of therapies. The neurological standards are based on Hoehn and Yahr and the UPDRS (Unified Parkinson's Disease Rating) scales. The last one is more precise and it will be used in this study. We would like to estimate disease progression in different groups of patients that were tested during three visits every half-year. Our method may lead to introduce more precise follow up and introduction of the possible internet-treatment.

2 Methods

All 62 PD patients were divided into three groups: BMT patients (only medication), and patients on medication and with implanted electrodes in the STN (subthalamic nucleus [3]) during our study: DBS group or before our study: POP group.

The Deep Brain Stimulation (DBS) surgery was performed in the Institute of Neurology and Psychiatry WUM. PD patients were tested in the following sessions: MedON/MedOFF sessions (sessions with or without medication). The other groups: DBS and POP patients were also tested in StimON/StimOFF session were DBS stimulation was switched ON or OFF. All combinations gave four sessions: (1) MedOFFStimOFF; (2) MedOFFStimON; (3) MedONStimOFF; (4) MedON-StimON. Details of these procedures were described earlier [2]. The UPDRS tests and neuropsychological tests were performed by neurologists from Warsaw Medical University. Fast eye movements (EM) - reflexive saccades (RS) were recorded as described in details before [1, 3]. The following parameters of RS were measured: the delay (latency) related to time difference between the beginning of the light spot movements and the beginning of the eye movement; saccade's amplitude in comparison to the light spot amplitude; max velocity of the eye movement; duration of saccade defined as the time from the beginning to the end of the saccade.

2.1 Theoretical Basis

Our data mining analysis follows rough set (RS) theory after Zdzislaw Pawlak [4]) because RS gave the best results in PD symptoms classifications in comparison to other methodologies [1]. Our data are represented as a decision table where rows represented different measurements (may be obtained from the same or different patients) and columns were related to different attributes. An information system [4] is as a pair $S = (U, A)$, where U, A are finite sets: U is the universe of objects; and A is the set of attributes. The value $a(u)$ is a unique element of V (where V is a value set) for $a \in A$ and $u \in U$.

A decision table for S is the triplet: $S = (U, C, D)$ where: C, D are condition and decision attributes [5]. Each row of the information table gives a particular rule that connects condition and decision attributes for a single measurements of a particular patient. As there are many rows related to different patients and sessions, they gave many particular rules. Rough set approach allows generalizing these rules into universal hypotheses that may determine optimal treatment options for an individual PD patient. Different rules' granularities (abstraction) are similar to complex objects recognition [2] and may simulate association processes of the 'Golden Neurologist'.

In the present study, we are trying to use data from different groups of patients for training and testing. The purpose was to find what are limits of rules that may predict symptoms development of patients with different treatments in different disease stages.

We have used the RSES 2.2 (Rough System Exploration Program) [6] with implementation of RS rules to process our data.

3   Results

All 62 PD patients were divided into three groups: BMT patients (only medication), and patients on medication and with implanted electrodes in the STN (subthalamic nucleus [3]) during our study: DBS group or before our study: POP group.

In 23 patients of BMT group the mean age was 57.8+/− 13 (SD) years; disease duration was 7.1+/− 3.5 years, UPDRS was 36.1+/− 19.2. In 24 patients of DBS group the mean age of 53.7+/− 9.3 years, disease duration was 10.25+/− 3.9 years (stat. diff. than BMT-group: p < 0.025), UPDRS was 62.1+/− 16.1 (stat. diff. than BMT-group: p < 0.0001). In 15 patients of POP group the mean age was 56.2+/− 11.3 (SD) years and disease duration was 13.5+/− 3.6 years (stat. diff. than DBS-group: p < 0.015), UPDRS was 59.2+/− 24.5 (stat. diff. than BMT-group: p < 0.0001).

These statistical data are related to the data obtained during the first visit for each group: so-called BMT W1 (visit one), DBS W1 (visit one) and POP W1 (visit one).

3.1   BMT Patients' Rules for the Disease Progression

The BMT patients (only on medication) were tested in two sessions (session 1: without, and session 3: with medication) three times every half-year.

We have used ML and rough set theory [6] in order to obtain rules determining decision and condition attributed for the first visit BMTW1. On the basis of these rules we have predicted the UPDRS values obtained during the second (half -year later W2 – BMTW2) and the third (one year later BMTW3) visits. UPDRS was optimally divided by RSES into 4 ranges: "(−Inf, 24.0)", "(24.0, 36.0)", "(36.0, 45.0)", "(45.0, Inf)" for both visits (W2 and W3) the global coverage was 1.0 and the global accuracy was 0.7. Example of rules from BMTW1:

$$(Ses = 3)\&(PDQ39 = "(-Inf, 50.5)") => (UPDRS = "(-Inf, 33.5)"[12])\ 12 \quad (1)$$

$$(dur = "(-Inf, 5.65)")\&(Ses = 3)\&(Epworth = "(-Inf, 14.0)")$$
$$=> (UPDRS = "(-Inf, 33.5)"[7]) \, 7 \tag{2}$$

$$(dur = "(5.65, Inf)")\&(Ses = 3)\&(Epworth = "(14.0, Inf)")$$
$$=> (UPDRS = "(-Inf, 33.5)"[4]) \, 4 \tag{3}$$

In the first rule (1) if the session number 3 and PDQ39 = (−Inf, 50.5) then UPDRS was (−Inf, 33.5) in 12 cases. The second rule (2) was fulfilled in 7 cases and the third one (3) in 4 cases. There were 70 rules.

3.2   DBS and POP Patients' Rules for the Disease Progression

As **DBSW1** had only 2 sessions (before surgery) we could only predict session **DBSW3** on the basis of **DBSW2** (half of the year earlier) (Table 1).

Table 1. Confusion matrix for UPDRS of DBSW3 by rules obtained from DBSW2.

Predicted

		"(46.0, 72.0)"	"(38.0, 46.0)"	"(19.5, 38.0)"	"(72.0, Inf)"	"(Inf, 19.5)"	ACC
	"(46.0, 72.0)"	12	5	2	5	1	0.48
Actual	"(38.0, 46.0)"	2	5	1	2	2	0.42
	"(19.5, 38.0)"	0	4	13	3	7	0.48
	"(72.0, Inf)"	4	0	0	12	0	0.75
	"(-Inf, 19.5)"	0	0	4	0	12	0.75
	TPR	0.67	0.4	0.65	0.55	0.6	

TPR: True positive rates for decision classes; ACC: Accuracy for decision classes: the global coverage was 1 and the **global accuracy was 0.562**

POP patients' rules for the disease progression. As above, we have predicted UPDRS for visits **POPW2** and **POPW3** on the basis of visit **POPW1** with total accuracy: 0.667 and 0.793 with a coverage: 1 and 0.967.

3.3   BMT Patients' Rules for Estimation of DBS Patients' Disease Progression

As BMT patients have only two sessions (S1 – MedOff, and S3 – MedON) and DBS patients four sessions (see Methods) we have divided them to two sets: one with StimON set-up and another one with StimOFF set-up. We were not successful in prediction SimOFF sessions as DBS patients were in more advanced stage than BMT group. Our UPDRS predictions for **DBSW1** had global accuracy 0.64 (coverage 0.5);

for **DBSW2** - global accuracy was 0.85 (coverage 0.3); for **DBSW3** - global accuracy was 0.74 (coverage 0.6).

3.4 DBS Patients' Rules for Estimation of POP Patients' Disease Progression

We could not predict UPDRS of POP patients from rules obtained from DBS patients probably because many years of DBS have changed some brain circuits.

4 Discussion

There are novel technologies and data constantly improve PD patients' treatments, but are also still doubts if the actual procedures are optimal for a particular individual case. Our long time purpose is to use the data mining and machine learning in order to *compare different neurological protocols and their effectiveness*. We think that the best future approach will be to perform all tests automatically at home, process them with intelligent algorithms and to submit results to the doctor for his/her decision. Another, more advanced approach that we were testing in this work, would be to create the standard treatment for each new case on the basis of already successfully treated patients and correct treatment as symptoms are developing in time. We have demonstrated that relatively easy to estimate symptoms and their time development in populations treated in a different ways (e.g. only medication treatment). This result may give the basic (locally optimal) follow-ups. If patient is doing significantly worse then others (rules), his/her treatment is not optimal, and should be changed. In the next step, we may use rules obtained from different clinics to get them even more universal and optimal. Our new approach is related not only to longitudinal study but also test different patient population with different treatments. Can we in this case find optimal way of different treatments? The second group of patients were in more advanced stage of disease so it was not possible to get 100% coverage like in the first case. The second group with longitudinal study had a new treatment (brain stimulation) that started from the second visit. We have tested if the same treatment in different populations gives similar results. Patients got two treatments: medication (medication ON and OFF) and electric brain stimulation (ON and OFF). We have analyzed these treatments as two different sets: (1) StimOFF: medication ON and OFF; (2) StimON: medication ON and OFF. As a result, it was not possible to get sufficient accuracy in the first situation, but we got good accuracy in the second case- with the brain stimulation. However, our third POP group was different than two other as we did not succeeded to obtain good prediction by rules obtained by other groups BMT or DBS. It maybe related to the longer period of brain stimulation (DBS) that has changed some central mechanisms. It is an important negative result that needs more study. In the near future, we may look for additional condition attributes in order to improve a global accuracy. The reason that our rules did not apply to symptoms of patients without brain stimulation might be related to the surgery. Inserting electrodes through the brain till the basal ganglia probably partly destroys some of these pathways. Functions of these connections are expressed by our rules, damaging them changes their functionality. We have demonstrated that the DBS (electric STN stimulation) procedure revoked and improved rules that became similar to rules of early stage Parkinson's disease patients.

5   Conclusions

This work is a continuation of our previous findings [1, 3], comparing classical approach used by most neurologists and based on their partly subjective experience and intuitions with the intelligent data processing (machine learning, data mining) classifications. We have demonstrated that the parameters of eye movements and neuropsychological data are sufficient to predict longitudinal symptom developments in different therapy related groups of PD patients.

Acknowledgements. This work was partly supported by projects Dec-2011/03/B/ST6/03816, from the Polish National Science Centre.

References

1. Przybyszewski, A.W., Kon, M., Szlufik, S., Szymanski, A., Koziorowski, D.M.: Multimodal learning and intelligent prediction of symptom development in individual parkinson's patients. Sensors **16**(9), 1498 (2016). doi:10.3390/s16091498
2. Przybyszewski, A.W.: Logical rules of visual brain: from anatomy through neurophysiology to cognition. Cogn. Syst. Res. **11**, 53–66 (2010)
3. Przybyszewski, A.W., Kon, M., Szlufik, S., Dutkiewicz, J., Habela, P., Koziorowski, D.M.: Data mining and machine learning on the basis from reflexive eye movements can predict symptom development in individual Parkinson's patients. In: Gelbukh, A., Espinoza, F.C., Galicia-Haro, S.N. (eds.) MICAI 2014, Part II. LNCS, vol. 8857, pp. 499–509. Springer, Cham (2014). doi:10.1007/978-3-319-13650-9_43
4. Pawlak, Z.: Rough sets: Theoretical Aspects of Reasoning About Data. Kluwer, Dordrecht (1991). p. 509. Springer (2014)
5. Bazan, J., Son, Nguyen, H., Trung, T., Nguyen, Skowron A., Stepaniuk, J.: Decision rules synthesis for object classification. In: Orłowska, E. (ed.) Incomplete Information: Rough Set Analysis, pp. 23–57. Physica–Verlag, Heidelberg (1998)
6. Bazan, J.G., Szczuka, M.: RSES and RSESlib - a collection of tools for rough set computations. In: Ziarko, W., Yao, Y. (eds.) RSCTC 2000. LNCS(LNAI), vol. 2005, pp. 106–113. Springer, Heidelberg (2001). doi:10.1007/3-540-45554-X_12

Adversarial Optimization of Indoor Positioning System Using Differential Evolution

Feroz Ahmad$^{(\boxtimes)}$ and Sreedevi Indu

Delhi Technological University, Delhi, India
ferozahmad_2k14@dtu.ac.in, s.indu@dce.ac.in

Abstract. This paper presents an adversarial approach to improve the accuracy of an indoor positioning system. In the present work, we propose a system, composed of two components which act as an adversary to each other while determining the accurate parameters in the equations governing the distance evaluations. Differential Evolution is employed to update the parameters in the continuous domain, in real-time by generating an adversarial relation using the two components. Distance evaluation using Time-of-Arrival (TOA) and Received Signal Strength (RSS) are the two strategies used to evaluate distances independently.

Keywords: Indoor positioning system · Indoor localization · Evolutionary computation · Differential evolution

1 Introduction

Large amount of work on indoor system has been done using several techniques in the past, but most of the works calibrate the unknown constants once before the operation of the experiment and then utilizes the evaluated constant values for their complete operation [1,3,5,9]. Despite the knowledge of constantly occurring subtle changes in the surrounding, the effect on the constants involved is neglected. In the present paper, we aim to update the involved constants regularly by an adversarial mechanism in the continuous domain of the constants and position coordinates.

Throughout the following text, the node whose position is to be evaluated is referred as Unknown node and the beacon nodes which emit ultrasonic signals and radiowave packet are referred as Reference nodes. The position of reference nodes is predetermined.

2 Background

2.1 Time-of-Arrival Technique

TOA (Time-of-Arrival) is a distance estimation technique. In this method, the distance between the Reference node and the Unknown node is calculated using transmission time of the signal and the speed of the signal as follows:

$$d_{TOA} = time \times speed \tag{1}$$

© Springer International Publishing AG 2017
B.U. Shankar et al. (Eds.): PReMI 2017, LNCS 10597, pp. 276–281, 2017.
https://doi.org/10.1007/978-3-319-69900-4_35

where d_{TOA} is the distance between the Reference node and the Unknown node measured using TOA, *time* is the duration of time taken by signal propagation from Reference node to Unknown node and *speed* is the speed of propagation of the signal. In TOA based systems only one way propagation time is recorded [4].

2.2   Received Signal Strength Technique

RSS (Received Signal Strength) based methods are also distance estimation techniques based on signal attenuation. It performs better in absence of LOS (Line of Sight) channel, which is the case in practical implementations. The signal path loss due to propagation is used to calculate the distance using the following relation [6,8]:

$$RSS(x = d) = -RSS(x = 1m) - 10n \log_{10}(d) + \delta \tag{2}$$

$$d_{RSS} = 10^{\frac{RSS(x=d)+A-\delta}{10 \cdot n}} \tag{3}$$

where $RSS(x = d)$ is RSS value at a d distance (in meters) from transmitter, A is RSS(x = 1m), d_{RSS} is the distance of Unknown node from the Reference node computed using RSS technique, n is the medium as well as location dependent signal propagation constant and δ corresponds to attenuation due to obstacles.

2.3   Trilateration

Trilateration is a geometrical positioning technique. In this method, reference distances from three non-collinear points is used to calculate physical position (x and y coordinates) of unknown node in 2D Cartesian Plane as indicated in Fig. 1 (adjusted Reference nodes according to proposed system) and Eqs. (4) and (5) [5].

$$x = \frac{d_A^2 + R^2 - d_B^2}{2R} \tag{4}$$

$$y = \frac{d_A^2 + R^2 - d_C^2}{2R} \tag{5}$$

where x and y are the respective coordinates in the assumed 2D plane, d_A is the distance of the Unknown node from Reference node A, d_B is the distance of the Unknown node from Reference node B, d_C is the distance of the Unknown node from Reference node C, R is the distance between Reference node A and Reference Node B (also Reference node A and Reference Node C).

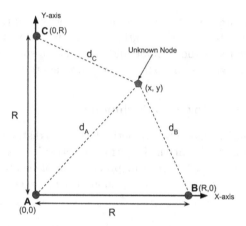

Fig. 1. Technique of trilateration adapted and used in the experiment (Red Circle - Reference Node, Green Pentagon - Unknown Node) (Color figure online)

2.4   Differential Evolution

Differential Evolution [7] is an optimization algorithm under evolutionary computation. Under the given set of constraints and optimization objective function, the values of decision variables can be calculated by iterative attempt to improve a candidate solution generated by the algorithm. This algorithm requires three parameters: NP - population size, F - a parameter to control the mutation, and CR - crossover probability. The procedure of this algorithm can be divided as: Initialization, Mutation, Crossover and Selection.

DE initializes a population P with individuals x_i, where i ϵ {1, 2,.., NP} and x_i being a t-dimensional vector. Mutation step in this algorithm is achieved by (6), that is to generate a mutant vector $v_{i,G}$ for each population vector $x_{i,G}$ where G corresponds to generation of the population.

$$v_{i,G+1} = x_{r_1,G} + F(x_{r_2,G} - x_{r_3,G}) \tag{6}$$

where r_1, r_2, r_3 are random indices such that r_1, r_2, r_3 ϵ {1, 2,.., NP} and

Recombination of population is performed using Crossover operation. A uniform crossover in (7) involves combination of parent vector $x_{i,G}$ and the mutant vector $v_{i,G+1}$ to yield trial vector $u_{i,G+1}$ according to following criteria:

$$u_{j,i,G+1} = \begin{cases} v_{j,i,G+1} & \text{if } random(0,1) < CR \text{ or } j == d_i \\ x_{j,i,G} & \text{otherwise} \end{cases} \tag{7}$$

where u is the trial vector, v is the mutant vector, j is dimension index and j ϵ {1, 2,.., t} (t is the total number of dimensions or components in the individual population vector $x_{i,G}$, G is the generation of the population, i is population index, $random(0,1)$ generates a float random number between 0 and 1, d_i ϵ {1, 2,.., t} is a randomly chosen index. The selection strategy on each population element concludes the iteration. If $f(u_{i,G+1}) < f(x_{i,G})$, then $x_{i,G+1} = u_{i,G+1}$ otherwise $x_{i,G}$, where f is the fitness or objective function.

3   Proposed System

The aim of the system is to predict the indoor location of Unknown node, by updating the constants involved in Eqs. (1) and (3) in real-time during the operation. Our proposed system consists of two components capable of measuring the distances which are employed to act as an adversary to each other. The first component is the technique corresponding to Time-of-Arrival (TOA) which uses ultrasonic signals to compute the duration of time of propagation. The second component is the technique using RSS (Received Signal Strength) of radiowave packets from Reference nodes.

3.1   RSS Value Stabilization

It is a very common problem to record highly fluctuating values of Received Signal Strength (RSS). However, the RSS values can be stabilized using the following update rule in (8), using a control factor γ.

$$sRSS_t = \gamma \cdot sRSS_{t-1} + (1 - \gamma) \cdot RSS_t \qquad (8)$$

where sRSS is the stabilized RSS value, RSS_t is the RSS value recorded from the communication module. (8) is applicable only in cases where the motion of Unknown node is continuous in the 2D plane domain and not abrupt.

3.2   Adversarial Optimization to Update Constants

The idea is to measure the distance of the Unknown node from Reference nodes A, B and C: d_A, d_B and d_C using two techniques. The first technique being TOA, we record time duration from the point Unknown node requests an ultrasonic signal packet by radio communication to the point of arrival of ultrasonic signal at Unknown node. This evaluation is done for all the Reference nodes A, B and C, obtaining TOA_A, TOA_B, TOA_C. The second technique of RSS is employed to the beacon packets coming from Reference nodes A, B and C to Unknown node, obtaining RSS_A, RSS_B, RSS_C. These RSS values are stabilized using (8). Substituting these obtained values in the objective function $f(A, \delta, n, c)$ for every Reference node, we run differential evolution to obtain optimal values of A, δ, n and c.

The objective function f is absolute value of the difference of distances calculated by two techniques (1) and (3) between the Reference node and the Unknown node, $f = |d_{k,RSS} - d_{k,TOA}|$, where $k \in \{A, B, C\}$. This choice of objective function definition gives rise to adversarial nature in the proposed approach. The objective function f subject on A, δ, n, c is as follows:

$$f(A, \delta, n, c) = \left| \left(10^{\frac{-(RSS(x=d) + A - \delta)}{10 \cdot n}} \right) - \left(TOA \times c \right) \right| \qquad (9)$$

Each individual of the population in Differential Evolution algorithm encodes A, δ, n, c in their inherent information. In this application, the values of A, δ, n, c are constrained to their respective ranges ($\pm 10\%$ of the constant value evaluated in the beginning of the experiment) due to physical phenomena.

3.3 Update of Position

The final aim of the system is to provide position coordinates of the Unknown node, with respect to assumed Cartesian plane as in Fig. 1. We have utilized the second component of the system to report final coordinates of the particular cycle. Using the new values of A, δ, n and the latest stabilized RSS values in (3), we compute d_A, d_B and d_C. Applying trilateration (4), (5) using these three distance values, we report the coordinates of Unknown node.

Error is calculated as the distance between estimated position coordinate (x,y) and real position coordinate (x_0,y_0).

4   Experiment and Results

The experiment is conducted in an indoor environment with a predetermined 2D Cartesian plane of dimension $5\,\text{m} \times 5\,\text{m}$. The Reference and Unknown nodes communicate via. ZigBee (IEEE 802.15.4-based suite of high-level communication protocols) [2]. Each node is equipped with ultrasonic transmitter/receiver. All the nodes are computationally powered by NXP JN5168 ZigBee microcontroller. The setup in case of Unknown node is mounted over a movable bot to fulfill the purpose of a movable node, whose position is determined in continuous manner. The experimental setup of the nodes is equivalent to the scheme in the Fig. 1.

Table 1. Performance Comparison

Algorithm	Ours				Naive RSS
	NP = 10		NP = 20		
	$\gamma = 0.4$	$\gamma = 0.6$	$\gamma = 0.4$	$\gamma = 0.6$	
Minimum Deviation(cm)	2.98	3.12	2.76	2.61	4.51
Maximum Deviation(cm)	19.03	18.71	16.94	16.18	23.77
Average Deviation(cm)	8.92	8.51	8.39	8.25	11.19
Root Mean-Square Error(cm)	5.83	5.62	5.51	5.48	9.37

Due to limited computation power of JN 5168 microcontroller the differential evolution algorithm in the experiment has been executed on a population size (NP) of 10 & 20, and for 10 generations only. These parameters have been decided after establishing a suitable trade off between computation time and reliability of results. The experiment is conducted for 2 values of γ as 0.4 and 0.6 for RSS stabilization. $\gamma = 0.6$ for being more inertial towards the previous RSS values.

Table 1 compares our technique with naive RSS technique. The naive RSS technique employs constants evaluated once at the beginning of the experiment in the above described setup. It is evident from the comparison of Root Mean-Square Error of both the techniques that our technique is superior by employing update of parameter values in real-time. Further, our proposed techniques performs better for $NP = 20$ due to more exhaustive optimization.

5 Conclusion

An indoor positioning system which can update its functional parameters in real-time was successfully proposed and its performance was verified. Currently there is one disadvantage associated with the system, as it might not be very practical in its usecase but this paper successfully proposes a model which can update its parameters by an adversarial approach. Further work to replace or modify first component of TOA is required to improve this system for more practical purposes.

References

1. Alarifi, A., Al-Salman, A., Alsaleh, M., Alnafessah, A., Al-Hadhrami, S., Al-Ammar, M.A., Al-Khalifa, H.S.: Ultra wideband indoor positioning technologies: analysis and recent advances. Sensors **16**(5), 707 (2016)
2. Farahani, S.: ZigBee wireless networks and transceivers. Newnes (2011)
3. Liu, H.H., Yang, Y.N.: Wifi-based indoor positioning for multi-floor environment. In: TENCON 2011–2011 IEEE Region 10 Conference, pp. 597–601. IEEE (2011)
4. Medina, C., Segura, J.C., De la Torre, A.: Ultrasound indoor positioning system based on a low-power wireless sensor network providing sub-centimeter accuracy. Sensors **13**(3), 3501–3526 (2013)
5. Oguejiofor, O.S., Aniedu, A.N., Ejiofor, H.C., Okolibe, A.U.: Trilateration based localization algorithm for wireless sensor network. Int. J. Sci. Mod. Eng. (IJISME) **1**(10), 2319–6386 (2013)
6. Seidel, S.Y., Rappaport, T.S.: 914 mhz path loss prediction models for indoor wireless communications in multifloored buildings. IEEE Trans. Antennas Propag. **40**(2), 207–217 (1992)
7. Storn, R., Price, K.: Differential evolution-a simple and efficient adaptive scheme for global optimization over continuous spaces, vol. 3. ICSI Berkeley (1995)
8. Tian, H., Wang, S., Xie, H.: Localization using cooperative aoa approach. In: International Conference on Wireless Communications, Networking and Mobile Computing, WiCom 2007, pp. 2416–2419. IEEE (2007)
9. Zhang, D., Xia, F., Yang, Z., Yao, L., Zhao, W.: Localization technologies for indoor human tracking. In: 2010 5th International Conference on Future Information Technology (FutureTech), pp. 1–6. IEEE (2010)

Fast Convergence to Near Optimal Solution for Job Shop Scheduling Using Cat Swarm Optimization

Vivek Dani$^{(\boxtimes)}$ ⓘ, Aparna Sarswat ⓘ, Vishnu Swaroop ⓘ, Shridhar Domanal ⓘ,
and Ram Mohana Reddy Guddeti ⓘ

Department of Information Technology, National Institute of Technology Karnataka,
Surathkal, Mangalore, India
`vivekpdani@gmail.com, sarswataparna@gmail.com, visalpha@gmail.com,`
`shridhar.domanal@gmail.com, profgrmreddy@gmail.com`

Abstract. Job Shop Scheduling problem has wide range of applications. However it being a NP-Hard optimization problem, always finding an optimal solution is not possible in polynomial amount of time. In this paper we propose a heuristic approach to find near optimal solution for Job Shop Scheduling Problem in predetermined amount of time using Cat Swarm Optimization. Novelty in our approach is our non-conventional way of representing position of cat in search space that ensures advantage of spatial locality is taken. Further while exploring the search space using randomization, we never explore an infeasible solution. This reduces search time. Our proposed approach outperforms some of the conventional algorithms and achieves nearly 86% accuracy, while restricting processing time to one second.

Keywords: Job Shop Scheduling · Cat Swarm Optimization · NP-Hard · Makespan

1 Introduction

Job Shop Scheduling is a NP-Hard problem; thereby it cannot be assured that optimal solution would be achieved in finite amount of time. In most of the real world applications, finding near optimal solution in small finite amount of time is more preferable than spending huge amount of time in finding optimal solution. In job shop scheduling problem (JSSP) we have a set of jobs and a set of machines on which these jobs have to be executed in optimal manner. We refer Fig. 1 as an example. Each job has some sub-task (to which we call as operations) represented as nodes in each row. Number inside each node is written in 'p.q' format indicating that it is q^{th} operation of pth job. Next to each node we have mentioned machine on which that node has to run and for how much amount of time it has to run. Here every i^{th} operation of every job has to be completed before $(i+1)^{th}$ operation of that job is started. On any machine M_x, only one operation can be executed at a time. Any operation of job j can

© Springer International Publishing AG 2017
B.U. Shankar et al. (Eds.): PReMI 2017, LNCS 10597, pp. 282–288, 2017.
https://doi.org/10.1007/978-3-319-69900-4_36

be executed before any operation of job k, (where $j \neq k$). Every job has exactly one operation for every machine. Preemption is not allowed between operations. Goal here is to find an order in which operations should be assigned to each machine so that the total amount of time required to complete all operations of all jobs (i.e. makespan) is minimum. In order to solve this problem we use cat swarm optimization (CSO) [2] technique.

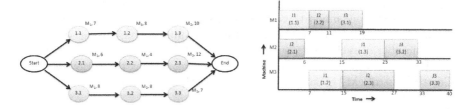

Fig. 1. Graphical representation of JSSP   **Fig. 2.** Gantt chart

JSSP has many heuristic approaches of solving it to near optimal solution. The most noted is the shifting bottle neck heuristic which uses branch and bound algorithm. Good accuracy is observed in [1], which uses CSO however the time for convergence ranges from 1 sec to 3000 sec, depending upon instance of dataset used. In [7] 3.96% relative error was observed, however 1000 iterations were used every time. Artificial fish swarm optimization was used in [3], they used 100 iterations and tried to find near optimal solution. However the highest accuracy they achieved was 73.33% and average accuracy is much lower than it. Ant colony optimization was used in [4], where approach used was parallel. For getting optimal solution, as number of jobs increases number of ants were increased there by causing load on system. Also the number of iterations used is large along with the disadvantage of getting trapped in local optima. Thus, a good amount of work has been done in this area but none of the existing approach finds suboptimal solution in real time with 86% accuracy. Major difference between our approach and approach used in [1] is the way of representing position of cat. Below are the key contributions of this paper and as per our knowledge this is first work which uses CSO in fast convergent manner over reduced search space for finding solution of JSSP.

- Proposed method utilizes the topological ordering of JSSP graph to extract the valid random solution every time within the search space.
- Further, the representation of a cat's position is novel that takes advantage of spatial locality and thereby reducing the computation time.

2 Proposed Methodology

In our further discussion, j would be number of jobs, m would be number of machines, '$totalOp$' would be total number of operations in a job and $O(p,q)$ would be p^{th} operation of qth job. All jobs have equal number of operations.

2.1   Finding Solution for JSSP Using CSO

In this sub-section we describe entire work flow of finding near optimal solution of JSSP using CSO. In CSO each cat has four attributes, which are 'current position', 'current velocity', 'best position seen so far' and 'mode' which can be 'seeking' or 'tracing'.

1. Initialize position of cats. Keep some cats in seeking mode and some in tracing mode.
2. If cat is in seeking mode then conventional method in seeking mode is to get new position of cat by adding a random value to its current position. M_{size} number of such positions are generated. M_{size} is seeking memory pool size i.e. number of positions that a cat can remember at time. However we directly generate M_{size} number of random positions for the cat, using method described in Subsect. 3.2.
3. If cat is in tracing mode then follow below steps:
   (a) Calculate difference between two positions of cat using method described in Subsect. 3. X_{best} is best position among positions explored by all the cats and $X_{current}$ is current position of cat

   $$X_{\mathrm{dif}} = X_{\mathrm{best}} - X_{\mathrm{current}} \qquad (1)$$

   (b) Calculate new velocity of cat as

   $$V_{\mathrm{new}} = V_{\mathrm{old}} * inr + sc * r * X_{\mathrm{dif}} \qquad (2)$$

   where 'inr' is inertia, tendency of cat to retain its old velocity, 'sc' is scaling factor and 'r' is random number.
   (c)
   $$X_{\mathrm{new}} = X_{\mathrm{current}} + V_{\mathrm{new}}. \qquad (3)$$

   Method of adding velocity to position is described in Subsect. 3.1.
4. Update X_{best} to be the best position among all the positions explored till now. Smaller makespan are considered better.
5. Go to step 2.1 if stopping condition isn't met, which in our case is maximum number of iterations.

2.2   Representing Position of Cat

Table 1 is made referring to Fig. 1. In Table 1 'Id' is nothing but a unique identity given to each column. Position of cat can be defined as vector of Id's. Equation (4) represents a valid solution for JSSP (i.e. position of cat) according to convention used in [1]. We call this representation as 'format-1'. In [1] while assigning initial position to each cat, they generate a random vector and check if its a valid solution, if it is, then they assign it to a cat, else they rearrange the elements in vector to convert it to a valid solution. Disadvantage of this representation is that more than one representation refers to a same solution. Solution 1 and 2 in (4) are different representations of the same solution corresponding to gantt

Table 1. Information matrix

Id		1	2	3		4	5	6		7	8	9
Job Id		1	1	1		2	2	2		3	3	3
Operation sequence	1	2	3		1	2	3		1	2	3	
Machine Id	1	3	2		2	1	3		1	2	3	
Service time	7	8	10		6	4	12		8	8	7	

Table 2. Sub-lists and index mapping

Value of sub-list	Index
[1, 2, 3]	1
[1, 3, 2]	2
[2, 1, 3]	3
[2, 3, 1]	4
[3, 1, 2]	5
[3, 2, 1]	6

chart in Fig. 2. It doesn't restrict us from representing an infeasible solution, as shown in (5) solution 3 is an infeasible solution. Method that we use to represent position of a cat is based on order in which operations are assigned to each machine. Solution in (4) can be represented as $[[1, 2, 3], [2, 1, 3], [1, 2, 3]]$. This is our representation of position of cat to which we call as 'format-2'. It is a list of m sub-lists. Each sub-list corresponds to each machine. First sub-list i.e. $[1, 2, 3]$ corresponds to order in which operations would be assigned to machine M_1. Similarly for M_2 and M_3. We exploit the fact that any machine M_x will be required by exactly one operation in each job i.e. there will be no two operations of same job to be executed on same machine. Numbers 1, 2, 3 in every sub-list denotes job Id. Referring to Figs. 1 and 2, we now discuss how to interpret sub-lists. On Machine M_1, first operation of job with job Id=1 will be executed (i.e. operation 1.1), followed by operation of job with job Id=2 (i.e. operation 2.2) and finally operation of job with job Id=3 (i.e. operation 3.1). If we use the format-1 for position of cat that is used in [1], then size of search space would be $(m * j)!$ and size of search space if our representation (format-2) is used, would be $m * (j!)$, which is lesser than $(m * j)!$. From format-2 representation, we can easily reproduce gantt chart as in Fig. 2 by calculating the start time (ts) when an operation starts its execution on a machine. This can be done by referring to order of operations in sub-lists and adhering to restrictions of JSSP that are defined in Sect. 1.

$$Solution1 = \begin{bmatrix} 1 \ 4 \ 2 \ 5 \ 7 \ 3 \ 6 \ 8 \ 9 \end{bmatrix}, Solution2 = \begin{bmatrix} 1 \ 4 \ 5 \ 2 \ 3 \ 7 \ 6 \ 8 \ 9 \end{bmatrix} \quad (4)$$

$$Solution3 = \begin{bmatrix} 9 \ 8 \ 7 \ 6 \ 5 \ 4 \ 3 \ 2 \ 1 \end{bmatrix} \quad (5)$$

3   Computing Distance Between Two Positions of Cat

The way in which we compute distance between two positions of cat is novel. Position of cat represents a solution for JSSP. Thus if two cats are near then intuitively the solutions should also have similar makespan. If we have m machines then we will have m sub-lists in every solution. And if there are j jobs then each sub-list will have j elements. All possible values that a sub-list can have, when we have 3 jobs is shown in Table 2. Values are arranged in ascending order and to each sub-list an index is given. We calculate difference between two sub-lists as:

$$IndexOf(sL_p) - IndexOf(sL_q) \text{ where } sL_p, sL_q \text{ are sub-lists} \qquad (6)$$

For example difference between $[1, 3, 2]$ and $[3, 1, 2]$ would be $2 - 5 = -3$. Consider three positions of cat $P1 = [[1,2,3],[2,1,3],[1,2,3]]$, $P2 = [[3,2,1],[2,1,3],[1,2,3]]$ and $P3 = [[1,3,2],[2,1,3],[1,2,3]]$

$$P1 - P2 = [IndexOf([1,2,3]) \ IndexOf([2,1,3]) \ IndexOf([1,2,3])]$$
$$-[IndexOf([3,2,1]) \ IndexOf([2,1,3]) \ IndexOf([1,2,3])]] \qquad (7)$$

Difference between two positions of a cat is an m dimensional vector. Makespan of P1, P2 and P3 are 40, 52 and 40 respectively. In Table 3 we can observe that magnitude of difference in makespan ($|dif\_mp|$) and magnitude of difference in cats position ($|dif\_cp|$) are correlated. This property can be used increase convergence rate. Let the ith element of sublist be O(p,q). Smaller the value of i, more will be its impact on change in makespan. This is because change in i^{th} element of a sub-list will affect all elements after i^{th} element in same sub-list and in other sub-lists.

Table 3. Difference in cat position versus difference in makespan

	dif_cp	$|dif\_cp|$	$|dif\_mp|$
P1 - P2	[1 3 1] - [6 3 1] $=[-5\ 0\ 0]$	$\sqrt{((-5)^2 + 0^2 + 0^2)}$ =5	$|40 - 52| = |-12| = 12$
P1 - P3	[1 3 1] - [2 3 1] $=[-1\ 0\ 0]$	$\sqrt{((-1)^2 + 0^2 + 0^2)}$ =1	$|40 - 40| = 0$

3.1 Adding Velocity to Position of Cat

Let velocity $V = [1\ 1\ 1]$, position $X = [1\ 3\ 1]$
X_{new}(in vector form) $= X + V = [1\ 3\ 1] + [1\ 1\ 1] = [2\ 4\ 2]$
As in our example we have only 3 machines, maximum value that an element in sub-list can have is 3. Hence we change X_{new} from $[2\ 4\ 2]$ to $[2\ 3\ 2]$.
$X_{new} = [sublistAt(2) \ sublistAt(3) \ sublistAt(2)] = [[1,3,2][2,1,3][1,3,2]]$
(where sublistAt() is a method that converts an index to a sublist, refer Table 2)

3.2 Generating Random Position of Cat

To assign initial position to a cat in [1] a random vector was generated. This vector can be an invalid solution. Hence extra efforts have to be put in, to convert it to a valid solution. Also after some rearrangement (as in [1]) several different invalid solutions may get converted to same valid solution, leading to several cats getting same initial position. This affects the convergence speed. In our method we make sure that position assigned to any cat, is a valid position. Initially a valid solution in form of format-1 is generated using steps shown in Algorithm 1. Then we convert it in the form of format-2.

Algorithm 1. Generate valid random position for a cat

1: **function** GENERATERANDPOS
2:     nextPossibleOp = list of first operations of all jobs   ▷ nextPossibleOp keeps track of all operations that can be executed next
3:     position=[ ]   ▷ Current position of cat is initially empty
4:     totalOp=j*m   ▷ total number of operations
5:     i=0
6:     **while** $i < totalOp$ **do**
7:         O(p, q) = randomly select one operation out of nextPossibleOp
8:         nextPossibleOp= nextPossibleOp - O(p, q)
9:         position[i++]= O(p, q)
10:        **if** $p <$ number of operations in job p **then**
11:            $nextPossibleOp = nextPossibleOp \cup O(p + 1, q)$
12:        **end if**
13:    **end while**
14:    **return** position
15: **end function**

Table 4. Experimental results

D	j*m	A	B	Error %	D	j*m	A	B	Error %
LA01	10 * 5	666	805	20.8709	Orb1	10*10	1059	1383	30.5949
LA02	10 * 5	655	776	18.4733	Orb2	10*10	888	896	0.9009
LA03	10 * 5	597	620	3.8526	Orb3	10*10	1005	1201	19.5025
LA04	10 * 5	590	659	11.6949	Orb4	10*10	1005	1144	13.8308
LA05	10 * 5	593	627	5.73356	Orb5	10*10	888	899	1.23874
LA10	15*5	958	1029	7.41127	Orb6	10*10	1010	1282	26.9307
LA11	20*5	1222	1317	7.77414	Orb7	10*10	397	459	15.6171
LA12	20*5	1039	1190	14.5332	Orb8	10*10	899	1069	18.9099
LA13	20*5	1150	1330	15.6522	Orb9	10*10	934	1196	28.0514
LA14	20*5	1292	1292	0	Orb10	10*10	944	1089	15.3602
LA15	20*5	1207	1428	18.3099	Abz5	10*10	1234	1326	7.45543
LA16	10*10	946	946	0	Abz7	20*15	654	748	14.3731
LA17	10*10	789	820	3.92902	Abz8	20*15	634	717	13.0915
LA18	10*10	848	892	5.18868	Abz9	20*15	656	730	11.2805
LA19	10*10	842	870	3.32542	Ft06	6*6	55	62	12.7273
LA20	10*10	902	944	4.65632	Ft10	10*10	930	1038	11.6129
LA30	20*10	1355	1618	19.4096	Ft20	20*5	1165	1561	33.9914
LA31	30*10	1784	2022	13.3408	LA32	30*10	1850	2082	12.5405
LA33	30*10	1719	2091	21.6405	LA34	30*10	1721	2117	23.0099
LA35	30*10	1888	2336	23.7288					
Average percentage error									13.6037

4 Experiment

We tested our approach on 40 instances of OR-Library [8] (benchmark data set). System used had Intel Core i5-2430M CPU at 2.40 GHz with 4 GB RAM. We set number of cats in seeking mode as 11 and in tracing mode as 11, seeking memory pool size as 8, scaling factor (sc) as 0.2, initial velocity as [1 1 ... 1] and inertia (inr) as 0.8. In Table 4 column 'A' denotes 'Best known solution', 'B' denotes 'Solution that we have got' and 'D' denotes 'Instance in dataset'. We calculate error % as $\frac{(B-A)*100}{A}$. We achieved 86% accuracy despite of restricting number of iterations to 10, which consumed nearly one sec, thereby reaching faster towards suboptimal solution (i.e. better convergence rate).

5 Conclusion

We used CSO to solve NP-Hard problem of JSSP. Novelty in our approach was in the way in which we represented position of cat, method for selecting initial position of cats and the method for updating current cats position in seeking and tracing mode so as to achieve faster convergence. This enabled finding suboptimal solution in small interval of time. This approach can be used for many practical time critical applications. In future work we aim to increase the accuracy, without compromising with processing time.

References

1. Bouzidi, A., Riffi, M.E.: Cat swarm optimization to solve job shop scheduling. In: Third IEEE International Colloquium in Information Science and Technology (CIST) (2014)
2. Chu, S.-C., Tsai, P., Pan, J.-S.: Cat swarm optimization. In: Yang, Q., Webb, G. (eds.) PRICAI 2006. LNCS, vol. 4099, pp. 854–858. Springer, Heidelberg (2006). doi:10.1007/978-3-540-36668-3_94
3. Pythaloka, D., Wibowo, A.T., Sulistiyo, M.D.: Artificial fish swarm algorithm for job shop scheduling problem. In: 3rd International Conference on Information and Communication Technology (ICoICT), 2015. IEEE (2015)
4. Turguner, C., Sahingoz, O.K.: Solving job shop scheduling problem with ant colony optimization. In: IEEE 15th International Symposium on Computational Intelligence and Informatics (CINTI), 2014. IEEE (2014)
5. Lihong, W., Haikun, T., Guanghua, Y.: A hybrid genetic algorithm for job-shop scheduling problem. In: IEEE 28th Canadian Conference on Electrical and Computer Engineering (CCECE), 2015. IEEE (2015)
6. Ma, P.C., et al.: A hybrid particle swarm optimization and simulated annealing algorithm for job-shop scheduling. In: IEEE International Conference on Automation Science and Engineering (CASE), 2014. IEEE (2014)
7. Flrez, E., Gmez, W., Bautista, L.: An ant colony optimization algorithm for job shop scheduling problem. arXiv preprint arXiv:1309.5110 (2013)
8. Brunel University London, 20 February 2016. http://people.brunel.ac.uk/mastjjb/jeb/orlib/files/jobshop1.txt

Music-Induced Emotion Classification from the Prefrontal Hemodynamics

Pallabi Samanta[1], Diptendu Bhattacharya[2], Amiyangshu De[1],
Lidia Ghosh[1](✉) (ORCID), and Amit Konar[1]

[1] Electronics and Tele-communication Engineering, Jadavpur University,
Kolkata, India
pallabi.samanta18@gmail.com, amiyangshu_de@yahoo.com,
lidiaghosh.bits@gmail.com, konaramit@yahoo.co.in
[2] Computer Science and Engineering, National Institute of Technology Agartala,
Agartala, India
diptendu1@gmail.com

Abstract. Most of the traditional works on emotion recognition utilize manifestation of emotion in face, voice, gesture/posture and bio-potential signals of the subjects. However, these modalities of emotion recognition cannot totally justify its significance because of wide variations in these parameters due to habitat and culture. The paper aims at recognizing emotion of people directly from their brain response to infrared signal using music as the stimulus. A type-2 fuzzy classifier has been used to eliminate the effect of intra and inter-personal variations in the feature-space, extracted from the infrared response of the brain. A comparative analysis reveals that the proposed interval type-2 fuzzy classifier outperforms its competitors by classification accuracy as the metric.

Keywords: Emotion classification · Functional near-infrared spectroscopy · Interval type-2 fuzzy set classifier · Evolution algorithm

1 Introduction

In recent times, brain computer interface (BCI) has earned immense popularity for its inherent advantages in understanding the biological basis of cognitive processes, involving perception, memory, emotion and sensory-motor coordination. Emotion is regarded as the conscious experience concerning the pleasure, neutrality and displeasure levels of cognitive reaction of the brain in response to external stimulation.

Among different types of brain stimulation, music is one of the common modalities [4] of emotion arousal. Although no scientific justification on the role of music to emotion arousal is known till date, it is noticed that slow tempos, minor harmonies and a fixed pitch of a music is responsible of arousal of sadness [5]. Similarly, fast tempos, cacophonous and a wide range of pitch and dynamics have correlation with arousal of fear. Similar characterizations of stimuli for arousal of specific emotion has been ascertained by different research groups [6].

© Springer International Publishing AG 2017
B.U. Shankar et al. (Eds.): PReMI 2017, LNCS 10597, pp. 289–295, 2017.
https://doi.org/10.1007/978-3-319-69900-4_37

Most of the existing techniques attempt to classify emotion experienced by a subject based on the external manifestation of his/her emotion, such as change in facial expressions, voice qualities and physiological characteristics (like body temperature and skin conductance). A few well-known works that need special mention in this regard are listed below.

Das *et al.* [2] and Halder *et al.* [1] report novel techniques of emotion recognition using facial expression, voice and EEG analysis [9]. Wu *et al.*reported the change in brain wave synchronization during listening to music [3]. Furthermore, Mathur *et al.* [5] demonstrate the role of Indian classical music structure in emotional arousal. Banerjee *et al.* [6] studied the effect of music in human brain and body.

However understanding the cognitive underpinnings of emotional arousal needs more studies based on brain-imaging and cellular neuro-dynamics. We, here, employ functional Near Infra-Red Spectroscopy (fNIRs 1100) device to capture the pre-frontal brain response during emotion arousal with an aim to recognize the emotion from the brain response along with interpreting the involved brain regions [7]. The main focus of the present study is to model intra-personal and inter-personal uncertainty in the feature space of the fNIRS data obtained from the subjects, when the subjects experience musical stimuli. The uncertainty captured by the model is used later by an interval type-2 fuzzy set induced pattern classifier to recognize emotion. Besides, the results of emotion classification for given fNIRS features obtained from one or more voxels in the pre-frontal regions explains the engagement of the brain modules in the arousal process of emotion.

The paper is divided into four sections. Section 2 presents all the main steps, including normalization and pre-processing of the fNIRS signals, feature extraction, feature selection and the proposed Interval Type-2 fuzzy classifier for emotion recognition. Section 3 deals with experiments on feature selection and classifier performance. Conclusions are listed in Sect. 4.

2   Principles and Methodologies

This section reports all the required tools and techniques to resolve the proposed problem. The following steps are performed to classify hemodynamics responses associate with emotional arousal from music: (1) Scaling of the raw data, (2) Processing of the raw data and artifact removal, (3) Feature extraction from the oxyhemoglobin (HbO) and de-oxyhemoglobin (HbR) data obtained from fNIRS signals, (4) Feature selection based on evolutionary algorithm and (5) Classification of hemodynamic features using Interval Type-2 Fuzzy classifier.

2.1   Scaling of the Raw Data and Artifact Removal

The scaling of the raw data is performed using a max-min technique adopted from the protocol of De *et al.* [4]. Such transformation returns normalized HbO and HbR in $[0, 1]$.

Different physiological and environmental artifacts are removed by means of elliptical IIR low-pass filter with cut-off frequency o 0.5 Hz [7,8].

2.2 Feature Extraction

We use an fNIRs system having four sources and ten detectors that forms (4 sources) × (4 detectors) = 16 channels. The temporal hemodynamics in 16 channels is represented by (i) HbO and (ii) HbR absorption curve.

In the present scheme we used music to induce emotions, and these measured HbO(t) and HbR(t) at t = kT, where T is the samples interval, and k = 0, 1, 2, ... Here we have taken the HbO(t) and HbR(t) responses for 90 s, which are divided into 6 time-windows of 15 s each. We select a sampling rate of 2 Hz, i.e., 2 samples/second. Thus for 15 s duration, we have (15 × 2) = 30 samples denoted by HbO(t) and HbR(t) for k = 0 to 29; and T = 0.5 s.

Features: We have taken difference d(t) = HbO(t) - HbR(t) per window and obtain the Static Features [7] Mean(m), Variance(v), Skewness(sk), Kurtosis(ku) and Average Energy(E) from the standard definitions. To obtain the dynamic behavior, we compute the change in m, var, sk, ku and E over the transitions between each consecutive window of 15 s in a time frame of 90 s. For 5 transitions of windows we have (5 × 5) = 25 features. Coinciding Static and Dynamic features together, we have as many as (30 + 25) = 55 features. Thus for 16 voxels we have (16 × 55)= 880 features.

2.3 Feature Selection

We adopt an evolutionary algorithm based feature selection [10] to reduce 880 features into 200 features. The algorithm used for feature selection attempts to maximize inter-class separation and minimize intra-class separation. The following two objectives are designed to attain the above requirements. It is given that $\vec{a}_i^x = \vec{a}_{i,1}^x, ..., \vec{a}_{i,R}^x$ is the i-th feature vector having R numbers of components falling in class x, b_j^x and b_j^y denote the component of class centroids for class x and y respectively, the two objective functions are as

$$J_1 = \sum_{c=1}^{P}\sum_{i=1}^{Q}\sum_{j=1}^{R}|a_{i,j}^x - b_j^x| \quad (1) \qquad J_2 = \sum_{y=1,y\neq c}^{P} \sum_{c=1}^{P}\sum_{j=1}^{R}|b_j^x - b_j^y| \quad (2)$$

where P represents the number of classes, Q the number of data points, and R is the number of features. We have attempt to optimize $J = J_1 - J_2$ using evolutionary algorithm.

2.4   Fuzzy Classification

For the present emotion recognition problem, we considered 30 subjects and have performed repeated experiments of 10 times per subject. Let f_i be a feature. Then its ten instances are $f_i^1, f_i^2, ..., f_i^{10}$. We take the mean and variance of $f_i^1, f_i^2, ..., f_i^{10}$ and denote them by m_i and σ_i. We adopt Gaussion membership function to represent the membership of feature f_i. Now, for 30 experimental subjects we have 30 such Gaussion membership functions (MF) for a given feature f_i. We take the maximum and minimum of these 30 MFs to obtain the Interval Type- 2 Fuzzy set (IT2FS) [1].

Classifier Rule:
$Rule_i$: If f_1 is closed to its center, f_2 is closed to its center,......, and f_n is closed to its center, then class $= emotion_i$.

To resolve the classification problem, we determine the degree of firing strength of all the classifier rules. The rule having the highest firing strength represents the true emotion class.

Firing strength Computation: Let $f_1, f_2, ..., f_n$ be the measurement points. We obtain

$$LFS_i = Min(\underline{\mu}_{\tilde{A}_1}(f_1), \underline{\mu}_{\tilde{A}_2}(f_2), ..., \underline{\mu}_{\tilde{A}_n}(f_n)) \tag{3}$$

$$UFS_i = Min(\overline{\mu}_{\tilde{A}_1}(f_1), \overline{\mu}_{\tilde{A}_2}(f_2), ..., \overline{\mu}_{\tilde{A}_n}(f_n)) \tag{4}$$

where LFS_i and UFS_i denote the lower and upper firing strength of the i-th rule. We take the average of LFS_i and UFS_i to denote the average strength of firing of the rule i. We denote this by FS_i.

Thus for n classes, we need to fire n rules with the same measurements and determine their firing strength FS_i, $i = 1$ to n. Let the i-th rule have the different firing strength, i.e.; $FS_j > FS_k$ for all $k \neq i$. Then we declare the j-th emotion class as the solution for the classification task (Fig. 1).

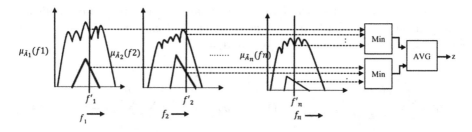

Fig. 1. Computing firing strength of an activated IT2FS induced rule

3   Experiments and Results

This section reports experimental protocols, the results from experimental instances and the inference derived from the experimental analysis.

3.1 Experimental Setup

30 right handed student volunteers, whose ages are between 20 to 27 took part in this experiment. Musical stimulus (Indian classical music) is presented by the head-phones mounted over the ears over a period of 90 s. Each participant undergoes 10 trials for each kind of music and a total set of six songs. 15 s interval, which generates maximum emotional depth, is considered as classification winsow. The hemodynamic data is recorded after removal of the base line.

3.2 Biological Inference of Hemodynamics in Emotion

Experimental analysis reports different emotion induced activations in prefrontal brain region. We adopt voxel plot approach from De *et al.* [11] (Fig. 3) using MATLAB 2015b to detect the spatial brain activation considering the mean HbO concentration during the specified 15 sec window of emotional activation. Here, we observe the least activation of the DorsoLateral Pre-frontal Cortex (DLPFC) [4] in happiness. The activation tends to rise in processing sadness and becomes highest in fear. Orbito-Frontal Cortex (OFC) shows a similar trend. The voxel plot for three emotions: (a) happiness, (b) sadness and (c) fear, is presented in Fig. 3 (due to lack of space the voxel plot of disgust is omitted). It also helps us to classify the different spatial pattern of brain activation due to emotional exposure from music.

3.3 Experiment 1: Feature Selection by Evolutionary Algorithm

Here, the feature dimension is reduced by using Evolutionary Algorithm. The best 200 features are selected among total 880 features. Figure 2 shows the discrimination of the selected 200 features by their relative amplitudes for each of the four classes: c_1 describing Happiness, c_2 describing Sadness, c_3 defining Fear and c_4 representing Disgust.

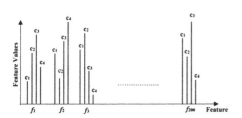

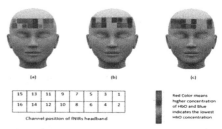

Fig. 2. Testing discrimination level of selected features

Fig. 3. Voxel plot of average HbO concentration

3.4   Experiment 2: Classifier Performance Analysis

To study the performance analysis, we compare the relative performance of the proposed IT2FS algorithm with three traditional emotion classification algorithms like Type-1 Fuzzy Classifier, multiclass Support Vector Machine (m-SVM) Classifier, Multi-layer Perceptron (MLP) algorithm. Table-I reveals that the final measure of the classification accuracy is the highest for the IT2FS method.

Table 1. Average Ranking of IT2FS over Three Traditional Classifiers according to their mean classifier accuracy

Emotion	IT2FS	Type-1 Fuzzy classifier	m-SVM	MLP
Happiness	83%	72%	67%	80.12%
Sadness	92%	80.67%	70%	82.12%
Fear	84%	75%	68.34%	81.45%
Disgust	78.89%	70%	65%	78.22%
Average ranking by Friedman test	1	3	4	2

3.5   Experiment 3: Statistical Comparison of Classifier Performance Using Friedman Test

To validate the importance of the work, we examine the performance of the classifier algorithms (IT2FS, Type-1 Fuzzy classifier, m-SVM and MLP) on four different databases using Friedman test. The Friedman Statistic used in this test has the standard definition as mentioned in [1]. The Friedman Statistic score is computed as $\chi_F^2 =11.095$ with $N = 4$ and $k = 4$, which is greater than $\chi_{3,0.05}^2 = 7.815$. Thus, the null hypothesis is rejected at 3 degree of freedom with 78% accuracy suggesting that the classifier performance can be ranked according to their mean accuracy percentages. The average ranking of the classifiers computed using Friedman test is given in Table 1.

4   Conclusion

The paper introduces a novel approach to recognize music-induced emotion of subjects from their pre-frontal IR response. It is evident from the experimental results that the evolutionary algorithm based feature selection and the IT2FS induced classification approach together outperforms other conventional techniques. The IT2FS-induced classifier classifies the reduced 200 dimensional feature vectors into 4 emotion classes: happiness, sadness, fear and disgust with classification accuracies 83%, 92%, 84% and 78.89% respectively. The justification of IT2FS induced classifier is apparent due to its significance in intra-class and inter-class feature variation in the fNIRS signals. Experimental results further reveal that the DLPFC and OFC region of the brain is least activated during stimulation of happiness; the activation grows in sadness to disgust and with the highest response in fear.

References

1. Halder, A., Konar, A., Mandal, R., Chakraborty, A., Bhowmik, P., Pal, N.R., Nagar, A.K.: General and interval type-2 fuzzy face-space approach to emotion recognition. IEEE Trans. Syst. Man Cybern. Syst. **43**(3), 587–605 (2013)
2. Das, S., Halder, A., Bhowmik, P., Chakraborty, A., Konar, A., Janarthanan, R.: A support vector machine classifier of emotion from voice and facial expression data. In: World Congress on Nature and Biologically Inspired Computing: (NaBIC 2009) (2009)
3. Wu, J., Zhang, J., Ding, X., Li, R., Zhou, C.: The effects of music on brain functional networks: a network analysis. Nueroscience **250**, 49–59 (2013)
4. Schmidt, L.A., Traino, L.J.: Frontal brain electrical activity (EEG) distinguishes valence and intensity of musical emotions. Cogn. Emot. **15**(4), 487–500 (2001)
5. Mathur, A., Vijayakumar, S.H., Chakrabarti, B., Singh, N.C.: Emotional responses to Hindustani raga music: the role of musical structure. Front. Psychol. **30**, 1–11 (2015)
6. Banerjee, A., Sanyal, S., Sengupta, R., Ghosh, D.: Music and its effect on body, brain/mind: a study on indian perspective by nuero-physical approach. iMedPub J. **1**(1:2), 1–11 (2015)
7. Naseer, N., Hong, K.S.: fNIRS-based brain-computer interfaces: a review. Front. Hum. Neurosci. **28**, 1–15 (2015)
8. Herff, C., Heger, D., Fortmann, O., Hennrich, J., Putze, F., Schultz, T.: Mental workload during n-back task-quantified in the prefrontal cortex using fNIRS. Front. Hum. Neurosci. **7**, 1–9 (2013). Article no 935
9. Chakraborty, A., Konar, A., Halder, A., Kim, E.: Emotion control by audio-visual stimulus using fuzzy automata. In: IEEE International Conference on Fuzzy Systems (FUZZ), pp. 1–8. IEEE, July 2010
10. Lahiri, R., Rakshit, P., Konar, A., Nagar, A.K.: Evolutionary approach for selection of optimal EEG electrode positions and features for classification of cognitive tasks. In: IEEE Congress on Evolutionary Computation (CEC), pp. 4846–4853, July 2016
11. De, A., Konar, A., Samanta, A., Biswas, A., Ralescu, A.L., Nagar, A.K.: Cognitive load classification tasks from hemodynamic responses using type-2 fuzzy sets. In: Fuzz IEEE (2017)

Speech and Natural Language Processing

Analysis of Features and Metrics for Alignment in Text-Dependent Voice Conversion

Nirmesh J. Shah$^{(\boxtimes)}$ (iD) and Hemant A. Patil$^{(\boxtimes)}$ (iD)

Speech Research Lab, DA-IICT, Gandhinagar, India
{nirmesh88_shah,hemant_patil}@daiict.ac.in

Abstract. Voice Conversion (VC) is a technique that convert the perceived speaker identity from a source speaker to a target speaker. Given a source and target speakers' parallel training speech database in the text-dependent VC, first task is to align source and target speakers' spectral features at frame-level before learning the mapping function. The accuracy of alignment will affect the learning of mapping function and hence, the voice quality of converted voice in VC. The impact of alignment is not much explored in the VC literature. Most of the alignment techniques try to align the acoustical features (namely, spectral features, such as Mel Cepstral Coefficients (MCC)). However, spectral features represents both speaker as well as speech-specific information. In this paper, we have done analysis on the use of different speaker-independent features (namely, unsupervised posterior features, such as, Gaussian Mixture Model (GMM)-based and Maximum A Posteriori (MAP) adapted from Universal Background Model (UBM), i.e., GMM-UBM-based posterior features) for the alignment task. In addition, we propose to use different metrics, such as, symmetric Kullback-Leibler (KL) and cosine distances instead of Euclidean distance for the alignment. Our analysis-based on % Phone Accuracy (PA) is correlating with subjective scores of the developed VC systems with 0.98 Pearson correlation coefficient.

Keywords: Gaussian Mixture Model · Spectral features · Posterior features

1 Introduction

The use of text-to-speech (TTS) systems in the commercial applications has increased recently. Voice Conversion (VC) is being used to develop personalized TTS in a cost effective manner. VC is a technique that modifies the speech signal uttered by a source speaker in such way that it is perceived as if it was uttered by a target speaker. Based on the nature of training corpus (i.e., parallel, non-parallel or cross-lingual), VC can be broadly classified into *text-dependent* VC (for parallel corpus) and *text-independent* VC (for non-parallel corpus) [18].

The alignment of source and target spectral features' before learning the *mapping* or *transformation* function is a key issue. In the case of parallel corpus,

© Springer International Publishing AG 2017
B.U. Shankar et al. (Eds.): PReMI 2017, LNCS 10597, pp. 299–307, 2017.
https://doi.org/10.1007/978-3-319-69900-4_38

dynamic time warping (DTW) algorithm is used [15] and in the case of text-independent VC, state-of-the-art algorithm Iterative combination of a Nearest Neighbor search step and a Conversion step Alignment (INCA) algorithm [4] is used. The impact of alignment on the quality of converted voice is less explored in the VC literature. However, the significance of alignment is much explored in speech recognition [15], audio search [21] and speech synthesis [10,16,19,20]. The initial attempt in [6] has clearly demonstrated that the alignment accuracy affects quality of converted voice. In addition, it has shown that misaligned pairs will result into outliers that deteriorate the quality of converted voice [12].

In the literature, posterior features have been extensively used for keyword detection [1,9,13,21], template-based speech recognition task [2]. In this paper, we propose to use unsupervised Gaussian posterior features to find the warping path between speech utterances from source and target speaker. In addition, we have also explored various spectral features for the alignment, such as, Mel Cepstral Coefficients (MCC) features and standard Mel Frequency Cepstral Coefficients (MFCC) and posterior features derived from these features. The key issue with alignment techniques in VC is that they try to minimize the Euclidean distance between acoustic features for alignment. However, same phoneme uttered by two different speakers will not have the minimum Euclidean distance. Hence, we have explored various metric techniques, such as, cosine similarity, Euclidean distance and symmetric Kullback-Leibler (KL) distance. Results are shown in terms of % phonetic accuracies after the aligned pairs and the subjective evaluation on the developed VC systems.

2   Alignment Technique

2.1   Motivation

The alignment of source and target speakers' spectral features is the key issue before learning the mapping function as the both speakers have spoken utterances with the different speaking rate or speaking style. Figure 1 shows the block diagram of a proposed system. First, the spectral features and the excitation source features, which represents the speaker-related information are extracted. Once the alignment of the spectral features is done, the next task is to learn the mapping function among these aligned pairs. The unknown spectral features from the source speaker is converted using the mapping function. Finally, the vocoder is used to get speech signal from converted features. If the corresponding pairs are wrongly aligned, it will deteriorate the quality of a converted voice. Hence, one should have accurate phone boundaries to align the spectral features. In this paper, we are applying different features and distance metrics to obtain warping path, which will be used for the alignment as shown in Fig. 1.

2.2   Dynamic Time Warping (DTW)

Dynamic Time Warping (DTW) is considered as state-of-the-art method for aligning spectral features in case of parallel data. The main objective of DTW

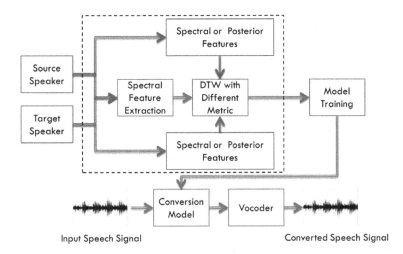

Fig. 1. A schematic block diagram of proposed VC system for the parallel corpus. Dotted box indicates the contribution in this paper.

is to find an optimal warping path between speech patterns X and Y. Let $X = \{x_1, x_2, ..., x_N\}$ and $Y = \{y_1, y_2, ..., y_M\}$ are the short-time spectral feature vector sequence corresponding to the training speech utterances, where N and M are the length of the two feature sequences. DTW minimizes the overall distance $d(X, Y)$, which is the sum of local distance $d(x_{w_x(k)}, y_{w_y(k)})$ computed over warping path w_x and w_y. Hence, DTW can be explained as [15]:

$$DTW(X, Y) = \min_{w_x, w_y} \sum_{k=1}^{K} d(x_{w_x(k)}, y_{w_y(k)}). \tag{1}$$

The above mentioned objective function is optimized by using the four standard constraints as given in [15]. $d(X, Y)$ in Eq. (1) is the metric applied between the features to calculate similarity. In the literature, $d(X, Y)$ is taken as the Euclidean distance [7]. Similar to the study reported in image processing and computer vision literature, namely, Euclidean distance may not correlate well with the perceptual distance of two patterns in a feature space [8]. Hence, we have explored Euclidean distance, cosine similarity and symmetric KL distance for spectral and posterior features in Eq. (1).

2.3 Mel Cepstral Coefficients (MCC) *vs.* Mel Frequency Cepstral Coefficients (MFCC)

In the literature, MFCC is considered as the standard features in speech recognition. The details of MFCC and MCC can be found in [3,5], respectively. MFCC exploits perceptually-motivated auditory filterbank (such as, Mel scale filterbank). However, MCC is using allpass transform to approximate Mel scale as shown in Fig. 2. Hence, MCC and MFCC are different features.

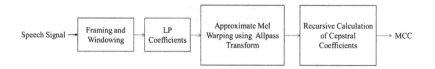

Fig. 2. Block diagram to calculate MCC. After [5].

DCT is not applied at the end of MCC as shown in Fig. 2 and hence, it makes it less suitable in Euclidean space. In this paper, we have explored both the features MFCC and MCC for the alignment task.

3   Proposed Posterior Features

3.1   Gaussian Posterior Features

First, the unsupervised Gaussian Mixture Model (GMM) is trained on the TIMIT database [14]. Gaussian posterior features are the posterior probability vectors for a given Gaussian mixture components [21]. For a given speech utterances, $X = (x_1, x_2, ..., x_n)$, Gaussian posterior features are defined as $GP(X) = (r_1, r_2, ..., r_n)$. Here, r_i can be calculated as:

$$r_i = (P(C_1|x_i), P(C_2|x_i), ..., P(C_m|x_i)), \qquad (2)$$

where C_i represents the ith Gaussian mixture component. Once the posterior feature is obtained, the P_{min} threshold is applied (i.e., set probability value zero if its value is less than P_{min}). Posterior probability vector is re-normalized to ensure that the summation of each dimension to be one [21]. Here, we have taken $P_{min} = 0.001$. In this paper, posterior features for the source and target speakers' utterances have been calculated and these features are used to find optimum warping path using DTW.

3.2   GMM-UBM Posterior Features

The GMM learned using unsupervised technique on TIMIT database may not represent well the given source and target speaker pair in terms of posterior features. Hence, we applied maximum a posteriori (MAP)-based adaptation technique to adapt the estimated GMM on TIMIT database (which can be considered as Universal Background Model (UBM)) to the given source target speaker pair [14]. Given training data (from source and target speakers) and UBM (learned on TIMIT), first calculate probabilistic alignment of training vectors, i.e.,

$$Pr(i|x) = \frac{\omega_i p_i(x_t)}{\sum_{j=1}^{M} \omega_j p_j(x_t)}. \qquad (3)$$

Sufficient statistics from a given training data for weight, mean and variance parameters are given by $n_i = \sum_{t=1}^{T} Pr(i|x_t)$, $E_i(x) = \frac{1}{n_i}\sum_{t=1}^{T} Pr(i|x_t)x_t$,

$E_i(x^2) = \frac{1}{n_i} \sum_{t=1}^{T} Pr(i|x_t)x_t^2$, respectively [14]. Update equations for i^{th} mixture is given by [14]:

$$\hat{\omega}_i = [\alpha_i^{\omega} n_i / T + (1 - \alpha_i^{\omega})]\gamma, \tag{4}$$

$$\hat{\mu}_i = \alpha_i^m E_i(x) + (1 - \alpha_i^m)\mu_i, \tag{5}$$

$$\hat{\sigma}_i^2 = \alpha_i^v E_i(x^2) + (1 - \alpha_i^v)(\sigma_i^2 + \mu_i^2) - \hat{\mu}_i^2, \tag{6}$$

where $\alpha_i^\rho = \frac{n_i}{n_i + r}$, $\rho \in \{\omega, m, v\}$, where r is a relevance factor. The updated GMM will be used to calculate posterior features for training data and it is used to calculate warping path.

4   Experimental Results

In this paper, the CMU-ARCTIC database have been taken for developing VC systems using different alignment techniques. 100 parallel utterances for each speaker have been taken from the speaker pairs, BDL-RMS (male-male), BDL-SLT (male-female), CLB-RMS (female-male) and CLB-SLT (female-female). 25-D MCC and MFCC (including the 0th coefficient) with 5 ms frame shift have been estimated. In order to calculate posterior features, number of mixture components have been varied, for example, $\{m = 2, 4, 8, 16, 32, 64, 128, 256, 512, 1024\}$.

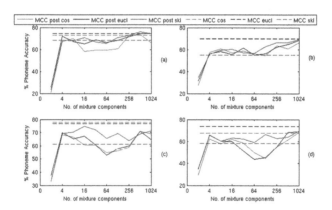

Fig. 3. % Phone accuracy for TIMIT Posterior with MCC features: (a) BDL-RMS (b) BDL-SLT (C) CLB-SLT and (d) CLB-RMS, where, MCC: Mel cepstral Coefficients, Post: Posterior features, EUCL: Euclidean distance, SKL: symmetric KL distance, COS: cosine distance.

The relative analysis of the different features with different metrics is presented here. Results are presented in terms of the % Phoneme Accuracy (PA) obtained after estimating warping path for different configurations. The ground truth for CMU-ARCTIC database is available, which is obtained using training speaker-dependent Hidden Markov Model (HMM) over 1132 utterances for each speaker.

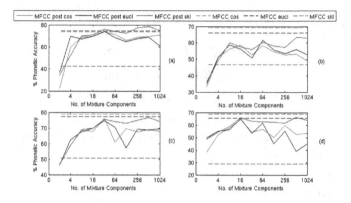

Fig. 4. % Phone accuracy for TIMIT Posterior with MFCC features: (a) BDL-RMS (b) BDL-SLT (C) CLB-SLT and (d) CLB-RMS.

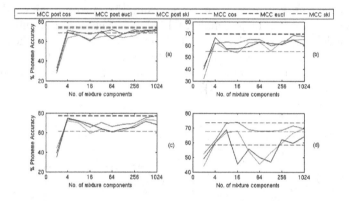

Fig. 5. % Phone accuracy for TIMIT-ARCTIC GMM-UBM Posterior with MCC features: (a) BDL-RMS (b) BDL-SLT (C) CLB-SLT and (d) CLB-RMS, where, MCC: Mel cepstral Coefficients, Post: Posterior features, EUCL: Euclidean distance, SKL: symmetric KL distance, COS: cosine distance.

Figures 3 and 4 shows the % PA for four different systems with three different distance metrics using MCC, MFCC and their posterior features obtained using TIMIT database, respectively. In all the cases, posterior features with symmetric KL distance performs better than Euclidean or cosine scoring distance.

Figures 5 and 6 shows similar observation. In addition, we can see that MFCC features with cosine distance performs better than Euclidean or symmetric KL distance. However, MCC features performs better with Euclidean distance only. Furthermore, one can observe that posterior features obtained using TIMIT database are not performing better than the spectral features. This may be due to the fact that TIMIT database consists of unbalanced gender proportion which leads to unbiased posterior representations. In particular, TIMIT database consists of 192 female and 438 male speakers' speech data. Hence, models are

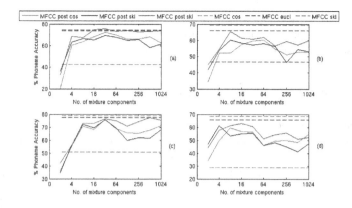

Fig. 6. % Phone accuracy for TIMIT-ARCTIC GMM-UBM Posterior with MFCC features: (a) BDL-RMS (b) BDL-SLT (C) CLB-SLT and (d) CLB-RMS.

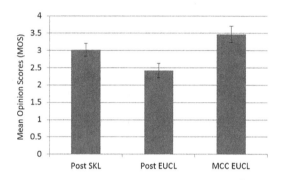

Fig. 7. MOS analysis along with 95% confidence intervals for VC systems.

biased towards male speakers' data. Thus, we can see that posterior features perform better only in case of male-male system. For the case of GMM-UBM posterior features, we can observe that posterior features perform similar to the spectral features as compared to the TIMIT posterior features.

Here, we have developed three different VC systems using posterior features and symmetric KL distance, MCC Euclidean distance and posterior Euclidean distance for each possible speaker pairs (i.e., total 12 VC systems). The Mean Opinion Score (MOS) test has been selected for the subjective evaluation. Subjects were asked to evaluate randomly played utterances for the speech quality on the scale of 1 to 5 (1 very bad, 2 bad, 3 average, 4 good and 5 very good). Figure 7 shows the MOS obtained from the 12 subjects (with no known hearing impairments with the age between 23 to 30 years), 2 females and 10 males from total 264 samples. The posterior features with the symmetric KL distance performs better as compared to the Euclidean distance. The MOS are correlating with the % PA of developed system with 0.98 Pearson correlation coefficient. Here, we have not presented MCD scores as it is found that it does not correlate well with subjective scores in VC literature [11,17].

5   Summary and Conclusions

In this study, we presented analysis of spectral and posterior features for the alignment tasks in text-dependent VC system with different distance metrics. We have done comparison-based on the % PA obtained after aligning the features-based on the estimated warping path. We found that posterior features perform better with symmetric KL distance than the Euclidean and cosine distance. Furthermore, we observed that MFCC performs better with cosine distance than the Euclidean distance. However, Euclidean distance works well with MCC. Hence, our analysis will be useful to select appropriate distance metric for particular features. Our analysis is correlating with subjective scores.

References

1. Aradilla, G., Bourlard, H., Magimai-Doss, M.: Posterior features applied to speech recognition tasks with user-defined vocabulary. In: Proceeding ICASSP, Taipei, pp. 3809–3812 (2009)
2. Aradilla, G., Vepa, J., Bourlard, H.: Using posterior-based features in template matching for speech recognition. In: INTERSPEECH, Pittsburgh, pp. 1–5 (2006)
3. Davis, S., Mermelstein, P.: Comparison of parametric representations for mono-syllabic word recognition in continuously spoken sentences. IEEE Trans. Acoust. Speech Signal Process. **28**(4), 357–366 (1980)
4. Erro, D., Moreno, A., Bonafonte, A.: INCA algorithm for training voice conversion systems from nonparallel corpora. IEEE Trans. Audio Speech Lang. Process. **18**(5), 944–953 (2010)
5. Fukada, T., Tokuda, K., Kobayashi, T., Imai, S.: An adaptive algorithm for mel-cepstral analysis of speech. In: ICASSP, San Francisco, California, USA, pp. 137–140 (1992)
6. Helander, E., Schwarz, J., Nurminen, J., Silen, H., Gabbouj, M.: On the impact of alignment on voice conversion performance. In: INTERSPEECH, Brisbane, Australia, pp. 1–5 (2008)
7. Kain, A., Macon, M.W.: Spectral voice conversion for text-to-speech synthesis. In: Proceeding ICASSP, Seattle, WA, pp. 285–288 (1998)
8. Kulis, B., et al.: Metric learning: a survey. Found. Trends® Mach. Learn. **5**(4), 287–364 (2013)
9. Madhavi, M.C., Patil, H.A.: Modification in sequential dynamic time warping for fast computation of query-by-example spoken term detection task. In: SPCOM, Bangalore, India, pp. 1–5 (2016)
10. Patil, H.A., Patel, T., Talesara, S., Shah, N., Sailor, H., Vachhani, B., Akhani, J., Kanakiya, B., Gaur, Y., Prajapati, V.: Algorithms for speech segmentation at syllable-level for text-to-speech synthesis system in Gujarati. In: Oriental COCOSDA, New Delhi, India, pp. 1–7 (2013)

11. Rajpal, A., Shah, N.J., Zaki, M., Patil, H.A.: Quality assessment of voice converted speech using articulatory features. In: Proceeding ICASSP, New Orleans, pp. 5515–5519 (2017)
12. Rao, S.V., Shah, N.J., Patil, H.A.: Novel pre-processing using outlier removal in voice conversion. In: 9th ISCA Speech Synthesis Workshop, Sunnyvale, CA, USA, pp. 147–152 (2016)
13. Reddy, P.R., Rout, K., Murty, K.S.R.: Query word retrieval from continuous speech using GMM posteriorgrams. In: SPCOM, Banglore, India, pp. 1–6 (2014)
14. Reynolds, D.A., Quatieri, T.F., Dunn, R.B.: Speaker verification using adapted Gaussian mixture models. Digit. Signal Process. **10**(1–3), 19–41 (2000)
15. Sakoe, H., Chiba, S.: Dynamic programming algorithm optimization for spoken word recognition. IEEE Trans. Acoust. Speech Signal Process. **26**(1), 43–49 (1978)
16. Shah, N.J., Vachhani, B.B., Sailor, H.B., Patil, H.A.: Effectiveness of PLP-based phonetic segmentation for speech synthesis. In: Proceeding ICASSP, Florence, Italy, pp. 270–274 (2014)
17. Shah, N.J., Patil, H.A.: Novel amplitude scaling method for bilinear frequency warping based voice conversion. In: Proceeding ICASSP, New Orleans, USA, pp. 5520–5524 (2017)
18. Sündermann, D., Bonafonte, A., Ney, H., Höge, H.: A first step towards text-independent voice conversion. In: International Conference on Spoken Language Processing (ICSLP), South Korea, pp. 1–4 (2004)
19. Talesara, S., Patil, H.A., Patel, T., Sailor, H., Shah, N.: A novel Gaussian filter-based automatic labeling of speech data for TTS system in Gujarati language. In: Proceeding IALP, Urumqi, China, pp. 139–142 (2013)
20. Zaki, M., Shah, N.J., Patil, H.A.: Effectiveness of multiscale fractal dimension-based phonetic segmentation in speech synthesis for low resource language. In: Proceeding IALP, Kuching, Borneo, Malaysia, pp. 103–106 (2014)
21. Zhang, Y., Glass, J.R.: Unsupervised spoken keyword spotting via segmental DTW on Gaussian posteriorgrams. In: IEEE Workshop on Automatic Speech Recognition & Understanding (ASRU), Merano, Italy, pp. 398–403 (2009)

Effectiveness of Mel Scale-Based ESA-IFCC Features for Classification of Natural *vs.* Spoofed Speech

Madhu R. Kamble[(✉)] and Hemant A. Patil[(✉)]

Speech Research Lab, Dhirubhai Ambani Institute of Information and Communication Technology (DA-IICT), Gandhinagar, Gujarat, India
{madhu_kamble,hemant_patil}@daiict.ac.in

Abstract. The performance of biometric systems based on Automatic Speaker Verification (ASV) degrades due to spoofing attacks, generated using different speech synthesis (SS) and voice conversion (VC) techniques. Results of recent ASV spoof 2015 challenge indicate that spoof-aware features are a possible solution, rather than focusing on a powerful classifier. In this paper, we investigate the effect of various frequency scales (such as, ERB, Mel and linear) applied on a Gabor filterbank. The output of filterbank was used to exploit the contribution of instantaneous frequency (IF) in each subband energy via Teager Energy Operator-based Energy Separation Algorithm (TEO-ESA) to capture possible changes in spectral envelope of spoofed speech. The IF is computed from narrow-band components of the speech signal and Discrete Cosine Transform (DCT) is applied on deviations in IF, which are referred to as Instantaneous Frequency Cosine Coefficients (IFCC). The classification results on static features shows an EER of 1.32% with Mel frequency scale and 1.87% with linear. The results with delta feature of linear frequency scale gets reduced further to 1.39% whereas, with Mel scale, it increased by 0.64% on development set of ASV spoof 2015 challenge database.

Keywords: Automatic Speaker Verification · Energy Separation Algorithm · Teager Energy Operator · Gabor filterbank · Spoofed speech

1 Introduction

Spoofing attacks replicate a person's identity from his or her voice to get access to a sensitive or protected system. Automatic Speaker Verification (ASV) or voice biometric system deals with a great threat from speech technology related to SS and VC. The literature includes various spoofing attacks, namely, replay, impersonation, SS, VC and twins [11]. Replay attack deals with playback of pre-recorded speech. An impersonation is an approach where an attacker tries to mimic a genuine target speaker. Likewise, twins are considered as imitation based on physiological characteristics. The other machine-generated techniques vulnerable to ASV systems include Text-to-Speech (TTS) synthesis and VC.

© Springer International Publishing AG 2017
B.U. Shankar et al. (Eds.): PReMI 2017, LNCS 10597, pp. 308–316, 2017.
https://doi.org/10.1007/978-3-319-69900-4_39

A novel feature set was used that decomposes speech into various subbands and exploit contributions of IF in each subband via discrete Energy Separation Algorithm (ESA). In this paper, we study the effect of various frequency scales, namely, Equivalent Rectangular Bandwidth (ERB), Mel and linear for classification of natural *vs.* spoofed speech. The Gabor filterbank was used as it is smooth and compact in both time and frequency domains (due to Heisenberg's uncertainty principle in signal processing framework). The earlier studies shows accurate estimation of amplitude and frequency with Gabor filter. The decomposition of a speech signal was done with Teager Energy Operator (TEO)-based ESA. Nonlinear energy operator is used by ESA to track the instantaneous energy of the source generating signal and separate it into its amplitude and frequency components. Here, we exploit the contribution of instantaneous frequency (IF) in each subband energy via ESA. The estimation of IF was carried out with ERB, Mel and linear frequency scale. The dependency of frequency scales shows the importance to extract the IF as the scales are different, the cutoff frequency will also be different and hence, the IF. The scale of ERB and Mel are more or less similar and follows the auditory motivated scales. The ERB and Mel have the pattern of increasing bandwidth as the frequency increases. Comparing both ERB and Mel itself have difference, i.e., at higher frequency, ERB has more higher bandwidth than the Mel scale. The linear frequency scale shows the constant effect of bandwidth throughout all the frequencies. Experiments are done on ASV spoof 2015 challenge database [12].

2   Multiband Filtering and Demodulation

A real Gabor bandpass filter is used to extract the speech resonance from the speech signal. In the literature, it was shown that Gabor filter optimally acts as compact and smooth both in time and frequency domains (because Fourier transform of Gaussian is a Gaussian) and thus, provides accurate amplitude and frequency estimates in the demodulation stage. The impulse response $h(t)$ and frequency response $H(f)$ of Gabor filter is given as [2]:

$$h(t) = exp(-a^2t^2)cos(2\pi vt), \tag{1}$$

$$H(f) = \frac{\sqrt{\pi}}{2\alpha}\left[exp\left(-\frac{\pi^2(f-v)^2}{\alpha^2}\right) + exp\left(-\frac{\pi^2(f+v)^2}{\alpha^2}\right)\right], \tag{2}$$

where v is the center frequency (in Hz) of the filter chosen equal to various frequency scales, i.e., ERB, Mel and linear scale. The frequency scale for Mel and ERB is given as [1] and [2]:

$$Mel(v) = 2595log_{10}(1 + v/700), \tag{3}$$

$$ERB(v) = 6.23(v/1000)^2 + 93.39(v/1000) + 28.52. \tag{4}$$

Maragos *et al.* developed ESA to demodulate speech signal into amplitude envelope $a(n)$ and instantaneous frequency $w(n)$ [6]. The energy operator that tracks energy of source producing an oscillation signal $x(n)$ is defined as [5]:

$$E_n = \Psi_d\{x(n)\} = x^2(n) - x(n-1)x(n+1) \approx A^2\omega^2. \qquad (5)$$

The ESA amplitude and frequency estimates are [7]:

$$a[n] \approx \frac{2\Psi_d\{x[n]\}}{\sqrt{\Psi_d\{x[n+1]) - x[n-1]\}}}, \qquad (6)$$

$$\omega_i[n] \approx arcsin\sqrt{\frac{\Psi_d\{x[n+1] - x[n-1]\}}{4\Psi_d\{x[n]\}}}. \qquad (7)$$

Equations (6) and (7) are w.r.t. symmetric approximation of derivative, i.e., $y[n] = \frac{x(n+1)-x(n-1)}{2}$. Similar equations and algorithm exists in continuous time-domain. The ESA is simple, computationally efficient and has excellent time resolution (due to high time resolution property of TEO [3]).

3 ESA-IFCC Feature Set

As proposed in our earlier work Fig. 1 shows the block diagram of Energy Separation Algorithm-Instantaneous Frequency Cosine Coefficients (ESA-IFCC) feature set [4,8,9]. Here, the input speech is first split into N frequency subband signals, i.e., Gabor filterbank was used to obtain N subband signals with ERB, Mel and linear frequency scales. The ESA is applied using TEO onto each N bandpass (subband)-filtered signals to obtain corresponding AEs and IFs. Furthermore, we have taken only IF and computed for each of the narrowband components in order to emphasize the spectral envelope of genuine *vs.* spoofed speech. The IF are segmented into overlapping short frames of 20 ms, shifted by 10 ms, and the temporal average is computed to obtain N-dimensional IFCs for every frame. The redundancy among IFCs is exploited to obtain a low-dimensional representation by employing DCT that has energy compaction property and thus, retaining first few DCT coefficients that are referred as Instantaneous Frequency Cosine Coefficients (IFCC). Algorithm for extracting ESA-IFCC feature set is given in Algorithm 1.

3.1 Spectrographic Analysis

Figure 2 shows spectral energy density obtained at the output of Gabor filterbank with different frequency scales (i.e., ERB, Mel and linear) upto 4000 Hz. It was observed that in lower frequency regions more information is captured in terms of formants, F_0 and harmonics of a speech signal with all the frequency scales. However, only with linear frequency scale, it was observed that it provides more significant speaker-specific information in lower as well as in higher frequency

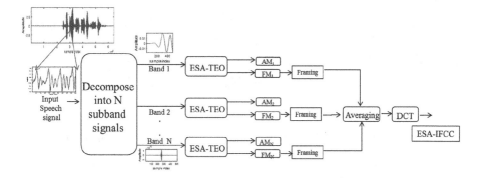

Fig. 1. Schematic diagram of ESA-IFCC feature extraction.

Algorithm 1. The ESA-IFCC feature extraction from speech signals.

1: $x(n)$= speech signal.
2: Consider an N channel with ERB or Mel or linearly spaced Gabor filterbank in time-domain.
3: **for** i=1 to N **do**
4:    Perform narrowband filtering of $x(n)$ through i^{th} filter; $x_i(n)$.
5:    Compute TEO from $x_i(n)$ as in Eq. (5)
6:    Compute ESA and extract IF $\omega_i(n)$ as in Eq. (7).
7: **end for**
8: Segment $\omega_i(n)$, $i = 1, 2.....N$ into short-time frames of duration as 20 ms, shifted by 10 ms in time-domain.
9: Average IF for each frame to obtain N-dimensional IFCs.
10: Apply DCT on ESA-IFCs and retain first few coefficients to get ESA-IFCCs.

---

regions. The key difference for Mel and linear frequency scales is obtained in lower frequency region (i.e., spectral energy density with Mel scale is darker and have better resolution in lower frequency regions as compared to linear scale that possibly makes it to perform better to classify natural and spoofed signals).

3.2   Filterbank Scale Analysis

The Gabor filterbank with 40 subband filters and bandwidth of 1.09 Hz is kept for ERB, Mel and for linear, it is 100 Hz are shown in Fig. 3. It can be observed from filterbank response in Fig. 3(a) and (b) that filterbank obtained with ERB and Mel scales are more compressed at lower frequency regions. However, both indeed shows the difference in the higher frequencies regions, i.e., for ERB, the bandwidth increases at higher frequency regions, which makes it less reliable to extract the IF [10]. The filterbank obtained with linear frequency scale has the almost equal bandwidth for all the frequency regions that makes it relatively more convenient to extract the IF properly with equal emphasis on each sub-bands. The effect of the different frequency scales obtained with 40 subband

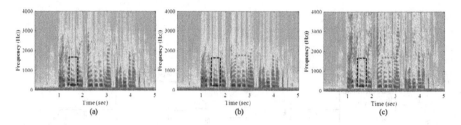

Fig. 2. Spectral energy density obtained with 40 subband filter signals for (a) ERB (b) Mel and (c) linear frequency scale. The black and green color dotted rectangle in Fig. 2(b) indicates that spectral energy density is darker (i.e., more energy) in lower frequency regions than that of Fig. 2(c). (Color figure online)

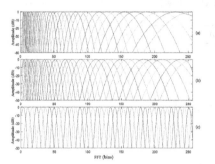

Fig. 3. Gabor filterbank with 40 subband filters and bandwidth 1.09 for various scales (a) ERB (b) Mel and (c) linear.

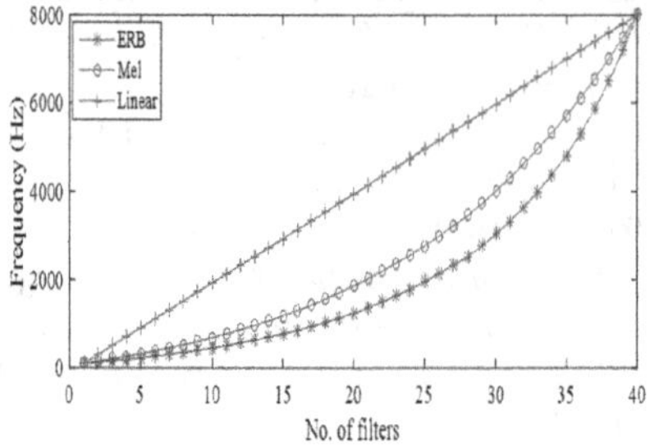

Fig. 4. Comparison of frequency scales.

filters and with maximum frequencies of 8000 Hz was shown in Fig. 4 with a standard Gabor filterbank.

4   Experimental Results

The experiments are conducted on the development set of ASV spoof 2015 challenge database [12], which consists of speech data collected from 106 speakers (45 male and 61 female) and three subsets with non-overlapping speakers. Table 1 summarizes speaker and utterance information for each subset [12].

4.1   Experimental Setup

The ESA-IFCC features were extracted using 40 subbands Gabor filterbank with ERB, Mel and linearly-spaced frequency scale with a frequency range of 10–8000 Hz. For each narrowband component, TEO-based ESA was applied for computing AM-FM components. IF were computed for each of the narrowband components. Furthermore, these IFs were averaged over short-time windows of

Table 1. Number of speakers and utterances in different datasets

Subset	# Speakers		# Utterances	
	Male	Female	Genuine	Impostor
Training	10	15	3750	12625
Dev	15	20	3497	49875
Eval	20	26	9404	184000

Table 2. Results of ESA-IFCC with 13 dimension feature vector in % EER on development set with Gabor filterbank having different frequency scale.

Scale	Static	S+Δ	S+Δ+$\Delta\Delta$
ERB	35.66	31.85	30.93
Mel	**1.32**	1.96	2.52
linear	1.86	**1.39**	2.23

20 ms duration, shifted by 10 ms, to obtain 13-D ESA-IFCC features. The ESA-IFCC were obtained by applying DCT on IFCs and retaining the first 13 coefficients in the transformed-domain. Another state-of-the-art feature set, namely, Mel Frequency Cepstral Coefficients (MFCC) was used to perform score-level fusion (extracted with same parameters as used to extract for ESA-IFCC).

Model training and score-level fusion. We have used Gaussian Mixture Model (GMM) with 128 mixtures for modeling the classes. Final scores are represented in terms of log-likelihood ratio (LLR). The decision of test speech being genuine or impostor is based on the LLR, i.e.,

$$LLR = log(LLK\_Model1) - log(LLK\_Model2), \quad (8)$$

where LLK_Model 1 and 2 are the likelihood scores from the GMM for the genuine and impostor trials. To explore the possible complementary information captured by MFCC and ESA-IFCC feature set, we use their score-level fusion, i.e.,

$$LLK_{combine} = (1 - \alpha)LLK_{feature1} + \alpha LLK_{feature2}, \quad (9)$$

where α equal to weight of fusion, LLK feature score for individual feature set.

4.2 Results on Development Set

Table 2 shows the results on development set in % EER. The ESA-IFCC features were extracted with various frequency scales. EER with frequency scale of ERB have an EER of 35.66% with S (static) feature vector as it has increased bandwidth with higher frequency that makes less reliable to extract IF from narrowband signal. Furthermore, the EER reduces to 31.85% and 30.93% with S+Δ (Δ delta) and S+Δ+$\Delta\Delta$ ($\Delta\Delta$ double delta). The EER for Mel and linear frequency scale are 1.32% and 1.86%, respectively, with static feature vector. The bandwidth for ERB, Mel and linear is kept as 1.019 Hz and 100 Hz, respectively. for linear. Figure 5 shows the plot of DET curves for individual systems with all feature vector, i.e., S, S+Δ and S+Δ+$\Delta\Delta$.

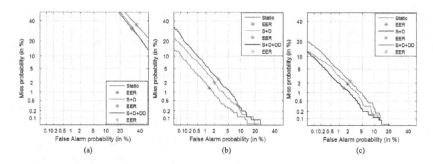

Fig. 5. DET curves on development set for (a) ERB, (b) Mel and (c) linear frequency scale with static, static+delta and static+delta+double-delta.

Effect of Score-Level Fusion on Development Set: Results for MFCC and ESA-IFCC feature set are shown in Table 3. From the results, proposed feature set captures speaker-specific information embedded in natural speech. Table 3 shows that the ESA-IFCC features produce much lower % EER than MFCC alone with Mel and linear frequency scale. Furthermore, the score-level fusion of MFCC and ESA-IFCC features was done as per Eq. (9). It was observed that ESA-IFCC feature with ERB frequency scale do not show any performance improvement when fused with MFCC. The result of fusion with ESA-IFCC feature along with Mel frequency shows much interesting results. For the static feature vector (with $\alpha = 0.7$) the fusion of MFCC and ESA-IFCC reduces to 1.01%. Similar pattern was observed for Δ and $\Delta\Delta$ features. Similarly, ESA-IFCC feature with linear scale it reduces to 1.44% from MFCC and ESA-IFCC. The contribution of particular system is decided by the weight of fusion (i.e., α). From Table 3, it is observed that most of the system contribution was done with ESA-IFCC features as the parameter α most of time was biased towards

Table 3. Results in EER (%) on development set score-level fusion of MFCC ($\alpha = 0$) and ESA-IFCC ($\alpha = 1$) with 13-D static feature dimension (FD) (as per Eq. 9)

Freq. scale	EER (%) for varying α										
	FD	0	0.1	0.2	0.3	0.4	0.5	0.6	0.7	0.8	0.9	1
ERB	S(static)	**6.98**	8.71	13.14	17.89	21.95	25.48	28.35	30.74	32.62	34.22	35.66
	D(S+Δ)	**6.75**	6.83	8.78	11.46	14.75	18.34	21.56	24.64	27.43	29.79	31.85
	D+$\Delta\Delta$	6.14	**5.90**	8.72	12.26	16.16	19.75	22.95	25.65	27.74	29.52	30.93
Mel	S	6.98	4.35	2.99	2.10	1.59	1.27	1.08	**1.01**	1.03	1.16	1.32
	D	6.75	3.99	2.70	2.01	1.67	1.46	**1.35**	1.44	1.57	1.75	1.96
	D+$\Delta\Delta$	6.14	3.56	2.37	1.76	1.51	**1.50**	1.59	1.78	1.96	2.23	2.52
linear	S	6.98	6.01	5.09	4.28	3.53	2.84	2.23	1.86	1.59	**1.44**	1.86
	D	6.75	5.82	4.99	4.17	3.38	2.69	2.13	1.64	1.24	**1.14**	1.39
	D+$\Delta\Delta$	6.14	5.48	4.64	3.92	3.31	2.75	2.24	1.91	**1.67**	1.73	2.23

Table 4. Results in terms of % EER on Evaluation dataset for each spoofing attack. Results for Known and unknown attacks. A:ESA-IFCC

Features	Known attacks						Unknown attacks						All Avg.
	S1	S2	S3	S4	S5	Avg	S6	S7	S8	S9	S10	Avg	
MFCC	2.34	9.57	0.00	0.00	9.01	4.18	7.73	4.42	0.3	5.17	52.99	14.12	9.15
A:ERB	25.57	29.74	23.74	24.32	52.35	31.14	49.04	35.14	4.42	37.07	13.00	27.73	29.43
A:linear	0.85	1.85	0.00	0.00	3.03	1.14	13.01	1.63	0.23	1.89	33.37	10.02	5.58

ESA-IFCC. Therefore, it can be said that the ESA-IFCC features have more contribution in decreasing the % ERR. Hence, the ESA-IFCC features capture the *complementary* information that was not captured from MFCC alone.

4.3   Results on Evaluation Set

Table 4 shows the results on evaluation set with known and unknown spoofing attacks. It was observed that SS attacks (S3, S4) were easily detected for known attacks while S10 (MARY TTS) in unknown attacks was most difficult to detect. It was observed that with ERB scale of ESA-IFCC feature S10 was classified better than MFCC and ESA-IFCC (linear scale). However, other spoofing attacks (S1–S9) perform better to classify spoof speech with linear scale of ESA-IFCC. These results show that performance degrades significantly in the face of unknown attacks however, the average performance for unknown attacks is dominated by S10 then the performance of known attacks.

5   Summary and Conclusions

In this work, we studied the effect of frequency scale for estimation of ESA-IFCC with different frequency scales motivated by auditory filter scale with Gabor filterbank. However, it is found with spectrographic analysis that more spectral information are emphasized in lower frequency regions with ERB, Mel and linear frequency scales. Although the ERB and Mel frequency scales are very much similar having difference in higher frequency (i.e., for ERB the bandwidth increases for higher frequency than that for Mel scale). The experimental results on development set of ASV spoof 2015 challenge database shows Mel scale-based feature extraction of ESA-IFCC perform better than linear and ERB scales. In future, we would like to explore effect of various filterbank and effect of different bandwidth for exploiting IF for classification problem.

References

1. Davis, S., Mermelstein, P.: Comparison of parametric representations for mono-syllabic word recognition in continuously spoken sentences. IEEE Trans. Acoust. Speech Sig. Process. **28**(4), 357–366 (1980)

2. Dimitrios, D., Petros, M., Alexandros, P.: Auditory Teager energy Cepstrum coefficients for robust speech recognition. In: INTERSPEECH, pp. 3013–3016 (2005)
3. Kaiser, J.F.: On a simple algorithm to calculate the energy of a signal. In: International Conference on Acoustics, Speech, and Signal Processing (ICASSP), pp. 381–384, Albuquerque, New Mexico, USA (1990)
4. Kamble, M.R., Patil, H.A.: Novel energy separation based instantaneous frequency features for spoof speech detection. In: Accepted in European Signal Processing Conference (EUSIPCO), Kos Island, Greece, 28 August–2 September 2017
5. Maragos, P., Kaiser, J.F., Quatieri, T.F.: Energy separation in signal modulations with application to speech analysis. IEEE Trans. Sig. Process. **41**(10), 3024–3051 (1993)
6. Maragos, P., Kaiser, J.F., Quatieri, T.F.: On separating amplitude from frequency modulations using energy operators. In: International Conference on Acoustics, Speech, and Signal Processing (ICASSP), vol. 2, pp. 1–4, San Francisco, California, USA (1992)
7. Maragos, P., Kaiser, J.F., Quatieri, T.F.: On amplitude and frequency demodulation using energy operators. IEEE Trans. Sig. Process. **41**(4), 1532–1550 (1993)
8. Patil, H.A., Kamble, M.R., Patel, T.B., Soni, M.H.: Novel variable length Teager energy separation based if features for replay detection. In: INTERSPEECH (2017, accepted)
9. Sailor, H.B., Kamble, M.R., Patil, H.A.: Unsupervised representation learning using convolutional restricted Boltzmann machine for spoof speech detection. In: INTERSPEECH (2017, accepted)
10. Vijayan, K., Reddy, P.R., Murty, K.S.R.: Significance of analytic phase of speech signals in speaker verification. Speech Commun. **81**, 54–71 (2016)
11. Wu, Z., Evans, N., Kinnunen, T., Yamagishi, J., Alegre, F., Li, H.: Spoofing and countermeasures for speaker verification: a survey. Speech Commun. **66**, 130–153 (2015)
12. Wu, Z., Kinnunen, T., Evans, N.W.D., Yamagishi, J., Hanilci, C., Sahidullah, M., Sizov, A.: ASVspoof 2015: the first automatic speaker verification spoofing and countermeasures challenge. In: INTERSPEECH, pp. 2037–2041, Dresden, Germany (2015)

Novel Phase Encoded Mel Filterbank Energies for Environmental Sound Classification

Rishabh N. Tak⊙, Dharmesh M. Agrawal⊙, and Hemant A. Patil⁽⊠⁾⊙

Speech Research Lab, Dhirubhai Ambani Institute of Information
and Communication Technology, (DA-IICT), Gandhinagar, India
hemant_patil@daiict.ac.in

Abstract. In Environment Sound Classification (ESC) task, only the magnitude spectrum is processed and the phase spectrum is ignored, which leads to degradation in the performance. In this paper, we propose to use phase encoded filterbank energies (PEFBEs) for ESC task. In proposed feature set, we have used Mel-filterbank, since it represents characteristics of human auditory processing. Here, we have used Convolutional Neural Network (CNN) as a pattern classifier. The experiments were performed on ESC-50 database. We found that our proposed PEFBEs feature set gives better results compared to the state-of-the-art Filterbank Energies (FBEs). In addition, score-level fusion of FBEs and proposed PEFBEs have been carried out, which leads to further relatively better performance than the individual feature set. Hence, the proposed PEFBEs captures the complementary information than FBEs alone.

Keywords: Sound classification · Phase encoded spectrogram · Score-level fusion · CNN

1 Introduction

Environmental Sound Classification (ESC) is an important research problem due to its application in various field, such as, hearing aids, road surveillance system, security and safety purpose, etc. ESC task was earlier attempted using mel frequency cepstral coefficients (MFCCs) feature set and GMM classifier [3]. Recently, deep learning -based approaches are used for ESC task, such as, Convolutional neural network (CNN)-based classification built for end-to-end system for ESC on CNN framework [9].

In this paper, we propose the new phase-based approach for ESC task. In particular, we propose the phase encoded Mel Filterbank energies with CNN as a back-end for ESC task. In this paper, we explore importance of phase in audio processing task. To the best of the authors knowledge, this is the first approach in the literature that used phase encoded feature sets for ESC task. Results shows that the phase encoded based feature set perform better than the state-of-the-art feature namely, Mel-filterbank energies (FBEs). The score-level fusion of PEFBEs and FBEs gives the significant performance jump in classification accuracy.

© Springer International Publishing AG 2017
B.U. Shankar et al. (Eds.): PReMI 2017, LNCS 10597, pp. 317–325, 2017.
https://doi.org/10.1007/978-3-319-69900-4_40

2   Phase Encoded Feature Set

2.1   Motivation

In speech processing, the phase spectrum of a speech signal has gained lesser attention than the magnitude spectrum. There are mainly two issues due to which phase information is discarded. First, the computationally complex phase unwrapping task during processing of phase spectrum [8]. Second, perceptually, magnitude spectrum is more relevant than the phase spectrum [8]. In addition, the very often used features, such as, mel cepstral frequency coefficients (MFCC), linear prediction cepstral coefficients (LPCC), frequency domain linear predicted (FDLP) coefficients etc., are derived from the magnitude spectrum of speech [8]. Recent studies have reported using FT phase-based features, such as, Modified Group Delay (MGD) [15], Relative Phase Shift (RPS) [10], Cosine-Phase [14], etc. Motivated by these studies, we propose a novel phase-based features. These features are derived from very recent findings of phase encoding in the magnitude spectrum of speech signal. It results into magnitude spectrum that contains both magnitude as well as phase information in it. The algorithm of phase encoding is developed for new class of signals known as Causal Delta Dominant (CDD) signal. By making a signal as a CDD signal, we can reconstruct back original signal from its magnitude spectrum alone [11,12]. An interesting aspect of this work is that, there are no constraints on the signal, i.e., it is not necessary for signal to be minimum-phase or need not to have rational system function ($H(\mathcal{Z})$) or corresponding frequency response $H(e^{j\omega})$ Fig. 1. The block diagram of phase encoding scheme for signal reconstruction is shown below.

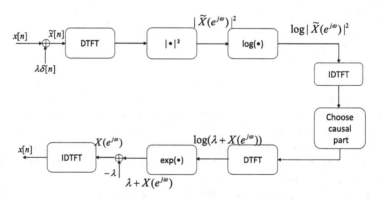

Fig. 1. Block diagram of phase encoded spectrogram and signal reconstruction. After [11].

2.2   Mel Filternbank Energies (FBEs)

Mel frequency analysis of speech is based on human perception experiments. It is observed that human ear acts as a bank of subband filters (i.e., filterbank). It concentrates on only certain frequency components (primarily due to the place

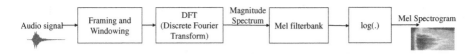

Fig. 2. Block diagram of Mel spectrogram of an audio signal. After [2].

theory of hearing). These filters are overlapped and non-uniformly spaced on the frequency-axis. In audio processing, it is shown that within 10–30 ms duration, the signal is considered to be the stationary and hence, smaller duration window is selected [4] (Fig. 2).

2.3   Phase Encoded Filterbank Energies (PEFBEs)

To use the phase-encoded approach for speech-related applications, it is necessary to derive a set of features. As shown in Fig. 3, a Kronecker delta impulse of λ amplitude is origin at each frame of a signal. Next, we take DFT of every frame and apply the normalization on each FFT-bins. Then, calculate the power spectrum of individual frames. This identifies frequencies that are present in a given the frame. Mel filterbank is applied to the power spectra, which gives the total energy present in each subband filter. Then, we apply log-operation on subband energies. We refer these subband energies as *phase encoded filterbank energies (PEFBEs)*. We set number of FFT bins as total number of samples per frame. The proposed algorithm to extract PEFBEs features from the speech signal is given in Algorithm 1.

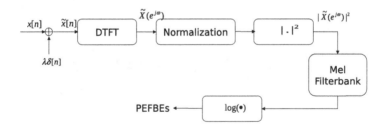

Fig. 3. Block diagram of proposed PEFBEs feature extraction scheme.

2.4   Importance of λ

To justify the importance of λ, an experiment was conducted on 1000 utterances of natural, VC and SS randomly selected from ASV spoof 2015 challenge database [16]. For each of the utterance, its corresponding reconstructed signal back (using the approach shown in Fig. 1) for $\lambda = 0$ and $\lambda \neq 0$ is estimated.

Table 1. Mean log-spectral distortion (LSD) values of 1000 utterances for various λ values from ASVspoof 2015 database

Speakers	$\lambda = 0$	$\lambda \neq 0$	Relative difference (%)
Natural	2.02	0.381	81.13
VC	2.053	0.360	82.46
SS	2.115	0.381	81.90

The log-spectral distortion (LSD) is calculated for $\lambda = 0$ and $\lambda \neq 0$, and compared with the LSD values for natural, VC and SS speech signals.

From Table 1, it is observed that result of relative difference between LSD values for $\lambda = 0$ and $\lambda \neq 0$ is found to be approximately 81–82%. Thus, it indicates encoding of phase in the magnitude spectrum captures better signal reconstruction capability (i.e., synthesis) of the speech pattern. The key difference between Figs. 1 and 3 is the normalization block. It is observed that, with normalization, formants and harmonics are more visible as compared to without normalization. Hence, normalization increases the energy variations which is useful for ESC.

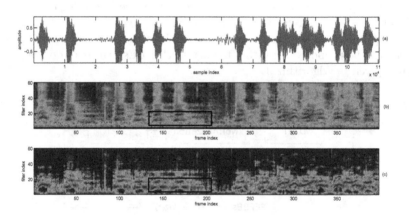

Fig. 4. Spectrographic analysis: (a) raw audio signal of dog sound, (b) Mel filterbank spectrogram, (c) phase encoded spectrogram. The regions indicated by blackboxes shows the differences between spectrum representation in (b) and (c).

As shown in Figs. 4(b) and (c), the proposed PEFBEs (Fig. 4(c)) has better representation in lower frequency region than FBEs (Fig. 4(b)). However, PEFBEs has slightly lower resolution in higher frequency regions as compared to the FBEs. Such representation observed improvement in classification accuracy of classes, such as, harmonic sounds, transient sounds, etc.

Algorithm 1. Proposed PEFBEs Feature Extraction Algorithm

1: Take a speech signal $x[n]$.
2: Apply framing on the signal, let $(x_t)_{t\epsilon[1,P]}$ is the tth frame with 20 ms window size and 10 ms window shift.
3: Add Kronecker impulse delta of λ amplitude to each speech frame at the origin, $\tilde{x}_t[n] = x_t[n] + \lambda\delta[n]$.
4: Take DFT of each frame, such as, $\tilde{X}_t^i(e^{j\omega}) = \lambda + X_t^i(e^{j\omega})$, where $X_t^i(e^{j\omega})$ indicates i^{th} FFT-bin, $\forall\ t\epsilon[1,P]$.
5: Perform the normalization on each FFT-bin.

$$S_t^i(e^{j\omega}) = \frac{\tilde{X}_t^i(e^{j\omega}) - mean(\tilde{X}_t^i(e^{j\omega}))}{std(\tilde{X}_t^i(e^{j\omega}))}$$

6: Perform absolute squaring that results in power spectra.
7: Apply Mel filterbank on power spectra.
8: Apply log(.) on Mel spectrum energies.

3 Experimental Setup

3.1 Dataset

In this paper, we have used the publicly available database ESC-50 [7] for the ESC task. The ESC-50 dataset consists of 2000 short (5 sec) environmental recordings. These recordings are divided into 50 equally balanced classes. These 50 classes are divided into five major groups, namely, animals, natural soundscapes and water sounds, human non-speech sounds, interior/domestic sounds and exterior/urban noises. The files are pre-arranged in 5-folds for comparable cross-validation. Due to this reason, the results of the experiments can be directly compared to the baseline results and with the previous approaches.

3.2 Convolutional Neural Network (CNN) Classifier

We have used the CNN classifier with the architecture as proposed in [6] for the ESC task. However, we have not used data augmentation technique. Since the objective of this paper is to compare the performance of the front-end feature representation, we have not used the augmentation to analyze as to how these features perform for all the classes. Before feature extraction for CNN classifier, we first pre-process the audio signal. All the audio files were downsampled to 22.05 kHz. To extract features, the audio files were divided into frames by using 25 ms Hamming window with 50% overlap. Then, we applied silence removal algorithm. For silence removal, we first check for more than three consecutive silence frames (approximately, 50 ms duration). If silence is present in more than three frames, then we remove the silence frames, else we keep those frames. Simple energy thresholding algorithm was used to remove the silence regions. Mel Filterbank Energies (FBEs) are used as the baseline features. 60-D FBEs, and PEFBEs were extracted from files of audio frames. The short segments of

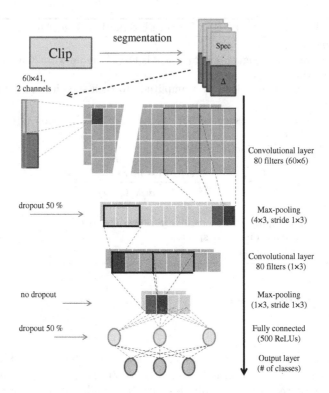

Fig. 5. CNN architecture for ESC task. After [6].

41 frames were used as the input to the CNN. The segments were extracted with 50% overlap from the audio files.

Figure 5 shows the details of each layer in the CNN architecture that we have used in ESC task. The network was implemented using Keras [1] with theano back-end on NVIDIA Titan-X GPU. A mini-batch implementation with 200 batch size was used to train the network. Network parameters were similar to as used in [6]. The learning rate of 0.002, L^2 regularization with the coefficient 0.001 and network was trained for 300 epochs. At the testing time, the class of the test audio files were using the probability prediction scheme [6]. We performed score-level fusion of different feature sets as used in [5].

4   Experimental Results

To evaluate the performance of various feature sets, 5-fold cross-validation was performed on ESC-50 dataset. We compare the performance of PEFBEs with FBEs. The overall results of the proposed method and baseline feature sets are summarized in Table 2 with CNN as classifier. It can be observed that PEFBEs perform significantly better than FBEs with an absolute improvement of 5.45%

in classification accuracy. Moreover, to investigate the possibility of any complementary information captured by different feature sets, we have done their score-level fusion. The score-level fusion of PEFBEs with FBEs improves the performance. However, the score-level fusion of FBEs (73.25%) and PEFBEs (67.80%) achieved the best accuracy of 84.15% in this paper. This shows that the proposed PEFBEs contains highly complementary information over the FBEs, which is helpful in the ESC task. Our proposed work is also compared with the other studies reported in the literature in (as shown Table 3). Again, it can be observed from Table 3 that, PEFBEs performs significantly better than CNN with FBEs [6,13]. In [13], filterbank is learned from the raw audio signal using CNN as an end-to-end system. The EnvNET [13] performs better when combining with log Mel CNN. However, our proposed PEFBEs outperform EnvNET [13] even without the system combination indicating the significance of phase for the ESC task.

Table 2. % Classification accuracy of ESC-50 dataset with different feature sets and its score-level fusion. The $\oplus$ sign and α indicate score-level fusion and fusion factor, respectively.

Feature Sets	α	Accuracy (%)
FBEs	-	67.80
PEFBEs	-	**73.25**
FBEs $\oplus$ PEFBEs	0.5	**84.15**

Table 3. Comparison of classification accuracy of ESC-50 dataset in the literature. The $\otimes$ sign indicated system combination before soft-max.

Feature Sets	Accuracy (%)
PEFBEs (proposed)	**73.25**
FBEs $\oplus$ PEFBEs (proposed)	**84.15**
Piczak FBEs-CNN [6]	64.50
Human [7]	81.30
EnvNET [13]	64.00
logmel-CNN [13]	66.5
logmel-CNN $\otimes$ EnvNet [13]	71.00

5   Summary and Conclusions

In this study, we use the state-of-the-art feature set FBEs, and proposed PEFBEs for ESC task. Performance of ESC system was compared with FBEs on publicly available dataset, ESC-50. The proposed PEFBEs feature set gave better results for this application with the same parametrization as that of state-of-the-art ESC system. Moreover, the results suggested that using score-level fusion of FBEs and proposed PEFBEs gave better accuracy than the individual feature set. This indicates that the proposed PEFBEs contains complementary information than FBEs alone. Our future work plan includes the use of proposed PEFBEs feature set for different datasets, such as, UrbanSound8K and RWCP datasets.

References

1. Chollet, F.: Keras. https://github.com/fchollet/keras. Accessed on 26 Feb 2017
2. Davis, S., Mermelstein, P.: Comparison of parametric representations for monosyllabic word recognition in continuously spoken sentences. IEEE Trans. Acoust. Speech Signal Process. **28**(4), 357–366 (1980)
3. Elizalde, B., Lei, H., Friedland, G., Peters, N.: An i-vector based approach for audio scene detection. In: IEEE AASP Challenge on Detection and Classification of Acoustic Scenes and Events (2013)
4. Eronen, A.J., Peltonen, V.T., Tuomi, J.T., Klapuri, A.P., Fagerlund, S., Sorsa, T., Lorho, G., Huopaniemi, J.: Audio-based context recognition. IEEE Trans. Audio Speech Lang. Process. **14**(1), 321–329 (2006)
5. Li, J., Dai, W., Metze, F., Qu, S., Das, S.: A comparision of deep learning methods for environmental sound detection. In: IEEE International Conference on Acoustics, Speech and Signal Process. (ICASSP), New Orleans, USA, pp. 126–130 (2017)
6. Piczak, K.J.: Environmental sound classification with convolutional neural networks. 25th International Workshop on Machine Learning for Signal Processing (MLSP), MA, USA, Boston, pp. 1–6 (2015)
7. Piczak, K.J.: ESC: Dataset for environmental sound classification. In: Proceedings of the 23rd International Conference on Multimedia, Brisbane, Australia, pp. 1015–1018 (2015)
8. Raitio, T., Juvela, L., Suni, A., Vainio, M., Alku, P.: Phase perception of the glottal excitation and its relevance in statistical parametric speech synthesis. Speech Commun. **81**, 104–119 (2016)
9. Salamon, J., Bello, J.P.: Deep convolutional neural networks and data augmentation for environmental sound classification. IEEE Signal Process. Lett. **24**(3), 279–283 (2017)
10. Saratxaga, I., Sanchez, J., Wu, Z., Hernaez, I., Navas, E.: Synthetic speech detection using phase information. Speech Commun. **81**, 30–41 (2016)
11. Seelamantula, C.S.: Phase-encoded speech spectrograms. In: INTERSPEECH, San Francisco, USA, pp. 1775–1779 (2016)
12. Shenoy, B.A., Mulleti, S., Seelamantula, C.S.: Exact phase retrieval in principal shift-invariant spaces. IEEE Trans. Signal Process. **64**(2), 406–416 (2016)
13. Tokozume, Y., Harada, T.: Learning environmental sound with end-to-end convolutional neural network. In: IEEE International Conference on Acoustics, Speech and Signal Process (ICASSP), New Orleans, USA, pp. 2721–2725 (2017)
14. Wu, Z., Siong, C.E., Li, H.: Detecting converted speech and natural speech for anti-spoofing attack in speaker recognition. In: INTERSPEECH, Portland, Oregon, USA, pp. 1700–1703 (2012)

15. Yegnanarayana, B., Saikia, D., Krishnan, T.: Significance of group delay functions in signal reconstruction from spectral magnitude or phase. IEEE Trans. Acoust. Speech Signal Process. **32**(3), 610–623 (1984)
16. Zhizheng, Kinnunen, T., Evans, N.W.D., Yamagishi, J., Hanilçi, C., Sahidullah, M., Sizov, A.: ASVspoof 2015: the first automatic speaker verification spoofing and countermeasures challenge, In: INTERSPEECH, Dresden, Germany, pp. 2037–2041 (2015)

An Adaptive i-Vector Extraction for Speaker Verification with Short Utterance

Arnab Poddar[1(✉)], Md Sahidullah[2], and Goutam Saha[1]

[1] Department of Electronics and Electrical Communication Engineering, Indian Institute of Technology, Kharagpur, India
arnabpoddar@iitugp.ac.in
[2] School of Computing, University of Eastern Finland, Joensuu, Finland

Abstract. A prime challenge in automatic speaker verification (ASV) is to improve performance with short speech segments. The variability and uncertainty of intermediate model parameters associated with state-of-the-art i-vector based ASV system, extensively increases in short duration. To compensate increased variability, we propose an adaptive approach for estimation of model parameters. The pre-estimated *universal background model* (UBM) parameters are used for adaptation. The speaker models i.e., i-vectors are generated with the proposed adapted parameters. The ASV performance with the proposed approach considerably outperformed conventional i-vector based system on publicly available speech corpora, NIST SRE 2010, especially in short duration, as required in real-world applications.

Keywords: i-vector · Short utterance · Duration variability · Baum-Welch statistics

1 Introduction

Automatic speaker verification (ASV) is the process of recognizing the identity claimed by a person through speech samples. I-vector based ASV are considered as the state-of-the-art technology for its high performance, low complexity, and easy session/channel compensation. The applications of ASV in important sectors like banking, finance, forensic, defense etc., often constrain the duration of speech data [1,4,7]. The performance of ASV rapidly degrades in short duration [6,7]. To overcome the deficiency with short utterances, the work in [2] has attempted to model variability caused by short duration segments in i-vector domain. The short utterance problem is also addressed in other application of speech processing like language identification where an alternate estimation of i-vector was introduced treating all supervector dimensions with equal in the i-vector modeling [11].

The main challenge for short utterances is the increased intra-speaker variability in estimated parameters due to variability in lexicon and speech duration [3]. Utterance duration is associated with the uncertainty in i-vector point

© Springer International Publishing AG 2017
B.U. Shankar et al. (Eds.): PReMI 2017, LNCS 10597, pp. 326–332, 2017.
https://doi.org/10.1007/978-3-319-69900-4_41

estimation [8]. In i-vector based system, the intermediate parameters *i.e*, Baum Welch statistics, totally represent the extracted features from speech [2,6]. The zero-order BW statistics, i.e., the probabilistic counts, define the co-variance matrix of the posterior distribution given the utterance [8]. An analysis on BW statistics, presented in this work, showed increased intra-speaker variability due to sparse nature of estimated parameters in limited duration. To mitigate the sparsity and uncertainty in the estimated parameters, we have proposed a method of adapting them with information from pre-estimated background model parameters. Consequently, a comparative analysis on uncertainty of conventional and proposed adapted i-vector is presented which showed reduced uncertainty of proposed adapted i-vectors in different duration conditions. Considerable improvement of performance is noted in different duration condition on speaker recognition evaluation (SRE) corpora, NIST SRE 2010. In the rest of the paper, we briefly describe i-vector GPLDA and proposed modifications system in Sects. 2 and 3 respectively. Subsequently, we describe the experimental setup, results in Sect. 4 and draw the conclusion in 5.

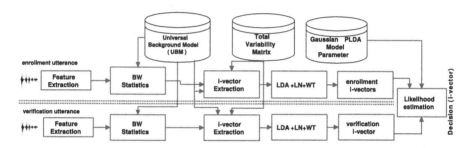

Fig. 1. Block Diagram showing i-vector GPLDA based ASV system.

2 Descriptions of i-Vector ASV System

Figure 1 shows the block diagram of i-vector based ASV system. An i-vector is a fixed-dimensional representation of a speech signal in factor analysis framework [1]. The i-vector ($\mathbf{y}$) decomposes *Gaussian mixture model* (GMM) *supervector* of $s - th$ speaker (μ_s) into a low-dimensional subspace [1] as, $\mu_s = \bar{\mu} + \mathbf{\Phi y_s}$, where $\mathbf{\Phi}$ is a low-rank *total variability* (TV) matrix defining the speaker and channel independent space, (μ) is used from GMM universal background model (UBM). The GMM-UBM is mathematically represented as $\lambda_{\text{UBM}} = \{w_i, \bar{\mathbf{m}}_i, \bar{\mathbf{\Sigma}}_i; i = 1, 2, \ldots, C\}$ where C is the Gaussian components, w_i is the prior of i-th component (w_i satisfies $\sum_{i=1}^{C} w_i = 1$), $\mathbf{m}_i$ and $\mathbf{\Sigma}_i$ are the mean and co-variance matrix [9]. The i-vectors are estimated using zeroth and first order BW statistics N_i and $\mathbf{E}_i$, respectively, from an utterance ($\mathbf{X}$) with T frames $\mathbf{X} = \{\mathbf{x}_1, \mathbf{x}_2, \ldots, \mathbf{x}_T\}$ as,

$$N_i = \sum_{t=1}^{T} P(i|\mathbf{x}_t, \lambda_{UBM}), \, and \, \mathbf{E}_i(\mathbf{X}) = \frac{1}{N_i} \sum_{t=1}^{T} P(i|\mathbf{x}_t, \lambda_{UBM})\mathbf{x}_t, \qquad (1)$$

where P corresponds to the posterior probability of Gaussian component i generating the vector $\mathbf{x}_t$ [1]. The posterior distribution of $\mathbf{E}$, conditioned on the i-vector $\mathbf{y}$ is hypothesized to be $p(\mathbf{E}|\mathbf{y}) = \mathcal{N}(\mathbf{\Phi}\mathbf{y}, \mathbf{N}^{-1}\mathbf{\Sigma})$. The i-vectors, $i.e,$ MAP estimate of $\mathbf{y}$ is given by

$$\mathbb{E}(\mathbf{y}|\mathbf{E}) = (\mathbf{I} + \mathbf{\Phi}^{\top}\mathbf{\Sigma}^{-1}\mathbf{N}\mathbf{\Phi})^{-1}\mathbf{\Phi}^{\top}\mathbf{\Sigma}^{-1}\mathbf{N}(\mathbf{E} - \bar{\mathbf{m}}) \qquad (2)$$

The i-vectors are further projected on subspaces to reduce the session and channel variability. For session and channel compensation, we have used widely used Gaussian probabilistic LDA (GPLDA) to compute recognition scores as likelihood ratio [4].

3   Analysis and Proposed Modification

From Eq. 1, it can be shown that N depends on the number of speech frames (T) in the utterance, $\sum_{i=1}^{C} N_i = \sum_{i=1}^{C}\sum_{t=1}^{T} Pr(i|\mathbf{x}_t) = T$ Therefore, N is normalized with T. *Normalized zero-order Baum-Welch statistics* (NBS) for the i-th Gaussian component is shown as, $\tilde{N}_i = \dfrac{1}{T}\sum_{t=1}^{T} Pr(i|\mathbf{x}_t)$. We use duration independent NBS for further analysis.

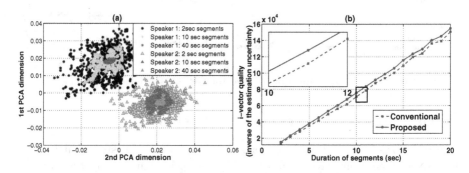

Fig. 2. (a) Scatter plot of PCA projected NBS ($\tilde{N}$) for two speakers. (b) Comparison of i-vector estimation quality as inverse of the estimation uncertainty in conventional and proposed system. The segments of different duration conditions are truncated from a long utterance of a speaker in NIST 2010 corpus.

Scatter plots of principal component (PCA) projected NBS ($\tilde{N}$) for two speakers are shown in Fig. 2(a). 1st two principal components for different truncated segments of 2sec, 10sec and 40sec are shown here. The PCA projection matrix is estimated from 1000 truncated segments from long duration segments of approximately 2.5 min of 2 male speakers from NIST 2008. It can be observed that the NBS show higher variability in short utterances. Larger variation in NBS for short duration condition incorporates higher uncertainty in i-vector estimation. This can be explained by i-vector estimation, i.e., in Eq. 2. It is known from the theory of i-ivector that the co-variance of the estimated i-vector is defined by $(\mathbf{I} + \mathbf{\Phi}^\top \mathbf{\Sigma}^{-1} \mathbf{N} \mathbf{\Phi})^{-1}$ [5]. For short utterances, $\mathbf{N}$ becomes lower and as a consequence, the uncertainty in i-vector estimation increases. In this work, we attempt to improve the zero-order statistics $\mathbf{N}$ estimation by adapting background model parameters, estimated with sufficiently large speech data. We propose the modified NBS (N_i^{adp})as,

$$N_i^{adp} = T \times [\beta \tilde{N}_i + (1 - \beta)w_i] \; where \, 0 \leq \beta \leq 1 \tag{3}$$

where β controls the adaptation of NBS. Hence the modified i-vector extraction equation is given by:

$$\mathbb{E}(\mathbf{y}|\mathbf{E}) = (\mathbf{I} + \mathbf{\Phi}^\top \mathbf{\Sigma}^{-1} \mathbf{N^{adp}} \mathbf{\Phi})^{-1} \mathbf{\Phi}^\top \mathbf{\Sigma}^{-1} \mathbf{N^{adp}} (\mathbf{E} - \bar{\mathbf{m}}) \tag{4}$$

In Fig. 2(b), we show the comparison of i-vector estimation quality for both conventional and proposed NBS adapted i-vector system in different duration condition using a quality measure based on the i-vector posterior covariance [8]. The posterior distribution of i-vector $\mathbf{y}$ is Gaussian with covariance matrix $\mathbf{y}_\Sigma = (\mathbf{I} + \mathbf{\Phi}^\top \mathbf{\Sigma}^{-1} \mathbf{N} \mathbf{\Phi})^{-1}$ [1,8]. The quality measure $Q(\mathbf{y}_\Sigma)$ is calculated as $Q(\mathbf{y}_\Sigma) = \frac{1}{tr(\mathbf{y}_\Sigma)}$, where $tr(\cdot)$ is the trace operator. Higher value of quality measure $Q(\mathbf{y}_\Sigma)$ indicates lower uncertainty and vice-versa. It compares the quality metric $Q(\mathbf{y}_\Sigma)$ of conventional and proposed i-vectors of segments in different segment duration. For this, the value of adaptation parameter β is kept at 0.5. observations from Fig. 2(b) suggests that the quality metric has improved for the proposed adapted NBS based system over the conventional i-vector based system in different duration condition.

Table 1. Summary of speech corpora used in the experiments.

Specifications	#target model	#test segments	#genuine trials	#imposter trials
NIST 2010	489	351	353	13307
Other specifications: Features and Development parameters				
MFCC	Dimension: 19+19Δ+19$\Delta\Delta$; 20 filterbank, 20ms Hamming window			
GMM-UBM	Dimension: 512; Data: NIST SRE '04, '05, Switchboard II			
TV (Φ) Matrix	Dimension: 400; Data: NIST SRE '04, '05, '06, Switchboard II			
GPLDA	Dimension: 150; Data: NIST SRE '04, '05, '06, Switchboard II			

4   Experimental Results and Discussion

In ASV experiments, we use mel-frequency cepstral coefficients (MFCC) appending delta (Δ) and double-delta ($\Delta\Delta$) coefficients. The non-speech frames are rejected using a voice activity detector (VAD) as in [10]. Subsequently, cepstral mean and variance normalization (CMVN) is utilized as feature normalization [10]. A gender-specific UBM is trained by *expectation maximization* (EM) algorithm. We carried out the ASV experiments on NIST 2010 *core-core*[1] speaker recognition evaluation (SRE) corpus on the *telephone-telephone* part of male speakers. The summary of the databases, development parameters and features are detailed in Table 1. We truncate the long speech segments in 2 sec (200 active frames), 5 sec (500 active frames), 10 sec (1000 active frames) duration, rejecting prior 500 active speech frames after VAD to diminish phonetic similarity in initial salutation in conversation to avoid text-dependence as in [2]. The ASV performance is observed in *equal error rate* (EER) and *detection cost function* (DCF) [6,10].

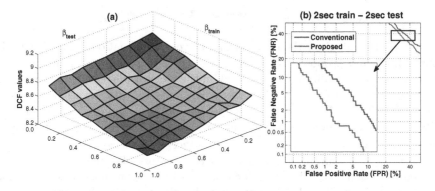

Fig. 3. (a) Surface plot of DCF obtained by varying the adaptation parameter $(\beta_{train}, \beta_{test})$ in *5 sec train - 5 sec testing* condition for in NIST SRE 2010, (b) Detection error trade-off (DET) curve for NIST 2010 *2sec train-2sec test* condition.

In this work, NBS $(\tilde{N}_i)$ is adapted with the information from UBM weight (w_i) to diminish the effect of duration variability (Eq. 3). In order to observe the effect of adaptation parameter (β) on ASV, its value is varied between 0 and 1 in steps of 0.1 for both train and test segments. In Fig. 3(a), the surface plot of the DCF values for $5sec - 5sec$ condition is presented. The blue regions denotes the lower values of DCF indicating optimal operating region of adaptation parameters β_{train} and β_{test} for a particular duration condition. The process is followed for different duration condition separately to estimate optimal β_{train} and β_{test}. In a separate experiments with *full training − truncated test* condition, the NBS of only truncated segment is adapted. For the 6 different duration conditions, the optimal value of β in Table 2 is shown along with the performance of the conventional and the proposed i-vector based system. The adaptation of NBS improves the performance in different duration conditions. In Fig. 3(b), the detection error trade off (DET) curve for 2sec train-2sec test condition is

---

[1] https://www.nist.gov/sites/default/files/documents/itl/iad/mig/
   NIST_SRE10_evalplan-r6.pdf.

Table 2. ASV performance with baseline and proposed i-vector based system on NIST 2010 (*core-core*).

Train-Test Condition	EER[%] (baseline)	EER[%] (proposed)	DCF×100 (baseline)	DCF×100 (proposed)	β_{train}	β_{test}
(a) **Truncated training - Truncated testing**						
2sec-2sec	37.67	**34.27**	9.98	**9.81**	0.7	0.9
5sec-5sec	25.95	**24.07**	9.01	**8.39**	0.8	0.8
10sec-10sec	14.44	**13.31**	6.52	**6.38**	0.3	0.4
(b) **Full training - Truncated testing**						
Full-2sec	21.81	**20.11**	8.52	**8.07**	-	0.9
Full-5sec	12.72	**12.00**	5.51	**5.36**	-	0.6
Full-10sec	7.36	**7.08**	3.72	**3.69**	-	0.3

presented for both conventional and proposed i-vector based system. The results reported in Table 2 are shown for best values of adaptation parameters computed by extensive experimentation. We observe that optimal value of β for different duration condition decreases with the increase in test segment duration. This suggests that adaptation is more effective for short utterances.

5 Conclusion

Considerable ASV performance with limited duration speech is a major requirement for real-world application. We found that the variability of zero-order Baum-Welch statistics and uncertainty associated with the i-vector increases considerably in shorter duration speech. For better estimation of i-vector, we propose adaptation of zero-order statistics using the information from pre-estimated UBM parameter. The proposed approach reduced the uncertainty associated with the i-vector computation. The performance of state-of-the-art ASV system with proposed adaptation has considerably improved especially in short duration condition.

References

1. Dehak, N., Kenny, P., Dehak, R., Dumouchel, P., Ouellet, P.: Front-end factor analysis for speaker verification. IEEE Trans. Audio Speech Lang. Process. **19**(4), 788–798 (2011)
2. Kanagasundaram, A., Dean, D., Sridharan, S., Gonzalez-Dominguez, J., Gonzalez-Rodriguez, J., Ramos, D.: Improving short utterance i-vector speaker verification using utterance variance modelling and compensation techniques. Speech Commun. **59**, 69–82 (2014)
3. Kanagasundaram, A., Vogt, R., Dean, D.B., Sridharan, S., Mason, M.W.: i-vector based speaker recognition on short utterances. In: Proceedings of INTERSPEECH, pp. 2341–2344. ISCA (2011)

4. Kenny, P.: Bayesian speaker verification with heavy-tailed priors. In: The Speaker and Language Recognition Workshop, Odyssey, p. 14. ISCA (2010)
5. Kenny, P., Ouellet, P., Dehak, N., Gupta, V., Dumouchel, P.: A study of inter-speaker variability in speaker verification. IEEE Trans. Audio Speech Lang. Process. **16**(5), 980–988 (2008)
6. Poddar, A., Sahidullah, M., Saha, G.: Performance comparison of speaker recognition systems in presence of duration variability. In: Annual IEEE India Conference (INDICON), pp. 1–6. IEEE (2015)
7. Poddar, A., Sahidullah, M., Saha, G.: Speaker verification with short utterances: a review of challenges. trends and opportunities. In: IET Biometrics (accepted with minor) (2017)
8. Poorjam, A.H., Saeidi, R., Kinnunen, T., Hautamäki, V.: Incorporating uncertainty as a quality measure in i-vector based language recognition, Odyssey, pp. 74–80 (2016)
9. Reynolds, D.A., Quatieri, T.F., Dunn, R.B.: Speaker verification using adapted Gaussian mixture models. Digit. Signal Process. **10**(1), 19–41 (2000)
10. Sahidullah, M., Saha, G.: Design, analysis and experimental evaluation of block based transformation in MFCC computation for speaker recognition. Speech Commun. **54**(4), 543–565 (2012)
11. Van Segbroeck, M., Travadi, R., Narayanan, S.S.: Rapid language identification. IEEE Trans. Audio Speech Lang. Process. **23**(7), 1118–1129 (2015)

Spoken Keyword Retrieval Using Source and System Features

Maulik C. Madhavi[1]($^{(\boxtimes)}$) (iD), Hemant A. Patil[1]($^{(\boxtimes)}$) (iD), and Nikhil Bhendawade[2] (iD)

[1] Dhirubhai Ambani Institute of Information and Communication Technology (DA-IICT), Gandhinagar, India
{maulik_madhavi,hemant_patil}@daiict.ac.in
[2] Texas A&M University, College Station, TX, USA
nikhilbhendawade@gmail.com

Abstract. In this paper, a novel excitation *source-related* feature set, *viz.*, Teager Energy-based Mel Frequency Cepstral Coefficients (T-MFCC) is proposed for the task of spoken keyword detection. Experiments are carried out on TIMIT database for spoken keyword detection. Furthermore, state-of-the-art feature set, *viz.*, MFCC is used as the *baseline* spectral feature set to represent implicitly vocal tract (i.e., system) information. The idea is to exploit the vocal-source (and its *nonlinear coupling* with formant) and *system-related* information embedded in the spoken query. Experimental results show % EER of *17.23* and *22.58* for MFCC and proposed T-MFCC features, respectively. However, the significant reduction in % EER, i.e., by *1.8* % (as compared to MFCC) is observed when evidences from T-MFCC and MFCC are *combined* using *score-level fusion*; indicating that proposed feature set captures *complementary* linguistic information (in the spoken keyword) than MFCC alone.

Keywords: Speech Source Information · T-MFCC · Phonetic representation · Spoken Term Detection · Dynamic String Matching

1 Introduction

Recently, technological improvements have allowed recording and storing of vast collections of speech data with various contents. Audio mining within such speech collections has many commercial and military applications. Current speech archives are mostly prohibitive in terms of duration for human-based spoken audio mining approaches. Thus, it is important to seek for automatic, reliable and fast solutions to mine large collections of speech. In the context of *audio mining*, Spoken Term Detection (STD) is concerned to detect all the occurrences of queried terms within a speech database. NIST started evaluation called Spoken Term Detection (STD) in 2006 [1] to search a term into spoken database. Speech recognition-based architecture generates word-based lattices [1]. However, such a recognizer has to deal with an issue of Out-of-Vocabulary (OOV). Therefore, subword-based speech sound units are important to handle this issue

B.U. Shankar et al. (Eds.): PReMI 2017, LNCS 10597, pp. 333–341, 2017.
https://doi.org/10.1007/978-3-319-69900-4_42

as subwords capture small duration task of information. STD problem can be attempted as a phonetic symbol search. The speech utterance under the test is converted into the sequence of phonetic symbols whereas text query is converted into a phonemic string (from the *pronunciation dictionary*) [19]. This phonemic symbol representation of the query is used to find probable match into test data.

In this paper, a phonetic search-based approach is used for keyword detection in a speech signal. The novelty of the paper is to exploit *source* and *system* information from the speech for this search task. In addition, the effect of phonetic string representation, *viz.*, broad (*Phoneset10*) and narrow (*Phoneset39*) is also examined. The primary motivation behind using *Phoneset10* is to capture broad category of speech sounds. For example, unvoiced fricative (*ufr*) sounds (such as /s/ and /sh/) are confused with each other, while they are less confused among other vowels like /aa/. This, in turn, reduced the miss detection by avoiding the much-confused sounds at the cost of false alarm. On the contrary, *Phoneset39* takes care of the inadequate information, and thus, it is expected to capture the detailed linguistic information better than the coarser information. Hence, complementary information is combined to enhance the performance. In this paper, Mel Frequency Cepstral Coefficients (MFCC) is used as a spectral parametric representation of the speech signal in order to capture linguistic information [2]. In addition, Teager energy-based MFCC (T-MFCC) is used to capture the vocal *source-related* information [14]. The score-level fusion of *source* and *system* feature is found to improve the performance the person recognition system [13]. The combination of posteriorgram at a different sound unit-level (such as phone and grapheme level) has been found to be effective in STD task [18]. This is a fusion of evidence obtained via different speech sound unit. In addition, for spoken word recognition task, *spectral* and amplitude and frequency *modulation* information are combined together. Here, template matching approach was employed to analyze the effectiveness of spoken word recognition experiment [5]. In this paper, a possible fusion of their complementary information is explored to detect the phonetic string for query detection task.

The organization of rest of the paper is as follows: Sect. 2 discusses the indexing and searching subsystems. Section 3 gives details of feature extractions. Section 4 presents experimental setup used. Section 5 presents the experimental results. Finally, Sect. 6 gives a summary of present work along with future research directions.

2   Architecture of STD System

2.1   Indexing Subsystem

Indexing subsystem converts the spoken database into phonetic symbols. The *Phoneset10* and *Phoneset39* were earlier used for phone recognition task [3,9]. They represent broad and narrow phonetic classes, respectively. The list of a phonetic symbol used in this paper is mentioned in Table 1. Indexing subsystem first takes the phonetically-labeled data from TIMIT training database. Open source Hidden Markov Model (HMM) Toolkit (HTK) is used to build the HMM

Table 1. The list of phonetic symbols of TIMIT database.

Phonelist	Phonetic symbols
Phonelist 10	sil (silence), ucl (unvoiced closure), vcl (voiced closure), ubt (unvoiced burst), vbt (voiced burst), ufr (unvoiced fricative), vfr (voiced fricative), nas (nasal), svl (semivowel), vow (vowel)
Phonelist 39	sil, iy, ih, eh, ae, ax, uw, uh, ao, ey, ay, oy, aw, ow, er, l, r, w, y, m, n, ng, v, f, dh, th, z, s, zh, jh, ch, b, p, d, dx, t, g, k, hh

models [20]. Every phonetic unit is modeled by 3 states of HMM. The observation from each HMM states follows Gaussian Mixture Model (GMM) in the feature space (number of mixture model in *Phoneset10* and *Phoneset39* are taken as 64 and 4, respectively). Context-independent monophones are considered as phonetic symbols during indexing process.

2.2 Search Subsystem

The HMM decoder converts the test utterance into a phonetic string; hypothesized string. The phonetic strings are sequence of monophones (i.e., either *Phoneset39* or *Phoneset10*). To detect the query term in speech test data, phonetic transcription of query term could directly be searched through the hypothesis phonetic string. Approximate string matching has been employed via *Dynamic String Matching* (DSM) operation for searching the query into test data. Query phonetic string is aligned dynamically to decode test phonetic string using Dynamic Programming (DP)-based algorithm [16]. The matching score is computed to decide the presence of query within test utterance. Consider hypothesis and query, which contains m and n phonetic symbols, respectively. An example showing the DSM operation is shown in Fig. 1.

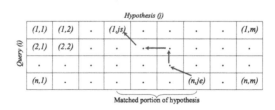

Fig. 1. A schematic example showing the dynamic string matching (DSM) operation.

3 Feature Extraction

In this paper, two feature sets, *viz.*, MFCC [2,14] and T-MFCC are used. To extract MFCC and T-MFCC feature vectors, speech is first passed through pre-processing stage, which involves, frame blocking, Hamming windowing and pre-emphasis. The dimension of feature vector is *39* (*13*-dimensional static and their dynamic Δ and $\Delta - \Delta$ coefficients).

Teager suggested that the *nonlinear* vortex-flow is the key source in the speech production and developed nonlinear energy tracking algorithm. Teager Energy Operator (TEO) [7] for discrete-time signal $x[n]$ is defined as $\Psi(x[n]) = x[n]^2 - x[n-1]x[n+1]$. TEO is expected to capture the running estimate of *temporal* energy in terms of instantaneous *amplitude* and instantaneous *frequency* [7]. To examine the important source-related information captured by TEO consider an utterance taken from CMU-ARCTIC database [8]. Figure 2 shows time-domain waveform, its differenced electroglottograph (EGG) plot and TEO profile.

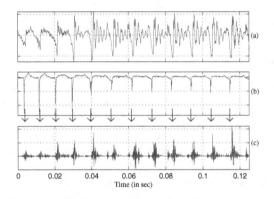

Fig. 2. (a) Time-domain waveform, (b) its differenced EGG signal and (c) TEO of time-domain waveform. Arrow indicates location of GCI in (b) and in (c).

From Fig. 2, it can be seen that the TEO peaks mostly corresponds to the GCI instances (obtained from the differenced EGG plot which serves as the ground truth). Thus, TEO is expected to capture the source related to pitch harmonics information. Moreover, TEO profile of speech show *bumps* within every GCI. If speech production model would have been a linear system, then the impulse response (for each formant) of each 2nd order resonator (whose cascade approximates vocal tract transfer function) would have been damped sinusoid and then corresponding TEO profile would have been exponentially decaying function [12,15]. However, TEO of such damped sinusoids in real speech shows the presence of bumps within glottal cycle, indicating the speech production process is not only due to the linear model; rather there is significant contribution of nonlinear effects (captured through TEO profile and this may not be captured well through linear model alone) which is referred to as *aeroacoustic* contribution [15],[17]. The presence of these bumps may represent a nonlinear coupling between glottal flow and formants which in turn depends on both linguistic information (to a certain extent). The idea behind proposed T-MFCC is to capture this nonlinear coupling via MFCC framework. T-MFCC feature set uses the Teager energy instead of conventional l^2 energy. Details of T-MFCC feature extraction is given in [14] and given in Fig. 3.

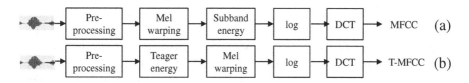

Fig. 3. A schematic block diagram for feature extraction (a) MFCC and (b) T-MFCC.

As TEO profile corresponds to GCI, T-MFCC is expected to capture the vocal source-related information more dominantly. Earlier Teager energy-based features are found to be effective for speech recognition task. In particular, AM-FM-based features are used as a hybrid feature with MFCC to improve the speech recognition task [4]. *Nonlinear* and non-parametric behavior of speech signal can be modeled through joint Amplitude Modulation-Frequency Modulation (AM-FM) technique [11]. Fusion in such techniques is at feature-level. TEO-based cepstral features (TEOCEP) have been used for speech recognition task under signal degradation condition [6]. The present paper focuses TEO at to capture source-related information estimated from speech and compute cepstral features from the signal which correlates with GCI locations.

Table 2. The statistics of query word used. (The number in the braces indicates the count for their occurrences (#a) in the test data and number of pronunciations used in *Phoneset10* (#b) and *Phoneset39* (#c))

Query words	#a	#b	#c	Query words	#a	#b	#c
Age	10	1	1	Organizations	7	5	5
Artists	7	1	4	Problem	9	6	6
Children	15	5	8	Surface	7	1	2
Development	8	4	6	Warm	8	2	2
Money	17	2	2	Year	177	3	7

4   Experimental Setup

In this paper, we used *10* queries are selected from database which are listed in the Table 2. These queries are selected such that they are expected to have a variety of numbers of syllables. Different pronunciation variations in queries

(using TIMIT test reference transcription) are used to search the relevant phonetic string. In the searching, *genuine* scores are pulled from the utterance where
the query is present. It means the searching problem is posed as to detect the
utterance which contains the query. The performance evaluation of the experiment was done by NIST DET (Detection Error Tradeoff) curve [10] and %
Equal Error Rate (EER) is used as an evaluation metric. Here, complete detection is not performed via threshold setting, since operating point may deviate.
For example, in order to achieve the same false alarm rate and miss detection
rate, a threshold is set to the score value at % EER point. In this experimental
setup, a lattice is not used to avoid unnecessary computational cost in DSM
operation. For *phoneset10*, the only single best path is chosen, since it has less
confusion across phonetic symbols. For *phoneset39*, 5 best paths are chosen for
every decoded utterance in order to consider multiple alternatives.

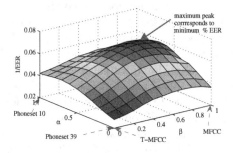

Fig. 4. A surface plot showing an inverse of % EER w.r.t. different score-level and
phoneset-level of fusion. In particular, peaks in surface plot indicates minimum % EER.

5   Experimental Results

Experiment 1: *The effect of different phonesets: Phoneset10* may be useful
in eliminating the miss detection of the query as it contained only *10* phonetic
symbols which have less confusion among them. On the counter side, *Phoneset39*,
contains more detailed phonetic information. Hence, it eliminates the false alarm
at the cost of missing the correct events. The linear combination of the scores
from *Phoneset10* and *Phoneset39* is,

$$S_p = \alpha S_{P10} + (1 - \alpha)S_{P39}, \tag{1}$$

where S_{P10}, S_{P39} and S_P are the edit distance scores from *Phoneset10*, *Phone-
set39* and their linear combination, respectively. In addition, α is the weights of
the linear combination, which varies from *0* to *1*.

Experiment 2: *Score-level fusion of MFCC and T-MFCC:* In the previous
section, TEO profile is expected to capture the excitation source-like information

and which is important for the phonetic event detection. In this section, the scores obtained from the source and system features are fused at score-level.

Figure 4 shows the performance of detection task when the score-level fusion is employed. In particular,

$$S_F = \beta S_M + (1 - \beta) S_T, \tag{2}$$

where S_M, S_T and S_F are the edit distance scores from MFCC, T-MFCC and their score-level fusion, respectively. β is the weights of the fusion, which varies from 0 to 1. The effectiveness of score-level fusion and proposed phoneset weights are shown in Fig. 4. The *surface* plot of an inverse of % EER is plotted. An inverse of % EER is used for better visualization in terms of peaks in the curve. The peak of the curve corresponds to minimum % EER. It is evident from Fig. 4 that % EER is less for weights $\alpha = 0.7$ in case of MFCC and T-MFCC. This may be due to the fact that phonetic information captured in *Phoneset10* is more compact. However, it represents broad phonetic representation. The performance is further improved if score-level fusion is employed. It can be observed that for score-level fusion $\beta = 0.7$ and $\alpha = 0.6$, % EER is minimum. The score-level fusion of source-system features indeed reduces % EER and thus, improve the overall detection performance. Let us consider two cases, namely, (i) $\alpha = 0.7$ optimum values for MFCC and T-MFCC and their score-level fusion for $\beta = 0.7$ and (ii) $\alpha = 0.6$ and $\beta = 0.7$, optimum % EER in the score-level fusion and linear combination. The results are shown in Table 3. DET curves obtained from these both cases are shown in Fig. 5. Based on different fusion coefficients and linear weights, the optimum performance is obtained for $\alpha = 0.6$, $\beta = 0.7$ (i.e., % EER = *15.43%*). DET curve shows that the score-level fusion of MFCC and T-MFCC performs better at most of the operating points on the DET curve than MFCC alone (Fig. 5(a)). The result indicates that proposed feature set (namely, T-MFCC) captures the *complementary* information in spoken query than MFCC-alone. The accuracy of monophone MFCC is *66.41%* and T-MFCC

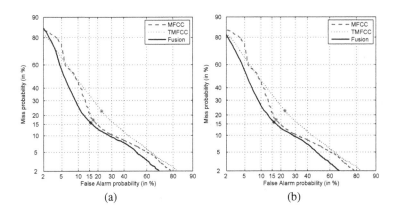

(a)   (b)

Fig. 5. A Detection Error Trade-off (DET) curve for the query detection task (a) *case 1* and (b) *case 2*.

Table 3. Optimum % EER for different feature sets, namely, MFCC, T-MFCC and their score-level fusion.

Feature set	% EER
MFCC ($\alpha = 0.7$)	17.23
T-MFCC ($\alpha = 0.7$)	22.58
Score-level Fusion ($\alpha = 0.7, \beta = 0.7$)	15.81
Score-level Fusion ($\alpha = 0.6, \beta = 0.7$)	**15.43**

is *39.62%*. The performance of MFCC is better than T-MFCC alone, which was shown in DET curves. However, there might be complementary information captured by MFCC and T-MFCC so that they together improve the performance.

6   Summary and Conclusions

In this paper, vocal source information (captured via T-MFCC) is fused with vocal tract information (captured via MFCC) to improve the spoken query detection task. In addition, a linear combination of different phonetic representation, i.e., phone-sets improves the query detection performance. In particular, how the spoken keyword detection system behaves w.r.t. to different phone-sets and signal representation were analyzed.

References

1. The Spoken Term Detection (STD) 2006 Evaluation Plan (2006). http://www.itl. nist.gov/iad/mig/tests/std/2006/docs/std06-evalplan-v10.pdf. Accessed 20 Jan 2016
2. Davis, S., Mermelstein, P.: Comparison of parametric representations for monosyllabic word recognition in continuously spoken sentences. IEEE Trans. Audio Speech Lang. Process. **28**(4), 357–366 (1980)
3. Dhananjaya, N., Yegnanarayana, B., Suryakanth, V.G.: Acoustic-phonetic information from excitation source for refining manner hypotheses of a phone recognizer. In: Proceedings of ICASSP, Prague, pp. 5252–5255. IEEE (2011)
4. Dimitriadis, D., Maragos, P., Potamianos, A.: Robust AM-FM features for speech recognition. IEEE Signal Process. Lett. **12**(9), 621–624 (2005)
5. Gopalan, K., Chu, T.: Keyword word recognition using a fusion of spectral, cepstral and modulation features. In: Proceedings of CONIELECOMP, Cholula, pp. 234–238. IEEE (2012)
6. Jabloun, F., Cetin, A.E., Erzin, E.: Teager energy based feature parameters for speech recognition in car noise. IEEE Signal Process. Lett. **6**(10), 259–261 (1999)
7. Kaiser, J.F.: On a simple algorithm to calculate the energy' of a signal. In: Proceedings of ICASSP, Albuquerque, pp. 381–384. IEEE (1990)
8. Kominek, J., Black, A.W.: The CMU ARCTIC databases for speech synthesis (2003). http://www.festvox.org/cmu_arctic. Accessed 20 Jan 2016

9. Lee, K.F., Hon, H.W.: Speaker-independent phone recognition using hidden Markov models. IEEE Trans. Acoust. Speech Signal Process. **37**(11), 1641–1648 (1989)

10. Martin, A., Doddington, G., Kamm, T., Ordowski, M., Przybocki, M.: The DET curve in assessment of detection task performance. In: Proceedings of EUROSPEECH, Rhodes, pp. 1895–1898 (1997)

11. Narayana, K.V.S., Sreenivas, T.V.: Comparison of AM-FM based features for robust speech recognition. In: Proceedings of INTERSPEECH, Brighton, pp. 1545–1548 (2008)

12. Patil, H.A., Parhi, K.K.: Development of TEO phase for speaker recognition. In: Proceedings of SPCOM, pp. 1–5 (2010)

13. Patil, H.A., Parhi, K.K.: Novel variable length teager energy based features for person recognition from their hum. In: Proceedings of ICASSP, Dallas, pp. 4526–4529. IEEE (2010)

14. Patil, H.A., Basu, T.K.: The teager energy based features for identification of identical twins in multi-lingual environment. In: Pal, N.R., Kasabov, N., Mudi, R.K., Pal, S., Parui, S.K. (eds.) ICONIP 2004. LNCS, vol. 3316, pp. 333–337. Springer, Heidelberg (2004). doi:10.1007/978-3-540-30499-9_50

15. Quatieri, T.F.: Discrete-time Speech Signal Processing: Principles and Practice. Pearson Education (2006). http://books.google.co.in/books?id=UMR9ByupVy8C

16. Sakoe, H., Chiba, S.: Dynamic programming algorithm optimization for spoken word recognition. IEEE Trans. Audio Speech Lang. Process. **26**(1), 43–49 (1978)

17. Teager, H.M., Teager, S.M.: Evidence for nonlinear sound production mechanisms in the vocal tract. In: Hardcastle, W.J., Marchal, A. (eds.) Speech Production and Speech Modelling. NATO ASI Series, vol. 55. Springer, Dordrecht (1990). doi:10.1007/978-94-009-2037-8_10

18. Tejedor, J., Wang, D., King, S., Frankel, J., Colás, J.: A posterior probability-based system hybridisation and combination for spoken term detection. In: Proceedings of INTERSPEECH, Brighton, pp. 2131–2134 (2009)

19. Wallace, R., Vogt, R., Sridharan, S.: A phonetic search approach to the 2006 NIST spoken term detection evaluation. In: Proceedings of INTERSPEECH, Antwerp, pp. 2385–2388 (2007)

20. Young, S., Evermann, G., Gales, M., Hain, T., Kershaw, D., Liu, X.A., Moore, G., Odell, J., Ollason, D., Povey, D., et al.: The HTK book (for HTK version 3.4) (2006)

Novel Gammatone Filterbank Based Spectro-Temporal Features for Robust Phoneme Recognition

Ankit Nagpal$^{(\boxtimes)}$ⓘ and Hemant A. Patilⓘ

Dhirubhai Ambani Institute of Information and Communication Technology,
Gandhinagar, Gujarat, India
{ankit_nagpal,hemant_patil}@daiict.ac.in

Abstract. Recently, Automatic Speech Recognition (ASR) technology is being used in practical scenarios and hence, robustness of ASR is becoming increasingly important. State-of-the-art Mel Frequency Cepstral Coefficients (MFCC) features are known to be affected by acoustic noise whereas physiologically motivated features such as spectro-temporal Gabor filterbank (GBFB) features intend to perform better in signal degradation conditions. The spectro-temporal GBFB feature extraction incorporates mel filterbank to mimic frequency mapping in the Basilar Membrane (BM) in the inner ear. In this paper, Gammatone filterbank is used and a comparison is done between GBFB with mel filterbank (GBFB$_{mel}$) features and GBFB with Gammatone filterbank (GBFB$_{Gamm}$) features. MFCC features and Gammatone Frequency Cepstral Coefficients (GFCC) features are concatenated with GBFB$_{mel}$ and GBFB$_{Gamm}$ features, respectively, to improve recognition performance. Experiments are carried out to calculate phoneme recognition accuracy (PRA), on TIMIT database (without '*sa*' sentences), with additive white, volvo and high frequency noises at various SNR levels from -5 dB to *20* dB. Results show that, with acoustic modeling only, proposed feature set (GBFB$_{Gamm}$+GFCC) performs better (in terms of PRA %), than GBFB$_{mel}$+MFCC features by an average of *1%*, *0.2%* and *0.8%* for white, volvo and high frequency noises, respectively.

Keywords: Robust ASR · Gabor filterbank (GBFB) features · Gammatone filterbank · MFCC · Acoustic model · Language model

1 Introduction

Automatic Speech Recognition (ASR) is being used in practical scenarios which involves various noises and channel effects. Decades of research has brought several methods to improve performance of ASR system by increasing robustness against variability of speech signals. Methods include capturing of temporal cues from the speech signal (TempoRAl Patterns (TRAPS) [1]), spectral information from the speech signal (Mel Frequency Cepstral Coefficients (MFCC) [2] and Perceptual Linear Prediction (PLP) [3]). MFCC features are concatenated with their

© Springer International Publishing AG 2017
B.U. Shankar et al. (Eds.): PReMI 2017, LNCS 10597, pp. 342–350, 2017.
https://doi.org/10.1007/978-3-319-69900-4_43

first and second order temporal derivatives (i.e., delta and double-delta features), to capture temporal dynamics in the speech signal. It resulted in improvement in ASR performance and hence became a big motivation to use joint spectro-temporal features for ASR task. Another motivation to use spectro-temporal features in ASR is the fact that our brain responds to joint spectro-temporal patterns in the speech signal rather than temporal-only or spectral-only patterns [10]. Biological studies indicate that neurons in the primary auditory cortex ($A1$) of mammals are explicitly tuned to spectro-temporal patterns [4] and different neurons are excited by different spectro-temporal patterns depending upon their Spectro-Temporal Receptive Fields (STRFs). Hence, it would be worthwhile to explore and analyze spectro-temporal features of speech signal since these features are physiologically motivated and it is already known that human speech recognition system is better than any ASR system. The shape of STRF of a neuron looks like a 2-D Gabor filter as shown in Fig. 1(b) [8]. Arrow indicates highly varying 2-D impulse response region, where red and blue colors indicate region of strongly excitatory and suppressed responses. The stages of speech processing, from the signal entering the ear, till brain, is shown in Fig. 1(a) [7]. The final output of the speech processing is the response of the neuron in the $A1$, known as cortical representation, which the brain understands. The neural response is the convolution of the input time-frequency representation of speech signal with the STRF of the neuron (called as the cortical stage).

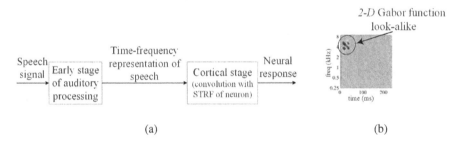

Fig. 1. (a) Speech processing stages in humans. (b) STRF of a neuron in $A1$. Adapted from [8]. All figures in the paper are best viewed in color.

Schadler *et al.* [4] tried to mimic speech recognition of mammals, in ASR task. Algorithm takes log-mel spectrogram (spectro-temporal patterns as input to neurons in $A1$) and passes it through a bank of 2-D Gabor filters (real part of Gabor filters, as 2-D impulse response of neurons known as STRFs) to generate corresponding time-frequency representations, known as the cortical representations. In this paper, Gammatone filters [5] are used instead of mel filters to generate spectro-temporal Gabor filterbank (GBFB) features with Gammatone filterbank (GBFB$_{Gamm}$), in contrast to spectro-temporal Gabor filterbank (GBFB) features with mel filterbank (GBFB$_{mel}$). Gammatone Frequency Cepstral Coefficients (GFCC) are seen to perform better than MFCC [6] and hence, are concatenated with GBFB$_{Gamm}$ features to improve recognition performance. We have analyzed the performance of the proposed features (i.e., GBFB$_{Gamm}$+GFCC) on TIMIT database [9] with different additive noises such as white, volvo and high frequency noises, at various SNR levels. Performance of features is compared with GBFB$_{mel}$+MFCC features and MFCC features alone. Experiments are carried out taking into consideration the effectiveness of Language Model (LM), with HTK as back end [12].

The rest of the paper is organized as follows. Section 2 describes the spectro-temporal feature extraction algorithm in detail. Section 3 contains the experimental results and finally, Sect. 4 concludes the paper along with future research directions.

2   Spectro-Temporal Feature Extraction

Figure 2 shows the architecture for spectro-temporal feature extraction from the speech signal. Log-Gammatone spectrogram is passed through 2-D Gabor filterbank to generate time-frequency representations corresponding to the Gabor filters. These time-frequency representations are combined and dimensionality is reduced to form GBFB with Gammatone filterbank (GBFB$_{Gamm}$) features.

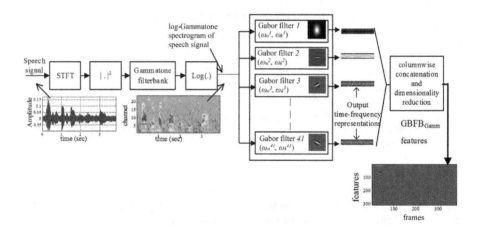

Fig. 2. Architecture for spectro-temporal feature extraction.

2.1   Log-Gammatone Spectrogram as Input to Gabor Filterbank

Gammatone filterbank is commonly used filterbank to simulate the motion of the basilar membrane in the cochlea. Slaney's Auditory toolbox [5] is used to generate the Gammatone filterbank. Spectrogram is expressed as:

$$S(k,\tau) = \sum_{n=0}^{N-1} x[n]w[n,\tau]\exp^{-j2\pi kn/N}, \tag{1a}$$

$$X(k, \tau) = |S(k, \tau)|^2, \tag{1b}$$

where $x[n]$ is the speech signal, $w[n]$ is the window function, τ is the time frame, N is the window length in samples and $S(k, \tau)$ is the short-time Fourier transform (STFT). Spectrogram is represented by $X(k, \tau)$. Figure 3 shows log-Gammatone spectrogram for the segment of clean speech signal, dr1_fdacl_sx394_te from TIMIT database (with sampling frequency 16 kHz) and for additive white noise with 5 dB SNR. Parameters used for calculating log-Gammatone spectrogram are window (Hanning) length = 25 ms, window shift = 10 ms, number of channels/subband filters in Gammatone filterbank = 23, with center frequencies ranging from 100 Hz to 8000 Hz. Figure 3 clearly indicates that joint spectro-temporal intensity pattern in the noisy signal has varied significantly from that of the clean version and thus recognizing speech from a noisy speech signal is indeed a challenging task.

2.2   Gabor Filterbank

The localized complex Gabor filters are defined in (2a), b and c, with the channel and time-frame variables k and n, respectively; ω_k and ω_n the spectral and the temporal modulation frequencies respectively; v_k and v_n the number of semi-cycles under the envelope in spectral and temporal dimension. A Gabor filter is the product of a complex sinusoid carrier (2b) with the corresponding modulation frequencies ω_k and ω_n, and an envelope function defined in (2a).

$$h_b(x) = \begin{cases} 0.5 - 0.5\cos(2\pi x/b), 0 < x < b \\ 0, else \end{cases}, \tag{2a}$$

$$s_\omega(x) = e^{j\omega x}, \tag{2b}$$

$$g(n, k) = s_{\omega_k}(k)s_{\omega_n}(n)h_{\frac{v_k}{2\omega_k}}(k - p)h_{\frac{v_n}{2\omega_n}}(n - q), \tag{2c}$$

where p and q represent the shift in the envelope of the Gabor filter to align the filter at the origin. The above definition would lead to infinite support for purely temporal or purely spectral modulation ($\omega_k = 0$ or $\omega_n = 0$) filters. Thus, filter size is limited to 69 channels and 40 time frames.

There is a linear relationship between the modulation frequency and the extension of the envelope (Eq. (2a), b and c) and hence all the filters with same values for v_k and v_n are constant Q (i.e., quality factor) filters. DC bias of each filter is removed since relative energy fluctuations are important for speech classification. Mean removal on a logarithmic scale is same as dividing on a linear scale and thus this corresponds to a normalization. While cepstral coefficients normalize spectrally, and RASTA (Relative Spectra) [11] processing and discrete derivatives normalize temporally, DC-free Gabor filters naturally normalize in both directions.

Temporal modulation frequencies up to 16 Hz and spectral modulation frequencies up to 0.5 cycle/channel are most sensitive to humans [10] and therefore, best performance is attained if maximum modulation frequencies of the filters are

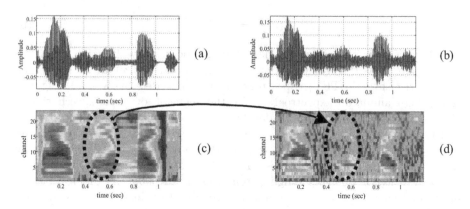

Fig. 3. (a) Segment of the clean speech signal dr1_fdac1_sx394_te from TIMIT database (Fs = *16* kHz), (b) signal in (a) with additive white noise at *5* dB SNR-level, (c) log-Gammatone spectrogram of clean signal, (d) log-Gammatone spectrogram of the noisy speech signal.

around these values. Empirically, we found that maximum modulation frequencies of *12.5* Hz and *0.25* cycle/channel produced the best performance. With the aim of evenly covering the modulation transfer space, modulation frequencies of the filterbank are decided as in (3a, b).

$$\omega_x^{i+1} = \omega_x^i \frac{1 + c/2}{1 - c/2}, \tag{3a}$$

$$c = d_x \frac{8}{v_x}, \tag{3b}$$

where d_x (in x-domain) is the distance factor between the two adjacent filters. Gabor filters with following frequencies are considered.

$$\omega_k = -0.25, -0.12, -0.06, -0.03, 0, 0.03, 0.06, 0.12, 0.25,$$
$$\omega_k = 0, 3.09, 4.92, 7.84, 12.5,$$

in cycles/channel and Hz, respectively. Hence, *41* unique 2-D spectro-temporal Gabor filters are achieved whose real parts are used to process the log-Gammatone spectrogram of the speech signal. The parameters for Gabor filterbank used here are given in Table 1. These parameters, empirically, found to perform the best and are thus used for the speech recognition task considered in this paper.

2.3   Output of the Gabor Filter

2-D convolution of log-Gammatone spectrogram is done with the real part of the Gabor filter to get time-frequency representation that contains patterns matching the modulation frequencies associated with the filter (Fig. 4). The dimension

Table 1. Parameters used for Gabor filterbank

Parameter	ω_n (max)	ω_k (max)	v_n	v_k	d_n	d_k
Value	12.5	0.25	3.5	3.5	0.2	0.3

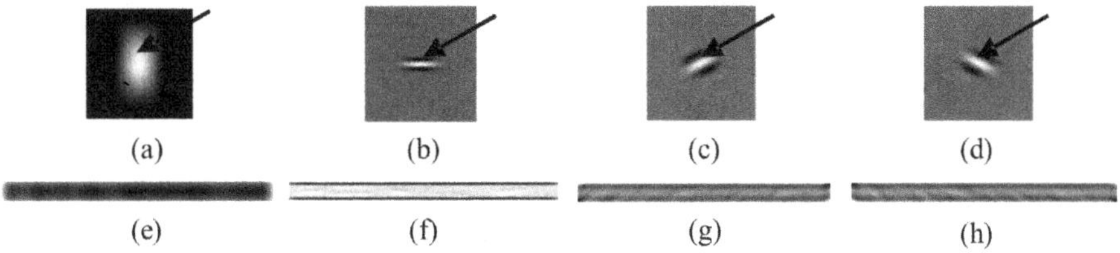

(a)

(b)

(c)

(d)

(e)

(f)

(g)

(h)

Fig. 4. Four Gabor filters with (ω_n, ω_k) as $(0,0)$, $(0,0.12)$, $(3.09,-0.06)$, $(3.09,0.06)$ in (a), (b), (c) and (d), respectively. Corresponding output using log-Gammatone spectrogram of speech signal dr1_fdac1_sx394_te from TIMIT database, with white noise added at 5 dB SNR, in (e), (f), (g) and (h). Gabor filters parameters used are $v_n = v_k = 3.5$, $d_n = 0.2$ and $d_k = 0.3$.

of single filter's output time-frequency representation is same as that of the log-Gammatone spectrogram of the speech signal, i.e., 23 (number of Gammatone channels) × number of frames of the speech signal. Outputs of all the 41 Gabor subband filters are concatenated columnwise to form the features. Figure 4 shows some Gabor filters with different combinations of modulation frequencies (ω_n, ω_k) and corresponding outputs of noisy speech signal (generated by adding white noise at 5 dB SNR, to clean speech signal from TIMIT database). The orientation of the Gabor filters are depicted by arrows, indicating that different combination of modulation frequencies (ω_n, ω_k) leads to different orientation of the Gabor filter.

The resultant concatenated output would be quite high-dimensional ($23 \times 41 = 943$). To reduce computational complexity, dimensionality needs to be reduced. Dimensionality is reduced by exploiting the fact that the filter output between adjacent channels is highly correlated when the subband filter has a large spectral extent. Thus, channel selection scheme as discussed in [4] is applied to the complete feature matrix and dimensionality is reduced to 311. Since, Gabor filter size is limited to 40 time frames, these features encode upto 400 ms (40 × 10 ms window duration) context while MFCC features encode upto 45 ms context. To improve recognition performance, GFCC features [6] are concatenated with GBFB$_{Gamm}$ features to give GBFB$_{Gamm}$+GFCC features which results in the dimension of 350 (i.e., $311 + 39 = 350$).

3 Experimental Results

Recognition experiments are conducted on TIMIT database with additive white, volvo and high frequency noises at various SNR levels ranging from 20 dB to −5 dB. Core training sentences (3696) and core testing sentences (192) of TIMIT

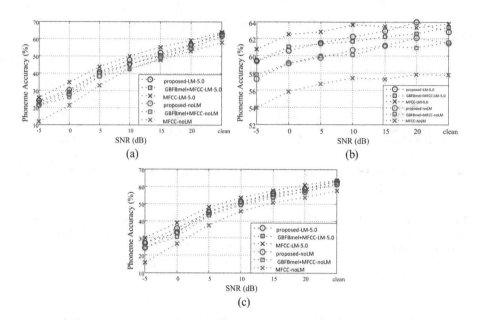

Fig. 5. Comparison of phoneme-level accuracy (in %) between the proposed features, GBFB$_{mel}$+MFCC features and MFCC features for LM *5.0* and with no LM, for additive white, volvo and high frequency noises at various SNR levels in (a), (b) and (c), respectively.

database are used in the experiments. For our experiments, training and testing environments are kept same. Hidden Markov Model (HMM) is used as the back end and phoneme-level accuracy, as given in (4), is used as the performance measure with one phoneme modeled by *5* states and each state modeled by mixture of *8* Gaussians. HTK is used to carry out the experiments. The % phoneme recognition accuracy (*PRA*) is defined as [12]:

$$\%PRA = \frac{N - D - S - I}{N} \times 100, \tag{4}$$

where N is the total number of labels (phonemes) in the reference transcriptions, S is the substitution errors, D is the deletion errors and I is the insertion errors. A comparison between proposed features, i.e., GBFB$_{Gamm}$ concatenated GFCC (GBFB$_{Gamm}$+ GFCC, dimension = *350*) features, GBFB$_{mel}$ concatenated MFCC (GBFB$_{mel}$+MFCC, dimension = *350*) features and MFCC features (dimension = *39*) is shown in Fig. 5, for additive white, volvo and high frequency noises, for various SNR levels. Experiments are conducted with *5.0* weighted LM and for without LM. When experimented with *5.0* weighted language model (LM), it is found that MFCC features perform better than the other two features for clean and noisy environments with SNR ranging from *20* dB to −*5* dB. For SNR = ∞ (clean conditions), *20* dB, *15* dB, *10* dB, *5* dB,

0 dB, −*5* dB, MFCC features perform better (in terms of *PRA* %) than the proposed features by an average (computed over various SNR levels from −*5* dB to *20* dB) of *2.6%*, *1%* and *2.3%* and perform better than GBFB$_{mel}$+MFCC by an average of *3.5%*, *1.2%* and *2.5%*, for additive white, volvo and high frequency noise, respectively. Thus, with *5.0* LM, the proposed features perform better than GBFB$_{mel}$+MFCC by an average of *0.9%* for white noise and *0.2%* for volvo and high frequency noises. When experimented without incorporating LM, it is seen that the proposed features outperform both MFCC and GBFB$_{mel}$+MFCC under signal degradation conditions. For signal degradation conditions, the proposed features perform better than MFCC by an average of *4.6%*, *3.5%* and *5.4%* and perform better than GBFB$_{mel}$+MFCC by an average of *1%*, *0.2%* and *0.8%* for white, volvo and high frequency noise, respectively. Under clean conditions, without LM, the proposed features perform almost similar to GBFB$_{mel}$+MFCC features but perform better than MFCC features by *3.7%*. It can be observed that, with acoustic modeling only, spectro-temporal Gabor filterbank (GBFB) features (whether incorporating Gammatone filterbank or mel filterbank) when concatenated with cepstral coefficients perform better than the state-of-the-art MFCC features in clean conditions as well as in the presence of various additive noises. This is because GBFB features are able to capture more local joint spectro-temporal information in the speech signal. In addition, when Gammatone filterbank is used instead of mel filterbank, to extract GBFB features, the recognition performance under signal degradation conditions (SNR ranging from *20* dB to −*5* dB), is improved.

4   Summary and Conclusions

With acoustic modeling only, the spectro-temporal GBFB features when concatenated with cepstral coefficients perform better than the state-of-the-art MFCC features because of the fact that GBFB features are able to capture more local joint spectro-temporal information in the speech signal (by passing spectrogram of speech through various *2-D* Gabor subband filters aligned at modulation frequencies important for speech intelligibility). Thus, spectro-temporal features are preferred for the languages/ databases which do not have enough accurate language models (due to scarcity of training data). When Gammatone filterbank is used instead of the standard mel filterbank, the recognition performance of the spectro-temporal features is improved. Future work will be to reduce the dimension of such high-dimensional spectro-temporal features and to see the effect of context window of the features (defined by temporal dimension of the Gabor filter) on the recognition performance.

References

1. Hermansky, H., Sharma, S.: Temporal patterns (TRAPS) in ASR of noisy speech. In: Proceedings of International Conference on Acoustics, Speech and Signal Processing (ICASSP), Phoenix, Arizona, USA, vol. 1, pp. 289–292 (1999)

2. Davis, S.B., Mermelstein, P.: Comparison of parametric representation for monosyllabic word recognition in continuously spoken sentences. IEEE Trans. Acoust. Speech Signal Process. **28**(4), 357–366 (1980)

3. Hermansky, H.: Perceptual linear predictive (PLP) analysis of speech. J. Acoust. Soc. Am. **87**(4), 1738–1752 (1990)

4. Schadler, M., Meyer, B., Kollmeier, B.: Spectro-temporal modulation subspace spanning filter bank features for robust automatic speech recognition. J. Acoust. Soc. Am. **131**(5), 4134–4151 (2012)

5. Slaney, M.: Auditory Toolbox, version 2. http://engineering.purdue.edu/malcolm/interval/1998-010/. Accessed 7 Apr 2015

6. Shao, Y., Jin, Z., Wang, D., Srinivasan, S.: An auditory-based feature for robust speech recognition. In: Proceedings of International Conference on Acoustics, Speech and Signal Processing (ICASSP), Taipei, Taiwan, pp. 4625–4628 (2009)

7. Chi, T., Ru, P., Shamma, S.A.: Multiresolution spectrotemporal analysis of complex sounds. J. Acoust. Soc. Am. **118**(2), 887–906 (2005)

8. Depireux, D.A., Ru, P., Shamma, S.A., Simon, J.Z.: Response-field dynamics in the auditory pathway. In: Computational Neuroscience, pp. 1–6 (1998)

9. Lee, K., Hon, H.: Speaker-independent phone recognition using hidden Markov Models. IEEE Trans. Acoust. Speech Signal Process. **37**(11), 1642–1648 (1989)

10. Chi, T., Gao, Y., Gutyon, M.C., Ru, P., Shamma, S.A.: Spectro-temporal modulation transfer functions and speech intelligibility. J. Acoust. Soc. Am. **106**(5), 2719–2732 (1999)

11. Hermansky, H., Morgan, N.: RASTA processing of speech. IEEE Trans. Speech Audio Process. **2**(4), 578–589 (1994)

12. Young, S.J., Evermann, G., Gales, M.J.F., et al.: The HTK book for HTK version 3.4. Microsoft Corporation (2006)

Neural Networks Compression
for Language Modeling

Artem M. Grachev[1,2]([✉]) [iD], Dmitry I. Ignatov[2] [iD], and Andrey V. Savchenko[3] [iD]

[1] Samsung R&D Institute Rus, Moscow, Russia
grachev.art@gmail.com
[2] National Research University Higher School of Economics, Moscow, Russia
[3] Laboratory of Algorithms and Technologies for Network Analysis, National
Research University Higher School of Economics, Nizhny Novgorod, Russia

Abstract. In this paper, we consider several compression techniques
for the language modeling problem based on recurrent neural networks
(RNNs). It is known that conventional RNNs, e.g., LSTM-based networks in language modeling, are characterized with either high space
complexity or substantial inference time. This problem is especially crucial for mobile applications, in which the constant interaction with the
remote server is inappropriate. By using the Penn Treebank (PTB)
dataset we compare pruning, quantization, low-rank factorization, tensor train decomposition for LSTM networks in terms of model size and
suitability for fast inference.

Keywords: LSTM · RNN · Language modeling · Low-rank
factorization · Pruning · Quantization

1 Introduction

Neural network models can require a lot of space on disk and in memory. They
can also need a substantial amount of time for inference. This is especially important for models that we put on devices like mobile phones. There are several
approaches to solve these problems. Some of them are based on sparse computations. They also include pruning or more advanced methods. In general, such
approaches are able to provide a large reduction in the size of a trained network, when the model is stored on a disk. However, there are some problems
when we use such models for inference. They are caused by high computation
time of sparse computing. Another branch of methods uses different matrix-
based approaches in neural networks. Thus, there are methods based on the
usage of Toeplitz-like structured matrices in [1] or different matrix decomposition techniques: low-rank decomposition [1], TT-decomposition (Tensor Train
decomposition) [2,3]. Also [4] proposes a new type of RNN, called uRNN
(Unitary Evolution Recurrent Neural Networks).

In this paper, we analyze some of the aforementioned approaches. The
material is organized as follows. In Sect. 2, we give an overview of language

B.U. Shankar et al. (Eds.): PReMI 2017, LNCS 10597, pp. 351–357, 2017.
https://doi.org/10.1007/978-3-319-69900-4_44

modeling methods and then focus on respective neural networks approaches. Next we describe different types of compression. In Sect. 3.1, we consider the simplest methods for neural networks compression like pruning or quantization. In Sect. 3.2, we consider approaches to compression of neural networks based on different matrix factorization methods. Section 3.3 deals with TT-decomposition. Section 4 describes our results and some implementation details. Finally, in Sect. 5, we summarize the results of our work.

2   Language Modeling with Neural Networks

Consider the language modeling problem. We need to compute the probability of a sentence or sequence of words $(w_1, \ldots, w_T)$ in a language L.

$$P(w_1, \ldots, w_T) = P(w_1, \ldots, w_{T-1})P(w_T|w_1, \ldots, w_{T-1})$$

$$= \prod_{t=1}^{T} P(w_t|w_1, \ldots, w_{t-1}) \quad (1)$$

The use of such a model directly would require calculation $P(w_t|w_1, \ldots, w_{t-1})$ and in general it is too difficult due to a lot of computation steps. That is why a common approach features computations with a fixed value of N and approximate (1) with $P(w_t|w_{t-N}, \ldots, w_{t-1})$. This leads us to the widely known N-gram models [5,6]. It was very popular approach until the middle of the 2000s. A new milestone in language modeling had become the use of recurrent neural networks [7]. A lot of work in this area was done by Thomas Mikolov [8].

Consider a recurrent neural network, RNN, where N is the number of timesteps, L is the number of recurrent layers, $x_{\ell-1}^t$ is the input of the layer ℓ at the moment t. Here $t \in \{1, \ldots, N\}$, $\ell \in \{1, \ldots, L\}$, and x_0^t is the embedding vector. We can describe each layer as follows:

$$z_\ell^t = W_\ell x_{\ell-1}^t + V_\ell x_\ell^{t-1} + b_l \quad (2)$$
$$x_\ell^t = \sigma(z_\ell^t), \quad (3)$$

where W_ℓ and V_ℓ are matrices of weights and σ is an activation function. The output of the network is given by

$$y^t = \text{softmax}\left[W_{L+1} x_L^t + b_{L+1}\right]. \quad (4)$$

Then, we define

$$P(w_t|w_{t-N}, \ldots, w_{t-1}) = y^t. \quad (5)$$

While N-gram models even with not very big N require a lot of space due to the combinatorial explosion, neural networks can learn some representations of words and their sequences without memorizing directly all options.

Now the mainly used variations of RNN are designed to solve the problem of decaying gradients [9]. The most popular variation is Long Short-Term Memory

(LSTM) [7] and Gated Recurrent Unit (GRU) [10]. Let us describe one layer of LSTM:

$$i_\ell^t = \sigma \left[W_l^i x_{l-1}^t + V_l^i x_l^{t-1} + b_l^i \right] \qquad \text{input gate} \qquad (6)$$

$$f_\ell^t = \sigma \left[W_l^f x_{l-1}^t + V_l^f x_l^{t-1} + b_l^f \right] \qquad \text{forget gate} \qquad (7)$$

$$c_\ell^t = f_l^t \cdot c_l^{t-1} + i_l^t \tanh \left[W_l^c x_{l-1}^t + U_l^c x_l^{t-1} + b_l^c \right] \qquad \text{cell state} \qquad (8)$$

$$o_\ell^t = \sigma \left[W_l^o x_{\ell-1}^t + V_l^o x_l^{t-1} + b_l^o \right] \qquad \text{output gate} \qquad (9)$$

$$x_\ell^t = o_\ell^t \cdot \tanh[c_l^t], \qquad (10)$$

where again $t \in \{1, \ldots, N\}$, $\ell \in \{1, \ldots, L\}$, c_ℓ^t is the memory vector at the layer ℓ and time step t. The output of the network is given the same formula 4 as above.

Approaches to the language modeling problem based on neural networks are efficient and widely adopted, but still require a lot of space. In each LSTM layer of size $k \times k$ we have 8 matrices of size $k \times k$. Moreover, usually the first (or zero) layer of such a network is an embedding layer that maps word's vocabulary number to some vector. And we need to store this embedding matrix too. Its size is $n_{vocab} \times k$, where n_{vocab} is the vocabulary size. Also we have an output softmax layer with the same number of parameters as in the embedding, i.e. $k \times n_{vocab}$. In our experiments, we try to reduce the embedding size and to decompose softmax layer as well as hidden layers.

We produce our experiments with compression on standard PTB models. There are three main benchmarks: Small, Medium and Large LSTM models [11]. But we mostly work with Small and Medium ones.

3 Compression Methods

3.1 Pruning and Quantization

In this subsection, we consider maybe not very effective but still useful techniques. Some of them were described in application to audio processing [12] or image-processing [13,14], but for language modeling this field is not yet well described.

Pruning is a method for reducing the number of parameters of NN. In Fig. 1. (left), we can see that usually the majority of weight values are concentrated near zero. It means that such weights do not provide a valuable contribution in the final output. We can set some threshold and then remove all connections with the weights below it from the network. After that we retrain the network to learn the final weights for the remaining sparse connections.

Quantization is a method for reducing the size of a compressed neural network in memory. We are compressing each float value to an eight-bit integer representing the closest real number in one of 256 equally-sized intervals within the range.

Pruning and quantization have common disadvantages since training from scratch is impossible and their usage is quite laborious. In pruning the reason

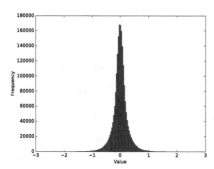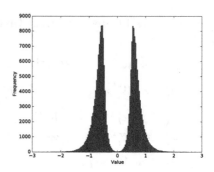

Fig. 1. Weights distribution before and after pruning

is mostly lies in the inefficiency of sparse computing. When we do quantization, we store our model in an 8-bit representation, but we still need to do 32-bits computations. It means that we have not advantages using RAM. At least until we do not use the tensor processing unit (TPU) that is adopted for effective 8- and 16-bits computations.

3.2   Low-Rank Factorization

Low-rank factorization represents more powerful methods. For example, in [1], the authors applied it to a voice recognition task. A simple factorization can be done as follows:

$$x_\ell^t = \sigma \left[W_\ell^a W_\ell^b x_{\ell-1}^t + U_l^a U_l^b x_\ell^{t-1} + b_l \right] \tag{11}$$

Following [1] require $W_l^b = U_{\ell-1}^b$. After this we can rewrite our equation for RNN:

$$x_l^t = \sigma \left[W_l^a m_{l-1}^t + U_l^a m_l^{t-1} + b_l \right] \tag{12}$$

$$m_l^t = U_l^b x_l^t \tag{13}$$

$$y_t = \text{softmax} \left[W_{L+1} m_L^t + b_{L+1} \right] \tag{14}$$

For LSTM it is mostly the same with more complicated formulas. The main advantage we get here from the sizes of matrices W_l^a, U_l^b, U_l^a. They have the sizes $r \times n$ and $n \times r$, respectively, where the original W_l and V_l matrices have size $n \times n$. With small r we have the advantage in size and in multiplication speed. We discuss some implementation details in Sect. 4.

3.3   The Tensor Train Decomposition

In the light of recent advances of tensor train approach [2,3], we have also decided to apply this technique to LSTM compression in language modeling.

The tensor train decomposition was originally proposed as an alternative and more efficient form of tensor's representation [15]. The TT-decomposition (or TT-representation) of a tensor $A \in \mathbb{R}^{n_1 \times \ldots \times n_d}$ is the set of matrices $G_k[j_k] \in \mathbb{R}^{r_{k-1} \times r_k}$, where $j_k = 1, \ldots, n_k$, $k = 1, \ldots, d$, and $r_0 = r_d = 1$ such that each of the tensor elements can be represented as $A(j_1, j_2, \ldots, j_d) = G_1[j_1]G_2[j_2] \ldots G_d[j_d]$. In the same paper, the author proposed to consider the input matrix as a multidimensional tensor and apply the same decomposition to it. If we have matrix A of size $N \times M$, we can fix d and such $n_1, \ldots, n_d$, $m_1, \ldots, m_d$ that the following conditions are fulfilled: $\prod_{j=1}^{d} n_j = N$, $\prod_{i=1}^{d} m_i = M$. Then we reshape our matrix A to the tensor A with d dimensions and size $n_1 m_1 \times n_2 m_2 \times \ldots \times n_d m_d$. Finally, we can perform tensor train decomposition with this tensor. This approach was successfully applied to compress fully connected neural networks [2] and for developing convolution TT layer [3].

In its turn, we have applied this approach to LSTM. Similarly, as we describe it above for usual matrix decomposition, here we also describe only RNN layer. We apply TT-decomposition to each of the matrices W and V in Eq. 2 and get:

$$z_\ell^t = \mathrm{TT}(W_i)x_{\ell-1}^t + \mathrm{TT}(V_l)x_\ell^{t-1} + b_\ell. \tag{15}$$

Here $\mathrm{TT}(W)$ means that we apply TT-decomposition for matrix W. It is necessary to note that even with the fixed number of tensors in TT-decomposition and their sizes we still have plenty of variants because we can choose the rank of each tensor.

4   Results

For testing pruning and quantization we choose Small PTB Benchmark. The results can be found in Table 1. We can see that we have a reduction of the size with a small loss of quality.

For matrix decomposition we perform experiments with Medium and Large PTB benchmarks. When we talk about language modeling, we must say that the embedding and the output layer each occupy one third of the total network size. It follows us to the necessity of reducing their sizes too. We reduce the output layer by applying matrix decomposition. We describe sizes of **LR LSTM 650-650** since it is the most useful model for the practical application. We start with basic sizes for W and V, 650×650, and 10000×650 for embedding. We reduce each W and V down to 650×128 and reduce embedding down to 10000×128. The value 128 is chosen as the most suitable degree of 2 for efficient device implementation. We have performed several experiments, but this configuration is near the best. Our compressed model, **LR LSTM 650-650**, is even smaller than **LSTM 200-200** with better perplexity. The results of experiments can be found in Table 2.

In TT decomposition we have some freedom in way of choosing internal ranks and number of tensors. We fix the basic configuration of an LSTM-network with two 600-600 layers and four tensors for each matrix in a layer. And we perform a grid search through different number of dimensions and various ranks.

We have trained about 100 models with using the Adam optimizer [16]. The average training time for each is about 5–6 h on GeForce GTX TITAN X

Table 1. Pruning and quantization results on PTB dataset

Model	Size	No. of params	Test PP
LSTM 200-200 (Small benchmark)	18.6 Mb	4.64 M	117.659
Pruning output layer 90% w/o additional training	5.5 Mb	0.5 M	149.310
Pruning output layer 90% with additional training	5.5 Mb	0.5 M	121.123
Quantization (1 byte per number)	4.7 Mb	4.64 M	118.232

Table 2. Matrix decomposition results on PTB dataset

	Model	Size	No. of params	Test PP
PTB benchmarks	LSTM 200-200	18.6 Mb	4.64 M	117.659
	LSTM 650-650	79.1 Mb	19.7 M	82.07
	LSTM 1500-1500	264.1 Mb	66.02 M	78.29
Ours	LR LSTM 650-650	16.8 Mb	4.2 M	92.885
	TT LSTM 600-600	50.4 Mb	12.6 M	168.639
	LR LSTM 1500-1500	94.9 Mb	23.72 M	89.462

(Maxwell architecture), but unfortunately none of them has achieved acceptable quality. The best obtained result (**TT LSTM 600-600**) is even worse than **LSTM-200-200** both in terms of size and perplexity.

5   Conclusion

In this article, we have considered several methods of neural networks compression for the language modeling problem. The first part is about pruning and quantization. We have shown that for language modeling there is no difference in applying of these two techniques. The second part is about matrix decomposition methods. We have shown some advantages when we implement models on devices since usually in such tasks there are tight restrictions on the model size and its structure. From this point of view, the model **LR LSTM 650-650** has nice characteristics. It is even smaller than the smallest benchmark on PTB and demonstrates quality comparable with the medium-sized benchmarks on PTB.

Acknowledgements. This study is supported by Russian Federation President grant MD-306.2017.9. A.V. Savchenko is supported by the Laboratory of Algorithms and Technologies for Network Analysis, National Research University Higher School of Economics. D.I. Ignatov was supported by RFBR grants no. 16-29-12982 and 16-01-00583.

References

1. Lu, Z., Sindhwan, V., Sainath, T.N.: Learning compact recurrent neural networks. In: Acoustics, Speech and Signal Processing (ICASSP) (2016)
2. Novikov, A., Podoprikhin, D., Osokin, A., Vetrov, D.P.: Tensorizing neural networks. In: Advances in Neural Information Processing Systems 28: Annual Conference on Neural Information Processing Systems 2015, pp. 442–450 (2015)
3. Garipov, T., Podoprikhin, D., Novikov, A., Vetrov, D.P.: Ultimate tensorization: compressing convolutional and FC layers alike. CoRR/NIPS 2016 Workshop: Learning with Tensors: Why Now and How? abs/1611.03214 (2016)
4. Arjovsky, M., Shah, A., Bengio, Y.: Unitary evolution recurrent neural networks. In: Proceedings of the 33rd International Conference on Machine Learning, ICML 2016, pp. 1120–1128 (2016)
5. Jelinek, F.: Statistical Methods for Speech Recognition. MIT Press, Cambridge (1997)
6. Kneser, R., Ney, H.: Improved backing-off for m-gram language modeling. Proc. IEEE Int. Conf. Acoust. Speech Sig. Process. **1**, 181–184 (1995)
7. Hochreiter, S., Schmidhuber, J.: Long short-term memory. Neural Comput. **9**(8), 1735–1780 (1997)
8. Mikolov, T.: Statistical Language Models Based on Neural Networks. Ph.D. thesis, Brno University of Technology (2012)
9. Hochreiter, S., Bengio, Y., Frasconi, P., Schmidhuber, J.: Gradient flow in recurrent nets: the difficulty of learning long-term dependencies. In: Kremer, S.C., Kolen, J.F. (eds.) A Field Guide to Dynamical Recurrent Neural Networks (2001)
10. Cho, K., van Merrienboer, B., Bahdanau, D., Bengio, Y.: On the properties of neural machine translation: Encoder-decoder approaches. arXiv preprint 2014f (2014). arXiv:1409.1259
11. Zaremba, W., Sutskever, I., Vinyals, O.: Recurrent neural network regularization. Arxiv preprint (2014)
12. Han, S., Mao, H., Dally, W.J.: Deep compression: Compressing deep neural networks with pruning, trained quantization and Huffman coding. In: Acoustics, Speech and Signal Processing (ICASSP) (2016)
13. Molchanov, P., Tyree, S., Karras, T., Aila, T., Kaut, J.: Pruning convolutional neural networks for resource efficient transfer learning. arXiv preprint (2016). arXiv:1611.06440
14. Rassadin, A.G., Savchenko, A.V.: Compressing deep convolutional neural networks in visual emotion recognition. In: Proceedings of the International Conference on Information Technology and Nanotechnology (ITNT), vol. 1901, pp. 207–213. CEUR-WS (2017)
15. Oseledets, I.V.: Tensor-train decomposition. SIAM J. Sci. Computing **33**(5), 2295–2317 (2011)
16. Kingma, D., Ba, J.: Adam: a method for stochastic optimization. In: The International Conference on Learning Representations (ICLR) (2015)

A Metaphor Detection Approach Using Cosine Similarity

Malay Pramanick$^{(\boxtimes)}$ and Pabitra Mitra

Department of Computer Science and Engineering, Indian Institute of Technology,
Kharagpur 721302, WB, India
malay.pramanick@iitkgp.ac.in

Abstract. Metaphor is a prominent figure of speech. For their preva-
lence in text and speech, detection and analysis of metaphors are required
for complete natural language understanding. This paper describes a
novel method for identification of metaphors with word vectors. Our
method relies on the semantic distance between the word and the corresponding object or action it is applied to. Our method does not target
any particular kind of metaphor but tries to identify metaphors in general. Experimental results on the VU Amsterdam Metaphor Corpus show
that our method gives state of the art results as compared to previous
reported works.

Keywords: Metaphor detection · Word embedding/Word vectors ·
Cosine similarity · VUAMC

1 Introduction

Metaphor is a figure of speech, that shows similarities between one thing
and another or between actions. Metaphors are so abundant in any language
that their identification and interpretation would benefit the Natural Language
Processing (NLP) methods like paraphrasing, summarization, machine translation, language generation etc.

For any metaphor, to be analysed and interpreted, it has to be identified
first. Some of the existing computational methods for metaphor detection use
heirarchical organisation of conventional metaphors or conventional mappings of
subject-verb, verb-object, subject-object or selectional restrictions as provided
in lexical resources available, or domain mapping of the word and its context [17].

We tackle the problem of detection of metaphor in a given sentence irrespective of its type, and without using lexical resources like WordNet. For this we
come up with a novel method using word embeddings, even when embeddings
were not meant for this purpose. The method for detection of metaphor thus
described in this paper uses similarity metrics for vectors, with the vector representation of words. With the similarity, thus obtained, as features, Decision
Tree Classifier is used to classify whether any metaphor is present in the given
sentence. Experiments with the VU Amsterdam Metaphor Corpus show better
results compared to strong baselines.

© Springer International Publishing AG 2017
B.U. Shankar et al. (Eds.): PReMI 2017, LNCS 10597, pp. 358–364, 2017.
https://doi.org/10.1007/978-3-319-69900-4_45

2   Related Works

There have been many works on detection of metaphors computationally, supervised as well as unsupervised. Shutova [17] has a comprehensive review of computational metaphor detection. Following are some of the works that are related to our approach.

To determine whether a sentence contains a metaphor Wilks et al. [21] extracted all verbs along with the subject and direct object arguments for each verb using the Stanford Parser. Extracting the verbs from the sentence, they checked for preference violations with the help of WordNet [6,14] and VerbNet [16]. If there is a violation, they mark it as 'Preference Violation metaphor'. They also take into consideration the 'conventional metaphors' and determine them by the senses in WordNet. Klebanov et al. [9] used the logistic regression classifier to detect metaphor using unigrams, part of speech, concreteness and topic models as features. Klebanov et al. [8], to improve their previous work, tuned the weight parameter to represent concreteness of information, including the difference of concreteness. Su et al. [20], based on the theory of meaning, presented a metaphor detection technique, considering the difference between the source and target domains in the semantic level rather than the categories of the domains. They extract subject-object pair by a dependency parser, which they refer to as 'concepts-pair'. Then they compare the cosine similarity of the concepts-pair and from the WordNet find out whether the subject is hypernym or hyponym of the object. When the cosine similarity is below a particular threshold and 'concept-pair' does not have a hypernym-hyponym relation, it is categorized as metaphorical, otherwise literal. But they target only nominal metaphors ('IS-A' metaphors) aka Type I metaphors [11], whereas our method is general and does not look for any particular type of metaphor.

3   Motivation

Many real-world NLP systems treat words as atomic units because of simplicity, robustness and the observation that simple models trained on huge amounts of data outperform complex systems trained on less data [12]. Motivation behind the proposed approach is that other methods treat words as atomic units but words can have multiple degrees of similarity [13] and many word embeddings acknowledge that fact.

4   Proposed Metaphor Detection Approach

Flow diagram for our approach is shown in Fig. 1.

4.1   Vector Representation of Words

The method proposed in this paper uses vector representation of words already made available to it. We have used the open-source Google Word2Vec[1] system,

---

[1] Available at https://code.google.com/archive/p/word2vec/.

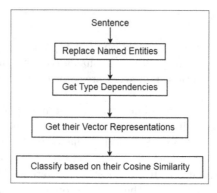

Fig. 1. Flow Diagram

and for training it, we have used text corpus from the latest English Wikipedia dump[2], preprocessed with the Perl script of Matt Mahoney[3].

For training as well as testing purposes, one might come across words for which embeddings are not provided. For such scenarios, we map those to a constant vector of the same dimension as of the word vectors provided.

4.2   Feature Extraction

Replacing Named Entities: First we normalize the sentences with Normalization Form KD (NFKD) [3]. This is required because in presence of non-ascii characters, the Stanford NLP Softwares[4] sometime produce characters which are originally not there in the input.

We replace the Named Entities because we cannot get the vector representation for many proper nouns, and the chances increase for the unpopular ones. Also the replacement is required for unification of similar proper nouns under the same category. For example, different companies have different names, but unification is required for them to be treated similarly. So we use Stanford Named Entity Recognizer (NER) [7] for that purpose. Once the entities are recognized, the names are replaced by the entities. So "Montenegro's sudden rehabilitation of Nicholas 's memory is a popular move" (VU Amsterdam Metaphor Corpus) becomes "LOCATION's sudden rehabilitation of PERSON 's memory is a popular move".

Getting Type Dependencies: We parse the sentences with NER replaced with the Stanford PFCG Lexical Parser [10] to get the parse trees and also the typed dependencies (Stanford Typed Dependencies) [4]. Of all the dependencies identified, we keep a subset of the dependencies along with their types.

---

[2] Available at https://dumps.wikimedia.org/enwiki/latest/.

[3] Available at http://www.mattmahoney.net/dc/textdata.html.

[4] http://nlp.stanford.edu/software/.

We decide, the types that we choose to include in our subset, in such a way that they may contain a metaphor. Wilks et al., [21], consider *agent, nsubj, xsubj, dobj* and *nsubjpass* as they look for metaphor surrounding a verb. We choose a larger subset. For example, we also consider *acomp* (adjectival complement) [5], as it may result in metaphors as in 'he looks green'.

4.3 Training

The system has to be provided with an annotated metaphor corpus, a corpus with sentences having metaphors and some without, marked positive and negative respectively, for training purpose. It gets the cosine similarity of the dependent word pairs, and then distributes the cosine similarities according to the class of the sentence they come from, i.e., the cosine similarities of dependent words of a metaphor containing sentences are put in the positive class and those coming from sentences not containing any metaphor are put in the negative class.

4.4 Classification

The default class of a sentence is negative. Then one by one the cosine similarities are classified with CART [1], which is a Decision Tree Classifier. If atleast one of them is classified to be positive, the sentence is marked positive.

5 Experiments

5.1 Dataset

The **VU Amsterdam Metaphor Corpus** (VUAMC)[5] [19] is one of the "largest available corpus hand-annotated for all metaphorical language use, regardless of lexical field or source domain". It is based on "a systematic and explicit metaphor identification protocol" [18] with inter-annotator reliability of $\kappa > 0.8$.

5.2 Baselines

We compare our method with two baselines, one that does not use word embedding and one that does, which are explained as follows.

Baseline 1 (UPT+CUpDown+DCUpDown model)

As one of our baselines, we use the results from Klebanov et al. [8]. They also report on the VUAMC other than the 'Essay Data'. We consider the average of VUAMC (VUA in [8]) for comparison. We choose their best reported results achieved by using the method known as UPT+CUpDown+DCUpDown model.

---

[5] Available at http://ota.ahds.ac.uk/headers/2541.xml.

Baseline 2 (CRF (with SF+CF+AF+XF))

As our next baseline, we use the results from Rai et al. [15]. They also report on the VUAMC. For comparison, we choose their best reported results achieved by using CRF with feature set of SF+CF+AF+XF on overall VUAMC dataset across every genre (Dataset2 in [15]).

Baseline 3 (SVM (with word embeddings))

For each of the sentences, after replacing NERs, we get the typed dependencies. For each of the pairs of words, we append word vector of the second word in the (ordered) pair to the vector representation of the first and thus obtain the feature vectors. For a sentence containing metaphor, the feature vectors derived from the (typed) dependent pairs are placed in positive class and those sentences which do not contain metaphor, their feature vectors are placed in negative class. By default, for classification, a sentence is put in a negative class and if atleast one of its feature vectors is classified by Support Vector Classifier [2] to be positive, the sentence is marked positive for metaphor.

5.3   Evaluation

For training and testing purpose, we consider the VU Amsterdam Metaphor Corpus and performed a 10-fold cross validation on it.

We compare our method against the baselines on the basis of precision, recall and F_1-score. For their calculation, sentences containing metaphors are considered to constitute the positive class, irrespective of the number of metaphors in the sentence and sentences not having metaphors constitute the negative class.

Table 1. VU Amsterdam Metaphor Corpus.

Method	Precision	Recall	F_1-score
UPT+CUpDown+DCUpDown model	0.438	0.669	0.511
CRF (with SF+CF+AF+XF)	0.633	0.587	0.609
SVM (with word embeddings)	0.606	0.982	0.749
The proposed method	0.617	0.982	0.758

6   Results and Discussions

As shown in Table 1, the proposed method outperforms the baselines. Our method surpasses each of the criteria considered for comparison of the methods. For the VU Amsterdam Metaphor Database, Klebanov et al. [8] report an average F_1-score of 0.511 and Rai et al. [15] report F-measure of 0.609. The proposed approach gives an F_1-score of 0.758.

Some of the typed dependencies are ignored so as to speed up the process and decrease the volume of the data to be examined for detection procedure. Considering all of them does not improve the results significantly, but increase the overheads.

Analysing the false positives, we found out that over-fitting of the positive class is due to the presence of common pairs in the typed dependencies of *dobj*(direct object), *nsubj*(nominal subject) and the alikes. We observed in our experiments that if we do not consider those dependencies, the F_1-score falls drastically.

Our system gives a larger number of false positives compared to false negatives, which we believe to be the better option. Metaphor interpretation, comes after metaphor recognition. For false negatives, the metaphors will be treated literally and interpreted in ways they were not intended. But for the cases of false positives, we search for the analogies, if any analogy is not found, we can always return to the literal meaning.

7   Conclusion

In this paper we proposed a novel approach for metaphor detection which uses cosine similarity as its main component. We compared our results on a standard dataset and showed superior performance. In future, we intend to use the proposed method in downstream applications like paraphrasing and summarization.

References

1. Breiman, L., Friedman, J., Stone, C.J., Olshen, R.A.: Classification and Regression Trees. CRC Press (1984)
2. Cortes, C., Vapnik, V.: Support-vector networks. Mach. Learn. **20**(3), 273–297 (1995)
3. Davis, M., Dürst, M.: Unicode normalization forms (2001)
4. De Marneffe, M.-C., MacCartney, B., Manning, C.D., et al.: Generating typed dependency parses from phrase structure parses. In: Proceedings of LREC, vol. 6, pp. 449–454 (2006)
5. De Marneffe, M.-C., Manning, C.D.: Stanford typed dependencies manual. Technical report, Technical report, Stanford University (2008)
6. Fellbaum, C.: WordNet. Wiley Online Library (1998)
7. Finkel, J.R., Grenager, T., Manning, C.: Incorporating non-local information into information extraction systems by gibbs sampling. In: Proceedings of the 43rd Annual Meeting on Association for Computational Linguistics, pp. 363–370. Association for Computational Linguistics (2005)
8. Klebanov, B.B., Leong, C.W., Flor, M.: Supervised word-level metaphor detection: experiments with concreteness and reweighting of examples. In: NAACL HLT 2015, p. 11 (2015)
9. Klebanov, B.B., Leong, C.W., Heilman, M., Flor, M.: Different texts, same metaphors: unigrams and beyond. In: Proceedings of the Second Workshop on Metaphor in NLP, pp. 11–17 (2014)

10. Klein, D., Manning, C.D.: Accurate unlexicalized parsing. In: Proceedings of the 41st Annual Meeting on Association for Computational Linguistics, vol. 1, pp. 423–430. Association for Computational Linguistics (2003)
11. Krishnakumaran, S., Zhu, X.: Hunting elusive metaphors using lexical resources. In: Proceedings of the Workshop on Computational Approaches to Figurative Language, pp. 13–20. Association for Computational Linguistics (2007)
12. Mikolov, T., Chen, K., Corrado, G., Dean, J.: Efficient estimation of word representations in vector space. arXiv preprint arXiv:1301.3781 (2013)
13. Mikolov, T., Yih, W.-T., Zweig, G.: Linguistic regularities in continuous space word representations. In: HLT-NAACL, vol. 13, pp. 746–751 (2013)
14. Miller, G.A.: Wordnet: a lexical database for english. Commun. ACM **38**(11), 39–41 (1995)
15. Rai, S., Chakraverty, S., Tayal, D.K.: Supervised metaphor detection using conditional random fields
16. Schuler, K.K.: Verbnet: a broad-coverage, comprehensive verb lexicon (2005)
17. Shutova, E.: Models of metaphor in NLP. In: Proceedings of the 48th Annual Meeting of the Association for Computational Linguistics, pp. 688–697. Association for Computational Linguistics (2010)
18. Steen, G.J., Dorst, A.G., Berenike Herrmann, J., Kaal, A., Krennmayr, T., Pasma, T.: A Method for Linguistic Metaphor Identification: From MIP to MIPVU, vol. 14. John Benjamins Publishing (2010)
19. Steen, G.J., Dorst, A.G., Berenike Herrmann, J., Kaal, A.A., Krennmayr, T.: Vu amsterdam metaphor corpus (2010)
20. Su, C., Huang, S., Chen, Y.: Automatic detection and interpretation of nominal metaphor based on the theory of meaning. Neurocomputing (2016)
21. Wilks, Y., Galescu, L., Allen, J., Dalton, A.: Automatic metaphor detection using large-scale lexical resources and conventional metaphor extraction. In: Proceedings of the First Workshop on Metaphor in NLP, pp. 36–44 (2013)

Named Entity Identification Based Translation Disambiguation Model

Vijay Kumar Sharma$^{(\boxtimes)}$ and Namita Mittal

Malaviya National Institute of Technology Jaipur, Jaipur, India
{2014rcp9541,nmittal.cse}@mnit.ac.in

Abstract. Machine Translation (MT) systems are in growing state for Indian languages, where either a translation or transliteration mechanism is used for a word or phrase. Identifying whether a word needs translation or transliteration mechanism, is still a challenge. Since the Named Entity (NE) terms have a property of similar pronunciation across the languages. So the Named Entity Identification (NEI) will be very useful for disambiguating the word in favor of either translation or transliteration. Term Frequency Model (TFM), i.e., a Cross-Lingual Information Retrieval (CLIR) model is used to evaluate the NEI based translation disambiguation model.

1 Introduction

The Named Entity Identification (NEI) is a task of identifying whether the term is a Named Entity (NE), i.e., the name of a person, location, and organization or not. Machine Translation (MT) system is a long standing research area and a lot of research has been done in MT for foreign languages, but the challenges are still not resolved for Indian languages. An issue of improper term translation or transliteration, i.e., whether a term needs to be translated or transliterated, is addressed in this paper. Most of the previous MT systems not address this issue and suffer from poor quality translations.

The proposed NEI translation disambiguation model is evaluated with Cross-Lingual Information Retrieval (CLIR). Dictionary and parallel/comparable corpus-based approaches are the traditional CLIR approaches. In this paper, a recently proposed parallel/comparable corpus-based Term Frequency Model (TFM) is used for evaluation [10]. Our contribution in this work for the Hindi language is to: (i) Collect and prepare the named entity annotated data and gazetteer list; Develop an NEI model with some linguistic patterns. (ii) Analysis and evaluation of an NEI model with TFM; Is NEI translation disambiguation model suitable for resolving improper term translation or transliteration issue? The paper structure is like; Sect. 2 represents literature review. Proposed approach is discussed in Sect. 3. Experiment results and discussions are presented in Sect. 4. Conclusion and future work is discussed in Sect. 5.

© Springer International Publishing AG 2017
B.U. Shankar et al. (Eds.): PReMI 2017, LNCS 10597, pp. 365–372, 2017.
https://doi.org/10.1007/978-3-319-69900-4_46

2   Literature Review

The NEI techniques are broadly categorized into (i) Rule-Based (RB) approaches, and (ii) Machine Learning (ML) approaches. RB approaches contain a set of rules which are based on grammar, gazetteer list and lists of trigger words. A lot of grammatical knowledge and experience about a particular language is required to write such rules which is the main deficiency of the RB approaches. The phonetic matching technique is based on the similar sounding property [1,6]. The Maximum Entropy Model (Max-Ent) combined with language specific rules and gazetteer list [2] are used to identify NE. The ML approaches need a lot of NE annotated data which is not available and very cumbersome to construct manually. Wikipedia's links are transformed into NE annotations [3]. The Conditional Random Fields (CRF) and Support Vector Machine (SVM) are the ML approaches and CRF is superior to SVM [4]. Wikipedia inter-wiki links among English and other languages are used in a language independent way to identify NE [5]. The RB and ML approaches are discussed and showed that the CRF is better than the RB and Max-Ent ML approach [7].

The direct translation, i.e., dictionary based, corpora based, MT, and indirect translation, i.e., Cross-Lingual Latent Semantic Indexing (CL-LSI), Cross-Lingual Latent Dirichlet Allocation (CL-LDA), Cross-Lingual Explicit Semantic Analysis (CL-ESA) are the Cross-Lingual Information Retrieval (CLIR) approaches [8]. A dictionary is used for translation. A transliteration mining algorithm is used to handle the Out Of Vocabulary (OOV) words [9]. The Term Frequency Model (TFM) includes the concept of a set of comparable sentences and cosine similarity [10]. The dual semantic space based translation models CL-LSI, CL-LDA are effective but not efficient [11]. A Statistical Machine Translation (SMT) system is trained on aligned comparable sentences [12]. The transliteration generation or mining techniques are used to handle the OOV words [13]. The CRF model is used to generate the OOV words transliterations [14,15].

3   Proposed Approach

User queries contain three types of terms which are stop words, terms which need translation, and terms which need transliteration. The proposed approach is represented in Fig. 1. Stop words are removed in the preprocessing step and the remaining terms are tested against the NEI module and TFM module.

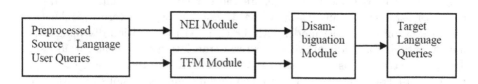

Fig. 1. NEI translation disambiguation based proposed approach

3.1 Named Entity Identification (NEI)

The CRF algorithm is better than other ML algorithms [4,7]. The CRF based Stanford Named Entity Recognizer[1] (SNER) is used to train the NEI system.

Table 1. Web sources of named entities

Named Entity	Sources
List of First Names	http://www.studentsoftheworld.info/penpals/stats.php3?Pays=IND
	http://babynames.extraprepare.com/
	http://www.indiaexpress.com/specials/babynames/
	http://www.babynames.org.uk/indian-boy-baby-names.htm
	http://www.newlyborn.org/most-popular-names/hindu-names.htmAahna
List of Middle Names	http://www.cs.colostate.edu/~malaiya/middlenames
	http://www.indianchild.com/indian_middle_names.htm
	http://www.top-100-baby-names-search.com/girl-middle-names.html
List of Last Names	https://en.wikipedia.org/wiki/Category:Indian_family_names
	http://surnames.behindthename.com/names/usage/indian
	https://en.wiktionary.org/wiki/Appendix:Indian_surnames
	http://blogs.transparent.com/hindi/common-surnames-in-india/
	http://www.indianhindunames.com/indian-surnames-origin-meaning.htm
	http://indiachildnames.com/surname/
List of Location in India	https://en.wikipedia.org/wiki/List_of_cities_and_towns_in_India_by_population
	https://en.wikipedia.org/wiki/List_of_state_and_union_territory_capitals_in_India
List of Suffixes	http://www.irfca.org/docs/place-names.html (Locations)
List of Organization	https://en.wikipedia.org/wiki/Category:Organisations_based_in_India
	https://en.wikipedia.org/wiki/List_of_Indian_government_agencies

---

[1] http://nlp.stanford.edu/software/CRF-NER.shtml.

SNER needs a lot of NE annotated training data which is not available for the Hindi language. So the NE annotated dataset and gazetteer lists need to be prepared to train the SNER.

An available NE tagged dataset[2] contains around 17000 sentences. This dataset is parsed by Shallow parser[3] developed by IIIT Hyderabad to obtain the Part Of Speech (POS) tags. Further NE tags and POS tags are merged, and an annotated dataset is prepared for training the SNER system. Any standard gazetteer list for NEI is not available. Various Indian named entity terms are collected from the Web to prepare a gazetteer list. The named entity terms and their sources are listed in Table 1. A testing word is classified into four categories, i.e., Person Name (NEP), Location (NEL), Organization (NEO) and non-NE terms (NOP). Various stop-word phrases are analyzed, and six phrases are identified as patterns. These patterns are like *Word1 Stop-word Word2*, and if any word in the identified patterns is an NE then another word is also an NE with the same NE tag. The proposed patterns are presented in Table 2.

Table 2. Stop-word phrases

S.no.	Stop-Word	Example Patterns
1	और	हरियाणा और दिल्ली. पांडिचेरी और मुम्बई
2	एवं	महाभारत एवं रामायण. हिंदी एवं उर्दू
3	तथा	विष्णुगुप्त तथा कौटिल्य. गंगा तथा ब्रह्मपुत्र
4	या	राजग या एनडीए. देवी या दुर्गा
5	व	जम्मू कश्मीर व उत्तराखंड. नारायणपुर व बीजापुर
6	अथवा	महाराष्ट्र अथवा उड़ीसा. सिलीगुड़ी अथवा कोलकाता

3.2   Term Frequency Model (TFM)

A brief discussion on TFM module is presented in Fig. 2. A term frequency matrix is constructed from a set of comparable sentences which are selected based on the source language query terms. Cosine Similarity Score (CSS) is used to select the top-n target language translations. CSS is computed between two term's vectors $A = a_1, a_2, ..., a_N$ and $B = b_1, b_2, ..., b_N$ as.

$$CSS = \frac{\sum_{i=1}^{N} A_i B_i}{\sqrt{\sum_{i=1}^{N} A_i^2}\sqrt{\sum_{i=1}^{N} B_i^2}} \tag{1}$$

---

[2] http://ltrc.iiit.ac.in/ner-ssea-08/index.cgi?topic=5.
[3] http://ltrc.iiit.ac.in/analyzer/hindi/run.cgi.

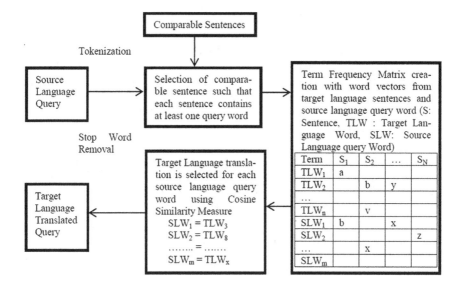

Fig. 2. NEI translation disambiguation based proposed approach

Algorithm 1. NEI translation disambiguation algorithm

Input:	**Word's NEI tag and Top-n translations**
Output:	**Proper translation/transliteration**
Step1:	if(word's NE Tag != NOP): // NOP: non-NE terms
Step2:	R_word = word's Romanized form
Step3:	R_trans = find Longest Common Subsequence (LCS) score between R_word and all Top-n translations and select the translation with maximum LCS score
Step4:	if(LCS score(R_trans)>=.60): Then R_trans is proper transliteration
Step6:	else: select the maximum CSS scorer translations
Step7:	else: select the maximum CSS scorer translations

3.3   Disambiguation

Disambiguation module collects NE tag from NER module and top-n translations from TFM module. A named entity word's transliteration is also present in top-n translations if word's transliteration is available in a comparable corpus, but that word's transliteration has very low translation CSS. So a disambiguation algorithm is proposed in Algorithm 1 to select the proper translation or transliteration. Longest Common Subsequence (LCS) score between two strings S_1 and S_2 is computed by Eq. 2.

$$LCS(S_1, S_2) = \frac{Longest\_common\_string(S_1, S_2)}{Maximum(length(S_1), length(S_2))} \qquad (2)$$

4   Experiment Results and Discussions

The proposed approach is evaluated with FIRE 2010 and 2011 datasets which contain a topic set of 50 Hindi language queries and a set of target English language documents. Topic set includes ⟨title⟩, ⟨desc⟩, and ⟨narr⟩ tag field in each query. We are experimenting with only ⟨title⟩ tag field. A preprocessed source language query is passed through NEI module and TFM module separately. The outcome of NEI module, i.e., an NE tagged query and the outcome of TFM module, i.e., top-5 translations are passed through the disambiguation module. Target language queries are the resultant outcome of the proposed approach. Vector Space Model (VSM) is used to retrieve query relevant target language documents. NEI disambiguation technique with CLIR system is evaluated by using Recall and Mean Average Precision (MAP). The recall is the fraction of relevant documents that are retrieved. MAP for a set of queries is the mean of the average precision score of each query. Precision is the fraction of retrieved documents that are relevant to the query. The experiment results are presented in Table 3.

The inclusion of NEI disambiguation module degrades the performance of CLIR system because at many instances the translation versions are more popular than the transliteration, so the proposed approach achieves low MAP than the TFM only in both the cases of Fire 2010 and 2011. The significant differences between the popularity of the term's translation and transliteration are presented in Table 4. NEI alone is not sufficient to select the proper translation or transliteration because term's popularity decides whether it needs either translation or transliteration.

Table 3. Comparative result analysis

Approach	FIRE 2010		FIRE 2011	
	Recall	MAP	Recall	MAP
TFM Only	0.8315	0.2888	0.6838	0.1688
Proposed Approach	0.7963	0.2782	0.6685	0.1589

Table 4. Effectiveness of NEI technique

Terms	NE Tag	Translite ration	Trans lation	Is NEI effec tive? Y/N
भारत	NEP	Bharat	India	N
प्रतिभा	NEP	Pratibha	Talent	Y
नगर	NEL	Nagar	City	N
भारतीय नौसेना	NEO	Bhartiya Nausena	Indian Navy	N

5   Conclusion and Future Work

NEI technique is analyzed to resolve the improper translation or transliteration issue. Indian languages suffer from a lack of availability of NE annotated data and Gazetteer list. The NE annotated data is prepared with the help of IIIT Hyderabad's NE corpus and shallow parser. Gazetteer lists are prepared from different web sources. Stanford NER is trained on NE annotated data and gazetteer list. The proposed linguistic patterns are used to improve the NEI system. TFM module is used to select the top-n translations against a query word. Disambiguation module selects the proper translation and transliteration based on the outcome of NEI and TFM module. The proposed approach achieves low MAP than the TFM only. NEI alone is not sufficient to select the proper translations or transliterations because term's popularity decides the translation or transliteration more effectively. In future, term's popularity will be used to identify that whether a term needs to be translated or transliterated.

References

1. Nayan, A., Rao, B.R.K., Singh, P., Sanyal, S., Sanyal, R.: Named entity recognition for Indian languages. In: IJCNLP, pp. 97–104 (2008)
2. Saha, S.K., Chatterji, S., Dandapat, S., Sarkar, S., Mitra, P.: A hybrid approach for named entity recognition in Indian languages. In: Proceedings of the IJCNLP-08 Workshop on NER for South and South East Asian languages, pp. 17–24 (2008)
3. Nothman, J., Curran, J.R., Murphy, T.: Transforming Wikipedia into named entity training data. In: Proceedings of the Australian Language Technology Workshop, pp. 124–132 (2008)
4. Maxwell, C.J., Krishnarao, A.A., Gahlot, H., Srinet, A., Kushwaha, D.S.: A comparative study of named entity recognition for Hindi using sequential learning algorithms. In: Advance Computing Conference, 2009, IACC 2009, IEEE International, pp. 1164–1169. IEEE (2009)
5. Bhagavatula, M., GSK, S., Varma, V.: Language-independent named entity identification using Wikipedia. In: Proceedings of the First Workshop on Multilingual Modeling, Association for Computational Linguistics, pp. 11–17 (2012)
6. Mathur, S., Saxena, V.P.: Hybrid approach to English-Hindi name entity transliteration. In: IEEE Students' conference on Electrical, Electronis and Computer Science (2014)
7. Prasad, G., Fousiya, K.K.: Named entity recognition approaches: a study applied to English and Hindi language. In: International Conference on Circuit, Power and Computing Technologies (ICCPCT), 2015, pp. 1–4. IEEE (2015)
8. Sharma, V.K., Mittal, N.: Cross Lingual Information Retrieval (CLIR): Review of tools, challenges and translation approaches. In: Information System Design and Intelligent Application, pp. 699–708 (2016)
9. Sharma, V.K, Mittal, N.: Cross lingual information retrieval: a dictionary based query translation approach? In: Advances in Intelligent Systems and Computing (2016)
10. Sharma, V.K., Mittal, N.: Exploiting parallel sentences and cosine similarity for identifying target language translation. J. Procedia Comput. Sci. **89**, 428–433 (2016)

11. Vulic, I., de Smet, W., Moens, M.-F.: Cross-language information retrieval models based on latent topic models trained with document-aligned comparable corpora. Inf. Retrieval **16**(3), 331–368 (2013)
12. Jagarlamudi, J., Kumaran, A.: Cross-Lingual information retrieval system for Indian languages. In: Peters, C., Jijkoun, V., Mandl, T., Müller, H., Oard, D.W., Peñas, A., Petras, V., Santos, D. (eds.) CLEF 2007. LNCS, vol. 5152, pp. 80–87. Springer, Heidelberg (2008). doi:10.1007/978-3-540-85760-0_10
13. Saravanan, K., Udupa, R., Kumaran, A.: Crosslingual information retrieval system enhanced with transliteration generation and mining. In: Forum for Information Retrieval Evaluation (FIRE-2010) Workshop (2010)
14. Surya, G., Harsha, S., Pingali, P., Verma, V.: Statistical transliteration for cross language information retrieval using HMM alignment model and CRF. In: Proceedings of the 2nd Workshop on Cross Lingual Information Access (2008)
15. Shishtla, P., Surya, G., Sethuramalingam, S., Varma, V.: A language-independent transliteration schema using character aligned models at NEWS 2009. In: Proceedings of the 2009 Named Entities Workshop: Shared Task on Transliteration, Association for Computational Linguistics, pp. 40–43 (2009)

LEXER: LEXicon Based Emotion AnalyzeR

Shikhar Sharma$^{(\boxtimes)}$ ⓘ, Piyush Kumar ⓘ, and Krishan Kumar ⓘ

Department of Computer Science and Engineering, National Institute
of Technology Uttarakhand, Srinagar Garhwal, India
{shikhar01.cse14,kpiyush26.cse14,kkberwal}@nituk.ac.in

Abstract. The huge population of India poses a challenge to government, security and law enforcement. What if we could know beforehand the consequences of any events. Social spaces, such as Twitter, Facebook, and Personal blogs, enable people to show their thoughts regarding public issues and topics. Public emotion regarding future and past events, like public gatherings, governmental policies, shows public beliefs and can be deployed to analyze the measure of support, disorder, or disrupted in such situations. Therefore, emotion analysis of Internet content may be beneficial for various organizations, particularly in government, law enforcement, and security sectors. This paper presents an extension to state-of-art-model for lexicon-based sentiment analysis algorithm for analysis of human emotions.

Keywords: Emotion detection · Natural language processing · Security · Prediction

1 Introduction

Social spaces, the Internet is one of the most important personal view exchange portals in the current era. The social media, such as Reddit, Blogs, and Pinterest etc. and the Internet, supply a very suitable platform for communicating with each other and sharing views with everyone. Accordingly, the part of the Internet in crime prevention and investigation has promptly increased. The Internet is rapidly becoming a way of preventing chaos by providing information for warning systems in concern of public safety. Sentiment study has already been used in various areas [1], non-secure area to forecast and monitor common views. Grabner et al. [2] deployed a domain based lexicon for classifying Twitter reviews. Sentiment examination is also executed on Twitter for forecasting box-office collections of movies [3]. Along with increasing interest in "Affective Computing", the task of "Emotion Detection" using text has also gained more attention during recent years. However, very little efforts are done in the detection of multiple emotion at the same time. Instead, most of the previous works assumed that emotions are mutually exclusive and focused on multi-class classification. But, the human emotions are much more complicated than that: emotions have connections, some occur together simultaneously, while some are opposite of each other, while resonate and create other emotional states [4,5].

© Springer International Publishing AG 2017
B.U. Shankar et al. (Eds.): PReMI 2017, LNCS 10597, pp. 373–379, 2017.
https://doi.org/10.1007/978-3-319-69900-4_47

The focus of the above work is mostly classifying emotion of document sources or processing the tweets around the event into a single type of emotion. However, they do not provide insights into how to characterize person's multiple emotion, which is the main contribution of this work. Perhaps the closest work to us is [5–8]. In contrast, we provide a fully automated and principled solution. The salient features of our work are stated as follows:

- LEXER technique can be employed to analyze the emotions behind the tweets (*anger, disgust, sadness, surprise, fear, joy, neutral*) over the Internet.
- A fuzzy set function is used to complement the emotional value of a negated word. This in comparison to polarity reversal is more realistic and reliable. Therefore, it can help to prevent the public outrages, communal riots in stipulated time.
- From the point of view of tweets, analysis, an efficient multi-emotion analyzer has not been applied to the best of our understanding. The proposed principled solution still has good emotion analyzing capabilities in comparison to previous works.

The manuscript is structured as follows, details of the work are discussed in Sect. 2, results are shown in Sects. 3 and 4 concludes the work.

2   Proposed Method

The approaches in sentiment examination can be grouped into two categories. Using lexicon is one of them. It demands calculation of the sentiment based on the semantic orientation of words or expression that happen in the text. From this perspective, a vocabulary comprising of negative and positive expressions is used, Moreover, a value is allotted to each word that can be either negative or positive called sentimental value [7]. In our model, we tried to extend this approach to analyze the emotions of the users.

Instead of having a dictionary of negative and positive words, we created a dictionary has different emotion values for words. Normally saying, the lexicon-based perspective uses a snippet of text that can be understood as **bag of words** [8]. Ensuring this understanding, emotion values from the vocabulary are allotted to every expression that being used in the text. The different values are combined together using a function known as combining function, such as average or sum, to make the end most prognosis relating to the comprehensive emotion for the text. Apart from the emotion estimate, the thought of the local context of the expression is also important, like intensification, inversion and downtoning.

The availability of labeled training set is very scarce. Thus, the work resolute in implementing a lexicon-based expertise. The dependency on the labeled data is the main drawback of machine learning algorithms. Also, the sufficiency and correctness of labeled data are extremely difficult to ensure. Besides this, the ease of modification and understanding for the human in case lexicon-based procedure gives an advantage over traditional machine learning expertise.

Thus, this can be contemplated as a notable merit of our work. We discovered that there is an ease in the generation of an efficient vocabulary in comparison to the collection and labeling relevant corpus. Moreover, lexicon based approaches are easily transformable into different languages.

2.1 Emotion Lexicon

The emotion lexicon constructed to consist of 3000 words. It is manually generated using movie reviews as the baseline. Each element of the vocabulary is given six values depicting different emotions, i.e. Anger, disgust, sadness, surprise, fear, joy. The values vary in the range of 0 (no dominance) to 100 (most dominating). From the knowledge of human psychology, it knows that sometimes we human exhibit emotions which are a mixture of different emotions like anger and disgust. For example, sentence *Corruption in India is increasing day by day* represents anger as well as disgust. It may be wrong in such cases to decide between anger and disgust. To overcome such issues, we tried to classify the emotion into multiple emotions.

2.2 Intensitifiers and Downtoners

Intensifiers are the words like definitely, really, too, etc. These words can be defined as words that increase the dominance of a particular emotion over the other. They can be classified into two categories [8,9], namely downtoners (rarely, never) and amplifiers (really, too) as decreasing and increasing the intensity of emotions respectively. In our work, all the intensifiers were sorted on the basis of frequency and the 25 most frequently used intensifiers were selected and then, these intensifiers were subdivided into two classes, namely downtoners and intensifiers. By means of experimentation, we concluded that downtoners can decrease the value of the emotion by half.

2.3 Inversion

The most widely used technique for handling inversion in lexicon-based expertise is to reverse the polarity of an item in the vocabulary. It applies to words that are preceded by a negator in a sentence [10,11], for example, happy: 87 and not happy: -87. In our work, we decided to use a different procedure for inversion. Instead of reversing the emotion value, we employed a complementing function which complements the value of recognized words, for e.g. happy: 80 and not happy: 20. At first, a lexicon comprising of 20 negating words is created manually. Following this, we used the Twitter corpus was used to select the most frequent inversion of adjectives and verb expressions. Then, we applied the concept of complementing a fuzzy set. Since each emotion value can be treated as membership value, its complement can solve the problem.

The main merit of using the complementing function instead of the polarity reversion is better accuracy in allotting the emotional values of expressions.

For example, in the sentence: *I don't enjoy the ride.*, the emotion which will be allotted to the sentence using the traditional polarity reversal procedure would be sadness (opposite of joy is sadness) and the sentence will be the dominance of sadness as emotion. In fact, it will be same as *I felt this ride saddening.*, which is contradictory to real world scenarios. But using the complement function as shown in Eq. 1 would give better results.

$$F_n = 100 - F_e \qquad (1)$$

Moreover, no intensifiers and negators are included in emotion lexicon. Also, if they are surrounded only by neutral emotion, they are considered as neutral words as proposed by Jurek et al. [8].

2.4   Combining the Results: Combining Function

After the identification of all the expressions in the text, the local context of these expressions is verified. The combining function is then applied to obtain the endmost value. In our work, there is the requirement of a function that can be applied to the single expression. It returns the absolute value of each emotion from the text normalized to $0 - 100$. This resulted in better efficiency to analyze the emotion with respect to intensity. Accordingly, it also determined how strongly emotion dominates in a sentence. So, we deployed the function from [8]. Firstly, an average is calculated for each emotion within a message. Then, the value of each emotion is calculated as shown in Eq. 2.

$$F_e = min\{\frac{A_e}{2 - log(3.5 \times W_e)}, 100\} \qquad (2)$$

Where, F_e denotes the value of that emotion, A_e stands for the average emotion value for each emotion, W_e stands for the count of that emotion.

2.5   Emotion Classification

After calculation of endmost value between 0 and 100 for each class of emotion, the dominant emotions are identified. If the value of the emotion is more than 30, it returns that emotion or 0. If there are words only pertaining to a specific emotion in the message, then it is selected as final emotion. If the two or more emotion values are at a sufficient distance (the difference between the values is sufficient) then, the emotions having values greater than 30 are selected. Otherwise, the text is treated as neutral [12,13].

3   Experiment and Discussion

The proposed method was tested for various real-time inputs (self-made Facebook comments dataset), movie reviews dataset (manually labeled) as well as the Twitter dataset. As proposed by Jurek et al. [8], the accuracy of the model increased dramatically with normalization of the values. The same trends are obtained in the proposed method too. The following three sub-sections show in details the result of the method.

3.1 Qualitative Analysis

Table 1 depicts the accuracy of the model for the Twitter dataset (self-labeled), movie reviews dataset (the part which is not used in labeling) and the self-made dataset by using the Facebook comments. The model also classified texts having more than one emotion correctly. For e.g., *Stop it!* can be interpreted having disgust, anger in the voice of the speaker. Our model produces the positive results regarding the issue in lesser time as compared to machine learning models.

Table 1. Accuracy over different labeled datasets

Dataset	Accuracy (%)
Twitter dataset	69.1
Movie reviews dataset	65.7
Self made Facebook dataset	67.2

3.2 Quantitative Analysis

Table 2 shows the confusion matrix for the Twitter dataset (all the texts were labeled having one emotion only). It contains 100 anger, 100 disgust, 100 sadness, 100 surprise, 100 fear, 100 joy manually labeled samples.

Table 2. Confusion matrix for different emotions

Assigned emotion	Labelled emotion						
	Anger	Disgust	Sadness	Surprise	Fear	Joy	Neutral
Anger	69	12	09	15	05	18	10
Disgust	11	70	11	08	03	12	05
Sadness	03	04	72	07	02	00	03
Surprise	07	06	01	68	11	01	07
Fear	02	05	02	00	62	02	05
Joy	00	01	05	01	09	65	08
Neutral	08	02	00	01	08	02	62

3.3 Computational Complexity

The proposed model was implemented on the standard desktop computer with 2.7 GHz dual core CPU has 4 GB RAM. The time required by the method to compute the results is shown in Table 3.

Table 3. Time requirement for different datasets

Dataset	Time (Sec)
Twitter dataset	5.12
Movie reviews dataset	6.67
Self made Facebook dataset	4.89

4 Conclusion

Social spaces, the Internet is one of the most important personal view exchange portals in the current era. The social media, such as Reddit, Blogs, and Pinterest etc. and the Internet, supply a very suitable platform for communicating with each other and sharing views with everyone. Accordingly, the part of the Internet in crime prevention and investigation has promptly increased. The Internet is rapidly becoming a way of preventing chaos by providing information for warning systems in concern of public safety. So, we deployed a model to automatically predict the emotional state of the user. This could prevent many negative events which can cause a great loss of life and wealth. Public outrages and riots in a country having such a large population can be disruptive. Hence, a model like ours can become a great aid in time of need.

References

1. Maite, T., et al.: Lexicon-based methods for sentiment analysis. Comput. Linguist. **37**(2), 267–307 (2011)
2. Gräbner, D., Zanker, M., Fliedl, G., Fuchs, M.: Classification of customer reviews based on sentiment analysis. In: Fuchs, M., Ricci, F., Cantoni, L. (eds.) Information and Communication Technologies in Tourism 2012, pp. 460–470. Springer, Vienna (2012)
3. Krauss, J., et al.: Predicting movie success and academy awards through sentiment and social network analysis. In: European Conference on Information Systems (2008)
4. Ovesdotter, A., et al.: Emotions from text: machine learning for text-based emotion prediction. In: Conference on Human Language Technology and Empirical Methods in Natural Language Processing. Association for Computational Linguistics (2005)
5. Duc-Anh, P., et al.: Multiple emotions detection in conversation transcripts. PACLIC **30**, 85 (2016)
6. Garcia, A., et al.: A lexicon based sentiment analysis retrieval system for tourism domain. Expert Syst. Appl. Int. J. **39**, 9166–9180 (2012)
7. Efstratios, K., et al.: Ontology-based sentiment analysis of twitter posts. Expert Syst. Appl. **40**(10), 4065–4074 (2013)
8. Anna, J., et al.: Improved lexicon-based sentiment analysis for social media analytics. Secur. Inf. **4**(1), 9 (2015)
9. Thelwall, M., Buckley, K.: Topic-based sentiment analysis for the social web: the role of mood and issue-related words. J. Am. Soc. Inf. Sci. Technol. **64**(8), 1608–1617 (2013)

10. Casey, W., et al.: Using appraisal groups for sentiment analysis. In: 14th ACM International Conference on Information and Knowledge Management. ACM (2005)
11. Andrius, M., et al.: Combining lexicon and learning based approaches for concept-level sentiment analysis. In: ACM Sentiment Discovery and Opinion Mining (2012)
12. Erik, C., et al.: New avenues in opinion mining and sentiment analysis. IEEE Intell. Syst. **28**(2), 15–21 (2013)
13. Awais, A.: Sentiment analysis of citations using sentence structure-based features. In: ACL 2011 Student Session (2011)

Lexical TF-IDF: An n-gram Feature Space for Cross-Domain Classification of Sentiment Reviews

Atanu Dey$^{(\boxtimes)}$ ⓘ, Mamata Jenamani ⓘ, and Jitesh J. Thakkar ⓘ

E-Business Centre of Excellence Lab (ECO), Department of Industrial and Systems Engineering, Indian Institute of Technology Kharagpur, Kharagpur 721302, India
`atanu.dey@iitkgp.ac.in`, `{mj,jt}@iem.iitkgp.ernet.in`

Abstract. Feature extraction and selection is a vital step in sentiment classification using machine learning approach. Existing methods use only TF-IDF rating to represent either unigram or n-gram feature vectors. Some approaches leverage upon the use of existing sentiment dictionaries and use the score of a *unigram* sentiment word as the feature vector and ignore TF-IDF rating. In this work, we construct n-gram sentiment features by extracting the sentiment words and their intensifiers or negations from a review. Then the score of an n-gram constructed from lexicon of semantic *unigram* and its *intensifier* or *negation* is multiplied to *TF-IDF* rating to determine the feature score. We experiment with two benchmark data sets for sentiment classification using *Support Vector Machine* and *Maximum Entropy* method with cross domain validation by considering training and testing data from two different sets and obtain a substantial improvement in terms of various performance measures compared to existing methods. Cross-domain validation ensures proposed method can be applied for sentiment classification of data sets where example patterns are not available, which typically is the case with commercial data sets.

Keywords: Sentiment analysis · n-gram · Cross-domain · Maximum Entropy (ME) · Support Vector Machine (SVM) · Lexical TFIDF

1 Introduction

Sentiment analysis, the process of identifying the opinion polarity of a piece of text, is used to analyze the user generated contents from various web resources such as product reviews, movie reviews, citizen opinion of public policies etc. It helps the consumers to research on products or services before making a purchase decision and the organizations to gather data on customer satisfaction

---

This work was supported by *Ministry of Human Resource Development*, [Sanction Letter Number: F. No. 5-5/2014-TS.VII, Dt; 04-09-2014], Department of Higher Education, New Delhi, India.

© Springer International Publishing AG 2017
B.U. Shankar et al. (Eds.): PReMI 2017, LNCS 10597, pp. 380–386, 2017.
https://doi.org/10.1007/978-3-319-69900-4_48

and critical feedback to improve upon. There are two broad approaches for sentiment analysis: lexicon based and machine learning based. The lexicon based approaches use natural language processing tools to extract sentiment words from the reviews then find the overall polarity by using sentiment lexicons such as SentiWordNet, SenticNet, VADER (Valence Aware Dictionary for sEntiment Reasoning) [1]. In order to use machine learning based approaches one has to first create lots of example patterns by getting the positive or negative sentiments of real users on reviews of a specific domain; extract the features using natural language tools; find the numeric value of the features using certain mechanism such as TF-IDF rating; train the classifiers such as Nave Bayes (NB) [2], Support Vector Machine (SVM) [3], Maximum Entropy (ME) [4]; and finally use the trained classifiers to determine sentiment polarity of unrated reviews.

Though the machine learning approach shows better performance in many cases [2,5], it suffers from two problems; first, creating training patterns from real users which is time consuming and expensive [5,6]; second, selection of right features and their numeric value [5,7]. To deal with the first problem, many researchers advocate for cross domain validation approach [7], where the training and testing patterns are from two unrelated datasets. To deal with the second problem, many methods are proposed to create feature vectors such as (1) use of TF-IDF rating associated with unigrams, bigrams or in general n-grams, and (2) lexicon-based approach where sentiment score of the feature is used.

In the proposed work, we present a new approach called *Lexical TFIDF* for creating a feature vector. We construct sentiment n-grams by collecting the appropriate words from the review in consultation with a sentiment dictionary and create senti n-grams by using the intensifier and negation specified in [8]. This is a contrast with the earlier approaches where the features can be any word or n-gram not limited to sentiment words. Specifically, the score of the sentiment lexicon, intensifier and negation are adopted from different sources [1,8]. Then this score is multiplied with TF-IDF rating to determine the feature weight. Experiment with two benchmark data sets, IMDb (2004), Epinion product reviews; and two classifiers support vector machines and maximum entropy method shows substantial improvement in terms of accuracy and other performance measures for cross-domain validation when compared with existing methods like Mudinas et al. [7] and Tripathy et al. [5].

Rest of the paper is organized as follows. Next section presents the literature review. In Sect. 3, proposed approach is explained. Section 4 represents the experimental results. Section 5 concludes the paper and shows the future scope.

2   Literature Survey

As discussed above selection of right features and their scores is the key to improve the performance of machine learning based approach. TF-IDF and count vectorizer are generally used as features for the text classification [5]. A Few researchers use lexicon based approaches for feature extraction and decide the scores in combination with count vectorizer [7]. Cross-domain validation ensures applicability of sentiment analysis approach to the real world data sets where training patterns are not available or expensive to obtain. In this regard, many attempts have been made in the recent past. In the cross-domain learning problem, the training data set and the target data set are from different sources. For example, Mudinas et al. [7] used training data from Browser(Customer) dataset and testing data from Miscellaneous(Editor) dataset of CNETs software download website.

3   Proposed Approach

Before applying the proposed approach the reviews undergo few NLP steps where (1) stop words such as punctuations, article, etc.; (2) symbols such as @, $, %, etc.; (3) hyperlink and numeric numbers are removed. For example applying these steps, we get only relevant words as shown in Table 1 for three reviews.

Table 1. Reviews for preprocessing

Reviews	Before preprocessing	After preprocessing
Review 1	The movie is awesome, feeling very happy	['movie', 'awesome', 'feeling', 'very', 'happy']
Review 2	The movie is fine, but not very good	['movie', 'fine', 'but', 'not', 'very', 'good']
Review 3	The movie is not good	['movie', 'not', 'good']

Figure 1 is the pictorial representation of the proposed approach with six steps. Detailed explanation of these steps are as follows:

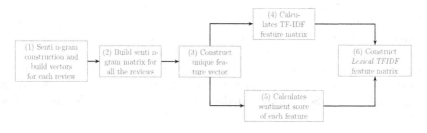

Fig. 1. Block diagram of Lexical TF-IDF

Step 1. Senti n-gram construction and build vectors for each review:
When an intensifier (e.g., 'very') or negation (e.g., 'not') appears before a semantic unigram (e.g., 'happy') then we merge them and construct a bigram

(e.g., 'very happy' and 'not happy'). Similarly, we construct a trigram if two intensifiers or negations consecutively appears before a semantic unigram (e.g., 'not very good'). The n-gram word vector for the example reviews in Table 1 are as follows:

Review 1: ["awesome", "feeling", "very happy"], Review 2: ["fine", "not very good"], Review 3: ["not good"]

Step 2. Build senti n-gram matrix for all the reviews: The n-gram word vectors obtained in step 1 are used to construct a matrix (M) taking all the reviews together as shown in below.

$$M = \begin{bmatrix} awesome & feeling & very\,happy \\ fine & not\,very\,good & - \\ not\,good & - & - \end{bmatrix}$$

Step 3. Construct unique feature vector: The unique senti n-grams extracted from the above matrix are treated as the feature. Continuing with our example the feature vector for the review data set in Table 1 is as follows:

Feature-Vector = ['awesome', 'feeling', 'fine', 'not good', 'not very good', 'very happy']

Step 4. Calculates TF-IDF feature matrix: TF-IDF feature matrix is generated using the above features as columns and reviews as the rows. TF-IDF taring matrix for our problem is:

$$TF - IDF = \begin{bmatrix} 0.577 & 0.577 & 0 & 0 & 0 & 0.577 \\ 0 & 0 & 0.707 & 0 & 0.707 & 0 \\ 0 & 0 & 0 & 1 & 0 & 0 \end{bmatrix}$$

Step 5. Calculates sentiment score of each feature: The sentiment score of each unigram feature is fetched from VADER lexicon [1] and the scores of other n-grams (Bigrams and Trigrams) are calculated using SO-CAL (Semantic Orientation CALulator) approach [9].

For example, unigram like "awesome", "feeling", "fine" having sentiment scores are 3.1, 0.5, 0.8 respectively. For bigrams and trigrams, the well-established lexicon is not available. The SO-CAL approach is used to avoid this situation [9] with a list of intensifiers (amplifier and downtoner) [8], having individual percentage scores. For negation, a constant value 4 is used to shift the semantic word to its opposite polarity.

An example of score calculation for a bigram "very happy". Suppose, sentiment score of "happy" is "+2.7", and percentage score of "very" (intensifier) is +25%. Then, the score of "very happy" would be: $+2.7 \times (100\% + 25\%) = +3.375$. For the example problem the score vector (S) is as follows:

$$S = \begin{bmatrix} Features: & 'awesome' & 'feeling' & 'fine' & 'not good' & 'not very good' & 'very happy' \\ Score: & 3.1 & 0.5 & 0.8 & -2.1 & -1.625 & +3.375 \end{bmatrix}$$

Step 6. Construct _Lexical TFIDF_ feature matrix: Each feature column of TF-IDF feature matrix is multiplied with the sentiment score of that feature to obtain the _Lexical TFIDF_. The final _Lexical TFIDF_ matrix for the example problem is:

$$Lexical\,TFIDF = \begin{bmatrix} 1.789 & 0.289 & 0 & 0 & 0 & 1.947 \\ 0 & 0 & 0.566 & 0 & -1.149 & 0 \\ 0 & 0 & 0 & -2.1 & 0 & 0 \end{bmatrix}$$

This matrix can be used as input to supervised machine learning algorithms for training. Here, we use two algorithms: ME and SVM. In ME, the feature matrix of training data is generally used to set constraints. The characteristics of training data are then expressed by these constraints which are used for testing [4]. SVM method takes a decision by drawing the hyper-planes boundary between two classes in an optimal way [3]. Many papers show SVM and ME outperform other algorithms [2,5]. Proposed feature selection approach along with above two classifiers is compared to three existing methods in terms of four performance metrics: accuracy, precision, recall, F1_Score.

Table 2. Performance evaluation for cross-domain (IMDb (2004) and Epinion) classification among different approaches

Training dataset	Testing dataset	Performance measure	Proposed approach		pSenti [7]	Tripathy et al. [5]		TF-IDF	
			ME	SVM		ME	SVM	ME	SVM
IMDb (2004)	Epinion cars	Accuracy	*0.84*	0.80	0.7	0.64	0.54	0.52	0.44
		Precision	*0.81*	0.78	0.81	0.60	0.54	0.51	0.46
		Recall	*0.88*	0.84	0.52	80.0	0.52	0.60	0.64
		F1_Score	*0.85*	0.81	0.63	0.69	0.53	0.56	0.53
IMDb (2004)	Epinion computers	Accuracy	0.84	*0.86*	0.76	0.78	0.56	0.64	0.48
		Precision	*0.87*	0.82	0.84	0.72	0.80	0.64	0.48
		Recall	0.80	*0.92*	0.64	0.92	0.16	0.64	0.44
		F1_Score	0.83	*0.87*	0.73	0.81	0.27	0.64	0.46
Epinion books and cars	Epinion computers	Accuracy	*0.82*	0.78	0.58	0.70	0.66	0.80	0.70
		Precision	*0.94*	0.94	0.75	0.66	0.75	0.80	0.63
		Recall	0.68	0.60	0.24	0.84	0.48	0.80	*0.98*
		F1_Score	0.79	0.73	0.36	0.74	0.59	*0.80*	0.76
Epinion computers	IMDb (2004)	Accuracy	*0.74*	0.60	0.54	0.54	0.52	0.42	0.44
		Precision	0.83	*0.86*	0.75	0.52	0.57	0.43	0.45
		Recall	0.60	0.24	0.12	*0.98*	0.16	0.48	0.52
		F1_Score	*0.70*	0.38	0.21	0.69	0.25	0.45	0.48

4   Experimental Result

We experiment with two real world data sets and two classifiers as discussed above. The data sets are IMDb (2004) and Epinion. *IMDb (2004)* is polarity dataset consisting of 1000 positive and 1000 negative movie reviews [10]. Where as, *Epinion* is a collection of 400 reviews of 8 different products: cars, books, cookware, computers, movies, hotels, phones and music. Each category contains 25 positive and 25 negative reviews [11]. For experiment purpose we consider the reviews corresponding to books, cars and computers. We use Python 3.5 with NLTK (for pre-processing) and Sklearn (for feature discovery and classification).

Table 2 shows the comparison of cross-domain classification where our method outperforms other methods 81.25% times considering all the performance measures. However, in all of the experiments, the proposed approach achieves highest accuracy and precision using ME or SVM.

5 Conclusion

In this work, we construct n-gram sentiment features by first extracting the sentiment words and their intensifiers from reviews. The scores corresponding to these features are obtained from the existing sentiment lexicons. Proposed *Lexical TFIDF* matrix is constructed by multiplying TF-IDF rating with feature score. We experiment with two benchmark data sets and two well known classifiers with cross domain validation shows our approach outperforms in 81.25% cases considering all the performance measures, hence, can be used for real data sets where example patterns are not available. In future, we plans to improve upon the proposed method, mathematically analyze the robustness of the method and apply to real case studies.

References

1. Hutto, C.J., Gilbert, E.: Vader: a parsimonious rule-based model for sentiment analysis of social media text (2014)
2. Pang, B., Lee, L., Vaithyanathan, S.: Thumbs up?: sentiment classification using machine learning techniques. In: Proceedings of the ACL 2002 Conference on Empirical Methods in Natural Language Processing, vol. 10, pp. 79–86 (2002)
3. Hsu, C.-W., Chang, C.-C., Lin, C.-J., et al.: A practical guide to support vector classification (2003)
4. Nigam, K., Lafferty, J., McCallum, A.: Using maximum entropy for text classification. In: IJCAI 1999 Workshop on Machine Learning for Information Filtering, vol. 1, pp. 61–67 (1999)
5. Tripathy, A., Agrawal, A., Rath, S.K.: Classification of sentiment reviews using n-gram machine learning approach. Expert Syst. Appl. **57**, 117–126 (2016)
6. Matsumoto, S., Takamura, H., Okumura, M.: Sentiment classification using word sub-sequences and dependency sub-trees. In: Ho, T.B., Cheung, D., Liu, H. (eds.) PAKDD 2005. LNCS (LNAI), vol. 3518, pp. 301–311. Springer, Heidelberg (2005). doi:10.1007/11430919_37
7. Mudinas, A., Zhang, D., Levene, M.: Combining lexicon and learning based approaches for concept-level sentiment analysis. In: Proceedings of the First International Workshop on Issues of Sentiment Discovery and Opinion Mining, p. 5. ACM (2012)
8. Brooke, J.: A semantic approach to automated text sentiment analysis. Ph.d. thesis, Simon Fraser University (2009)
9. Taboada, M., Brooke, J., Tofiloski, M., Voll, K., Stede, M.: Lexicon-based methods for sentiment analysis. Comput. Linguist. **37**(2), 267–307 (2011)

10. Pang, B., Lee, L.: A sentimental education: sentiment analysis using subjectivity summarization based on minimum cuts. In: Proceedings of the 42nd Annual Meeting on Association for Computational Linguistics, p. 271 (2004)
11. Taboada, M., Grieve, J.: Analyzing appraisal automatically. In: Proceedings of AAAI Spring Symposium on Exploring Attitude and Affect in Text (AAAI Technical Report SS-04-07), Stanford University, CA, pp. 158–161. AAAI Press (2004)

A Method for Semantic Relatedness Based Query Focused Text Summarization

Nazreena Rahman[1]([✉])(iD) and Bhogeswar Borah[2](iD)

[1] Department of Computer Science and Engineering, Assam Kaziranga University,
Jorhat 785006, Assam, India
nazreena@kazirangauniversity.in
[2] Department of Computer Science and Engineering, Tezpur University,
Sonitpur 784028, Assam, India
bgb@tezu.ernet.in

Abstract. In this paper, a semantic relatedness based query focused text summarization technique is introduced to find relevant information from single text document. This semantic relatedness measure extracts the related sentences according to the query. The query focused text summarization approach can work on short query when the query does not contain enough information. Better summaries are produced by this method with increased number of query related sentences included. Experiments and evaluation are done on DUC 2005 and 2006 datasets and results show significant performance.

Keywords: Semantic relatedness · Query focused text summarization · Relevant information · Short query

1 Introduction

Text summarization finds information rich sentences for readers. The research area of text summarization is increasingly becoming popular due to the availability of huge amount of information. Text summarization presents the significant content to minimizing time and cost. It is considerably different from human summarization. Human summary can include significantly rich content and themes which is very difficult to include in case of automatic text summary. To find out the linguistic meaning of words and relations with other words, semantic measure is applied. Text summarization can be generic or user focused; generic summary summarizes the important content and query focused summary gives the summary specifically for user's interest. Extractive and abstractive methods are used to make summary. Abstractive method needs reformulation of sentences while extractive method extracts the sentences present in input text documents [1]. Here, we propose one semantic relatedness based text summarization method to extract semantically related sentences with the query.

Luhn in 1958 [2] first introduced text summarization by finding significant words from a text. Significant words are found by calculating the occurrence

© Springer International Publishing AG 2017
B.U. Shankar et al. (Eds.): PReMI 2017, LNCS 10597, pp. 387–393, 2017.
https://doi.org/10.1007/978-3-319-69900-4_49

of a word in a text file. Based on the presence of significant words, sentences are ranked and extracted for summarization. In some recent approaches, Abadi et al. [3] (2015) used linguistic knowledge and expansion of content words. Content words includes noun, verb, adjective and adverb. The method finds semantic similarity between the content words along with the word-order similarity. Finally, they used combination model to select relevant sentences to the input query and also the sentences which are semantically very similar to the other high scoring sentences. We introduce semantic relatedness based query focused text summarization (SRQ) method to get well-defined summary according to the user's need. This SRQ method can work when the query words are not present in the input text. Present method can also perform when the query is short or does not contain enough information.

2   Proposed Semantic Relatedness Based Query Focused Text Summarization (SRQ Method)

Semantic relatedness measure: On the basis of semantic relatedness measure, important sentences are selected for summary purpose. In linguistics, semantics is the study of meaning and semantic relatedness gives the measure of how two words are related to each other. It is different from semantic similarity measure. Semantic similarity gives the measure of alikeness of two words or concepts and semantic relatedness gives more general concept than semantic similarity. For example, hand and finger are not semantically similar but they are semantically related. To find semantic relatedness between content words, WordNet is used. WordNet is a database used to find semantic relations (Miller 1998) [4] for English words. WordNet contains semantic network that defines different relations for content words. The following Table 1 gives different semantic relations for each content word present in WordNet database.

Hirst and St-Onge (HSO) [5] proposed one path based semantic relatedness measure using WordNet. Two words can be related in many ways like 'is-a', 'part-of', 'member-of' relations. For example, in Wordnet, hand and fingers are semantically related with 'part-of' relation. Semantic relatedness between two words includes all types of relations that are present in WordNet and finds the shortest path from the various semantic networks. They find the semantic relation between two content words by measuring the shortest path between them along with number of changes of direction in the shortest path. The following Fig. 1 shows the 'is-a' relation where shortest path and number of changes of direction between two words are (Hemorrhagic_fever and Respiratory_tract_infection) as found in WordNet:

Semantic relatedness between two words: Initially, pre-process the content words by doing stemming. The required method for finding semantic relatedness between two words is given in Eq. 1.

$$Score\,(w1, w2) = 2 * c - path\,length\,between\,w1\,and\,w2 - k\,*\,number\,of$$
$$direction\,changes\,between\,w1\,and\,w2 \tag{1}$$

Table 1. Different semantic relations in WordNet

Different relations for Noun:

Relation-type	Meaning	Example
Hypernym	Gives superordinate term	flower → angiosperm
Hyponym	Gives subordinate term	flower → african_daisy
Member Meronym	From group to their member	university → graduate_ school
Part Meronym	From whole to part	house → loft
Has-Instance	From concept to instance	wood → lignin
Member Holonym	From member to group	people → world
Part Holonym	From part to whole	face → head
Stuff-Of	From instance to concept	wood → beam
Antonym	Gives the opposite word	winner → looser

Different relations for Verb:

Relation-type	Meaning	Example
Hypernym	From a verb to superordinate verb	run → travel_rapidly
Troponym	Gives manner relation	sleep → nap
Entails	A verb follows logically another verb	step → walk
Antonym	Gives the opposite word	start → stop

Different relations for Adjective:

Relation-type	Meaning	Example
Antonym	Gives the opposite word for adjective	able → unable

Different relations for Adverb:

Relation-type	Meaning	Example
Antonym	Gives the opposite word for adverb	kindly → unkindly

Here, $c = 8$ and $k = 1$ are considered as constants. If two words are same then the maximum semantic relatedness value of HSO will be 16 and minimum value is 0 [6]. We tested semantic relatedness score with different threshold values. Based on performance, the method uses average or higher semantic relatedness score by taking the threshold value as 8.

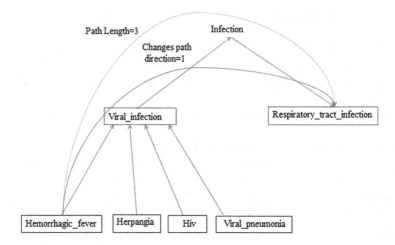

Fig. 1. Fragment WordNet concept hierarchy showing the path and direction changes of paths between *Hemorrhagic_fever* and *Respiratory_tract_infection*

Semantic relatedness between two sentences: To find out the semantic related two sentences, semantic relatedness is calculated for each of the content word of the first sentence S_1 with all the content words present in the second sentence S_2 and the maximum score is taken. After finding score for every word in the sentence S_1 with the words in S_2, we take maximum score as the score for S_1. The method to find semantic relatedness for the sentence S_1 with respect to S_2 is given in Eq. 2:

$$Score\,(S_1, S_2) = \max_{w1 \in S_1, w2 \in S_2} (score\,(w1, w2)) \qquad (2)$$

Important sentence selection: Now, in query focused text summarization, we have a query with input text documents. Before applying semantic relatedness in SRQ method, we give priority to the sentences on the basis of following nine criteria to be considered as important sentences for the text summarization purpose. Semantic relatedness is calculated only for the important sentences.

Title Word Matching: If the words present in a sentence also occur in the title or heading of a text document, then that sentence can be considered as an important one.

Proper Noun: Proper noun or entity name gives more importance to a sentence. Hence, we take out the proper noun containing sentences.

Numerical Data: Presence of numerical data in a sentence always contains rich information.

Thematic Word: Thematic word means word that occur in a text file more frequently. Presence of thematic word makes the sentence important. We find top ten most frequent words from the text file and take out those sentences where any thematic word is present.

Noun Phrase: Presence of noun phrases in a sentence makes the sentence important. The method uses chunkparser to find noun phrases [7].

Font-based Word: Sentences containing words appearing as uppercase, bold, italics or underlined fonts are normally considered as more meaningful.

Cue Phrase: Sentences containing any cue phrase such as in conclusion, this letter, this report, summary, argue, purpose, development are most likely to be in summary.

Sentence Length: It is considered as longer sentence contains more information.

Sentence Position: Important sentences are usually present at the first and the last of the paragraph. We consider the first and the last sentences from paragraphs.

Semantic relatedness is calculated between the input text title (S_t) and an important sentence (S_i) present in input text document by using Eqs. 1 and 2. Again semantic relatedness is measured between query (S_q) and an important sentence (S_i) using the same Eqs. 1 and 2. We will consider those sentences where score is equal or above the defined threshold value.

Extracting Summary: To create the summary, common sentences are obtained from calculating semantic relatedness between text title and important sentences $(score\,(S_t, S_i))$ and query and important sentences $(score\,(S_q, S_i))$. To find out the set of sentences related to the title, the method uses Eq. 3.

$$T = \{s \mid s \in S_i,\ score\,(S_t, S_i) \geq 8\} \tag{3}$$

Similarly, to find out the set of sentences related to the query, the method uses Eq. 4.

$$Q = \{s \mid s \in S_i,\ score\,(S_q, S_i) \geq 8\} \tag{4}$$

Finally, summary can be found using the following method:

$$Summary_{sentences} = T \cap Q \tag{5}$$

3   Experiments

We use DUC 2005 and DUC 2006 datasets (http://duc.nist.gov), where each topic contains a query and a set of input text documents. Each text document contains newspaper or newswire information in English. DUC 2005 and 2006 datasets are particularly used for query-based text summarization purpose. Queries are based on real world complex questions, where answers not only contain date, name or quantity. Here, each dataset contains 50 documents and length of each summary has been restricted to 250 words only.

To evaluate the performance of SRQ method with other existing methods, ROUGE toolkit [8] is used. ROUGE compares similarity between candidate summary and reference summary. Candidate summary means summary produced from different methods and reference summary comes from DUC datasets.

This ROUGE consists of set of metrics, such as ROUGE-N (n-gram co-occurrence statistics), ROUGE-L (longest common subsequence), ROUGE-W (weighted longest common subsequence), ROUGE-S (skip-bigram co-occurrence statistics) and ROUGE-SU4 (skip-bigram based on maximum skip distance of 4, plus unigram). We compare our results with top-performing DUC 2005 and 2006 systems where systems have done their experiments particularly for query-based text summarization. Here, recall value of ROUGE-1 (unigram-based), ROUGE-2 (bigram-based) and ROUGE-SU4 are used for our experiment purpose. The following Figs. 2 and 3 shows the comparison of different ROUGE values of existing systems with SRQ method and finds that SRQ performs well in comparison with these existing systems.

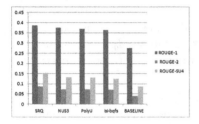

Fig. 2. Experimental results on DUC 2005 datasets

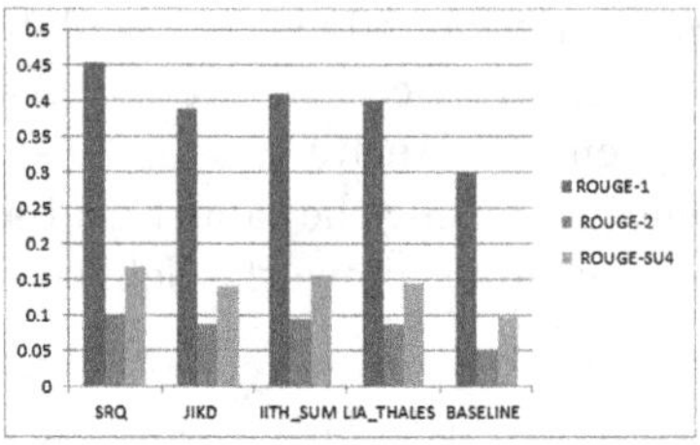

Fig. 3. Experimental results on DUC 2006 datasets

4   Conclusion and Future Work

The paper has presented a query focused text summarization method based on semantic relatedness. This SRQ method performs well for short query. The method is tested with different participating methods in DUC 2005 and DUC 2006 and gives better results. In future we can incorporate effective redundancy removal technique to get more query relevance and information rich summary.

References

1. Damova, M., Koychev, I.: Query-based summarization: a survey (2010)
2. Luhn, H.P.: The automatic creation of literature abstracts. IBM J. Res. Dev. **2**(2), 159–165 (1958)
3. Abdi, A., Idris, N., Alguliyev, R.M., Aliguliyev, R.M.: Query-based multi-documents summarization using linguistic knowledge and content word expansion. Soft Comput. **21**(7), 1–17 (2015)
4. Miller, G.A., Beckwith, R., Fellbaum, C., Gross, D., Miller, K.J.: Introduction to wordnet: an on-line lexical database. Int. J. Lexicography **3**(4), 235–244 (1990)
5. Hirst, G., St-Onge, D., et al.: Lexical chains as representations of context for the detection and correction of malapropisms. In: WordNet: An Electronic Lexical Database, vol. 305, pp. 305–332 (1998)

6. Patwardhan, S., Banerjee, S., Pedersen, T.: Using measures of semantic relatedness for word sense disambiguation. In: Gelbukh, A. (ed.) CICLing 2003. LNCS, vol. 2588, pp. 241–257. Springer, Heidelberg (2003). doi:10.1007/3-540-36456-0_24
7. Bird, S., Klein, E., Loper, E.: Natural Language Processing with Python: Analyzing Text with the Natural Language Toolkit. O'Reilly Media Inc., Sebastopol (2009)
8. Lin, C.-Y.: Rouge: a package for automatic evaluation of summaries. In: Text Summarization Branches Out: Proceedings of the ACL-2004 Workshop, vol. 8, Barcelona, Spain (2004)

Bioinformatics and Computational Biology

Efficient and Effective Multiple Protein Sequence Alignment Model Using Dynamic Progressive Approach with Novel Look Back Ahead Scoring System

Sanjay Bankapur$^{(\boxtimes)}$ ⓘ and Nagamma Patil$^{(\boxtimes)}$

National Instititue of Technology Karnataka, Surathkal 575025, India
sanjaybankapur.mit@gmail.com, nagammapatil@nitk.ac.in

Abstract. Multiple protein sequence alignment is the elementary hurdle towards addressing further challenges like prediction of protein structure and its functions, protein sub-cellular localization, drug discovery etc. For the last 3 decades numerous models have been proposed to address this challenge however the models are either computationally complex or not effective with respect to aligned results. In this paper, a computationally efficient and effective model is proposed to solve multiple protein sequence alignment. Our proposed model follows dynamic progressive global alignment approach in which a sequence pair is merged dynamically based on novel scoring system, named Look Back Ahead (LBA). Proposed model results were validated with aligned reference results on benchmark datasets (PREFAB4refm and SABrem), using four metrics: Sum-of-Pairs (SP), Total Gap Penalty (TGP), Column Score (CS) and Total Mutation Count Pair-wise (TMCP). Experimental results demonstrate that the proposed method outperforms benchmark reference results in any three evaluation metrics by 77.46% and 68.65% for PREFAB4refm and SABrem datasets respectively.

Keywords: Multiple protein sequence alignment · Progressive alignment · Global alignment · Look back ahead scoring system

1 Introduction

Multiple Protein Sequence Alignment is a tool which aligns more than two peptide sequences (Proteins) based on minimum distance or maximum similarity. The correctly aligned sequences help in predicting protein structure and its functions, predicting subcellular localization and drug discovery [18].

General Problem Statement: Given a set of N unaligned protein sequences S: $\{s_1, s_2, ..., s_N\}$ of variable length $L_1, L_2, ..., L_N$ respectively, which are defined over 20 amino acid's alphabet set $\Sigma = \{A, C, D, E, F, G, H, I, K, L, M, N, P, Q, R, S, T, V, W, Y\}$. Multiple protein sequence alignment for given set of sequences S is defined as S': $\{s'_1, s'_2, ..., s'_N\}$, where the length of all N sequences are same

© Springer International Publishing AG 2017
B.U. Shankar et al. (Eds.): PReMI 2017, LNCS 10597, pp. 397–404, 2017.
https://doi.org/10.1007/978-3-319-69900-4_50

and these aligned sequences should possess biological relevance. S' is defined on the same alphabet set with an additional symbol '-' termed as gap, i.e. S' defined over Σ U {-}.

A good example of multiple protein sequence alignment is shown in Table 1, where five input unaligned sequences of varying length is aligned in a manner, in which all aligned sequences length are equal. A gap(-) is introduced at respective position, not only to make all sequences length equal but also to make aligned sequences biologically meaningful. A gap is coined as indel (insertion-deletion). Permanent alterations of one or more Amino Acid Molecules (AAM) such as indels or substitutions are called mutation.

Table 1. Multiple protein sequence alignment example

Unaligned input sequences	Aligned output sequences
s_1: NKYLS (5)	s_1': NKYLS (5)
s_2: NYLS (4)	s_2': N-YLS (5)
s_3: NFLS (4)	s_3': N-FLS (5)
s_4: NKLS (4)	s_4': NK-LS (5)
s_5: NFS (3)	s_5': N- -FS (5)

In this post-genomic era, optimized next-generation high-end machines for genome sequencing such as Illumina [12] produces large gene sequences in a short time. In a linear time, these generated gene sequences are converted to protein sequences with negligible error. Due to this, the current scenario demands for an effective and efficient alignment model to handle large unaligned protein data.

The reminder of this paper is structured as follows: In Sect. 2, we discuss about related works. In Sect. 3, we introduce the proposed model and also the evaluation criteria for comparison. The Sect. 4 explains performance analysis which includes runtime environment setup, datasets used, results and analysis. Finally, Sect. 5 concludes the paper with the prospects of future work.

2   Related Works

Many techniques are applied to solve the sequence alignment, however, there is dearth of models to compute biologically accurate alignment [10]. Existing models for sequence alignment are mainly categorized into three approaches namely: classical, progressive and iterative.

Global alignment and local alignment methods are considered as classical alignment approaches. These alignment methods follows dynamic programming technique which computes all possible cases to obtain an optimal alignment. In global alignment (Needleman-Wunsch), sequences are aligned over their whole length [9]. In contrast, local alignment (Smith-Waterman) identifies similar regions within a sub sequence [15]. These approaches are best suited for few number of biological sequences are to be aligned. However, as the number of unaligned sequences increases, alignment process becomes exponentially expensive in computation. Hence, sequence alignment is a NP-Complete problem [19].

This limitation of classical approach leads to progressive alignment approach. Progressive alignment approach makes use of dynamic programming technique and consists mainly of three steps: First, calculate distance matrix or similarity matrix for all pair of given N unaligned sequences of variable length. Second, construct a guide tree based on the distance or similarity matrix and third, progressively combine pair-wise alignment using guide tree to obtain the final alignment of multiple sequences. Accordingly, the time complexity of progressive approach is $O((N^2 * L^2) + O(N * log(N)) + O(N^3 + N * L^2)$ which is approximately equal to $O(N^3 + N * L^2)$. Many researchers have contributed to progressive approach and among them Clustal W [16], Clustal O [14], Kalign [8] and MUSCLE [4] are more popular and widely used. In progressive approach, the authors [5] proved that "once a gap, always a gap". This is the major limitation of the progressive approach which leads to a local optima.

To overcome the local optima trap, iterative approaches were developed over the last decade. Iterative methods follow stochastic techniques to align multiple sequences by running limited number of iterations. Optimum alignment for a given set of sequences might converge using iterative approach by running maximum iterations with trade-off of time. Recently published methods are MSAGMOSA [7] which uses genetic algorithm, IMSA [1] which uses immunology approach, MOMSA [20] which uses evolutionary algorithm, H4MSA [13] which uses memetics approach. For alignment, although these methods are effective in aligned results they are extremely inefficient in computation time [20].

To address multiple protein sequence alignment problem for large protein sequences, even though both classical and iterative approach are effective, they are inefficient. In this paper, we propose an efficient and effective multiple protein sequence alignment model using dynamic progressive approach with LBA scoring system.

3   Proposed Model

3.1   Proposed Algorithm

Considering the known limitation of progressive alignment approach, we propose a modified and dynamic variant of progressive alignment with LBA scoring system to overcome local optima.

Step 1 executes N-1 times and each time it performs NC_2 combinations to select the best pair from available set of pairs. Similarity Score for a given pair of sequences is calculated using Look Back Ahead (LBA) scoring system. Step 2 executes N-1 times. In each iteration, a pair of aligned sequences are merged into a single consensus sequence by creation of a $20*L$ matrix which stores all the information for a pair sequence without any loss. Here, 20 represents all amino acid molecules and L indicates the length of the merged sequence. As a sequence is reduced by merging, value of N is also reduced in Step 3. Time complexity

---

Algorithm 1. Proposed Algorithm

Input: N unaligned protein sequences of variable length, where $N > 2$
Output: Aligned N protein sequences of fixed length enclosing biological relavance.
1:    For a given N input sequences, perform global pair-wise alignment for all possible combinations (NC_2) and choose an aligned pair which has maximum similarity score.
2:    Merge chosen aligned pair to make a single consensus sequence.
3:    Reduce N by one i.e. $N=(N-1)$ and loop back to step 1 until N becomes one.

---

of proposed model is: $O((N-1) * NC_2 * L^2 + (N-1) + (N-1))$ which is approximately equals to $O(N^3 * L^2)$.

We adopted global alignment approach and modified similarity scoring weightage factor for residue match/mismatch. The proposed LBA scoring system, which follows heuristic approach, scores a given pair of residue based on three things: (i) current residue match/mismatch score - looked up from mutation matrix such as PAM [2] or BLOSUM [6], (ii) similarity score till previous residue, and (iii) status score of previous residue. Given a pair of unaligned sequences say s_1 and s_2 with length L_1 and L_2 respectively, global alignment approach generates a 2-dimentional table of size $L_1 * L_2$, to explore all possible cases to obtain best possible alignment. From left to right and top to bottom fashion, each cell in the table is scored using LBA scoring system. Right bottom most cell provides the optimum similarity score for a given unaligned pair.

Let X be a table, a score of ith residue from sequence s_1 ad j^{th} residue from sequence s_2 is given in Eq. 1.

$$Score(X_{i,j}) = \max\{A, B, C\} \tag{1}$$

where A, B & C are defined in Eqs. 2, 3 and 4 respectively.

$$A = (Score(X_{i,j-1}) - gappenalty) - D \tag{2}$$

$$B = (Score(X_{i-1,j-1}) + m(AAM_i, AAM_j)) - E \tag{3}$$

$$C = (Score(X_{i-1,j}) - gappenalty) - F \tag{4}$$

where, $Score(X_{i,j-1})$, $Score(X_{i-1,j})$ and $Score(X_{i-1,j-1})$ are the scores of previous cells i.e. left, top and top-left-diagonal (diagonal) respectively. $gappenalty$ is a predefined value, $m(AAM_i, AAM_j)$ is a value obtained from mutation matrix and in the experiment, PAM250 has been considered. AAM_i is the ith residue from s_1 and AAM_j is the jth residue from s_2. Here D, E and F are the scores which are calculated on previous residue status. Each previous cell can have any one status among $diagonalnongap$, $leftgap$ and $topgap$. Where, $leftgap$ indicates a gap in sequence s_1, $topgap$ indicates a gap in sequence s_2 and $diagonalnongap$ indicates no gap in any of the sequences. D, E and F are defined as follows:

$$D = \begin{cases} 0 & \text{if } Status(X_{i,j-1}) = leftgap \\ gapopenpenalty & \text{otherwise} \end{cases} \tag{5}$$

$$E = \begin{cases} 0 & \text{if } Status(X_{i-1,j-1}) = diagonalnongap \\ gapclosepenalty & \text{otherwise} \end{cases} \tag{6}$$

$$E = \begin{cases} 0 & \text{if } Status(X_{i-1,j}) = topgap \\ gapopenpenalty & \text{otherwise} \end{cases} \tag{7}$$

where, *gapopenpenalty* and *gapclosepenalty* both are predefined values. In the experiment, *gappenalty*, *gapopenpenalty* & *gapclosepenalty* are the predefined configured values which are in the ratio of *1:4:1*. In order to select *gapopenpenalty* value, we have tested the following values: *2, 4, 6, 8, 10* & *12*. Finally, the best configuration value was *gapopenpenalty* = *6*. In the model, predefined values are defined as:

gappenalty is a penalty when gap occurs in current position from either of sequences.

gapopenpenalty is a penalty when gap occurs in current position and no gap in previous position from either of the sequences.

gapclosepenalty is a penalty when no gap in current position and gap in previous position from either of the sequences.

Once the maximum score is obtained for $X_{i,j}$, $Status(X_{i,j})$ will be set to *leftgap* or *diagonalnongap* or *topgap* only if maximum score is equal to A or B or C respectively.

3.2 Evaluation Criteria

Over the years, multiple metrics are proposed and these are used either in scoring system or in fitnness functions to improve the quality (Q) [17] of the alignment. Here we considered most commonly used metrics such as Sum-of-Pair (SP) [1,11, 13,20], Total Gap Penalty (TGP) [7,13,20] and Column Score (CP) [4]. Also we proposed a new metric called Total Mutation Count Pair-wise (TMCP). These metrics are used for evaluation of the proposed model.

Total Mutation Count Pair-wise: Even though TGP depicts the biological evolution process, we infer it is not sufficient enough to conclude the measured alignment. This is mainly due to the individual value for *gapopen* and *gapextend* is not universally the same. Further the ratio between these two values is still debatable. Hence, we propose a new metric called total mutation count pair-wise which is more biologically relevant and TMCP is defined as:

$$TMCP(S') = \sum_{i=1}^{N-1} \sum_{j=i+1}^{N} MC(s'_i, s'_j) \tag{8}$$

$MC(s'_i, s'_j)$ is total number of mutations for a given pair of aligned sequence i.e. s'_i and s'_j. A column or set of consecutive columns are considered to be one mutation only if respective column molecules are not identical. For example: From Table 2, s'_1 and s'_2 are two aligned sequences, MC is mutation count for the given pair; hence, the total mutation count for the given pair is 3. Lower the value of TMCP, better is the alignment.

Table 2. Example of mutation count for a pair

S1	A	C	F	N	L	Y	S	D	F	N	K	D	F	C	V	V	I	S	F	C
S2	-	C	F	N	L	Y	R	V	-	S	-	-	F	C	V	-	-	-	-	-
MC	1	0					1					0				1				

4 Performance Evaluation

4.1 Experiment Setup

Runtime Environment: All experiments were conducted on an Intel(R) Core(TM) i5 2.30GHz CPU with 4GB RAM and running on 64-bit Ubuntu 16.10 Operating System. The proposed model has been implemented in Java, Eclipse Platform 3.8.1.

Datasets: Experimental analysis has been done on two benchmark datasets i.e. PREFAB4refm & SABrem. For both datasets, input unaligned sequence sets and aligned reference result sets are from [3].

4.2 Result and Analysis

In earlier section, we demonstrated that the proposed model is efficient. Next, to analyze and demonstrate the effectiveness of the proposed model, experiments were conducted on benchmark datasets (PREFAB4refm and SABrem). SP, TGP, CS and TMCP values are captured from the aligned results and compared with the benchmark aligned reference sets. All the four evaluation metrics are highly dependent on each other i.e. any efforts to improve one metric, rest of the metrics get affected. Table 3 represents the list of metrics that were considered for their respective alignment.

Table 3. Algorithms and their metrics

Algorithm	SP	TGP	CS	TMCP	Time efficient
Clustal W [16]	✓	✓	X	X	✓
Clustal O [14]	✓	✓	✓	X	✓
Kalign [8]	✓	✓	X	X	✓
MUSCLE [4]	✓	✓	✓	X	✓
MSAGMOSA [7]	✓	✓	✓	X	X
MOMSA [13]	✓	✓	X	X	X
IMSA [1]	✓	✓	✓	X	X
H4MSA [20]	✓	✓	✓	X	X
Proposed	✓	✓	✓	✓	✓

Table 4. Comparision of proposed model results with reference results

Dataset	Total # of sets	Improvement in at-least any 2 EM	Effective % in any 2 EM	Improvement in at-least any 3 EM	Effective % in any 3 EM
PREFAB4refm	692	684	98.84	536	77.46
SABrem	303	296	97.69	208	68.65

PREFAB4refm: As shown in Table 4, contains 692 sets. The proposed alignment model results are 98.84% and 77.46% improved when compared to aligned benchmark results with respect to any two Evaluation Metrics (EM) and three EM respectively.

SABrem: As shown in Table 4, contains 303 unaligned sequence sets. The proposed alignment model results are 97.69% and 68.65% improved when compared to aligned benchmark results with respect to any two EM and any three EM respectively.

5 Conclusion and Future Work

Multiple protein sequence alignment is still an open challenge. Existing alignment techniques need continuous improvement in order to bridge the gap between large unaligned protein sequences and extremely time inefficient alignment models. In order to address this gap, we proposed a dynamic and effective multiple protein sequence model. The proposed LBA novel scoring system enhances the effectiveness of the proposed dynamic alignment model. Further, along with the state-of-the-art metrics, we have defined a new biologically more meaningful evaluation metric to measure and compare the proposed model results with aligned reference results. The proposed model is tested on benchmark datasets and all the metric results are promising and efficient.

Based on the results obtained from the proposed model, in future, we want to improve the model by (1) Efficient: by making the model parallel to reduce the run time and (2) Effective: by introducing a light weight optimizer for the four metric objectives which enhances the quality (Q) of aligned results with the trade-off of acceptable additional running time.

References

1. Cutello, V., Nicosia, G., Pavone, M., Prizzi, I.: Protein multiple sequence alignment by hybrid bio-inspired algorithms. Nucleic Acids Res. **39**(6), 1980–1992 (2011)
2. Dayhoff, M., Schwartz, R., Orcutt, B.: 22 a model of evolutionary change in proteins. In: Atlas of protein sequence and structure, vol. 5, pp. 345–352. National Biomedical Research Foundation Silver Spring, MD (1978)
3. Edgar, R.: http://www.drive5.com/bench/

4. Edgar, R.C.: Muscle: multiple sequence alignment with high accuracy and high throughput. Nucleic Acids Res. **32**(5), 1792–1797 (2004)
5. Feng, D.F., Doolittle, R.F.: Progressive sequence alignment as a prerequisiteto correct phylogenetic trees. J. Mol. Evol. **25**(4), 351–360 (1987)
6. Henikoff, S., Henikoff, J.G.: Amino acid substitution matrices from protein blocks. Proc. Natl. Acad. Sci. **89**(22), 10915–10919 (1992)
7. Kaya, M., Sarhan, A., Alhajj, R.: Multiple sequence alignment with affine gap by using multi-objective genetic algorithm. Comput. Methods Programs Biomed. **114**(1), 38–49 (2014)
8. Lassmann, T., Sonnhammer, E.L.: Kalign-an accurate and fast multiple sequence alignment algorithm. BMC Bioinform. **6**(1), 298 (2005)
9. Needleman, S.B., Wunsch, C.D.: A general method applicable to the search for similarities in the amino acid sequence of two proteins. J. Mol. Biol. **48**(3), 443–453 (1970)
10. Notredame, C.: Recent evolutions of multiple sequence alignment algorithms. PLoS Comput. Biol. **3**(8), e123 (2007)
11. Ortuno, F., Florido, J.P., Urquiza, J.M., Pomares, H., Prieto, A., Rojas, I.: Optimization of multiple sequence alignment methodologies using a multiobjective evolutionary algorithm based on nsga-ii. In: 2012 IEEE Congress on Evolutionary Computation (CEC), pp. 1–8. IEEE (2012)
12. Oyola, S.O., Otto, T.D., Gu, Y., Maslen, G., Manske, M., Campino, S., Turner, D.J., MacInnis, B., Kwiatkowski, D.P., Swerdlow, H.P., et al.: Optimizing illumina next-generation sequencing library preparation for extremely at-biased genomes. BMC Genom. **13**(1), 1 (2012)
13. Rubio-Largo, Á., Vega-Rodríguez, M.A., González-Álvarez, D.L.: A hybrid multiobjective memetic metaheuristic for multiple sequence alignment. IEEE Trans. Evol. Comput. **20**(4), 499–514 (2016)
14. Sievers, F., Wilm, A., Dineen, D., Gibson, T.J., Karplus, K., Li, W., Lopez, R., McWilliam, H., Remmert, M., Söding, J., et al.: Fast, scalable generation of high-quality protein multiple sequence alignments using clustal omega. Mol. Syst. Biol. **7**(1), 539 (2011)
15. Smith, T.F., Waterman, M.S.: Identification of common molecular subsequences. J. Mol. Biol. **147**(1), 195–197 (1981)
16. Thompson, J.D., Higgins, D.G., Gibson, T.J.: Clustal w: improving the sensitivity of progressive multiple sequence alignment through sequence weighting, position-specific gap penalties and weight matrix choice. Nucleic Acids Res. **22**(22), 4673–4680 (1994)
17. Thompson, J.D., Plewniak, F., Poch, O.: A comprehensive comparison of multiple sequence alignment programs. Nucleic Acids Res. **27**(13), 2682–2690 (1999)
18. Thompson, J.D., Poch, O.: Multiple sequence alignment as a workbench for molecular systems biology. Curr. Bioinform. **1**(1), 95–104 (2006)
19. Wang, L., Jiang, T.: On the complexity of multiple sequence alignment. J. Comput. Biol. **1**(4), 337–348 (1994)
20. Zhu, H., He, Z., Jia, Y.: A novel approach to multiple sequence alignment using multiobjective evolutionary algorithm based on decomposition. IEEE J. Biomed. Health Inf. **20**(2), 717–727 (2016)

Classification of Vector-Borne Virus Through Totally Ordered Set of Dinucleotide Interval Patterns

Uddalak Mitra and Balaram Bhattacharyya$^{(\boxtimes)}$

Department of Computer and System Sciences, Visva Bharati University,
Santiniketan 731235, India
balaramb@gmail.com

Abstract. In genome analysis, common approach to all word methods is use of long words to improve precision in biological findings. However, arbitrary increment in word length cannot always be fruitful, rather causing increase in space-time complexity. We observe that instead of mere increase in length, integration of word intervals along with order and frequency of their occurrence have great impact in extracting sequence information with much smaller word length and devise a method, Dinucleotide Interval Patterns (DIP), for entropy retrieval from ordered sets of dinucleotide intervals. Experiments on natural sequences of Flaviviridae virus with length 9 to 12 kbp establish that only word size of 2bp is capable of deriving precise taxonomic classification of the virus. This is in sharp contrast to standard word-based methods requiring a minimum of 6bp word size to achieve nearly 30% Topological Similarity in comparison to 60% score by DIP with only 2bp.

Keywords: Dinucleotide pattern entropy · Genome grouping · Flaviviridae classification · Vector identification

1 Introduction

In recent years, word-frequency methods become standard tools for analysis and comparison of DNA sequences. Principal advantage of these methods over alignment, viz. NCBI-BLAST family of software [1], is better scaling of computation times with sequence length. In the studies of clustering of taxonomic units, subtyping and likes, standard word frequency methods [2–4] have delivered a reliable means to analyze DNA sequences. But their performance falls through in several cases, viz., determination of genomic distance between two DNA sequences, identification of conserved regions like short DNA motifs [5]. Major cause behind the difference is lying with how the method views the sequence. Word-frequency methods completely neglect positional information and interpret a sequence as a bag of words. Limitation is thus non-capturing of entropy variation over biological changes incurred in sequence. In contrast, alignment-based methods consider exact position and quality of similarity of every part of the sequence that reflect

© Springer International Publishing AG 2017
B.U. Shankar et al. (Eds.): PReMI 2017, LNCS 10597, pp. 405–410, 2017.
https://doi.org/10.1007/978-3-319-69900-4_51

compositional structure with higher precision. However, scalability of alignment-based methods is an open challenge. Hence, initiatives on word-based method with new techniques are in the literature for scalable sequence analysis. Efforts are on to improve precision of outcome of word methods through inclusion of more descriptive information about compositional structure of DNA. Composition vector [6] is a way to enrich feature frequency profiles by subtracting the random background from frequency count of each word using a Markov model of order (k-2). that diminish the influence of random neutral mutations. An alternative to word frequency statistics is accounting probabilistic appearance of common words between two sequences, popularly known as D2 statistics. The statistical dependence between adjacent occurrences of common words among sequences is taken care of using a technique called spaced-word [7]. However, use of larger word size in all these methods generates huge number of possible words that significantly increase space time complexity. Hence, reduction in word size without sacrificing the precision is a need. Instead of continually increasing the length of words, the present work focuses on the patterns of their successive appearance over the sequence. It incorporates intervals and orders of their occurrence into the method. This result in extraction of word entropy to such an extent that optimum level of entropy is achieved with only dinucleotide words for taxonomic classification of Flaviviridae Virus (FV).

2   Method

With an alphabet $\Sigma = \{A, C, G, T\}$ and $L \in N$, let S is a biological sequence of length L over Σ^L. A subsequence of length 2 over the sequence S is designated as a dinucleotide. With four nucleotide symbols in Σ, the set of all possible dinucleotides are {AA,AC,AG,AT,CA,CC,CG,CT,TA,TC,TG,TT}. Let the $j^{th}(1 \leq j \leq 16)$dinucleotide w^j occurs at locations l_i^j, i=1(1)m, m being the maximum number of occurrence of the dinucleotide over the sequence S. We define the set of intervals between each successive locations of the jth dinucleotide, w^j, as $D^j = \{d_1^j, d_2^j, \cdots d_m^j\}$: where

$$d_i^j = l_{i+1}^j - l_i^j, i \leq m \tag{1}$$

To characterize the order of occurrence of intervals of the jth dinucleotide w^j, we impose the concept of totally ordered set T^j over the set D^j. Mathematically, a total order set is a set with a relation on the set (called the total order) that satisfies the conditions for partial order with an additional condition called comparability condition. A relation $\leq$ is a total order on a set T if the following properties hold, Reflexivity: a le a for all a $\in$ T, Antisymmetric: a $\leq$ b and b $\leq$ a implies a=b, Transitivity: a $\leq$ b and b $\leq$ c implies a $\leq$ c, Comparability (trichotomy law): For any a, b $\in$ T either a $\leq$ b or b $\leq$ a hold. To apply the relation $\leq$ we define the elements of the totally order set T^j over the set D^j of intervals of the dinucleotide w^j as

$$t_i^j = \sum_{i=1}^{r} d_i^j, 1 \leq r \leq m \tag{2}$$

The totally order set of intervals T^j, of jth dinucleotide w^j, is independent of other dinucleotides. Given the set T^j we can obtain information about the occurrence frequency along with distribution pattern and occurrence order of the dinucleotide w^j over the sequence S. The entropy of a totally order set of intervals can reflect the importance of position (both location and its order of occurrence) of a dinucleotide over the sequence. We construct a discrete probability mass function $P^j = \{p_1^j, p_2^j, \cdots, p_m^j\}$ where $p_i^j = t_i^j / \sum_{i=1}^{m} t_i^j$. The Shannon's entropy h^j is thus can be defined

$$h^j = -\sum_{i=1}^{m} t_i^j * log_2(t_i^j) \tag{3}$$

Entropies of all the dinucleotides form the representation vector of the given sequence S as in feature space of dinucleotide distribution as $H = (h^1, h^2, \cdots, h^r)$, r=16. The representation vector H can be used as the transformed presentation for the given sequence S in feature space on which we can apply a distance measures to compute similarity/dissimilarity with other sequences.

2.1   Distance Measure between sequences in feature space

To measure the distance between two biological sequences in feature space (H^i and H^j) we use Euclidean distance between given pair of sequences, as follows

$$\sigma_{ij} = \sqrt{\sum_{i=1}^{r} (h_i^r - h_j^r)^2} \tag{4}$$

3   Experiment

3.1   Vector Identification

Vector identification is primary issue to control epidemic situation owing to viral infection. For instance, infection of Dengue, a species of Flaviviridae, could lead to a disastrous state, had the mosquito Aedes aegypti not been identified as its carrier. Flaviviridae is a family of fast evolving RNA viruses that can infect mammals, birds and invertebrates (ticks and mosquitoes) organisms. For these viruses, transmission mode (vectors) plays a vital role in their life cycle in order to cause infection to respective hosts and thus identification of respective vectors can lead to framing strategies for controlling the virus.

Biological segregation of Flaviviridae into three genera, viz., Flavivirus, Hepacivirus and Pestivirus has carried out on criteria like host-range and outcome of infection. Genus Flavivirus are transmitted to their respective hosts only by different arthropod vectors like mosquitoes, ticks or insects via blood sucking. The second genus, Hepacivirus, infect only mammals mainly transmitted by blood contact, while the genus Pestivirus infects several non-human mammals via oral-fecal or respiratory routes. Another ecological lineage of viruses,

NKV (non-known vector), for which no arthropod is yet known as vector, cause infection similar to Flavivirus. Thus, identifying families of these viruses through study of phylogeny will help in identifying possible vectors for unknown cases.

Molecular phylogeny is a technique to group genetically similar sequences. Life cycle of virus is interesting and a motivation for phylogeny study. Interaction between FVs and their vectors is a continuous process involving both immune system of vectors and escape mechanism of viruses. Viruses mimic vector-specific genomic pattern in course of the interaction, subjected to vector-induced pressures [8]. Thus, common patterns, in virus genomes captured by molecular phylogeny, are indication of vectorspecificity in Flaviviridae.

Flavivirus phylogeny

Dataset: Test datasets are compiled with 34 Flaviviridae virus genomes (Table 1) collected from the freely available repository of National Center of Biotechnology Information (https://www.ncbi.nlm.nih.gov/). These virus genomes vary from 9 to 12 kbp in length. Sequences with label D1-D12 are mosquito-borne, D13-D15 are insectborne, D16-D21 are tick-borne, D22-D28 are NKV, D29-D31 are Hepaciviruses and D32-D34 are Pestiviruses.

Table 1. Flaviviridae virus genomes

Label	Accession no	Label	Accession no	Label	Accession no	Label	Accession no
D1	NC_001471	D10	NC_000943	D19	NC_005062	D28	NC_003996
D2	NC_001474	D11	NC_002031	D20	NC_001809	D29	NC_001710
D3	NC_001475	D12	NC_008719	D21	NC_001672	D30	NC_009823
D4	NC_002640	D13	NC_008604	D22	NC_005039	D31	NC_001655
D5	NC_009026	D14	NC_001564	D23	NC_008718	D32	NC_001461
D6	NC_009028	D15	NC_005064	D24	NC_004119	D33	NC_002032
D7	NC_001563	D16	NC_006974	D25	NC_003675	D34	NC_025677
D8	NC_001437	D17	NC_003687	D26	NC_003635	-	-
D9	NC_066551	D18	NC_003690	D27	NC_003676	-	-

We apply the proposed method (DIP) to devise genomic distance among the viruses enlisted in Table 1. It transforms each genome sequence into feature space through entropy extraction of 16 dinucleotide (2bp) patterns. DIP next computes the distance matrix, elements of which are simply pair wise distances between all possible genome pairs in feature space. Phylogeny tree (Figure 1) that reflects the taxonomic classification of the enlisted Flaviviridae viruses is computed using the hierarchical clustering algorithms UPGMA.

Clear segregation of FVs into three known genera, Hepacivirus (D29-S31), Pestivirus (D32-S34) and Flavivirus (D1-S28) based on genomic distances as captured by DIP is observed. Further, insect-borne (D13-S15), tick-borne (D16-S21) and mosquitoborne (D1-S12) viruses are alienated into subgroups under Flaviviruses group. Such distinct groups in the phylogeny patterns drawn by DIP

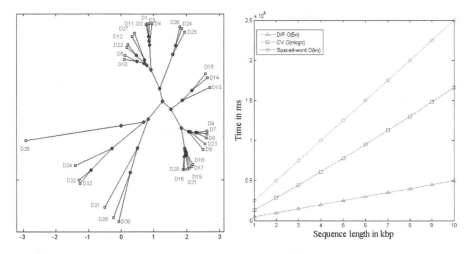

Fig. 1. Cladogram tree of FV (Table 1) using 2bp

Fig. 2. Comparing performance and scalability

indicates that viruses with common vectors are near classified together, reflecting their vector-specificity. DIP thus offers a way for vector identification under health hazard situation. It is interesting to note in Fig. 1 that viruses GBV-B (D29) and GBV-C (D31) are grouped into the same class with Hepacivirus. This is identical with earlier report [9] from polyprotein-based study. These are accepted candidate of Hepacivirus by the International Committee on Taxonomy of Viruses (ICTV). Moreover, NKV viruses, D22, D23 and D27 are paraphyletic with mosquito-borne viruses, whereas others NKV viruses, D24, D25, D26 and D28, are in a separate subgroup that is paraphyletic with Pestiviruses, indicating blood sucking non-mosquito pests as their possible vectors.

3.2   Performance and scalability

The phylogeny tree of Flaviviridae (Table 1) by Clustal Omega (www.ebi.ac.uk/Tools/msa/clustalo) is taken as reference for comparison with two alignment-free methods, composition vector (tlife.fudan.edu.cn/cvtree) and spaced word (http://spaced.gobics.de/). Topological Similarity (TS) computed following the method in (www.mas.ncl.ac.Uk/ntmwn/compare2trees). Results are reported in Table 2.

Figure 2 presents a comparative study on performance and scalability, showing excellence of DIP in addition to biological consistence of knowledge retrieved. Highest TS score obtained by DIP proves that appropriate statistical feature is more powerful than mere length of word in extracting information from natural sequence.

Table 2. Comparing the proposed method with existing

Method	Space complexity (in bytes)	Time complexity	Word size	TS-score
Clustal Omega	34 × 12500	14.24 min	Not applicable	Ref. tree
Composition vector	34 × 4^6	12.75sec	6	35.0%
Space word	34 × 4^7	50.46sec	7	31.8%
DIP	34 × 4^2	0.5304sec	2	60.1%

4   Conclusion

We present a concept of inducting interval and order of occurrence of words with frequency to capture minute changes in nucleotide patterns and develop a method for entropy computation. From patterns of dinucleotides only, the method builds taxonomic classification for Flaviviridae virus with higher precision. Advantages of introducing the concept are twofold: accuracy in result and economy in computation as longer words are not required.

Viruses with common vectors are genetically closer in terms of arrangements of dinucleotides. As the proposed method can classify viruses on the basis of their dinucleotide patterns, genetic closeness of a new virus to a class can lead to tracing its possible vector.

References

1. Altschul, S.F., Gish, W., Miller, W., Myers, E.W., Lipman, D.J.: Basic local alignment search tool. J. Mol. Biol. **215**, 403–410 (1990)
2. Sims, G.E., Jun, S.R., Wu, G.A., Kim, S.H.: Whole-genome phylogeny of mammals: evolutionary information in genic and nongenic regions. Proc. Nat. Acad. Sci. U.S.A. **106**(40), 17077–17082 (2009)
3. Sims, G.E., Kim, S.H.: Whole-genome phylogeny of Escherichia coli/Shigella group by feature frequency profiles (FFPs). Proc. Nat. Acad. Sci. U.S.A. **108**(20), 832–934 (2011)
4. Gao, L., Qi, J.: Whole genome molecular phylogeny of large dsDNA viruses using composition vector method. BMC Evol. Biol. **7**, 41 (2007)
5. Alsop, E.B., Raymond, J.: Resolving prokaryotic taxonomy without rRNA: Longer oligonucleotide word lengths improve genome and metagenome taxonomic classication. PLoS ONE **8**, e67337 (2013)
6. Hao, B.L., Qi, J., Wang, B.: Prokaryotic phylogeny based on complete genomes without sequence alignment. Mod. Phys. Lett. B **2**, 1–4 (2003)
7. Leimeister, C.A., Boden, M., Horwege, S., Lindner, S.: Fast alignment-free sequence comparison using spaced-word frequencies. Bioinformatics **30**(14), 1991–1999 (2014)
8. Lobo, F.P., Mota, B.E.F., Pena, S.D.J., Azevedo, V., Macedo, A.M., et al.: Virus-Host coevolution: common patterns of nucleotide motif usage in flaviviridae and their hosts. PLoS ONE **4**(7), e6282 (2009). doi:10.1371/journal.pone.0006282

A Quasi-Clique Mining Algorithm for Analysis of the Human Protein-Protein Interaction Network

Brijesh Kumar Sriwastava[1] (ID), Subhadip Basu[2(✉)] (ID),
and Ujjwal Maulik[2] (ID)

[1] Department of Computer Science and Engineering,
Government College of Engineering and Leather Technology,
Kolkata 700098, India
[2] Department of Computer Science and Engineering, Jadavpur University,
Kolkata 700032, India
subhadip@cse.jdvu.ac.in

Abstract. The fundamental of complete interaction system of all living cell is protein- protein interactions (PPI). A protein-protein interactions network (PPIN) can be viewed as an intricate system of proteins. The proteins are linked by interactions between themselves. In this work, we developed a new algorithm to find largest quasi-cliques in human PPIN. We also identify significant clusters of proteins for subsequent pathway analysis. In the current experimental setup, we have mined 49 quasi-cliques from the human PPIN, with the largest quasi-clique having size 29. Each of these protein clusters are analysed with KEGG pathway analysis. The algorithm has been compared with the *state-of-the art* available in this field. We observe that our method is better than other methods available in this domain and finds larger quasi-cliques with higher size.

Keywords: Protein-Protein interaction · Network analysis · Quasi-clique · Pathway analysis

1 Introduction

Proteins interact with other proteins to accomplish biological functions. The transient or more permanent complexes are formed due to such interactions. These interaction networks facilitate biological processes. To study its biological function, it is essential to recognize its probable interaction with other proteins. A PPI network can be thought as a complex system of proteins base on interactions between themselves. Wagner et al. [1] have demonstrated the PPI network as an undirected graph. The nodes are used to represent proteins and edges are used to represent the interaction among proteins. A substantial biological knowledge at the molecular level of interacting proteins can be obtained by PPINs [2]. Important directions for study of biological pathways and protein function can be obtained by mining these networks [3].

© Springer International Publishing AG 2017
B.U. Shankar et al. (Eds.): PReMI 2017, LNCS 10597, pp. 411–417, 2017.
https://doi.org/10.1007/978-3-319-69900-4_52

In order to discover the cluster of protein complexes in PPINs, lots of techniques have been used by researchers. These include clustering of sub-graph, finding dense regions [4–6], or clique finding [7]. The concept of maximum quasi-clique problem (MQP) is introduced by Matsuda et al. [8]. It is a constrained association of vertices in a graph. It leads to a γ-quasi-clique.

Subsequently, Pie et al. [9] have proposed a mining algorithm (Crochet) to discover all quasi-cliques. Further, they have upgraded their algorithm and proposed *Crochet*[+] for the same purpose [10]. These methods have some restrictions for discovering all quasi-cliques. Brunato et al. [11] have proposed another definition for quasi-clique with a pair of parameters. Bhattacharyya et al. [12] have presented an algorithm to find the biggest quasi-cliques in PPIN of H*omo sapiens*.

In view of above facts, it is evident that there is an increasing necessity to localize those significant clusters of protein in an interaction network. The existing algorithms for determination of quasi-cliques are not sufficient to address the complexity of many networks. In case of homo-sapiens, simple analysis of tightly coupled cliques from the protein-protein networks may not be sufficient for investigation of key disease pathways. Therefore, we have tried to relax the constraints in an attempt to find all possible maximal quasi-cliques in the networks. The work presented here is found to be computationally efficient from the earlier works Quick [13] and Cocain [14] and the experimental results validates our claims.

In this work, we attempt to search for the largest PPI cluster using a new quasi-clique algorithm (qCliP). In the following, we first described the important preliminaries. After that method is presented along with detailed pathway analysis.

2 Methods

Here, some basic definitions and preliminaries of Maximal Quasi-clique Problem is first described. The graph indicate undirected labelled simple graph. A graph G is defined by tuples (V, E), where V is set of vertices and E is set of edges in between the pair of vertices. Our objective is to search for all possible maximal quasi-cliques in PPINs. A PPIN can be defined by tuples (P, I), where P denotes protein set and I denotes set of interactions. So, we have direct analogy between (V, E) and (P, I).

γ-quasi-clique graph: For $(0 < \gamma \leq 1)$, if each vertices of the graph G has at least degree $\lceil \gamma \times (|V| - 1) \rceil$ then such graph G is called γ-quasi-clique graph.

An algorithm to find the largest quasi-clique is presented in the following. The proposed method finds quasi-cliques in large protein-protein interaction networks.

Algorithm to Find the Largest Quasi Clique in a Graph

Input: PPIN as a graph G; γ, where $(0 < \gamma < 1)$
Output: All maximal quasi-cliques: C_m, for m −quasi-clique

---

1. $i=0$
2. Max = maximum number of nodes reachable from any node
3. **for** ($j=Max$ **to** 3 **step** -1) **do**
4. $d= j$ // d=cardinality of quasi-clique
5. $A = \emptyset$
6.   qCliP$(A, 0, d)$
7. **end for**

$qCliP(A, i, d)$

---

1. **if** $(i = d$ and $(degree_{a_k} \geq 2, \forall\ a_k \in A)\ )$ **then**
2. A is a d −quasi-clique in G
3. **else**
4. $i = i + 1$
5.   **if** ($i \leq d$) **then**
   // creating C_i which is set of all candidate vectors for i −quasi-clique
6.   **if** $(A = \emptyset)$ **then**
7. .   Add each node $n_j \in V$ in the singleton vector c_j of candidates list C_i
8.   **else**
9.   //permute all candidate vectors, satisfying the property of C_i
10.   Compute $G_m = \lceil \gamma \times (A_{size} - 1)\rceil$
11.   **for** $(\forall\ node\ n_j \in (V - A), degree_{n_j} \geq 2)$ **do**
12. $adj = \sum_k adjacency(n_k, n_j), \forall\ n_k \in A$
13.   **if** $(adj \geq 1$ and $adj \geq G_m$) **then**
14.   create a new vector c_l in C_i by joining
                     vector A and node n_j from $(V - A)$
15.   **end if**
16.   **end for**
17.   **end if**
18. **end if**
19. **if** $(C_i \neq \emptyset)$ **then**
20. **for** $(\forall\ c_k \in C_i$) **do** //where c_k is the kth candidate vector of C_i
21.   call $qCliP(c_k, i, d)$ //backtrack for d −quasi-clique
22. **end for**
23. **end if**
24. **end if**

---

3 Results and Discussion

In this work, we have first started with 1831 distinct human proteins involving 2252 interactions (dip20100614) [15]. Then we have filtered the given data so that each entry has a valid Uniprot id, complete primary sequence annotation and 3D information (PDB id). So after this filtration the data size reduced to 1007 interactions with 857 distinct proteins [16]. This database is used for performance evaluation of the proposed algorithm, to identify all possible maximal quasi-cliques from this PPIN, and subsequent pathway analyses.

We have first executed our proposed algorithm for nine different values of γ starting from 0.9 to 0.1 with an interval of 0.1. In this experiment, we observed that proposed method provides largest quasi-clique with cardinality of 23 for γ is 0.1. In the second stage, we executed the novel algorithm for finer γ values in the range (0, 0.1) with an interval of 0.01. We finally observed that algorithm mines largest quasi-clique of size 29 when γ is 0.07. Considering the value of the $\gamma = 0.07$, we got 49 different maximal quasi-cliques with size ranging from 3 to 29.

For pathway analysis of the clustered proteins, obtained by our proposed algorithm, we have used the web server (http://david.abcc.ncifcrf.gov/tools.jsp), where we first converted proteins ids from Uniprot id to gene id and then analysed all the corresponding genes on KEGG pathway analysis [17]. Our algorithm identifies 46 clusters

Table 1. KEGG Pathway for some quasi-cliques obtained from our proposed algorithm

Quasi clique number	Cardinality	KEGG id	KEGG pathway	P value
1	29	hsa04110	Cell cycle	1.34E−10
2	11	hsa04110	Cell cycle	5.18E−10
3	10	hsa04630	Jak-STAT signaling pathway	9.29E−05
4	10	hsa04622	RIG-I-like receptor signaling pathway	4.17E−06
5	10	hsa04062	Chemokine signaling pathway	3.57E−15
6	8	hsa04623	Cytosolic DNA-sensing pathway	4.19E−07
7	8	hsa04623	Cytosolic DNA-sensing pathway	4.07E−05
8	6	hsa05220	Chronic myeloid leukemia	1.22E−05
9	6	hsa05220	Chronic myeloid leukemia	1.22E−05
10	6	hsa05200	Pathways in cancer	0.001013
11	6	hsa05220	Chronic myeloid leukemia	1.22E−05
12	6	hsa05200	Pathways in cancer	0.004149
13	5	hsa05130	Pathogenic Escherichia coli infection	1.23E−04
14	4	hsa05212	Pancreatic cancer	2.72E−06
15	3	hsa05211	Renal cell carcinoma	0.013766

for KEGG pathway. The Table 1 shows the KEGG pathway of some quasi-cliques along with their respective p-values.

We have compared the performance of the proposed algorithm with the available prior works in this domain. For evaluation of the system performances, the execution time for finding non-redundant disjoint maximal quasi-cliques is considered as one of the key criteria. Two other algorithms, viz., Quick [13] and Cocain [14], are compared with our method on an uniform hardware platform with Intel 2.4 GHz CPU computer having 2 GB internal memory. As discussed before, the performance of our proposed algorithm is optimised for $\gamma = 0.07$. But during comparison of the method with other algorithms, we have considered a wide spectrum of γ values as 0.01, 0.07, 0.1, 0.5 and 0.9, within the range (0, 1). The detailed results of all methods for all considered γ values are given in the Table 2. It has been found that our novel algorithm identifies the largest maximal quasi-cliques of cardinality 29 particularly when γ is 0.07. Overall, our method identifies 49 mutually-exclusive, maximal quasi-cliques from the PPIN and the experiment is completed in 352 s.

Table 2. Comparative performance analysis of all four methods for different Gamma (γ) values is shown. Please note that DA identifies only the maximum quasi-clique and Cocain works only with the γ range (0.5, 1). Quick executes faster but extracts many overlapping quasi-cliques from the PPIN.

Gamma (γ)	Methods	Execution time (s)	Number of quasi-clique	Cardinality quasi-clique
0.01	Proposed method	150	67	12
	Quick	0.009	1426	26
	Cocain	-	-	-
0.07	Proposed method	352	49	29
	Quick	258.834	4471088	15
	Cocain	-	-	-
0.1	Proposed method	129	94	23
	Quick	89.199	3382024	12
	Cocain	-	-	-
0.5	Proposed method	15	61	7
	Quick	0.015	2489	7
	Cocain	0.110002	1455	3
0.9	Proposed method	7	61	5
	Quick	0.003	81	5
	Cocain	0.060001	699	2

The Cocain algorithm works only for γ values in the range $(0.5, 1)$. Though it takes minimum time for execution in such a specific range, but the major limitation is that the method is not producing significant quasi-cliques for the PPIN. Most of the quasi-cliques are of cardinality 2 or 3 and the total number of quasi-cliques generated by Cocain method ranges in thousands within its allowable γ range. A detailed comparative analysis of the above mentioned methods is given in the Table 2.

4   Conclusion

In the current work, a new algorithm is presented to find all possible non overlapping non redundant maximal quasi-cliques and also the largest size quasi-clique in the huge PPI networks. Subsequently, we apply this approach on huge PPIN and find important clusters of proteins. We have analysed these protein clusters based KEGG pathway analysis. In this work, we have attempted to cluster interactive human proteins within the PPIN using the developed algorithm and also compared its performance with other available works in this domain. It may be observed that this algorithm is better than other algorithm for identifying non-overlapping, non-redundant maximal quasi-cliques. The performance of the algorithm can be improved when applied over more robust network and also it will be biologically more important.

Acknowledgement. This work is partially supported by the CMATER research laboratory of the Computer Science and Engineering Department, Jadavpur University, India, PURSE-II and UPE-II project and Research Award (F.30-31/2016(SA-II)) from UGC, Government of India.

References

1. Wagner, A.: How the global structure of protein interaction networks evolves. Proc. Roy. Soc. London Ser. B Biol. Sci. **270**, 457–466 (2003)
2. Du, D., Pardalos, P.M.: Handbook of Combinatorial Optimization. Springer, New York (1998). doi:10.1007/978-1-4613-0303-9
3. Bomze, I.M., Budinich, M., Pardalos, P.M., et al.: The maximum clique problem. In: Handbook of Combinatorial Optimization, vol. 4, no. 1, pp. 1–74 (1999)
4. Altaf-Ul-Amin, M., Shinbo, Y., Mihara, K., et al.: Development and implementation of an algorithm for detection of protein complexes in large interaction networks. BMC Bioinform. **7**(1), 207 (2006)
5. Brohee, S., Van Helden, J.: Evaluation of clustering algorithms for protein-protein interaction networks. BMC Bioinform. **7**(1), 488 (2006)
6. Pereira-Leal, J.B., Enright, A.J., Ouzounis, C.A.: Detection of functional modules from protein interaction networks. Proteins Struct. Funct. Bioinform. **54**(1), 49–57 (2003)
7. Spirin, V., Mirny, L.A.: Protein complexes and functional modules in molecular networks. Proc. Natl. Acad. Sci. U.S.A. **100**(21), 12123–12128 (2003)
8. Matsuda, H., Ishihara, T., Hashimoto, A.: Classifying molecular sequences using a linkage graph with their pairwise similarities. Theoret. Comput. Sci. **210**(2), 305–325 (1999)
9. Pei, J., Jiang, D., Zhang, A.: On mining cross-graph quasi-cliques. In: Proceedings of the Eleventh ACM SIGKDD International Conference on Knowledge Discovery in Data Mining, pp. 228–238 (2005)

10. Jiang, D., Pei, J.: Mining frequent cross-graph quasi-cliques. ACM Trans. Knowl. Discovery Data (TKDD) **2**(4), 16 (2009)
11. Brunato, M., Hoos, Holger H., Battiti, R.: On effectively finding maximal quasi-cliques in graphs. In: Maniezzo, V., Battiti, R., Watson, J.-P. (eds.) LION 2007. LNCS, vol. 5313, pp. 41–55. Springer, Heidelberg (2008). doi:10.1007/978-3-540-92695-5_4
12. Bhattacharyya, M., Bandyopadhyay, S.: Mining the largest quasi-clique in human protein interactome. In: International Conference on Adaptive and Intelligent Systems, ICAIS 2009, pp. 194–199 (2009)
13. Liu, G., Wong, L.: Effective pruning techniques for mining quasi-cliques. In: Daelemans, W., Goethals, B., Morik, K. (eds.) ECML PKDD 2008. LNCS, vol. 5212, pp. 33–49. Springer, Heidelberg (2008). doi:10.1007/978-3-540-87481-2_3
14. Zeng, Z., Wang, J., Zhou, L., et al.: Coherent closed quasi-clique discovery from large dense graph databases. In: Proceedings of the 12th ACM SIGKDD International Conference on Knowledge Discovery and Data Mining, pp. 797–802 (2006)
15. Salwinski, L., Miller, C.S., Smith, A.J., et al.: The Database of Interacting Proteins: 2004 Update. Nucleic Acids Res. **32**, D449–D451 (2004)
16. Sriwastava, B.K., Basu, S., Maulik, U., et al.: PPIcons: identification of protein-protein interaction sites in selected organisms. J. Mol. Model. **19**(9), 4059–4070 (2013)
17. Huang, D.W., Sherman, B.T., Lempicki, R.A.: Systematic and integrative analysis of large gene lists using DAVID bioinformatics resources. Nat. Protoc. **4**(1), 44–57 (2008)

Prediction of Thyroid Cancer Genes Using an Ensemble of Post Translational Modification, Semantic and Structural Similarity Based Clustering Results

Anup Kumar Halder[iD], Pritha Dutta[iD], Mahantapas Kundu[iD],
Mita Nasipuri[iD], and Subhadip Basu[✉][iD]

Department of Computer Science and Engineering, Jadavpur University,
Kolkata 700032, India
anup21.halder@gmail.com, prithadutta90@gmail.com, mahantapas@gmail.com,
mitanasipuri@gmail.com, bsubhadip@gmail.com

Abstract. Thyroid cancer is one of the most prevalent cancers which affects a large population all over the world. To find effective therapeutic measures against thyroid cancer, it is necessary to identify potential genes which lead to this disease. In this paper, we consider an ensemble of structural, semantic and post translational modification (PTM) similarities based clustering of human genes using known thyroid cancer genes as seeds. Our purpose is to identify potential genes which may be responsible for thyroid cancer from the clusters.

Keywords: Thyroid cancer · PTM similarity · Semantic similarity · Structural similarity · Clustering

1 Introduction

Thyroid cancer is caused by malignancy of thyroid cells. Thyroid cancer is of the following types: Papillary thyroid cancer (PTC), Follicular thyroid cancer (FTC), Medullary thyroid cancer (MTC) and Anaplastic thyroid cancer (ATC). PTC is the most prevalent thyroid cancer which is seen in 75% to 85% cases. The number of people affected with thyroid cancer has significantly increased in the past few years (worldwide 213,000 people). Thus, it has become urgent to understand the mechanism behind the malignancy of thyroid cells to discover effective therapeutic measures. For this, we need to identify the genes responsible for this disease so that effective therapeutic measures can be adopted. For some cancer genes missense mutations based clustering is used to identify new candidates. Stehr et al. [9] and Ryslik et al. [8] used 3D structural information in missense mutations clustering to predict new cancer genes. In [6], Kurubanjerdjit et al. has proposed a clique percolation based clustering in identification of cancer associated proteins. In this paper, we present an ensemble of PTM, semantic and structural similarities based clustering of human genes using known thyroid cancer genes (CNC) as seeds and predict novel genes which may cause thyroid cancer.

© Springer International Publishing AG 2017
B.U. Shankar et al. (Eds.): PReMI 2017, LNCS 10597, pp. 418–423, 2017.
https://doi.org/10.1007/978-3-319-69900-4_53

2   Methodology

In this paper, we present an ensemble of similarities based clustering approach to predict potential thyroid cancer causing genes in *Homo sapiens* using the information of known thyroid cancer genes. We use PTM similarity, semantic similarity and structural similarity to assess the similarity of two genes.

2.1   PTM Similarity

To determine the PTM similarity, we first find the number of occurrences of interactions between different PTM types along with the particular residue at which the modification occurs. Then, for each protein pair we determine whether their respective PTM types together with the modified residues are present in the PTM interaction list. If present, we score (normalize in the range (0,1]) the PTM similarity of the protein pair with the occurrence of the PTM interaction.

2.2   Semantic Similarity

The semantic similarity between two proteins is estimated by considering the similarities between their all pairs of annotating Gene Ontology (GO) terms belonging to a particular ontology (molecular function (MF), biological process (BP), cellular component (CC)). Similarity between a pair of GO terms is assessed on the basis of topological properties of the GO graph and the average information content (IC) of the disjunctive common ancestors (DCAs) of the GO terms [3].

2.3   Structural Similarity

We use two scoring metrics, TM-score [12] and RMSD [5], to measure the structural similarity of two proteins. TM-score gives a value in the range (0, 1], where 1 indicates a perfect match in topological similarity of two protein structures. We use the TM align algorithm [12] for comparing the structures of two proteins. This algorithm identifies the best structural alignment between two proteins. After the optimal superposition, RMSD represents the root mean squared deviation of all the equivalent atom pairs of two protein structures. In general, lower RMSD indicates better superposition. A RMSD value 3Åindicates a high degree of structural similarity. However, a lower RMSD and higher TM-score indicates a better structural similarity, thus they are inversely related. Finally, we incorporate both the scoring metrics to quantify the structural similarity as,

$$StructSim(p,q) = \frac{1}{2}\{(1 - \frac{RMSD}{3}) + TMscore\} \tag{1}$$

Here we restrict the RMSD score up to 3Å for higher structural similarity. In Eq. 1, any RMSD value less than 3Å will contribute positively with TM-score. In addition, RMSD value 0 and TM-score 1 represents optimal structural similarity.

2.4   Cluster Ensembling

In this work, initially, clustering is performed using above three similarity metric at three different similarity thresholds ($\theta_{PTM}, \theta_{Semn}, \theta_{Struct}$). For a particular seed we ensemble all three cluster results and create a new set of cluster members for each seed. Finally, we consider each of the member of the new set as a member of the final cluster set if it is the member of at least 30% of the total clusters (seeds). The overall proposed procedure is shown in Fig. 1.

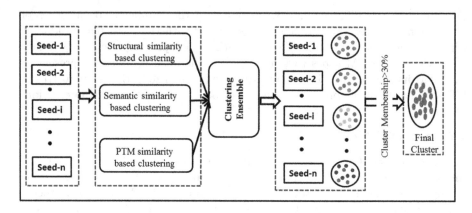

Fig. 1. The basic workflow of clustering result ensembling technique.

3   Dataset Description

We download the genes involved in all types of thyroid cancer from the Thyroid Cancer and Disorder Gene Database (TCGDB) [1] and KEGG and Human Protein Atlas database (CNC genes) [11]. We download protein-protein interactions (PPIs) from the iRefWeb database [10]. From this, we consider only those interactions in which both the proteins are present in both reviewed Uniprot and Protein Data Bank (PDB). Finally, we obtain 4726 PPIs and 4492 unique proteins which is used for validation. For the test dataset, we consider all reviewed human proteins from Uniprot whose structure information are available in PDB. We finally obtain a total of 1321 proteins in the test dataset. Ontology data and GO annotations are downloaded from the Gene Ontology database [2]. The PTM data and PTM interaction data are collected from the HPRD database [7].

4   Experimental Results and Discussion

In this paper, we present a clustering, based on an ensemble of structural, semantic and PTM similarities, of genes using 26 known thyroid cancer genes selected as the seeds. The purpose of this clustering is utilize known thyroid genes to

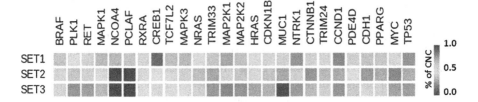

Fig. 2. Heatmap of CNC occurrence percentage over the seed based clustering results of three datasets.

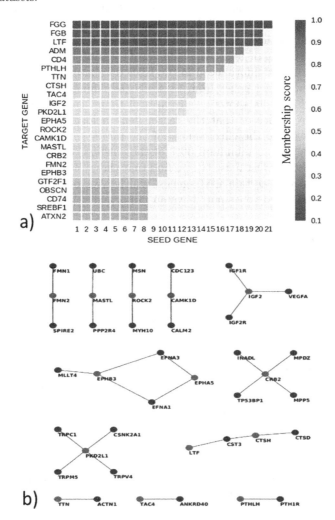

Fig. 3. (a) Membership of the predicted target genes to 21 clusters. A colored box represents that the target gene belongs to the respective cluster. (b) Network of predicted genes and their direct interaction partner genes having CNC annotations. Red nodes represent the predicted genes and blue nodes represent the CNC annotated genes.

predict new genes which may be responsible for thyroid cancer. In this work, total 4492 genes are considered as target genes that includes 297 thyroid cancer genes taken from Human protein Atlas database. To choose the appropriate thresholds $(\theta_{PTM}, \theta_{Semn}, \theta_{Struct})$ for all three clustering, we further sub divide the target genes into three subsets. Each subset contains equal number of CNC genes and equal number of non-CNC genes. These thresholds are set at a value such that the final clustering result has only CNC genes in the clusters. Figure 2 shows the heatmap of the seed based clustering result and percentage of CNC genes obtained from three different sets. CNC percentage ranges from 0 to 1 where 1 implies that all the cluster members are CNC annotated and 0 implies that none of the members have CNC annotation.

Depending on this threshold, we apply this ensemble clustering method over 1350 test data consisting of genes which do not have any Thyroid cancer annotations and have structure information in the PDB database. Using this approach we retrieve 18 new target genes from 21 seeds (remaining 5 seed genes create empty clusters). Figure 3a shows occurrences of target genes over the clusters where colored box indicates that the target gene belongs to the corresponding cluster. To evaluate the effectiveness of the target genes we consider only 14 genes which belong to minimum 30% of the clusters. Using the interaction dataset from the String Database [4], we find that these 14 predicted genes have direct interaction with certain CNC genes, which have been shown in Fig. 3b Thus, these 14 predicted genes may have an important role in thyroid cancer.

5 Conclusion

In this paper, we present a clustering, based on an ensemble of structural, semantic and PTM similarities, of human genes with 26 known thyroid cancer genes as seeds. In this method, we first select appropriate thresholds for structural similarity, semantic similarity and PTM similarity based clustering separately. The thresholds are selected such that after applying this clustering method on the validation dataset, the clusters contain only CNC genes as members. We then use this ensemble clustering method to predict potential thyroid cancer genes. Our clustering result predicts 14 genes with no CNC annotations, but which have direct interactions with CNC annotated genes. From the results, we can summarise that these 14 predicted genes may be responsible for Thyroid cancer since they are directly associated with Thyroid cancer causing genes.

Acknowledgement. This project is partially supported by the CMATER research laboratory of the Computer Science and Engineering Department, Jadavpur University, India, PURSE-II and UPE-II project and Research Award (F.30-31/2016(SA-II)) from UGC, Government of India and Visvesvaraya PhD scheme for ELECTRONICS & IT from DeitY, Government of India.

References

1. Bansal, A., Ramana, J.: TCGDB: a compendium of molecular signatures of thyroid cancer and disorders. J. Cancer Sci. Ther. **7**, 198–201 (2015)
2. Gene Ontology Consortium, et al.: The gene ontology (GO) database and informatics resource. Nucleic Acids Res. **32**(suppl 1), D258–D261 (2004)
3. Dutta, P., Basu, S., Kundu, M.: Assessment of semantic similarity between proteins using information content and topological properties of the gene ontology graph. IEEE/ACM Trans. Comput. Biol. Bioinform. (2017). doi:10.1109/TCBB. 2017.2689762
4. Franceschini, A., Szklarczyk, D., Frankild, S., Kuhn, M., Simonovic, M., Roth, A., Lin, J., Minguez, P., Bork, P., Von Mering, C., et al.: String v9. 1: protein-protein interaction networks, with increased coverage and integration. Nucleic Acids Res. **41**(D1), D808–D815 (2013)
5. Kabsch, W.: A discussion of the solution for the best rotation to relate two sets of vectors. Acta Crystallogr. Sect. A Crystal Phys. Diffr. Theor. Gen. Crystallogr. **34**(5), 827–828 (1978)
6. Kurubanjerdjit, N., Huang, C.H., Ng, K.L.: Identification of lung cancer associated protein by clique percolation clustering analysis. In: 2013 13th International Symposium on Communications and Information Technologies (ISCIT), pp. 737–740. IEEE (2013)
7. Prasad, T.K., Goel, R., Kandasamy, K., Keerthikumar, S., Kumar, S., Mathivanan, S., Telikicherla, D., Raju, R., Shafreen, B., Venugopal, A., et al.: Human protein reference database2009 update. Nucleic Acids Res. **37**(suppl 1), D767–D772 (2009)
8. Ryslik, G.A., Cheng, Y., Cheung, K.H., Bjornson, R.D., Zelterman, D., Modis, Y., Zhao, H.: A spatial simulation approach to account for protein structure when identifying non-random somatic mutations. BMC Bioinform. **15**(1), 231 (2014)
9. Stehr, H., Jang, S.H.J., Duarte, J.M., Wierling, C., Lehrach, H., Lappe, M., Lange, B.M.: The structural impact of cancer-associated missense mutations in oncogenes and tumor suppressors. Mol. Cancer **10**(1), 54 (2011)
10. Turner, B., Razick, S., Turinsky, A.L., Vlasblom, J., Crowdy, E.K., Cho, E., Morrison, K., Donaldson, I.M., Wodak, S.J.: iRefWeb: interactive analysis of consolidated protein interaction data and their supporting evidence. Database 2010, baq023 (2010)
11. Uhlén, M., Björling, E., Agaton, C., Szigyarto, C.A.K., Amini, B., Andersen, E., Andersson, A.C., Angelidou, P., Asplund, A., Asplund, C., et al.: A human protein atlas for normal and cancer tissues based on antibody proteomics. Mol. Cell. Proteomics **4**(12), 1920–1932 (2005)
12. Zhang, Y., Skolnick, J.: TM-align: a protein structure alignment algorithm based on the TM-score. Nucleic Acids Res. **33**(7), 2302–2309 (2005)

mRMR+: An Effective Feature Selection Algorithm for Classification

Hussain A. Chowdhury[ID] and Dhruba K. Bhattacharyya[(✉)][ID]

Department of Computer Science and Engineering, Tezpur University,
Sonitpur 784028, Assam, India
{hussain,dkb}@tezu.ernet.in

Abstract. This paper presents an empirical study using three entropy measures such as Shannon's entropy, Renyi's entropy, and Tsallis entropy, while calculating mutual information to select top ranked features. We evaluate the selected features using three established classifiers such as naive Bayes, IBK and Random Forest in terms of classification accuracy on five gene expression datasets. We observe that none gives consistent performance in ordering the features based on their rank. To address this issue, we propose a variant of mRMR, using ensemble approach based on our own weight function. The results establish that our method is significantly superior than its other counterparts in terms of feature selection and classification accuracy in most of the datasets.

Keywords: Entropy · Mutual information · Feature selection · mRMR

1 Introduction

A feature is an individual measurable property of a phenomenon being observed. The representation of raw input data uses many features, only some of which are relevant to the class. Feature selection for supervised classification can be accomplished on the basis of entropy information between features and classes. We use Shannon Entropy [10], Renyi's and Tsallis Entropy [6] to calculate mutual information [3] between feature and class or feature-feature in this work. It is found that mRMR [8] is a practical and superior algorithm for feature selection and classification, however it does not perform well if lesser number of attributes present in datasets [8]. The main motivation behind our work is to develop an enhanced feature selection algorithm that performs consistently well in all kinds of datasets. An ensemble method for entropy-based feature selection is developed and evaluated using common machine learning algorithms on a variety of UCI gene expression datasets. We carry out comparative study among existing entropy-based feature selection methods. Our method eliminates irrelevant and redundant data and in majority cases it improves the performance of learning algorithms.

© Springer International Publishing AG 2017
B.U. Shankar et al. (Eds.): PReMI 2017, LNCS 10597, pp. 424–430, 2017.
https://doi.org/10.1007/978-3-319-69900-4_54

2 Related Work

In the past two decades, a good number of MI-based feature selection algorithms have been introduced. Two main important aspects of feature selection are: (i) minimum redundancy in terms of number of features and (ii) maximum relevance of a feature with a given class label. Some well-known MI-based feature selection algorithms are: Information Gain [1], Gain Ratio [3], mRMR [8] and its variant [9]. InfoGain and GainRatio select features based on relevancy only, however other mentioned MI-based feature selection algorithms select most relevant and least redundant features. From our study, we observe that mRMR is appropriate for large number of applications having large numbers of features [8]. It performs well on both continuous and discrete data.

To achieve minimum redundancy - maximum relevance for categorical variables [5], most researchers consider that if the feature values are uniformly distributed in different classes, its mutual information with these classes is zero. If a feature is highly differentially expressed for different classes, it should have large mutual information. Thus, mutual information can be considered as a measure to estimate relevance of features.

The mRMR algorithm aims to select a feature set S, which shows maximum relevance to a given class (features provide maximum information about the class) and are of less redundant. mRMR considers the mutual information of each feature against the classes, but also subtracts the redundancy of each feature with the already selected ones. mRMR follows filter criterion based on mutual information estimation. Instead of estimating the mutual information between a whole set of features and the class labels, the authors estimate it for each one of the selected features separately. On one hand, they maximize the relevance $I(x_j; C)$ of each already selected individual feature and on the other hand they minimize the redundancy between x_j and the rest of selected features. This criterion can be expressed for selection of mth feature is:

$$max_{x_j \in X - S_{m-1}}[I(x_j; C) - \frac{1}{m-1} \sum_{x_i \in S_{m-1}} I(x_j; x_i)]. \qquad (1)$$

This criterion can be used by a greedy algorithm, which in each iteration takes a single feature and decides whether to add it to the selected feature set, or to discard it, and this process is repeated till required set S of K optimal features is obtained. This implies that the mth feature x_m will be selected only when a set of $(m-1)$ features i.e., S_{m-1} exits. We refer to the original mRMR method as $mRMR_{MI}$. Another variant of the mRMR criterion [9] also exists (referred here as $mRMR_{GR}$). In [9], it is reformulated using a different representation of redundancy. The authors propose to use a coefficient of uncertainty which consists of dividing the MI value between two features x_j and x_i by the entropy of $H(x_i)$, where $x_i \in S_{m-1}$. The equation is as given below.

$$max_{x_j \in X - S_{m-1}}[I(x_j; C) - \frac{1}{m-1} \sum_{x_i \in S_{m-1}} \frac{I(x_j; x_i)}{H(x_i)}] \qquad (2)$$

In this study, we use these two variants of mRMR algorithms in our experiments, analyze their pros and cons, and introduce another variant of mRMR which is an effective combination of above two variants.

3 $mRMR+$: The Proposed Ensemble $mRMR$ Algorithms

We carried out an exhaustive experimental study using the two variants of mRMR on benchmark datasets. Our observation is that the MI-based mRMR (i.e. $mRMR_{MI}$) does not perform well if the number of attributes in the dataset are less [8]. However, the second variant of mRMR can eliminate this disadvantage of $mRMR_{MI}$. But, we have found from our exhaustive experimentation that most of the time $mRMR_{GR}$ also performs poorly if the number of attributes is higher in the datasets.

Our proposal i.e., $mRMR+$ is an effective combination of the above two mRMR variants through a weight function. We performed an exhaustive experimentation to determine the proper weight function dynamically. We experimentally found that in most of the cases, if MI value between two variables is more than GR (gain ratio) than $mRMR_{MI}$ does not perform well. To eliminate this problem, we combine these two variants of mRMR (Eqs. 1 and 2) in such a way that the combination function performs consistently well for any number of variables. Our method performs well in almost all datasets than above discussed variants of mRMR. We perform a comparative analysis among all the three variants of mRMR using aforesaid three entropy measures. The proposed formulation of $mRMR+$ for the selection of the mth feature is as follows:

$$max_{x_j \in X - S_{m-1}}[I(x_j; C) - (\frac{l}{m-1} \sum_{x_i \in S_{m-1}} I(x_j; x_i) + \frac{1-l}{m-1} \sum_{x_i \in S_{m-1}} \frac{I(x_j; x_i)}{H(x_i)})].$$

(3)

Our method takes gene expression dataset as input and apply a discretization in preprocess step to eliminate noises from data. The value of weight function l is computed before finding out the top relevant feature based on MI value between feature and class. After that, using Eq. 3 we find out least redundant and maximum relevant feature from the remaining features and add one feature at a time to the selected feature list till requires K optimal features are selected.

Our proposed weight function take gene expression data as input and calculate $m = Max(MI(x_i, C))$ and $n = Max(GR(\frac{MI(x_i, C)}{H(C)}))$. If it is observed that $m \geq n$ then in our method weight (l) is calculated as $l = 1 - \frac{n}{m}$ else weight (l) is calculated as $l = \frac{m}{n}$. To select the mth feature, the computational complexity of this incremental search is $O(|S|.M)$ where M is the number of attributes in the dataset, which is similar to the MI-based mRMR algorithm [8].

4 Experimental Results

To evaluate the usefulness of the different variants of mRMR algorithm and different entropy measures, five UCI machine learning datasets of gene expression profiles having classes ≥ 2 were chosen and presented in Table 1. The accuracy of 10-fold cross validation of classification methods for all features are reported in Table 1 using three different classification methods viz., Naive Bayes (NB) [7], Random Forest (RF) [4] and IBK [2]. Generally, RF performed better than other classification methods due to its suitability for high dimensional data. To discretize the datasets, we use same discretization technique as used by the two mentioned variants of mRMR. Due to the space constrains we are unable to present detail results. Figure 1(a) presents classification accuracy of NB classifier on lung cancer dataset in forward direction. The average classification accuracies of Shanon, Renyi's and Tsallis entropy based MIs are 85.31%, 77.50%, 82.50%, respectively. Whereas, average classification accuracy of Shannon entropy based mRMR variants is 88.12% where our proposed method provides average 88.44% classification accuracy. Figure 1(b) reports results on colon tumor dataset based on NB classifier when we select top ranked features in forward direction. The average classification accuracies of Shanon, Renyi's and Tsallis entropy based MIs are 86.94%, 86.61%, 86.61%, respectively. Shannon entropy based mRMR dominates other entropy based mRMR results. We found average classification accuracy of 88.87% in case of Shannon Entropy based mRMR variants where our proposed method provides average 89.52% classification accuracy. Table 2 reports average classification accuracy for the top ten selected features using NB classifier of different entropy based $mRMR_{MI}$. We found that Shannon entropy based mRMR variants always dominate other entropy based mRMR variants. So, in remaining experimental results we only consider Shannon entropy based mRMR variants. Figure 1(c) reports classification accuracy of NB classifier on breast cancer dataset and the average classification accuracies of Shanon, Renyi's and Tsallis entropy based MIs for this dataset are same (i.e., 95.29%). In case of Shannon Entropy based mRMR variants, we observe that average classification accuracy is 95.81% where our method provides average 95.85% classification accuracy. Figure 1(d) presents classification accuracy of NB classifier on breast cancer dataset and average classification accuracy of Shanon, Renyi's and Tsallis entropy based MIs for this dataset are 90.37%, 90.467%, 89.90%, respectively. In case of Shannon entropy based mRMR, we found average classification accuracy is 90.97% among the three mRMR variants where our method provides average 91.03% classification accuracy. Figure 1(e), (f), (g) report results on NCI

Table 1. Dataset and accuracy (the 10-fold cross validation) classifiers

Datasets name	# instances	# features	# classes	NB	IBK	RF
Lung cancer	32	56	2	68.75	78.125	84.375
Colon tumar	62	2000	2	69.3548	69.3548	82.2581
Breast cancer	699	10	2	96.7096	95.1359	96.5665
Promoter	106	58	2	93.4579	79.4393	94.3925
NCI	61	9712	9	45	46.6667	43.3333

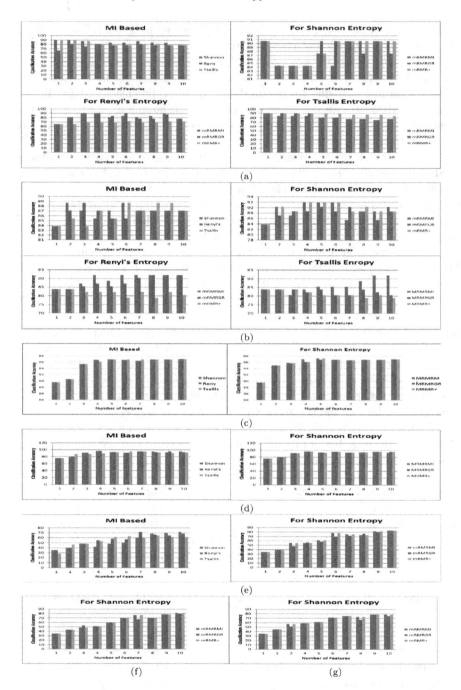

Fig. 1. (a) Accuracy of NB classifier on Lung Cancer. (b) Accuracy of NB classifier on Colon Tumor. (c) Accuracy of NB classifier on Breast Cancer. (d) Accuracy of NB classifier on Promoter. (e) Accuracy of NB classifier on NCI. (f) Accuracy of IBK classifier on NCI dataset. (g) Accuracy of RF classifier on NCI.

Table 2. Average classification accuracy of NB classifier in % for top 10 features

Dataset name	$mRMR_{MI}$ (USE)	$mRMR_{MI}$ (URE)	$mRMR_{MI}$ (UTE)	$mRMR+$(USE)
Lung cancer	87.81	82.81	81.62	88.43
Colon tumar	89.03	89.51	86.12	89.51
Breast cancer	95.85	95.22	95.15	95.85
Promoter	90.84	90.84	90.28	91.02
NCI	63.83	59.33	61.50	63.83

USE: Using Shannon Entropy, URE: Using Renyi's Entropy, UTE: Using Tsallis Entropy

dataset using NB, IBK and RF classifier respectively. The average classification accuracy of Shanon, Renyi's and Tsallis entropy based MIs for NCI dataset are 53.33%, 56.50%, 55.00%, respectively. $mRMR+$ shows higher average classification accuracies for NB, IBK and RF classifier.

Finally, we present the effectiveness of our method in Table 2. Table 2 shows that Shannon entropy based $mRMR_{MI}$ performs well in four out of five datasets than Renyi's entropy based $mRMR_{MI}$ and in all datasets than Tsallis entropy based $mRMR_{MI}$. On the other hand, our method $mRMR+$ based on Shannon entropy consistently performed well in all datasets in every aspect of our analysis.

5 Conclusions

Our method, referred to as $mRMR+$, performs significantly well in comparison to its competing mRMR and its variant algorithm over five benchmark datasets. Our study also includes an exhaustive empirical study on three well known entropy measures, while selecting relevant and non-redundant features to achieve best possible classification accuracy.

References

1. Abusamra, H.: A comparative study of feature selection and classification methods for gene expression data. Ph.d. thesis, King Abdullah University of Science and Technology (2013)
2. Aha, D.W., Kibler, D., Albert, M.K.: Instance-based learning algorithms. Mach. Learn. **6**(1), 37–66 (1991)
3. Bonev, B.: Feature selection based on information theory. Ph.d. thesis, University of Alicante, June 2010
4. Breiman, L.: Random forests. Mach. Learn. **45**(1), 5–32 (2001)
5. Ding, C., Peng, H.: Minimum redundancy feature selection from microarray gene expression data. J. Bioinform. Comput. Biol. **3**(2), 185–205 (2005)
6. Maszczyk, T., Duch, W.: Comparison of Shannon's, Renyi's and Tsallis entropy used in decision trees. In: Rutkowski, L., Tadeusiewicz, R., Zadeh, L.A., Zurada, J.M. (eds.) ICAISC 2008. LNCS, vol. 5097, pp. 643–651. Springer, Heidelberg (2008). doi:10.1007/978-3-540-69731-2_62
7. Murphy, K.P.: Naive Bayes classifiers. University of British Columbia (2006)

8. Peng, H., Long, F., Ding, C.: Feature selection based on mutual information criteria of max-dependency, max-relevance, and min-redundancy. IEEE Trans. Pattern Anal. Mach. Intell. **27**(8), 1226–1238 (2005)
9. Ponsa, D., López, A.: Feature selection based on a new formulation of the minimal-redundancy-maximal-relevance criterion. In: Martí, J., Benedí, J.M., Mendonça, A.M., Serrat, J. (eds.) IbPRIA 2007, Part I. LNCS, vol. 4477, pp. 47–54. Springer, Heidelberg (2007). doi:10.1007/978-3-540-72847-4_8
10. Shannon, C.E.: A mathematical theory of communication. ACM SIGMOBILE Mob. Comput. Commun. Rev. **5**(1), 3–55 (2001)

Topological Inquisition into the PPI Networks Associated with Human Diseases Through Graphlet Frequency Distribution

Debjani Bhattacharjee[1] ⓘ, Sk Md Mosaddek Hossain[2](✉) ⓘ, Raziya Sultana[2] ⓘ, and Sumanta Ray[2](✉) ⓘ

[1] Acharya Prafulla Chandra College, New Barrackpore, Kolkata 700131, West Bengal, India
[2] Department of Computer Science and Engineering, Aliah University, New Town, Kolkata 700156, West Bengal, India
mosaddek.hossain@gmail.com, sumanta.ray@aliah.ac.in

Abstract. In this article, we have proposed a new framework to compare topological structure of protein-protein interaction (PPI) networks constructed from disease associated proteins. Here, similarity of local topological structure between networks is discovered through the analysis of frequent sub-pattern occurred in them using a novel similarity measure based on graphlet frequency distribution. Graphlets are small connected non-isomorphic induced subgraphs in a network which provides detailed topological statistics of it. We have analyzed pairwise similarity of 22 disease associated PPI networks and compared topological and biological characteristics. It has been observed that the PPI networks associated with disease classes 'metabolic' and 'neurological' have the highest similarity scores. Higher similarity has also been observed for networks of disease classes 'bone' and 'skeletal'; 'endocrine' and 'multiple'; and 'gastrointestinal and respiratory'. Topological analysis of the networks also reveals that degree and betweenness centrality of proteins is strongly correlated for the network pairs with high similarity scores. We have also performed gene ontology and pathway based analysis of the proteins involved in the disease associated networks.

1 Introduction

Analyzing and understanding the intricate structure of Human Disease Network (HDN) is one of the most challenging fields in computational biology research [1]. Most human diseases are complex as they are not only associated with a single gene but a group of genes [2]. A comprehensive study on disease similarities provides new ideas about the cause of diseases and act as the key player in diagnosis and treatment of these complex diseases [3]. In [4], a disease phenotype network is constructed by performing a text mining approach to group common clinical terms. Goh et al. [1], first introduce the concept of human-disease network which provides a network of disorders and disease genes which are linked with known

© Springer International Publishing AG 2017
B.U. Shankar et al. (Eds.): PReMI 2017, LNCS 10597, pp. 431–437, 2017.
https://doi.org/10.1007/978-3-319-69900-4_55

gene disease association. Using this data Bandyopadhyay et al. [5] proposed an approach to find disease associated protein complexes in human PPI network. In [6], a novel framework is introduced to discover the similarity between two tissue or disease specific networks through multi-label graphlet counting. In [7], novel disease gene association is predicted by using RWR algorithm and functional similarity between protein complexes. A novel framework is proposed to compare biological networks using graphlet degree distribution in [8].

Here, we proposed a novel framework to compare the local structure of disease associated PPI networks using graphlet frequency. For this, first we have constructed 22 PPI networks from the 22 disease/disorder classes reported in [1]. Each PPI network consists of proteins associated with a particular disorder/disease class. We have found the occurrences of 3-, 4-, and 5-node graphlets in each of the networks and compare the occurrences to know the topological similarity between two networks. To count the occurrences of graphlets we have utilized a widely popular tool called G-trie Scanner [9]. In G-trie scanner a tree is constructed with set of sub graphs based on common structure or patterns in which nodes are connected. We have proposed a similarity measure which take the occurrences of graphlets and return a similarity score which signifies the similarity between the network structure. We have analyzed the similarity scores of each pair of networks, predict disease pairs having high similarity between the associated network structure. We have also analyzed topological properties of each network and conducted a gene ontology and pathway based analysis.

2   Method

This section describes the proposed framework to compare topological similarity between disease associated PPI Networks.

2.1   Dataset Preparation

We have downloaded the disease gene association database from Goh et al. [1]. The dataset is modeled by a bipartite network consisting of two disjoint sets of nodes: one set represents disease/disorder whereas the other sets corresponds to associated genes. The disorders/disease list and the responsible genes are collected from Online Mendelian Inheritance in Man (OMIM; [10]), a repository of human disease genes and phenotypes. In [1], all the disease/disorders are categorized into 22 broad classes. We have utilized this data and mapped all the disease associated proteins in human PPI network downloaded from Human Protein Reference Database (HPRD) [11]. Thus we get 22 PPI networks, each of which consists of proteins associated with a particular disease class. All the networks are highly sparsed and the density ranging from 6.9067e−06 to 1.0116e−04. We have utilized DAVID Functional Annotation Bioinformatics tool [12] for functional enrichment analysis.

2.2   Comparing the PPI Networks Using Graphlet Frequency

For each network, we have computed the occurrences of 29 graphlets using G-trie scanner [9]. Here, we have considered the graphlets of node size 3, 4 and 5 for comparison purpose as shown in Fig. 1-(a). We have computed similarities between two disease associated networks by comparing the occurrences of graphlets. Since the network size for each disease category is different, we normalized the occurrences by dividing each occurrence by its respective network size. Next, we arranged all the obtained graphlet frequencies in a 22×29 adjacency matrix, where we have 22 categories of diseases and frequency of 29 graphlets structure for each disease network. Let k be the number of graphlets (here, $k = 29$), $N_1(G_i)$ represents the occurrence of graphlet G_i in network N_1 and $N_2(G_i)$ represents the same for network N_2, then we have computed similarity score between two networks as:

$$sim(N_1, N_2) = \frac{\sum_{i=1}^{k} \frac{\min(N_1(G_i), N_2(G_i))}{\max(N_1(G_i), N_2(G_i))}}{k}. \tag{1}$$

The similarity scores sim is equal to 0 for two exactly same networks and maximum 1 for two networks having maximum disagreement in terms of graphlets occurrences. Network similarity is finally estimated by comparing the similarity score between the networks using the equation above. Thus we get a similarity matrix of dimension 22×22 which represents the pairwise similarity between two disease associated networks.

3   Results

3.1   Comparing Networks Using Similarity Score

We have compared the topological structure of the disease associated networks using the similarity score specified in Eq. (1). First, 22 PPI networks are formed from each disease associated protein set. Next, for each pair of networks, similarity score is identified. High score between two networks signifies that the 29 graphlets follows same patterns within the two networks. Similarly, low score represents that there is an inconsistency between the occurrences of the graphlets within two networks. We have computed the similarity scores between each pair of networks and depicted these in Fig. 1-(b) and (c) with a box plot. From this figure, it can be observed that the network associated with 'mascular' and 'cancer' disease classes have high and low similarity scores with other networks, respectively. This suggests that the topological structure of PPI network associated with cancer disease class is dissimilar to other disease associated networks. In Fig. 1-(b), we have shown a visualization of the similarity structure between networks using the similarity scores. For each network associated with a disease class, we have chosen top five networks having high similarity value and plotted these. Here, color and size of each circle is varying with disease class and similarity scores, respectively. From the Fig. 1-(b), it is observed that network structure of disease classes 'metabolic' and 'developmental' has high similarity value. Similarly the following network pairs have high similarity scores: 'bone-skeletal', 'endocrine-multiple', 'gastrointestinal-respiratory' and 'metabolic-neurological'.

3.2   Topological Analysis of Disorder Associated Proteins

To investigate whether the similarity scores are correlated with the topological features of the proteins involved within the networks, we find degree and betweenness centrality of each protein associated with the 22 disease associated networks. Here, degree of a protein signifies number of interactions it made within the whole human interactome. Betweenness centrality of a protein is also calculated by considering the whole human PPI network. We observe that degree and betweenness centrality is strongly correlated for the disease associated PPI networks with high similarity scores. Figure 1-(d–g), shows the scatter plots between degree and betweenness centrality of proteins associated with two disease classes. We have taken four pairs of disease associated networks with high similarity scores and plot degree vs. betweenness centrality of each nodes. It can be seen from the figure that disease pair 'metabolic-neurological' having the highest similarity score 0.67, has a strong correlation between degree and betweenness centrality of associated proteins($R^2 = 0.89$). The similar results can be observed for disease pairs: 'bone-skeletal' ($sim\_score = 0.583$, R^2 value 0.634), 'gastrointestinal-respiratory' ($sim\_score = 0.573$, R^2 value 0.741), and 'endocrine-multiple' ($sim\_score = 0.541$, R^2 value 0.89). To know whether there is any difference in degree or betweenness centrality of proteins associated with the similar disease pairs we plot these two metric for each protein which are associated with four similar disease pairs: 'bone-skeletal', 'endocrine-multiple', 'gastrointestinal-respiratory' and 'metabolic-neurological'. Figure 1-(h–i) show the box and jitter-plot of degree and betweenness centrality of those proteins. It can be observed from the figures that there is no distinguishable difference in degree and betweenness centrality of proteins associated with the similar disease pairs.

3.3   Functional Enrichment Analysis

Gene ontology based analysis is the most important and strong tool to identify the underlying biological meaning and functions of a set of proteins. Here, we have investigated the gene ontology terms and pathways which are associated with the proteins of the most similar disease associated network pairs: 'bone-skeletal', 'endocrine-multiple', 'gastrointestinal-respiratory' and 'metabolic-neurological'. In Table 1, the most significant GO-terms and KEGG pathway are listed. As can be seen from the table that similar disease pair like 'gastrointestinal-respiratory' is enriched in same biological process 'MAPK cascade'. Most of the disease associated proteins are enriched in cancer pathways.

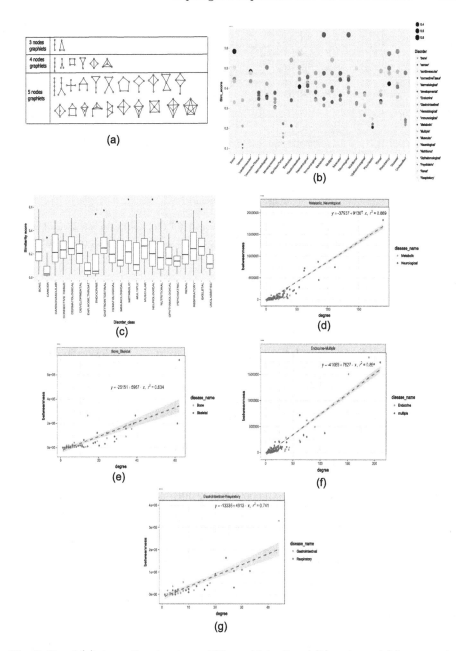

Fig. 1. Panel (a) shows the structure of 29 graphlets. Panel (b) and panel (c) represents dot plot and box plot of similarity scores of all the disorder classes with other classes, respectively. Color and size of the dots are varying with respect to the disorder class and similarity scores shown in the legends. Panel (d–g) represents scatter plots of correlations between degree and betweenness centrality of disease associated proteins for the disease pairs: 'bone-skeletal', 'endocrine-multiple', 'gastrointestinal-respiratory' and 'metabolic-neurological'. Panel-(h–i) represents Box and Jitter plots of the same for the four disease pairs.

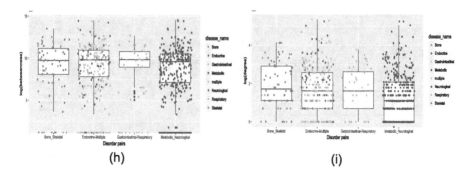

Fig. 1. (*continued*)

Table 1. Table shows the gene ontology terms and KEGG pathway associated with the proteins of most similar pair of disease classes: 'bone-skeletal', 'endocrine-multiple', 'gastrointestinal-respiratory' and 'metabolic-neurological'

Disease_class	GO-term_(GO-id)/p-value	KEGG_Pathway/ p-value
Bone	Extracellular matrix organization (GO:0030198)/1.60E−32	Pathways in cancer (6.50E−18)
Skeletal	Positive regulation of transcription from RNA polymerase II promoter (GO:0045944)/1.40E−36	Pathways in cancer (3.90E−32)
Endocrine	Positive regulation, of transcription from RNA polymerase II promoter (GO:0045944)/1.90E−69	Pathways in cancer (1.60E−32)
Metabolic	Positive regulation, of transcription from RNA polymerase II promoter (GO:0045944)/1.70E−27	Prostate cancer (1.80E−16)
Gastrointestinal	MAPK cascade (GO:0000165)/2.40E−14	ErbB, signaling pathway (1.80E−14)
Respiratory	MAPK cascade (GO:0000165)/8.40E−20	Proteoglycans in cancer (1.50E−20)
Neurological	Not found	Not found

4   Conclusions

In this paper, we have proposed a novel framework to compare the topological structure of disease associated PPI networks. It appears from the analysis that the PPI networks corresponding to the disease pair 'bone-skeletal', 'endocrine-multiple', 'gastrointestinal-respiratory' and 'metabolic-neurological' are similar with respect to their topological features. It is also observed from the topological analysis of the disease associated proteins that degree and betweenness centrality is strongly correlated for similar disease associated network pair. Functional enrichment analysis also reveals that the proteins associated with similar disease associated networks pair are enriched in same gene ontology terms. Further analysis and a proper investigation of biological properties of similar and dissimilar disease associated PPI networks may yield some new insights into the underlying structure of disease-gene association.

References

1. Goh, K., Cusick, M., Valle, D., Childs, B., Vidal, M., Barabasi, A.: The human disease network. PNAS **104**, 8685–8690 (2007)
2. Kanehisa, M., Goto, S., Furumichi, M., Tanabe, M., Hirakawa, M.: KEGG for representation and analysis of molecular networks involving diseases and drugs. Nucleic Acids Res. **38**(1), D355 (2010)
3. Yang, J., Wu, S.-J., Yang, S.-Y., Peng, J.-W., Wang, S.-N., Wang, F.-Y., Song, Y.-X., Qi, T., Li, Y.-X., Li, Y.-Y.: DNetDB: the human disease network database based on dysfunctional regulation mechanism. BMC Syst. Biol. **10**(1), 36 (2016)
4. Chen, Y., Zhang, X., Zhang, G.-Q., Xu, R.: Comparative analysis of a novel disease phenotype network based on clinical manifestations. J. Biomed. Inf. **53**, 113–120 (2015)
5. Bandyopadhyay, S., Ray, S., Mukhopadhyay, A., Maulik, U.: A multiobjective approach for identifying protein complexes and studying their association in multiple disorders. Algorithms Mol. Biol. **10**(24) (2014). doi:10.1186/s13015-015-0056-2
6. Sonmez, A.B., Can, T.: Comparison of tissue/disease specific integrated networks using directed graphlet signatures. In: Proceedings of the 7th ACM International Conference on Bioinformatics, Computational Biology, and Health Informatics, ser. BCB 2016, New York, NY, USA, pp. 533–534. ACM (2016)
7. Le, D.-H.: A novel method for identifying disease associated protein complexes based on functional similarity protein complex networks. Algorithms Mol. Biol. **10**(1), 14 (2015). https://doi.org/10.1186/s13015-015-0044-6
8. Pržulj, N.: Biological network comparison using graphlet degree distribution. Bioinformatics **23**(2), e177 (2007)
9. Ribeiro, P., Silva, F.: G-tries: a data structure for storing and finding subgraphs. Data Mining Knowl. Discov. **28**(2), 337–377 (2014)
10. Hamosh, A., Scott, A.F., Amberger, J.S., Bocchini, C.A., McKusick, V.A.: Online Mendelian Inheritance in Man (OMIM), a knowledgebase of human genes and genetic disorders. Nucleic Acids Res. **33**(Database issue), 514–517 (2005)
11. Prasad, T., Goel, R., Kandasamy, K.: Human protein reference database. Nucleic Acids Res. **37**, D767–D772 (2009)
12. Huang, D., Sherman, B., Tan, Q., Collins, J., Alvord, W., Roayaei, J., Stephens, R., Baseler, M., Lane, H., Lempicki, R.: The David gene functional classification tool: a novel biological module-centric algorithm to functionally analyze large gene lists. Genome Biol. **8**(9), R183 (2007)

Machine Learning Approach for Identification of miRNA-mRNA Regulatory Modules in Ovarian Cancer

Sushmita Paul$^{(\boxtimes)}$ and Shubham Talbar

Department of Bioscience and Bioengineering, Indian Institute
of Technology Jodhpur, Jodhpur, India
{sushmitapaul,talbar.1}@iitj.ac.in

Abstract. Ovarian cancer is a fatal gynecologic cancer. Altered expression of biomarkers leads to this deadly cancer. Therefore, understanding the underlying biological mechanisms may help in developing a robust diagnostic as well as a prognostic tool. It has been demonstrated in various studies the pathways associated with ovarian cancer have dysregulated miRNA as well as mRNA expression. Identification of miRNA-mRNA regulatory modules may help in understanding the mechanism of altered ovarian cancer pathways. In this regard, an existing robust mutual information based Maximum-Relevance Maximum-Significance algorithm has been used for identification of miRNA-mRNA regulatory modules in ovarian cancer. A set of miRNA-mRNA modules are identified first than their association with ovarian cancer are studied exhaustively. The effectiveness of the proposed approach is compared with existing methods. The proposed approach is found to generate more robust integrated networks of miRNA-mRNA in ovarian cancer.

Keywords: miRNAs · Genes · Mutual information · MRMS · Ovarian cancer

1 Introduction

Ovarian cancer has a distinctive biology and behavior at the clinical, cellular and molecular levels. It is the most prevalent and lethal female reproductive cancer, accounting for 5% of female cancer deaths. According to National Cancer Institute around 22,440 women will get diagnosed by this disease and 14,080 cases will die due to the disease by 2017 [14]. The five-year overall survival rate of this disease is 46.5% when untreated. Whereas, early detection of the disease with proper treatment can increase the overall survival rate of patients, that is, 92.5%. Therefore, it is important to understand the role of biomarkers like miRNAs and mRNAs in various pathways of ovarian cancer.

MicroRNA (miRNAs) are small non-coding RNAs of size $\sim$ 22-nucleotides. miRNA suppresses the expression of mRNA by binding to the $3'$ untranslated

© Springer International Publishing AG 2017
B.U. Shankar et al. (Eds.): PReMI 2017, LNCS 10597, pp. 438–447, 2017.
https://doi.org/10.1007/978-3-319-69900-4_56

region of the mRNA. They are found in many plants and animals. Extensive studies have been conducted to understand their role in different biological processes and diseases [1,6,10]. Studies related to the role of miRNAs and their targets in ovarian cancer is less studied. Only nine papers related to this topic are available in Pubmed. Therefore, there is dire need to conduct studies related to this topic. To come up with solutions for developing a diagnostic and prognostic tool against ovarian cancer. Existing methods usually use sequence data for identification of miRNAs and their targets. However, there exists a higher possibility of false positive rates. Therefore, few works have been done that used miRNA and mRNA expression data. However, few of them select miRNAs and mRNAs separately and then by using the correlation between the selected biomarkers reconstruction of regulatory modules take place. Other methods use regression methods they require more computational time. Hence, there is a need to develop a scalable approach for identification of miRNA-mRNA regulatory modules in ovarian cancer.

This paper presents a framework for selection of important miRNA-mRNA regulatory modules in ovarian cancer. For selection of regulatory modules, mutual information based maximum-relevance maximum-significance (MIM-RMS) [13] has been used. Here, a set of genes that are regulated by a particular miRNA is identified with MIMRMS. In the current study, the expression values of miRNAs are discretized and used them as class labels. Whereas, the expression values of genes are considered features. Mutual information between two variables here miRNA and mRNA suggests about the interdependency between them. The MIMRMS algorithm selects a set of genes for a particular miRNA by maximizing both relevance and significance of the gene. In this manner, a set of gene is selected that is both relevant and significant with respect to that miRNA. The miRNA information is used as a class label and mRNAs are later selected with the help of MIMRMS algorithm. For a particular miRNA, a set of 50 mRNAs is selected using the MIMRMS algorithm. The mRNAs of each module are evaluated further with the help of K-nearest neighbor classifier in order to reduce false positives. The effective mRNAs obtained represent a regulatory module, that is, a miRNA regulating a set of mRNAs. Next, to avoid irrelevant modules statistical significance of each module is computed using STRING database. Pathway enrichment analysis, and disease ontology enrichment analysis revealed the importance of selected modules with respect to ovarian cancer. The modules generated by MIMRMS are compared with the modules generated by mRMR algorithm as well as MatrixEQTL. From the results, it is revealed that the MIMRMS based approach generates more significant miRNA-mRNA regulatory modules for Ovarian cancer data.

2   Construction of miRNA-mRNA Modules

Automatic detection of miRNA-mRNA modules is very important to understand the underlying mechanism of the disease. This section describes the method that has been used for identification of miRNA-mRNA modules in ovarian cancer.

In the present work, the MIMRMS [12] has been used to identify miRNA-mRNA regulatory modules.

Provided the matrices of miRNA expression and gene expression a decision matrix is created first. A decision matrix contains a class label attribute and conditional attributes. Here, the expression values of each miRNA are discretized and later used it as class label. All the expression values of genes are considered as features or conditional attributes. The rows represent samples. Therefore, total 175 decision matrices are created each having dimension of 415 rows and 13,946 columns and one class label. For each miRNA, a set of mRNAs is selected by implementing MIMRMS algorithm. Next, the K-nearest neighbor algorithm is applied on the genes for each module for selecting an effective set of genes that generates high classification accuracy. Biologically it can be interpreted as those genes that are regulated by a particular miRNA. The aim of this study was to select a set of relevant as well as significant genes that can map on miRNA. Thus, generating a regulatory network that may potentially have some role in the onset and progression of ovarian cancer. Next, the existing MIMRMS algorithm and K-nearest neighbor algorithms are described.

2.1   The Gene Selection Algorithm

This section describes about the existing MIMRMS algorithm [12] that has been used in the current study. The MIMRMS generates a set of mRNAs by maximizing both relevance as well as significance. The MIMRMS algorithm is described next.

The MIMRMS algorithm selects a set of mRNAs Θ from a given microarray data set $\mathbb{C} = \{\mathscr{G}_1, \cdots, \mathscr{G}_i, \cdots, \mathscr{G}_j, \cdots, \mathscr{G}_m\}$ of m mRNAs. Relevance of a mRNA quantifies the correlation of the mRNA with respect to class label or miRNA. Also, it infers about the dependency of the class label $\mathbb{M}$ on an attribute. Here, the relevance of the mRNA $\mathscr{G}_i$ with respect to class labels /miRNAs $\mathbb{M}$ is defined as $\hat{f}(\mathscr{G}_i, \mathbb{M})$. Whereas, $\tilde{f}(\mathscr{G}_i, \mathscr{G}_j)$ is defined as the significance of the mRNA $\mathscr{G}_j$ with respect to the mRNA $\mathscr{G}_i$. In this study for calculation of both relevance and significance mutual information [11] is used [12].

The relevance $\hat{f}(\mathscr{G}_i, \mathbb{M})$ of a mRNA $\mathscr{G}_i$ with respect to the class label or miRNA $\mathbb{M}$ using mutual information can be computed as follows:

$$\hat{f}(\mathscr{G}_i, \mathbb{M}) = I(\mathscr{G}_i, \mathbb{M}), \tag{1}$$

where $I(\mathscr{G}_i, \mathbb{M})$ represents the mutual information between attribute $\mathscr{G}_i$ and miRNA or class label $\mathbb{M}$ that is given by

$$I(\mathscr{G}_i, \mathbb{M}) = H(\mathscr{G}_i) - H(\mathscr{G}_i \mid \mathbb{M}). \tag{2}$$

Here, $H(\mathscr{G}_i)$ and $H(v_i \mid \mathbb{M})$ represent the entropy of mRNA $\mathscr{G}_i$ and the conditional entropy of $\mathscr{G}_i$ given class label $\mathbb{M}$, respectively. The entropy is a measure of uncertainty.

Provided a set of attributes individual contribution of an attribute for calculation of dependency on decision attribute can be computed with the help of significance criterion. Hence, significance value of an attribute signifies its importance. Removal of an attribute from the set of condition attributes leads to change in dependency value. This change is the significance of the attribute. Its value ranges from 0 to 1. If its value is 0 (1), then the attribute is dispensable (indispensable).

Definition 1. Given $\mathbb{C}, \mathbb{M}$ and an attribute $\mathscr{G} \in \mathbb{C}$, the significance of the attribute $\mathscr{G}$ is defined as [12]:

$$\sigma_{\mathbb{C}}(\mathbb{M}, \mathscr{G}) = \hat{f}(\mathbb{C}, \mathbb{M}) - \hat{f}(\mathbb{C} - \{\mathscr{G}\}, \mathbb{M}) \tag{3}$$

The total relevance of all selected mRNAs and total significance among the selected mRNAs are, therefore, given by

$$\mathscr{J}_{\text{relev}} = \sum_{\mathscr{G}_i \in \Theta} \hat{f}(\mathscr{G}_i, \mathbb{M}) \qquad \mathscr{J}_{\text{signf}} = \sum_{\mathscr{G}_i \neq \mathscr{G}_j \in \Theta} \tilde{f}(\mathscr{G}_i, \mathscr{G}_j). \tag{4}$$

For identification of miRNA-mRNA module, first of all, a decision table is created for each miRNA. The decision table contains gene or mRNA as conditional attributes and miRNA as class label. The rows are samples. The MIMRMS algorithm is implemented on each decision table for identification of genes or mRNAs that are associated with that particular miRNA. The MIMRMS process starts by initializing $\mathbb{C} \leftarrow \{\mathscr{G}_1, \cdots, \mathscr{G}_i, \cdots, \mathscr{G}_j, \cdots, \mathscr{G}_m\}, \Theta \leftarrow \emptyset$. Next, it calculates relevance $\hat{f}(\mathscr{G}_i, \mathbb{M})$ of each mRNA $\mathscr{G}_i \in \mathbb{C}$ with respect to class label or miRNA. Most relevant mRNA $\mathscr{G}_i$ is selected having highest relevance value $\hat{f}(\mathscr{G}_i, \mathbb{M})$. In effect, $\mathscr{G}_i \in \Theta$ and $\mathbb{C} = \mathbb{C} \backslash \mathscr{G}_i$. The algorithm iteratively computes significance of each mRNA with respect to already selected mRNAs and selects the mRNA if it has maximum value for optimization function. As a result of that, $\mathscr{G}_j \in \Theta$ and $\mathbb{C} = \mathbb{C} \backslash \mathscr{G}_j$. This step occurs till the desired number of mRNAs are selected for corresponding miRNA or class label. The optimization function of the MIMRMS algorithm is

$$\hat{f}(\mathscr{G}_j, \mathbb{M}) + \frac{1}{|\Theta|} \sum_{\mathscr{G}_i \in \Theta} \tilde{f}(\mathscr{G}_i, \mathscr{G}_j). \tag{5}$$

Mutual information is used to compute both relevance and significance of a mRNA. The relevance and significance of a mRNA are calculated using (1) and (3), respectively.

The expression values of both miRNA and mRNA in a microarray data are continuous in nature. Continuous expression values of a miRNA and mRNA need to be discretized for calculation of relevance of a mRNA with respect to miRNA or clinical outcome using mutual information. The marginal probabilities and the joint probability are computed using discretized expression values of a mRNA and miRNA. These probabilities are later used to compute the mRNA-class/miRNA relevance. Therefore, discretization of continuous valued miRNAs and mRNAs is a very vital step in the current study. In the current study discretization method mentioned in [4] is used. This method discretizes expression values of a miRNA and mRNA using mean μ and standard deviation σ that are computed over n expression values of that particular miRNAs or mRNA. Next, the values bigger than $(\mu + \sigma)$ is represented as 1, the values between $(\mu - \sigma)$ and $(\mu + \sigma)$ as 0 and the values smaller than $(\mu - \sigma)$ as -1. The over-expression, baseline, and under-expression of the miRNAs or mRNAs correspond to these three values.

2.2 K-Nearest Neighbor Rule

The K-nearest neighbor (K-NN) rule [5] is a classifier. It is used to evaluate the efficiency of a set of reduced mRNAs. It classifies an unknown sample by considering its nearest or closest training samples in the feature space. A sample is classified by a majority vote of its K-neighbors, with the sample being assigned to the class most common amongst its K-nearest neighbors. The value of K, chosen for the K-NN, is the square root of the number of samples in training set. In the current study, the mRNAs of each miRNA-mRNA module obtained using the MIMRMS algorithm are further processed. For each miRNA-mRNA module, K-NN is implemented for selecting best mRNAs for a particular miRNA. The mRNAs in a particular module generating highest accuracy values are considered further. Biologically it can be inferred that the mRNAs finally selected for a particular module are regulated by the miRNA of that module.

3 Experimental Results

In the current study, the existing MIMRMS algorithm is used to identify regulatory modules. Fifty top-ranked mRNAs are selected using the MIMRMS algorithm for further analysis. For MatrixEQTL top 50 mRNAs of each module is directly used for further analysis as the ranking of the mRNAs was not sured. In a module filtering of mRNAs is further carried out to reduce false positives. Therefore, prediction accuracy of K-nearest neighbor (K-NN) rule along with leave-one-out cross-validation (LOOCV) is computed for the mRNAs of each module. Finally, the obtained modules are evaluated using STRING database [17], pathway enrichment analysis, and disease ontology. Both miRNA and mRNA expression data for serous ovarian cancer were downloaded through the Cancer Genomics Browser of UC Santa Cruz [3]. Both data contain exactly same samples, that is, 415. Whereas, the number of miRNAs and genes are 175, and 13,946, respectively. The effectiveness of the proposed approach is compared with the methods mentioned in Huang and Cai [7] and Matrix eQTL [15]. Huang and Cai used minimum redundancy maximum relevance criteria [4] for selection of modules.

3.1 Selection of Significant Regulatory Modules

Total 175 modules are generated by implementing the MIMRMS and K-NN rule. The leave one out accuracy of each module varied from 0% to 48.43%.

Next, STRING database [17] is used to generate connections between the genes of each module to check whether the genes of obtained modules are involved in same biological function or not. The database uses information from experimentally validated connections, prediction, text mining, and so forth for creating a connection between two genes or proteins. STRING database stores the information of protein-protein interaction. It also provides the statistical significance for a particular protein-protein interaction network (PPIN). The statistical significance of networks is quantified using P-value.

Table 1 represents the total number of significant regulatory networks (P-value < 0.05) generated by MatrixEQTL, mRMR, and MIMRMS algorithm. From the table, it is seen that MatrixEQTL, mRMR, and MIMRMS algorithms generate significant PPI network. However, only MatrixEQTL and MIMRMS algorithms generate Network with very low P-value $= 0$. The MatrixEQTL generates only one network with P-value $= 0$ whereas, the MIMRMS generates five highly significant P-value $= 0$ networks. The details of all six (one MatrixEQTL and five MIMRMS) modules are presented in Table 2. The images of few networks are provided in Fig. 1. From the figure, it is seen that the networks generated are highly inter-connected and compact. They also suggests that the MIMRMS based approach selects significant regulatory modules.

Table 1. Number of significant modules generated By MatrixEQTL, mRMR, and MIMRMS

Algorithms/Methods	Number of significant modules
MatrixEQTL	56
mRMR	8
MIMRMS	42

Table 2. Description of most significant modules

miRNA	No. of genes in module	Algorithm
hsa-mir-17	775	MatrixEQTL
hsa-mir-30e	40	MIMRMS
hsa-mir-100	50	MIMRMS
hsa-mir-181c	47	MIMRMS
hsa-let-7c	35	MIMRMS
hsa-mir-23a	36	MIMRMS

3.2   Pathway Enrichment Analysis

For the biological interpretation of highly significant modules P-value $= 0$, the Cytoscape [16] plug-in ClueGO [2] has been used to perform pathway enrichment

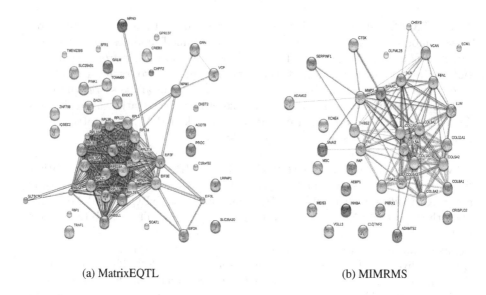

(a) MatrixEQTL   (b) MIMRMS

Fig. 1. PPINs generated by STRING for MatrixEQTL and MIMRMS algorithms

analysis. Genes of significant modules are used for pathway enrichment analysis. For the current analysis, the threshold for P-Value was set to 0.05 and the minimum number of genes associated with a term was set to 3. WikiPathways database [9] has been used as background database for the current study.

Figure 2 represents pathway terms obtained by MatrixEQTL and MIM-RMS. From the figure, it is seen that the module selected by MatrixEQTL contains genes that are mainly associated with the process of protein synthesis. It indicates that they are housekeeping genes. On the other hand, modules generated by MIMRMS algorithm generates modules whose members are more associated with pathways in cancer. However, two modules from MIMRMS algorithm selected housekeeping genes. The terms generated for MIMRMS modules like *miRNA targets in ECM and membrane receptors*, *Senescence and Autophagy in Cancer*, and so forth are cancer associated pathways.

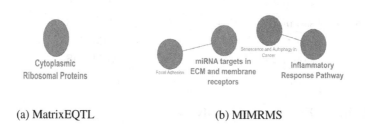

(a) MatrixEQTL   (b) MIMRMS

Fig. 2. Pathway enrichment analysis

3.3   Disease Ontology Enrichment Analysis

Further analysis of the most significant networks (one MatrixEQTL and 5 MIM-RMS) was done using disease ontology (DO) enrichment analysis. The R package DOSE [18] was used. This package identifies a statistically significant disease ontology term that is associated with a set of genes. Here, DO id's with P-value $<$ 0.05 are selected. Table 3 represents the DO terms and their respective P-values. From the table, it is seen that the MatrixEQTL do not generate any relevant DO term with respect to Ovarian cancer. Whereas, one of the modules of the MIMRMS generates DO term that is highly relevant to Ovarian cancer (bold text). The result indicates that the MIMRMS algorithm efficiently selects regulatory networks compare to other existing methods. According to miR2Disease [8] all the miRNAs mentioned (both MatrixEQTL and MIMRMS) in Table 2 are associated with ovarian cancer.

Table 3. Comparative analysis of association of modules with diseases

Algorithm	ID	Description	p.adjust	qvalue
MatrixEQTL	DOID:1342	Congenital hypoplastic anemia	2.05E-03	1.89E-03
MIMRMS-23	DOID:9588	Encephalitis	2.04E-05	1.65E-05
	DOID:1883	Hepatitis C	5.07E-05	4.10E-05
	DOID:8469	Influenza	2.50E-04	2.02E-04
	DOID:2237	Hepatitis	1.47E-03	1.19E-03
MIMRMS-95	DOID:1342	Congenital hypoplastic anemia	1.37E-02	1.33E-02
MIMRMS-142	DOID:1342	Congenital hypoplastic anemia	1.69E-02	1.65E-02
MIMRMS-159	DOID:5683	Hereditary breast ovarian cancer	2.94E-02	2.77E-02
MIMRMS-168	DOID:0060095	Uterine benign neoplasm	4.69E-04	3.36E-04
	DOID:13223	Uterine fibroid	4.69E-04	3.36E-04
	DOID:0060086	Female reproductive organ benign neoplasm	5.01E-04	3.59E-04
	DOID:0050622	Reproductive organ benign neoplasm	5.37E-04	3.85E-04
	DOID:0060085	Organ system benign neoplasm	5.62E-03	4.04E-03
	DOID:3713	**Ovary adenocarcinoma**	4.37E-02	3.14E-02
	DOID:1790	Malignant mesothelioma	4.79E-02	3.44E-02

4   Conclusions

The paper presents an integrative approach for automatic detection of regulatory network by applying the existing MIMRMS algorithm. The importance of MIMRMS algorithm over other existing algorithms is demonstrated in terms of identification of miRNA-mRNA regulatory modules. The MIMRMS algorithm generates more significant regulatory modules that are highly related to ovarian cancer. The obtained regulatory modules may be helpful for understanding the underlying etiology of the disease.

Acknowledgement. This work is partially supported by the seed grant program of the Indian Institute of Technology Jodhpur, India (grant no. I/SEED/SPU/20160010).

References

1. Alvarez-Garcia, I., Miska, E.A.: MicroRNA Functions in Animal Development and Human Disease. Development **132**(21), 4653–4662 (2005)
2. Bindea, G., Mlecnik, B., Hackl, H., Charoentong, P., Tosolini, M., Kirilovsky, A., Fridman, W.-H., Pags, F., Trajanoski, Z., Galon, J.: ClueGO: a cytoscape plug-in to decipher functionally grouped gene ontology and pathway annotation networks. Bioinformatics **25**(8), 1091 (2009)
3. Cline, M.S., Craft, B., Swatloski, T., Goldman, M., Ma, S., Haussler, D., Zhu, J.: Exploring TCGA pan-cancer data at the UCSC cancer genomics browser. Sci. Rep. **3**(2652), 1–6 (2013)
4. Ding, C., Peng, H.: Minimum redundancy feature selection from microarray gene expression data. J. Bioinform. Comput. Biol. **3**(02), 185–205 (2005)
5. Duda, R.O., Hart, P.E.: Pattern Classification and Scene Analysis. Wiley (1973)
6. He, L., Hannon, G.J.: MicroRNAs: small RNAs with a big role in gene regulation. Nat. Rev. Genet. **5**, 522–531 (2004)
7. Huang, T., Cai, Y.-D.: An information-theoretic machine learning approach to expression QTL analysis. PLoS ONE **8**(6), 1–9 (2013)
8. Jiang, Q., Wang, Y., Hao, Y., Juan, L., Teng, M., Zhang, X., Li, M., Wang, G., Liu, Y.: miR2Disease: a manually curated database for microrna deregulation in human disease. Nucleic Acids Res. **37**, D98 (2009)
9. Kutmon, M., Riutta, A., Nunes, N., Hanspers, K., Willighagen, E.L., Bohler, A., Mlius, J., Waagmeester, A., Sinha, S.R., Miller, R., Coort, S.L., Cirillo, E., Smeets, B., Evelo, C.T., Pico, A.R.: WikiPathways: capturing the full diversity of pathway knowledge. Nucleic Acids Res. **44**(D1), D488 (2016)
10. Li, J., Liu, Y., Wang, C., Deng, T., Liang, H., Wang, Y., Huang, D., Fan, Q., Wang, X., Ning, T., Liu, R., Zhang, C.-Y., Zen, K., Chen, X., Ba, Y.: Serum miRNA Expression profile as a prognostic biomarker of stage II/III colorectal adenocarcinoma. Sci. Rep. **5**(12921) (2015), doi:10.1038/srep12921
11. Maji, P.: Mutual information-based supervised attribute clustering for microarray sample classification. IEEE Trans. Knowl. Data Eng. **24**(1), 127–140 (2012)
12. Maji, P., Paul, S.: Rough set based maximum relevance-maximum significance criterion and gene selection from microarray data. Int. J. Approximate Reasoning **52**(3), 408–426 (2011)
13. Paul, S., Maji, P.: Gene expression and protein-protein interaction data for identification of colon cancer related genes using f-information measures. Nat. Comput. **15**(3), 449–463 (2016)
14. Quitadamo, A., Tian, L., Hall, B., Shi, X.: An integrated network of MicroRNA and gene expression in ovarian cancer. BMC Bioinform. **16**(5), S5 (2015)
15. Shabalin, A.A.: Matrix eQTL: ultra fast eQTL analysis via large matrix operations. Bioinformatics **28**(10), 1353 (2012)

16. Shannon, P., Markiel, A., Ozier, O., Baliga, N.S., Wang, J.T., Ramage, D., Amin, N., Schwikowski, B., Ideker, T.: Cytoscape: a software environment for integrated models of biomolecular interaction networks. Genome Res. **13**(11), 2498–2504 (2003)
17. Szklarczyk, D., Franceschini, A., Wyder, S., Forslund, K., Heller, D., Huerta-Cepas, J., Simonovic, M., Roth, A., Santos, A., Tsafou, K.P., Kuhn, M., Bork, P., Jensen, L.J., von Mering, C.: STRING v10: proteinprotein interaction networks, integrated over the tree of life. Nucleic Acids Res. **43**(D1), D447 (2015)
18. Yu, G., Wang, L.-G., Yan, G.-R., He, Q.-Y.: DOSE: an R/Bioconductor package for disease ontology semantic and enrichment analysis. Bioinformatics **31**(4), 608 (2015)

Data Mining and Big Data Analytics

K-Means Algorithm to Identify k_1-Most Demanding Products

Ritesh Kumar[1] (ID), Partha Sarathi Bishnu[2]([✉]) (ID), and Vandana Bhattacherjee[2] (ID)

[1] Deptartment of CSE, Cambridge Institute of Technology, Ranchi, India
bhritesh@gmail.com
[2] Deptartment of Computer Science & Engineering, Birla Institute of Technology,
Ranchi 834001, Jharkhand, India
psbishnu@gmail.com, bhattacherjeev@yahoo.co.in

Abstract. This paper attempts to identify k_1-most demanding products using K-Means clustering algorithm. A comparison of proposed algorithm with existing algorithms has been made. The experiments performed on synthetic and real datasets showed the effectiveness of our proposed algorithm.

Keywords: Data mining · Clustering · Decision support

1 Introduction

In real world the resources are generally inadequate and decisions regarding their allotment must be made judiciously based on the behavior of customers and producers. To predict the performance of the new (candidate) products (CP) among the customers (C) where few existing products (EP) are already present in the market [1,2], the company is trying to comprehend the profitability of the CP so that the company can set the line of advertising and marketing strategies.

The satisfaction bit strings [1] (SBS) of the existing and candidate products table (Table 1) which may be constructed using BMI index structure [1], displays the customer product relationship. The ep_1 to ep_3 are the existing products (EP), cp_1 to cp_9 are the candidate products (CP) and c_1 to c_8 are the customers (C). The entry value 1 or 0 implies that the customer is satisfied or not satisfied by the product respectively. For example, the content $\{1, 0, 1, 1, 1, 0, 1, 1\}$ of the existing product ep_1 indicates that the customers c_1, c_3, c_4, c_5, c_7, and c_8 are satisfied by the ep_1 and customers c_2 and c_6 are not. The probability that customer c_1 will select candidate product cp_4 is 1/9 (column 2, Table 1). It is assumed that customers select any product with equal probability [5]. The expected number of customers [1] for cp_4 is estimated by adding the probabilities for each customer $c_i \in C$ selecting [1] cp_4 as follows: $(1/9 + 1/7 + 0/7 + 0/6 + 0/8 + 0/6 + 0/6 + 1/8) = 0.3789$. Consider a set of existing products (EP) with multiple attributes $\{a_1, a_2, ..., a_d\}$. The customers (C) have demanded for few existing products (EP) and the company is launching a set of new products (CP). Now to take various managerial decisions the goal is to identify k_1-most

© Springer International Publishing AG 2017
B.U. Shankar et al. (Eds.): PReMI 2017, LNCS 10597, pp. 451–457, 2017.
https://doi.org/10.1007/978-3-319-69900-4_57

Table 1. The SBS of the existing and candidate products

$EP \cup CP$	c_1	c_2	c_3	c_4	c_5	c_6	c_7	c_8
ep_1	1	0	1	1	1	0	1	1
ep_2	1	1	1	1	0	1	0	0
ep_3	0	1	1	1	1	0	1	1
cp_1	0	0	0	0	1	1	0	0
cp_2	1	1	1	1	1	1	1	0
cp_3	1	1	1	1	1	1	1	1
cp_4	1	1	0	0	0	0	0	1
cp_5	1	0	0	0	0	1	1	1
cp_6	1	1	1	1	1	0	0	1
cp_7	1	1	1	0	1	1	1	1
cp_8	1	0	0	0	0	0	0	1
cp_9	0	0	0	0	1	0	0	0

demanding products (kCP). For example, the expected number of total customers [1] for cp_2, cp_3 and cp_7 are 1.0218, 1.1468, and 0.9802 respectively. The
expected number of total customers [1] for $\{cp_2, cp_3, cp_7\}$ is $(1.0218 + 1.1468 +
0.9802 =)$ 3.1488. The value 3.1488 is the highest value among all the combina-
tions consisting of 3 (k_1) candidates products. The k_1-most (here, k_1 is set to 3)
demanding products are $\{cp_2, cp_3, cp_7\}$.

The main objective of this paper is to identify the k_1-most demanding products
using K-Means [9] clustering algorithm. First, we apply K-Means algorithm to
identify the group, $CGkCP$, where the k_1-most candidate products may reside
in. Then we identify k_1-most demanding products from the $CGkCP$. To compare
the performance of our K-Means based k_1-most demanding products (CMDP)
algorithm ($\mathbf{C}$(clustering)$\mathbf{M}$(most)$\mathbf{D}$(demanding)$\mathbf{P}$(products)) experiments have
been conducted in which three other techniques [1] have been executed with
the help of synthetic and real datasets and results are compared. The CMDP
algorithm performs fairly well on all the datasets.

The outline of this paper is as follows: in Sect. 2 we present the proposed CMDP
algorithm. Section 3 presents the experiments. Finally in Sect. 4 we conclude this
paper.

2   Proposed CMDP Algorithm

2.1   Formal Problem Statement of k_1-most Demanding Products

First we discuss the simple K-most demanding products problem for the sake of
completeness [1,3,4,6–8]. Assume a set of customers $C = \{c_1, c_2, ..., c_{nc}\}$, where
$nc(\geq 1)$ is the number of customers, demanding some particular typical type of
products. $EP = \{ep_1, ep_2, ..., ep_{nep}\}$ are the existing products, which are already

popular among the set of customers C. A company is attempting to launch new products (candidate products) $CP = \{cp_1, cp_2, ..., cp_{ncp}\}$. Each product p_i, $p_i \in CP \cup EP$, consists of d number of features which are used to describe the quality of the products. Further we may assume that each customer $c_i \in C$ will definitely purchase one of the products (from CP or EP or from both) as per his/her requirements. Now our aim is to identify k_1, $1 \leq k_1 \leq ncp$, products from CP, such that the expected number of the total customer [1] for the k_1, $1 \leq k_1 \leq ncp$, products is maximized [1]. Let $kCP = \{kcp_1, kcp_2, ..., kcp_{k_1}\}$, denote a set of k_1, $1 \leq k_1 \leq ncp$, products which are selected from CP. Moreover, $N(EP, c_i)$ and $N(kCP, c_i)$ represent the total number of products in EP and kCP satisfying customer $c_i \in C, 1 \leq i \leq nc$ respectively. The probability $P(cp_i, c_j)$ of a customer $c_j, 1 \leq j \leq nc$, purchasing a product $cp_i \in kCP, 1 \leq i \leq k_1$ is as follows [1]:

$$P(cp_i, c_j) = \begin{cases} \frac{1}{N(EP, c_j) + N(kCP, c_j)} & : \quad \text{if } cp_i \text{ satisfies } c_j \\ 0 & : \quad \text{otherwise} \end{cases} \tag{1}$$

For a product $cp_i \in kCP, 1 \leq i \leq k_1$, the expected number of customers C, is $E(cp_i, C) = \sum_{j=1}^{nc} P(cp_i, c_j)$ (2) and the expected number of the total customers in C for the set kCP is $E(kCP, C) = \sum_{i=1}^{k_1} E(cp_i, C) = \sum_{i=1}^{k_1} \sum_{j=1}^{nc} P(cp_i, c_j)$ (3). The k_1-most demanding products are the k_1, $1 \leq k_1 \leq ncp$, from CP with the maximum $E(kCP, C)$. $E(\{cp_2, cp_3, cp_7\}, C)$ acquires the largest value ($2.3333 + 2.4167 + 2.6667 = 7.4167$), hence the set $\{cp_2, cp_3, cp_7\}$ is the best result of the 3-MDP discovering.

2.2 The CMDP Algorithm

For handling k_1-most demanding product problem, Lin et. al [1] suggested ($K - MDP$) four algorithms such as single product based greedy algorithm (SPG) [1], incremental based greedy algorithm (IG) [1], apriori based algorithm (APR) [1], and upper bound pruning algorithm (UBP) [1]. Now our goal is to increase the scalability of the existing SPG, IG, APR and UBP [1] algorithms. Before applying SPG, IG, APR and UBP algorithms, we apply K-Means algorithm to pre-process the input data and then identify a cluster group ($CGkCP$), which must contain the set kCP. The K-Means algorithm [9,10] is one of the oldest and the most popular clustering techniques whose applications span from data mining, image processing to recent machine intelligence and data analysis. The K-Means algorithm is a partition based clustering method. It is simple, robust and efficient clustering method in processing large data set.

Let $CG = cg_1, cg_2, ..., cg_K$ denote a set of cluster groups (The K-Means algorithm generates CG). For each cluster group calculate Ψ_{cg_i}, $1 \leq i \leq K$ and $\Psi_{cg_i} = \sum_{j=1}^{n_i} \sum_{l=1}^{nc} P(cp_j, c_l) = \sum_{l=1}^{nc} \sum_{j=1}^{n_i} P(cp_j, c_l) = \sum_{l=1}^{nc} \xi(cp_{cg_i}, c_l) = \sum_{l=1}^{nc} \frac{N(cp_{cg_i}, c_l)}{N(EP, c_l) + N(cp_{cg_i}, c_l)}$, (4) where $N(cp_{cg_i}, c_l) = N(kCP_i, c_l)/n_i, +N(cp_{cg_i} - kCP_i, c_l)/n_i$. where n_i is the number of data present in cg_i. Let cg_1 and cg_2 are two cluster groups which consist of $n_1 \geq k_1$ and $n_2 \geq k_1$ numbers of data respectively. We can prove that if the number of candidate products in $kCP_1 \subseteq cg_1$ satisfies customers C is more than or equal to the number of candidate products in $kCP_2 \subseteq cg_2$ satisfies C, then $\Psi_{cg_1} \geq \Psi_{cg_2}$.

Lemma 1. *Let cg_1 and cg_2 are two clusters and the sets $kCP_1 \subseteq cg_1$ and $kCP_2 \subseteq cg_2$ are two k_1-candidate products, where $kCP_1 \neq kCP_2$ and $kCP_1 \cap kCP_2 = \phi$. If $N(kCP_1, c_l)/n_1 \geq N(kCP_2, c_l)/n_2$ and $N(cp_{cg_1} - kCP_1, c_l)/n_1 \geq N(cp_{cg_2} - kCP_2, c_l)/n_2$, then $\xi(cp_{cg_1}, c_l) \geq \xi(cp_{cg_2}, c_l))$.*

Proof. Let $w = N(kCP_1, c_l)/n_1$, $x = N(cp_{cg_1} - kCP_1, c_l)/n_1$, $y = N(kCP_2, c_l)/n_2$, and $z = N(cp_{cg_2} - kCP_2, c_l)/n_2$, where n_1 and n_2 are the number of data present in cg_1 and cg_2 respectively. It is known that $w \geq y$ thus $(w - y) \geq 0$ and $x \geq z$ thus $(x - z) \geq 0$. $\xi(cp_{cg_1}, c_l) = \frac{(w+x)}{N(EP,c_l)+(w+x)} = \frac{(y+z)+(w+x)-(y+z)}{N(EP,c_l)+(y+z)+(w+x)-(y+z)} = \frac{(y+z)+(w-y)+(x-z)}{N(EP,c_l)+(y+z)+(w-y)+(x-z)} \geq \frac{(y+z)}{N(EP,c_l)+(y+z)} \geq \xi(cp_{cg_2}, c_l))$ (by applying proper fraction [1], here $(w - y) + (x - z)$ is a positive number)

Theorem 1. *Given two cluster groups cg_1 and cg_2, $kCP_1 \subseteq cg_1$ and $kCP_2 \subseteq cg_2$ are two sets of k_1 candidate products, where $kCP_1 \neq kCP_2$ and $kCP_1 \cap kCP_2 = \phi$. If $\xi(cp_{cg_1}, c_l)) \geq \xi(cp_{cg_2}, c_l))$ for each customer $c_l \in C$, then $\Psi_{cg_1} \geq \Psi_{cg_2}$.*

Proof. If $\xi(cp_{cg_1}, c_l)) \geq \xi(cp_{cg_2}, c_l))$ for all $c_l, 1 \geq l \geq nc$ (from Lemma 1), then $\sum_{l=1}^{nc} \xi(cp_{cg_1}, c_l)) \geq \sum_{l=1}^{nc} \xi(cp_{cg_2}, c_l))$ and $\Psi_{cg_1} \geq \Psi_{cg_2}$.

Example 1. Let there be eight customers, three existing products and nine candidate products as shown in Table 1. Suppose that the K value is set to 2 (number of clusters). The K-Means algorithm generates two groups cg_1 and cg_2. The first group consisting of data as follows: $cg_1 = \{cp_2, cp_3, cp_6, cp_7\}$ and the second group consisting of data $cg_2 = \{cp_1, cp_4, cp_5, cp_8, cp_9\}$. The calculated $\Psi_{cg_1} = 2.4240$ and $\Psi_{cg_2} = 1.0957$. The maximum $\Psi_{cg_1} = 2.4240$ value indicates that cluster group 1 is the $CGkCP$. Note that cluster group 1 consist of the data $\{cp_2, cp_3, cp_7\}$ which are 3-(k_1)-most demand products i.e., through maximum Ψ_i value we can identify the $CGkCP \in CG$.

We now present the steps of our proposed algorithm (Algorithm 1) as follows:
```
Algorithm 1: The CMDP Algorithm
Input: The SBS table, K and k1 value
Output: k1-most demanding products
Step 1: Apply K-Means algorithm to generate CG;
Step 2: Identify CGkCP ∈ CG using maximum Ψcgi value;
Step 3: Apply any k-MDP algorithm on CGkCP;
```

The steps of our proposed CMDP algorithm are as follows: step 1: apply K-Means algorithm where, number of clusters (K), is $K = ncp/(k_1 * p)$, where ncp is the number of candidate products (number of input data of the K-Means algorithm), k_1 is the number of most demanding products and p is the regulatory parameter, the typical value of p we set is 5. Now, we have to select appropriate K value so that $CGkCP$ must contains more than k_1 numbers of data. From the clusters, identify $CGkCP \in CG$ using maximum $\Psi_{cg_i}, 1 \leq i \leq K$ value. In step 2, apply any of the existing k-MDP algorithms (SPG, IG, APR or UBP) [1] on $CGkCP$ data to identify the k_1-most demanding products. Note that UBP algorithm always gives optimal solution [1].

3 Experiments

3.1 Experimental Analysis

For evaluation of our proposed CMDP algorithm two real datasets (car and auto data) from UCI machine learning repository (http://archive.ics.uci.edu/ ml/) have been used. The number of data are 1728 and 398 and the dimensions (we have selected) are 6 and 7 respectively. To construct the satisfaction bit string table (SBS), we have selected last 100 data as customer choice data and then we have constructed the SBS table. From the SBS table first 30 percent data we have selected as EP and rest of the data as CP. Data with missing values have been eliminated. The algorithm have been executed on different dimensions (nc), and sizes (ncp) (Figs. 1a and b). For comparison purpose we have implemented six programs, where SPG, IG, and UBP are the existing algorithms [1], and CSPG, CIG and CUBP are the algorithms with K-Means clustering (proposed CMDPs). For the real datasets (car data and auto data), we set $K = 10$ and 2 number of clusters respectively. For all the cases the k_1 value was 3. The algorithms were executed 10 times and the best result (lowest time) was reported. The K-Means algorithm was made to iterate 30 times (the convergence criteria of the K-Means clustering). All the programs (coded in Octave -3.2.4) were executed on a computer with an Intel Celeron processor, 1.30 GHz, and 1 GB of RAM running the Microsoft Windows XP operating system.

Table 2. Experiments on Real Datasets

Dataset	SPG	CSPG	IG	CIG	UBP	CUBP
Car data	8.8282	4.3751	16.6888	12.3438	87538.33	53.157
Auto data	1.4065	1.3281	3.1094	2.9063	50.235	4.5151

3.2 Results

To evaluate the scalability performance of our proposed algorithm we compare execution time with other existing algorithms. The performance (in terms of time) of CSPG, CIG, and CUBP algorithms (proposed) as compared with SPG, IG and UBP (UBP algorithm always gives optimal solution [1]) respectively are

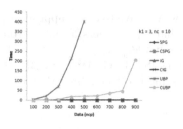
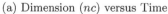
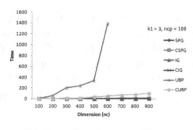

(a) Dimension (*nc*) versus Time   (b) Data (*ncp*) versus Time

Fig. 1. Performance comparisons

better for the real datasets (Table 2). The accuracy rates (AR) for CUBP and UBP are always 100 percent. The AR for CIG and IG are 100 percent (most of the time). But the AR for CSPG and SPG are not 100 percent. From the plot (using synthetic datasets)(Figs. 1a and b) it is seen that the times for our K-Means algorithm based CMDP algorithms are the best. It is also seen that the CMDP algorithms scale well in terms of dimension (*nc*) and size (*ncp*).

4   Conclusions

In this paper the efficiency of the existing k-MDP algorithm to find the k_1-most demanding products has been increased by incorporating the K-Means clustering algorithm. The experiments conducted for comparison with existing algorithms prove the effectiveness of our approach.

References

1. Lin, C.Y., Koh, J.L., Chen, A.L.P.: Determining k-most demanding products with maximum expected number of total customers. IEEE Trans. Knowl. Data Eng. **25**(8), 1732–1747 (2013)
2. Mankiw, N.G.: Principle of Economics, 5th edn. South Western College Publication, New York (2008)
3. Islam, M.S., Liu, C.: Know your customer: computing k-Most promising products for targeted marketing. VLDB J. **25**(4), 545–570 (2016)
4. Koh, J.L., Lin, C.Y., Chen, A.L.P.: Finding k most favorite products based on reverse top-t queries. VLDB J. **23**(4), 541–564 (2014)
5. Zhang, Z., Lakshmanan, L.V.S., Tung, K.H.: On domination game analysis for microeconomic data mining. ACM Trans. Knowl. Discov. Data (TKDD) **2**(4), 18–44 (2009)
6. Miah, M., Das, G., Hristidis, V., Mannila, H.: Determining attributes to maximize visibility of objects. Knowledge-Based Systems, IEEE Trans. Knowl. Data Eng. **21**(7), 959–973 (2009)
7. Peng, Y., Wong, R.C., Wan, Q.: Finding top-k preferable products. IEEE Trans. Knowl. Data Eng. **24**(10), 1774–1788 (2012)

8. Wan, Q., Wong, R.C., Peng., Y.: Finding top-k profitable products. In: ICDE, pp. 1055–1066 (2011)
9. MacQuuen, J.B.: Some methods for classification and analysis of multivariate observations. Proc. 5th Berkeley Symp. Math. Stat. Probab. **1**, 281–297 (1967). University of California Press, Berkeley
10. Han, J., Kamber, M.: Data Mining: Concepts and Techniques. Morgan Kaufmann, New York (2000)

Detection of Atypical Elements
by Transforming Task to Supervised Form

Piotr Kulczycki[1,2](✉) [ID] and Damian Kruszewski[1] [ID]

[1] Centre of Information Technology for Data Analysis Methods,
Polish Academy of Sciences, Systems Research Institute, Warsaw, Poland
kulczycki@ibspan.waw.pl, kulczycki@agh.edu.pl
[2] Division for Information Technology and Systems Research,
AGH University of Science and Technology,
Faculty of Physics and Applied Computer Science, Cracow, Poland

Abstract. The problem of identifying atypical elements in a data set presents many difficulties at every stage of analysis. For instance, it is not clear which traits should distinguish such elements, and what more we cannot know in advance of their natural pattern, which even if it did exist, would in its nature be significantly limited. The subject of the presented research is the procedure for transforming the problem of detection of atypical elements from an unsupervised task to a supervised one with equal-sized patterns. This allows a suitable analysis, in particular the use of diverse well-developed methods of classification. Elements are considered atypical by their rare occurrence, which when coupled with the application of nonparametric methodology enables their detection not only on the peripheries of the distribution, but also – in the multimodal case – potentially located inside.

Keywords: Atypical element · Rare element · Outlier · Atypical elements detection · Classification · Distribution-free methods

1 Introduction

Atypical elements (often rashly referred to as outliers) can intuitively be considered as significantly differing from the rest of a data set (Aggarwal 2013; Barnett and Lewis 1994). The immense diversity of interpretations of such an intuitive definition means that even the concept of an atypical element itself is ambiguous, from the trivial, where they are elements furthest away from the remaining population (outliers), to the functional, when they have the greatest – or rather excessive – influence on a system operation. This paper will apply the most universal frequency approach, whereby atypical elements are rare, i.e. the probability of their appearance is faint. Thanks to the application of distribution-free nonparametric methodology, we can identify atypical observations not only on the peripheries of the population, but in the case of multi-modal distributions with wide-spreading segments, also those lying in between such segments, even if close to the center of the set.

A different problem results from the unsupervised nature of the task, which manifests in the lack of a priori natural pattern of atypical elements. It is worth noting that

© Springer International Publishing AG 2017
B.U. Shankar et al. (Eds.): PReMI 2017, LNCS 10597, pp. 458–466, 2017.
https://doi.org/10.1007/978-3-319-69900-4_58

even if it existed, it would obviously occur significantly less than the pattern of typical ones. The subject of this paper is the transformation of an unsupervised task to a supervised one with equal-sized patterns, which in consequence enables the use of a well-developed valuable and distinctive classification apparatus.

The procedure investigated and presented here is ready-to-use without laborious research. Its easy and illustrative interpretation is particularly valuable.

Section 2 presents the distribution-free statistical kernel estimators methodology. Then, the basic formula of the procedure for identifying atypical, i.e. rarely occurring, elements is described in Sect. 3. Due to difficult conditioning, mainly stemming from a naturally very low number of elements considered atypical, the quality of the procedure is considerably improved in Sect. 4 by significantly increasing the set of elements representative for the population. Next, in Sect. 5, patterns of atypical and typical elements, equal in size, will be generated, which among others form the basis for the convenient application of classification methods, according to the researcher's preferences and specifics of the task under consideration. Final comments are shortly presented in Sect. 6.

A broader description of the concept worked out here and detailed results of empirical verification can be found in the paper (Kulczycki and Kruszewski 2017a). In the publication (Kulczycki and Kruszewski 2017b) the procedure design to submit the result in fuzzy and intuitionistic fuzzy forms is investigated.

2 Nonparametric Kernel Estimators

In the presented method, the characteristics of a data set will be defined using the nonparametric methodology of kernel estimators. It is distribution-free, i.e. the preliminary assumptions concerning the types of appearing distributions are not required. A broad description can be found in the monographs (Kulczycki 2005; Wand and Jones 1995). Exemplary applications for data analysis tasks are described in the publications (Kulczycki et al. 2012; Kulczycki and Charytanowicz 2016; Kulczycki and Kowalski 2016); see also (Kulczycki and Lukasik 2014).

Let the n-dimensional continuous random variable X be given, with a distribution characterized by the density X. Its kernel estimator $\hat{f} : \mathbb{R}^n \to [0, \infty)$, calculated using the experimentally obtained m-element random sample x_i for $i = 1, 2, \ldots, m$, in its basic form is defined as

$$\hat{f}(x) = \frac{1}{mh^n} \sum_{i=1}^{m} K\left(\frac{x - x_i}{h}\right), \tag{1}$$

where $m \in \mathbb{N}\backslash\{0\}$, the coefficient $h > 0$ is called a smoothing parameter, while the measurable function $K : \mathbb{R}^n \to [0, \infty)$ of unit integral $\int_{\mathbb{R}^n} \hat{f}(x)\mathrm{d}x = 1$, symmetrical with respect to zero and having a weak global maximum in this place, takes the name of a kernel.

The choice of the kernel form has – from a statistical point of view – no practical meaning and thanks to this, it becomes possible to take into account primarily properties of the estimator obtained or computational aspects, advantageous from the point of view of the applicational problem under investigation; for broader discussion see the books (Kulczycki 2005 – Sect. 3.1.3; Wand and Jones 1995 – Sects. 2.7 and 4.5). In the one-dimensional case (i.e. when $n = 1$) the normal (Gauss) kernel

$$K_j(x) = \frac{1}{\sqrt{2\pi}} \exp\left(-\frac{x^2}{2}\right) \tag{2}$$

and the uniform kernel

$$K_j(x) = \begin{cases} \frac{1}{2} & \text{dla } x \in [-1, 1] \\ 0 & \text{dla } x \notin [-1, 1] \end{cases} \tag{3}$$

will be used in the following. The normal kernel is generally held as basic. The uniform kernel has bounded support and assumes a finite number of values, which will be taken advantage of later in this paper. In the multidimensional case, a so-called product kernel will be applied in the following. The main idea here is the division of particular variables with the multidimensional kernel then becoming a product of n one-dimensional kernels for particular coordinates. Thus the kernel estimator (1) is then given as

$$\hat{f}(x) = \frac{1}{mh_1 h_2 \dots h_n} \sum_{i=1}^{m} K_1\left(\frac{x_1 - x_{i,1}}{h_1}\right) K_2\left(\frac{x_2 - x_{i,2}}{h_2}\right) \dots K_n\left(\frac{x_n - x_{i,n}}{h_n}\right), \tag{4}$$

where K_j $(j = 1, 2, \dots, n)$ denote one-dimensional kernels, e.g. (2) or (3), h_j $(j = 1, 2, \dots, n)$ are smoothing parameters individualized for particular coordinates, while assigning to coordinates

$$\begin{bmatrix} x_1 \\ x_2 \\ \vdots \\ x_n \end{bmatrix} \quad \text{and} \quad x_i = \begin{bmatrix} x_{i,1} \\ x_{i,2} \\ \vdots \\ x_{i,n} \end{bmatrix} \quad \text{for } i = 1, 2, \dots, m. \tag{5}$$

The above kernels fulfill the additional requirements of the particular procedures used in the following.

The fixing of the smoothing parameter has significant meaning for quality of estimation. Fortunately many suitable procedures for calculating its value on the basis of a random sample have been worked out. For the purposes of the research investigated here, the simplified method (Kulczycki 2005 – Sect. 3.1.5; Wand and Jones 1995 – Sect. 3.2.1) will be applied, according to which

$$h_j = \left(\frac{8\sqrt{\pi}}{3} \frac{W(K_j)}{U(K_j)^2} \frac{1}{m}\right)^{1/5} \hat{\sigma}_j \quad \text{for } j = 1, 2, \dots, n, \tag{6}$$

where $W(K_j) = \int_{-\infty}^{\infty} K_j(x)^2 dx$ and $U(K_j) = \int_{-\infty}^{\infty} x^2 K_j(x) dx$, while $\hat{\sigma}_j$ denotes the estimator of a standard deviation for the j-th coordinate:

$$\hat{\sigma}_j = \sqrt{\frac{1}{m-1} \sum_{i=1}^{m} x_{i,j}^2 - \frac{1}{m(m-1)} \left(\sum_{i=1}^{m} x_{i,j} \right)^2} \quad \text{for} \quad j = 1, 2, \ldots, n. \quad (7)$$

As shown in verification testing the presented procedure, this method seems to be sufficiently precise, and furthermore it is simple and fast. The functional values occurring in formula (6) are, respectively, for normal kernel (2)

$$W(K_j) = \frac{1}{2\sqrt{\pi}}, \; U(K_j) = 1 \quad (8)$$

and for uniform (3)

$$W(K_j) = \frac{1}{2}, \; U(K_j) = \frac{1}{3}. \quad (9)$$

For specific cases the more sophisticated yet effective plug-in method (Kulczycki 2005 – Sect. 3.1.5; Wand and Jones 1995 – Sect. 3.6.1) can be also proposed. It is provided for one-dimensional tasks but, of course, this method can be also applied in the n-dimensional case when a product kernel is used, sequentially n times for each coordinate.

In practice, various modifications and generalizations of the standard form of the kernel estimator presented above are possible, fitting its properties to specific realities. It is worth remembering however, that they increase complexity of formulas, their interpretation becomes more difficult and in consequence the problem is less convenient for potential users to solve. For many aspects concerning the kernel estimators method, see the classic monographs (Kulczycki 2005; Wand and Jones 1995).

3 Basic Version of Procedure

The basic idea of the presented procedure for identification of atypical elements stems from the significance test proposed in the work (Kulczycki and Prochot 2002). Thanks to the application of nonparametric methods it is unnecessary to introduce assumptions concerning distribution type for an examined population.

Let the set be given, with elements representative for the population

$$x_1, x_2, \ldots, x_m. \quad (10)$$

Treat these elements as realizations of the n-dimensional continuous random variable X with distribution having density f and calculate – in accordance with Sect. 2 (using a normal kernel) – the kernel estimator $\hat{f}$. Next consider the set of its value for elements of set (10), so

$$\hat{f}(x_1), \hat{f}(x_2), \ldots, \hat{f}(x_m). \tag{11}$$

It is worth noticing that, regardless of the dimension of the random variable X, the values of set (11) are real (one-dimensional).

Define now the number

$$r \in (0,1) \tag{12}$$

establishing sensitivity of the procedure for identifying atypical elements. This number will determine the assumed proportion of atypical elements in relation to the total population, therefore the ratio of the number of atypical to the sum of atypical and typical elements. In practice

$$r = 0.01, 0.05, 0.1 \tag{13}$$

is the most often used, with particular attention paid to the second option. In certain applications it is possible to use other, approximate values of the above parameter.

Let us treat set (11) as realizations of a real (one-dimensional) random variable and calculate the estimator for the quantile of the order r. The positional estimator of the second order (Parrish 1990) will be applied in the following, given by the formula

$$\hat{q}_r = \begin{cases} z_1 & \text{for} \quad mr < 0.5 \\ (0.5 + i - mr)z_i + (0.5 - i + mr)z_{i+1} & \text{for} \quad mr \geq 0.5 \end{cases}, \tag{14}$$

where

$$i = [mr + 0.5], \tag{15}$$

while $[d]$ denotes an integral part of the number $d \in \mathbb{R}$, and z_i is the i-th value in size of set (11) after its sorting, thus

$$\{z_1, z_2, \ldots, z_m\} = \{\hat{f}(x_1), \hat{f}(x_2), \ldots, \hat{f}(x_m)\} \tag{16}$$

with $z_1 \leq z_2 \leq \ldots \leq z_m$. Application of the positional quantile estimator guarantees its value does not exceed beyond support of the random variable under investigation, or rather to be more precise, thanks to the use of kernel (2) with positive values, the condition $\hat{q}_r > 0$ is fulfilled.

Generally there are no special recommendations concerning choice of sorting algorithm (Canaan et al. 2011) used for specifying set (16). However, let us interpret definition (14) and (15), taking into account condition (13). So, it is enough to sort only the $i+1$ smallest values in the set $\{z_1, z_2, \ldots, z_m\}$, therefore about 1-10% of its size. One can apply a simple algorithm that subsequently finds the $i+1$ smallest elements of the set $\{z_1, z_2, \ldots, z_m\}$.

Finally, if for a given tested element $\hat{x} \in \mathbb{R}^n$, the condition $\hat{f}(\tilde{x}) \leq \hat{q}_r$ is fulfilled, then this element should be considered atypical; for the opposite $\hat{f}(\tilde{x}) > \hat{q}_r$ it is typical. What is noteworthy is that for the correctly estimated quantities $\hat{f}$ and $\hat{q}_r$, the above guarantees obtaining the proportion of the number of atypical elements to total population at the assumed level r.

The above procedure for identifying atypical elements, combined with the properties of kernel estimators, allows in the multidimensional case for inferences based not only on values for specific coordinates of a tested element, but above all on the relations between them.

4 Extended Pattern of Population

Although, from a theoretical point of view, the procedure presented in the previous section seems complete, when the values r are applied in practice – see condition (13) – and the size m is not big, the estimator of the quantile $\hat{q}_r$ is encumbered with a large error, due to the low number of elements z_i smaller than the estimated value. To counteract this, a data set will be extended by generating additional elements with distribution identical to that characterizing the subject population, based on set (10).

The methodology for enlarging a set representative for the investigated population is suggested using von Neumann's elimination concept (Gentle 2003). This allows the generation of a sequence of random numbers of distribution with support bounded to the interval $[a, b]$, while $a < b$, characterized by the density f of values limited by the positive number c, i.e.

$$f(x) \leq c \text{ for every } x \in [a, b]. \tag{17}$$

In the multidimensional case, the interval $[a, b]$ generalizes to the n-dimensional cuboid $[a_1, b_1] \times [a_2, b_2] \times \ldots \times [a_n, b_n]$., while $a_j < b_j$ for $j = 1, 2, \ldots, n$.

First the one-dimensional case is considered. Let us generate two pseudorandom numbers u and v of distribution uniform to the intervals $[a, b]$ and $[0, c]$, respectively. Next one should check that

$$v \leq f(u). \tag{18}$$

If the above condition is fulfilled, then the value u ought to be assumed as the desired realization of a random variable with distribution characterized by the density f, that is

$$x = u. \tag{19}$$

In the opposite case the numbers u and v need to be removed and steps (18) and (19) repeated, until the desired number of pseudorandom numbers x with density f is obtained.

In the presented procedure the density f is established by the kernel estimators methodology, described in Sect. 2. Denote its estimator as $\hat{f}$. The uniform kernel will be employed, allowing easy calculation of the support boundaries a and b, as well as the parameter c appearing in condition (17). Namely:

$$a = \min_{i=1,2,\ldots,m} x_i - h \qquad (20)$$

$$b = \max_{i=1,2,\ldots,m} x_i + h \qquad (21)$$

$$c = \max_{i=1,2,\ldots,m} \left\{ \hat{f}(x_i - h), \hat{f}(x_i + h) \right\}. \qquad (22)$$

The last formula results from the fact that the maximum for a kernel estimator with the uniform kernel must occur on the edge of one of the kernels. It is also worth noting that calculations of parameters (20)–(22) do not require much effort. This is thanks to the appropriate choice of kernel form.

In the multidimensional case, von Neumann's elimination algorithm is similar to the previously discussed one-dimensional version. The edges of the n-dimensional cuboid $[a_1, b_1] \times [a_2, b_2] \times \ldots \times [a_n, b_n]$ are calculated from formulas comparable to (20)–(22) separately for particular coordinates. The kernel estimator maximum is thus located in one of the corners of one of the kernels; therefore

$$c = \max_{i=1,2,\ldots,m} \left\{ \hat{f} \left(\begin{bmatrix} x_{i,1} \pm h_1 \\ x_{i,2} \pm h_2 \\ \vdots \\ x_{i,n} \pm h_n \end{bmatrix} \right) \right\} \quad \text{following all combinations of } \pm . \qquad (23)$$

The number of these combinations is finite and equal to 2^n. Using the formula presented, n particular coordinates of pseudorandom vector u and the subsequent number v are generated, after which condition (18) is checked.

The results of verification presented in Sect. 6 show that for the properly extended set (10), the procedure investigated here for identifying atypical elements allows us to obtain a proportion of this type of element throughout the whole population, with great accuracy, sufficient from an applicational point of view.

5   Equal-Sized Patterns of Atypical and Typical Elements

Let us consider set (10) introduced in Sect. 3, consisting of elements representative for an investigated population, and extended as described in accordance with Sect. 4. In taking its subset comprising these observations x_i for which $\hat{f}(x_i) \leq \hat{q}_r.$, one can treat it as a pattern of atypical elements. Denote it thus:

$$x_1^{at}, x_2^{at}, \ldots, x_{m_{at}}^{at}. \qquad (24)$$

Similarly, the set of observations for which $\hat{f}(x_i) > \hat{q}_r$ may be considered as a pattern of typical elements:

$$x_1^{t}, x_2^{t}, \ldots, x_{m_t}^{t}. \qquad (25)$$

Sizes of the above patterns equal respectively m_{at} and m_t. Of course $m_{at} + m_t = m$; we also have

$$\frac{m_{at}}{(m_{at}+m_t)} \cong r \tag{26}$$

In this way, unsupervised in its nature, the problem of identifying atypical elements has been reduced to a supervised classification task, although with strongly unbalanced patterns – taking into account relation (26) with (13), set (24) is in practice around 10-100 times smaller than (25). Classification is relatively conveniently conditioned and can use many different well developed methods. However most procedures work much better if patterns are of similar or even equal sizes (Kaufman and Rousseeuw 1990). Using once again the algorithm presented in Sect. 5, the size of the set can be increased to m_t, so that $m_{at} = m_t$, thus equaling patterns of atypical (24) and typical (25) elements.

Finally, a method for the unsupervised identification of atypical elements, has been thus brought to supervised classification with two patterns of equal, relatively large size, thereby creating the conveniently conditioned task with rich and diverse methodology, allowing for the selection of the best procedure regarding the character of the problem and user preferences.

6 Final Comments

The operation of the procedure was tested in details. First with the use of generated data the quantitative aspects were verified, in particular suggestions for fixing parameters. Figure 1 presents an exemplary decision tree attained for the bimodal distribution:

$$N(-3,1) \quad 40\%, \qquad N(3,1) \quad 60\%. \tag{27}$$

This classification method offers an illustrative interpretation of a problem. Thanks to the equal-sized patterns, the results obtained in this way are close to those obtained with an unsupervised procedure of identification for atypical elements, however the potential fundamental analysis of decision trees brings great additional possibilities to enhance a model as information concerning its correctness is obtained, and flexibly adapt it to a changing environment.

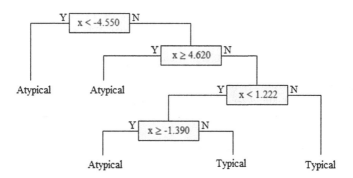

Fig. 1. Decision tree for bimodal distribution (27); $r = 0.1$, $m = 1,000$, $m^* = 10,000$.

Next, real experimental data taken from medicine (National Health and Nutrition Examination Survey 2016; National Cancer Institute 2016) were applied to demonstrate the comprehensive application of the presented procedure. The obtained results fully positively confirmed the correct functioning of the procedure presented in this paper. A detailed description of the experimental verification is presented in the paper (Kulczycki and Kruszewski 2017). The concept's independence from a distribution characterizing an analyzed set (in particular multimodality) as well as the dimensionality of a problem (within a reasonable range) should be underlined.

References

Aggarwal, C.C.: Outlier Analysis. Springer, New York (2013)

Barnett, V., Lewis, T.: Outliers in Statistical Data. Wiley, New York (1994)

Canaan, C., Garai, M.S., Daya, M.: Popular sorting algorithms. World Applied Programming 1, 62–71 (2011)

Gentle, J.E.: Random Number Generation and Monte Carlo Methods. Springer, New York (2003)

Kaufman, L., Rousseeuw, P.J.: Finding groups in data: An introduction to cluster analysis. Wiley, New York (1990)

Kulczycki, P.: Estymatory jądrowe w analizie systemowej. WNT, Warsaw (2005)

Kulczycki, P., Charytanowicz, M.: An algorithm for conditional multidimensional parameter identification with asymmetric and correlated losses of under- and overestimations. J. Stat. Comput. Simul. 86, 1032–1055 (2016)

Kulczycki, P., Charytanowicz, M., Kowalski, P.A., Lukasik, S.: The complete gradient clustering algorithm: properties in practical applications. J. Appl. Stat. 39, 1211–1224 (2012)

Kulczycki, P., Kowalski, P.A.: A complete algorithm for the reduction of pattern data in the classification of interval information. Int. J. Comput. Methods 13, 1650018 (2016)

Kulczycki, P., Kruszewski, D.: Identification of atypical elements by transforming task to supervised form with fuzzy and intuitionistic fuzzy evaluations. Appl. Soft Comput. 60, 623–633 (2017a)

Kulczycki, P., Kruszewski, D.: Detection of atypical elements with fuzzy andintuitionistic fuzzy evaluation. In: Mitkowski, W., Kacprzyk, J., Oprzedkiewicz, K., Skruch, P. (eds.) Trends in Advanced Intelligent Control, Optimization and Automation, pp. 774–786. Springer, Cham (2017b)

Kulczycki, P., Lukasik, S.: An algorithm for reducing dimension and size of sample for data exploration procedures. Int. J. Appl. Math. Comput. Sci. 24, 133–149 (2014)

Kulczycki, P., Prochot C.: Identyfikacja stanów nietypowych za pomocą estymatorów jądrowych. In: Bubnicki, Z., Hryniewicz, O., Kulikowski, R. (eds.) Metody i techniki analizy informacji i wspomagania decyzji. EXIT, Warsaw, pp. 57–62 (2002)

National Health and Nutrition Examination Survey, http://www.cdc.gov/nchs/nhanes.htm/. Accessed 10 May 2016

National Cancer Institute, http://ctep.cancer.gov/. Accessed 10 May 2016

Parrish, R.: Comparison of quantile estimators in normal sampling. Biometrics 46, 247–257 (1990)

Wand, M., Jones, M.: Kernel Smoothing. Chapman and Hall, London (1995)

Mining Rare Patterns Using Hyper-Linked Data Structure

Anindita Borah$^{(\boxtimes)}$ and Bhabesh Nath

Department of Computer Science and Engineering, Tezpur University,
Tezpur, Sonitpur 784028, Assam, India
anindita01.borah@gmail.com, bnath@tezu.ernet.in

Abstract. Rare pattern mining has emerged as a compelling field of research over the years. Experimental results from literature illustrate that tree-based approaches are most efficient among the rare pattern mining techniques. Despite their significance and implication, tree-based approaches become inefficient while dealing with sparse data and data with short patterns and also suffer from the limitation of memory. In this study, an efficient rare pattern mining technique has been proposed that employs a hyper-linked data structure to overcome the shortcomings of tree data structure based approaches. The hyper-linked data structure enables dynamic adjustment of links during the mining process that reduces the space overhead and performs better with sparse datasets.

Keywords: Frequent patterns · Rare patterns · Pattern mining · Data structure

1 Introduction

Over the years, pattern mining has played an imperative role in solving many data mining tasks. For a considerable period of time, pattern mining research was restricted only to the extraction of frequent patterns disregarding the mining of rare patterns. Rare patterns have proved to be of vital importance in a wide range of applications ranging from network anomaly detection, equipment failure, medicine to fraud detection. Considering the significance of rare patterns, research on rare pattern mining is increasing rapidly and a considerable amount of work has already been carried out for the extraction of these momentous patterns. The techniques of rare pattern mining available in the literature either follow a level-wise approach and generate candidates like Apriori [2] or use efficient data structure and extract rare patterns without generating candidates like FP-Growth [4]. Among the two, tree based approaches have been found to be more efficient in terms of performance compared to level-wise approaches.

Tree based approaches achieve good compression in case of dense datasets. As dense dataset contains many frequent items, sharing of nodes having common item prefixes will be more and hence compactness of the tree structure will also be higher. On the contrary, sparse datasets contain lesser number of frequent

© Springer International Publishing AG 2017
B.U. Shankar et al. (Eds.): PReMI 2017, LNCS 10597, pp. 467–472, 2017.
https://doi.org/10.1007/978-3-319-69900-4_59

items that reduces the compression ratio of the tree structure to a great extent. Also, it has been found that tree based approaches work well with data having long patterns but fails miserably when the data have short patterns. In this paper, an efficient rare pattern mining approach has been proposed that generates appreciable results in case of sparse datasets and data with long patterns and also requires less memory compared to the eminent tree based rare pattern mining approaches.

The remaining paper is systematized as follows:- Some prior works in the area of rare pattern mining have been discussed in Sect. 2. The proposed approach for solving the bottleneck of existing algorithms is presented in Sect. 3 followed by the experimental results in Sect. 4. Section 5 finally concludes the paper with some feasible future perspectives.

2   Related Work

Since its inception, an appreciable amount of work has been done for the extraction of rare patterns. This section illustrates the prior works in the area of rare pattern mining.

Liu et al. [6] made the initial attempt using an Apriori based approach to generate the rare patterns by assigning a minimum support to each item individually. ARIMA [8] and AfRIM [1] on the other hand, employed a single support threshold for extracting the rare patterns. Considering the shortcomings of Apriori based approaches, few other techniques have adopted a tree based approach. The primer method in this category is the Compressed FP-Growth (CFP-Growth) algorithm proposed in [5] where the extraction of rare patterns is based on a multiple minimum support framework. The most popular and efficient pattern growth approach for mining rare patterns is the Rare Pattern Tree (RP-Tree) Mining algorithm proposed in [9]. The algorithm uses two support thresholds and takes into account only those transactions that posses at least one rare item. RP-Tree algorithm is further enhanced for better performance using multiple support thresholds in [3].

3   Rare Pattern Mining Using Hyper-Linked Data Structure

As explained in previous sections, handling sparse datasets is a severe research issue that needs utmost attention. This work is therefore an attempt to resolve this issue in context of rare pattern mining. This section presents the proposed rare pattern mining approach called Hyper-Linked Rare Pattern Mining (Hyper-Linked RPM) with the help of a suitable example for better understandability.

The proposed approach employs a hyper-linked queue based data structure for extracting rare patterns [7]. Experimental results illustrate that it is faster and outperforms the pattern growth and level-wise approaches in many cases. This is because the proposed technique employs memory-based queue instead of a tree data structure that is more efficient in mining sparse datasets and has less space overhead. Also, the computational overhead for constructing tree structures is more as compared to simple queue data structures. The proposed technique of Hyper-Linked RPM is illustrated in Algorithm 1.

Algorithm 1. Hyper-Linked Rare Pattern Mining (Hyper-Linked RPM)

    Input : Transaction database DB
    Output: Complete set of rare patterns

1 Generate the support count(Sup) for all items I in DB.
2 **for** *each item* I $\in$ DB, **do**
3 if I.Sup $<$ *freq*Sup $\wedge$ I.Sup $>$ *rare*Sup
4 I $\rightarrow$ *RareItem*
5 **for** *each transaction* T $\in$ DB, **do**
6 if $\exists p$ such that $p \in$ *RareItem* $\wedge$ $p \in$ T
7 T $\rightarrow$ *RareItemTrans*
8 **end**
9 Create a header table H with three fields: item-id, hyper-link and support count to store the items of T.
10 Create separate queues, Q with two fields: hyper-link and item id to store the items of *RareItemTrans*. Link transactions with same first item using hyper-links.
11 For each item α in H, generate the rare item projections in the α-projected database.

The technique generates the support count or frequency of occurrence of every item during the initial scan of database. During the second scan, for building the hyper-linked data structure, only those transactions will be considered that involves at least one rare item. The reason being, transactions containing only frequent items have no contribution in the rare pattern mining process. To distinguish between frequent and rare items, two support thresholds *freq*Sup and *rare*Sup have been used. The support count of rare itemset (SupRareItem) must lie between these two support thresholds, i.e. *freq*Sup$>$ SupRareItem $>$*rare*Sup. The items of the reduced database will be stored in a header table H having three fields: item id, hyper-link and support count of items. It is to be noted that the support counts of the items in the header table will be their support counts in the original database. Support counts of items in the reduced database will not be considered. While loading the transactions into memory, transactions with the same first item are stored in queues and linked together using hyper-links. The heads of the queues will be represented by the items of the header table.

For example, a, b, c, d and e are the items of the reduced database. The data structure will perform mining on the following subsets of rare patterns: (i) patterns having only item a, (ii) patterns having item b but not a, (iii) patterns having item c but neither of a and b, (iv) patterns having item d but neither of

a, b and c (v) patterns having item e but neither of the former items. The first subset of rare patterns are obtained by mining the a-projected database having all the rare item projections that contain item a and are connected together through links in the a-queue. Mining of a-projected database is done by first creating a header table H_a, where the support count of each item is its corresponding frequency of occurrence with item a in the reduced database. Next the items satisfying $freq$Sup and $rare$Sup in the a-projected database are obtained upon traversal of the a-queue. The same procedure continues to mine the ab-projected database by creating Header Table H_{ab} and traversing the ab-queue. If none of the items in H_{ab} could satisfy the thresholds, no rare patterns will be generated and the search terminates for this path. Next the ac-projected database is considered to mine the rare patterns by traversing the ac-queue. If the items in the ac-projected database could not satisfy the thresholds, the search again terminates. The same process continues for other items of the a-projected database. Once the mining of a-projected database is complete, the procedure again starts for mining the next subset of rare patterns i.e. the b-projected database by adjusting the links.

4   Experimental Evaluation of Proposed Approach

To gauge the effectiveness of proposed approach, this section illustrates its performance evaluation on both real-life and synthetic sparse datasets. Real-life datasets Gazelle and Retail have been obtained from UCI repository while synthetic datasets T25I15D10k and T40I10D15K have been generated using synthetic dataset generation method described in [2]. Characteristics of each dataset are given in Table 1. The implementation has been done in Java on a machine of 2.90 GHz Intel i5 processor having 4 GB main memory and 64-bit Windows 8 Pro operating system.

The comparison has been carried out with two tree based approaches: a rare pattern mining algorithm called RP-Tree and a modified frequent pattern mining algorithm called FP-Growth. To generate only rare itemsets, FP-Growth algorithm has been revised by considering only those itemsets that satisfy $rare$Sup and pruning those that exceeds $freq$Sup. Keeping $rare$Sup constant at 5% and varying $freq$Sup threshold, the results obtained for the above datasets are shown

Table 1. Datasets used

Datasets	Number of items per transaction	Number of transactions	Category	Type
Gazelle	267	59,602	Real	Sparse
Retail	52	88,126	Real	Sparse
T25I10D10K	25	10,000	Synthetic	Sparse
T40I10D15K	40	15,000	Synthetic	Sparse

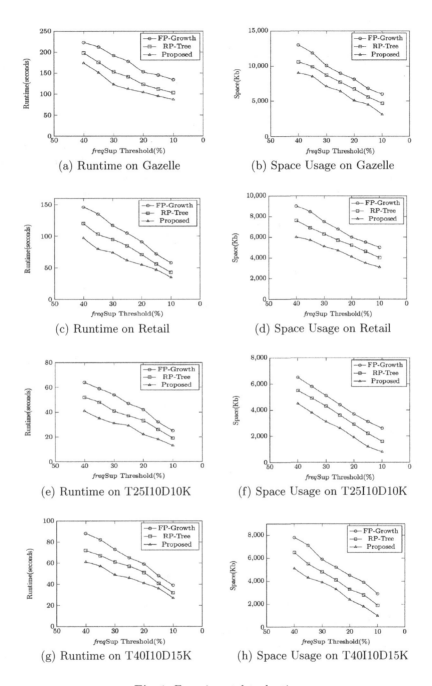

(a) Runtime on Gazelle

(b) Space Usage on Gazelle

(c) Runtime on Retail

(d) Space Usage on Retail

(e) Runtime on T25I10D10K

(f) Space Usage on T25I10D10K

(g) Runtime on T40I10D15K

(h) Space Usage on T40I10D15K

Fig. 1. Experimental evaluation

in Fig. 1. From the figure, it is evident that the proposed approach is faster and has less space requirement compared to FP-Growth and RP-tree.

5   Conclusion and Future Work

Rare pattern mining has established its significance in front of the data mining community. Pattern growth approaches are the most effective ones among the rare pattern mining techniques. However, they suffer from performance drawback while dealing with sparse data and data with short patterns. This paper, introduces a rare pattern mining method that employs a queue based hyper-linked data structure. The data structure automatically adjusts links while mining rare patterns and greatly reduces the memory overhead encountered by tree based approaches. Performance evaluation given in Sect. 4 elicits the fact that the proposed method is more space efficient and faster in dealing with sparse datasets unlike pattern growth approaches. However, for dense datasets, pattern growth approaches outperforms the proposed approach.

As a future work, the proposed approach can be integrated with some tree based approach to effectively handle dense datasets as well. Further study may also incorporate some database partitioning approach to enhance scalability of the proposed algorithm for handing large datasets.

References

1. Adda, M., Wu, L., Feng, Y.: Rare itemset mining. In: 2007 Sixth International Conference on Machine Learning and Applications, ICMLA 2007, pp. 73–80. IEEE (2007)
2. Agrawal, R., Srikant, R., et al.: Fast algorithms for mining association rules. In: Proceedings of 20th International Conference on Very Large Data Bases, VLDB, vol. 1215, pp. 487–499 (1994)
3. Bhatt, U., Patel, P.: A novel approach for finding rare items based on multiple minimum support framework. Proc. Comput. Sci. **57**, 1088–1095 (2015)
4. Han, J., Pei, J., Yin, Y., Mao, R.: Mining frequent patterns without candidate generation: a frequent-pattern tree approach. Data Min. Knowl. Discov. **8**(1), 53–87 (2004)
5. Hu, Y.H., Chen, Y.L.: Mining association rules with multiple minimum supports: a new mining algorithm and a support tuning mechanism. Decis. Support Syst. **42**(1), 1–24 (2006)
6. Liu, B., Hsu, W., Ma, Y.: Mining association rules with multiple minimum supports. In: Proceedings of the Fifth ACM SIGKDD International Conference on Knowledge Discovery and Data Mining, pp. 337–341. ACM (1999)
7. Pei, J., Han, J., Lu, H., Nishio, S., Tang, S., Yang, D.: H-Mine: hyper-structure mining of frequent patterns in large databases. In: 2001 Proceedings IEEE International Conference on Data Mining, ICDM 2001, pp. 441–448. IEEE (2001)
8. Szathmary, L., Napoli, A., Valtchev, P.: Towards rare itemset mining. In: 2007 19th IEEE International Conference on Tools with Artificial Intelligence, ICTAI 2007, vol. 1, pp. 305–312. IEEE (2007)
9. Tsang, S., Koh, Y.S., Dobbie, G.: RP-Tree: rare pattern tree mining. In: Cuzzocrea, A., Dayal, U. (eds.) DaWaK 2011. LNCS, vol. 6862, pp. 277–288. Springer, Heidelberg (2011). doi:10.1007/978-3-642-23544-3_21

Random Binary Search Trees for Approximate Nearest Neighbour Search in Binary Space

Michał Komorowski[(✉)] and Tomasz Trzciński

Institute of Computer Science, Warsaw University of Technology,
Nowowiejska 15/19, 00-665 Warsaw, Poland
michalkomorowski1984@gmail.com, t.trzcinski@ii.pw.edu.pl

Abstract. Approximate nearest neighbour (ANN) search is one of the most important problems in computer science fields such as data mining or computer vision. In this paper, we focus on ANN for high-dimensional binary vectors and we propose a simple yet powerful search method that uses Random Binary Search Trees (RBST). We apply our method to a dataset of 1.25M binary local feature descriptors obtained from a real-life image-based localisation system provided by Google as a part of Project Tango [7]. An extensive evaluation of our method against the state-of-the-art variations of Locality Sensitive Hashing (LSH), namely Uniform LSH and Multi-probe LSH, shows the superiority of our method in terms of retrieval precision with performance boost of over 20%.

Keywords: Approximate nearest neighbour search · Binary vectors · Random Binary Search Trees · Locality sensitive hashing

1 Introduction

The goal of nearest neighbour search is to find vectors from a database that lie close to a query vector. This is a common use case in disciplines such as computer vision [17] or data mining [15]. However, often finding the exact nearest neighbour is costly while retrieving approximate neighbours is sufficient. Therefore several successful solutions in the area of Approximate Nearest Neighbour Search (ANN) have been proposed and among them the two most prominent ones are hierarchical structure (tree) based methods [2,5] and hashing based methods [6,20].

One of the typical computer vision tasks where ANN search is used due to prohibitive amounts of data points is image-based localisation [4,13]. ANN search is typically used in this context to find similarities between local feature descriptors extracted from different images. The majority of works on ANN focus on descriptors that are vectors of real numbers [5,10,12,16]. However, extraction of real-valued descriptors is time consuming so they are often substituted with binary descriptors when real-time performance is required. At the same time methods suitable for real-valued descriptors do not seem to work equally well when applied to binary ones [18].

© Springer International Publishing AG 2017
B.U. Shankar et al. (Eds.): PReMI 2017, LNCS 10597, pp. 473–479, 2017.
https://doi.org/10.1007/978-3-319-69900-4_60

In this paper, we propose ANN search method that uses Random Binary Search Trees (RBST) to find similar vectors within a database of binary vectors. As a use case of our method we take image-based localisation problem and we evaluate our method on a real world dataset of over 1 million binary local feature descriptors obtained within the frames of Google Project Tango [7] collaboration. Our ANN search method outperforms the state of the art in terms of retrieval accuracy, while providing similar recall and memory consumption.

Several other types of trees have been proposed in the literature for indexing of binary descriptors e.g.: k-means trees, kd-trees, or vantage-points trees [8]. However, their application to binary descriptors leads to severe performance drops, as indicated in [18]. Therefore we compare our proposed Random Binary Search Trees method with Local Sensitivity Hashing method [6] and its further modifications: Uniform LSH [18] and Multi-probe LSH [11].

2   Random Binary Search Trees

In this section, we propose a simple yet powerful ANN method for indexing and searching a database of binary descriptors. We draw the inspiration for the method from standard Binary Search Trees (BST) [3]. These structures are well designed for speeding up search process and building up on their success, we propose a modified version of them, called Random Binary Search Trees. Our proposed RBST differ from standard Binary Search Trees in the following aspects.

Firstly, all paths from the root node to the leafs in our RBST have the same length. Secondly, the leafs of our RBST are used to store binary descriptors. The most important difference, however, is the fact that the nodes of our trees store a bit mask. It specifies which bit of a binary descriptor needs to be checked in order to decide if a given descriptor should be assigned to the left or to the right branch of a given node during indexing and search. Thanks to this setup RBST are extremely fast as no distances must be calculated in order to create and search them - the fast binary operation AND is used instead.

In the indexing stage, we use one or more Random Binary Search Trees to store the information about binary descriptors from our database. Each descriptor from the database traverses the tree from the root towards the leaves. While traversing the tree, the descriptor is assigned to left or right branch based on the output of the binary AND operation on the descriptor and the bit mask of the node. In the querying stage, we use those constructed trees to search for candidate nearest neighbours by traversing the trees with a query descriptor and retrieving candidates per each tree. The final set of candidates is returned as a union of candidates across the trees. In the last stage of search, candidate descriptors are sorted based on their Hamming distance to the query descriptor. We then retrieve N descriptors with the smallest distance.

Our Random Binary Search Trees algorithm is controlled by four parameters: N equals to number of approximate nearest neighbours retrieved with default $N = 10$, N_{tree} defines the number of RBST to be created, D specifies the maximum depth of a tree and N_{test} defines how many dimensions of a binary descriptor can be checked in a single tree. Although each node can check only one dimension, this parameter allows us to randomly subsample the space of binary dimensions across different binary trees and increases robustness of our method.

The randomness of our RBST stems from the fact that bits masks for nodes are selected randomly from a given set of bits. A similar idea is used in [9]. However, the trees proposed in [9] were not used to index binary descriptors, but to classify keypoints. A related method can also be found in [4] where trees are generated in supervised way using a stability metric. We evaluated application of this approach to our RBST, however, in our experiments trees proposed in [4] were up to 3 orders of magnitude slower than our Random Binary Search Trees. Our proposed RBST may also look similar to Randomised Binary Search Trees [14]. However, there are few differences. In comparison to our RBST data structure proposed in [14] associates a priority with every inserted key, use rotations to balance a tree and does not store list of keys (in our case descriptors) in leafs.

2.1 Bits Selection Metrics and Hash Codes

We also used the following bit metrics to weight the probability of a given bit to be selected for a mask in the nodes: Shannon entropy of a bit, its conditional entropy and its empirical stability. We define the empirical stability metric as a number of descriptors representing the same 3D point with equal value of a given bit to a total number of descriptors of the same 3D point. After calculating those bit metrics, we used their distribution as bias in the selection of a bit mask for each node. Bits with the higher values of bit metrics are used more often to generate RBST. In order to limit memory consumption, we also used hash codes of binary descriptors, instead of the raw vectors. For hashing the descriptors we used Semi-Supervised Hashing method [19] with various hash code lengths (32, 64, 128, 256 bits). Although in some cases bit metrics or hash codes increased the performance of our method, the improvement was rather negligible and, therefore, in the remainder of this paper, we rely on random bit selection for the node masks.

3 Evaluation

In this section, we evaluate the accuracy and efficiency of our RBST method and compare it with the state of the art. To increase robustness of our evaluation, we run our experiments 10 times, each time on a different subset of 100K descriptors extracted from dataset of 1.26M 512-dimensional binary FREAK descriptors [1]. This dataset was obtained from Google Project Tango [7] collaboration and was generated using state-of-the-art 3D reconstruction methods. As evaluation metrics, we use Precision@N defined as number of correctly retrieved nearest neighbours within the first N descriptors retrieved. Similarly, we compute Recall@N defined as the ratio of retrieved nearest neighbours describing the same 3D point within N returned descriptors versus all descriptors describing given 3D point. We also measure querying time and average the results over 10 runs. All experiments are run using a server with 32 GB of RAM and Intel(R) Xeon(R) 2.60 GHz CPU.

3.1 Initial Experiments

To validate our method and verify the appropriate range of parameters, we first run an initial set of experiments with the following set of parameters: $N_{tree} = \{1, 3, 6, 9, 12\}$, $D = \{20, 30, 40, 50\}$ and $N_{test} = \{64, 128, 256, 512\}$. Based on obtained results, we defined a default set of parameters to be evaluated against the state of the art in the next sections, as they give a good balance between the precision, the recall and the average query time: $D = \{30, 40, 50\}$ and $N_{test} = 256$.

We also discovered the following trends. Firstly, the higher value of N_{tree} the higher Precision@10, at the expense of the average query time. The dependence between N_{tree} and the average query time, assuming other parameters remain unchanged, is quasi-linear. Secondly, the lower value of D, the higher average query time. Shallower trees have leafs with higher number of descriptors and since the last step of search includes sorting candidate vectors, the more candidates we retrieve, the longer the sorting. The highest precision can be obtained for the trees with the highest depth, for which majority of leafs contain not more than a few nodes but at the cost of the recall. As to N_{test}, the higher value of this parameter the smaller average query time (even 2 times or more), because descriptors are spread across higher number of leafs. This, in turn, results from a fact that more bits are taken into account while generating trees.

3.2 Comparison with the State of the Art

In this section, we compare our RBST against the competitive approaches for ANN search in binary spaces. Figures 1 and 2 show the results of experiments. Following the evaluation protocol of [18] we plot Precision and Recall results obtained against average query times. We compare our method against 3 variants of Local Sensitive Hashing (LSH) algorithm, as they were shown to provide the best performances in [18]. We use our own implementation of those algorithms. The parameters of all the methods were optimised using grid search approach. In the case of RBST the evaluation was done for $N_{tree} = \{1, 3, 6, 9, 12\}$ trees. For the hashing methods, the number of hash tables used were equal to $\{1, 2, 4, 8, 16\}$. For LSH and Uniform LSH the hash length was 56 and for Multi-Probe 28. We report average memory consumption as memory required by the algorithms to build indexing structures for descriptors and not descriptors themselves.

Figure 1 shows that RBST provides better performance with respect to the state of the art hashing methods in terms of search precision, given equal query time. The performance boost is especially visible for lower average query times

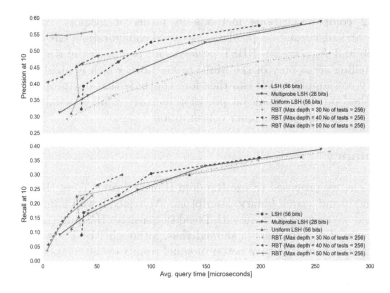

Fig. 1. Precision@10 and Recall@10 versus the average query time.

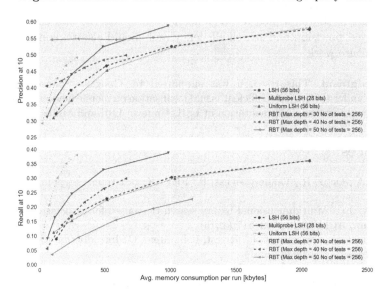

Fig. 2. Precision@10 and Recall@10 versus the average memory consumption.

($<50\,\mu s$), where our proposed RBST algorithm leads to over 20% precision increase over the next best Uniform-LSH method. At the same time, our evaluation shows that the precision increase does not lead to any significant recall drops. If we consider both Precision and Recall our RBST achieve the best results for $D = 40$ and $N_{test} = 256$.

Figure 2 compares various methods in terms of memory consumption. Although particular results depend on the tested configuration, one can see that for $D = 40$ and $N_{test} = 256$ RBST performs au pair with the state-of-the-art methods, falling short only of the Multi-probe LSH, which is highly optimised for memory consumption. We can therefore conclude that our proposed RBST search method provides significant precision increase, while remaining competitive in terms of recall and memory consumption.

4   Summary

In this article, we proposed to use Random Binary Search Trees (RBST) algorithm to index and search binary descriptors. We tested a wide range of configurations and we compared them with Locality Sensitive Hashing (LSH) and its two variations. The experiments showed that, although RBST are a relatively simple data structure, they give better or equal results to the competing hashing algorithms.

Future work on ANN search with our trees includes improving the linear search stage after retrieving the initial set of candidate descriptors, as this part remains a bottleneck of the algorithm. Furthermore, application of a more complex bit metric that can measure dependencies between the bits could lead to the improved precision and search efficiency and should also remain within the scope of future work.

Acknowledgment. This research was supported by Google's Sponsor Research Agreement under the project "Efficient visual localisation on mobile devices". We thank Oskar Dylewski for the implementation of LSH, Uniform LSH and Multi-probe LSH.

References

1. Alahi, A., Ortiz, R., Vandergheynst, P.: FREAK: fast retina keypoint. In: CVPR (2012)
2. Bentley, J.L.: Multidimensional binary search trees used for associative searching. Commun. ACM **18**(9), 509–517 (1975)
3. Cormen, T.H., Leiserson, C.E., Rivest, R.L., Stein, C.: Introduction to Algorithms. MIT Press, Cambridge (2001)
4. Feng, Y., Fan, L., Wu, Y.: Fast localization in large-scale environments using supervised indexing of binary features. IEEE Trans. Image Process. **25**(1), 343–358 (2016)
5. Fukunaga, K., Narendra, P.M.: A branch and bound algorithm for computing k-nearest neighbors. IEEE Trans. Comput. **100**(7), 750–753 (1975)
6. Gionis, A., Indyk, P., Motwani, R.: Similarity search in high dimensions via hashing. VLDB **99**(6), 518–529 (1999)
7. Google Tango. https://get.google.com/tango/
8. Kumar, N., Zhang, L., Nayar, S.: What is a good nearest neighbors algorithm for finding similar patches in images? In: Forsyth, D., Torr, P., Zisserman, A. (eds.) ECCV 2008. LNCS, vol. 5303, pp. 364–378. Springer, Heidelberg (2008). doi:10.1007/978-3-540-88688-4_27

9. Lepetit, V., Fua, P.: Keypoint recognition using randomized trees. IEEE Trans. Pattern Anal. Mach. Intell. **28**(9), 1465–1479 (2006)
10. Liu, T., Moore, A., Gray, A., Yang, K.: An investigation of practical approximate nearest neighbor algorithm. In: NIPS (2004)
11. Lv, Q., Josephson, W., Wang, Z., Charikar, M., Li, K.: Multi-probe LSH: efficient indexing for high-dimensional similarity search. In: VLDB (2007)
12. Nister, D., Stewenius, H.: Scalable recognition with a vocabulary tree. In: CVPR (2006)
13. Sattler, T., Leibe, B., Kobbelt, L.: Fast image-based localization using direct 2d-to-3d matching. In: ICCV (2011)
14. Seidel, R., Cecilia, R.A.: Randomized search trees. Algorithmica **16**(4), 464–497 (1996)
15. Shakhnarovich, G., Viola, P.A., Darrell, T.: Fast pose estimation with parameter-sensitive hashing. In: ICCV (2003)
16. Silpa-Anan, C., Hartley, R.: Optimised kd-trees for fast image descriptor matching. In: CVPR (2008)
17. Torralba, A., Fergus, R., Weiss, Y.: Small codes and large image databases for recognition. In: CVPR (2008)
18. Trzcinski, T., Lepetit, V., Fua, P.: Thick boundaries in binary space and their influence on nearest-neighbor search. Pattern Recogn. Lett. **33**(16), 2173–2180 (2012)
19. Wang, J., Kumar, S., Chang, S.F.: Semi-supervised hashing for large-scale search. IEEE Trans. Pattern Anal. Mach. Intell. **34**(12), 2393–2406 (2012)
20. Weiss, Y., Torralba, A., Fergus, R.: Spectral hashing. In: NIPS, vol. 21, pp. 1753–1760 (2009)

A Graphical Model for Football Story Snippet Synthesis from Large Scale Commentary

Anirudh Vyas, Sangram Gaikwad, and Chiranjoy Chattopadhyay[✉]

Indian Institute of Technology Jodhpur, Jodhpur, Rajasthan, India
anirudh2403@gmail.com, sangramga@gmail.com, chiranjoy@iitj.ac.in

Abstract. Sports Commentaries offer sparse and redundant information in a lengthy format. Patterns can be observed in news articles written by sports journalists. In this paper, we propose a graphical method to synthesise story snippet from football match commentaries. Our model effectively extracts important information from lengthy text documents. Experimental study reveals that our model closely matches with human expectations. Both qualitative and quantitative analysis proves the effectiveness of our proposed method.

Keywords: Summarization · Sports · Football · Graph based · Journalism

1 Introduction

Large number of football games are played on a daily basis around the globe. It is a challenge to write a news report instantly after the match or a session of match has completed. Portable mobile applications or web services in this field will revolutionise journalism and sports news. Also shorter text snippets, rather than long news articles, highlighting salient news of the match will attract a lot of sport fans. Huge amounts of live text commentary (unstructured) of the game is available in the web. In this paper, we consider a specific use case of football live text commentary to generate a short new article or snippet. However producing grammatically correct and human readable summaries is still a challenging task.

Existing extractive summarization consist of supervised learning and unsupervised learning approaches are surveyed extensively [5]. Existing algorithms of Lex Rank, Text Rank are unsupervised learning techniques for text summarization based on graph centrality and sentence similarity for ranking sentences and picking up the top ranked sentences as summaries [2]. Micro-opinions are concise and readable phrases in text to represent important opinions in the text using a novel unsupervised learning approach [4]. An automated method for implicitly crowd sourcing summaries of events using only status updates posted to Twitter as a source, also proved to be successful [8]. Application of supervised learning framework for constructing sports news from live text commentary is also being studied [9], which proves as a foundation for further study in our supervised learning approach. An ontology based approach was proposed in [1].

© Springer International Publishing AG 2017
B.U. Shankar et al. (Eds.): PReMI 2017, LNCS 10597, pp. 480–485, 2017.
https://doi.org/10.1007/978-3-319-69900-4_61

In this paper we show that entity graph based model produces better results than the supervised learning model. We compare our results with other existing techniques using standard metric, as well as human evaluators. We discuss our approach in Sect. 2. In Sect. 3, we describe the proposed Football Match Concept Graph (FMCG) model, followed by the smart symmetrization algorithm in Sect. 4. Experimental results are described in Sect. 5, while Sect. 6 concludes the paper.

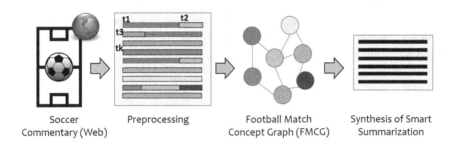

| Soccer Commentary (Web) | Preprocessing | Football Match Concept Graph (FMCG) | Synthesis of Smart Summarization |

Fig. 1. Framework diagram of the proposed smart football story snippet synthesis.

2 Methodology

Figure 1 depicts the overall framework of our proposed algorithm. We first obtain the football match commentary by parsing it from one of the many websites that provide live match commentaries. The data used in the research was scraped from websites that host live match commentaries (www.sportsmole.com). We scraped the commentaries for 60 matches that spanned two leagues and various teams. The raw data is then processed and cleaned. The text data is first tokenized into sentences which are then each assigned a time-stamp based on the time they are attributed to in the commentary. Sentences with only one word are removed. With the cleaned and processed data we generate a entity map that holds all the relevant and important information present in the commentary. With the cleaned and processed data we generate a concept map that holds all the relevant and important information present in the commentary. The detailed algorithm is discussed in Sect. 3. The graph is constructed on the basis of domain knowledge and cross referencing from a game information database. Named entity recognition and regular expressions are used to identify the entities like team names, venue, player names, time stamps etc. The goal is to achieve a snippet as closer to the gold standard summaries available, and that closely matches with the expectation of a common reader. The last part is the synthesis step. Once the graph is obtained, we parse the graph to generate a summary of the match. The parsing algorithm and the synthesis method is discussed in Sect. 4.

3   Football Match Concept Graph (FMCG) Creation

We propose a novel Football Match Concept Graph (FMCG) to capture the relationship among various entities across various entities in a football match. The nodes of the graph represent entities involved in the match. In a football match the entities are team names, players, goals scored, leagues, venue, player scoring the goals, full time and half time scores, and final result. The edges define the different relationships between the entities [6]. It is observed that the football match summary written by a sports journalist follows a structured flow of events. Our FMCG model, due its structure provides consistent results close to human readable summaries. Domain knowledge of football game is utilised in the construction of the FMCG.

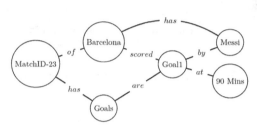

Villarreal tied the match against Barcelona in the la liga league with 1 goal(s) each. Villarreal was playing at home in their stadium Estadio de la Ceramica. The score at half time was Villarreal 0-0 Barcelona. Sansone scored a magnificent goal for Villarreal at 50 min. Messi scored a magnificent goal for Barcelona at 90 min. The score at the end of the match was Villarreal 1-1 Barcelona.

Fig. 2. Structure of graph for football match entities.

We have adapted a two phase approach to extract specific entities from a football commentary. First, named entities are recognized using [3]. Since [3] is not designed for football matches, it results in many false alarms. E.g. given a sentence "the newly-named Estadio de la Ceramica and it is a real cracker of an affair as an exciting Villarreal team", [3] detects "Villarreal" as person, and "Estadio de la Ceramica" as organization. However, the former is a team, while the later is a stadium. To rectify these errors, in phase 2, we parse the results using regular expressions and database from external sources consisting of team names, leagues, and stadiums; to cross reference the database with the available commentary data of the specific match. This helps us to achieve a correct name-entity mapping. Figure 2 depicts a typical FMCG.

4   Snippet Synthesis Algorithm

Once the graph is obtained we try to answer some specific questions to synthesize a snippet or summary of the match. They are: *1. Name of the league/ tournament? 2. The participating teams? 3. Venue and which team's home stadium is it? 4. Who was the winner? 5. The goal scorers and goal timing? 6. What was the score at half-time and full-time?* We obtain the answers to these questions by traversing the graph and searching for the relevant information. We implemented the Depth First Search (DFS) algorithm to search for information in the graph. So, for example if we need to find who scored the goal Goal 1 (shown in Fig. 2) and which team the player belonged to we first find Goal 1 through DFS, then we search for the player and team connected to our node Goal 1 and obtain the answer. Once the information is obtained we pass it on to the synthesis algorithm. The synthesis algorithm has predefined sentence formats that are filled in with the information to obtain the snippet. To synthesise a summary that is coherent and concise we have defined a logical sequence and format of the information to be presented. An example of the summary is as follows:

Villarreal tied the match against Barcelona in the la liga league with 1 goal(s) each. Villarreal was playing at home in their stadium Estadio de la Ceramica. The score at half time was Villarreal 0-0 Barcelona. Sansone scored a magnificent goal for Villarreal at 50 min. Messi scored a magnificent goal for Barcelona at 90 min. The score at the end of the match was Villarreal 1-1 Barcelona.

5   Experiments and Results

We used a total data-set of 60 matches with an average of 223 sentences in each commentary. For each commentary, there are time-stamps from 0–90 min, pointing out the occurrence of every sentence with respect to a match. For example the name of the teams and the league is mentioned at the start of the commentary in all the matches so we only need to search for it in the first 10 sentences. Sentences with only one word do not hold any useful information, so were removed during processing of the data.

5.1   Evaluation of Summaries

For evaluation, we have used two methods, the ROUGE Score and human evaluation of summaries. The ROUGE-N [7] metric to compare generated snippets to gold standards generated manually. The gold standards [8] used is game recap articles from a reliable website source. The recap articles provide a gold standard for reference to be used for evaluating the algorithm generated summaries using both ROUGE and human evaluation. Although studies have suggested that there is a correlation with ROUGE metric and manually generated summaries [7], however this evaluation is not perfect. Hence, we have used both the techniques to evaluate. Each of the three human evaluators then used a 5-level Likert scale to score the generated summaries on three dimensions: readability, syntax correctness, and interpreted meaning of the summary. To provide a baseline the three human evaluators also evaluated the recap gold standard articles.

5.2   Quantitative Results

Human evaluation of the summaries for readability, syntax correctness and semantic meaning compared to the gold standards in Table 1. Table 1 clearly indicate comparatively high readability, lower syntax errors in English, and higher

Table 1. 5-level Likert scale to score to Human evaluation of the summaries.
M = Mean, Mdn = Median, SD = Standard Deviation.

Method →	Gold standard			Graph based			Named Entity		
Metric	M	Mdn	SD	M	Mdn	SD	M	Mdn	SD
Readable	4.54	5.00	0.49	4.10	4.00	1.00	2.50	2.00	0.90
Correct Syntax	4.07	4.00	0.27	3.85	4.00	1.10	1.77	1.00	1.20
Content meaning	-	-	-	3.50	3	1.19	1.5	1	0.79

Table 2. Comparison of F-scores of the models that we implemented

Model	F-score	Recall	Precision
Lex rank	0.397	0.450	0.371
Supervised	0.358	0.303	0.491
Entity graph	0.362	0.325	0.512

content meaning interpreted in Entity Graph based summary as compared to
NER Stanford model using supervised learning (see Table 2). These result can
be attributed to the fact of inclusion of domain knowledge of a football, news
article writing in entity graph model as compared to supervised learning model.

5.3   Successful and Failure Scenarios

Our framework is effective on a use case with sufficient domain knowledge. Here,
we used the domain knowledge in football to create a graph that stores the
information of a match. The algorithm works as discussed when the teams are
in the database and the commentary has all the information needed to answer the
questions. If there is insufficient information the algorithm will return incomplete
snippets. For the creation of the graph, we use a database to extract information
from the commentaries, if there is a mention of a team or a player in a manner
different from that in the database we will not be able to extract that information
successfully. For example, players and teams are often mentioned in various
different ways: "Ronaldo" is sometimes mentioned as "CR7", while "Barcelona"
is mentioned as "Barca". These variations if not accounted for will cause errors.
Our algorithm fails in cases the team names are not present in the database.

5.4   Discussion

Our proposed model generates substantially better results than previous
approaches. The unsupervised lex-rank and text-rank approaches are good generalized methods but they do not take into account the domain information of
the commentary and thus give poor summaries. The supervised method is a good
approach for automating summaries and takes into account the domain knowledge as well. However, the summaries generated are not coherent since it extracts

important sentences rather than synthesizing. Thus the summaries generated do not score high on human readability. We have used a database to extract information rather than using named entity recognizers [3], which performs poorly. Therefore to generate information rich snippets that are coherent and score high on the human readability test we propose the above algorithm. The synthesis algorithm can be further improved to generate more organic summaries, which further resemble human written summaries. The graph creation algorithm can also be improved such that it relies less and less on domain knowledge and it automatically extracts important information.

6 Conclusion

Our proposed algorithm scored high on the human readability index and better than the previous models on the F-Score index. It generates coherent and information rich summaries and the summaries can be easily changed while keeping the entity graph the same. The algorithm can be adopted to different use cases and sports with sufficient domain knowledge. In future, we are planning to extend this work to provide instant news summaries by summarising commentary streams and thus save the journalists from the repetitive work of summarising matches. The proposed technique can also be clubbed with video symmetrization techniques to identify key events in sports videos.

References

1. Bouayad-Agha, N., Casamayor, G., Mille, S., Wanner, L.: Perspective-oriented generation of football match summaries: old tasks, new challenges. ACM Trans. Speech Lang. Process. **9**(2), 3:1–3:31 (2012)
2. Erkan, G., Radev, D.R.: Lexrank: graph-based lexical centrality as salience in text summarization. J. Artif. Intell. Res. **22**, 457–479 (2004)
3. Finkel, J.R., Grenager, T., Manning, C.: Incorporating non-local information into information extraction systems by gibbs sampling. In: Proceedings of the rd Annual Meeting on Association for Computational Linguistics, pp. 363–370, ACL 2005 (2005)
4. Ganesan, K., Zhai, C., Viegas, E.: Micropinion generation: an unsupervised approach to generating ultra-concise summaries of opinions. In: Proceedings of the 21st international conference on World Wide Web, pp. 869–878. ACM (2012)
5. Gupta, V., Lehal, G.S.: A survey of text summarization extractive techniques. J. Emerg. Technol. Web Intell. **2**(3), 258–268 (2010)
6. Jiang, Z., Li, P., Zhang, Y., Li, X.: Generating semantic concept map for MOOCs. In: International Conference on Educational Data Mining (2016)
7. Lin, C.Y.: Rouge: a package for automatic evaluation of summaries. In: Text Summarization Branches Out: Proceedings of the ACL-2004 Workshop, vol. 8, Barcelona, Spain (2004)
8. Nichols, J., Mahmud, J., Drews, C.: Summarizing sporting events using twitter. In: Proceedings of the 2012 ACM International Conference on Intelligent User Interfaces, pp. 189–198. ACM (2012)
9. Zhang, J., Yao, J.G., Wan, X.: Toward constructing sports news from live text commentary. In: Proceedings of ACL (2016)

An Efficient Approach for Mining Frequent Subgraphs

Tahira Alam$^{(\boxtimes)}$⍟, Sabit Anwar Zahin⍟, Md. Samiullah⍟,
and Chowdhury Farhan Ahmed⍟

Department of Computer Science and Engineering,
University of Dhaka, Dhaka, Bangladesh
tahiradu@gmail.com, sgtlaugh@gmail.com,
samiullah@cse.univdhaka.edu, farhan@du.ac.bd

Abstract. Graph-based data mining techniques, known as graph mining, are capable of modeling several real-life complex structures such as roads, maps, computer or social networks and chemical structures by graphs. Useful information can be mined by discovering the frequent subgraphs. However, the existing approaches to mine frequent subgraphs have significant drawbacks in terms of efficiency. In this paper, we focus on real-time frequent subgraph mining and propose an efficient customized data structure and technique to reduce subgraph isomorphism checking as well as a supergraph based optimized descendant generation algorithm. Extensive performance analyses prove the efficiency of our algorithm over the existing methods.

Keywords: Data mining · Knowledge discovery · Frequent patterns · Graph mining

1 Introduction

Real-life data and relationship among data can be conveniently modelled as a graph structure. For instance, in biological and chemical datasets, it is more appropriate to model them as graphs. Hence comes the need of mining interesting patterns from these graph datasets and mining frequent subgraph is one of the key research areas [1,4].

Existing methods to mine frequent subgraph patterns either use an Apriori approach [2,3] or a Pattern-Growth approach [5]. The Apriori approach results in redundant candidate generation which is very expensive. AGM [2] or FSG [3], the most common algorithms using the Apriori approach suffer from this overhead. The AGM [2] algorithm uses an iterative vertex-based candidate generation method that increases the substructure size by one vertex at each iteration. Two size-k frequent graphs are merged only if they have the same size-$(k$-$1)$ subgraphs. The newly formed candidate includes the size-$(k$-$1)$ subgraph in common and the additional two vertices from the two size-k patterns. On the other hand the FSG [3] algorithm adopts a similar edge-based candidate generation strategy

© Springer International Publishing AG 2017
B.U. Shankar et al. (Eds.): PReMI 2017, LNCS 10597, pp. 486–492, 2017.
https://doi.org/10.1007/978-3-319-69900-4_62

that increases the substructure size by one edge after each iteration. The popular Pattern-Growth algorithm gSpan adopts DFS search as opposed to BFS used inherently in Apriori-like algorithms like AGM or FSG. Each graph is assigned an unique minimum DFS Code, and a hierarchical search tree is constructed based on this. After a pre-order DFS traversal of this tree, gSpan discovers all frequent subgraphs satisfying the minimum support threshold.

For real-time decision making problems like automated traffic control and dynamic route teller system, fraud/anomaly detection etc., we need a subgraph mining algorithm that can mine the subgraphs very quickly. However, the search for a subgraph in a graph is an NP-Complete problem and requires extensive enumeration which is a huge overhead in existing methods, including gSpan. These factors motivated us to design an algorithm that can avoid redundant and false pattern checking as well as reducing costly isomorphism checking in order to discover all the resultant frequent subgraphs in real-time. The proposed algorithm in this paper, msiSpan (minimum sequential indexed Subgraph Pattern Mining), attempts to greatly reduce this overhead by indexing subgraphs with custom data structures.

2 Proposed Method

In this section, we propose $msiSpan$ algorithm for mining subgraphs from several graph transactions with necessary definitions and example.

Definition 1. Suppose D is a graph database with N number of graph transactions that is, $D = \{G_1, G_2, G_3,.....G_N\}$. The Minimum DFS Codes and corresponding DFS subscriptings of all the graph transactions are produced. The roots of all the base subscriptings are connected with a dummy root node. Now the dummy root node is labeled '0' and the whole supergraph is now traversed in pre-order and all the nodes are labeled according to their discovery time. Thus the $Minimum\ Supergraph$ is formed which represents the whole database.

Definition 2. A compact data structure called $Minimum\ Sequential\ Index$ is proposed to index the occurrences of the rightmost paths of the currently mined frequent subgraphs. For a particular subgraph S, the $Minimum\ Sequential\ Index$ of S is denoted as $MSI(S) = \{d_1, d_2, d_3,....d_k\}$, where k is the number of transactions in the graph database that contains S. Each d_i is a list containing the occurrences of the rightmost path of S in the $Minimum\ Supergraph$ for the corresponding graph transaction.

Consider a graph database, $D = \{G_1, G_2, G_3,.....G_N\}$. S_i is the set of subgraphs consisting only one edge and i is the lexicographical position of the DFS code of the subgraph. The steps of our proposed algorithm is as follows:

1. Find the Minimum DFS Code of all the graph transactions. The infrequent edges are replaced by insignificant edges. Once an edge is replaced by an insignificant edge, it is not considered for further analysis.

2. The frequent subgraphs with one edge are identified and arranged sequentially in increasing DFS lexicographic order.

3. The positions of the subgraphs found in step 2 are stored in *Minimum Sequential Index* as $MSI(S_i)$. Here, S_i are the subgraphs containing only one edge and $i = 1,2,3....,n$ where n is the number of frequent subgraphs containing one edge, sorted in increasing DFS lexicographic order.

4. The frequent 1 edge subgraphs are extended by adding forward edges to every node in the rightmost path and both backward and forward edges from the rightmost node in DFS lexicographic order. In our method, the number of extension candidates is significantly reduced with the help of *Minimum Sequential Index* and *Minimum Supergraph*. From the *MSI*, the positions of a node on the rightmost path can be retrieved. From the *Minimum Supergraph*, the adjacent nodes of any node in the rightmost path can be found. Only those frequent edges are used to extend nodes in the rightmost path which are adjacent to the corresponding node in the *Minimum Supergraph*.

5. If an edge can be added to a node on the rightmost path, then the node in the rightmost path of the newly formed subgraph is added to its *Minimum Sequential Index*. The number of lists in the *Minimum Sequential Index* is the support count of that subgraph. If it is greater than or equal to the minimum support threshold then it is added to the set of frequent subgraphs. Otherwise it is pruned since no frequent subgraphs can be generated by extending this subgraph.

   Checking the frequency from the *Minimum Sequential Index* is the most significant contribution of our work. This technique is efficient since it counts the frequency of a candidate subgraph after extending one edge at a time from the occurrences of its parent subgraph. On the other hand, gSpan checks for the whole subgraph in all transactions of the projected database and this is an NP-Complete problem.

6. After mining all the descendants of a subgraph, its children are extended in DFS lexicographic order. This recursive process continues following the extension rules mentioned above, until no more frequent subgraph can be mined. If a subgraph cannot be extended further then the recursive function backtracks.

7. After all the frequent subgraphs containing a subgraph S_i are mined, then all the edges labeled S_i in the *Minimum Supergraph* are replaced by insignificant edges. This essentially shrinks the *Minimum Supergraph* resulting in faster processing in the next steps.

It is known that if two graphs have the same Minimum DFS Code then they are isomorphic [5]. Thus when a subgraph with Minimum DFS Code equal to the Minimum DFS Code of any previously found subgraph is found, we prune it thereby avoiding duplicate subgraphs.

Let us consider the graph database in Fig. 1 (Let, Minimum Support Threshold, $\sigma = 2/3$). The edges representing single and double bonds are labelled as '1' and '2', respectively as shown in Fig. 2.

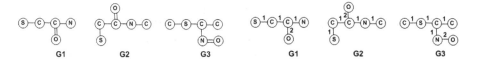

Fig. 1. A graph database.   **Fig. 2.** Graph database after labeling.

Base Subscripting:

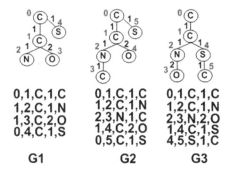

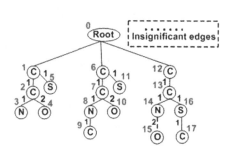

Fig. 3. Minimum DFS Code with their corresponding DFS Trees.

Fig. 4. Minimum Supergraph after removing the non-frequent edges.

The Minimum DFS Codes with the corresponding base subscriptings of the graph transactions are shown in Fig. 3. The constructed *Minimum Supergraph* after adding the roots of the base subscriptings with a common root and replacing the non-frequent edges with insignificant edges is shown in Fig. 4. The frequent subgraphs with one edge (in DFS lexicographically sorted order), their Minimum DFS Codes and *Minimum Sequential Indices* are shown in Fig. 5.

Figure 6 shows the generated descendants of subgraph S_a. Here, from $MSI(S_a)$, we see that the rightmost node 'C' occurred in the *Minimum Supergraph* in positions 1, 2, 6, 7, 12 and 13. From the *Minimum Supergraph* it can be seen that they are connected with the nodes labeled 'N', 'S', 'O'.

Frequent subgraphs With 1 edge:	Minimum DFS Code:	Minimum Sequential Index:
(S_a)	0,1,C,1,C	[{(1,2),(2,1)},{(6,7),(7,6), {(12,13),(13,12)}}]
(S_b)	0,1,C,1,N	[{(2,3)},{(7,8),(9,8)}, {(13,14)}]
(S_c)	0,1,C,1,S	[{(1,5)},{(6,11)},{(13,16), (17,16)}]
(S_d)	0,1,C,2,O	[{(2,4)},{(7,10)}]

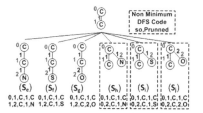

Fig. 5. Frequent subgraphs with 1 edge and their Minimum Sequential Indices (for msiSpan).

Fig. 6. Descendants of S_a in case of msiSpan.

Therefore, only those frequent edges from the rightmost node 'C' are extended. Likewise, the next rightmost node 'C' will be extended. Finally we get the descendant subgraphs S_e, S_f, S_g, S_h, S_i and S_j. Since the DFS Codes of S_h, S_i and S_j are not as same as their Minimum DFS Codes, they are pruned. The other three are found frequent. Here the frequency checking cost is significantly reduced as we only check at the occurrences of S_a from $MSI(S_a)$ in the *Minimum Supergraph*. This recursive process is continued until all the frequent subgraphs are mined.

3   Experimental Results

A comprehensive performance study is performed in our experiments on real life datasets (Chemical-340, MOLT-4 (Active) and MCF-7 (Active)) found from a website[1]. All experiments of our algorithm and gSpan have performed on a 2.40 GHz Intel Pentium Core 2 Duo PC with 2 GB RAM, running Windows 7 Operating System. Both algorithms were implemented using C/C++ and on the same environment and machine. Our experiments show that our proposed method is more efficient when compared with the well-known graph mining algorithm gSpan by an order of magnitude.

Figure 7(left) depicts the performance of our proposed method msiSpan against gSpan with scalability (dataset size vs time) for the Chemical-340 dataset. The dataset size is varied keeping the Minimum Support Threshold at 10%. The required processing time increases with the increasing dataset size as expected. Our proposed method is proved to be more efficient.

Figure 7(middle) depicts the performance of our proposed method msiSpan against gSpan with scalability (dataset size vs time) for the MOLT-4 (Active) dataset. Here, the dataset size is varied for a constant Minimum Support Threshold of 45%. Here also, the required processing time increases with the increasing dataset size as expected. Our proposed method is proved to be more efficient than the existing method.

In Fig. 7(right), the performance of msiSpan is compared with that of gSpan with respect to scalability (dataset size vs time) for the MCF-7 (Active) dataset. The dataset size is varied for a fixed Minimum Support Threshold of 40%. Again, the required processing time increases with the increasing dataset size. msiSpan is proved to be more efficient when compared to gSpan.

Figure 8(left) depicts the performance of our proposed method msiSpan against gSpan with efficiency (Minimum Support Threshold vs time) for the Chemical-340 dataset. The minimum support threshold is varied with respect to time as the dataset size is fixed. In case of both of the algorithms the required processing time decreases with increased Minimum Support Threshold as expected. msiSpan is proved to be more effective and efficient.

Figure 8(middle) depicts the performance of msiSpan against gSpan with efficiency (Minimum Support Threshold vs time) for the MOLT-4 (Active) dataset.

---

[1] https://www.cs.ucsb.edu/~xyan.

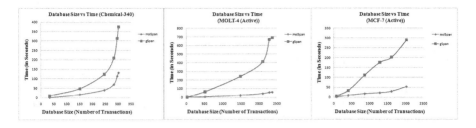

Fig. 7. Database Size vs Time (left:Chemical-340, middle:MOLT-4 (Active), right: MCF-7 (Active)).

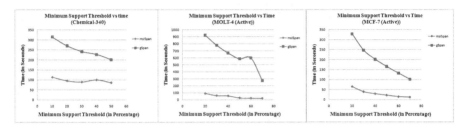

Fig. 8. Minimum Support Threshold vs Time(left:Chemical-340, middle:MOLT-4 (Active), right:MCF-7 (Active)).

The minimum support threshold is varied with respect to time as the dataset size is fixed. The required processing time decreases with increased Minimum Support Threshold. msiSpan is proved to be more efficient than the existing method.

In Fig. 8(right), the performance of msiSpan is compared with that of gSpan with respect to efficiency (Minimum Support Threshold vs time) for the MCF-7 (Active) dataset. The minimum support threshold is varied with respect to time as the dataset size is fixed. The required processing time decreases with increased Minimum Support Threshold. msiSpan is proved to be more efficient when compared to gSpan.

4   Conclusions

Our research objective is to propose a time-efficient algorithm that mines frequent subgraphs from a graph database and our proposed algorithm, msiSpan, achieves this goal in an efficient manner. We have implemented our algorithm successfully and compared its performance with respect to gSpan, the most widely used algorithm to mine frequent subgraphs. We present several experimental results analyzing the performance of our algorithm. We have a plan to use distributed memory to reduce the memory overhead as our future work.

References

1. Cheng, W., Yan, C.: A graph approach to mining biological patterns in the binding interfaces. J. Comput. Biol. **24**(1), 31–39 (2017)
2. Inokuchi, A., Washio, T., Motoda, H.: An apriori-based algorithm for mining frequent substructures from graph data. In: Zighed, D.A., Komorowski, J., Żytkow, J. (eds.) PKDD 2000. LNCS (LNAI), vol. 1910, pp. 13–23. Springer, Heidelberg (2000). doi:10.1007/3-540-45372-5_2
3. Kuramochi, M., Karypis, G.: Frequent subgraph discovery. In: ICDM 2001, USA, pp. 313–320 (2001)
4. Rao, B., Mishra, B.K.: An approach to clustering of text documents using graph mining techniques. IJRSDA **4**(1), 38–55 (2017)
5. Yan, X., Han, J.: gSpan: Graph-based substructure pattern mining. In: ICDM 2002, Japan (2002)

Image Annotation Using Latent Components and Transmedia Association

Anurag Tripathi[1][(✉)][iD], Abhinav Gupta[2][iD], Santanu Chaudhary[3][iD], and Brejesh Lall[1][iD]

[1] Department of Electrical Engineering, Indian Institute of Technology, New Delhi, India
eez128368@ee.iitd.ac.in
[2] ECE Department, JIIT, Noida, India
[3] CEERI, Pilani, India

Abstract. During the last decade, image collections have increased considerably. Searching these voluminous image databases over web requires either visual features or text available in form of captions or tags. Another issue with visual search is the ambiguity in tagging where same content is expressed in different words by different users. Therefore textual search, which is easier for representing information and reliable to access it, is generally used to explore huge database of images. Another issue with visual search is the ambiguity in tagging i.e. tagging of the same content using different words by different users. To address these issues, we propose a simple and effective image annotation model based on probabilistic latent component analysis (PLCA). In our framework, the probabilistic model serves two fold purpose: firstly to label various textual words against the images while the second being the identification of the visual features for tagging. In this paper, we resolve multi-tag problem against each image. This approach has been rigorously tested on LabelMe dataset and the results are found to be encouraging. This facilitates the multiple relevant tags to given input image.

Keywords: Expectation Maximization · Probabilistic latent component · Image annotation

1 Introduction

Image annotation is challenging but important task particularly for designing image retrieval systems. Annotation is defined as multi-label classification problem in which each image is associated to different number of different semantic keywords. Traditional solution is to manually annotate images and to search images based on these annotations. Due to large size of image corpus, automatic annotation of images is more reliable compared to manual tagging. However, automatic annotating is challenging task as it is difficult to establish correspondence between the keywords and image regions from the available training data. Several approaches exist in literature to address annotation task. Some authors

B.U. Shankar et al. (Eds.): PReMI 2017, LNCS 10597, pp. 493–500, 2017.
https://doi.org/10.1007/978-3-319-69900-4_63

consider annotation as translation from image instances to keywords. Yang and Mori [1], initially considered co-occurrence model for associating words against image regions. Different variants of this concept has been later published which differ particularly with respect to the association models. Further, translation model based approach proposed by Barnard et al. [2] represents each image as distribution of words. The links between visual words and tags were established using latent topic models like latent Dirichlet allocation (LDA). However, these latent topic models could not accurately model the underlying relationship between tags and words. Moreover, individual pixels or even image regions may be difficult to associate to tags. To this end, query expansion is a standard technique for reducing errors by associating context with individual tags.

Annotation can be performed manually using facilities like mechanical turk or automatically using intelligent algorithms. The reason is that the manual tagging of images may result in ambiguous tags i.e. annotating same content with different textual words. These errors are usually untraceable. On the other hand, automatic image annotation can be broadly categorized into two methodologies viz. visual similarity based labeling and semantic labeling. Visual similarity based labeling uses image similarities to transfer textual annotation from labeled images to unlabeled images under the assumption that similar images should have similar annotations [3]. While, semantic labeling makes correspondence between text and local image features under the assumption that similar local features should have similar annotations. The automatic image annotation based on visual similarity is ambiguous due to texture less regions.

In [4] the objective is to segment the photo into different classes. There may be ambiguity at local appearance at patch level e.g. a display unit may belong to TV, mobile, laptop etc. This ambiguity has been resolved fusing other contextual information from the surrounding for which [4] uses a CRF model. In [2,5–7] the LDA the statistical topic model approach has been extended to annotate the images. These approaches are used to learn the joint distribution between the image features and the corresponding tags associated with the images. These generative models employ latent variable to represent the underlying correlation between two modalities. Wherein these latent variables may be shared between the models or all the models can have their own set of latent variables. Liu et al. [8] propose a nonparametric approach for object recognition and scene parsing using label transfer. To segment and recognize the query image, the approach warps the pre-defined annotations and clubs multiple cues in MRF framework based on the dense scene correspondences obtained from SIFT flow. In the above discussion, we have investigated the drawback of both the methodologies of image annotation and propose a new methodology to overcome the drawbacks. In [10] PLCA is used in image for hierarchical classification in semi-supervised way. In [10] segmented object from the images of scene category is used to learn the model and these learned models are used for classification. We have extended this approach to image annotation. The main contribution of this paper is in adapting the probabilistic latent component analysis (PLCA) [11] for categorizing the images into multiple components. Here the components refer to the objects present in the image.

The major contributions of our work are:

1. In this approach, an image is described using visual components. These components are generated using low level features learned using probabilistic components.
2. The probability of components are used for representation compared to handcrafted features used in conventional approaches.
3. For extracting the latent relationship between components and tags, Expectation Maximization approach is used.

The paper is organized as follows. Section 2 describes the proposed framework. In Sect. 3 we present experimental results on image annotation and finally conclusions are given at the end.

2   Tag Prediction Using Latent Components

In this paper, novel tag prediction approach is proposed using latent component analysis. Visual words are extracted from input image using Probabilistic Latent Component Analysis (PLCA). PLCA is used for categorizing images into multiple components. Here the components refer to objects present in the image. The association between visual words (image features) and tags (referred to as textual words) is established by learning parameters using Expectation Maximization approach. The performance is further improved by finding visual co-occurrence of textual as well as visual features. This is done to showcase the fact that tree cannot occur in indoor images. Thus, probability of occurrence of tree with table will be significantly low. The detailed description of steps (see Fig. 1) involved are given below.

2.1   Preliminaries

For learning image annotation task, suppose we have N images $I = \{i_1, i_2 \ldots i_N\}$ and M semantic labels $L = \{l_1, l_2 \ldots l_M\}$. Features are extracted for each image (x_i) using bag of words model [12]. The spatial histogram of x_i is abstracted as a K-dimensional data point, where K corresponds to number of visual words in an image denoted as $\{c_1, c_2, \ldots, c_K\}$. Each image in the training set is associated with number of labels $(l \subset L)$. Each label vector $l_i \in \{0,1\}^N$ is a binary vector such that $l_i(k) = 1$ if x_i belongs to k^{th} semantic label and 0 otherwise.

2.2   Extracting Visual Words Using PLCA

This paper focuses on adapting probabilistic latent component analysis (PLCA) for categorizing image as mixture of latent components. The basic idea behind using latent variable analysis is the *Principle of local independence* i.e. if a latent

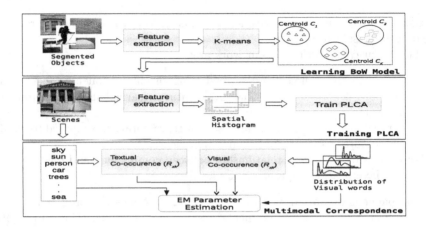

Fig. 1. Block diagram of proposed transmedia annotation model

variable causes a number of observed variables then the observed variables conditioned on that latent variable must be statistically independent. To find latent components from each image (x_i), we extract the dense image features from the corpus of images and quantize the feature space according to their statistics. In our approach we have used k-means clustering algorithm for quantization (Fig. 1). It may be noted that value of k depends on count of visual words [12]. The joint probability distribution $P(v, x_i)$ is given as

$$P(v, x_i) = \sum_z P(z)P(v|z)P(x_i|z) \tag{1}$$

where v represents visual words of image x_i and z is the latent variable corresponding to a given component. PLCA framework analyzes the underlying hidden structure of the given source image by characterizing the generative distribution. This is done by estimating the parameters of above equation from the observed $P(v, x_i)$. Parameter estimation is done by using expectation-maximization (EM) algorithm. In the learning stage, the multinomial distributions for each of the components is denoted by $P_s(w|z)$ and are learned for every source. The parameters $P_x(z)$ and $P_s(w|z)$ are randomly initialized and estimated iteratively using EM algorithm as given in Algorithm 1.

2.3   Visual and Textual Co-Occurrence

Textual co-occurrence based similarity define the closeness between two labels (for instance a and b). In this paper, textual co-occurrence between two labels is measured using cosine similarity, defined as

$$S_{ll}(a, b) = cos(l_a, l_b) = \frac{\langle l_a^T l_b \rangle}{||l_a|| ||l_b||} \tag{2}$$

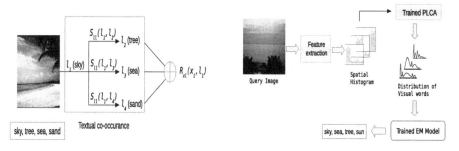

Fig. 2. Computing image to label correspondence using textual co-occurrence

Fig. 3. Illustrating tag prediction using proposed transmedia annotation model

where l_a is a binary vector and $\langle l_a^T l_b \rangle$ represents common images annotated to both a and b class. The label similarity matrix (S_{ll}) is symmetric.

In this paper, each image is represented as set of component probabilities (p_i) given as probability density function. The similarity between images (p, q) is defined using KL-divergence

$$S_{xx}(p, q) = \text{KL}(p, q) = \sum_i^K p(i) \log \frac{p(i)}{q(i)} \tag{3}$$

The similarity between images and labels is equal and symmetric (Fig. 2). Similarly, image to label similarity (R_{xl}) is defined for each image (i) that contains annotations $\{l_k | i \in l_k\}$,

$$R_{xl}(i, k) = \frac{\sum_{k' | i \in l_{k'}} S_{ll}(k, k')}{\sum_{k | i \in l_k} \sum_{k' | i \in l_{k'}} S_{ll}(k, k')} \tag{4}$$

The co-occurrence probabilities helps in assigning larger weights to words (visual and textual) that occur together for instance probability of word sun co-occurring with sky but vice versa might not be true.

2.4   Transmedia Association Model

After obtaining component probabilities against each image, machine translation model is designed from the training database to map visual topics to tags. To design the language translation model, each input image is represented as combined tuple of visual and textual words represented a

$$x_i = \{V_i, W_i\} = \{v_{i1}, v_{i2}, \ldots, v_{iK}, w_{i1}, w_{i2}, \ldots, w_{iL}\} \tag{5}$$

where v_{ij} is the probability of jth visual component in ith image and w_{ij} is the binary variable indicating whether the jth tag appears in image i. The significance of mapping model is to find the mixture by which jth visual word is associated to kth textual word. This association is established through the translation matrix (T). The probability of associating the jth textual word w_{ij} with kth visual component v_{ik} is defined as

$$p(W_i|V_i) = \prod_{l=1}^{L}(p(w_l|V_i))^{w_{il}} = \prod_{l=1}^{L}\left(\sum_{k=1}^{K}T_{lk}v_{il}\right)^{w_{il}} \tag{6}$$

The idea is to find the association between components and tags by upgrading the translation probabilities using all images in the training set. This is achieved by maximizing the likelihood, given as

$$L(X) = \prod_{i=1}^{N}L(x_i) = \prod_{i=1}^{N}L(W_i, V_i) = \prod_{i=1}^{N}p(W_i|V_i)p(V_i) = \prod_{i=1}^{N}\prod_{l=1}^{L}\left(\sum_{k=1}^{K}T_{lk}v_{il}\right)^{w_{il}} \tag{7}$$

The log likelihood function is maximized using

$$L(X) = \sum_{i=1}^{N}\sum_{l=1}^{L}\log\left(\sum_{k=1}^{K}T_{lk}v_{il}\right)^{w_{il}} \tag{8}$$

The expectation maximization approach is used to find the optimal association parameters (T). The probabilities are upgraded iteratively using

$$T_{jk} = \sum_{i} w_{ij}\left(\frac{R_{xl}(i,j)v_{ik}T_{jk}}{\sum_{k} v_{ik}t_{jk}}\right) \tag{9}$$

2.5   Tag Prediction

After estimating the optimal parameters (T), the probability of annotating a test image (y) with a textual word w_j is calculated as

$$p(w_j|V_y; T) \approx \sum_{k=1}^{m}T_{jk}v_{yk} \tag{10}$$

where V_y is set of visual words extracted from test image (y) using PLCA (see Fig. 3).

Algorithm 1. PLCA Training	**Algorithm 2.** Transmedia Association

Input: Test, Training images, no. of basis and Visual BOW
for $1,\ldots,maxiter_1$ **do**
  E-Step:
  $P_x(z\|w) = \frac{P_x(w\|z)P(z)}{\sum_z P_x(w\|z)P(z)}$
  M-Step:
  $P(z) = \frac{\sum_w P_x(w)P_x(z\|w)}{\sum_z \sum_w P_x(w)P_x(z\|w)}$
  $P(w\|z) = \frac{\sum_x P_x(w)P_x(z\|w)}{\sum_x \sum_w P_x(w)P_x(z\|w)}$
  Until Convergence
end for
Output: Component model
	Input: Components and Tags
	for $1,\ldots,maxiter_2$ **do**
	  E-Step:
	  $L(X) = \sum_{i=1}^{N}\sum_{l=1}^{L}\log\left(\sum_{k=1}^{K}T_{lk}v_{il}\right)^{w_{il}}$
	  M-Step:
	  $T_{jk} = \sum_i w_{ij}\left(\frac{R_{xl}(i,j)v_{ik}T_{jk}}{\sum_k v_{ik}t_{jk}}\right)$
	  Until Convergence
	end for
	Output: Optimal association parameter T

3   Experimental Results

To evaluate the performance of proposed automatic image annotation tool (Algorithms 1 and 2) we have used LabelMe dataset [13]. We have employed Lenovo P310 workstation with Intel Xenon $E3 - 1225v5@3.30$ GHz processor and 8 GB RAM for simulating our proposed approach. The MATLAB 2013a and LabelMe toolbox softwares are used. The dataset consists of 2689 images with annotations. For the purpose of evaluation, 80% images in the dataset is taken for training and the model is evaluated using remaining 20% of images. For the purpose of evaluation, results are analyzed with micro precision (Micro-P) and micro F1 (Micro-F1). Micro-P and Micro-F1 is defined as

$$\text{Micro-P} = \frac{\sum_{i=1}^{M} tp_i}{\sum_{i=1}^{M} tp_i + \sum_{i=1}^{M} fp_i} \tag{11}$$

$$\text{Micro-F1} = \frac{2PR}{P + R} \tag{12}$$

where P is precision, R is recall, tp are true positives, fp are false positives and fn are false negatives. Table 1 demonstrates comparative analysis of various tag prediction approaches and proves the efficacy of the proposed approach over state of the art approaches for tag prediction.

Table 1. Performance of various tag prediction approaches

Approach	Micro-P	Micro-F1
SVM	0.139	0.201
HF	0.127	0.106
RW	0.127	0.106
LS	0.136	0.138
I-BG [14]	0.210	0.311
LGC-BG1 [15]	0.503	0.532
LGC-BG2 [15]	0.506	0.537
Ours	**0.633**	**0.623**

4   Conclusion

In this paper we have proposed a probabilistic latent model approach for automatic image annotation using semi-supervised data. Our major contribution lies in implementing and using PLCA for image data which was previously used for audio. Further, the idea of associating visual words represented in form of components to textual words is achieved using translation model. This helps to achieve latent relationship between visual words present in the image to textual words.

The experiments are performed on LabelMe database and it is found that our approach outperforms state-of-the-art tag prediction approaches. This pioneers the applicability of the proposed approach in areas like scene understanding and tag recommendation.

References

1. Yang, W., Mori, G.: A discriminative latent model of image region and object tag correspondence. In: Proceedings of the 23rd International Conference on Neural Information Processing Systems (NIPS 2010), pp. 2397–2405. Curran Associates Inc., Red Hook (2010)
2. Barnard, K., Duygulu, P., Forsyth, D., Freitas, N., Blei, D.M., Jordan, M.I.: Matching words and pictures. J. Mach. Learn. Res. **3**, 1107–1135 (2003). doi:10.1162/153244303322533214
3. Makadia, A., Pavlovic, V., Kumar, S.: A new baseline for image annotation. In: Forsyth, D., Torr, P., Zisserman, A. (eds.) ECCV 2008. LNCS, vol. 5304, pp. 316–329. Springer, Heidelberg (2008). doi:10.1007/978-3-540-88690-7_24
4. Shotton, J., Winn, J., Rother, C., Criminisi, A.: TextonBoost: joint appearance, shape and context modeling for multi-class object recognition and segmentation. In: Leonardis, A., Bischof, H., Pinz, A. (eds.) ECCV 2006. LNCS, vol. 3951, pp. 1–15. Springer, Heidelberg (2006). doi:10.1007/11744023_1
5. Blei, D.M., Jordan, M.I.: Modeling annotated data. In: Proceedings of the 26th Annual International ACM SIGIR Conference on Research and Development in Information Retrieval. ACM (2003). doi:10.1145/860435.860460
6. Mcauliffe, J.D., Blei, D.M.: Supervised topic models. In: Advances in Neural Information Processing Systems (2008). doi:10.1109/ICDM.2015.148
7. Duangmanee, P., Attias, H.T., Nagarajan, S.S.: Topic regression multi-modal latent Dirichlet allocation for image annotation. In: IEEE Conference on Computer Vision and Pattern Recognition (CVPR). IEEE (2010). doi:10.1109/CVPR.2010.5540000
8. Liu, C., Yuen, J., Torralba, A.: Nonparametric scene parsing via label transfer. In: Hassner, T., Liu, C. (eds.) Dense Image Correspondences for Computer Vision, pp. 207–236. Springer, Cham (2016). doi:10.1007/978-3-319-23048-1_10
9. Shashanka, M., Raj, B., Smaragdis, P.: Probabilistic latent variable models as nonnegative factorizations. Comput. Intell. Neurosci. (2008). doi:10.1155/2008/947438
10. Atsumi, M.: Learning visual categories based on probabilistic latent component models with semi-supervised labeling. GSTF J. Comput. **2** (2012). doi:10.5176/2251-2179-ATAI20
11. Shashanka, M.: Latent variable framework for modeling and separating single-channel acoustic sources. Diss., Boston University, Boston (2007)
12. Tsai, C.F.: Bag-of-words representation in image annotation: a review. ISRN Artif. Intell. (2012). doi:10.5402/2012/376804
13. Russell, B.C., et al.: LabelMe: a database and web-based tool for image annotation. Int. J. Comput. Vision **77**, 157–173 (2008). doi:10.1007/s11263-007-0090-8
14. Wang, H., Huang, H., Ding, C.: Image annotation using bi-relational graph of images and semantic labels. In: CVPR 2011, Providence, RI, pp. 793–800 (2011). doi:10.1109/CVPR.2011.5995379
15. Pham, H.D., Kim K.H., Choi S.: Semi-supervised learning on bi-relational graph for image annotation. In: 22nd International Conference on Pattern Recognition, Stockholm, pp. 2465–2470 (2014)

Incremental Learning of Non-stationary Temporal Causal Networks for Telecommunication Domain

Ram Mohan[1(✉)], Santanu Chaudhury[2], and Brejesh Lall[2]

[1] R&D Department, Flytxt, Thiruvananthapuram, India
ram.mohan@flytxt.com
[2] Department of EE, Indian Institute of Technology, Delhi, India
{santanuc,brejesh}@ee.iitd.ac.in

Abstract. In today's competitive telecommunication industry understanding the causes that influence the revenue is of importance. In a continuously evolving business environment, the causes that influence the revenue keeps changing. To understand and quantify the effect of different factors we model it as a non-stationary temporal causal network. To handle the massive volume of data, we propose a novel framework as part of which we define rules to identify the concept drift and propose an incremental algorithm for learning non-stationary temporal causal structure from streaming data. We apply the framework on a telecommunication operator's data and the framework detects the concept drift related to changes in revenue associated with data usage and the incremental causal network learning algorithm updates the knowledge accordingly.

Keywords: Causes of effects · Incremental learning · Non-stationary causal networks

1 Introduction

Telecommunication operator needs to understand the factors that directly influence revenue, to stop any revenue loss. Factors for revenue loss can either be internal (Ex.: network quality issues) or external (Ex.: competitive offers). Traditional machine learning approaches are considered as black boxes. Modelling this as a causal network [5], helps us determine the various cause effect relationship amongst the variables, quantify how they impact the revenue and helps the domain expert to interpret (and validate) the learnt model. Most of the existing causal network learning algorithms require stationarity of time series, but in the telecommunication domain cause effect relationships undergoes changes with time and the learning algorithm should be able to capture the non-stationarity present, without which the causal network will be stale and forecasting of revenues will be less accurate. Also data volumes of the telecommunication subscriber database is huge and subscriber's call data records are continuous streams

© Springer International Publishing AG 2017
B.U. Shankar et al. (Eds.): PReMI 2017, LNCS 10597, pp. 501–508, 2017.
https://doi.org/10.1007/978-3-319-69900-4_64

and it is not possible to aggregate all the data available for learning at one go. Hence need arises for the learning algorithm to be incremental.

If we try to learn a global model for subscriber's usage to revenue mapping it is non-linear. Instead in data there are groups (clusters) of subscribers. Within the group, a model that maps recharge pattern and service utilization to revenue is actually linear. Hence we propose to use work of Ickstadt et. al [1] where it is shown how to learn non-parametric Bayesian network with infinite Gaussian mixture models (Bayesian network is a causal network if every edge displays cause effect relationship). It is well established that the mixture of multivariate Gaussian can approximate any density on R^d provided that the number of components can get arbitrarily large.

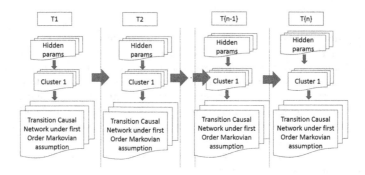

Fig. 1. Pictorial representation of non-stationary temporal causal model

To overcome the key challenges of non-stationarity and large volume of data, we model it as a non-stationary Temporal Causal Network (nsTCN - Fig. 1) and propose a incremental learning algorithm for learning nsTCN. Learning of a nsTCN involves learning the infinite Gaussian mixture model followed by learning transition causal network per cluster. We are learning the temporal network under first order Markovian assumption (FOMA), hence data record used for learning have variables from 2 successive time instances. Transition Causal network under first order Markovian assumption learns the cause effect relationship amongst the variables of current time instance along with the transition causal relationship between variables of previous time instance and current time instance. We have transition probabilities at cluster level to capture across cluster transition. We also associate hidden parameters with each of the clusters, which helps us model the hidden external factors (or confounding factors) influencing the cause effect relationship present within the cluster.

Our contributions for incremental learning of nsTCN are:

- Rules to determine concept drift, these rules are triggered on every batch of incoming data.
- A new algorithm to incrementally learn nsTCN's from streams of data, triggered only if a concept drift is detected.

More details on the solution are explained in the subsequent sections. Section 2 discusses about the related research, Sect. 3 discusses about the proposed solution, Sect. 4 discusses the experiments and its results, Sect. 5 is on future work and conclusion.

2   Related Research

Most causal discovery methods assume that cause effect relationship are static and try to learn it from the data. Pearl in her work [5] shows how causal inference in statistics can be modelled as a graphical model. We extend this to learn nsTCN in a incremental fashion.

Zhou et al. [6] modelled causal analysis in non-stationary setup as a Granger causality, instead we are interested in learning the causal network. Huang et al. [7] in their work, model a time-dependent causal network as part of which they model time as one of the causes for changing causal influences. They propose Gaussian Process regression for estimating the causal influence. Gaussian Process Regression learnt model has a memory requirement of $O(ND + N^2)$ which is quadratic in No. of training samples leading to a practical limit on No. of samples. Our work is different as (i) we propose an incremental learning algorithm (ii) we associate re-learning with identifying concept drift. (iii) we associate our cluster's with transition probabilities enabling it to forecast concept drift.

3   Proposed Solution

We cannot continuously learn from streaming data. Instead we first identify concept drift, if concept drift is detected then incrementally relearn nsTCN. Hence the proposed framework for incremental learning of nsTCN has following major tasks

- Rules to determine concept drift
- Algorithm to incrementally learn nsTCN

3.1   Rules to Identify Concept-Drift

A domain is non-stationary if it is associated with concept drift over time. Concept drift (CD) means that the statistical properties of the random variables have changed over time in unforeseen ways, leading to changes in cause effect relationship and the strength of their relationships.

Specific to nsTCN, rules are defined to determine the different types of concept drift, so that re-learning can be triggered accordingly.

- First type of concept drift: for new batch of data determine the KL divergence for subscriber record to cluster distribution, if the KL divergence is beyond a threshold then re-learning of type 1 is required.

– Second type of concept drift: For the new batch of data likelihood of the records associated with the clusters are determined. For any cluster if likelihood has dropped below a threshold re-learning of type 2 is required.

We use these rules in Algorithm 1. The information regarding type of relearning associated with each type is explained in the following section.

3.2   Algorithm to Incrementally Learn nsTCN

To learn clusters from streaming data we use work proposed by Huynh et al. [2]. We propose changes to conditional independence test equation used in PC-Stable Algorithm 3.2 to enable incremental learning of causal network per cluster.

Summarizing PC-Stable Algorithm with changes to partial correlation tests [4]

1. Learn skeleton by iteratively verifying pairwise conditional independence of variables given a set of observed variables $\{X^{(r)}; r \in k\}$. In each iteration the size of the set $\{X^{(r)}; r \in k\}$ (observed variables) is increased by 1.

2. To test whether $X^{(i)} \perp X^{(j)}|\{X^{(r)}; r \in k\}$ we compute Fisher's Z-Transform $Z(i,j|k) = \frac{1}{2}log\frac{1+\rho_{i,j|k}}{1-\rho_{i,j|k}}$

3. The partial correlation co-efficient $\rho_{i,j|k}$ can be learnt from pairwise correlation using dynamic programming as it has repetitive sub problem structure. $\rho_{i,j|k} = \frac{\rho_{i,j|k\backslash h}-\rho_{i,h|k\backslash h}\rho_{j,h|k\backslash h}}{\sqrt{(1-\rho_{i,h|k\backslash h}^2)(1-\rho_{j,h|k\backslash h}^2)}}$

4. When the observed variable set is of size 1 the partial correlation equation reduces to $\rho_{i,j|k} = \frac{\rho_{i,j}-\rho_{i,k}\rho_{j,k}}{\sqrt{(1-\rho_{i|k\backslash h}^2)(1-\rho_{j|k\backslash h}^2)}}$.

5. Equation 1 shows how $ci-suffStat$ collected per batch helps determine the partial correlation without having to visit the actual batch data

---

$$\rho_{i,j} = \frac{n\sum_{b\in batches}\sum X_b^{(i)}X_b^{(j)} - \sum_{b\in batches}\sum X_b^{(i)}\sum_{b\in batches}\sum X_b^{(j)}}{\sqrt{n\sum_{b\in batches}\sum X_b^{(i)^2}-(\sum_{b\in batches}\sum X_b^{(i)})^2} \cdot \sqrt{n\sum_{b\in batches}\sum X_b^{(j)^2}-(\sum_{b\in batches}\sum X_b^{(j)})^2}} \quad (1)$$

The key factor for designing an incremental algorithm is to identify additive operations and collect the required ci-sufficient stats. $ci-suffStat_{b_c} = (\sum X_b^{(i)}X_b^{(j)}, \sum X_b^{(i)}, \sum X_b^{(j)}, \sum X_b^{(i)^2}, \sum X_b^{(j)^2})$. Equation 1, show how using $ci-suffStat_{b_c}$ we determine the correlation between pair of variables, which in turn are rolled up to determine the skeleton.

The over all algorithm which incrementally learns the complete nsTCN from streaming (batchwise) data is presented in 1. The algorithm is triggered for every batch of data, which collects and caches the $ci-suffStat_{b_c}$ for every cluster,

---

Algorithmus 1. Algorithm to detect CD and update the causal networks

---

    procedure BATCHUPDATE($X = X_{t-1} \cup X_t$)
    cache the $ci - suffStat$ for the current batch $triggerRelearning = False$
    $relearningType = 1$ #1 for Just learning the causal structure, 2 to relearn the cluster and causal structure
4:    **if** $firstBatch$ **then**
        $triggerRelearning = True$
        $relearningType = 2$
    end if
    $conceptDrift, typeOfConceptDrift = Ruledriven$ #Populated based on the rules specified for concept drift
8:    **if** $conceptDrift$ **then**
        $triggerRelearning = true$
        $relearningType = typeOfConceptDrift$
    end if
12:    **if** $triggerRelearning$ and $relearningType == 1$ **then**
        for $cluster$: $clusters$ **do**
            if $cluster$ distribution has changed **then**

16:                PcAlgo as summarized in 3.2
                Update the parameters of the causal network.
            end if
        end for
20:    **end if**
    if $triggerRelearning$ and $relearningType == 2$ **then**
        $newClusters = null$
        for $cluster$: $clusters$ **do**
24:            Generate Data using the Causal network

            $newClusters$ =stream data to incremental clustering algorithm
        end for
28:        **for** $cluster$: $clusters$ **do**
            for $batch$: $batches$ **do**
                From the ci-suffStats of a batch Generate Data records.
                Identify new cluster allocation per record.
32:                Update ci-suffStats per batch per new cluster.
            end for
        end for
        $clusters = newClusters$
36:        **for** $cluster$: $clusters$ **do**
            Per cluster run PcAlgo as summarized in 3.2
            Update the parameters of the causal network.
        end for
        Cache the distribution for cluster to subscriber record mapping
40:    **end if**
    Forget the ci-suffStat associated with older
    end procedure

---

determines if concept drift has occurred and updates the causal network accordingly. We have different types of re-learning to be done as re-learning the cluster is computationally costly and type of relearning is determined by the concept drift rules.

4 Experimentation

For non-stationary causal analysis of ARPU (Average revenue per user) in telecommunication domain, raw data for the subscribers (.091 million) were collected, for a 8 month period (Aug 2016 to March 2017), from one of the leading Indian telecommunication service provider's database. The features are identified and a new dataset is built for the study. The dataset has a total of .7 million records (.091 million * 8 months) and around 32 features (one record includes subscriber's info from 2 successive time instance).

Except for GROSS ARPU and NET ARPU, all other features are resultants of a subscriber's transaction. A transaction is either of call made/received, sms sent, datausages and recharge. These transaction values are month-wise aggregated to form features. GROSS ARPU and NET ARPU are the operator determined values which represent the subscriber's overall monthly Revenue. Features are:

Decrement: value which is deducted per transaction from subscriber's core balance.

MrpOfRechargeDone: Market retail price of the recharge

TotalOgMou & TotalOgRev: Subscriber's out going call minutes and associated revenue generated for operator.

DataUsage, Data revenue & Data Arpu: data usage by subscriber and resultant revenue for the operator.

GrossArpu: GROSS average revenue per user. NetArpu: NET average revenue per user. StdOgMou & StdOgRev: national out going call minutes for the subscriber and resultant revenue for the operator.

TotalIcMou, TotalLocalIcMou & TotalStdIcMou: Overall, local and Std incoming call minutes for the subscriber.

LocalOnnetOgMou & LocalNetOgMou: within operator local outgoing call minutes for the subscriber.

As per the framework proposed, data is fed to the algorithm in batches, algorithm identified the cluster's and per cluster learnt associated causal network which explains how different usages affects the revenue. The framework also detected concept drift and updated required causal network accordingly.

As can be seen from the Fig. 2a the memory requirement for nsTCN is much lower than Huang et al.'s [7] GP Regression based causal analysis. The memory requirement for GP Regression is $O(ND + N^2)$ where as for nsTCN it is $O(KB(D^2) + KD^2)$ where N is the number of training records (samples), D is the number of features/random variables, K is the number of cluster identified and B is the number of batches for which the sufficient statistics are maintained.

Fig. 2. Comparisons

Now let us discuss results of the algorithm, which identified concept drift and associated nsTCN, on telecommunication domain's subscriber dataset. Figure 2b pictorially depicts cluster density distribution for top 3 clusters. It can be seen that for the month of December cluster 24 has seen an increase of 30% (from 21139 to 27724) subscriber records mapped to it, and the subscriber from the cluster 17 and cluster 15 have seen a drop in the subscriber mapped to them. The KL divergence was 0.09 above the threshold of 0.02.

In Cluster 17 the direct causal factors for Gross ARPU is Decrement. The direct causal factors for Decrement are TotalOgRev, DataRev, MrpOfRecharge-Done. Each of the revenues related to call, sms and data are influenced by respective usages. In Cluster 24 the data revenue did not contribute towards Gross ARPU of the subscriber.

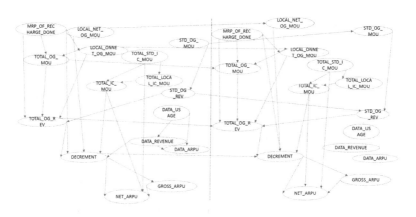

Fig. 3. Non-stationary temporal causal network associated with clusters'

Figure 3 shows the causal network for subscribers who underwent concept drift between the months of November and December. The complete disappearance of the edge suggests that the revenue dropped down to zero.

From the difference in causal network we can infer that the factors that caused the concept drift have to be related to subscriber's datausage. This heuristic matches with the launch of free services by a competitive Indian telecommunication operator in the month of December 2016 whose data related services were widely accepted by the subscribers. Using nsTCN to identify the concept drift and relearning, results in improvement for ARPU forecasting root mean square error (RMSE) to drop from 85.6 to 27.1.

5   Future Works and Conclusion

We propose a framework to incrementally learn nsTCN, as part of which we define rules to identify the concept drift and propose an algorithm to incrementally learn non-stationary temporal causal networks associated to a domain. We use our proposed framework to model real world telecommunication problem and identify the concept drift that occurred and see how non-stationary causal modelling helps us understand the impact on revenue. Also the Causal Networks provides us the insight that was very well matched with the dominant market forces.

As part of the future work without any modification to the algorithm we can add new variables in the dataset which captures seasonality and region, helping us to understand their influence on revenue. Also we can extend the algorithm to automate identification of hidden external factors based on the heuristic learnt.

References

1. Ickstadt, K., Bornkamp, B., Grzegorczyk, M., Wieczorek, J., Sheriff, M.R., Grecco, H.E., Zamir, E.: Nonparametric bayesian networks. In: Bayesian Statistics 9. Oxford University Press (2010)
2. Huynh, V., Phung, D.: Streaming clustering with Bayesian nonparametric models. Neurocomputing **258**, 52–62 (2017). Elsevier
3. Song, L., Kolar, M., Xing, E.: Time-varying dynamic Bayesian networks. In: Advances in Neural Information Processing Systems (2009)
4. Colombo, D., Maathuis, M.H.: Order-independent constraint-based causal structure learning. J. Mach. Learn. Res. **15**, 3921–3962 (2014)
5. Pearl, J.: Causal inference in statistics: an overview. Stat. Surv. **3**, 96–146 (2009)
6. Zhou, Y., Kang, Z., Zhang, L.: Costas Spanos causal analysis for non-stationary time series in sensor-rich smart buildings. In: Automation Science and Engineering (CASE) (2013)
7. Huang, B., Zhang, K., Scholkopf, B.: Identification of time-dependent causal model: a Gaussian process treatment. In: Proceedings of the Twenty-Fourth International Joint Conference on Artificial Intelligence (2015)

Effectiveness of Representation and Length Variation of Shortest Paths in Graph Classification

Asif Salim, S.S. Shiju, and S. Sumitra$^{(\boxtimes)}$

Department of Mathematics, Indian Institute of Space Science and Technology,
Thiruvananthapuram, India
asifsalim.16@res.iist.ac.in, {shijusnair.13,sumitra}@iist.ac.in

Abstract. Kernel methods are widely used for the classification of graphs. Different graph kernels have been proposed based on certain properties of graphs such as shortest paths, random walks, subtree patterns, subgraphs etc. Since shortest paths have been used for different graph kernel designs, we make a detailed analysis on the effectiveness of representation and effect of variation in length of shortest paths in classification of the node labeled graphs. We identified that certain modification in their conventional representation and resultant feature extraction gives better results and/or efficient feature representation rather than using them in their trivial definition mode. The effectiveness of resulting representations and length variations are analyzed with their ability to classify labeled graphs with an appropriate graph kernel design using support vector machines.

Keywords: Kernel methods · Shortest paths · Graph kernels · Support vector machines

1 Introduction

Graphs are considered to be universal data structure. It has a philosophical importance in the sense that any real world phenomena can be represented in the form of graphs [1]. Nowadays the usage of graphical tools in representing and analysing real world applications has been increased.

Kernel methods [2,3], which is based on statistical learning theory, have been applied successfully on various applications like classification of gene expression data, hand written recognition, text mining etc. The performance of kernel algorithms depends on the reproducing kernel used. The design of kernels that make use of the domain's nature and the geometry of data for complex non-vectorial points like graphs is a developing field of research. The first work on kernel designs on this direction was done by Haussler (1999) through his *R-convolution kernel* [4]. There after a lot graph kernels have been proposed whose designs are based on some particular properties of the graph [5–7].

© Springer International Publishing AG 2017
B.U. Shankar et al. (Eds.): PReMI 2017, LNCS 10597, pp. 509–516, 2017.
https://doi.org/10.1007/978-3-319-69900-4_65

2   Effect of Shortest Path Representations

We define a graph as a triplet $G = (\mathcal{V}, \mathcal{E}, l)$, where $\mathcal{V}$ is a set of nodes, $\mathcal{E}$ is a set of edges and l is a labeling function $l : \mathcal{V} \rightarrow \Sigma$ where Σ is an alphabet which contains all node labels. A *labeled graph* in this paper refers to an undirected graph having nodes being labeled according to l.

Let the shortest path of length n be represented as $\Pi(v_0, v_n) = \{v_0, v_1, v_2, ..., v_n\}$ where v_0 is the starting node, v_n is the destination node and v_i is the node encountering in i^{th} step.

Here we consider the labeled shortest paths for graph classification. The steps include identifying shortest paths and making a representation of the paths by constructing a string which constitutes the node labels that encounters at each node of the shortest path. We studied two ways of representation of the shortest paths and their representation capacity in classification problems are analyzed by defining an appropriate graph kernel as discussed below.

2.1   Trivial Representation

In this definition each shortest paths are represented as a string where i^{th} string component corresponds to the label of ith node encountered in the shortest path i.e., the paths are represented as

$$L_{SP}(\Pi) = \{l(v_0)l(v_1)l(v_2)\ldots l(v_n)\}$$

where $l(v_i)$ is the labeling function applied to node v_i.

2.2   Encoded Representation

We can think about another representation where we could count the presence of node labels rather than their order of occurrence as in trivial definition. It is obvious that this new encoded representation contains lesser number of features than previous. So in order to minimize the number of features we can introduce an encoding scheme to each L_{SP} as explained below.

First of all we define a dictionary D where elements of Σ is following a total ordering. Then separate total ordering is done according to the dictionary to each L_{SP} in two stages, (1) to the end nodes alone and (2) to the nodes that falls in between. Let $\mathcal{T}$ represents this two stage total ordering procedure. If a separate ordering is not given to end points, the shortest paths $\Pi(v_i, v_j)$ and $\Pi(v_j, v_i)$ between node v_i and v_j although same, will have two different representations and it results in an unnecessary increase in number of features.

An example is shown in the Fig. 1. Note that we have included zero length paths also as part of this feature representation. Zero length paths imply that the shortest path walker remains still in its starting position without any movements or equivalently it counts the occurrence of each node labels in the graph.

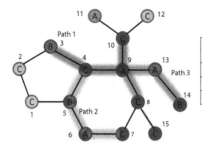

Shortest paths	Trivial representation	Encoded representation
Path 1-{3,4,9,10}	{B,C,A,C}	{B,A,C,C}
Path 2-{7,6,5,4}	{C,A,B,C}	{C,A,B,C}
Path 3-{8,9,13,14}	{C,A,A,B}	{B,A,A,C}

Fig. 1. Feature representation of certain shortest paths of length three corresponding to the highlighted portion of the graph (note that node labels are given inside circles). The table shows the node labels associated with these paths or trivial representation and their corresponding encoded representation (Color figure online)

2.3   Other Representation of Shortest Paths in the Literature

Shortest paths have been used widely for the classification purpose. Borgwardt et al. [6] used a shortest path representation (for the labeled graph) in the form of a triplet (v_1, v_2, l), where v_1 and v_2 are the labels of ordered end nodes and $l \in \mathcal{N}_0$ is the length of the path. Shervashidze et al. [7] applied this representation to their Wiesfeiler-Lehman graph kernel framework.

In the case of unlabeled graphs, Borgwardt et al. [6] represents the path as a scalar whose value is length of the shortest path. Note that this scalar representation can also be used in the case of labeled graphs (neglecting the labels). We compare the performance of our encodings with these above mentioned representations in Sect. 4.6.

2.4   Graph Kernel Definition

Now we apply the encoded representation given in Sect. 2.2 in an appropriate graph kernel to do the classification and compare the performance of other shortest path encodings as well as two other graph kernel definitions as explained in Sect. 4.6. The graph kernel is designed as follows.

Let $\Sigma_{G_i}^{P_k}, \Sigma_{G_j}^{P_k}$ be the sets containing all the strings produced by $\mathcal{T}$ applied to shortest paths of length k in graphs G_i and G_j.

For assessing the individual prediction capability we define the Labeled Shortest Path kernel(K_{LSP}) between graphs G_i and G_j as

$$K_{LSP}(G_i, G_j) = \sum_{k=1}^{p_{max}} \sum_{p \in \Sigma_{G_i}^{P_k}} \sum_{p' \in \Sigma_{G_j}^{P_k}} \delta(p, p')$$

where $p_{max} \in \mathcal{Z}_+$ is the maximum length of the path and δ is the Kronecker delta function.

Without loss of generality, same kernel definition can be applied to the strings produced by trivial representations of the graph where $\Sigma_{G_i}^{P_k}, \Sigma_{G_j}^{P_k}$ represents the strings produced by trivial representation of shortest paths.

Note that encoded representation gave better results in graph classification compared with trivial representation and it also resulted in a large reduction in number of features as discussed in Sects. 4.3 and 4.4.

3   Effect of Variation in Length of Shortest Paths

In this section we discuss about the effects of constraining shortest path lengths in graph classification. The overall idea is to compare whether the results got by using all length shortest paths have an improvement, once we restrict the shortest path length to a threshold.

The idea stems from the tottering effect observed in graph kernels [8]. It can be stated as: *"by iteratively visiting the same cycle of nodes (tottering), a walk can generate artificially high similarity values limiting the expressiveness of resultant kernel definition"*. Note that here we are not visiting a node more than once as per a single shortest path but when we consider several shortest paths this effect is more. Hence it is natural to limit the length of the shortest paths to a threshold before being used in the graph kernel definition in order to minimize tottering effect.

Considering this, we can make a modification in the graph kernel explained in previous section as explained below.

$$K_{LSP}(G_i, G_j) = \sum_{k=1}^{d} \sum_{p \in \Sigma_{G_i}^{P_k}} \sum_{p' \in \Sigma_{G_j}^{P_k}} \delta(p, p')$$

where $d \leq p_{max}$ is the length of the shortest paths upto which we have used for feature construction or threshold.

Note that the performance under this setting has improved compared with all shortest paths and the threshold d is fixed through cross validation.

4   Experiment

The efficiency of the proposed approaches was analyzed by subjecting them on real world data sets and compared its performance with graph kernels utilizing three shortest path representations mentioned in Sect. 2.3: Shortest Path (SP) kernel [6] for scalar and triplet representations, Weisfeiler-Lehman (WL)-SP [7] kernel (utilizing Borgwardt's [6] triplet representation in WL framework). We also compared kernel definition based on our encoding scheme with two other graph kernels namely: Random Walk (RW) kernel [5] (which makes use of random walks), and Weisfeiler-Lehman (WL)-subtree kernel [7] (which makes use of subtree patterns).

4.1   Datasets

The datasets used were MUTAG, PTC(MR), NCI1, NCI109 and PROTEINS. MUTAG [9] is a dataset of 188 mutagenic aromatic and heteroaromatic nitro compounds labeled according to whether or not they have a mutagenic effect on the Gramnegative bacterium Salmonella typhimurium. NCI1 and NCI109 [10] are two balanced datasets of chemical compounds (4110 and 4127 respectively) screened for activity against non-small cell lung cancer and ovarian cancer cell lines respectively. PTC(MR) [11] dataset describes the carcinogenicity of 344 chemical compounds for male rats. PROTEINS is a dataset of chemical compounds with two classes (enzyme and non-enzyme) introduced in [12].

4.2   Experimental Setup

The validation process were carried out in the following way. Using hold out technique 80% of the data points were assigned for training and the remaining for testing. 10 fold cross-validation was done on training data. The above process was repeated 30 times and the results reported were averaged over these 30 iterations to nullify the effects of fold assignments.

SVM is implemented using Libsvm [13]. The performance parameters used were accuracy and F-measure.

Accuracy is defined as the percentage of testing points predicted correctly.

$$Accuracy = \frac{TP + TN}{P + N}$$

where TP is "true positive" which is the count of correctly classified points in positive class, TN is "true negative" which is the count of correctly classified points in negative class, P and N is the number of testing points belonging to positive and negative class respectively. F-measure is defined as the harmonic mean between Precision and Recall, where

$$Precision = \frac{TP}{TP + FP} \ and \ Recall = \frac{TP}{P}$$

where FP is "false positive" which is the number of negative class data points misclassified into positive class.

4.3   The Effect of Shortest Path Encodings

Figure 2(a) shows the number of actual features and decrease in number of features when shortest path encoding is done.

It should be noted that although we are minimizing the number of features, it will not affect the classification performance. Figure 2(b) shows the accuracy with trivial features and encoded features using shortest paths of whole length (without applying any restriction on length of the path).

Note that the number of features getting reduced eventually depends on the number of unique labels associated with each graph in a dataset.

Dataset	Number of trivial features	Number of features via encoding
MUTAG	796	303
NCI1	134408	11280
NCI109	133269	11579
PTC(MR)	15575	3834
PROTEINS	89693	11092

a

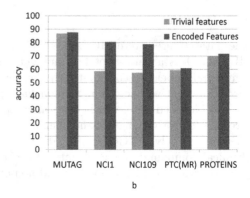

b

Fig. 2. The effect of shortest path encoding (a) comparison of number of features (b) comparison of accuracy with trivial features and encoded features

4.4   Effects of Choosing Paths of Different Length

The results in classification performance for varying shortest path lengths are given in Fig. 3. It is evident that limiting length of the path improves performance compared with the case where whole paths are used. It is noted that:

1. With shortest paths of length 1 alone accuracy increased to 89.78 from 87.58 in MUTAG dataset.
2. With shortest paths upto 9 length accuracy increased to 81.01 from 80.37 in NCI1 dataset.
3. With shortest paths upto 10 length accuracy increased to 80.32 from 78.51 in NCI109 dataset.
4. With shortest paths upto 7 length accuracy increased to 62.08 from 60.89 in PTC dataset.
5. With shortest paths upto 7 length accuracy increased to 71.97 from 71.56 in PROTEINS dataset.

4.5   Results

The accuracy and F-measure results are tabulated in Tables 1 and 2 respectively. The best results are given in bold letters.

4.6   Observations

The results reported under LSP kernel are for encoded representations and shortest path length limited by threshold identified through cross-validation. Proposed approach performs better than path/walk based kernels, RW kernel [5], Shortest Path kernel (with scalar and triplet representation) [6] and WL-Shortest Path kernel [7] and hence our encoding of shortest path performs better than other encodings. WL kernel [7] is based on subtree patterns and proposed framework comes second in performance where ever WL is better.

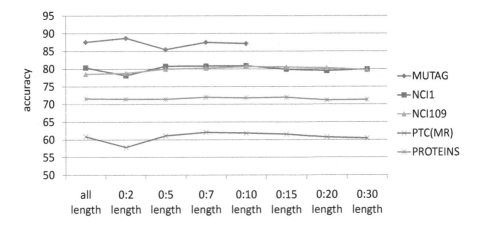

Fig. 3. The effect of variation in shortest path length in accuracy

Table 1. Accuracy of the proposed shortest path encoding based LSP kernel with other graph kernels

Kernel	MUTAG	NCI1	NCI109	PTC(MR)	PROTEINS
Kernels utilizing other encodings					
SP kernel[a]	88.68 ± 3.96	72.56 ± 1.74	71.73 ± 1.89	58.42 ± 5.87	57.56 ± 2.84
SP kernel[b]	87.84 ± 5.66	67.15 ± 1.63	70.63 ± 1.80	59.65 ± 6.02	73.83 ± 2.93
WL-SP	85.30 ± 5.08	83.54 ± 1.09	81.92 ± 1.88	59.60 ± 5.68	68.66 ± 3.15
Kernels utilizing other graph properties					
RW kernel	81.58 ± 2.67	65.57 ± 0.47	64.61 ± 0.37	53.64 ± 5.83	OUT OF TIME
WL-subtree	85.72 ± 5.81	**84.79 ± 1.11**	**83.81 ± 1.75**	60.93 ± 4.66	**74.67 ± 2.47**
LSP kernel	**89.78 ± 3.74**	81.01 ± 0.91	80.32 ± 1.14	**62.08 ± 4.01**	71.52 ± 2.36

[a]Shortest Path kernel applied with scalar representation
[b]Shortest Path kernel applied with triplet representation.

Table 2. F-measure of the proposed shortest path encoding based LSP kernel with other graph kernels

Kernel	MUTAG	NCI1	NCI109	PTC(MR)	PROTEINS
Kernels utilizing other encodings					
SP kernel[a]	89.57 ± 4.59	73.58 ± 2.15	72.44 ± 2.65	52.64 ± 5.84	62.45 ± 2.68
SP kernel[b]	88.76 ± 3.87	67.56 ± 1.78	71.59 ± 1.72	53.93 ± 7.23	77.74 ± 2.42
WL-SP	86.38 ± 5.42	83.48 ± 1.18	81.56 ± 1.85	52.18 ± 6.07	72.68 ± 3.03
Kernels utilizing other graph properties					
RW kernel	83.52 ± 5.61	65.76 ± 0.71	64.34 ± 0.49	46.40 ± 5.74	OUT OF TIME
WL-subtree	88.90 ± 4.35	**84.63 ± 1.18**	**83.41 ± 1.60**	52.21 ± 6.30	**78.40 ± 2.50**
LSP kernel	**91.58 ± 3.78**	81.00 ± 0.89	80.39 ± 1.16	**53.82 ± 5.73**	76.28 ± 2.24

[a]Shortest Path kernel applied with scalar representation
[b]Shortest Path kernel applied with triplet representation.

5   Conclusion

It has been identified that the shortest paths used in their trivial definition is not as effective as their encoded representation. It helps in decreasing the number of features to a greater extent. It is also identified that usage of higher lengthened paths are not contributing significantly to the classification tasks and limiting the shortest path length to a threshold improves the performance significantly. So a significant improvement in shortest path based approaches can be achieved by following the encoded representations and restriction on path length.

References

1. Dipert, R.R.: The mathematical structure of the world: the world as graph. J. Philos. **94**(7), 329–358 (1997)
2. Smola, A.J., Schölkopf, B.: Learning with Kernels. Citeseer (1998)
3. Shawe-Taylor, J., Cristianini, N.: Kernel Methods for Pattern Analysis. Cambridge University Press, Cambridge (2004)
4. Haussler, D.: Convolution kernels on discrete structures, Technical report. Citeseer (1999)
5. Vishwanathan, S.V.N., Schraudolph, N.N., Kondor, R., Borgwardt, K.M.: Graph kernels. J. Mach. Learn. Res. **11**, 1201–1242 (2010)
6. Borgwardt, K.M., Kriegel, H.-P.: Shortest-path kernels on graphs. In: Fifth IEEE International Conference on Data Mining (ICDM 2005), p. 8. IEEE (2005)
7. Shervashidze, N., Schweitzer, P., van Leeuwen, E.J., Mehlhorn, K., Borgwardt, K.M.: Weisfeiler-lehman graph kernels. J. Mach. Learn. Res. **12**, 2539–2561 (2011)
8. Mahé, P., Ueda, N., Akutsu, T., Perret, J.-L., Vert, J.-P.: Extensions of marginalized graph kernels. In: Proceedings of the Twenty-First International Conference on Machine Learning, p. 70. ACM (2004)
9. Debnath, A.K., Lopez de Compadre, R.L., Debnath, G., Shusterman, A.J., Hansch, C.: Structure-activity relationship of mutagenic aromatic and heteroaromatic nitro compounds. Correlation with molecular orbital energies and hydrophobicity. J. Med. Chem. **34**(2), 786–797 (1991)
10. Wale, N., Watson, I.A., Karypis, G.: Comparison of descriptor spaces for chemical compound retrieval and classification. Knowl. Inf. Syst. **14**(3), 347–375 (2008)
11. Toivonen, H., Srinivasan, A., King, R.D., Kramer, S., Helma, C.: Statistical evaluation of the predictive toxicology challenge 2000–2001. Bioinformatics **19**(10), 1183–1193 (2003)
12. Dobson, P.D., Doig, A.J.: Distinguishing enzyme structures from non-enzymes without alignments. J. Mol. Biol. **330**(4), 771–783 (2003)
13. Chang, C.-C., Lin, C.-J.: Libsvm: a library for support vector machines. ACM Trans. Intell. Syst. Technol. (TIST) **2**(3), 27 (2011)

An Efficient Encoding Scheme for Dynamic Multidimensional Datasets

Mehnuma Tabassum Omar$^{(\boxtimes)}$ (iD) and K.M. Azharul Hasan$^{(\boxtimes)}$ (iD)

Department of Computer Science and Engineering,
Khulna University of Engineering & Technology, Khulna, Bangladesh
misty2409@gmail.com, az@cse.kuet.ac.bd

Abstract. Big Data involve composite, undefined volume and unspecified rate of datasets [1]. The index array lags behind the conventional approaches to maintain the data velocity by allowing subjective expansion on the boundary of array dimension. The major concern of large volume applications like "Big Data" is to perceive data volume and high velocity for further operations. In this paper we offer a scalable encoding scheme that replaces data block allocation with segment allocation and reorganizes the n dimensions of array into 2 dimensions only. Hence it requires 2 indices for data encoding and offers low indexing cost.

Keywords: Array storage · Array indexing · Big data storage · Data encoding

1 Introduction

The territory of data volume progressively expands to terabytes and petabytes and expected to direct in Exascale computing [1]. Array based model like Conventional Multidimensional Array (CMA) can dominate other structures for their easy maintenance. But it is not scalable. The Index Array model [2, 3] solves this limitation by dynamically allocating memory during run time as form of subarrays (SA). But it cannot meet the expected demand of memory utilization as per the demand of data volume especially for "Big Data" applications [1] because of address space overflow. Again it is quite difficult to visualize the large volume of data. [4] mentions a structure which enhances the data volume capacity of Index Array by dealing address space overflow. The structure can also visualize the large volume of data by representing n dimension into 2 dimension only. But the most challenging task in large volume application is to get useful information as the volume entail sparsity [1]. Data encoding is an effective way to preserve only those cells that are meaningful and not-empty [5]. In this paper, we acclaim an encoding scheme based on SAI scheme [4]. The scheme is a segment based structure that encodes 2D indices of the SAI structure. We named the proposed encoding as Segment based Encoding Scheme and denoted as SES. The organization of the paper is as follows: Sect. 2 describes some related works. Section 3 revises the SAI model, Sect. 4 explains the proposed encoding scheme, Sect. 5 analyses the performances and Sect. 6 outlines the conclusion.

© Springer International Publishing AG 2017
B.U. Shankar et al. (Eds.): PReMI 2017, LNCS 10597, pp. 517–523, 2017.
https://doi.org/10.1007/978-3-319-69900-4_66

2 Related Work

Although large volume is the most needed property in various field of computation, the main challenge is to extract effective information from the volume due to sparsity. [6] deals sparsity in collaborative filtering using emotion and semantic based features. [7] handles sparsity for twitter sentiment analysis. The multi-dimensional indexed array based encoding scheme using history-offset has been initiated in [8] can also be found in [9, 10]. [11] shows an encoding scheme that undergoes indexing overhead and it can efficiently operate up to 4th dimension. [12] offers an encoding scheme where the compression ratio is not suitable for higher dimensional array. Most of the index model mentioned above demand nD indexing. In this paper, we represent a scalable segment based encoding scheme that utilize only 2D indices for an nD array. Therefore, can illustrate better performance than the other schemes.

3 Segment Based Array Indexing (SAI)

The proposed scheme is a 2D depiction of an nD array that allocates small segments. Consider an nD Conventional Multidimensional Array (CMA(n)) of size $A[l_1, l_2, \ldots, l_n]$. Then $<x_1, x_2, \ldots, x_n>$ be the Real nD Index (RnI); where l_i is the length of dimension d_i. Among CMA(n), $\lceil \frac{n}{2} \rceil$ number of odd dimensions fit along row direction d_1' and rest $\frac{n}{2}$ number of even dimensions fit along column direction d_2'. The CMA(n) is converted to $A'[l_1', l_2']$ and $<x_1', x_2'>$ be the Revised 2D Index (R2I) where l_1' and l_2' are the length of d_1' and d_2' respectively. So, $<x_1, x_2, \ldots, x_n>$ to $<x_1', x_2'>$ is done as follows:

$$x_1' = x_1 l_3 l_5 \ldots l_{n-3} l_r + x_3 l_5 \ldots l_{n-3} l_r + \ldots + x_r$$
$$x_2' = x_2 l_4 l_6 \ldots l_{n-3} l_c + x_4 l_6 \ldots l_{n-3} l_c + \ldots + x_c$$
$$r = \begin{cases} n-1, & \text{if n is even} \\ n, & \text{if n is odd} \end{cases} ; c = \begin{cases} n-1, & \text{if n is odd} \\ n, & \text{if n is even} \end{cases} \tag{1}$$

$$f(x_1', x_2') = \begin{cases} x_1' \times l_2' + x_2', & \text{if } d_1' \text{holds the SA} \\ x_2' \times l_1' + x_1', & \text{if } d_2' \text{holds the SA} \end{cases} \tag{2}$$
$$l_1' = l_1 \times l_3 \times \ldots \times l_r; \quad l_2' = l_2 \times l_4 \times \ldots \times l_c$$

For an extension along d_i, the SA size (saz) is calculated as $saz = \prod_{j=1}^{n} l_j (i \neq j)$, where l_j is the length of d_j. If the direction of SA is on d_2', then the segment size sgz is l_1', otherwise l_2' and the number of segment is calculated as $nos = \frac{saz}{sgz}$. Figure 1(a) shows a CMA(5) of size [2, 2, 2, 2, 2] by a SAI of $[l_1', l_2']$ or [8, 4]. The CMA index <1, 0, 1, 1, 0> is converted to SAI by <6, 1>. Figure 1(b) shows the segmentation of Fig. 1(a). Here, $saz = 32$, $l_2' = 4$ and the nos is $\frac{32}{4}$ or 8. The SAI includes five types of 2D Supplementary Tables (ST) for attaining scalability as: *History Table (HT)* stores construction history of the; *The Index Table (IT)* stores the initial index of the

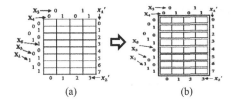

Fig. 1. Dimension transformation of a CMA(5)

corresponding extended dimension; *Extend Dimension (EDT)* tracks the scalable direction by assigning value 1 to n; *Multiplicative Coefficient Table (MCT)* stores co-efficient of x'_1 or x'_2 (Eq. 1); *Address Table (AT)* stores the first address of the first segment of SA.

Figure 2(a) shows a SAI after extending on d_2, d_1, d_4 respectively. The bold dotted SA shows an extension on d_2. Here, *saz* is 16 (*i.e* 2^4), *sgz* is 8 (*i.e* l'_1) and *nos* is 2 (*i.e* $\frac{16}{8}$). The 1st address of the 1st segment (*i.e* 32) is stored in $ST_2[1].AT$. The new history is stored in $ST_2[1].HT$. The new value of l_2 (i.e. 2) is stored in $ST_2[1].IT$ and d_2 is stored in $ST_2[1].EDT$ (i.e. 2). To retrieve a data, let, the row indexes are $(x_1, x_3, \ldots, x_r)$ and column indexes are $(x_2, x_4, \ldots, x_c)$. Let *max()* returns the maximum value and *Cmax()* returns the count of *max()*. Find $max_r = x_\alpha = max(x_1, x_3, \ldots, x_r)$, $m_r = Cmax(x_1, x_3, \ldots, x_r)$ and $max_c = x_\beta = max(x_2, x_4, \ldots, x_c)$, $m_c = Cmax(x_2, x_4, \ldots, x_c)$, where max_r is the maximum index value in row direction and x_α is the index position of α dimension in row direction that contains max_r and m_r is the count of the indexes that contain max_r. To find i (or j) from ST_1 (or ST_2) there can be two cases using m_r (or m_c) as follows:

  i. If $m_r = 1$, find i such that $ST_1[i].IT = max_r = x_\alpha$ and $ST_1[i].EDT = \alpha$

  ii. If $m_r > 1$, $m_r = a$. Let $i_1, i_2, \ldots, i_a$ contains max_r such that $ST_1[k].IT = max_r = x_\alpha$ and $ST_1[k].EDT = \alpha$ where $1 \leq k \leq a$. Now from $i_1, i_2, \ldots, i_a$ find $h_{max} = max(ST_1[i_1].HT, ST_1[i_2].HT, \ldots, ST_1[i_a].HT)$. Find i such that $h_{max} = ST_1[i].HT$.

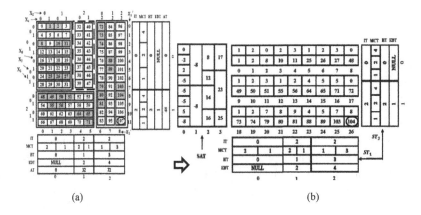

Fig. 2. A realization of a SES System

Find $H_{max} = \max(ST_1[i].HT, ST_2[j].HT)$ (SA direction) and recall x'_1, x'_2 as follows:

$$x'_1 = x_1 ST_1[i].MCT[0] + x_3 ST_1[i].MCT[1] + .. + x_r ST_1[i].MCT\left[\left[\frac{n}{2}\right] - 1\right]$$

$$x'_2 = x_2 ST_2[j].MCT[0] + x_4 ST_2[j].MCT[1] + .. + x_c ST_2[j].MCT\left[\frac{n}{2} - 1\right]$$

If $ST_1[i].MCT_{max}$ is the maximum MCT on ST_1, then find start index (sx'), segment number (SN), segment's first address (SFA) and value (VALUE) as follows:

$$sx' = \begin{cases} ST_1[i].IT \times ST_1[i].MCT_{max}, \text{when } SA \text{ exists on } d'_1 \\ ST_2[j].IT \times ST_2[j].MCT_{max}, \text{when } SA \text{ exists on } d_2 \end{cases} \quad (4)$$

$$SN = \begin{cases} x'_1 - sx', \text{when } SA \text{ exists on } d'_1 \\ x'_2 - sx', \text{when } SA \text{ exists on } d'_2 \end{cases} \quad (5)$$

$$SFA = \begin{cases} ST_1[i].AT[0] + SN \times l'_2, \text{when } SA \text{ exists on } d'_1 \\ ST_2[j].AT[0] + SN \times l'_1, \text{when } SA \text{ exists on } d'_2 \end{cases} \quad (6)$$

$$VALUE = \begin{cases} SFA + x'_2, \text{when } SA \text{ exists on } d'_1 \\ SFA + x'_1, \text{when } SA \text{ exists on } d'_2 \end{cases} \quad (7)$$

Let $(x_1, x_2, x_3, x_4, x_5) = (2, 2, 1, 2, 1)$. For row $max_r = 2$, $Cmax(2, 1, 1) = 1$ and $x_\alpha = x_1 = 2, \alpha = 1$. Select ST_1 index $i = 1$ ($ST_1[1].IT = 2$ and $ST_1[1].EDT = 1$). For column, $max_c = 2$, $Cmax(2, 2) = 2$. Select ST_2 index $j_1 = 1$, $j_2 = 2$ and $j = 2$ (j_2 is larger).

And $x'_1 = 2 \times 4 + 1 \times 2 + 1 \times 1 = 11$ and $x'_2 = 2 \times 1 + 2 \times 3 = 8$ (Eq. 1). $H_{max} = ST_2[2].HT$, $sx' = 2 \times 3 = 6$ (Eq. 4), $SN = 8 - 6 = 2$ (Eq. 5), $SFA = 72 + 2 \times 12 = 96$ (Eq. 6) and VALUE $= 96 + 11 = 107$ (Eq. 7).

4 Segment Based Encoding Scheme

In 2D SES scheme, the index that exhibits the SA direction is called major index and the rest is named as minor index. The 2D Address Table (AT) is replaced by a 1D Segment Address Table (SAT) that contains each segment's locations of a SA. For empty segments, it stores the negation of next available non-empty memory position. The SES representation of Fig. 2(a) (shaded empty cells) is shown in Fig. 2(b). The non-empty cells are replaced by its value and minor index. Consider the third segment of the first SA in Fig. 2(a). The minor index is x'_2. So three tuples <0, 8>, <2, 10> and <3, 11> will be stored by SES. The location of tuple <0, 8> will be pointed by SAT[0] [2]. As, the next segment is empty, it will store -5. To encode an array non-empty cell, the R2I, H_{max} and SN are calculated (see Sect. 3). The segment's first non-empty cell is located in SAT[H_{max}][SN]. Now, perform a binary search to find the minor index. Given an RnI $(x_1, x_2, x_3, x_4, x_5) = (2, 2, 0, 2, 0)$. The R2I, H_{max} and SN are <8,8>, 3,

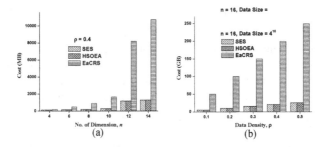

Fig. 3. Storage requirement

2 respectively. As SAT[H_{max}][SN] > 0, the segment is non-empty. Now, minor index x'_1 or 8 shows that the value is 104.

5 Performance Analysis

The analysis has been employed in Intel(R) Xeon(R) E5620 @ 2.40 GHz processor having 8 processors, 32 GB RAM, 1406 MB cache memory. The program is written in C and the data size is 8 Bytes. The analysis is linked with HSOEA [11], EaCRS [12]. The cost of EaCRS is always higher compared to others as it requires nD history and column information and n-1D row information for data encoding. Figure 3 illustrates the storage requirements. The SES and HSOEA scheme requires two parameters to encode nD data.

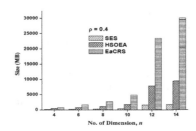

Fig. 4. Encoding cost

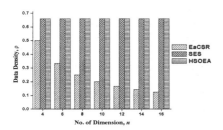

Fig. 5. Range of usability, υ

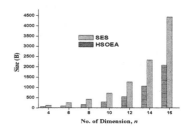

Fig. 6. Indexing overhead

Figure 3(a) shows storage requirement with varying dimensions and Fig. 3(b) shows storage requirement with varying data density $\rho = \frac{number\ of\ non-empty\ cells}{total\ number\ of\ cells}, 0 \leq \rho \leq 1$. Figure 4 shows the encoding costs. The HSOEA requires nD history, 2D segment number and 2D offset. The SES beats the others as it requires 2D indices to encode nD data. The range of usability (v) of an encoding scheme is the greatest ρ fit for the compression ratio ($\eta = \frac{size\ of\ compessed\ array}{size\ of\ uncompressed\ array} < 1$). The SES and HSOEA points the range of usability at $\rho = 0.66$, which is higher than EaCRS scheme as shown in Fig. 5. The SES and HSOEA monitors each segment's first address as the SA is divided into segments. The EaCRS does not offer segmentation. The HSOEA needs nD indices and extra metrics after 4th dimension. So, index overhead is less in SES as shown in Fig. 6.

6   Conclusion

The size of data to be needed is expanding gradually. Conversely, in real world the amount of effective data is very small for the presence of sparsity. It is very challenging to deal with sparsity while keeping the additional costs like data compression. Here, we present a 2D encoding scheme for nD array. We have shown that the proposed scheme can effectively encodes 66% data while reducing the indexing and encoding cost accordingly. It can be used in big data storage and parallel or multiprocessor environment.

References

1. Reed, D.A., Dongarra, J.: Exascale computing and big data. Commun. ACM **58**(7), 56–68 (2015). doi:10.1145/2699414
2. Rotem, D., Zhao, J.L.: Extendible arrays for statistical databases and OLAP applications. In: 8th International Conference on Scientific and Statistical Database Systems (SSDBM), pp. 108–117 (1996). doi:10.1109/SSDM.1996.506053
3. Otoo, E.J., Nimako, G., Ohene-Kwofie, D.: Chunked extendible dense arrays for scientific data storage. Parallel Comput. **39**(12), 802–818 (2013). doi:10.1016/j.parco.2013.08.006
4. Omar, M.T., Azharul Hasan, K.M.: Towards an efficient maintenance of address space overflow for array based storage system. In: Proceeding of the 17th International Conference on Parallel and Distributed Computing, Applications and Technologies (2016)
5. Hasan, K.M.A.: Compression schemes of high dimensional data for MOLAP. In: Evolving Application Domains of Data Warehousing and Mining: Trends and Solutions, Chap. 4, pp. 64–81 (2010). doi:10.4018/978-1-60566-816-1.ch004
6. Moshfeghi, Y., Piwowarski, B., Jose, J.M.: Handling data sparsity in collaborative filtering using emotion and semantic based features. In: SIGIR 2011, pp. 625–634 (2011). doi:10.1145/2009916.2010001
7. Saif, H., He, Y., Alani, H.: Alleviating data sparsity for Twitter sentiment analysis. In: 2nd Workshop on Making Sense of Microposts (#MSM2012): Big Things Come in Small Packages at the 21st International Conference on the World Wide Web (WWW 2012), 16 April 2012, Lyon, France, CEUR Workshop Proceedings, pp. 2–9 (2012). doi:10.1.1.309.6821

8. Hasan, K.M.A., Tsuji, T., Higuchi, K.: An efficient implementation for MOLAP basic data structure and its evaluation. In: Kotagiri, R., Krishna, P.Radha, Mohania, M., Nantajeewarawat, E. (eds.) DASFAA 2007. LNCS, vol. 4443, pp. 288–299. Springer, Heidelberg (2007). doi:10.1007/978-3-540-71703-4_26

9. Tsuchida, T., Tsuji, T., Higuchi, K.: Implementing vertical splitting for large scale multidimensional datasets and its evaluations. In: Cuzzocrea, A., Dayal, U. (eds.) DaWaK 2011. LNCS, vol. 6862, pp. 208–223. Springer, Heidelberg (2011). doi:10.1007/978-3-642-23544-3_16

10. Tsuji, T., Amaki, K., Nishino, H., Higuchi, K.: History-offset implementation scheme of xml documents and its evaluations. In: In 18th International Conference on Database Systems for Advanced Applications, pp. 315–330 (2013). doi:10.1007/978-3-642-37487-6_25

11. Sk, M., Masudul Ahsan, K.M., Hasan, A.: An efficient encoding scheme to handle the address space overflow for large multidimensional arrays. J. Comput. **8**(5), 1136–1144 (2013). doi:10.4304/jcp.8.5.1136-1144

12. Islam, R., Hasan, K.M.A., Tsuji, T.: EaCRS: an extendible array based compression scheme for high dimensional data. In: 2nd Symposium on Information and Communication Technology (SoICT 2011), pp. 92–99 (2011). doi:10.1145/2069216.2069237

Deep Learning

Stacked Features Based CNN for Rotation Invariant Digit Classification

Ayushi Jain[1]⬤, Gorthi R.K. Sai Subrahmanyam[2]⬤, and Deepak Mishra[1(✉)]⬤

[1] Department of Avionics, Indian Institute of Space Science and Technology,
Trivandrum 695547, Kerala, India
`ayushijain.168@gmail.com, deepak.mishra@iist.ac.in`
[2] Department of Electrical Engineering, Indian Institute of Technology,
Tirupati 517506, A.P., India
`rkg@iittp.ac.in`

Abstract. Covolutional neural networks extract deep features from input image. The features are invariant to small distortions in the input, but are sensitive to rotations, which makes them inefficient to classify rotated images. We propose an architecture that requires training with images having digits at one orientation, but is able to classify rotated digits oriented at any angle. Our network is built such that it uses any simple unit of CNN by training it with single orientation images and uses it multiple times in testing to accomplish rotation invariant classification. By using CNNs trained with prominent features of images, we create a stacked architecture which gives adequately satisfactory classification accuracy. We demonstrate the architecture on handwritten digit classification and on the benchmark mnist-rot-12k. The introduced method is capable of roughly identifying the orientation of digit in an image.

1 Introduction

Feature extraction and classification have become much more simpler and efficient with the aid of convolutional neural networks(CNN). They use a series of convolution, non-linear activation, sub-sampling and fully connected layers to extract deep hierarchical features from the input image. CNNs have extensively been applied for computer vision and classification tasks such as texture classification [1], image super resolution [2], medical image segmentation [3], etc.

CNN features are highly distinguishable and invariant to scale changes and distortions in the input. But they are sensitive to rotations in the image. Thus a CNN trained with images having digits at one orientation may fail to classify images with rotated digits. Nonetheless, attempts have been made to achieve rotation independent classification by rotating the training dataset at various angles and using large rotated dataset for training. This technique is called data augmentation and has been used in many works including [4,5]. But large training data requires larger training time. Also, augmented data contains rotated form of same image, thus it might have redundant features. Another approach for rotation invariant classification is Spatial Transformer Networks [6] in which

© Springer International Publishing AG 2017
B.U. Shankar et al. (Eds.): PReMI 2017, LNCS 10597, pp. 527–533, 2017.
https://doi.org/10.1007/978-3-319-69900-4_67

they introduce a STN module which has a localisation sub-network that learns the parameters of transformation from the input image and transforms the feature maps across a sampling grid using those parameters such that the overall cost function is minimized. But inserting a STN module in a network makes the training more complicated.

We introduce an architecture that is trained with images having digits at single orientation (say 0°) and is able to classify the digits rotated at any angle. We introduce multiple instance testing to accomplish the task, which uses a trained CNN architecture various times in testing and decides the final label based on the activations obtained from multiple CNNs. CNN has the ability to include different features in terms of maps to arrive at better classification or recognition and we have utilized this fact to improve the proposed basic architecture to achieve even better classification by replicating it with datasets derived from enhanced features such as edges, morphological operations, etc. The introduced architecture is also capable of estimating the approximate orientation of digit in the input image without any additional computations.

2   Proposed Architecture: RIMCNN

In various classification tasks such as digit classification, object classification, etc., the orientation of digit/object in an image is very crucial. An ideal classifier should be able to classify all digits irrespective of persons handwriting which can be erect or slanted. Also, it might benefit automated readability of scanned documents, as documents scanned in any direction can be correctly read.

We design an architecture that can identify rotated digits at all angles without any complexity in training. It can achieve rotation invariant digit classification using multiple instances in training. We will use the abbreviated form of the architecture 'RIMCNN' throughout the paper. The architecture has two stages: (a) Training (b) Testing

2.1   Training

As mentioned above, the proposed architecture requires simple training, as is done for any CNN. We construct or choose an existing CNN architecture which is efficient enough to classify test data having images with digits without rotations, and train it with available data. We do not introduce any rotation or modification in the network during training. The selected CNN is trained with stochastic gradient descent (SGD) approach. This trained network is then used in testing.

2.2   Testing

This is the essential phase of our architecture that differs from other methods which merely evaluate the trained network with test dataset. It is quiet obvious and proven that the network trained with images having non-oriented digits is able to classify the non-oriented test images successfully. But when tested with rotated images, the network becomes inefficient. We build a rotation invariant CNN architecture by using a basic CNN unit multiple times in testing.

The CNN trained in the training phase is used in parallel for N times. The inputs to CNNs are N rotated versions of original image i.e. original image rotated at N angles $(L_1, L_2, ..., L_N)$. Thus each test image is rotated N times and each rotated version is fed to a parallel instance of trained CNN. The motivation behind the selected approach is that the CNN unit which gets that rotated version of test image that has orientation closer to that of training data, will always produce correct label. Also, it is observed that the activation produced by that CNN for correct label will always be higher than the activations produced by all other CNNs for all labels. Thus by selecting the label corresponding to maximum response is decided as the final label. Thus if we have C classes, then each CNN will generate $C \times 1$ output. Now if we use N rotations in testing, then we get $N \times C$ responses at the output of RIMCNN. Now final label is the one which generates the maximum response among $N \times C$ outputs.

For handwritten digit classification, LeNet-5 architecture introduced in [7] is a very efficient architecture. Thus we use the same for evaluating our results. The RIMCNN test architecture with LeNet is shown in Fig. 1.

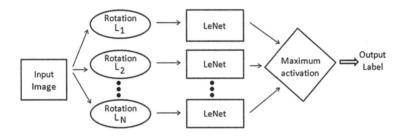

Fig. 1. RIMCNN test phase

Number of CNN Units and Rotation Angles. The number of CNN units(N) and rotation angles$(L_1, L_2, ..., L_N)$ depend on the application. The rotation angles should be selected such that they span the entire range of rotation in the test data, say (L_{min}, L_{max}). If rotations in test data are not known in prior, the angles can be uniformly spaced between $0°$ to $360°$. Higher is the number of CNN units selected(N), higher is the accuracy for all rotations, but more is the testing time. so there is always a trade-off between N and classification error.

Orientation of Digit in Test Image. The highest response is obtained from the angle (say L_k) that brings the digit closer to the orientation that was included in the training dataset, thus negative of the angle L_k gives the approximate orientation of the digit in the test image. Now if we wish to get more accurate orientation, then we can use another stage of RIMCNN that has rotation angles sampled around L_k. Thus, without any additional complexity, we can obtain the rough estimation of digit-orientation.

3   Modified-RIMCNN

The basic RIMCNN discussed above is a simple approach with fair results, but selecting the final label is merely based on the maximum activation, which might not be always reliable. To further improve the accuracy in classification, we apply RIMCNN for some of the enhanced features of the original images, such as edges, morphological features, etc. However, these features independently do not improve classification. But when stacked together, they boost up the performance of RIMCNN. We extract edges from the original MNIST dataset to obtain edge dataset. Also, we dilate the original dataset to obtain dilated dataset. Now we train two different LeNet architectures with edge and dilated datasets respectively. RIMCNN is applied using three LeNets trained individually with original, edges and dilated images. Now instead of selecting the class corresponding to maximum activation as the final class, we select the class based on the outputs of all three LeNets. We find the vector sum of output activations from three LeNets, for each rotation, and decide the final label as the class which gives the maximum sum. The modified architecture is shown in Fig. 2.

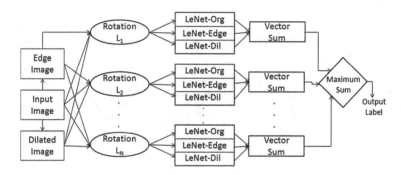

Fig. 2. Modified RIMCNN with edges and dilation. Lenet-Org, LeNet-Edge and LeNet-Dil are the LeNet-5 architectures trained on Original, Edges and Dilated datasets respectively

4   Simulation Results

We applied our architecture for handwritten digit classification using LeNet-5 as the basic CNN unit and observe that it performs better than LeNet for rotated test data. All simulations have been performed using a high-level neural networks library Keras(1.0.5) running on top of Theano(0.8.2). Intel(R) Xeon(R) X5675 computer with 24 GB RAM and NVIDIA Quadro 6000 graphics card is used. We evaluated our architecture on two datasets:

(i) MNIST [8]
(ii) mnist-rot-12k [9]

4.1 Performance Evaluation on MNIST Dataset

MNIST dataset consists of 60000 handwritten digits images divided into 50000 images for training and 10000 images for testing. We rotate the test dataset at different angles to analyse rotation independent abilities of our network. To account for the boundary distortions caused on rotating an image, we center the original 28×28 image in larger image(52×52). Also, on rotation between $0°$ to $360°$, the class-9 and 6 images may look similar, so we discard all images belonging to class 9 to avoid any ambiguity in classification. Thus the resultant 9-class dataset contains 54000 images for training and 9000 test images rotated across center, at steps of $10°$ between $0°$ to $360°$ for testing. We train the LeNet-5 architecture with 54000 images and use it in RIMCNN for testing with 36 rotated versions of 9000 test images. The results obtained from RIMCNN and Modified-RIMCNN with $N = 12$ on modified MNIST dataset and its comparison with LeNet is shown in Fig. 3.

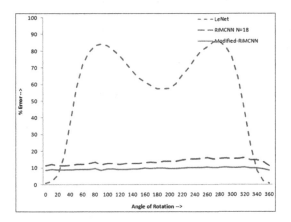

Fig. 3. Comparison of classification error (Y-axis) between RIMCNN and LeNet for MNIST test data rotated at various angles (X-axis)

4.2 Performance Evaluation on Mnist-rot-12k Dataset

The dataset mnist-rot-12k [9] is derived by rotating the images of MNIST dataset at random angles between $0°$ to $360°$. It has 12000 training images and 50000 test images containing rotated digits. As our architecture has an advantage that it doesn't require rotations for training, thus we can use the already existing model trained with MNIST dataset for testing rotated dataset as well. On using the same model, as was used in Sect. 2 on MNIST dataset, in RIMCNN with $N = 13$ and rotations uniformly sampled between $0°$ to $360°$, we achieve the classification accuracy of 86.73% on test images. RIMCNN takes 649.65 s for testing the given set of images. On applying modified RIMCNN introduced in Sect. 3 on the same dataset, accuracy is further improved to 89.36%. We demonstrate test error for different configurations of RIMCNN in Table 1.

Table 1. Test error comparison for different configurations of RIMCNN trained with original MNIST dataset (without rotation) and tested with mnist-rot-12k test data

RIMCNN-N	% test error
RIMCNN-6	18.66
RIMCNN-10	14.9
RIMCNN-13	13.27
Mod-RIMCNN-13	10.64

[10] compare their results with other architectures for mnist-rot dataset created by them. The approach they use to create their dataset is similar to that used for mnist-rot-12k, thus both datasets, more or less, are comparable. Almost all state-of-the-art architectures use rotated data for training. Since our architecture is not trained with rotated samples, whereas all other methods use rotated samples in some form, our results on classification accuracy cannot be directly compared with those obtained using state-of-the art methods. For fair comparison of our approach with state of the art methods, we include their results when they are **trained on the original training set (without rotation) and tested with rotated images**. ORN [10] achieves the lowest error of 16.21% against 55.59% error by STN [6], when trained without rotations and tested with rotated images. We manage to achieve the lowest possible error rates of 13.27% and 10.64% using RIMCNN and Modified RIMCNN respectively.

From the training time comparison made in [10], we can observe that their baseline CNN takes the minimum time of 16.4 s per epoch, let us denote this time by T, then ORN ([10]) and STN [6] take $1.09 \times T$ and $1.14 \times T$ s respectively, whereas TI-Pooling [11] takes the maximum time i.e. $7.73 \times T$ for one epoch. If our method is compared with them, it uses only a baseline CNN (LeNet), thus will take the minimum time for training among all networks.

5   Conclusion and Future Work

The introduced architecture is able to classify handwritten digits even at higher degree of rotation. It requires minimal training and shows better performance than LeNet architecture. It has an additional advantage of using pre-trained deep networks without any fine-tuning.

Its ability to identify rotated digits makes it applicable for rotated CAPTCHA recognition. It can further be applied to various tasks which demand rotation invariant classification such as texture classification, object recognition, etc. It can estimate the orientation of objects in the image, thus can be used in robotics, object tracking, etc.

References

1. Gonzalez, D.M., Volpi, M., Tuia, D.: Learning rotation invariant convolutional filters for texture classification. CoRR, abs/1604.06720 (2016)

2. Dong, C., Loy, C.C., He, K., Tang, X.: Image super-resolution using deep convolutional networks. IEEE Trans. Pattern Anal. Mach. Intell. **38**(2), 295–307 (2016)
3. Kayalibay, B., Jensen, G., van der Smagt, P.: CNN-based segmentation of medical imaging data. CoRR, abs/1701.03056 (2017)
4. Dieleman, S., Willett, K.W., Dambre, J.: Rotation-invariant convolutional neural networks for galaxy morphology prediction. Monthly Not. R. Astron. Soc. **450**(2), 1441–1459 (2015)
5. Tivive, F.H.C., Bouzerdoum, A.: Rotation invariant face detection using convolutional neural networks. In: King, I., Wang, J., Chan, L.-W., Wang, D.L. (eds.) ICONIP 2006. LNCS, vol. 4233, pp. 260–269. Springer, Heidelberg (2006). doi:10.1007/11893257_29
6. Jaderberg, M., Simonyan, K., Zisserman, A., Kavukcuoglu, K.: Spatial transformer networks. CoRR, abs/1506.02025 (2015)
7. LeCun, Y., Bottou, L., Bengio, Y., Haffner, P.: Gradient-based learning applied to document recognition. Proc. IEEE **86**(11), 2278–2324 (1998)
8. LeCun, Y., Cortes, C.: MNIST handwritten digit database. AT&T Labs (2010). http://yann.lecun.com/exdb/mnist
9. Larochelle, H., Erhan, D., Courville, A., Bergstra, J., Bengio, Y.: An empirical evaluation of deep architectures on problems with many factors of variation. In: Proceedings of the 24th International Conference on Machine Learning, ICML 2007, pp. 473–480, New York, NY, USA. ACM (2007)
10. Zhou, Y., Ye, Q., Qiu, Q., Jiao, J.: Oriented response networks. CoRR, abs/1701.01833 (2017)
11. Laptev, D., Savinov, N., Buhmann, J.M., Pollefeys, M.: TI-POOLING: transformation-invariant pooling for feature learning in convolutional neural networks. CoRR, abs/1604.06318 (2016)

Improving the Performance of Deep Learning Based Speech Enhancement System Using Fuzzy Restricted Boltzmann Machine

Suman Samui[(⊠)], Indrajit Chakrabarti, and Soumya K. Ghosh

Indian Institute of Technology Kharagpur, West Bengal 721302, India
samuisuman@atdc.iitkgp.ernet.in

Abstract. Supervised speech enhancement based on machine learning is a new paradigm for segregating clean speech from background noise. The current work represents a supervised speech enhancement system based on a robust deep learning method where the pre-training phase of deep belief network (DBN) has been conducted by employing fuzzy restricted Boltzmann machines (FRBM) instead of regular RBM. It has been observed that the performance of FRBM model is superior to that of RBM model particularly when the training data is noisy. Our experimental results on various noise scenarios have shown that the proposed approach outperforms the conventional DNN-based speech enhancement methods which use regular RBM for unsupervised pre-training.

Keywords: Speech enhancement · Deep learning · Deep neural network · Restricted Boltzmann machine (RBM) · Fuzzy restricted Boltzmann machine (FRBM) · Unsupervised pre-training · Speech quality · Speech intelligibility

1 Introduction

Speech enhancement has received a considerable amount of attention in recent years as it is often used as an essential pre-processing stage of various speech communication-based application, including mobile communication and hearing-aid design. Traditionally, it is performed in the spectral domain by employing statistical model based single-channel methods. A detailed study of all these methods can be found in [6,7]. However, recent development in *computational auditory scene analysis* [8] and deep learning have introduced new techniques [5,10,12,13] which have outperformed the conventional classical methods.

In the current work, we have mainly focused on the learning algorithm of deep neural architecture in the context of speech enhancement application and further investigated how the performance of these systems can be improved by employing more robust learning method. The DNN often suffers from *vanishing gradient problem*. In order to resolve this issue, Hinton *et al.* introduced a powerful multi-layer generative model namely, DBN which can be layer-wise pre-trained by stacking multiple Restricted Boltzmann Machines (RBM) [4]. Although this

© Springer International Publishing AG 2017
B.U. Shankar et al. (Eds.): PReMI 2017, LNCS 10597, pp. 534–542, 2017.
https://doi.org/10.1007/978-3-319-69900-4_68

technique of initialization of network weights using DBN has been found to be quite effective in various applications in computer vision and in speech processing [3], recently many works in single-channel speech separation [5,11,13] avoided the pre-training phase because they found that the pre-training of DNN using stacked regular RBM does not significantly improve the performance. One of the possible reasons may be the constraints due to the structure of regular RBM, that may lead to many problems: (i) Firstly, the parameters (biases and weights between hidden and visible units) of regular RBM are assumed to be constants. As a result, the representation capability of RBM is downgraded by this constraint, (ii) the RBM cannot be considered to be adequately robust when noisy training data are used to train the system, (iii) the learning process of parameters in RBM is confined in a comparatively small space which is in conflict with the benefits of deep learning.

The above observations have motivated us to employ more robust deep learning algorithm with robust acoustic features so that the generalization capability of the DNN-based speech enhancement system (SES) can be enhanced further. The major contributions of the present work are as follows:

- A DNN-based SES has been proposed where instead of using regular RBM, the generative training of DBN has been conducted by using fuzzy restricted Boltzmann machines (FRBM) [1], which has been found to be more effective when the training data are noisy [1].
- Experimental results have shown that DNN pre-trained with FRBM model can provide 26.22% improvement in speech quality and 18.33 % in speech intelligibility compared to a DNN-based SES pre-trained by stacking multiple regular RBMs.

This paper is organized as follows. In Sect. 2, we present the basic design methodology of a DNN-based SES with a discussion of relevant training targets and feature extraction process. Section 3 introduces FRBM model and further elaborates the learning mechanism of FRBM model. The experimental results are presented in Sect. 4. Finally, Sect. 5 concludes the paper.

2 DNN-Based Speech Enhancement System

The current work has considered a masking-based continuous training target *Ideal Ratio Mask* (IRM) [9] which is proven to be more effective over binary targets.

2.1 IRM Construction

The audio mixtures are first fed into a 64-channel gammatone filterbank, with center frequencies equally spaced in the range of 50 Hz-8000 Hz on the *equivalent rectangular bandwidth* (ERB) rate scale. The output in each channel is then segmented into 20 ms frames with 50% overlapping between successive frames.

This way of processing would produce a time-frequency representation of the audio mixture, termed as *Cochleagram*. The IRM is can be defined as [9]:

$$IRM(n,k) = \left(\frac{||S(n,k)||^2}{||S(n,k)||^2 + ||D(n,k)||^2} \right)^\alpha \tag{1}$$

where $||S(n,k)||^2$ and $||D(n,k)||^2$ denote the clean speech energy and the noise energy, respectively, contained within T-F unit (n, k). α is a tunable parameter and it has been empirically set to 0.5.

2.2   Acoustic Features and Network Architecture

Each frame is transformed into a complementary subset of various T-F unit level discriminative features inspired by [2,10]. The feature set includes (i) 31-D Mel Frequency Cepstral Coefficients (MFCC), (ii) 13-D Relative Spectral Transform-Perceptual Linear Prediction (RASTA-PLP), (iii) 15-D Amplitude Modulation Spectrogram (AMS), and (iv) 64-D Gammatone filter bank (GFB) features. In addition, velocity (delta feature) and acceleration (double-delta feature) coefficients are computed and appended with the raw features in the conventional way. A context window of two previous and two future frames are used, hence 1845-dimensional feature vector from each frame is utilized for training. Furthermore, zero mean and unit variance normalization are applied to all feature vectors. We have trained a total 64 sub-band DNNs, one for each sub-band channel as shown in Fig. 1. Each sub-band DNN follows a feed-forward architecture with input units equal to the feature dimension and contains 4 hidden layers with 1024 units in each layer, and an output layer with 1 output unit. The rectified linear unit and the sigmoid function are used as the activation functions for the hidden units and the output unit, respectively.

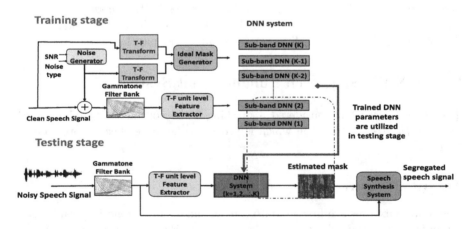

Fig. 1. Framework of a deep neural network based speech enhancement system

3   Training of DNN Using Fuzzy RBM

The effective training strategy of deep architectures consists in greedy layer-wise unsupervised *pre-training* followed by supervised *fine-tuning*. The main purpose of unsupervised pre-training using the generative model like DBN is to initialize the model to a point in parameter space which would make the optimization process more effective and fast [3]. To mitigate the flaws of regular RBM (as discussed in Introduction section) and enhance the deep learning capability, all the sub-band DNNs used in our system are pre-trained by stacking multiple FRBMs. This pre-training can be conducted in a greedy layer-wise fashion as shown in Fig. 2(b). Just like a regular RBM, the FRBM is also represented by an undirected stochastic graphical model, originally proposed in [1] as illustrated in Fig. 2(a). Unlike RBM, all the parameters $\bar{\phi} = \{\bar{b}, \bar{c}, \bar{w}\}$ of the FRBM model have been replaced by fuzzy numbers. In speech processing application, two variants of FRBM architectures: BBFRBM and GBFRBM are used to construct the DBN. As all the acoustic features extracted from the speech signal are real-valued, the input layer of the DBN is constructed by GBFRBM. The BBFRBM are used to form the subsequent layers of the DBN. In BBFRBM, both the visible and the hidden units follow Bernoulli distribution i.e. $(v, h) \in \{0,1\}^{m+n}$, whereas in GBFRBM, the visible units are continuous and follow a normal distribution and the hidden units follow binary distribution i.e. $v \in \{-\infty, \infty\}^m$ and $h \in \{0,1\}^n$. The probability distribution of regular RBM is represented as a function of energy function:

$$P(\mathbf{v}, \mathbf{h}, \theta) = \frac{\exp(-E(\mathbf{v}, \mathbf{h}, \theta))}{Z} \tag{2}$$

where $E(\mathbf{v}, \mathbf{h}, \theta)$ represent the energy function associated with RBM model and $\theta = \{\mathbf{b}, \mathbf{c}, \mathbf{W}\}$ is the parameter set. The parameter Z denotes the partition function. It is necessary to define the fuzzified energy functions [1] to introduce FRBM model:

$$E(\mathbf{v}, \mathbf{h}, \bar{\theta}) = -\sum_{i=1}^{m} \bar{b}_i v_i - \sum_{j=1}^{n} \bar{c}_j h_j - \sum_{i=1}^{m}\sum_{j=1}^{n} \bar{w}_{ij} v_i h_j \tag{3}$$

$$E(\mathbf{v}, \mathbf{h}, \bar{\theta}) = -\sum_{i=1}^{m} \frac{(v_i - \bar{b}_i)^2}{2\sigma_i^2} - \sum_{j=1}^{n} \bar{c}_j h_j - \sum_{i=1}^{m}\sum_{j=1}^{n} \bar{w}_{ij} h_j \frac{v_i}{\sigma_i^2} \tag{4}$$

where v_i and h_j denote the state of the ith visible unit and j^{th} hidden unit, respectively. w_{ij} represent the weight between them. Similarly, b_i and c_j are the bias terms related to the ith visible unit and j^{th} hidden unit respectively. The fuzzy energy functions for BBFRBM and GBFRBM are defined in (3) and (4), respectively. The fuzzy parameter set for both BBFRBM and GBFRBM is $\bar{\theta} = \{\bar{\mathbf{b}}, \bar{\mathbf{c}}, \bar{\mathbf{W}}\}$. The parameter σ_i^2 in (4) denotes the variance of the visible units and it is typically set to one, subjected to that all the visible units are normalized. Hence, this variance term has not been considered as the fuzzy RBM parameters.

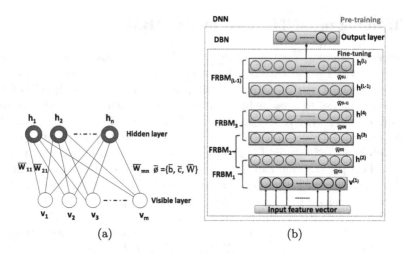

Fig. 2. (a) FRBM model. (b) Generative and discriminative training of DBN using stacked FRBM model.

In the learning process of FRBM model, the *fuzzy free energy function* (FFEF) needs to be defuzzified before defining the probability distribution. EFEF [1] can be defined by $\bar{F}(\mathbf{v}, \bar{\theta}) = -\log \sum_{\tilde{h}} e^{-\bar{E}(v, \tilde{h}, \bar{\theta})}$. Using the extension principle of fuzzy function, one can derive the fuzzy free energy function from the crisp energy function as: $\mathcal{F}(\mathbf{v}, \theta) = -\log \sum_{\tilde{h}} e^{-E(v, h, \theta)}$. The FFEF cannot be directly applied to define probability, because then we will end up with a fuzzy probability. The goal of training the FRBM is to find out optimal fuzzy parameter set $\bar{\theta}$ that maximizes the probability of data. So, the optimization process in FRBM learning process becomes a maximum-likelihood problem. We need to transform the fuzzy energy function into a crisp energy function. By employing, the centre of area method of defuzzification, the following can be obtained as [1]:

$$\mathcal{F}_c(\mathbf{v}, \bar{\theta}) = \frac{\int \theta \mathcal{F}(v, \theta) d\theta}{\int \mathcal{F}(v, \theta) d\theta}, \theta \in \bar{\theta} \tag{5}$$

Then, the probability can be defined by $P_c(\mathbf{v}, \bar{\theta}) = \dfrac{e^{-\mathcal{F}_c(v, \bar{\theta})}}{\mathcal{Z}}$, where for BBRBM $Z = \sum_{\tilde{v}} e^{-F_c(\tilde{v}, \bar{\theta})}$ and for GBRBM $Z = \int \sum_{\tilde{v}} e^{-F_c(\tilde{v}, \bar{\theta})}$. In FRBM model, the negative of log-likelihood function is considered as the objective function which can be given as:

$$\mathcal{L}(\bar{\theta}, \mathcal{T}_{\mathcal{D}}) = -\sum_{v \in \mathcal{T}_{\mathcal{D}}} log[P_c(v, \bar{\theta})] \tag{6}$$

where $\mathcal{T}_{\mathcal{D}}$ is the training dataset. The ultimate goal of the learning algorithm is to determine the optimal solutions of parameters which would minimize the objective function. So, the optimization problem can be defined as

$$\bar{\theta}^* = \underset{\bar{\theta}}{\operatorname{argmin}} \ \mathcal{L}(\bar{\theta}, \mathcal{T}_{\mathcal{D}}) \tag{7}$$

We have employed the SGD method combined with Monte Carlo Markov chain (MCMC) technique to train the FRBM model as described in [1]. For more insight and understanding of the learning algorithm of the FRBM, please refer to [1].

4 Experimental Results

We have created the training and test-stimuli by contaminating 720 Harvard sentences from IEEE corpus[1] by five types of noises: babble, street, transport, cafeteria and speech-shaped noise (SSN). These noise instances have been taken from a real-world noise database DEMAND (Diverse Environments Multichannel Acoustic Noise Database) corpus[2] except SSN. In order to create the mixture, each sentence is mixed with 6 different noise instances at six different SNR levels (-10, -5, 0, $+5$, $+10$ and $+15$ dB). The training set uses 500 sentences, validation set uses 100 sentences and test set uses 120 sentences. The noise segments used for creating those datasets are also completely different. It ensures

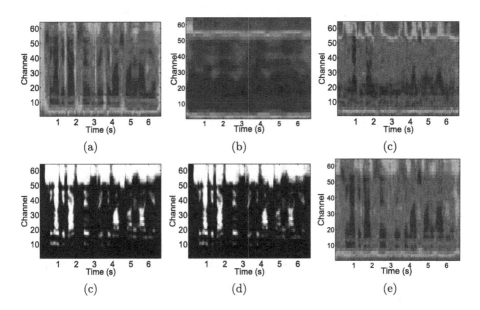

Fig. 3. A speech Separation illustration for an IEEE utterance mixed with babble noise using Cochleagrams: (a) the clean speech. (b) Babble noise. (c) Cochleagram of the mixture (0 dB SNR). (d) Ideal ratio mask. (e) Estimated ratio mask.(f) Estimated clean speech.

---

[1] http://www.cs.columbia.edu/hgs/audio/harvard.html.
[2] http://parole.loria.fr/DEMAND/.

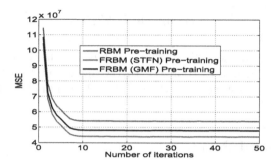

Fig. 4. Reconstruction error during Pre-training phase

that there is no overlapping between train, validation and test datasets. An example of the separation results are illustrated in Fig. 3.

To evaluate the effectiveness of DNN pre-training using FRBM model, we have created three DNN-based speech enhancement systems, all of which have the same architecture (as given in Section) and all are trained by the same aforementioned dataset. The only difference is that the pre-training of one DNN is conducted by using RBM model, denoted as DNN(RBM) and for the other two, FRBM is used for pre-training. In these two DNN systems, two different types of fuzzy RBM are used: (i) the FRBM with *Symmetric Triangular Fuzzy Number*, denoted by DNN(*FRBM-STFN*) and (ii) the FRBM with Gaussian Membership Function, denoted by DNN(*FRBM-GMF*). The mean square errors, generated in the pre-training learning phase are illustrated in Fig. 4. It is quite evident that the FRBM-STFN model generates less reconstruction error as compared to the RBM model. It indicates that the representation and learning capabilities of FRBM-model are more accurate than that of the

Table 1. Comparison of average PESQ and STOI Scores for different systems tested on test dataset (represented as PESQ(STOI) score)

System	SNR (in dB)			
	−10	−5	0	+5
Noisy mixture	1.125(0.332)	1.256(0.467)	1.438(0.682)	1.683(0.729)
DNN (No pre-training)	1.672(0.398)	1.964(0.604)	2.083(0.712)	2.316(0.848)
DNN(RBM)	1.797(0.408)	2.061(0.684)	2.353(0.793)	2.651(0.848)
Proposed DNN(FRBM-GMF)	1.897(0.468)	2.564(0.714)	2.921(0.827)	**3.316(0.892)**
Proposed DNN(FRBM-STFN)	**2.072(0.518)**	**2.944(0.764)**	**3.065(0.882)**	3.125(0.828)
DNN(RBM)-SVM	1.717(0.458)	2.169(0.654)	2.483(0.793)	2.571(0.838)

conventional RBM model. The performance of the SES has also been assessed by using standard objective measures such as: PESQ (*Perceptual Evaluation of Speech Quality*) and STOI (*Short-Time Objective Intelligibility*) metrics which are highly correlated with the subjective listening test. Comparative study of average PESQ and STOI scores that are obtained from different systems at various test SNR levels have been shown in Table 1. It implies that DNN pre-trained with FRBM-STFN model can provide 26.22% improvement in PESQ and 18.33 % in STOI compared to DNN(RBM) model.

5   Conclusions

In this article, we have pointed out some of the short-comings of unsupervised deep learning using regular RBM. We have employed FRBM for the pre-training phase of DNN since the FRBM model has the ability to represent the probability distribution of data much accurately than the regular RBM, particularly when training data are noisy. This benefit comes from the fact that the relationships between the visible and hidden units are defined by the fuzzy functions. Objective evaluations have shown that the performance of DNN-based SES can be improved significantly when it is pre-trained by FRBM.

References

1. Chen, C., Zhang, C.Y., Chen, L., Gan, M.: Fuzzy restricted boltzmann machine for the enhancement of deep learning. IEEE Trans. Fuzzy Syst. **23**(6), 2163–2173 (2015)
2. Chen, J., Wang, Y., Wang, D.: A feature study for classification-based speech separation at low signal-to-noise ratios. IEEE/ACM Trans. Audio Speech Lang. Process. **22**(12), 1993–2002 (2014)
3. Erhan, D., Bengio, Y., Courville, A., Manzagol, P.A., Vincent, P., Bengio, S.: Why does unsupervised pre-training help deep learning? J. Mach. Learn. Res. **11**, 625–660 (2010)
4. Hinton, G.E., Osindero, S., Teh, Y.W.: A fast learning algorithm for deep belief nets. Neural Comput. **18**(7), 1527–1554 (2006)
5. Kolbk, M., Tan, Z.H., Jensen, J.: Speech intelligibility potential of general and specialized deep neural network based speech enhancement systems. IEEE/ACM Trans. Audio Speech Lang. Process. **25**(1), 153–167 (2017)
6. Loizou, P.C.: Speech Enhancement: Theory and Practice. CRC Press (2013)
7. Samui, S., Chakrabarti, I., Ghosh, S.K.: Improved single channel phase-aware speech enhancement technique for low signal-to-noise ratio signal. IET Signal Proc. **10**(6), 641–650 (2016)
8. Wang, D., Brown, G.J.: Computational Auditory Scene Analysis: Principles, Algorithms, And Applications (2006)
9. Wang, Y., Narayanan, A., Wang, D.: On training targets for supervised speech separation. IEEE/ACM Trans. Audio Speech Lang. Process. **22**(12), 1849–1858 (2014)
10. Wang, Y., Wang, D.: Towards scaling up classification-based speech separation. IEEE Trans. Audio Speech Lang. Process. **21**(7), 1381–1390 (2013)

11. Williamson, D.S., Wang, Y., Wang, D.: Estimating nonnegative matrix model activations with deep neural networks to increase perceptual speech quality. J. Acoust. Soc. Am. **138**(3), 1399–1407 (2015)
12. Xu, Y., Du, J., Dai, L.R., Lee, C.H.: A regression approach to speech enhancement based on deep neural networks. IEEE/ACM Trans. Audio Speech Lang. Process. **23**(1), 7–19 (2015)
13. Zhang, X.L., Wang, D.: A deep ensemble learning method for monaural speech separation. IEEE/ACM Trans. Audio Speech Lang. Process. **24**(5), 967–977 (2016)

A Study on Deep Convolutional Neural Network Based Approaches for Person Re-identification

Harendra Chahar[(✉)] [iD] and Neeta Nain

Malaviya National Institute of Technology, Jawahar Lal Nehru Margh, Jaipur, India
hchahar616@gmail.com, nnain.cse@mnit.ac.in

Abstract. Person re-identification is a process to identify the same person again viewed by disjoint field of view of cameras. It is a challenging problem due to visual ambiguity in a person's appearance across different camera views. These difficulties are often compounded by low resolution surveillance images, occlusion, background clutter and varying lighting conditions. In recent years, person re-identification community obtained large size of annotated datasets and deep learning architecture based approaches have obtained significant improvement in the accuracy over the years as compared to hand-crafted approaches. In this survey paper, we have classified deep learning based approaches into two categories, i.e., image-based and video-based person re-identification. We have also presented the currently ongoing under developing works, issues and future directions for person re-identification.

Keywords: Person re-identification · Convolutional neural network

1 Introduction

In automated multi-camera video-surveillance, person re-identification is defined as whether the same person has been already observed at another place by different camera field of view. It is used for behaviour recognition, person tracking, image retrieval and safety purpose at public place. For humans to manually monitor video-surveillance systems to identify a probe accurately and efficiently is a difficult task. It is vary challenging problem due to variation in a person's appearance across different cameras. Therefore, person observed at multi-camera views have small inter-class variations and large ambiguities in intra-class variations.

For person re-identification, few surveys have been already exist [1–4]. In recent years, the availability of large size annotated person re-identification datasets and great success of deep learning in computer vision for image classification and object recognition also have made great influence in person re-identification. In this survey paper, we have presented the deep learning based approaches for person re-identification on both image and video datasets.

Section 2 present various deep learning approaches for person re-identification on image datasets. Section 3 describes different types of deep learning approaches for person re-identification on video datasets and various currently ongoing issues and future works. In Sect. 4, we have drawn conclusion.

© Springer International Publishing AG 2017
B.U. Shankar et al. (Eds.): PReMI 2017, LNCS 10597, pp. 543–548, 2017.
https://doi.org/10.1007/978-3-319-69900-4_69

2 Deep Learning Based Person Re-identification Approaches on Image Datasets

In year 2012, convolutional neural network based deep learning model has been presented by Krizhevsky et al. [7] in ILSVRC'12 competition. They won this competition with a large margin in accuracy. Since then convolutional neural network based deep learning models have been becomes more popular in computer vision comunity. Yi et al. [5] have been proposed a deep metric learning approach for person re-identification using a siamese convolutional neural network with a symmetry structure comprising two sub-networks connected by a cosine layer. A pair of images is used as a input, extracts features from each image separately and then uses their cosine distance for similarity matching. In [6] authors have been proposed a siamese architecture wherein a patch-matching layer is used which multiplies convolutional feature responses from the two inputs at a variety of horizontal stripes and uses product to compute patch similarity in similar latitude. Varior et al. [8] have been presented a method by inserting a gating function after each convolutional layer into the network to find effective subtle patterns in testing of paired images. In [9], a soft attention based model has been integrated with a siamese neural network to adaptively focus on the important local parts of paired input images. Cheng et al. [10] have been presented a triplet loss function, wherein a triplet of three images as input has been created. Each image is partitioned into four overlapping body parts after the first convolutional layer and fusion of all as a final one has been done in the fully-connected layer. In [12] authors have proposed a pipeline for learning generic feature representations from multiple domains. They combine all the datasets together and train a designed convolutional neural network from scratch on combined dataset and a softmax loss is used in the classification. In [13] authors has presented an approach wherein they construct a single fisher vector [14] for each image by using SIFT and color histograms aggregation. They have used fisher vectors as a input and build a fully connected network and linear discriminative analysis is used as an objective function. In [22] authors have proposed a deep

Table 1. Statistics of benchmark image datasets for person re-identification

Dataset	Time	#ID	#Image	#Camera	Label
VIPeR [18]	2007	632	1264	2	Hand
iLIDS [17]	2009	119	476	2	Hand
GRID [19]	2009	250	1275	8	Hand
CUHK01 [20]	2012	971	3884	2	Hand
CUHK02 [21]	2013	1816	7264	10	Hand
CUHK03 [6]	2014	1467	13164	2	Hand/DPM
PRID 450S [34]	2014	450	900	2	Hand
Market-1501 [32]	2015	1501	32668	6	Hand/DPM

Table 2. Rank-1 accuracy of different deep learning approaches for person re-identification on various image datasets, i.e., (VIPeR, CUHK-01, CUHK-03, PRID, iLIDS and Market-1501)

Authors/Year	Evolution	VIPeR	CUHK-01	CUHK-03	PRID	iLIDS	Market-1501
Yi [5] (2014)	CMC	28.23%	–	–	–	–	–
Li [6] (2014)	CMC	–	27.87%	20.65%	–	–	–
Wu [15] (2016)	CMC/mAP	–	71.14%	64.80%	–	–	37.21%
Xiao [12] (2016)	CMC	38.6%	66.6%	75.33%	64.0%	64.6%	–
Chi-Su [11] (2016)	CMC/mAP	43.5%	–	–	22.6%	–	39.4%
Liu [9] (2016)	CMC/mAP	–	81.04%	65.65%	–	–	48.24%
Varior [8] (2016)	CMC/mAP	37.8%	–	68.1%	–	–	65.88%
Wang [16] (2016)	CMC	35.76%	71.80%	52.17%	–	–	–
Geng [22] (2016)	CMC/mAP	**56.3%**	–	**85.4%**	–	–	**83.7%**

transfer learning approach wherein one stepped fine-tuning for large person re-identification datasets (Imagenet → Market-1501) and two stepped fine-tuning for small datasets (Imagenet → Market-1501 → VIPeR) have been used. We have taken all the result from existing approaches and observed overwhelming advantage of deep learning [22] in rank-1 accuracy on largest datasets CUHK03 and Market-1501 so far (Tables 1 and 2).

3   Deep Learning Based Person Re-identification Approaches on Video Dataset

The deep learning approaches for person re-identification on video datasets are [23,25,31] wherein appearance features have been used as the starting point into RNN to obtain the time flow information between frames. McLaughlin et al. [31] have been presented a framework wherein convolutional neural network is used to extract features from consecutive video frames and fedded through a recurrent final layer. In [23] authors have proposed the gated recurrent unit and an identification loss based recurrent neural network. Yan et al. [25] and Zheng et al. [33] have proposed a model in which each input video sequence is classifies into their respective subject by using the identification model. Color and local binary pattern features are fedded into LSTM cells. Wu et al. [24] has proposed a model to build a hybrid network by fusing color and LBP features to extract both spatial-temporal and appearance features from a video sequence. In [30] authors have presented a method to extract a compact and discriminative appearance features representation from selected frames based on flow energy profile instead of the whole sequence (Tables 3 and 4).

Computer vision community is always looking for annotated large size datasets for supervised learning. This is a challenging problem in person re-identification. Assigning an id to a pedestrian is not trivial. Open-world person re-identification can be viewed as a person verification task. Zheng et al. [35] has

Table 3. Statistics of benchmark video datasets for person re-identification

Dataset	Time	#ID	#Track	#Bbox	#Camera	Label
ETHZ [26]	2007	148	148	8580	1	Hand
3DPES [27]	2011	200	1000	200 k	8	Hand
PRID-2011 [28]	2011	200	400	40 k	2	Hand
iLIDS-VID [29]	2014	300	600	44 k	2	Hand
MARS [33]	2016	1261	20715	1 M	6	DPM&GMMCP

Table 4. Rank-1 accuracy of deep learning based approaches for person re-identification on different datasets, i.e.,(iLIDS-VID and PRIQ-2011)

Authors/Year	Evaluation	iLIDS-VID	PRIQ-2011
Wu [23] (2016)	CMC	46.1%	69.0%
Yan [25] (2016)	CMC	49.3%	58.2%
McLaughlin [31] (2016)	CMC	58%	70%
Zhang [30] (2017)	CMC	**60.2%**	**83.3%**

been presented a method to achieve low false and high true target recognition. Liao et al. [36] has proposed a method having two stages, in the first stage, it finds whether a query subject is present in the gallery or not. In second stage, assigns an id to the accepted query subject. Open-world person re-identification is still challenging task as evidenced by the low recognition rate under low false accept rate as shown in [35,36]. Therefore, there is need to design an efficient methods to improve both accuracy and efficiency of the person re-id systems.

4 Conclusion

Increasing the demand of saftey at public places gain more interest for person re-identification. In this survey paper, we have presented deep learning approaches in both image and video datasets. Solving the data volume issue, re-identification re-ranking methods, and open world re-identification systems are some important open issues that may attract further attention from the community.

References

1. D'Orazio, T., Grazia, C.: People re-identification and tracking from multiple cameras: a review. In 19th IEEE International Conference on Image Processing (ICIP), pp. 1601–1604 (2012)
2. Bedagkar-Gala, A., Shah, S.K.: A survey of approaches and trends in person re-identification. Image Vis. Comput. **32**(4), 270–286 (2014)
3. Gong, S., Cristani, M., Yan, S., Loy, C.C. (eds.): Person Re-Identification. ACVPR, vol. 1. Springer, London (2014). doi:10.1007/978-1-4471-6296-4

4. Satta, R.: Appearance descriptors for person re-identification: a comprehensive review. arXiv preprint arXiv1307.5748 (2013)
5. Yi, D., Lei, Z., Liao, S., Li, S.Z.: Deep metric learning for person re-identification. In: Proceedings of International Conference on Pattern Recognition, pp. 2666–2672 (2014)
6. Li, W., Zhao, R., Xiao, T., Wang, X.: Deepreid: deep filter pairing neural network for person re-identification. In: Proceedings of the IEEE Conference on Computer Vision and Pattern Recognition, pp. 152–159 (2014)
7. Krizhevsky, A., Sutskever, I., Hinton, G.E.: Imagenet classification with deep convolutional neural networks. In: Advances in Neural Information Processing Systems, pp. 1097–1105 (2012)
8. Varior, R.R., Haloi, M., Wang, G.: Gated Siamese convolutional neural network architecture for human re-identification. In: Leibe, B., Matas, J., Sebe, N., Welling, M. (eds.) ECCV 2016. LNCS, vol. 9912, pp. 791–808. Springer, Cham (2016). doi:10.1007/978-3-319-46484-8_48
9. Liu, H., Feng, J., Qi, M., Jiang, J., Yan, S.: End-to-end comparative attention networks for person re-identification, arXiv preprint arXiv:1606.04404 (2016)
10. Cheng, D., Gong, Y., Zhou, S., Wang, J., Zheng, N.: Person re-identification by multi-channel parts-based CNN with improved triplet loss function. In: Proceedings of the IEEE Conference on Computer Vision and Pattern Recognition, pp. 1335–1344 (2016)
11. Su, C., Zhang, S., Xing, J., Gao, W., Tian, Q.: Deep attributes driven multi-camera Person re-identification. In: Leibe, B., Matas, J., Sebe, N., Welling, M. (eds.) ECCV 2016. LNCS, vol. 9906, pp. 475–491. Springer, Cham (2016). doi:10.1007/978-3-319-46475-6_30
12. Xiao, T., Li, H., Ouyang, W., Wang, X.: Learning deep feature representations with domain guided dropout for person re-identification. In: Proceedings of the IEEE Conference on Computer Vision and Pattern Recognition, pp. 1249–1258 (2016)
13. Wu, L., Shen, C., van den Hengel, A.: Deep linear discriminant analysis on fisher networks: a hybrid architecture for person re-identification. Pattern Recognit. (2016)
14. Perronnin, F., Sánchez, J., Mensink, T.: Improving the fisher kernel for large-scale image classification. In: Daniilidis, K., Maragos, P., Paragios, N. (eds.) ECCV 2010. LNCS, vol. 6314, pp. 143–156. Springer, Heidelberg (2010). doi:10.1007/978-3-642-15561-1_11
15. Wu, L., Shen, C., Hengel, A.V.D.: Personnet: person re-identification with deep convolutional neural networks. arXiv preprint arXiv:1601.07255 (2016)
16. Wang, F., Zuo, W., Lin, L., Zhang, D., Zhang, L.: Joint learning of single-image and cross-image representations for person re-identification. In: Proceedings of the IEEE Conference on Computer Vision and Pattern Recognition, pp. 1288–1296 (2016)
17. Wei-Shi, Z., Shaogang, G., Tao, X.: Associating groups of people. In: Proceedings of the British Machine Vision Conference, pp. 23.1–23.11 (2009)
18. Gray, D., Tao, H.: Viewpoint invariant pedestrian recognition with an ensemble of localized features. In: Forsyth, D., Torr, P., Zisserman, A. (eds.) ECCV 2008. LNCS, vol. 5302, pp. 262–275. Springer, Heidelberg (2008). doi:10.1007/978-3-540-88682-2_21
19. Loy, C.C., Xiang, T., Gong, S.: Multi-camera activity correlation analysis. In: IEEE Conference on Computer Vision and Pattern Recognition, pp. 1988–1995. IEEE (2009)

20. Li, W., Zhao, R., Wang, X.: Human reidentification with transferred metric learning. In: Lee, K.M., Matsushita, Y., Rehg, J.M., Hu, Z. (eds.) ACCV 2012. LNCS, vol. 7724, pp. 31–44. Springer, Heidelberg (2013). doi:10.1007/978-3-642-37331-2_3
21. Li, W., Wang, X.: Locally aligned feature transforms across views. In: Proceedings of the IEEE Conference on Computer Vision and Pattern Recognition, pp. 3594–3601 (2013)
22. Geng, M., Wang, Y., Xiang, T., Tian, Y.: Deep transfer learning for person re-identification. arXiv preprint arXiv:1611.05244 (2016)
23. Wu, L., Shen, C., Hengel, A.V.D.: Deep recurrent convolutional networks for video-based person re-identification: an end-to-end approach. arXiv preprint arXiv:1606.01609 (2016)
24. Wu, Z., Wang, X., Jiang, Y.G., Ye, H., Xue, X.: Modeling spatial-temporal clues in a hybrid deep learning framework for video classification. In: Proceedings of the 23rd ACM International Conference on Multimedia, pp. 461–470 (2015)
25. Yan, Y., Ni, B., Song, Z., Ma, C., Yan, Y., Yang, X.: Person re-identification via recurrent feature aggregation. In: Leibe, B., Matas, J., Sebe, N., Welling, M. (eds.) ECCV 2016. LNCS, vol. 9910, pp. 701–716. Springer, Cham (2016). doi:10.1007/978-3-319-46466-4_42
26. Ess, A., Leibe, B., Van Gool, L.: Depth and appearance for mobile scene analysis. In: IEEE 11th International Conference on Computer Vision, pp. 1–8 (2007)
27. Baltieri, D., Vezzani, R., Cucchiara, R.: 3DPeS: 3D people dataset for surveillance and forensics. In: Proceedings of the 2011 Joint ACM Workshop on Human Gesture and Behavior Understanding, pp. 59–64 (2011)
28. Hirzer, M., Beleznai, C., Roth, P.M., Bischof, H.: Person re-identification by descriptive and discriminative classification. In: Heyden, A., Kahl, F. (eds.) SCIA 2011. LNCS, vol. 6688, pp. 91–102. Springer, Heidelberg (2011). doi:10.1007/978-3-642-21227-7_9
29. Wang, T., Gong, S., Zhu, X., Wang, S.: Person re-identification by video ranking. In: Fleet, D., Pajdla, T., Schiele, B., Tuytelaars, T. (eds.) ECCV 2014. LNCS, vol. 8692, pp. 688–703. Springer, Cham (2014). doi:10.1007/978-3-319-10593-2_45
30. Zhang, W., Hu, S., Liu, K.: Learning compact appearance representation for video-based person re-identification. arXiv preprint arXiv:1702.06294 (2017)
31. McLaughlin, N., Martinez del Rincon, J., Miller, P.: Recurrent convolutional network for video-based person re-identification. In: Proceedings of the IEEE Conference on Computer Vision and Pattern Recognition, pp. 1325–1334 (2016)
32. Zheng, L., Shen, L., Tian, L., Wang, S., Wang, J., Tian, Q.: Scalable person re-identification: a benchmark. In: Proceedings of the IEEE International Conference on Computer Vision, pp. 1116–1124 (2015)
33. Zheng, L., Bie, Z., Sun, Y., Wang, J., Su, C., Wang, S., Tian, Q.: MARS: a video benchmark for large-scale person re-identification. In: Leibe, B., Matas, J., Sebe, N., Welling, M. (eds.) ECCV 2016. LNCS, vol. 9910, pp. 868–884. Springer, Cham (2016). doi:10.1007/978-3-319-46466-4_52
34. Roth, P.M., Hirzer, M., Köstinger, M., Beleznai, C., Bischof, H.: Mahalanobis distance learning for person re-identification. In: Gong, S., Cristani, M., Yan, S., Loy, C.C. (eds.) Person Re-Identification. ACVPR, pp. 247–267. Springer, London (2014). doi:10.1007/978-1-4471-6296-4_12
35. Zheng, W.S., Gong, S., Xiang, T.: Towards open-world person re-identification by one-shot group-based verification. IEEE Trans. Pattern Anal. Mach. Intell. **38**(3), 591–606 (2016)
36. Liao, S., Mo, Z., Zhu, J., Hu, Y., Li, S.Z.: Open-set person re-identification. arXiv preprint arXiv:1408.0872 (2014)

Two-Stream Convolutional Network with Multi-level Feature Fusion for Categorization of Human Action from Videos

Prateep Bhattacharjee$^{(\boxtimes)}$ ⓘ and Sukhendu Das ⓘ

Department of Computer Science and Engineering, Indian Institute
of Technology Madras, Chennai, Tamil Nadu, India
prateepb@cse.iitm.ac.in, sdas@iitm.ac.in

Abstract. This paper presents the results of the exploration of a two-stream Convolutional Neural Network (2S-CNN) architecture, with a novel feature fusion technique at multiple levels, to categorize events in videos. The two streams are a combination of dense optical flow features with: (a) RGB frames; and (b) salient object regions detected using a fast space-time saliency method. The main contribution is in the design of a classifier moderated method to fuse information from the two streams at multiple stages of the network, which enables capturing the most discriminative and complimentary features for localizing the spatio-temporal attention for the action being performed. This mutual auto-exchange of information in local and global contexts, produces an optimal combination of appearance and dynamism, for enhanced discrimination, thus producing the best performance of categorization. The network is trained end-to-end and subsequently evaluated on two challenging human action recognition benchmark datasets viz. UCF-101 and HMDB-51, where, the proposed 2S-CNN method outperforms the current state of the art ConvNets by a significant margin.

Keywords: Action recognition · Two-stream networks · Deep learning

1 Introduction

Although significant success have come in the area of image recognition domain through the use of Convolutional Neural Networks (CNNs), the field of videos still remain unconquered. As the traditional hand-crafted features failed to produce acceptable classification accuracy for action from videos, CNNs and other recurrent architectures emerged recently as part of the deep learning (DL) trend. These models try to learn a set of optimal features for accurate classification in a supervised manner, hence shifting the research from design of features to building complex deep networks.

This paper offers a novel value addition to the existing two-stream architectures by providing an adaptive and controlled multi-stage fusion strategy between the two pathways. The mutual exchange of information occurs in two

© Springer International Publishing AG 2017
B.U. Shankar et al. (Eds.): PReMI 2017, LNCS 10597, pp. 549–556, 2017.
https://doi.org/10.1007/978-3-319-69900-4_70

contexts: (a) **local** and (b) **global**. The local context fusion captures the spatio-temporal cues in a small window of optical flow features centered around an RGB frame or the saliency map extracted from it, whereas the global fusion aims to integrate all these local operations and fix any errors accumulated during the local stage by using a projective Long Short Term Memory (LSTM) architecture [14] with added residual pathways. The local stage also incorporates controlled intermediate classification to automatically capture the spatio-temporal features for better inter-class discrimination. Experimentations on the popular real world datasets UCF-101 [16] and HMDB-51 [11] show considerable performance gain for the proposed model over the most current state-of-the-art techniques. Recently, deep learning techniques have achieved great success in the field of object recognition from images. Effective applications include [4,10,15,17] the use of volumetric or 3D CNNs, Trajectory-Pooled Deep-Convolutional Descriptors, Factorized Spatio-Temporal CNNs and recurrent networks consisting of LSTM modules.

The proposed Two-Stream Convolutional Neural Network (2S-CNN) architecture works by computing the optical flow and saliency map using sufficiently fast and accurate methods. Use of motion features along with the pixel values of the input frames allow the model to automatically learn the action being performed in each frame. 2S-CNNs have been proposed by Simonyan and Zisserman [15] based on the primary assumption that action in videos can be decomposed into spatial and temporal parts. Although they split the network in two parts, fusion of information takes place only after the class scores are predicted. Our model aims to rectify this by introducing fusion nodes at multiple stages of the network for facilitating controlled exchange of information at various scales of the input, which is a significant contribution of the paper.

2   Two-Stream Multi-level Fusion Architecture

The input to the network (see Fig. 1a) combines stacked optical flow features with: (a) RGB frames and (b) saliency maps extracted from individual frames.

Optical Flow Stream. Optical flow information is first computed based on the method proposed by Brox *et al.* [1]. Affine flow vector compensates the noise comes from [8]. This can be modeled at a point $p = (x, y)$ at time t, as

$$w_{aff}(p_t) = \begin{bmatrix} c_1(t) \\ c_2(t) \end{bmatrix} + \begin{bmatrix} a_1(t) \ a_2(t) \\ a_3(t) \ a_4(t) \end{bmatrix} \begin{bmatrix} x_t \\ y_t \end{bmatrix}, \tag{1}$$

where, c_i and a_i represents the translation, rotation and scaling parameters. The affine flow vector extracted using Eq. 1 is then subtracted from the original flow vector w_{flow}, to obtain the final corrected flow field w_{cor}, as:

$$w_{cor}(p_t) = w_{flow}(p_t) - w_{aff}(p_t) \tag{2}$$

The obtained flow information between two frames F_t and F_{t+1} comprises of w_{cor}^x and w_{cor}^y, the horizontal and vertical components of the flow field respectively. These two fields are stacked over C number of frames to obtain $2C$ input channels, such that they efficiently encode motion information at every point of the input frame.

Saliency Map Stream. As the proposed architecture aims for categorizing actions from video data, a fast but accurate saliency method is used which considers both the spatial (appearance) and temporal information, as proposed by Zhou et al. [21]. The saliency is computed by first over-segmenting the input video into color coherent Spatio-Temporal Regions (STR) and subsequently computing three feature vectors encoding the color statistics, normalized histogram of the flow magnitude and the distribution of flow orientation respectively.

RGB Stream. The RGB stream gets a RGB frame F_t as its input. This captures the overall visual features from the frame, and is aided at multiple levels by the optical flow stream to focus its attention to the desired localization of action in frames.

2.1 Multi-level Feature Fusion in 2S-CNN

The proposed architecture incorporates fusion at three levels as shown in Fig. 1a. These nodes at the intermediate stages capture information from the two streams and aid the later part of the network in identifying finer details to classify the actions more accurately. In the proposed model, the fusion of the two streams is done adaptively in two modes: (a) **Local context** and (b) **Global context**.

Local Context Fusion. This fusion strategy works on a sequence of optical flow frames $\{w_{cor}^t \pm C\}$ centered at RGB frame F_t at time t. This fuses the information in a context of $2C$ clips. Intuitively, the spatial (RGB/Saliency) stream captures the position of the target motion whereas the temporal (Optical flow) stream identifies the motion pattern in the local window. The main idea behind this exchange of information at a local level is to place the pixel-wise feature responses from the two parallel networks in harmony. The proposed 2S-CNN architecture uses convolutional fusion guided by internal as well as final classifiers to achieve this feat, as shown by the blocks FConv 1, FConv 2 and the penultimate Fully Connected layer in Fig. 1a.

Also, as the model is very deep (51 convolutional layers), residual connections have been used to ease the training process. Residual networks attain this by the use of skip connections inserted throughout the network. These units are represented as: $X_{l+1} = f(X_l + \mathcal{F}; \mathcal{W}_l)$, where, X_l and X_{l+1} denotes the input and output of the lth layer respectively, $\mathcal{F}$ is a nonlinear residual mapping denoted by the filter weights $\mathcal{W}_l$.

During back propagation, these skip connections help the gradients to propagate directly from the loss layers to any of the previous layers bypassing the intermediate ones, resulting in vastly diminished chance of vanishing gradients.

The fusion operation can be thought of as a function $f : P_a, P_b \longrightarrow Q$ where $P_a, P_b, Q \in \mathbb{R}^{h \times w \times d}$, and h, w and d denote the height, width and depth of the feature maps respectively. The convolution based fusion application stacks the two corresponding sets of feature maps from the respective streams and applies a series of convolutional operations to produce the output. In the architecture shown in Fig. 1a, the stacked output of the fusion node is fed to two convolutional layers having receptive fields of 1×1 and 3×3. The purpose of inclusion of the 1×1 convolution kernels is to introduce a non-linearity without altering the size of the feature maps. All the convolutions are followed by a ReLU activation function [6] and Local Response Normalization (LRN), which aims to imitate biological neurons by implementing a type of lateral inhibition in the network. The fusion operation is finalized by normalizing the input batches spatially.

Global Context Fusion. Although the local context fusion captures the correspondences between the spatial and temporal streams for recognizing action, it often under-performs if the input video has sudden viewpoint changes, unpredictable camera motion or jittery frames. These disturbing artifacts result in erroneous learning of spatio-temporal features and as the fusion is applied at several levels, the error gets accumulated resulting in incorrectly classified action. To overcome this the proposed method globally fuses the information obtained from several local context fusion stages over the entire video. This global information fusion is achieved by the use of stacked deep LSTM units [7] with projection layers.

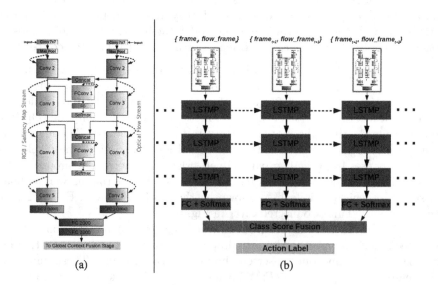

(a)   (b)

Fig. 1. (a) The two-stream multilevel local context fusion model. The dotted arrows denote the residual connections between two convolutional blocks. (b) The global context fusion stage. Dotted arrows between the LSTMP layers indicate hidden state outputs. The global stage aggregates all the input video clips and predicts the action label by pooling the final softmax scores over the entire input video.

As the training of LSTM layers are computationally expensive for large models, the proposed method uses Long Short-Term Memory Projected (LSTMP) architecture [14]. The computational complexity of learning LSTM models per time step is O(N) and is dominated by the factor $n_c \times (4 \times n_c + n_o)$ where n_c and n_o are respectively the number of memory cells and output units. Hence in a large network similar to the proposed one, the learning time becomes infeasible for even a moderate number of output dimensions and cells. The LSTMP architecture reduces the computational cost by inserting a projection or recurrent layer after the normal LSTM unit and forwarding the output to the input module. In this case, the cost of computation is dominated by $n_r \times (4 \times n_c + n_o)$ where n_r denotes the number of projection layer units. This use of projection layer results in reduced number of parameters from the LSTM module by a factor of $\frac{n_r}{n_c}$ and helps to increase the memory capacity of the model substantially.

3   Experimentation and Results

Rigorous experimentations are done for comparison of the performance for the 2S-CNN architecture with multi-level fusion on two real-word moderately large datasets: (a) **UCF-101**[16] and (b) **HMDB-51**[11].

3.1   Evaluation of Performance

The selection of fusion stages. The network is first trained in the local context level mentioned in Sect. 2.1 using multiple combinations of fusions at several stages, separately over the two datasets described above. The results, listed in Table 1 follow the trend observed in [4], that fusing information at the earlier stages show less impact on the overall classification accuracy. Amongst the different experimental combinations the highest performance gain was noticed by implementing the fusion before three levels in the network, viz. Conv 2, Conv 3 and the final fully connected layer, as shown in Fig. 1a. Table 1 compares the performance of the network under different combination of local fusion with and without the auxiliary classifiers introduced.

Training the Global Context Level. The global context stage is implemented using 1, 2 and 3 levels of LSTMP layers to capture the motion over the whole video. Comparison of the results in Tables 2 and 3 exhibit that the addition of this global fusion strategy achieves superior performance gain over classification accuracy using only the extracted local features (see Sect. 2.1) from the short chunks of the input. As the gain in accuracy was insignificant in case of inserting the third LSTMP layer over the previous case of two stacked LSTMP layers and also due to the high computational cost of BPTT for deeper recurrent networks, experimentation with more layers were not performed.

As evident from Tables 1 and 3, the global context fusion provides a significant improvement on predicting actions in the HMDB-51 dataset over the local stage of the network. Reason behind this is the fact that for HMDB-51 videos have high intra-class variations and several challenges in the form of camera

Table 1. Classification accuracy achieved on different combinations of feature fusion at several stages of the network, by the local context fusion stage. Results are shown on the split 1 of UCF-101 dataset [16]. Similar trend was observed on the HMDB-51 dataset [11] too.

Fusion Stages	Conv 3	Conv 4	Conv 5	FC 1	Conv 1 + Conv 4	Conv 2 + Conv 3	Conv 2 + Conv 3 + FC 1
Accuracy (without auxiliary classifiers)	81.82%	82.64%	84.01%	84.98%	85.17%	88.11%	**90.72%**
Accuracy (with auxiliary classifiers)	82.27%	83.34%	84.92%	85.44%	86.01%	88.89%	**91.25%**

Table 2. Results for the local fusion network using combination of flow features with saliency maps and RGB frames. All the results are on split 1 of UCF-101 and HMDB-51.

Method	UCF-101	HMDB-51
Optical flow + RGB frames	94.19%	70.36%
Optical flow + Saliency maps	94.79%	70.96%

Table 3. Classification accuracy for the global context network using several levels of LSTMP units.

Method	UCF-101	HMDB-51
Fusion + 1-LSTMP	91.91%	67.32%
Fusion + 2-LSTMP	93.87%	69.95%
Fusion + 3-LSTMP	94.19%	70.36%

motion, jitter and low quality. As the features get fine tuned at the local stage, the final global fusion module takes the advantage of temporal modeling of the learned features to better discriminate them.

Combination of Optical Flow with Saliency Maps. The model was trained both using the RGB and saliency maps obtained using the methodology described in Sect. 2. For both the datasets, using the saliency maps coupled with optical flow features result in better performance (as in Table 2) than the use of plain RGB frames. This is due to the fact that the segmented salient regions give a clue for the model to localize the distinguishing features better from those parts, while suppressing noisy areas which otherwise would have contributed to outliers, thus reducing the classification accuracy.

Finally, results in Table 4 compare the performance of the proposed architecture with other state-of-the-art and recent methods, utilizing hand-crafted and deep learned features, revealing the superiority of performance on both the challenging datasets.

Table 4. Comparison of the proposed 2S-CNN architecture with the state-of-the-art methods. (*) corresponds to methods using Improved Dense Trajectory (IDT) features. Missing numbers indicate unavailability of performance data or the corresponding method in the published article on the particular dataset.

Method	UCF-101	HMDB-51
Hybrid + BoW* [13]	87.9%	61.1%
Multi-resolution CNN [10]	65.4%	–
Two-stream CNN [15]	88.0%	59.4%
Long-term recurrent convolutional network [2]	82.9%	–
Factorized spatio-temporal CNN [17]	88.1%	59.1%
Multi scheme feature tracking [12]	89.1%	65.1%
Actions $\sim$ transformations Siamese CNN [19]	92.0%	62.0%
3D CNN* [9]	90.4%	–
Rank pooling [5]	–	63.7%
TDD* [18]	91.5%	65.9%
Adaptive multi-stream fusion [20]	92.6%	–
Stacked FVs + FV [13]	–	66.8%
Two-stream CNN with 3D pooling* [4]	93.5%	69.2%
Spatio-temporal residual net* [3]	94.6%	70.3%
Ours	**94.79**%	**70.96**%
Ours*	**95.81**%	**73.76**%

4 Conclusion

The two-stream CNN along with adaptive fusion strategy incorporated at different contextual levels shows best performance on two of the most popular and challenging action datasets. A controlled and adaptive multi-level fusion strategy at both local and global context is the highlight of this paper. Use of saliency maps with a combination of optical flow provides performance gain over the use of direct RGB frames as evident from the results in Table 2. Also, incorporating the fusion of information at two contexts results in significant improvement in performance.

References

1. Brox, T., Bruhn, A., Papenberg, N., Weickert, J.: High accuracy optical flow estimation based on a theory for warping. In: Pajdla, T., Matas, J. (eds.) ECCV 2004. LNCS, vol. 3024, pp. 25–36. Springer, Heidelberg (2004). doi:10.1007/978-3-540-24673-2_3
2. Donahue, J., Anne Hendricks, L., Guadarrama, S., Rohrbach, M., Venugopalan, S., Saenko, K., Darrell, T.: Long-term recurrent convolutional networks for visual recognition and description. In: CVPR, pp. 2625–2634 (2015)

3. Feichtenhofer, C., Pinz, A., Wildes, R.P.: Spatiotemporal residual networks for video action recognition. arXiv preprint arXiv:1611.02155 (2016)
4. Feichtenhofer, C., Pinz, A., Zisserman, A.: Convolutional two-stream network fusion for video action recognition. arXiv preprint arXiv:1604.06573 (2016)
5. Fernando, B., Gavves, E., Oramas, J.M., Ghodrati, A., Tuytelaars, T.: Modeling video evolution for action recognition. In: CVPR, pp. 5378–5387 (2015)
6. Hahnloser, R.H., Sarpeshkar, R., Mahowald, M.A., Douglas, R.J., Seung, H.S.: Digital selection and analogue amplification coexist in a cortex-inspired silicon circuit. Nature **405**(6789), 947–951 (2000)
7. Hochreiter, S., Schmidhuber, J.: Long short-term memory. Neural Comput. **9**(8), 1735–1780 (1997)
8. Jain, M., Jegou, H., Bouthemy, P.: Better exploiting motion for better action recognition. In: CVPR, pp. 2555–2562 (2013)
9. Ji, S., Xu, W., Yang, M., Yu, K.: 3D convolutional neural networks for human action recognition. T-PAMI **35**(1), 221–231 (2013)
10. Karpathy, A., Toderici, G., Shetty, S., Leung, T., Sukthankar, R., Fei-Fei, L.: Large-scale video classification with convolutional neural networks. In: CVPR, pp. 1725–1732 (2014)
11. Kuehne, H., Jhuang, H., Garrote, E., Poggio, T., Serre, T.: Hmdb: a large video database for human motion recognition. In: ICCV, pp. 2556–2563 (2011)
12. Lan, Z., Lin, M., Li, X., Hauptmann, A.G., Raj, B.: Beyond Gaussian pyramid: multi-skip feature stacking for action recognition. In: CVPR, pp. 204–212 (2015)
13. Peng, X., Zou, C., Qiao, Y., Peng, Q.: Action recognition with stacked fisher vectors. In: Fleet, D., Pajdla, T., Schiele, B., Tuytelaars, T. (eds.) ECCV 2014. LNCS, vol. 8693, pp. 581–595. Springer, Cham (2014). doi:10.1007/978-3-319-10602-1_38
14. Sak, H., Senior, A.W., Beaufays, F.: Long short-term memory recurrent neural network architectures for large scale acoustic modeling. In: ISCA (2014)
15. Simonyan, K., Zisserman, A.: Two-stream convolutional networks for action recognition in videos. In: NIPS, pp. 568–576 (2014)
16. Soomro, K., Zamir, A.R., Shah, M.: Ucf101: a dataset of 101 human actions classes from videos in the wild. arXiv preprint arXiv:1212.0402 (2012)
17. Sun, L., Jia, K., Yeung, D.-Y., Shi, B.E.: Human action recognition using factorized spatio-temporal convolutional networks. In: ICCV, pp. 4597–4605 (2015)
18. Wang, H., Schmid, C.: Action recognition with improved trajectories. In: ICCV, pp. 3551–3558 (2013)
19. Wang, X., Farhadi, A., Gupta, A.: Actions ∼ transformations. arXiv preprint arXiv:1512.00795 (2015)
20. Wu, Z., Jiang, Y.-G., Wang, X., Ye, H., Xue, X., Wang, J.: Fusing multi-stream deep networks for video classification. arXiv preprint arXiv:1509.06086 (2015)
21. Zhou, F., Bing Kang, S., Cohen, M.F.: Time-mapping using space-time saliency. In: CVPR, pp. 3358–3365 (2014)

Learning Deep Representation for Place Recognition in SLAM

Aritra Mukherjee$^{(\boxtimes)}$ ⓘ, Satyaki Chakraborty ⓘ, and Sanjoy Kumar Saha ⓘ

Department of Computer Science and Engineering,
Jadavpur University, Kolkata, India
kalpurush1601@gmail.com

Abstract. Closing loops for pose graph optimization, by recognising previously mapped places is an essential step for performing Simultaneous Localisation and Mapping (SLAM). The traditional approaches for recognising known places follow a feature-based bag-of-words model while discarding certain geometric and structural information. In order to improve real-time query performance, we take a slightly different approach by learning low-dimensional global representation vectors using a deconvolution net. Proposed 12-layer deconvolution net encodes and decodes an image to itself and in the process learns a representation of the image in a reduced feature space, it is then used for comparing one image with another to identify loop closures. Sequences from KITTI Visual Odometry dataset are used for evaluation and performance is compared with state-of-the-art techniques. Perceptual aliasing common in most place recognition approaches, is considerably less in ours.

Keywords: SLAM · Loop closure detection · Deconvolution net

1 Introduction

In the context of robot navigation with vision, the task of Simultaneous Localization And Mapping (SLAM) is an important task. The entire SLAM process relies on recognizing the places the robot has already visited to achieve visual loop closure detection. The major tasks are like representing the frames with the help of visual descriptors and subsequently judging the similarity between the frames based on the descriptors. It is to be noted that in the context of this work place recognition refers to recognising whether a place has been visited previously or not. Various approaches have been followed by the researchers. Some of the major approaches are as follows.

1.1 BoW Based Approaches

The BoW (Bag-of-words) approach was first successfully applied to image classification and retrieval [19]. Here, a fixed size vocabulary is used as a vector quantizer to classify descriptors in an image frame. The vectors consists of

© Springer International Publishing AG 2017
B.U. Shankar et al. (Eds.): PReMI 2017, LNCS 10597, pp. 557–564, 2017.
https://doi.org/10.1007/978-3-319-69900-4_71

image patches which acts as features and are generally chosen randomly from image patches with textured neighbourhood. The FABMAP model [4] considers a sequence of non-overlapping frames and checks if each frame belongs to an already visited place. It suffers from the problem of perceptual aliasing. In order to deal with the issue of perceptual aliasing as prevalent in FABMAP, methods like SeqSLAM [15] perform correlation-based matching on short sequences of images instead of depending directly on individual image frames. Voting based methods [9,13,20] perform a nearest neighbour search on the image descriptor space to identify potential matches. It is quite similar to the original bag of words approach. Sometimes image descriptors like SIFT [12], BRISK [11] or FREAK [1] are also used to form the descriptor vector. For fast and accurate nearest neighbour search in loop closure detection, it is essential to reduce the feature dimensions. Several Methods [2,13] have been presented in this direction. By means of majority voting, similar images are identified and loop closure is detected by thresholding on the similarity value.

1.2   Deep Learning Based Approaches

Convolutional neural network (CNN) based approaches have been developed for loop closure detection. Chen et al. [3] used the Overfeat network [17] trained on the ImageNet dataset to extract features from the image frames. Using a sequence of convolution and pooling operations, it is possible to obtain dense representations of the images and perform search on the low dimensional vector space. However, in this approach the network was pre-trained on the ImageNet dataset [5] and thus it is optimized mainly for object recognition and not oriented towards place recognition as desired for loop closure detection. Denoising autoencoders (DA) have also been used for localization tasks [18]. It uses a denoising autoencoder with fully connected layers to extract features for comparing structural similarity of two images.

Designing the descriptors suitable for loop closure detection is quite challenging. It depends on the scenes and conditions under consideration. It has motivated us to rely on deep learning that can automatically extract the features and can be utilized for place recognition. The paper is organized as follows. Brief introduction and survey is followed by proposed methodology in Sect. 2. Experimental result and conclusion are placed in Sects. 3 and 4 respectively.

2   Proposed Methodology

In this work we propose an autoencoder based deep learning network that extracts a lower dimensional vector representation of an image. With an autoencoder trained to encode and decode an image, the task of loop detection reduces to finding the distance between the encoded vectors of the query image and the input image. Whenever the distance falls below a certain threshold a loop closure can be reported. The value of the threshold can be either learned or tuned based on previous experience about the alteration limits of the environment.

The reconstruction process in this case uses the concept of switch matrix which holds the position of the pixel selected during a pooling layer of the encoder so that proper mapping can be done during decoding. The methodology is detailed in the subsequent subsections.

Some of the important aspects of our research are:

- Our 12 layer architecture with LCA layers reduces the input image of 96×336 i.e. 32256 pixels to only 200 dimensional feature vectors
- The quality of reconstruction from the decoder part of the network ensures that the 200 features extracted by our method capture important structural properties of the image.
- While detecting loop closures, it is often encountered that the objects of a place we had previously visited, have shifted by a few metres (or pixels) by the time we are arriving back at that place. Also, the camera poses of the two time instants are likely to be different. Hence, it is important that the features extracted from the image are translationally invariant to some extent, which is guaranteed by the pooling layers of the encoder network.
- Compared to traditional approaches of computing expensive features from an image, our deep features are generated by a series of dot products, non-linearities and pooling operations, which boosts real time performance significantly.

2.1   Architecture

At the heart of the proposed architecture lies a deconvolution net. It is further modified by adding a layer of locally connected autoencoders to map an image frame into a representation vector of n dimensions. The higher the value of n, the greater is the capability of the vector to encode unique macro level features of the scene in each of its elements. The choice of optimal size for the vector is subjected to further research. The value of n is empirically chosen as 200 in this work. We discuss the architecture in the following two subsections.

Deconvolution Net: Deep autoencoders were initially studied by Hinton et al. [8] for reducing the dimensionality of raw input data with neural networks. This approach was later extended for image [10] and document retrieval [7] tasks. But when working with images, fully connected autoencoders ignore local 2D image structure and hence suffer from a redundancy in learning the parameters. The visual field of the features are made to span the entire input thus destroying local structural information. In this case enforcing local connectivity and weight sharing [14,21] not only scales well for realistic image sizes, but also removes redundancies in the input to model discriminative representations.

Proposed architecture is essentially a 12 layer deep deconvolution net with only the middle layer as a layer of locally connected autoencoders. The first six layers are for encoding and the last six layers are for reconstructing the input which structurally is the mirror image of the encoding network. The features of the 6th layer (the layer of locally connected autoencoders) are used as representations for the image frames. Here, the stride of both convolution and pooling layers defines the number of pixels the kernel shifts. The pad defines the number of extra zero value pixels padded on the boundary after convolution or pooling. In our case we have chosen the zero-pad as 1, stride for convolution as 1 and kernels of dimensions 3×3, similar to the architecture of Noh et al. [16].

As deep learning involves huge amount of matrix computation, to speed up the process without significant loss of accuracy pooling technique is used. The image size to next convolution layer is diminished by selecting one pixel value of the next layer input, from a patch of the output image of the previous convolution layer. Max-pooling selects the pixel value which is maximum within the patch. Table 1 presents the complete architecture in tabular form.

Table 1. Description of the proposed network: The first half consists of convolution (conv) and pool layers, followed by encoding and decoding (LCA) and finally a number of deconvolution (deconv) and unpooling layers.

Layer	Kernel size	Stride	Pad	Output dim.
Input	–	–	–	$1 \times 96 \times 336$
Conv-1	3×3	1	1	$2 \times 96 \times 336$
Conv-2	3×3	1	1	$3 \times 96 \times 336$
Pool-1	2×2	2	0	$3 \times 48 \times 168$
Conv-3	3×3	1	1	$5 \times 48 \times 168$
Conv-4	3×3	1	1	$8 \times 48 \times 168$
Pool-2	2×2	2	0	$8 \times 24 \times 84$
Conv-5	3×3	1	1	$5 \times 24 \times 84$
Pool-3	2×2	2	0	$5 \times 12 \times 42$
LCA-enc	–	–	–	5×40
LCA-dec	–	–	–	$5 \times 12 \times 42$
Unpool-1	2×2	2	0	$5 \times 24 \times 84$
Deconv-1	3×3	1	1	$8 \times 24 \times 84$
Unpool-2	2×2	2	0	$8 \times 48 \times 168$
Deconv-2	3×3	1	1	$5 \times 48 \times 168$
Deconv-3	3×3	1	1	$3 \times 48 \times 168$
Unpool-3	2×2	2	0	$3 \times 96 \times 336$
Deconv-4	3×3	1	1	$2 \times 96 \times 336$
Deconv-5	3×3	1	1	$1 \times 96 \times 336$

Locally Connected Autoencoders: The feature maps at the output of the 6th layer are passed through a layer of locally connected autoencoders (LCA) to learn a further lower dimensional representation. An LCA is a fully connected 2 layer feedforward neural network where the number of input neurons is equal to the number of output neurons and the number of hidden neurons is equal to the dimension of the autoencoder, which in this case is 40. Each of the 5 feature maps are passed through an autoencoder and projected into a representation vector of 40 dimensions. All such representations are stacked on top of one another to form the 200 dimensional representation of the image frame. Using local connections instead of using a fully connected layer not only helps capturing distinguishing features from each feature map separately but also reduces the number of parameters to be learned.

Proposed approach is to some extent similar to the approach presented in [18]. But instead of a fully-connected autoencoder, in the proposed architecture deconvolution net is used for following reasons: (a) weight sharing (as done in convolution layers) extracts more meaningful and significant features when dealing with raw image data, (b) The features extracted by the proposed model are six layers deep and hence are more abstract compared to the features extracted by their 1 layer deep denoising autoencoder, (c) More importantly, pooling operations in the encoder of the deconvolution net introduce some translational invariance in the features extracted which is a very essential characteristic for detecting loop closures.

2.2   Training Methodology

The training is the commonly used two stage process [8] namely, *greedy layer-wise unsupervised pretraining* and *global fine-tuning*. The greedy unsupervised pretraining proceeds in a layerwise fashion. Keeping in mind the difficulty of jointly training a deep neural network architecture with respect to a global objective, at this stage, each layer is pretrained in an unsupervised fashion by taking the output of the previous layer and producing a new representation as output. This phase is called layer-wise because only the parameters of one layer are updated at a time keeping the others fixed. Normally fine tuning phase is supervised. However it has been shown [8] that for autoencoder networks, test accuracy improves significantly when the fine tuning phase is also unsupervised. Based on that observation, we have also adopted unsupervised fine tuning. Once the full autoencoder network is trained with respect to a global objective, the output of the LCA (locally connected autoencoder) layer are used as the learnt representations of the images in the dataset.

3   Results and Analysis

In order to carry out the experiment we have worked with the KITTI Odometry dataset [6]. For training, we used Sequences 0–4 with dataset augmentation (approximately, 100,000 images). Sequences 9 and 10 are used for validation and tested with sequences 5–8. Total time taken to train the network, was approximately 3.5 days for pretarining and 1.5 days for fine tuning, on an NVidia Quadro M5000 GPU with 8 GB VRAM. It is to be mentioned that during test, proposed method can process approximately 150 frames per second. On a machine with

1.4 Ghz Intel i5 CPU with 4 GB RAM, FABMAP has a maximum speed of 40FPS whereas our method operates at 110FPS, image dimension being 336×96.

For each of the test sequences 5, 6, 7 and 8, the generated confusion matrices are shown in Fig. 1 at a scale of 0 to 255. It shows the Euclidean distance between the learnt representation vector of the images in the sequence. It may be noted that along the diagonal the distance should be zero (as it is the distance with itself). By applying a threshold on the distances (similarity)loop closure is detected. The threshold on distance should be low enough to avoid the false detection. It has to be chosen keeping in mind that when the robot revisits the place there may be change in illumination, angle of view or even dynamic objects may also get shifted. In our experiment, it is empirically taken as 5. Image vectors with a distance less than the threshold qualify for a loop closure. In KITTI dataset, sequence 5 contains loop closure. Hence we have tested with the same and compared the outcome with OpenFabmap [4] and OpenSeqSlam [15]. The loop closure detection matrices are shown in Fig. 2. White denotes loop closure. It is clear in Fig. 2 that like others proposed methodology detects the closures successfully. It is to be noted that OpenSeqSlam suffers from over detection and significant miss is also present in both OpenSeqSlam and OpenFabmap. On the other hand, miss and false detection both are less for the proposed methodology. It may be noted that comparison was done by thresholding and then comparing it with ground truth confusion matrix on a pixel to pixel basis.

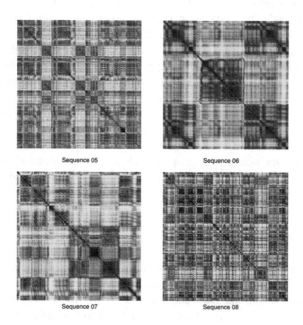

Fig. 1. Confusion matrices for sequences 5, 6, 7 and 8 of KITTI dataset. Darker the value, images are more similar.

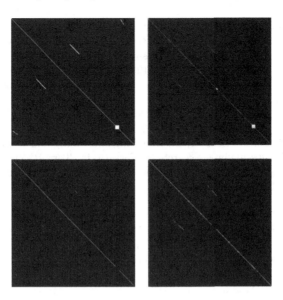

Fig. 2. Loop Closure Detection: ground truth matrix (top left) matrices for proposed methodology (top right), OpenSeqSlam [15] (bottom left) and OpenFabmap [4] (bottom right).

4   Conclusion

In this work we have proposed a deep learning autoencoder network that can represent an image with significantly lower dimension. But it preserves considerably the contextual and spatial information. As a result such representation becomes useful for applications like loop closure detection in SLAM. In our approach, we tried to combine the best of both the deep learning approaches (weight sharing in CNNs and unsupervised feature learning in DAs) in a deconvolution net. The advantage of this approach is that vectors generated for two frames of the same scene which differ geometrically but are similar contextually and by content, are quite close to each other. Thus the approach works in general place recognition tasks also and holds the promise to be extended to context and content based image matching problems.

References

1. Alahi, A., Ortiz, R., Vandergheynst, P.: Freak: fast retina keypoint. In: CVPR, pp. 510–517. IEEE (2012)
2. Bosse, M., Zlot, R.: Keypoint design and evaluation for place recognition in 2D lidar maps. Robot. Auton. Syst. **57**(12), 1211–1224 (2009)
3. Chen, Z., Lam, O., Jacobson, A., Milford, M.: Convolutional neural network-based place recognition. arXiv preprint arXiv:1411.1509 (2014)
4. Cummins, M., Newman, P.: Fab-map: probabilistic localization and mapping in the space of appearance. Int. J. Robot. Res. **27**(6), 647–665 (2008)

5. Deng, J., Dong, W., Socher, R., Li, L.-J., Li, K., Fei-Fei, L.: Imagenet: a large-scale hierarchical image database. In: CVPR, pp. 248–255. IEEE (2009)
6. Geiger, A., Lenz, P., Stiller, C., Urtasun, R.: Vision meets robotics: the KITTI dataset. Int. J. Robot. Res. **32**, 1231–1237 (2013)
7. Hinton, G., Salakhutdinov, R.: Discovering binary codes for documents by learning deep generative models. Top. Cogn. Sci. **3**(1), 74–91 (2011)
8. Hinton, G.E., Salakhutdinov, R.R.: Reducing the dimensionality of data with neural networks. Science **313**(5786), 504–507 (2006)
9. Jegou, H., Douze, M., Schmid, C.: Hamming embedding and weak geometric consistency for large scale image search. In: Forsyth, D., Torr, P., Zisserman, A. (eds.) ECCV 2008. LNCS, vol. 5302, pp. 304–317. Springer, Heidelberg (2008). doi:10.1007/978-3-540-88682-2_24
10. Krizhevsky, A., Hinton, G.E.: Using very deep autoencoders for content-based image retrieval. In: ESANN (2011)
11. Leutenegger, S., Chli, M., Siegwart, R.Y.: Brisk: binary robust invariant scalable keypoints. In: ICCV, pp. 2548–2555. IEEE (2011)
12. Lowe, D.G.: Object recognition from local scale-invariant features. In: ICCV, vol. 2, pp. 1150–1157. IEEE (1999)
13. Lynen, S., Bosse, M., Furgale, P., Siegwart, R.: Placeless place-recognition. In: 2014 2nd International Conference on 3D Vision, vol. 1, pp. 303–310. IEEE (2014)
14. Masci, J., Meier, U., Cireşan, D., Schmidhuber, J.: Stacked convolutional autoencoders for hierarchical feature extraction. In: Honkela, T., Duch, W., Girolami, M., Kaski, S. (eds.) ICANN 2011. LNCS, vol. 6791, pp. 52–59. Springer, Heidelberg (2011). doi:10.1007/978-3-642-21735-7_7
15. Milford, M.J., Wyeth, G.F.: SeqSLAM: visual route-based navigation for sunny summer days and stormy winter nights. In: ICRA, pp. 1643–1649. IEEE (2012)
16. Noh, H., Hong, S., Han, B.: Learning deconvolution network for semantic segmentation. In: ICCV, pp. 1520–1528 (2015)
17. Sermanet, P., Eigen, D., Zhang, X., Mathieu, M., Fergus, R., LeCun, Y.: OverFeat: integrated recognition, localization and detection using convolutional networks. arXiv preprint arXiv:1312.6229 (2013)
18. Shantia, A., Timmers, R., Schomaker, L., Wiering, M.: Indoor localization by denoising autoencoders and semi-supervised learning in 3D simulated environment. In: 2015 Internatioal Joint Conference on Neural Networks (IJCNN), pp. 1–7. IEEE (2015)
19. Sivic, J., Zisserman, A.: Video Google: a text retrieval approach to object matching in videos. In: ICCV, pp. 1470–1477. IEEE (2003)
20. Stewénius, H., Gunderson, S.H., Pilet, J.: Size matters: exhaustive geometric verification for image retrieval accepted for ECCV 2012. In: Fitzgibbon, A., Lazebnik, S., Perona, P., Sato, Y., Schmid, C. (eds.) ECCV 2012. LNCS, pp. 674–687. Springer, Heidelberg (2012). doi:10.1007/978-3-642-33709-3_48
21. Zeiler, M.D., Krishnan, D., Taylor, G.W., Fergus, R.: Deconvolutional networks. In: CVPR, pp. 2528–2535. IEEE (2010)

Performance of Deep Learning Algorithms vs. Shallow Models, in Extreme Conditions - Some Empirical Studies

Samik Banerjee$^{(\boxtimes)}$ ⓘD, Prateep Bhattacharjee ⓘD, and Sukhendu Das ⓘD

Indian Institute of Technology Madras, Chennai 600036, India
{samik,prateepb}@cse.iitm.ac.in, sdas@iitm.ac.in

Abstract. Deep convolutional neural networks (DCNN) successfully exhibit exceptionally good classification performance, despite their massive size. The effect of a large value of noise term, as irreducible error in Expected Prediction Error (EPE) is first discussed. Through extensive systematic experiments, we show how in extreme conditions the traditional approaches fare at par with large neural networks, which generalize well in practice. Specifically, our experiments establish that state-of-the-art convolutional networks trained for classification barely fit a random labeling of the training data as an extreme condition to learn. This phenomenon is quantitatively unaffected even if we train the CNNs with completely inseparable data. This can be due to large degree of corruption of the entire data by random noise or random labels associated with data due to observation error. We corroborate these experimental findings by showing that depth six CNN (VGG-6) fails to overcome large noise in image signals.

Keywords: Convolutional neural networks · Noise · Classification · SVM · EPE

1 Introduction

Convolutional neural network (CNN) models have become the state-of-the-art to solve hard classification problems and have significantly improved the accuracy for classifications. Traditional statistical machine learning methods require a human domain expert that can construct a good set of features as input dataset, while deep learning models waives the requirement of a hand crafted feature set. Hence it is more powerful and suitable for hard Artificial Intelligence tasks such as speech recognition or visual object classification. CNN based machine learning models can learn a hierarchy of features with complex and overlapping distributions on its own within the first few convolutional layers of CNN model, without any hand crafting of the raw input data. In the deepest layer of the model, a weighted set of selected features for each output is used to generate a prediction. Deep learning (DL) often outperforms traditional approaches [18],

© Springer International Publishing AG 2017
B.U. Shankar et al. (Eds.): PReMI 2017, LNCS 10597, pp. 565–574, 2017.
https://doi.org/10.1007/978-3-319-69900-4_72

for those hard classification problems in terms of performance accuracy, since the inevitable human error in feature selection can be easily avoided.

In the recent past, researchers have reported exciting results in various domains of computer vision and machine learning using convolutional neural networks (CNN). Still two questions [21] remains as the major interest about CNNs. The first question is about the power of the architecture − which classes of functions can it approximate well? The second question is; are good minima easier to find in deep rather than in shallow networks? In this paper we provide a set of experimental results for empirical evaluation, of both CNN and shallow methods, that puts some light into answers as to why and when deep networks fail or perform at par with the traditional shallow algorithms in complex and extreme conditions of data distributions. We define an extreme condition in labeled data, where the distributions overlap and nearest neighbors are randomly available with equal probability for all classes.

This paper compares shallow algorithms with deep networks, when we train both of them with different data distributions. The logic of the paper is as follows:

- Both shallow algorithms and deep networks are universal, that is they can approximate arbitrarily well any continuous function of d variables on a compact domain, but both of them fail to learn approximations with massive overlap.
- Many natural signals such as images and text require compositional algorithms that can be well approximated by Deep Convolutional Networks due to the basic properties of scalability and shift invariance. Of course, there are many situations that do not require shift invariant, scalable algorithms. For many functions that are not compositional do we expect any advantage of deep convolutional networks? [21]

Although difficult to prove this analytically, in spite of recent advances in concepts of Statistical Learning theory and deep artificial neural network analytics, we are forced to take the help of empirical studies to justify our logic and show-case the performance of CNN in extreme conditions. Recent reports by Thomas Poggio [21,22] reveal that DL algorithms for CNN are scalable and shift-invariant, and can approximate functions better than shallow methods. A recent work [1] shows that deep-CNN cannot handle distribution variations in the context of Transfer Learning and Domain Adaptation. None of these report any results of performance for deep learning algorithms on extreme conditions. This has been the main motivation of our work.

2   Related Work

Most publications on DL these days start with Hinton's back-propagation [17] and with Lecun's convolutional networks [19] (see [18] for a nice review). The works proposed in [24–26] mainly deal with a multi-stage complex system, which take the convolutional features obtained from their model and then use PCA

(Principal Component Analysis) for dimensionality reduction, followed by classification using SVM. Other significant works in this area are [1,4,14,16,17,20,23], which use CNN for object recognition, video classification, image captioning and character recognition tasks.

Several popular Machine Learning (ML) techniques had been originally designed and proposed for the solution of binary classification problems. Traditionally among them, one can mention the Support Vector Machines (SVMs) [7], the Perceptron [13] and the RIPPER algorithms [5]. Many algorithms developed by the machine learning community focus on learning in pre-defined feature spaces. However, many real-world classification tasks exist that involve features where such algorithms could not be applied [11]. This paper also reports that Naive Bayes' outperformed C4.5 induction algorithm based on empirical evaluations. In such cases, the non-parametric classification algorithms like k-NN perform better. Currently very few work focuses on the traditional culture (predominant in Digital Signal/Image Processing and Communications field) of performance degradation in the presence of noise. One assumes that training may provide the system the power to overcome noise or overlapping distributions of data. But, is it really so? There lies the motivation and focus of our work.

3   Analysis Using Expected Prediction Error (EPE)

Based on the concept of Bias-variance decomposition [12], one can write $EPE(Y|X) = \sigma^2 + B^2 + V$; where σ^2 is the irreducible error due to noise and the two other terms (Bias and Variance) are model and dimension dependent. In the presence of a large amount of noise ($\sigma >> 1$, say) in data, the error dominates resulting in degraded accuracy. In such a case, the prediction will generate random output in most cases. Figure 1 shows the EPE plot as demonstrated in [3]. For highly complex models (assuming for large orders, this metric is hypothetically equivalent to the 'power' of a deep-CNN) the error reaches 50% asymptotically. From a performance perspective, this can be visualized to be $EPE(Y|X) = B_n^2 + V_n$, where $B_n >> B$ and $V_n >> V$; *i.e.* a system randomly produces accurate results at most only for half of the cases ($\simeq 50\%$). We show this empirically using performance analysis of deep and shallow networks.

Noise is the unavoidable component of the loss, incurred independently of the learning algorithm. One always favor a more complex model if we assess that the 'goodness' of a model fits on the training data, as a more complex model will be able to capture small, random trends in the data due to noise [10]. Too large a model complexity/order causes overfitting. Overfitting occurs when an estimator is too flexible, allowing it to capture illusory trends in the data. These illusory trends are often the result of the noise in the observations. Its reasonable to assume that CNN models have extremely large complexity/order to deal with large variations of training samples. The above synthetic curve (Fig. 1) shows that for large order the test error will asymptotically touch 50%. The gap between total error and variance is due to noise in signal/data and perhaps so even for kernel based models (theoretical proof open for researchers). This

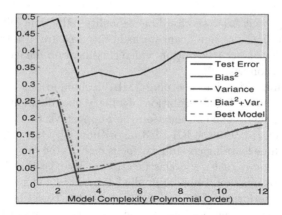

Fig. 1. Bias-variance trade-off (courtesy [3]).

trend should definitely be followed by all statistical classifiers [3] and even kernel models (e.g. SVM). The question remains, can CNN with its heavy training requirements overcome this and reduce the performance gap due to irreducible error. No formal proof is available, but one can empirically test to verify this, as for now.

For large noise, will performance of shallow models be weaker than CNN? How do you simulate this large noise? Either perturb the data samples or their class labels. We did this in an alternative way - make data points of two classes (binary classification problem) to overlap by a large extent. This in effect can be thought to be equivalently simulating a scenario of heavy noise on class labels. The noise level however cannot be quantified, other than a completely different mode of theoretical analytics, which is beyond the scope of the current paper. We quantify this noise by the amount of data overlap, with 100% data overlap indicating the maximum level of noise ($SNR \simeq 0$) where one may assume to have completely over-corrupted the input data (both class-wise distributions of training and testing data completely overlap with similar distributions).

Anyway, noise can play a significant role in the EPE as per bias-variance analysis. Indeed, according to Domingos [10], with the 0/1 loss the noise is linearly added to the error with a coefficient equal to $2P_D(f_D(x) = y) - 1$. Hence, if the classifier is accurate, that is, if $P_D(f_D(x) = y) >> 0.5$, then the noise $N(x)$, if present, influences the expected loss. In the opposite situation also, with very bad classifiers, that is when $P_D(f_D(x) = y) << 0.5$, the noise influences the overall error in the opposite sense: it reduces the expected loss. If $P_D(f_D(x) = y) \approx 0.5$, that is if the classifier provides a sort of random guessing, then $2P_D(f_D(x) = y) - 1 \approx 0$ is the estimate of the noise in real data sets (as shown in [10]). A straightforward approach simply consists in disregarding it, but in this way we could overestimate the bias. Some heuristics are proposed in [15], but the problem remains substantially unresolved. Given these unanswered questions, we resort to empirical studies, as also suggested in [10] with noise.

4   Details of CNN and Datasets Used

The '*Wt. layer*' in VGG-6 network [23] consists of a convolutional layer with the same *kernel size* and *number of filters* as proposed by the authors. The *FC* layers corresponds to the fully connected layers of the network. with two 50% *Dropout* layers. This moderately deep network is used for the empirical verification of the data. VGG-6 has been used for the object recognition tasks in [23].

4.1   Synthetic Scatter Dataset

Experimentations have been carried on two separate sets of data to study the effect of noise on the deep learning model compared with vanilla shallow supervised as well as non-parametric algorithms. The first set consists of two-class synthetically generated random data distributions, while the second consists of the Chars74K dataset [9].

Synthetic Data - To test the accuracy of the different algorithms, we have synthetically generated random data belonging to two classes. The distribution is considered to be elliptical for scatter generation (see Fig. 2) For a 2-class classification problem, dataset is generated as: (a) *50-dimensional data* and (b) *100-dimensional data*. The scatter is generated randomly and produced with 7 levels of overlap (difficulty) as described below (illustrated using 3-d scatters):

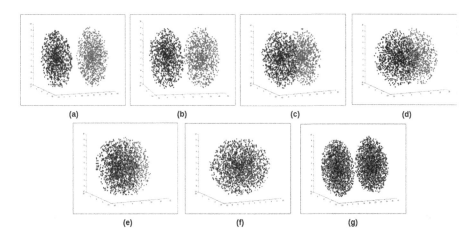

Fig. 2. Scatter Plots showing $3D$ Data: (a) Non-overlapping; (b) Barely touching; Overlap of: (c) 25%; (d) 50%; (e) 75%; (f) Fully Overlapping; (g) Random class labels (best viewed in color).

- **Non-overlapping (Fig. 2(a))** - The scatter for classes are completely separated, and they are separated from each other. This is the most easiest and favorable case.

- **Adjacent (Fig. 2(b))**- The data are completely separated, but they are touching each other at a single point.
- **Overlap (25%) (Fig. 2(c))**- 25% of the data from both classes overlap.
- **Overlap (50%) (Fig. 2(d))**- 50% of the data from both classes overlap.
- **Overlap (75%) (Fig. 2(e))**- 75% of the data from both classes overlap.
- **Completely overlapping (Fig. 2(f))**- The entire data from bothy classes (of decision regions) completely overlaps with each other. The class means, variances and boundaries are all identical.
- **Random (Fig. 2(g))**- The data is separated in 2 clusters as in non-overlapping case, but each cluster have a complete mixture of the two class labels randomly.

The extreme conditions are in Figs. 2(e)-(g). These are considered the most extreme and hard to solve by a machine. The datasets used are partitioned in a 10-fold cross-validation setting using $\{60 : 30 : 10\}$ as *train, test & validation* sets. For both the $50D$ and $100D$ data, 1 million data points/class are generated for the two class problem.

The Chars74K dataset [9] - Invariance of the CNN model to noise is further experimented on a benchmark real-world dataset for character recognition with 62992 synthesized characters from computer fonts (refer Fig. 3 for samples in the dataset). The dataset has 62 classes ($0 - 9, A - Z, a - z$). The VGG-6 model is trained on all these 62992 characters. The testing set is generated using Additive White Gaussian Noise (AWGN) [2] as shown in Fig. 4.

$$0 \quad \square \quad \boldsymbol{O} \quad 0 \quad \mathcal{3} \quad \boldsymbol{7} \quad \mathbf{B} \quad \mathsf{w} \quad \mathbb{M} \quad \boldsymbol{U}$$

Fig. 3. A few examples from the Chars74K dataset [9].

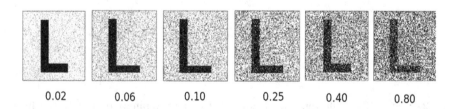

| 0.02 | 0.06 | 0.10 | 0.25 | 0.40 | 0.80 |

Fig. 4. An example showing the effect of AWGN on a character template, with increasing variance of noise.

5   Experimental Results

Experiments have been carried on the the synthetic datasets using SVM [6], k-NN, Naive Bayes and VGG-6 [23]. Figure 5(A) shows the accuracy of the traditional shallow learning methods for $50D$ data along with the VGG-6 CNN model. The plot reveals a constant drop in accuracy of the classification with increasing amount of overlap. The experiments are studied in 10-fold cross-validation mode. We observe the performance with increasing extremity (*i.e.* more overlap and similar boundaries of scatters). The *Completely overlapping (CO)* and the *Random (RM)* cases exhibit the poorest performance of the classifier since the accuracy of the binary classifier is around 50%, indicating the presence of extreme distribution overlap in the data over a pair of classes. Similar setup has been experimented on the $100D$ data where the deep VGG-6 model shows a similar trend in Fig. 5(B) along with the other classifiers. Note here that, the non-parametric classifier though performs worse than deep-CNN at low levels of overlap in class-wise data distributions, catches up quite well to produce a similar degraded performance under extreme overlap (CO and RM) conditions. A recognition accuracy of $\approx 50\%$ at *(f)* and *(g)* indices in Fig. 5(B) show that deep-CNN has no advantage over other simple shallow classifier in extreme conditions. This is one of the main outcomes of this empirical study. At full overlap (labels are random) the CNN performs similar to the shallow learning algorithms.

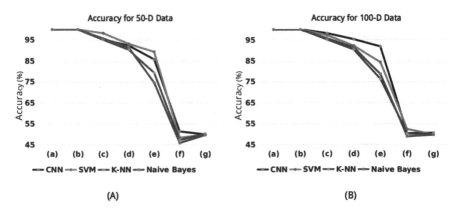

Fig. 5. Plots for accuracies of (A) $50D$ and (B) $100D$ data on the 7 different data distributions as shown in Fig. 2; (a) Non-overlapping; (b) Barely touching; Overlap of: (c) 25%; (d) 50%; (e) 75%; (f) Fully Overlapping; and (g) Random class labels.

The VGG-6 model is trained on the clear images of the Chars74K dataset and tested on the images with added noise (see Fig. 3). Figure 6(A) shows plots of accuracy of classification obtained by the VGG-6 model with increasing number of epochs (during training), when tested with image samples of low noise levels of perturbations of the image signal. Figure 6(B) shows the decrease in accuracy of the SVM (based on the HOG [8] feature extracted on the images) and VGG-6 models with increase in the variance of noise incorporated in the images. For natural images, we can infer that the CNNs are barely competent than shallow methods even when a small amount of noise degrades the images, and the performance of the CNN also falls rapidly with increasing levels of noise in data.

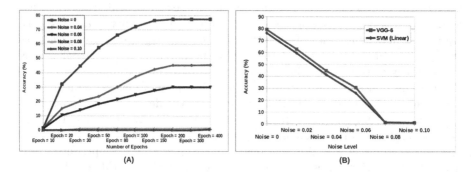

(A)   (B)

Fig. 6. Curve showing (A) the effect of noise with increasing number of Epochs in training the *VGG-6*; (B) effect on the accuracy of classification using SVM and VGG-6 (after *400 epochs*) with increasing levels of noise; on the Chars74K dataset [9].

6   Conclusion

This paper reveals that many state-of-the-art classifiers provide equivalently degraded performance under extreme conditions of the data. When the data is corrupted by large levels of noise or overlapping scatter distributions, even a recent state-of-the-art CNN model randomly classifies the data. In case of Natural images, the DL methods cannot handle extreme conditions (large noise). Being a supervised technique, the CNN models need a mechanism to overcome noise in the data to approximate and classify them more accurately.

References

1. Banerjee, S., Das, S.: Soft-margin learning for multiple feature-kernel combinations with domain adaptation, for recognition in surveillance face dataset. In: Proceedings of the IEEE Conference on Computer Vision and Pattern Recognition Workshops (CVPRW) on Biometrics, pp. 169–174 (2016)
2. Bergmans, P.: A simple converse for broadcast channels with additive white gaussian noise (corresp.). IEEE Trans. Inf. Theory **20**(2), 279–280 (1974)
3. Blog, C.M.: Model selection: underfitting, overfitting, and the bias-variance tradeoff (2013)
4. Chen, J.C., Zheng, J., Patel, V.M., Chellappa, R.: Fisher vector encoded deep convolutional features for unconstrained face verification. In: 2016 IEEE International Conference on Image Processing (ICIP), pp. 2981–2985, September 2016

5. Cohen, W.W.: Fast effective rule induction. In: Proceedings of the Twelfth International Conference on Machine Learning, pp. 115–123 (1995)
6. Cortes, C., Vapnik, V.: Support-vector networks. Mach. Learn. **20**(3), 273–297 (1995)
7. Cristianini, N., Scholkopf, B.: Support vector machines and kernel methods: the new generation of learning machines. AI Mag. **23**(3), 31 (2002)
8. Dalal, N., Triggs, B.: Histograms of oriented gradients for human detection. In: IEEE Computer Society Conference on Computer Vision and Pattern Recognition, CVPR 2005, vol. 1, pp. 886–893. IEEE (2005)
9. de Campos, T.E., Babu, B.R., Varma, M.: Character recognition in natural images. In: VISAPP (2), pp. 273–280 (2009)
10. Domingos, P.: A unified bias-variance decomposition. In: Proceedings of 17th International Conference on Machine Learning, pp. 231–238. Morgan Kaufmann, Stanford (2000)
11. Dougherty, J., Kohavi, R., Sahami, M., et al.: Supervised and unsupervised discretization of continuous features. In: Proceedings of the Twelfth International Conference on Machine Learning, vol. 12, pp. 194–202 (1995)
12. Friedman, J., Hastie, T., Tibshirani, R.: The Elements of Statistical Learning. Springer Series in Statistics, vol. 1. Springer, Berlin (2001)
13. Haykin, S.: Multilayer perceptrons. Neural Netw. Compr. Found. **2**, 156–255 (1999)
14. Hoffman, J., Guadarrama, S., Tzeng, E.S., Hu, R., Donahue, J., Girshick, R., Darrell, T., Saenko, K.: LSDA: Large scale detection through adaptation. In: Advances in Neural Information Processing Systems (NIPS), pp. 3536–3544 (2014)
15. James, G.M.: Variance and bias for general loss functions. Mach. Learn. **51**(2), 115–135 (2003)
16. Karpathy, A., Toderici, G., Shetty, S., Leung, T., Sukthankar, R., Fei-Fei, L.: Large-scale video classification with convolutional neural networks. In: Proceedings of the IEEE Conference on Computer Vision and Pattern Recognition, pp. 1725–1732 (2014)
17. Krizhevsky, A., Sutskever, I., Hinton, G.E.: Imagenet classification with deep convolutional neural networks. In: Advances in Neural Information Processing Systems, pp. 1097–1105 (2012)
18. LeCun, Y., Bengio, Y., Hinton, G.: Deep learning. Nature **521**(7553), 436–444 (2015)
19. LeCun, Y., Boser, B., Denker, J.S., Henderson, D., Howard, R.E., Hubbard, W., Jackel, L.D.: Backpropagation applied to handwritten zip code recognition. Neural Comput. **1**(4), 541–551 (1989)
20. Mao, J., Xu, W., Yang, Y., Wang, J., Huang, Z., Yuille, A.: Deep captioning with multimodal recurrent neural networks (m-rnn). arXiv preprint arXiv:1412.6632 (2014)
21. Mhaskar, H., Liao, Q., Poggio, T.: Learning functions: when is deep better than shallow. arXiv preprint arXiv:1603.00988 (2016)
22. Poggio, T., Mhaskar, H., Rosasco, L., Miranda, B., Liao, Q.: Why and when can deep-but not shallow-networks avoid the curse of dimensionality: a review. arXiv preprint arXiv:1611.00740 (2016)
23. Simonyan, K., Zisserman, A.: Very deep convolutional networks for large-scale image recognition. arXiv preprint arXiv:1409.1556 (2014)

24. Sun, Y., Wang, X., Tang, X.: Deep learning face representation from predicting 10,000 classes. In: Proceedings of the IEEE Conference on Computer Vision and Pattern Recognition (CVPR), pp. 1891–1898 (2014)
25. Taigman, Y., Yang, M., Ranzato, M., Wolf, L.: Deepface: closing the gap to human-level performance in face verification. In: Proceedings of the IEEE Conference on Computer Vision and Pattern Recognition (CVPR), pp. 1701–1708 (2014)
26. Zhu, Z., Luo, P., Wang, X., Tang, X.: Recover canonical-view faces in the wild with deep neural networks. arXiv preprint arXiv:1404.3543 (2014)

Deep Learning in the Domain of Multi-Document Text Summarization

Rajendra Kumar Roul[1]([⊠]) (ID), Jajati Keshari Sahoo[2] (ID), and Rohan Goel[1] (ID)

[1] Department of Computer Science, BITS-Pilani,
Goa Campus, Zuarinagar 403726, Goa, India
rkroul@goa.bits-pilani.ac.in, rohangoel0296@gmail.com
[2] Department of Mathematics, BITS-Pilani, Goa Campus,
Zuarinagar 403726, Goa, India
jksahoo@goa.bits-pilani.ac.in

Abstract. Text summarization is the process of generating a shorter version of the input text which captures its most important information. This paper addresses and tries to solve the problem of extractive text summarization which works by selecting a subset of phrases or sentences from the original document(s) to form a summary. Selections of such sentences are done based on certain criteria which formulates a feature set. Multilayer ELM (Extreme Learning Machine) which is based on the underlying deep network architecture is trained over this feature set to classify the sentences as important or unimportant. The used approach is unique and highlights the effectiveness of Multilayer ELM and its stability for usage in the domain of text summarization. Effectiveness of Multilayer ELM is justified by the experimental results on DUC and TAC datasets wherein it significantly outperforms the other well known classifiers.

Keywords: Deep learning · Extractive · ML-ELM · Rouge score · Summarization

1 Introduction

In this data driven world, more than 2.5 quintillion bytes of data are generated every day. However, since this huge quantity of data requires tremendous amount of processing, most of the data is never analyzed and we are still learning to make sense out of it. A large fraction of this data is in the form of text documents ranging from news articles to e-books. Often these documents are verbose and require long reading time which one typically wants to avoid. Hence, the need of summarizing these documents arises. Moreover, to process the large amount data efficiently, the technique of summarization needs to be automated. Two most common methods used for automatic text summarization are *Extractive* where important sentences and phrases are extracted from the original text without modifying the sentences themselves and *Abstractive* which involves paraphrasing parts of the original source text [1]. Multi-document summarization is

B.U. Shankar et al. (Eds.): PReMI 2017, LNCS 10597, pp. 575–581, 2017.
https://doi.org/10.1007/978-3-319-69900-4_73

a technique which can able to generate summaries from huge volume of documents. Many active research works have done in this domain [2–4]. This paper uses the extractive approach for the process of multi-document summarization. Given a corpus of documents, the proposed methodology gives a summary by extracting the most important sentences from the corpus using Multilayer ELM (ML-ELM), a classifier which is getting rapidly recognized in the machine learning domain having easy to implement and capable of handling large volume of data with high processing speed [5]. For generating the summaries algorithmically, the classifier is trained over a dataset and the trained model predicts the importance of the sentence in each document of the corpus. Identifying the feature set over which the training will occur is hence a crucial step in the process. Nine important features are identified by the proposed approach which are likely to be a part of a sentence in the summary. Experimental results on DUC and TAC datasets show that ML-ELM can outperform other traditional classifiers in the field of text summarization.

Remaining sections of the paper are as follows: Sect. 2 briefly discusses the basics of ML-ELM. The proposed approach is discussed in Sect. 3. Section 4 covers the experimental work and Sect. 5 concludes the paper.

2   Basic Preliminaries

2.1   Extreme Learning Machine

Huang et al. [6] suggested a feed forward neural network having single layer and named it as Extreme Learning Machine (ELM). Many important characteristics of ELM such as no back propagation, extremely fast learning speed, able to manage large dataset etc. make ELM more popular compared to other established classifiers.

Mathematically: Consider N different examples (x_i, y_i), where $x_i = [x_{i1}, x_{i2}, ..., x_{in}]^T \in R^n$ and $y_i = [y_{i1}, y_{i2}, ..., y_{im}]^T \in R^m$, such that $(x_i, y_i) \in R^n \times R^m$, $i = 1, 2, ..., N$. ELM has an activation function $g(\text{x})$ and L hidden layer nodes. Given input x, ELM output function can be written as

$$y_j = \sum_{i=1}^{L} \beta_i g(w_i \cdot x_j + b_i) \tag{1}$$

where $j = 1, ..., N$, w_i and b_i are randomly generated hidden node parameters. $w_i = [w_{i1}, w_{i2}, w_{i3}, ..., w_{in}]^T$ is the weight vector that joins the 'n' input nodes to the ith hidden node and b_i is the bias of the ith hidden node. β is the weight vector that connects each hidden node to every output node and is represented as $\beta = [\beta_1, ..., \beta_L]^T$. Equation 1 in a reduce form can be written as $H\beta = Y$, where Y and H are the output and hidden layer matrix respectively.

2.2 Multilayer ELM

An artificial neural network having multiple hidden layers called Multilayer ELM is proposed by Kasun et al. [7] which possesses all the properties of ELM since it combines ELM with ELM-autoencoder (ELM-AE). Parameters that represent ML-ELM are trained layer-wise using ELM-AE in an unsupervised manner. During the training time, no iteration takes place and hence the unsupervised training is very fast. The architectures of ELM-AE and ELM are almost similar except that ELM is supervised in nature, while ELM-AE is unsupervised and it can be stacked and trained in a progressive way. The stacked ELM-AEs will learn how to represent the data, the first level has a basic representation, the second level combines that representation to create a higher-level representation and so on. Using the Eq. 2, ML-ELM transfers the data between the hidden layers. The general architecture of ML-ELM is shown in Fig. 1.

$$H_i = g((\beta_i)^T H_{i-1}) \qquad (2)$$

where H_i is the ith hidden layer output matrix and β_i is the output weight vector of ELM-AE placed before the ith hidden layer. $i = 0$, represents the input layer $\mathbf{x}$. Regularized least square technique is used to calculate analytically the output weights of the connection between last hidden layer and nodes of the output layer.

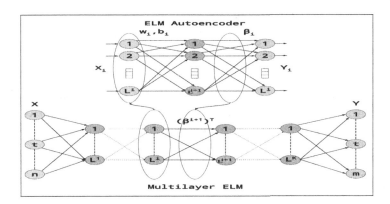

Fig. 1. Multilayer ELM and ELM Autoencoder

3   Proposed Approach

3.1   Identifying Important Features and Generating the Feature Vector

The proposed approach identified nine important features of a sentence which are described below. This nine-dimensional feature vector along with the class label form the feature vector for each sentence s of a document d belongs to the corpus C.

1. **Length of the sentence:** This feature is defined as how large a given sentence is by computing its size (i.e. the number of terms it contains).

2. **Weight of the sentence:** Term Frequency (TF) measures the frequency of a term t in d where as Inverse Document Frequency (IDF) measures the importance of t in the entire corpus C. TF-IDF value of a term is computed as $TF\text{-}IDF_{t,d} = TF_{t,d} \times IDF_t$. Score for a sentence s is computed by summing up the $TF\text{-}IDF$ values of all the terms belong to that sentence.

3. **Density of the sentence:** The density of a sentence s is computed by taking the ratio between the total count of keywords in s and the total count of words which includes all stop-words of s. For each $s \in d$:
   i. extract the keywords[1] from s and let the count of keywords be n.
   ii. compute the score as $\frac{n}{N}$, where N is number of words in s including stop-words.

4. **Presence of named entities in the sentence:** Named-entities are the terms which are generally proper nouns and they belong to the categories such as 'names of people', 'organization', 'locations' 'quantities' etc. Sentences having these named-entities are usually important because they tend to directly talk about an object. To detect the presence of such terms in a sentence, Stanford NER Tagger[2] is used. Score of a sentence is the number of named entities it contains.

5. **Presence of cue-phrases in the sentence:** In general, sentences that contain the phrases like 'in summary', 'our investigation', 'in conclusion', 'the paper describes' and the ones which highlight the quality such as 'important', 'the best', 'hardly', 'significantly', 'in particular' etc. are important because they happen to be a good source of significant information in a document. Sentences which contain such cue-phrases given a score of 1 and the rest are given 0. WordNet[3] has been used to find such words/phrases.

6. **Relative offset of the sentence:** Sentences that are located in the beginning or towards the end of a document tend to be more imperative as they carry relevant information like definitions and conclusions. Such sentences receive a score 1, otherwise 0.

7. **Presence of title words in the sentence:** A document is best described by those sentences that contain a part or all the words present in the title of that document and hence such sentences are considered as important. The score of sentence s is computed using Eq. 3.

$$\text{score of } s = \frac{\text{common words between the title and } s}{\text{total number of words in the title}} \tag{3}$$

8. **Presence of quoted text in the sentence:** Sentences which have a part of their text within quotation marks assert something specific and that information is important. For each $s \in d$, if it contains the words/phrases that reside within " " (double quotation) marks then it receives the score 1, otherwise 0.

---

[1] NLTK is used to extract the keywords.

[2] http://nlp.stanford.edu/software/CRF-NER.shtml.

[3] https://wordnet.princeton.edu/.

9. **Presence of upper-case words in the sentence:** This feature checks the presence of words/phrases that are upper-case in a sentence. These upper-case words/phrases are likely to refer the important acronyms, names, places, etc. Such sentences receive a score 1, otherwise 0.

3.2 Deciding the Class Label for Each Sentence

The class label for each sentence is either important (+1) or unimportant (-1). Those sentences of a document which are labeled as "important" will constitute the summary for that document.

4 Experimental Analysis

For ELM and ML-ELM, the code is run using different number of hidden nodes (n) and layers and only those number of nodes and layers are considered on which the best results are obtained. Every DUC[4] and TAC[5] datasets contain four human written gold summary. For DUC-2006 and 2007, ELM with $n =$ '175' achieved the maximum F-measure. For ML-ELM, n is considered as '50' and '30' respectively and the number of hidden layers $=$ '5' on which the best results is obtained. Tables 1 and 2 show the performance of different classifiers on these two DUC datasets. Similarly, for TAC-2008 and 2009, ELM with $n =$ '175' and ML-ELM using $n =$ '100' and hidden layers $=$ '5' achieved the maximum F-measure. The results on these two TAC datasets are shown in Tables 3 and 4 respectively. The Recall-Oriented Understudy for Gisting Evaluation (ROUGE) score[6] of ML-ELM with extractive gold summary and human-written gold summary on both datasets are shown in Tables 5 and 6 respectively. For unigram and bigram matching, recall computation is required and hence ROUGE-1 and ROUGE-2 are used. Similarly, another ROUGE score called ROUGE-SU4 [8] is also used for recall computation and it uses the technique "skip-bigram with unigram having maximum gap length of 4" for matching. As the human-written gold summaries most likely use words that are not a part of the original document and people tend to paraphrase them in their own way while using words, thus evaluating ROUGE scores using human-written gold summaries results low score as shown in Table 6. Since system generated summaries are extractive in nature, they strictly make use of the n-gram structure of the original set of documents. This results in a very less n-gram overlap between the human-written gold summaries and the system generated summaries. ROUGE essentially relies on the n-gram recall and hence the scores generated tend to be low. But if we create a set of extractive gold summaries using the human-written gold summaries and use them along with the system generated summaries, ROUGE scores tend to be good as shown in Table 5 because there is a sufficient n-gram recall between the two sets. From the tables, it is observed that F-measure (bold indicates the maximum) of ML-ELM is better than other established classifiers.

---

[4] http://www.duc.nist.gov.

[5] http://www.nist.gov/tac/data.

[6] http://www.berouge.com/Pages/default.aspx.

Table 1. DUC 2006 (train and test)   **Table 2.** DUC 2007 (train and test)

Classifier	Precision	Recall	F-measure	Classifier	Precision	Recall	F-measure
ELM	0.710	0.879	0.786	ELM	0.801	0.713	0.754
ML-ELM	0.748	0.853	**0.797**	ML-ELM	0.795	0.730	**0.761**
SVM (LinearSVC)	0.743	0.795	0.768	SVM (Linear SVC)	0.764	0.730	0.746
SVM (Linear kernel)	0.687	0.692	0.689	SVM (Linear kernel)	0.702	0.711	0.706
Decision tree	0.657	0.667	0.662	Decision tree	0.711	0.649	0.679
M-NB	0.713	0.833	0.768	M-NB	0.791	0.687	0.735
B-NB	0.646	0.656	0.651	B-NB	0.708	0.648	0.677
G-NB	0.702	0.693	0.697	G-NB	0.712	0.694	0.703
kNN	0.726	0.736	0.731	k-NN	0.763	0.654	0.704
Random forest	0.745	0.692	0.718	Random forest	0.726	0.718	0.722
Gradient boosting	0.738	0.715	0.726	Gradient boosting	0.694	0.674	0.684
Extra trees	0.734	0.698	0.716	Extra trees	0.735	0.702	0.718

Table 3. TAC 2008 (train and test)   **Table 4.** TAC 2009 (train and test)

Classifier	Precision	Recall	F-measure	Classifier	Precision	Recall	F-measure
ELM	0.732	0.785	0.758	ELM	0.732	0.797	0.763
ML-ELM	0.737	0.806	**0.77**	ML-ELM	0.731	0.806	**0.767**
SVM (LinearSVC)	0.682	0.842	0.754	SVM (Linear SVC)	0.703	0.810	0.753
SVM (Linear kernel)	0.683	0.675	0.678	SVM (Linear kernel)	0.728	0.711	0.719
Decision tree	0.657	0.653	0.655	Decision tree	0.661	0.69	0.675
M-NB	0.726	0.742	0.734	M-NB	0.749	0.730	0.739
B-NB	0.663	0.734	0.697	B-NB	0.704	0.652	0.677
G-NB	0.683	0.702	0.692	G-NB	0.724	0.701	0.712
k-NN	0.705	0.710	0.707	k-NN	0.714	0.700	0.707
Random forest	0.674	0.663	0.668	Random forest	0.701	0.689	0.695
Gradient boosting	0.653	0.645	0.649	Gradient boosting	0.684	0.693	0.688
Extra trees	0.677	0.694	0.685	Extra trees	0.708	0.703	0.705

5   Conclusion

This paper discussed an automatic text summarization technique using ML-ELM. The proposed approach has identified nine important features of a sentence to form the feature vector. ML-ELM is used on test datasets to find out

Table 5. ROUGE of ML-ELM (Extractive gold summary)

Table 6. ROUGE of ML-ELM (Human-written gold summary)

Dataset	ROUGE-1	ROUGE-2	ROUGE-SU4
DUC 2006	0.684	0.469	0.501
DUC 2007	0.715	0.482	0.515
TAC 2008	0.73	0.500	0.533
TAC 2009	0.711	0.494	0.523

Dataset	ROUGE-1	ROUGE-2	ROUGE-SU4
DUC 2006	0.097	0.041	0.051
DUC 2007	0.121	0.050	0.062
TAC 2008	0.062	0.027	0.032
TAC 2009	0.061	0.026	0.032

those sentences which are important for building the summary. For experimental purpose, different DUC and TAC datasets are used. ROUGE scores in terms of average F-measure are calculated using ML-ELM and the results show that ML-ELM performs better than other classifiers. This demonstrates that deep learning has high influence on summarization of textual data. This work can be extended by using the proposed technique to built a recommendation system for different electronic devices. Also, by combining the feature space of ML-ELM with other classifiers will improve the classification results further.

References

1. Ganesan, K., Zhai, C., Han, J.: Opinosis: a graph-based approach to abstractive summarization of highly redundant opinions. In: Proceedings of the 23rd International Conference on Computational Linguistics. Association for Computational Linguistics, pp. 340–348 (2010)
2. Yang, G., Wen, D., Chen, N.-S., Sutinen, E., et al.: A novel contextual topic model for multi-document summarization. Expert Syst. Appl. **42**(3), 1340–1352 (2015)
3. Valizadeh, M., Brazdil, P.: Exploring actor–object relationships for query-focused multi-document summarization. Soft Comput., 1–13 (2014)
4. Luo, W., Zhuang, F., He, Q., Shi, Z.: Exploiting relevance, coverage, and novelty for query-focused multi-document summarization. Knowl.-Based Syst. **46**, 33–42 (2013)
5. Roul, R.K., Asthana, S.R., Kumar, G.: Study on suitability and importance of multilayer extreme learning machine for classification of text data. Soft. Comput. **21**(15), 4239–4256 (2017)
6. Huang, G.-B., Zhu, Q.-Y., Siew, C.-K.: Extreme learning machine: theory and applications. Neurocomputing **70**(1), 489–501 (2006)
7. Kasun, L.L.C., Zhou, H., Huang, G.-B., Vong, C.M.: Representational learning with extreme learning machine for big data. IEEE Intell. Syst. **28**(6), 31–34 (2013)
8. Lin, C.-Y.: Rouge: a package for automatic evaluation of summaries. In: Text Summarization Branches Out: Proceedings of the ACL 2004 Workshop, vol. 8, pp. 74–81 (2004)

Space-Time Super-Resolution Using Deep Learning Based Framework

Manoj Sharma$^{(\boxtimes)}$ ⓘ, Santanu Chaudhury ⓘ, and Brejesh Lall ⓘ

Department of Electrical Engineering, Indian Institute of Technology,
Delhi 110016, India
mksnith@gmail.com, schaudhury@gmail.com, brejesh@ee.iitd.ac.in

Abstract. This paper introduces a novel end-to-end deep learning framework to learn space-time super-resolution (SR) process. We propose a coupled deep convolutional auto-encoder (CDCA) which learns the non-linear mapping between convolutional features of up-sampled low-resolution (LR) video sequence patches and convolutional features of high-resolution (HR) video sequence patches. The upsampling in LR video refers to tri-cubic interpolation both in space and time. We also propose a H.264/AVC compatible video space-time SR framework by using learned CDCA, which enables to super-resolve compressed LR video with less computational complexity. The experimental results prove that the proposed H.264/AVC compatible framework performs better than the state-of-art techniques on space-time SR in terms of quality and time complexity.

Keywords: Deep learning · Image and video super-resolution · Space-time super-resolution · H.264/AVC

1 Introduction

Super-resolution (SR) of videos can be categorized into spatial SR and temporal SR. The recovery of HR video frames from LR video frames is termed as spatial SR. On the other hand, temporal SR is the retrieval of those dynamic events which occur faster than provided frame-rate by predicting mid-frame information. Although much work has been done on natural images SR [1–4] and spatial SR [5–8] of videos, but few advancement have been made to achieve simultaneous space-time SR. This problem is more interesting and useful in many computer vision and biomedical tasks for pre-processing of videos. One class of space-time SR methods [9,10] takes multiple LR video sequences at the input. Another class of space-time SR methods is to super-resolve video in space and time using only single video [11]. Existed work on space-time SR from single LR video doesn't provide significant improvement. There is still much scope for simultaneous space-time resolution enhancement.

In this paper, we propose a novel deep learning based method which we call *coupled deep convolutional auto-encoder (CDCA)* to learn the relationship

ⓒ Springer International Publishing AG 2017
B.U. Shankar et al. (Eds.): PReMI 2017, LNCS 10597, pp. 582–590, 2017.
https://doi.org/10.1007/978-3-319-69900-4_74

between up-sampled (both in space and time by tri-cubic interpolation) LR and corresponding HR video sequence spatial patches. The proposed method simultaneously calculates the convolutional feature map of up-sampled LR and HR video frame spatial patches using convolutional auto-encoder (CAE) and learns the relationship between these feature maps using the convolutional neural network. Our framework is motivated by an machine learning-based method [2] for natural images SR, we adopt similar framework with some major improvement for space-time SR. In contrast to autoencoder used by Zeng et al. [2] that computed intrinsic features, convolutional auto-encoder (CAE) was used in our framework to extract the features since CAE provides a better representation of image patches [12] in comparison to simple auto-encoder. Additionally, in our framework, the convolutional neural network is used to learn the mapping between convolutional features of LR and HR patches. We learn the mapping between spatial patches of up-sampled LR and HR video sequences instead of 3D space-time patches for the optimization of computation complexity. Learning on 3D space-time patches will provide better high temporal frequency information at the cost of high computational complexity. We also extend the use of CDCA to propose H.264/AVC compatible framework, which enables to super-resolve videos in a compressed domain with less computing complexity. Existing works on video super-resolution were limited to raw videos, but almost all of the videos on the web and other sources are encoded (compressed) due to bandwidth and memory limitation. First, one has to convert encoded video into the raw video, then that video can be super-resolved. But, our proposed architecture can directly super-resolve encoded video during the decoding (decompression) process with less computational complexity, which makes it more suitable for real-time space-time video SR.

2   Space-Time Super-Resolution Using CDCA

Our LR video sequence has a dimension (W × L × T) and corresponding HR video sequence and up-sampled LR have a dimension (S.W × S.L × S.T). Here S is the space-time SR factor. The CDCA given in Fig. 1 has a three-stage architecture. In Fig. 1, we term up-sampled LR frame as LR frame. The first and third stage consist of two convolutional auto-encoder (CAE) to learn the convolutional feature map of up-sampled LR (both in space and time) and corresponding HR video frame spatial patches, respectively. This results in weights/filters of CAE to learn useful features which can reconstruct back the original video frame spatial patches. After that, we make the algorithm to learn the non-linearities between LR and HR video frame spatial patches convolutional feature map by using simple one layer convolutional neural network (CNN) in the second stage. Here, weights/filters are learned to obtain the map between convolutional feature map of LR and HR video frame spatial patches. After having learned weights/filters of all stages, we put all three stages together to form one network as shown in Fig. 1. Then this network is fine-tuned on space-time super-resolution dataset which has up-sampled LR video frame spatial patches as input and HR video frame spatial patches as the target.

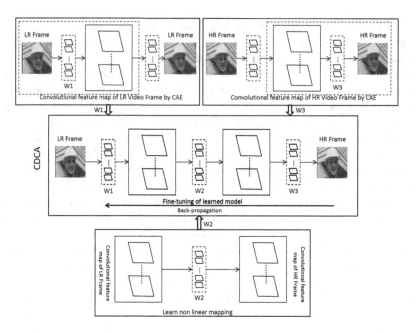

Fig. 1. Block Diagram of CDCA

We consider the up-sampled LR video frame spatial patches Y_i and learn mapping with corresponding HR video frame patches $X_i : \forall i = 1, 2..n$ where n is the total number of patches in training database. As a pre-processing step, we normalize the patch elements between [0 1]. Then convolutional feature map for LR video frame spatial patches is given by,

$$f_{i,L}^k = max(0, W_1^k * Y_i + b_1^k) \tag{1}$$

and, LR video frame spatial patches are reconstructed back by convolutional feature map as,

$$\hat{Y_i} = max(0, \sum_{k \in N} f_{i,L}^k * W_1^{'k} + c_1) \tag{2}$$

by, minimizing the loss function,

$$loss_{LR} = \frac{1}{n} \sum_{i=1}^{n} \frac{1}{2} \parallel Y_i - \hat{Y_i} \parallel_2^2 \tag{3}$$

Here N is the total number of feature maps of LR video frame spatial patches. Similarly, convolutional feature maps for HR video frame spatial patches is given by,

$$f_{i,H}^k = max(0, W_3^{'k} * X_i + b_3^k) \tag{4}$$

reconstruction of HR video frame patches as,

$$\hat{X}_i = max(0, \sum_{k \in M} f_{i,H}^k * W_3^k + c_3) \tag{5}$$

by, minimizing the loss function,

$$loss_{HR} = \frac{1}{n} \sum_{i=1}^{n} \frac{1}{2} \parallel X_i - \hat{X}_i \parallel_2^2 \tag{6}$$

here, M is the total number of convolutional feature maps of HR video frame spatial patches. M should be lesser than $N(M << N)$ to enforce sparsity and the relation between f_L^k and f_H^k is represented as,

$$\hat{f}_{i,H}^k = max(0, W_2^k * f_{i,L}^k + b_2^k) \tag{7}$$

Mapping between f_L^k and f_H^k is learned by minimizing the loss function,

$$loss = \frac{1}{n} \sum_{i=1}^{n} \frac{1}{2} \parallel f_{i,H}^k - \hat{f}_{i,H}^k \parallel_2^2 \tag{8}$$

After having pre-trained CDCA parameters $W_1, W_2, W_3, b_1, b_2, c_3$, we fine-tune all the parameters of combined framework CDCA on space-time SR data-set.

2.1 H.264/AVC Compatible Framework for Space-Time SR

We propose a novel H.264/AVC Compatible video SR framework which is using space-time SR algorithm, motion vector, spatial prediction parameters and residual error information to get HR video sequence from compressed LR video bit-stream. The proposed framework is given in Fig. 2. Our proposed video space-time SR framework uses different approaches for super-resolving I slices and P/B slices macro-blocks for optimization of computational cost. The working of this framework is described below:

1. In Fig. 2, encoded LR video bit-steam is the input for the standard H.264 decoder.
2. The motion vector (MV), residual error, spatial parameter and previously stored frame information are extracted from standard H.264 video decoder and are given to video space-time SR module.
3. All macro-blocks of I-slices and intra-predicted macro-blocks of P and B-slices are spatially super-resolved by applying spatial SR module block after spatial compensation process as given in lower part of video SR module. These macro-blocks are super-resolved by adding residues to the spatially compensated macro-blocks and then, followed by spatial SR module (i.e. CDCA learned on SRCNN [1] training dataset).

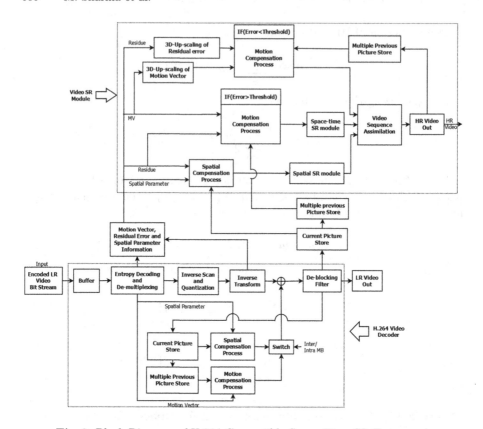

Fig. 2. Block Diagram of H.264 Compatible Space-Time SR Framework

4. The P and B-slices inter-predicted macro-blocks are super-resolved in space and time by using information of residue, MV, and space-time SR module as given in Fig. 2.
5. If the residue is greater than the threshold (as shown by middle part of video SR module), then the HR macro-blocks sequences are inter-predicted by adding residues to motion compensated macro-blocks sequences, and then followed by space-time SR module (input to space-time SR module is 3D up-sampled LR macro-blocks sequences).
6. If the residue is less than a threshold (as given in upper part of video SR module), MV and residue are up-scaled (both in space and time). HR macro-blocks sequences are predicted by adding re-scaled residues to the motion compensated macro-blocks sequences.
7. All HR macro-blocks sequences are arranged together to form a super-resolved video sequence.
8. Super-resolved I frame are stored as a reference frame, to be used as a reference for future P and B-frames.

The framework is also compatible with HEVC encoding scheme since HEVC has almost similar compression and decompression framework as H.264 with some extra features like adaptive Loop Filter, more number of intra-predicted modes and DCT based interpolation for luminance etc.

3 Results

Video sequences are taken from [11] to generate training data-set. LR video sequences are generated by 3D (space-time) down-sampling of HR video sequences. For the comparison of the qualitative performance of our H.264/AVC compatible framework with the existing state-of-the-art video spatial super-resolution methods, we take test sequences similar to those used in [7] to compute the results. To verify the effectiveness of proposed framework for spatial video SR, we conducted experiments on different standard video sequences. We compared proposed framework with state-of-the-art video SR algorithms as shown in

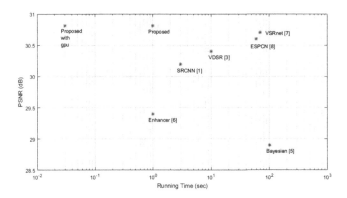

Fig. 3. Comparison between performance and runtime of different algorithms

Table 1. Average PSNR and SSIM comparison of different Video SR algorithms for different sequences

Sequence	Scale	Bayesian [5]	–	Enhancer [6]	–	VSRnet [7]	–	ESPCN [8]	–	Proposed	–
–	–	PSNR	SSIM	PSNR	SSIM	PSNR	SSIM	PSNR	SSIM	PSNR	SSIM
Myanmar	2	35.56	0.9515	35.94	0.9588	**38.48**	**0.9679**	38.37	0.9605	38.42	0.9612
Myanmar	3	32.20	0.9203	32.50	0.9099	34.42	0.9247	34.31	0.9239	**34.50**	**0.9288**
Myanmar	4	30.68	0.8895	30.23	0.8681	31.85	0.8834	31.53	0.8816	**31.98**	**0.8871**
Videoset4	2	29.69	0.9055	30.40	0.9141	31.30	0.9278	31.14	0.9237	**31.34**	**0.9300**
Videoset4	3	25.82	0.8328	26.34	0.7948	**26.79**	**0.8098**	26.44	0.8023	26.74	0.8097
Videoset4	4	25.06	0.7466	24.55	0.6877	24.84	0.7049	24.79	0.7008	**25.09**	**0.7178**
Foreman	2	35.88	0.9652	37.22	0.9693	38.52	0.9738	38.29	0.9721	**38.59**	**0.9758**
Foreman	3	33.81	0.9098	34.12	0.9105	35.74	0.9243	35.62	0.9234	**35.82**	**0.9334**
Foreman	4	33.26	0.8787	33.76	0.8808	34.69	0.8926	34.46	0.8879	**34.76**	**0.9095**

Table 1. Results show that proposed framework is comparable with state-of-the-art techniques. The experiment was conducted with a Linux work-station containing an Intel Xeon E5-2687W v3 processor with 3.1 GHz and 64 GB RAM. The graphics card used was NVIDIA GeForce GTX 980 with 2084 cores. In Fig. 3, we plot the average PSNR and run-time of different SR algorithms to 3× super-resolve per frame from the Myanmar and Videoset4 test sequence with a 704 × 576 resolution. Figure 3 clearly shows reduced computing complexity of our proposed framework in comparison of existing state-of-the-art video space-time SR techniques.

Motion aliasing occurs when the camera frame rate is lower than the temporal frequency of a fast moving object in video sequences. Observed object seems to be in false trajectory or distorted. Wagon wheel effect given in [11] is one of the best examples of motion aliasing effect; here the fan seems to be rotating in

Fig. 4. Temporal SR comparison (3×) between Bayesian approach (left) and our approach (right) [upper and lower one are key frames and mid frames are predicted one]

Fig. 5. Temporal SR (3×) on Flag sequence using (a) Tri-cubic interpolation. (b) [11]. (c) Proposed.

counter clock-wise direction [look at upper and lower key frames] but the actual rotation is in a clock-wise direction. This effect can be reduced by predicting mid-frame information. In Fig. 4, we show the comparison of our space-temporal SR approach with a Bayesian approach to reduce motion aliasing effect. We can easily visualize that quality of mid-frame is better and accurate in our approach. Some-times fast moving objects results in bad object shapes and blurriness along their motion trajectory. This effect becomes more prominent with an increase in object motion speed. It can be reduced by improving space-temporal SR. In Fig. 5, we show the comparison of different temporal SR approaches. Our framework is providing more visually pleasing video frames in comparison of exiting work and helps in reducing fast motion effects like, blurring and shape distortion.

4   Conclusions

We have proposed CDCA to learn space-time SR process and H.264/AVC compatible video space-time SR framework. Proposed H.264/AVC compatible framework outperforms all existing approaches for video spatial SR and space-time SR. The proposed framework drastically reduces the implementation complexity of space-time super-resolution learning algorithm in videos. This reduction in complexity and its implementation in GPU results in real-time space-time up-scaling of videos with improved quality.

References

1. Dong, C., Loy, C.C., He, K., Tang, X.: Learning a deep convolutional network for image super-resolution. In: Fleet, D., Pajdla, T., Schiele, B., Tuytelaars, T. (eds.) ECCV 2014. LNCS, vol. 8692, pp. 184–199. Springer, Cham (2014). doi:10.1007/978-3-319-10593-2_13
2. Zeng, K., Yu, J., Wang, R., Li, C., Tao, D.: Coupled deep auto-encoder for single image super-resolution. IEEE Trans. Cybern. **47**(1), 27–37 (2015)
3. Kim, J., Lee, J.K., Lee, K.M.: Accurate image super-resolution using very deep convolutional networks. In: CVPR (2016)
4. Mao, X.-J., Shen, C., Yang, Y.-B.: Image restoration using very deep convolutional encoder-decoder networks with symmetric skip connections. In: NIPS (2016)
5. Liu, C., Sun, D.: On bayesian adaptive video super-resolution. IEEE Trans. Pattern Anal. Mach. Intell. **36**(2), 346–360 (2014)
6. Faroudja, Y.C.: Video Enhancer, Patent App. PCT/US1993/001,907 (1993)
7. Kappeler, A., Yoo, S., Dai, Q., Katsaggelos, A.K.: Video super-resolution with convolutional neural networks. IEEE Trans. Comput. Imaging **2**(2), 109–122 (2016)
8. Shi, W., Caballeso, J.: Real time single image and video super-resolution using an efficient sub-pixel convolutional neural networks. In: CVPR (2016)
9. Shechtman, E., Caspi, Y., Irani, M.: Space-time super-resolution. IEEE Trans. Pattern Anal. Mach. Intell. **27**(4), 531–545 (2005)
10. Mudenagudi, U., Banerjee, S., Kalra, P.K.: Space-time super-resolution using graph cut optimization. IEEE Trans. Pattern Anal. Mach. Intell. **33**(5), 995–1008 (2011)

11. Themelis, K.E., Rontogiannis, A.A., Koutroumbas, K.D.: Space-time super-resolution from a single video. In: CVPR (2011)
12. Du, B., Xiong, W., Wu, J., Zhang, L., Tao, D.: Stacked convolutional de-noising auto-encoders for feature representation. IEEE Trans. Cybern. **47**(4), 1017–1027 (2016)

A Spatio-temporal Feature Learning Approach for Dynamic Scene Recognition

Ihsan Ullah[1,2(✉)] 🆔 and Alfredo Petrosino[1] 🆔

[1] CVPR Lab, Department of Science and Technology,
University of Naples Parthenope, Naples, Italy
{ihsan.ullah,petrosino}@uniparthenope.it
[2] Department of Computer Science, University of Milan, Milan, Italy

Abstract. The dynamic scene in a video comprises of a specific spatio-temporal pattern. A mask can learn the features efficiently compared to a sliding kernel approach as in a convolutional neural network that shrinks many parameters with respect to non-sliding or fully connected neural networks. In this paper, *3DPyraNet-F* a discriminative approach of spatio-temporal feature learning is proposed for dynamic scene recognition. It performs transfer learning by considering the highest layer of the learned network structure and combines it with a linear-SVM classifier, in a way that enhances dynamic scenes in videos. Encouraging results are achieved despite the lower computational cost, fewer parameters, and camera-induced motion. It outperforms the state-of-the-art for MaryLand-in-the-wild and shows a comparable result for YUPPEN dataset.

1 Introduction

Dynamic natural scene recognition (e.g. Beach, Storms, Fire, etc.) in a video clip is a highly researched area of computer vision (CV) and machine learning (ML) having applications in robotics and autonomous cars etc. Despite advances in image classification, recognition of dynamic scene (DS) from one single frame is unfeasible as it is insufficient information. Incorporating temporal information – that is considering consecutive frames – can improve the effectiveness of classifiers, but remains challenging as motion is often correlated with many artifacts: shadows, lighting variations, specular effects, camera-induced motion and more. Some of the well-known temporal models are reported in [1–3]. All these and many other recent papers claim 90+% efficiency on specifically focused scenarios. However, this performance is overly optimistic, as scenes change dramatically from one frame to the next due to occlusions and illumination in the surrounding environment.

The recent trend for dynamic scene recognition (DSR) [4,5] is to build deep neural networks (DNN) by learning more discriminative and flexible features. These models received great attention due to their huge success on large-scale datasets [5,6] and due to the idea that they can perform well for scene recognition

© Springer International Publishing AG 2017
B.U. Shankar et al. (Eds.): PReMI 2017, LNCS 10597, pp. 591–598, 2017.
https://doi.org/10.1007/978-3-319-69900-4_75

as well as other recognition tasks [4,5]. The key characteristic of convolutional *DNN* models is its kernel sharing and learning methodology. In comparison to fully connected *NN* models, this features decreases parameters as well as their discriminative power while considering large input frames from a video.

While many classical *CV* approaches use a coarse to fine refinement approach, recent deep learning (*DL*) models do not. The idea underlying the refinement is to build a hierarchy of features – a pyramid – and to finally select the most discriminative ones for the classification step as used in different feature extractors/descriptors, e.g. Steerable/Laplacian pyramids [7], SIFT [8], SPM [9] and more. Similarly, previously most models were following biological plausible pyramidal structure [10,11]. On the contrary, recent (*DNN*) models do not, resulting in an increase in convergence time, ambiguity, and number of parameters.

The key features of proposed *3DPyraNet-F* model are: (a) *3DPyraNet* is adopted in combination with linear-*SVM* classifier to learn and classify spatiotemporal features, (b) the weighting scheme is more suitable for learning the features from videos containing camera induced motion, and (c) the proposed model can be applied in multiple applications (with slight tuning), unlike handcrafted features. The paper is structured as: a motive behind 3d model is given in Sect. 2. Further, its sub-sections explain the present techniques, which are extended to proposed model. Section 3 explains proposed *3DPyraNet-F*. Section 4 discuss datasets and achieved results whereas, Sect. 5 concludes this work.

2   3DPyraNet

3DPyraNet is based on the concept of coarse to fine refinement or the decision making pyramidal structure of a brain [12]. This approach is widely used in *NN* models [10,13–15]. In addition, the structure of image pyramids and *NN* is quite similar. *3DPyraNet* shows that following/designing models in pyramidal structure enhance performance in-comparison to non-pyramidal despite simple configuration, less feature maps and hidden layers. *3DPyraNet* model consists of three main hidden layers as shown in Fig. 2. The given input is pre-processed i.e. normalized in zero mean unit variance. *3DPyraNet* key features i.e. weighting scheme, 3D correlation and pooling layers makes it different than *3DCNN* [2].

Weighting Scheme. *3DPyraNet* has a weight matrix that has equal size as input image/feature map at a lower layer [12]. To calculate an output neuron, a unique 3D partially shared kernel is extracted from the 3D weight matrix with the help of calculated receptive field as shown in Fig. 1. Parameter sharing may not be so useful in some cases [16], however, in *DSR* e.g. beach, where clouds or sky is always expected on upper position with sandy texture and water waves on the bottom, it is better to avoid the traditional sharing scheme, and use a partial sharing scheme that may give additional power to the model as proposed in [12]. Basic *3DPyraNet* consists of mainly two *3DCORR*, a *3DPOOL*, and a *FC* layer as shown in Fig. 2. It's extensions includes a linear classifier layer (SVM) which is discussed in Sect. 3.

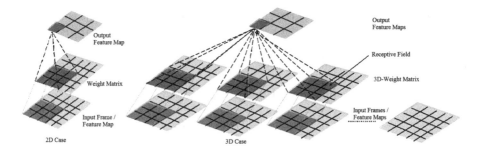

Fig. 1. Weighted scheme for 2D vs our 3D scheme

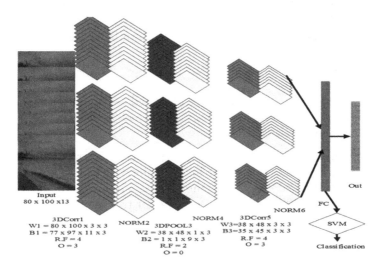

Fig. 2. Proposed 3DPyraNet-F (3DCorr (blue), Normalization (gray), Pool (brown) represents Pool, and bright blue represents FC layer) (Color figure online)

3D Correlation (3DCorr) Layer. A *DS* can be recognized by similar structure. Correlation operation with the ability to learn similarity and the proposed 3D weighting scheme is most suitable in this scenario due to the existence of correlation among consecutive frames. The output neuron $y_{u,v,z}^{l_n}$ on z feature map in the l_n layer is given by the Eq. 1.

$$y_{u,v,z}^{l_n} = f_{l_n} \left(\sum_{d=1}^{D} \sum_{(i,j,m) \in R_{(u,v,z)}^{l_n,d}} \left(\left(w_{(i,j,d)}^{l_n} \cdot y_{(i,j,m)}^{l_{n-1}} \right) + b_{(u,v,z)}^{l_n} \right) \right) \quad (1)$$

Where f_{l_n} represents an activation function used at current layer l_n. In these models, 'D' is equal to 3. The output neuron position is represented by (u,v) at the current output feature map z. This z is generated by a set of input maps (represented by m) in the temporal direction, where m is calculated by '$d+z-1$' from layer l_{n-1} as shown in Eq. 2 third row. Where d_{low} and d_{high} are set equal to 1 and D, respectively. i, j in the current map m at the lower layer is calculated by $R^{l_n,m}_{(u,v,z)}$, the receptive field for each neuron (u, v) in z output map. Here, r_{l_n} in Eq. 2. represents the size of receptive field. *3DPyraNet* use one bias for each neuron in an output feature map.

$$R^{l_n,d}_{(u,v,z)} = \left\{ \begin{array}{c} (i,j,m) \mid (u-1)+1 \leq i \leq (u-1)+r_{l_n}; \\ (v-1)+1 \leq j \leq (v-1)+r_{l_n}; \\ (d_{low}+z-1) \leq m \leq (d_{high}+z-1) \end{array} \right\} \qquad (2)$$

3D Temporal Pooling Layer *3DPOOL*. *3DPyraNet* performs *3DPOOL* (max-pooling) that helps in reducing the dimensionality not only in spatial domain, but also in the temporal domain. In traditional pooling layers where there are no weight parameters or bias's, *3DPyraNet* model consists of a weight parameter for each output maximum value as shown by Eq. 3.

$$y^{l_n}_{u,v,z} = f_{l_n}\left(\left(w^{l_n}_{u,v} \cdot \max_{1 \leq d \leq D}\left(\max_{(i,j,m) \in R^{l_{n-1},d}_{u,v,z}} \left(y^{l_{n-1}}_{i,j,m} \right) \right) \right) + b^{l_n}_{u,v,z} \right) \qquad (3)$$

The size of the receptive field (RF also represented as 'r_{l_n}' in Eq. 2) is different than the receptive field of *3DCorr* layer. In current model, the RF and O is taken as 2 and 0 in *3DPOOL3* layer.

Fully Connected (FC) Layer. Maps from *(NORM6)* layer are converted into a 1D column vector that consists of motion information encoded in multiple adjacent frames. The size of this feature vector rely on the input size, total number of layers (L), RF, O, and D. Read [12] for training the model.

3 Proposed *3DPyraNet-F* a Spatio-temporal Feature Learning Approach

The position oriented features of *3DPyraNet* can capture the required spatial information as a whole for recognizing DS in the videos [17], It generates sparse features as compared to the convolutional kernel and are learned using modified back-propagation. A variety of deep architectures can be designed from *3DPyraNet* based on its application, input image size, the number of layers, or a combination of multiple models to enhance the performance. However, here a global fusion based feature extraction technique is adopted which is an inspiration from the work done in [5]. Mainly, we have added a linear-SVM with *3DPyraNet* and enlarged the network size by giving large size input compare to input given to *3DPyraNet* in [12].

3DPyraNet-F Architecture. Selecting an optimal architecture is a challenging problem [17]. A general model is shown in Fig. 2. It consists of two *3DCORR* layers, a *3DPOOL*, a *FC* layer, and a linear-SVM classifier layer. When the model is trained, feature vectors from the last *Norm6* layer are extracted and fused in a single column feature vector. This fusion approach is similar to early or global fusion that provides a balanced mixture of spatial and temporal information. This spatio-temporal information is progressively assessed by *SVM*. The trained *SVM* model is ultimately used to classify the feature vectors produced by the trained model. Binary classification of One-vs-rest approach is adopted. The size of the network (depth and width) and the resulting size of the feature vector rely on the given input, *RF*, and overlap (*O*).

4   Results and Discussion

In this work, *3DPyraNet-F* is further assessed with videos recorded with camera-induced motion unlike [17]. It is compared to state-of-the-art handcrafted and features learning methods for *DS* recognition. The input size is large compared to previous model used in [12], i.e. $64 \times 48 \times 13$ and similar to the size used in [17] i.e. $80 \times 100 \times 13$ resulting in a feature vector of size 33075. We have a stride of 7 frames, resulting in fewer frames compared to previous models [3,4]. As an example, [4] used $128 \times 171 \times 16$ frames in a clip. From each frame, few random crops of size $112 \times 112 \times 16$ are extracted to augment the data. A mini batch of size 100 clips are used to train the model with SGD approach. The learning rate is taken as 0.000015, initially. It is decayed after every 4 epochs by multiplying it with 0.9. Early stopping criteria is adopted where the stop criteria are based on non-improvement of testing/validation performance.

Datasets. *DS* are categorized by a collection of dynamic patterns and their spatial layout, as recorded in small video clips. *DSR* in videos, recorded by moving cameras has proven to be more challenging as compared to static cameras. *YUPENN* and *MaryLand* are two *DSR* benchmarks. The videos are recorded in the real world with a static camera and a camera-induced motion, respectively. *YUPENN* has 420 fixed size videos of 14 type of scenes, i.e. beach, city street, etc. Similarly, *MaryLand* consists of 130 nonfixed size videos of 13 scene categories e.g. Avalanche, Boiling Water, etc.

Results. *3DPyraNet* shows good performance for *MaryLand* dataset despite the camera-induced motion. In multi-class problem, *3DPyraNet* gave almost similar accuracy as [18] with only 0.7% difference as shown in Table 1. In case of *YUPENN* dataset, *3DPyraNet* didn't perform as expected. One of the reasons could be that *3DPyraNet* performs better when there is a presence of motion in the videos as it is the case in *MaryLand* dataset. Another reason could be that the model needs further tuning to give optimal results in the case of the *YUPENN* dataset. *3DPyraNet-F* resulted in 96.2134% accuracy for *YUPENN* in 25 epochs. However, the resulting mean one-vs-all mean classification accuracy is 93.67% [17]. The results show optimal performance in comparison to [18,19], still it has 5.33% fewer accuracy than [20]. One of the reasons could be that the model in [20] combined complex pre-processing and feature extraction techniques (PCA, LLC, GMM, IFV, static pooling and their proposed dynamic spacetime pyramid pooling in SPM) that overcome even previous optimal results provided by *C3D*. Further, in comparison to *C3D*, one possible reason is the fact that *C3D*

Table 1. Accuracy's for Dynamic Scene Recognition (YUPENN and MaryLand) datasets, Layers represents main layers, Parameters are in million, and size is in MB

Model (Classifier)	YUPENN	MaryLand	Layers	Parameters in millions (Size in MB)
C3D (SVM) [4]	98.1	87.7	15	17.5 (305.14)
ImageNet [4]	96.7	87.7	8	17.5 (305.14)
3DPyraNet	45	67	4	0.83 (14.58)
3DPyraNet-F	93.67	**94.83**	4	0.83 (14.58)
Christoph's (SVM) [20]	**99**	80	-	-
Christoph's (SVM) [3]	96.2	77.7	-	-
Christoph's (SVM) [18]	86.0	67.7	-	-

[4] has high resolution, uses augmentation, and it is trained on Sports 1-Million videos dataset [5], whereas *3DPyraNet-F* is trained on the same small dataset. Yet, *3DPyraNet-F* gave proportionate results, i.e. 93.67%; a strong motivation for future evaluation of *3DPyraNet-F* on a big dataset. Christoph's et al. model [3] performance, as shown in Table 1 is better than ours by 1.5%, but their result is based on majority voting for video classification. Unlike ours, whereas in our case each clip is individually classified.

Secondly, *3DPyraNet-F* is tested with *MaryLand* dataset that includes camera induced motion. Despite camera motion, we achieved a state-of-the-art accuracy of 94.83% as shown in Table 1, representing the discriminative power of the proposed model. *3DPyraNet-F* outperforms state-of-the-art method [4] by 7.17%. Whereas, state-of-the-art model in-terms of *YUPENN* by 14.87%. Classes such as Boiling water, fountain, iceberg collapse, whirlpool shows slight poor results. A reason could be that all the classes contain some sort of similarity, i.e. water, which brings ambiguity making it hard to classify correctly.

Parameters Reduction. Immense parameters (in a trained model) requires more disk space, hence it is a substantial issue in application space [4,6,16,21,22]. A separate consideration should be made about the reduction of parameters. We compare our model against a state-of-the-art *C3D* model in terms of performance and fewer parameters. *C3D* has about 17.5M parameters, whereas this model consists of 0.83M parameters. Disk occupancy is very low in comparison to *C3D* model as shown in Table 1; it can be of great aid where memory is a problem e.g. in embedded systems and mobile devices.

5   Conclusion

3DPyraNet-F, due to its biologically inspired pyramid structure is a deep model that is capable to learn effective features in fewer layers and far fewer parameters as compared to its recent deep competitors, despite camera induced motion. It has been shown here that a good architecture can achieve competitive results even with a limited amount of data on different video analysis benchmarks for *DSR*. In the future, the widespread applicability of *3DPyraNet-F* will be verified by validating it on further challenging datasets. Based on our experience, we expect that it will give high performance regardless of the difficulty of the focus task.

References

1. Liu, W., Wang, Z., Tao, D., Yu, J.: Hessian regularized sparse coding for human action recognition. In: He, X., Luo, S., Tao, D., Xu, C., Yang, J., Hasan, M.A. (eds.) MMM 2015. LNCS, vol. 8936, pp. 502–511. Springer, Cham (2015). doi:10. 1007/978-3-319-14442-9_55
2. Ji, S., Yang, M., Yu, K.: 3D convolutional neural networks for human action recognition. PAMI **35**(1), 221–31 (2013)
3. Feichtenhofer, C., Pinz, A., Wildes, R.: Bags of spacetime energies for dynamic scene recognition. In: Proceedings of the CVPR, pp. 2681–2688 (2014)
4. Tran, D., Bourdev, L., Fergus, R., Torresani, L., Paluri, M.: Learning spatiotemporal features with 3D convolutional networks. In: ICCV (2015)
5. Karpathy, A., Leung, T.: Large-scale video classification with convolutional neural networks. In: CVPR, pp. 1725–1732 (2014)
6. Krizhevsky, A., Sutskever, I., Hinton, G.E.: ImageNet classification with deep convolutional neural networks. In: Advances in NIPS, pp. 1097–1105 (2012)
7. Beil, W.: Volume image processing (VIP'93) steerable filters and invariance theory. Patt. Recogn. Lett. **15**(5), 453–460 (1994)
8. Lowe, D.G.: Distinctive image features from scale-invariant keypoints. Int. J. Comput. Vis. **60**(2), 91–110 (2004)
9. Lazebnik, S., Schmid, C.: Beyond bags of features: spatial pyramid matching for recognizing natural scene categories. CVPR **2**, 2169–2178 (2006)
10. Cantoni, V., Petrosino, A.: Neural recognition in a pyramidal structure. IEEE Trans. Neural Netw. **13**(2), 472–480 (2002)
11. Phung, S.L., Bouzerdoum, A.: A pyramidal neural network for visual pattern recognition. ITNN **18**(2), 329–343 (2007)
12. Ullah, I., Petrosino, A.: A strict pyramidal deep neural network for action recognition. In: Murino, V., Puppo, E. (eds.) ICIAP 2015. LNCS, vol. 9279, pp. 236–245. Springer, Cham (2015). doi:10.1007/978-3-319-23231-7_22
13. Fernandes, B.J.T., Cavalcanti, G.D.C., Ren, T.I.: Lateral inhibition pyramidal neural network for image classification. IEEE Trans. Cybern. **43**(6), 2082–2091 (2013)
14. Chen, L.C., Papandreou, G., Kokkinos, I., Murphy, K., Yuille, A.L.: Semantic image segmentation with deep convolutional nets and fully connected CRFS (2015)
15. Wang, P., Cao, Y., Shen, C., Liu, L., Shen, H.: Temporal pyramid pooling based convolutional neural network for action recognition. IEEE TCSVT **PP**, 1 (2016)
16. Pang, Y., Sun, M., Jiang, X., Li, X.: Convolution in convolution for network in network, 1–9 (2016)
17. Ullah, I., Petrosino, A.: Spatiotemporal features learning with 3DPyraNet. In: Blanc-Talon, J., Distante, C., Philips, W., Popescu, D., Scheunders, P. (eds.) ACIVS 2016. LNCS, vol. 10016, pp. 638–647. Springer, Cham (2016). doi:10.1007/ 978-3-319-48680-2_56

18. Feichtenhofer, C., Pinz, A., Wildes, R.P.: Spacetime forests with complementary features for dynamic scene recognition. In: BMVC (2013)
19. Theriault, C., Thome, N., Cord, M.: Dynamic scene classification: learning motion descriptors with slow features analysis. In: IEEE CVPR, pp. 2603–2610, June 2013
20. Feichtenhofer, C., Pinz, A., Wildes, R.: Dynamic scene recognition with complementary spatiotemporal features. PAMI **PP**(99), 1 (2016)
21. Han, S., Pool, J., Tran, J., Dally, W.J.: Learning both weights and connections for efficient neural networks. CoRR abs/1506.02626 (2015)
22. Szegedy, C., Liu, W., Jia, Y., Sermanet, P., Reed, S., Anguelov, D., Erhan, D., Vanhoucke, V., Rabinovich, A.: Going deeper with convolutions. In: CVPR, USA, 7–12 June, pp. 1–9 (2015)

Spatial Data Science and Engineering

Spatial Distribution Based Provisional Disease Diagnosis in Remote Healthcare

Indrani Bhattacharya$^{(\boxtimes)}$ (iD) and Jaya Sil (iD)

Department of Computer Science and Technology,
Indian Institute of Engineering Science and Technology, Shibpur, India
indrani.84@hotmail.com, jayaiiests@gmail.com

Abstract. Patients in rural India cannot able to enquire about their health using appropriate disease related keywords, submitted as query. Lack of domain knowledge prevents the patients to refine the query using well-known feedback mechanism. Moreover, due to scarcity of doctors in rural India, the health assistants who run the health centers do not have enough knowledge to treat the patients based on the imprecise query. In the paper, we propose an autonomous provisional disease diagnosis system by classifying the query, which has been expanded using semantic of the domain knowledge. First, we apply spatial distribution based nearest neighbor spacing distribution (NNSD) on the disease related medical document corpus (MDC) to find the relevant terms, mostly symptoms with respect to different diseases. We frame a symptom vocabulary (SV) with the unique terms present in different diseases, known apriori. Each query is expanded as bag of symptoms (BoS) using 5-gram collocation model and log likelihood ratio (LLR) to measure the association between the query and the terms in the MDC. The terms in the BoS may not exactly match with the symptoms in the SV but have contextual similarity. We propose a novel approach to know which symptoms in the SV are nearest in context to the corresponding terms in the BoS. The feature vector is obtained by encoding the SV with respect to (w.r.t.) each BoS, which is sparse in nature. We apply sparse representation based classifier (SRC) to classify the query into a particular disease. Proposed nearest neighbor spacing distribution based sparse representation classifier (NNSD-SRC) shows promising performance considering MDC dataset and we validate the results with the doctors showing negligible error.

Keywords: Spatial distribution · Provisional diagnosis · Sparse classifier

1 Introduction

The goal of query classification is to identify the category label known a priori that best represents the domain of the keywords submitted in a query. However, the performance of a query based classifier largely depends on the keywords submitted by the users which often do not express the underlying information is searched for. Such keywords are called noise terms and cannot unambiguously represent the actual context of the query, resulting error in classification. Selection of more appropriate keywords, represent the context of the query enhances performance of the classifier.

© Springer International Publishing AG 2017
B.U. Shankar et al. (Eds.): PReMI 2017, LNCS 10597, pp. 601–607, 2017.
https://doi.org/10.1007/978-3-319-69900-4_76

In most of the cases, feedback mechanism [1] performs well when user can modify the query based on the suggestions provided by the search engine. However, there is no scope of query refinement using feedback when the user does not have any domain knowledge and this scenario is very common in rural healthcare sector of India. The healthcare services to remote villages face real challenge due to scarcity of doctors. Generally, health assistants manage the rural health centers but they have lack of expertise to refine the patient's query containing noise terms. In [2], a query classification system has been proposed for diagnosis of the disease at primary level by processing the imprecise query keywords with the help of experts' knowledge base. Therefore, the aim of the paper is to develop an autonomous provisional disease diagnosis system using statistical and computational methods, which effectively can monitor the health of the rural people.

It has been observed that the relevant words are spatially distributed while irrelevant words are randomly distributed in the document. Therefore, there is enormous difference in the pattern of occurrences between the relevant and the non-relevant terms in the document. A spatial distribution based method has been proposed for obtaining the symptoms related terms from the disease-related document corpus. In level statistical analysis of quantum disordered system, "energy level" of a word within an "energy spectrum" is considered as spatial distribution of the word to extract the relevant words whose energy levels attract each other [3]. In this paper, we propose a nearest-neighbour spacing distribution (NNSD) based approach to obtain symptoms w.r.t the disease-classes, known apriori. A symptom vocabulary (SV) is constructed using the unique symptoms present in the disease-classes [4]. We build a disease-symptom matrix (DSM) consisting of number of symptoms present in the SV and the number of corresponding diseases where each element of the matrix denotes tf-score [5] of the respective symptom, considering the disease related MDC. The DSM is built by extracting knowledge from the MDC and sparse in nature.

After knowledge extraction, the imprecise query submitted by the patient is expanded using the terms, which have strong association with the query keyword. For measuring association, suitable adaptive technique is needed which represent context of the query more precisely. In this paper, for expanding the query 5-gram collocation model and log-likelihood ratio (LLR) are employed to measure the association [6]. For a query keyword five co-occurred terms are considered as expanded query, called bag-of-symptoms (BoS). Each term in the BoS might not exactly match with the terms in the SV, though semantically or contextually similar. Here, we propose a novel approach for finding the most similar terms in the SV w.r.t each term in the BoS using distributional similarity measure. Finally, the SV is encoded with tf value of the terms in the BoS and considered as the feature vector (FV). Since the terms in a BoS are very specific, the FV is sparse and used as the test pattern for predicting the disease. We utilize sparse DSM and sparse test pattern for predicting the disease of a patient by applying Sparse Representation based Classifier(SRC) [7]. The proposed system is described in Fig. 1.

This paper is divided into four sections. Section 2 describes the methodology. Results are summarized in Sect. 3 and conclusions are arrived at Sect. 4.

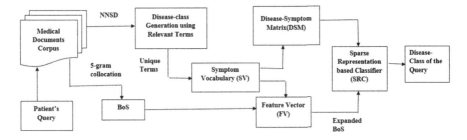

Fig. 1. Architecture of the proposed system

2   Methodology

In the paper, we propose an autonomous provisional disease identification system based on the patient's query keyword which is often imprecise consisting of noise terms. First contribution of the paper is knowledge extraction by analyzing the pre-defined disease related document corpuses collected from different medical sources.

2.1   Disease-Class Generation

Here, we utilize NNSD of words (or symptoms) over the documents for finding the relevant symptoms to a disease. The spacing distribution $P(d)$ of a word w is obtained as the normalized histogram of the set of distances or spacing $(d_1, d_2, ..., d_m)$ between consecutive occurrences of a word w in the documents, where m is the number of times the word w occurs in the document [4]. It has been observed that a non-relevant word like "and" is placed at random in the document, whereas a relevant word like "angina" appears in the "heart-disease" related document following spatial distribution $P(d)$. Therefore, the level of attraction of relevant words is higher than the level of attraction of irrelevant words. The relevance of a word is defined using the parameter ρ where

$\rho = \dfrac{\sigma}{d}, \overline{d}$ is the average distance and σ is the standard deviation $\sqrt{\overline{d^2} - \overline{d}^2}$ for distribution

$P(d)$. For different words, ρ value is used for comparing the distributional similarity. When the words are uncorrelated they follow Poisson distribution.

The relevant words follow a correlated spatial distribution and form a group w.r.t a disease based on ρ. In this paper, we obtain group of relevant words as symptoms for each disease class by applying NNSD to each word in the document. From Fig. 2 it is evident that the relevant words "heart", "angina" and "Palpitation" follow similar type of distribution with different mean and standard deviation while the non-relevant term "called" and "high" follow random distribution.

The symptoms in different disease classes are thus obtained and a Symptom Vocabulary (SV) is built with k number of unique symptoms ($n << k$) present in n different disease-classes. A disease-symptom-matrix (DSM)$n \times k$ is built as measurement space, each element of which is calculated using Eq. (1),

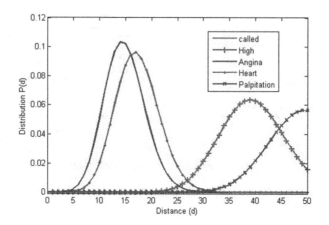

Fig. 2. Distribution of different keywords

$$\text{DSM } [ij] = log(1 + f_{w,D}); \text{ if } j^{\text{th}} \text{ term of SV presents in disease - class } i$$
$$= 0, \text{ otherwise} \tag{1}$$

Where $f_{w,D}$ is the count of the term w in D [5].

The DSM is a sparse matrix as most of the symptoms are unique for a disease and used to classify the query keyword submitted by the patient.

2.2 Query Expansion Model

In the proposed query expansion model, the query of a patient has been expanded using 5-gram collocation by consulting the same MDC. We find the co-occurred terms of the query keyword using LLR as association measure. It has been observed that beyond 5-gram, the co-occurred terms are redundant [8]. The expanded query consisting of five co-occurred terms and defined as bag-of- symptoms (BoS). The BoSs are not unique and there may be multiple BoSs for each keyword due to associations with different words throughout the document. From multiple BoSs the highest LLR scored BoS has been chosen as expanded query. For example, if a patient enquires about "heart" related problems, the keyword "heart" is expanded and the top scored BoS: **(heartbeat angina heart disease nausea)** is considered as expanded query.

Each BoS is used to generate the feature vector (FV) by comparing each term of the BoS with the symptoms in SV depending on the ρ value. The symptom in the SV, which is closest to the term of a BoS is encoded with the *tf* score [5] of the respective term. In case multiple terms of a BoS are mapped to the same symptom of the SV, highest *tf* score is used to encode the respective symptom. Remaining elements of the SV are set to zero and so the FV is sparse in nature.

2.3 Sparse Representation Based Classification of Query

The FV is represented by vector **y**, which is sparse and we apply SRC to classify the query by reconstruction using Eq. (2).

$$\mathbf{y}^T = \mathrm{DSM}^T * \mathbf{W} \tag{2}$$

Where **W** is the co-efficient vector and is sparse since not all elements of the disease-classes contribute to reconstruct the query sample **y**.

The sparsest solution can be obtained by solving the following optimization problem, given in Eq. (3),

$$\widehat{\mathbf{W}}_0 = \arg\min\|\mathbf{W}_0\|, \text{ subject to } DSM^T * \mathbf{W} = \mathbf{y}^T \tag{3}$$

Where $\|.\|_0$ is the L_0 - norm, counting the number of non-zero entries in the co-efficient vector. This problem has been solved in polynomial time by standard linear programming algorithm [8]. After the sparsest solution say, $\widehat{w}_1$ is obtained, the SRC [7] is performed in the following way.

For each disease-class i, let $\partial_i : \mathbb{R}^S \to \mathbb{R}^S$ be the characteristic function that selects the co-efficient associated with the ith class. Using only the co-efficient associated with the ith class, reconstruction has been performed for a given test sample **y** as ${\mathbf{y}_{new}^i}^T = DSM^T * \partial_i\left(\widehat{\mathbf{W}}_1\right)$ where $\mathbf{y}_{new}^i$ is called the prototype of class i with respect to the sample **y**. Equation (4) calculates the residual distance between the actual and its proto-type of class i,

$$r_i(y) = \left\|y - y_{new}^i\right\|_2 \tag{4}$$

The SRC decision rule: If $r_m(\mathbf{y}) = \min_i r_i(\mathbf{y})$, **y** is assigned to the class m [9].

Example

Step1. The BoS corresponding to the patient's keyword 'Angina' is (**Fatigue Coronary Palpitation Heart Nausea]**^{T}

Step2: Encode the expanded query as test pattern **y** using SV (1×70). The term "Coronary" is not present in SV, so replace "Coronary" with most similar symptom "Heart" by comparing ρ value. FV **y** is given as follows:
$\mathbf{y}_{(1\times70)} = [\ 0, 0. \ldots, 0, 1.27, \ldots, 0, 0, \ldots, 0, 0.3, \ldots, 0, 0, \ldots, 0, 0.3, \ldots, 0, 0, \ldots,$
$0, 0.9, \ldots, 0, 0\ ]^T$

Step3: Considering **y** as the encoded test sample and DSM (4 × 70) as training set, obtain the sparse coding vector $\mathbf{W}_{4\times1}$ using following Eq. (3)
$\mathbf{W}_{4\times1} = [0.12\ 0.03\ -0.04\ -0.005]^T$

Step4: Reconstruct **y** ($\mathbf{y}_{new}^i$) for every non-zero coefficient in $\mathbf{W}_i$ for the ith disease class label.

Step5: Residual distance for each class i is given using Eq. (4).
$r_i = [1.88\ 1.97\ 2.03\ 2]^T$

Step6: Minimum residual distance is 2.01 corresponding to $i = 1$. Therefore, the query is classified as disease-class "Heart-Disease".

3 Results and Discussions

In our experiment, a large medical document corpus (MDC) is prepared by consulting several medical websites (webmd.com, mayoclinic.org, healthcare.com) and literatures [10]. There are 260 documents divided into four sub-corpuses representing diseases, namely "Heart-disease", "Diabetes", "Diarrhea" and "Lung-disease".

The NNSD-SRC method has been applied on four different sub-corpuses to extract the relevant terms, which are symptoms and the dimension of the SV is 70. We sample 200 patients' query from a rural health kiosk in a span of one week and classify the query using 10-fold cross validation technique. NNSD-SRC method shows significant improvement in accuracy and guarantees lower rate of misclassification while

Table 1. Comparisons using different classifiers

Classifiers	Accuracy (%)	Precision	Recall	F-measure	Specificity
NB	94	0.94	0.94	0.94	0.98
MLP	90	0.9	0.9	0.9	0.97
SVM	86	0.87	0.86	0.86	0.96
RT	84	0.84	0.83	0.83	0.95
NNSD-SRC	**96**	**0.97**	**0.98**	**0.98**	**0.96**

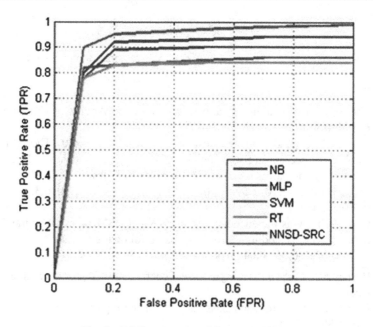

Fig. 3. ROC curve using different classifiers

comparing with other classifiers, as given in Table 1. High precision and recall value ensures that NNSD-SRC performs better than other classifiers. ROC curves for different classifiers are given in Fig. 3, which demonstrates best performance of the NNSD-SRC.

4   Conclusions

The proposed NNSD-SRC based provisional disease diagnosis method, which minimizes the experts' involvement. The patient's query has been expanded moderately based on 5-gram collocation approach. For classification of the query sparse representation based classifier (SRC) is employed which utilizes sparsity of the feature vector and the DSM matrix. The SRC based classifier outperforms other classifiers showing significant improvement in accuracy and sensitivity on different data sets. In the work, we prepare a benchmark data set MDC of medical documents related to "Heart-disease", "Diabetes", "Diarrhea" and "Lung-disease" and verified with the experts. The performance of the system is satisfactory and used in rural healthcare in India where scarcity of doctors is a real challenge.

Acknowledgement. This research was supported by grants from Information Technology Research Academy (ITRA), under the Department of Electronics and Information Technology (DeitY), Government of India.

References

1. Carpineto, C., Romano, G.: A survey of automatic query expansion in information retrieval. ACM Comput. Surv. (CSUR) **44**(1), 1 (2012)
2. Sil, J., Bhattacharya, I.: Patient classification based on expanded query using 5-gram collocation and binary tree. In: IEEE International Conference on Data Science and Advanced Analytics (DSAA), 2015 36678 2015, pp. 1–10. IEEE (2015)
3. Mehta, M.L.: Random Matrices, vol. 142. Academic Press, Amsterdam (2004)
4. Carpena, P., Bernaola-Galván, P., Hackenberg, M., Coronado, A.V., Oliver, J.L.: Level statistics of words: Finding keywords in literary texts and symbolic sequences. Phys. Rev. E **79**(3), 035102 (2009)
5. Ramos, J.: Using TF-IDF to determine word relevance in document queries. In: Proceedings of the First Instructional Conference on Machine Learning (2003)
6. Pauls, A., Klein, D.: Faster and smaller N-gram language models. In: Proceedings of the 49th Annual Meeting of the Association for Computational Linguistics: Human Language Technologies, vol. 1, pp. 258–267. Association for Computational Linguistics (2011)
7. Yang, J., Chu, D., Zhang, L., Xu, Y., Yang, J.: Sparse representation classifier steered discriminative projection with applications to face recognition. IEEE Trans. Neural Netw. Learn. Syst. **24**(7), 1023–1035 (2013)
8. Donoho, D.L., Tsaig, Y.: Fast solution of-norm minimization problems when the solution may be sparse. IEEE Trans. Inf. Theor. **54**(11), 4789–4812 (2008)
9. Bhattacharya, I., Sil, J.: Query classification using LDA topic model and sparse representation based classifier. In: 2016 Proceedings of the 3rd IKDD Conference on Data Science, p. 24. ACM, March 2016
10. Harrison's Principles of Internal Medicine, vol. 2. McGraw-Hill Medical, New York (2008)

Extraction of Phenotypic Traits for Drought Stress Study Using Hyperspectral Images

Swati Bhugra$^{(\boxtimes)}$ ⓘ, Nitish Agarwal ⓘ, Shubham Yadav ⓘ, Soham Banerjee ⓘ, Santanu Chaudhury ⓘ, and Brejesh Lall ⓘ

Department of Electrical Engineering, Indian Institute of Technology, Delhi, India
{eez138301,ee1130477,ee1130499,ee1130502,santanuc,brejesh}@ee.iitd.ac.in

Abstract. High-throughput identification of digital traits encapsulating the changes in plant's internal structure under drought stress, based on hyperspectral imaging (HSI) is a challenging task. This is due to the high spectral and spatial resolution of HSI data and lack of labelled data. Therefore, this work proposes a novel framework for phenotypic discovery based on autoencoders, which is trained using Simple Linear Iterative Clustering (SLIC) superpixels. The distinctive archetypes from the learnt digital traits are selected using simplex volume maximisation (SiVM). Their accumulation maps are employed to reveal differential drought responses of wheat cultivars based on t-distributed stochastic neighbour embedding (t-SNE) and the separability is quantified using cluster silhouette index. Unlike prior methods using raw pixels or feature vectors computed by fusing predefined indices as phenotypic traits, our proposed framework shows potential by separating the plant responses into three classes with a finer granularity. This capability shows the potential of our framework for the discovery of data-driven phenotypes to quantify drought stress responses.

Keywords: Autoencoders · SLIC superpixels · Hyperspectral · Drought stress · t-SNE · Deep learning · SiVM

1 Introduction

Drought stress is a major limiting factor for crop productivity. To select high yielding cultivars under drought conditions, current strategies depend on both (a) genotypic data of the cultivar and (b) quantification of its physiological and structural characteristics (phenotypic data) [1]. In this context, digital traits based on hyperspectral imaging (HSI) data have the potential to reveal changes in the plant's internal structure non-destructively [1]. Previous studies are based on extraction of single vegetation indices computed using two or three spectral bands. However, using single vegetation indices only quantifies specific changes to detect drought stress [2]. Behmann et al. [3] formulated a feature based on fusion of all the vegetation indices to characterise different stages of leaf senescence, whereas Römer et al. [4] used the entire spectra of the pixels in the HSI data. Since the stress labels for the pixels are not available, extracting digital traits to

© Springer International Publishing AG 2017
B.U. Shankar et al. (Eds.): PReMI 2017, LNCS 10597, pp. 608–614, 2017.
https://doi.org/10.1007/978-3-319-69900-4_77

study drought is an unsupervised task. Behmann et al. employed a framework combining k-means to extract drought clusters and based on these cluster labels, used Support Vector Machine (SVM) for drought stress classification. Here, the number of cluster centres and annotation of each cluster centre to its corresponding drought level was performed manually by an expert. Similarly, Römer et al. employed simplex volume maximisation (SiVM) to extract archetypes from the raw spectra of the pixels. To avoid the selection of noisy spectra as an archetype, an expert manually extracted only the spectrum belonging to plant pixels based on the domain knowledge.

Recent establishment of phenotyping platforms provides automated imaging of large number of experimental plants for drought stress study [1]. Since, the aforementioned approaches rely on experts, these will scale badly to this growing amount of data and are also prone to human bias. Thus, RGB imaging modules available in these platforms have been frequently exploited in contrast to HSI for drought analysis [1]. But, HSI data can capture intricate phenotypic information as compared to the corresponding RGB representations of the plant canopy [1]. Therefore, we propose a framework based on single-layer and multi-layer stacked autoencoders (AE) [5] to learn shallow and deep features respectively from HSI data in an unsupervised manner. The compact representations obtained from these networks were utilized to select distinctive archetypes using SiVM [6]. To identify different clusters that represent different degrees of drought stress level using the agglomerative representation computed from these archetypes for each HSI data, t-SNE [7] was employed. The separability of these clusters was quantified using Silhouette coefficient [8]. Although many methods have been proposed for the purpose of drought stress identification [9,10], but to the best of our knowledge, this is the first work that utilizes deep networks on HSI data to learn an implicit representation of features for drought stress characterization. To show the eligibility of our proposed approach based on the separation of different responses effectively, we empirically compared the silhouette coefficient with the (a) classical approach of using raw pixel spectra [4] and (b) feature comprising of different indices [3].

The rest of the paper is organised as follows: In Sect. 2 the dataset is described, Sect. 3 explains the methodology and in Sect. 4 the results are discussed.

2   Dataset

The drought experiment was conducted on wheat pots at the Plant Phenomics Facility, Indian Agricultural Research Institute (IARI), Pusa, New-Delhi during Rabi season of 2016. To examine the differential responses of drought, two genotypes of wheat crop: C-306 (drought tolerant) and HD-2967 (drought sensitive) were investigated for a period of 5 continuous days. Both genotypes were divided into three groups (six replicates each) in terms of water intensity i.e. well-watered, reduced watered and unwatered. HSI data was captured in the spectral range of 400 nm to 1000 nm at equal wavelength intervals resulting in

(a) C-306 (pseudo image)   (b) Segmented image   (c) Superpixel image   (d) Archetype-1   (e) Archetype-2

Fig. 1. Selected archetypes representation on C-306 (control)

108 bands and a corresponding pseudo colour image was also collected along the side view.

3   Methodology

The steps of the proposed framework to study the temporal dynamics of drought stress are explained in the following subsections.

3.1   Pre-processing Step

The HSI data contains wheat canopy and non-canopy elements such as soil, water and background. The segmentation of pseudo image is obtained graph-cut algorithm [11]. In addition to using the color features for each pixel as an input to the graph-cut, texture features [12] are also computed. The texture response is given by: $f(I; \beta, r, \sigma_H, \sigma_L) = \exp(\beta/(H_r * I_i + (G_{\sigma_H} * I_j - G_{\sigma_L} * I_j)))$ where, I is the pseudo image, G_{σ_H} and G_{σ_L} are Gaussian filters with σ_H and σ_L respectively, difference of the Gaussian kernels highlights high texture regions, H_r is a uniform circular filter with radius r that highlights the smooth regions in the image and β is the fall-off rate. The segmented pseudo image is used as a mask to extract the plant pixels from all the hyperspectral bands. Due to the highly correlated spectra of the neighbouring pixels in the segmented HSI data, superpixels based on Simple Linear Iterative Clustering (SLIC) [13] are extracted. The homogeneous regions obtained using SLIC computes a better representative spectra with less noise than the use of raw pixel spectra for subsequent analysis.

3.2   Feature Learning

The superpixels extracted from the HSI data were used to train the autoencoder and stacked autoencoder to learn shallow and deep features respectively in an unsupervised manner. The autoencoder (AE) [5] comprises of an encoder and a decoder. The encoder obtains the latent representation of dimension $H < M$ from the input features $x \in \mathbb{R}^M$ given by: $h = \phi(\mathbf{P}x + b)$, where $\mathbf{P} \in \mathbb{R}^{H \times M}$ is a matrix of learned weights, $b \in \mathbb{R}^H$ is bias vector and ϕ is an activation function. We used logistic sigmoid function as the activation function. A decoder reconstructs the input features $\hat{x}$ using the latent representation given by: $\hat{x} = \epsilon(\mathbf{P}'h + b')$, where ϵ is a logistic sigmoid activation function, $\mathbf{P}'$ is the weight matrix and b' the bias vector. Beginning with random initialisation of $\{\mathbf{P}, \mathbf{P}', b, b'\}$, the training process is formulated as an unsupervised optimisation of a cost function which measures the error between the input and its reconstruction given by: $\theta = argmin_\theta \mathbf{L}(x, \hat{x})$ with respect to the parameters $\theta = \{\mathbf{P}, \mathbf{P}', b, b'\}$, where $\mathbf{L}$ is defined as the squared difference between x and $\hat{x}$. The weights are updated with stochastic gradient descent which can be efficiently implemented using the Back-Propagation algorithm. In order to avoid over-fitting, a standard $L2$ norm weight regularisation [14] is employed for the elements of $\mathbf{P}$. For H hidden nodes, N training examples and M features (spectral bands) in the training data, this is given by:

$$\eta_w = \sum_h^H \sum_j^N \sum_i^M (w_{ji}{}^h)^2 \tag{1}$$

Using the Kullback-Leibler (KL) divergence, sparsity regularisation [15] is included with sparsity ($\rho = .5$) and is computed as shown below:

$$\eta_s = \sum_i^H \rho \, log\left(\frac{\rho}{\hat{\rho}_i}\right) + (1 - \rho) \, log\left(\frac{1 - \rho}{1 - \hat{\rho}_i}\right) \tag{2}$$

The cost function for the unsupervised optimisation problem is given by:

$$\mathbb{E} = \frac{1}{N} \sum_j^N \eta_j + \lambda \eta_w + \beta \eta_s \tag{3}$$

where, η_j is the squared error for the jth training data, λ and β is set to .01 and .5 respectively.

Stacked autoencoders (SAE) [5] are constructed using greedy layer wise strategy on the learnt AE. The learnt representation h of the input feature x is used as an input to another autoencoder which learns a latent representation v and so on. A deep network is obtained by stacking the layer wise trained autoencoders. The latent representation obtained from both the aforementioned architectures is then employed to quantify drought stress response, as explained in the next subsection.

3.3   Drought Stress Quantification

At the pixel level, well defined labels to denote different drought stress responses (DSR) are not available. Thus, to obtain distinctive archetypes characterising drought stages from the learnt features, SiVM is employed. SiVM extracts the archetypes by fitting a simplex with the maximum volume to the data. It selects the archetypes from the data matrix $\mathbf{V}$. Thus, the matrix $\mathbf{W}$ is defined as $\mathbf{W} = \mathbf{VG}$ with n data points and k selected archetypes where, $\mathbf{G} \in \mathbb{R}^{n \times k}$ and is restricted to unary column vectors and $\mathbf{H}$ is restricted to convexity. The number of extreme archetypes is chosen based on the increase in the accumulated maps of the selected archetypes [4]. If $\mathbf{W}_m$ is the matrix of selected m archetypes, h_{dm} is the normalised aggregation (belongingness histogram) of $\mathbf{H}_{dm}$ of dth HSI data where $d = 1, 2, \cdots, N$ images, then $(m + 1)^{th}$ archetype is added to $\mathbf{W}_m$, if $\mathbb{E}[h_{d(m+1)} - h_{dm}] \geq 0.1$. Thus, only those archetypes are selected which results in significant accumulation of the plant pixels in all HSI data. Belongingness histogram are represented in a 2D space using t-SNE [7] to study the clusters or patterns in terms of drought responses. t-SNE maps a high dimensional data into a lower dimension space by computing pair-wise similarity matrix and simultaneously preserving local and global structure of the data, whereas other classical approaches such as principal component analysis (PCA) [7], multidimensional scaling (MDS) [7] may not capture the non-linear relationship in high dimensional data. The stress responses obtained from t-SNE are evaluated using silhouette coefficient [8]. It is used to quantify the separability of different responses.

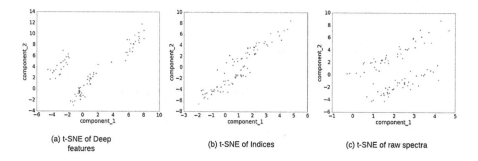

(a) t-SNE of Deep features

(b) t-SNE of Indices

(c) t-SNE of raw spectra

Fig. 2. Drought stress characterisation

4   Results

The segmented pseudo image, with the corresponding SLIC superpixels is shown in Fig. 1(b) and (c) respectively. $160,000$ superpixels obtained from six images belonging to different irrigation treatments were used to train the autoencoder. The autoencoder was trained in an unsupervised manner and no supervised fine tuning was applied. To improve the convergence of the training algorithms, data was normalised, i.e. the spectral band with zero mean and the spectral values normalised to unit variance. The learning rate was kept low i.e. 10^{-4}. In the first AE, the 108 spectral bands were mapped to a latent representation in a subspace with a hidden layer of 80 nodes. For a deep representation of the input spectra, the latent representation obtained was used to train the second AE. The hidden layer of this second AE was estimated to be 30, based on the small reconstruction error. The trained model was validated based on mean square error of the test data, which was of the order of 10^{-2} and lower as compared to the first AE. Thus for the subsequent drought stress analysis, stacked AE model was employed. The representation obtained for the SLIC pixels, was used as an input to SiVM and four archetypes were selected automatically based on the aforementioned criteria in Sect. 3.3. The visualisation of the accumulation map of C-306 cultivar (control day 1) corresponding to the 1st and 2nd archetype is shown in Fig. 1(d) and (e) respectively. The pixels belonging to high intensity shows high similarity to the archetype. The 1st latent representation selected encapsulates the spectra of the healthy leaves and the 2nd representation captures the leaves with senescence. This illustrates the effectiveness of the autoencoder to separate the different drought responses within the plant canopy based on unsupervised dimensionality reduction. Although training the weight matrix requires a large amount of computation time, but once the trained model is obtained the encoding of the data to extract the compact features is fast.

Since drought symptoms do not manifest over local regions but the entire plant (as shown in Fig. 1), aggregated belongingness for all the pixels in each HSI data represents the overall stress response of the plant. To uncover the different set of drought responses captured using these learnt features, t-SNE (with perplexity $= 5$) was employed and silhouette coefficient was used to validate the separability. The t-SNE computed for the learnt feature is shown in Fig. 2(a). The significance of the groups was obtained by linking image to the genotype and drought/control day. It was discovered that in Fig. 2(a), one cluster consisted of the plants belonging to the control group, the second cluster belonged to the C-306 replicates at drought days $3, 4, 5$ and the third clusters comprised of the HD-2967 replicates at the same drought days (silhouette coefficient .811). This shows a statistical difference between the drought response of both the varieties on the same day of drought stress, which was successfully captured using the learnt features. On the other hand, based on the archetypes selected from (a) raw spectra [4] and (b) the feature vector comprising of indices [3], only two distinct clusters: control and drought (with silhouette coefficient 0.711 and 0.69 respectively) were identified. This finer granularity in classification shows the potential of our framework to reveal data-driven phenotypic patterns.

5   Conclusion

In this article, we presented a novel framework that provides phenotypic expression of drought stress based on deep learning and based on these expressions, captured the phenotypic difference between a drought susceptible cultivar (HD-2967) and a drought tolerant cultivar (C-306). The findings contribute to the ongoing studies to predict drought stress based on phenotypic traits. The application of deep networks for drought study based on HSI data is largely unexplored, thus more investigations of the learnt features and its relation to different physiological responses in plants is essential for an accurate and high throughput drought characterization.

References

1. Humplík, J.F., Lazár, D., Husičková, A., Spíchal, L.: Automated phenotyping of plant shoots using imaging methods for analysis of plant stress responses–a review. Plant Meth. 11(1), 29 (2015)
2. Thenkabail, P.S., Smith, R.B., De Pauw, E.: Hyperspectral vegetation indices and their relationships with agricultural crop characteristics. Remote Sens. Environ. 71(2), 158–182 (2000)
3. Behmann, J., Steinrücken, J., Plümer, L.: Detection of early plant stress responses in hyperspectral images. ISPRS J. Photogrammetry Remote Sens. 93, 98–111 (2014)
4. Römer, C., Wahabzada, M., Ballvora, A., Pinto, F., Rossini, M., Panigada, C., Behmann, J., Léon, J., Thurau, C., Bauckhage, C., Kersting, K.: Early drought stress detection in cereals: simplex volume maximisation for hyperspectral image analysis. Funct. Plant Biol. 39(11), 878–890 (2012)
5. Palm, R.B.: Prediction as a candidate for learning deep hierarchical models of data, vol. 5. Technical University of Denmark (2012)
6. Thurau, C., et al.: Yes we can: simplex volume maximization for descriptive web-scale matrix factorization, pp. 1785–1788. ACM (2010)
7. van der Maaten, L., Hinton, G.: Visualizing data using t-SNE. J. Mach. Learn. Res. 9, 2579–2605 (2008)
8. Bolshakova, N., Azuaje, F.: Cluster validation techniques for genome expression data. Signal Process. 83(4), 825–833 (2003)
9. Singh, A., Ganapathysubramanian, B., Singh, A.K., Sarkar, S.: Machine learning for high-throughput stress phenotyping in plants. Trends Plant Sci. 21(2), 110–124 (2016)
10. Bhugra, S., Anupama, A., Chaudhury, S., Lall, B., Chugh, A.: Phenotyping of xylem vessels for drought stress analysis in rice. In: Fifteenth IAPR International Conference on Machine Vision Applications (MVA), pp. 428–431 (2017)
11. Boykov, Y., Veksler, O., Zabih, R.: Fast approximate energy minimization via graph cuts. IEEE Trans. Pattern Anal. Mach. Intell. 23(11), 1222–1239 (2001)
12. Minervini, M., Abdelsamea, M.M., Tsaftaris, S.A.: Image-based plant phenotyping with incremental learning and active contours. Ecol. Inf. 23, 35–48 (2014)
13. Achanta, R., Shaji, A., Smith, K., Lucchi, A., Fua, P., Süsstrunk, P.: SLIC superpixels compared to state-of-the-art superpixel methods. IEEE Trans. Pattern Anal. Mach. Intell. 34(11), 2274–2282 (2012)
14. Møller, M.F.: A scaled conjugate gradient algorithm for fast supervised learning. Neural Netw. 6(4), 525–533 (1993)
15. Olshausen, B.A., Field, D.J.: Sparse coding with an overcomplete basis set: a strategy employed by V1. Vis. Res. 37(23), 3311–3325 (1997)

Spatio-Temporal Prediction of Meteorological Time Series Data: An Approach Based on Spatial Bayesian Network (SpaBN)

Monidipa Das[(✉)] and Soumya K. Ghosh

Department of Computer Science and Engineering,
Indian Institute of Technology Kharagpur, Kharagpur 721302, India
monidipadas@hotmail.com, skg@iitkgp.ac.in

Abstract. This paper proposes a *space-time model* for prediction of meteorological time series data. The proposed prediction model is based on a *spatially extended Bayesian network* (SpaBN), which helps to *efficiently* model the *complex spatio-temporal dependency* among large number of spatially distributed variables. Validation has been made with respect to prediction of daily *temperature, humidity,* and *precipitation rate* around the spatial region of *Kolkata, India.* Comparative study with the benchmark and state-of-the-art prediction techniques demonstrates the superiority of the proposed spatio-temporal prediction model.

Keywords: Space-time model · Time series prediction · Spatial Bayesian network · Meteorology

1 Introduction

Spatio-temporal data are ubiquitous in the nature. The meteorological time series data, as collected from spatially distributed weather stations or from sensor networks, are one of the prominent examples in this respect. Prediction of meteorological time series is essential not only to anticipate the weather condition for taking adequate measures, but also it helps in proper management of energy [6]. However, the major challenge in meteorological time series prediction is the complex spatio-temporal inter-relationships among the variables. Modeling such space-time dependency becomes more complicated when the number of spatially distributed influencing variables becomes considerably large. For the same reason, the effectiveness of many of the existing space-time prediction models, especially those are based on graph-based approaches, are significantly hindered.

In the present work, we have proposed an improved, graph-based, probabilistic model, so as to handle such spatio-temporal prediction scenario. The approach is based on the *spatial Bayesian network* (SpaBN) [3], which can efficiently model the influence from large number of spatially distributed variables. Previously, SpaBN has shown encouraging performance in the domain of hydrology [3]. In the present work, we have applied SpaBN as the base technology behind our proposed space-time model for meteorological time series prediction.

© Springer International Publishing AG 2017
B.U. Shankar et al. (Eds.): PReMI 2017, LNCS 10597, pp. 615–622, 2017.
https://doi.org/10.1007/978-3-319-69900-4_78

1.1   Problem Statement and Contributions

The relevant prediction problem can be formally stated as follows:

- Given, the historical daily time series data set over n meteorological variables in $M = \{m_1, m_2, \cdots, m_n\}$, corresponding to a set of l spatial locations $L = \{l_1, l_2, \cdots, l_l\}$ for previous t years: $\{y_1, y_2, \cdots, y_t\}$. The problem is to determine the daily times series of the variables in M, for any location $x \in (L \cup Z)$, for future q years $\{y_{(t+1)}, y_{(t+2)}, ..., y_{(t+q)}\}$, where, $(Z \cap L) = \phi$ and q is a positive integer.

In this context, spatio-temporal prediction of any meteorological variable $m \in M$ needs to consider influences of its co-located variables in M, from several spatially distributed locations in L. Though the graphical models, like Bayesian networks, are highly suitable for modeling such influences [2], however, considering separate influencing nodes corresponding to each location $l_i \in L$ makes the graphical structure as well as the analysis process extremely complex.

Present work attempts to address this issue by utilizing the effective modeling ability of the spatial Bayesian network (SpaBN). The major contributions in this regard are as follows:

- Exploring the *spatial Bayesian network* (SpaBN) analysis in *multivariate prediction* of meteorological time series data;
- Proposing SpaBN based *spatio-temporal prediction model* which is capable of *efficiently modeling* complex inter-variable dependency over space and time;
- Validating the proposed space-time model with respect to prediction of daily *temperature, humidity* and *precipitation rate* around Kolkata, India;
- Demonstrating the *effectiveness* of the proposed prediction model in comparison with benchmark and state-of-the-art space-time prediction techniques;

The remainder of the paper is organized as follows. The details of the proposed space-time model has been illustrated in Sect. 2. The results of empirical study have been reported in Sect. 3. Finally, we conclude in Sect. 4.

2   Proposed Space-Time Model

As depicted in the Fig. 1, the proposed prediction model comprises of three key steps: (i) *data pre-processing*, (ii) *spatial weight calculation*, and (iii) *spatio-temporal prediction*. Each of these steps are illustrated below:

2.1   Data Pre-processing

The main objective of the data pre-processing step is to discretize the continuous meteorological variables, so as to make these suitable for the discrete Bayesian analysis of SpaBN in the subsequent steps. The discretization is performed by considering maximum and minimum observed value ($max(m_i)$ and $min(m_i)$) in the historical time series for each continuous variable $m_i \in M$, and then dividing the whole range into appropriate number (R) of bins or sub-ranges of desired size $size(subRange) = \frac{max(m_i) - min(m_i)}{R}$. The value of R is determined empirically.

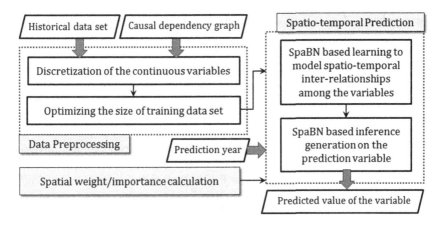

Fig. 1. Framework of the proposed spatio-temporal prediction model

Moreover, in the pre-processing step we also optimize the size of training data set with consideration to the temporal variability of the meteorological variables within short period of time. For example, in general, rainfall shows monthly variation. Therefore, in order to make prediction for a particular day, the rainfall data of the associated month is considered rather than considering the rainfall data of the whole year.

2.2 Spatial Weight/Importance Calculation

This step aims at determining the *spatial importance* or *spatial weight* (SW_i) of each location $l_i \in L$, with respect to the prediction location. The spatial weight SW_i is measured based on the *spatial distance* (SD_i) and the *correlation between the time series of each variable* in the neighborhood locations and that in the prediction location. Suppose, $NCorr^i_{m_j}$ is the *normalized correlation* value between the time series of variable m_j in the i-th neighborhood location and that in the prediction location, such that $NCorr^i_{m_j} \in [0,1]$. Then, the spatial weight of the location is determined as follows:

$$
SW_i = \frac{\sum_{j=1}^{|M|} NCorr^i_{m_j} + NISD_i}{\sum_{k=1}^{|L|}(\sum_{j=1}^{|M|} NCorr^k_{m_j} + NISD_k)}
\tag{1}
$$

where, $NISD_i$ is the normalized *inverse spatial distance* of i-th location from the prediction location, such that $NISD_i \in [0,1]$.

2.3 Spatio-Temporal Prediction

During the prediction process in the proposed space-time model, the effect of spatial influence of the meteorological variables are learnt with the help of SpaBN analysis. In order to describe the learning process, let's consider an example scenario, where M_1, M_2 and M_3 are three arbitrary meteorological variables. Also let M_1 is independent, M_2 is influenced by M_1, and M_3 is influenced by M_1 and M_2. Now, because of the inherent spatio-temporal inter-relationships among these variables, variable at one location is also influenced by the variables in its neighborhood locations. Therefore, considering a causal dependency graph, comprising of the representative variables from all the neighboring locations, will ultimately lead to a complex graphical structure for capturing spatio-temporal inter-relationships among the variables (refer Fig. 2a).

In such scenario, *spatial Bayesian network* (SpaBN) can be an appropriate tool for modeling these spatio-temporal inter-relationships in an efficient manner. As shown in the SpaBN structure (refer Fig. 2b), all the standard/classical nodes associated with the same but spatially distributed variable have been replaced with *composite nodes*, denoted by double lined circles. The replacement of all such standard nodes with a single composite node reduces both the structural and the algorithmic complexity in Bayesian analysis to a great extent.

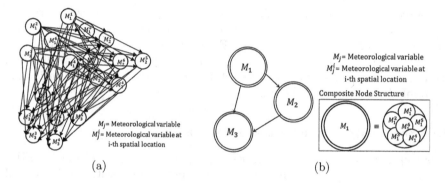

(a)   (b)

Fig. 2. Graph based modeling of spatio-temporal inter-relationships among the three meteorological variables: (a) a complex causal dependency graph of standard BN, (b) equivalent SpaBN structure [considering no. of locations $|L| = 6$]

Let $|L|$ be the number of neighboring locations considered. Then, according to the principle of SpaBN, the marginal and conditional probabilities of the variables in Fig. 2b are estimated in following fashion:

$$P(M_1) = \gamma \cdot \left[\sum_{i=1}^{|L|} P(M_1^i) \cdot SW_i \right] \tag{2}$$

$$P(M_2) = \gamma \cdot \left[\sum_{i=1}^{|L|} P(M_2^i) \cdot SW_i \right] \tag{3}$$

$$P(M_3) = \gamma \cdot \left[\sum_{i=1}^{|L|} P(M_3^i) \cdot SW_i \right] \tag{4}$$

$$P(M_2|M_1) = \gamma \cdot \left[\sum_{i=1}^{|L|} \frac{n(M_1^i, M_2^i)}{n(M_1^i)} \cdot SW_i \right] \tag{5}$$

$$P(M_3|M_1, M_2) = \gamma \cdot \left[\sum_{i=1}^{|L|} \frac{n(M_1^i, M_2^i, M_3^i)}{n(M_1^i, M_2^i)} \cdot SW_i \right] \tag{6}$$

where, SW_i is the spatial weight/importance of the i-th neighboring location with respect to the prediction location; γ is the normalization constant; and $n(< \cdot >)$ is the count of observation for the variable value combination $< \cdot >$.

Now, in order to capture the *temporal evolution* of the inter-variable dependencies, the SpaBN based learning process (as described above) is performed with historical data of each year separately, and finally the probabilistic estimates are combined in a weighted manner, so as to achieve the probability distributions corresponding to the inter-variable dependencies in the prediction year. Higher temporal weight (tw) is assigned to a year which is temporally nearer to the prediction year. The overall process of space-time learning is summarized through Algorithm 1, considering immediately next prediction year $y_{(t+1)}$.

Algorithm 1. Space-time learning using SpaBN

1: **Input:** Historical data set $H = \{H_{y_1}, \cdots, H_{y_t}\}$ for the past t years: $\{y_1, \cdots, y_t\}$; Causal dependency graph over all meteorological variables $m \in M$

2: **Output:** Probabilistic relationships among the meteorological variables for the prediction year.

3: P_F^m = Final probability estimate for a variable m.

4: P_i^m = Probability estimate corresponding to the the variable m, for the training year y_i

5: **for** each training year y_i, $(0 \leq i \leq t)$ **do**

6:     Apply SpaBN analysis to learn the probabilistic relationships among the variables using H_{y_i}.

7:     **for** each considered meteorological variable m **do**

8:         **for** each probability estimate P_i^m in the probability table of m **do**

9:             $d_i = [y_{(t+1)} - y_i]$; /* calculating temporal distance of y_i from prediction year */

10:            $tw_i = \left(\frac{\frac{1}{d_i}}{\sum_{j=1}^{t} \frac{1}{d_j}} \right)$; /* Estimating temporal weight/importance for the year y_i */

11:            $P_F^m = P_F^m + (tw_i \times P_i^m)$; /* probability updating for the prediction year */

12:         **end for**

13:     **end for**

14: **end for**

15: **return** P_F^m for all m in the causal dependency graph of SpaBN

Once the parameter learning is over, the inference is generated as per SpaBN by utilizing the spatial weights (SW_i). For example, let the observed/ evidence variables are: M_1 and M_2, from which the value of M_3 is to be inferred.

Then, as per the principle of SpaBN,

$$Inferred\,value\,of\,M_3 = \sum_{i=1}^{|L|} P(M_3^i|M_1^i, M_2^i) \cdot SW_i \tag{7}$$

where the value for $P(M_3^i|M_1^i, M_2^i)$ can be determined from the conditional probability table for the variable M_3. Among these inferred values, the predicted value becomes the one corresponding to the maximum probability.

3   Experimental Evaluation

This section describes the empirical study carried out for evaluating our proposed space-time prediction model.

3.1   Data Set and Study Area

The proposed prediction model has been validated by forecasting daily time series of three primary meteorological variables, namely *Temperature, relative Humidity*, and *Precipitation rate*, around *Kolkata [22.57° N, 88.36° E], India*. The corresponding historical daily time series data have been collected from the FetchClimate Explorer [4] for a span of 10 years (2006–2015). Predictions have been carried out for two locations (*Loc-1* [22.93°N, 87.25°E] and *Loc-2* [22.82°N, 88.29°E]), for the year 2016 (refer Fig. 3).

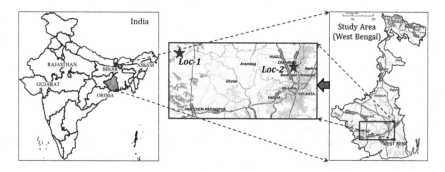

Fig. 3. *Study Area* around *Kolkata* [22.57°N, 88.36°E] in *West Bengal (India)*

3.2   Results

The comparative study has been made with benchmark prediction techniques, like *automated ARIMA* (R-Tool), *standard BN* (SBN), ANN (MATLAB nnTool) etc. and state-of-the-art space-time models, namely *hierarchical Bayesian autoregressive* (HBAR) model [5], and *spatio-temporal ordinary Kriging* (ST-OK) [1]. The prediction performance has been measured in terms of *four* popular statistical measures, namely *normalized root mean square deviation* (NRMSD) [3], *Pearson's correlation coefficient* (CC), *mean absolute error* (MAE), and *mean absolute percentage error* (MAPE) [2]. The best-fit between the observed and predicted value yields NRMSD = 0, CC = 1, MAE = 0 and MAPE = 0. The results of prediction have been summarized in Tables 1, 2 and 3.

Discussions: On analyzing the results, presented in Tables 1, 2 and 3, the following inferences can be drawn:

Table 1. Comparative study of *Temperature* prediction

Prediction approaches	Loc-1				Loc-2			
	Prediction metrics				Prediction metrics			
	NRMSD	MAE	MAPE	CC	NRMSD	MAE	MAPE	CC
A-ARIMA	0.329	3.219	7.463	0.098	0.211	3.064	7.278	0.137
ANN	0.212	1.771	3.698	0.711	0.569	0.761	2.529	0.929
SBN	0.099	1.035	0.147	0.935	0.951	1.028	0.085	0.929
HBAR	0.203	2.245	2.336	0.756	0.221	2.371	3.899	0.687
ST-OK	0.191	2.175	0.179	0.778	0.248	2.300	0.179	0.805
Proposed approach	**0.098**	**1.003**	**0.038**	**0.937**	**0.101**	**0.997**	**0.072**	**0.936**

Table 2. Comparative study of *Relative humidity* prediction

Prediction approaches	Loc-1				Loc-2			
	Prediction metrics				Prediction metrics			
	NRMSD	MAE	MAPE	CC	NRMSD	MAE	MAPE	CC
A-ARIMA	0.323	8.333	2.187	0.603	0.325	8.873	2.093	0.606
ANN	0.158	3.038	4.068	0.942	0.252	6.077	6.524	0.791
SBN	0.077	1.976	2.029	0.980	0.171	2.850	4.080	0.922
HBAR	0.156	3.696	2.782	0.910	0.150	3.353	1.357	0.904
ST-OK	0.192	4.970	0.789	0.868	0.288	6.255	4.463	0.790
Proposed approach	**0.069**	**1.328**	**0.669**	**0.989**	**0.064**	**1.315**	**1.150**	**0.985**

- In all the cases, the proposed prediction model produces the least NRMSDs and MAEs, which are significantly lesser than the other prediction techniques considered. This indicates superiority of our SpaBN based prediction, compared to the others.
- The high values of CC ($\approx$1) (refer Tables 1, 2 and 3) reveals that the series predicted by our model have the best match with the observed time series.
- The least MAPE values corresponding to the proposed space-time prediction model also demonstrate its better efficacy in comparison with the others.

Moreover, the improvement in computation time of the proposed model, with respect to standard Bayesian network (SBN) based prediction, has also been studied considering number of neighboring location $|L| = 6$, and variable domain size $R = 3$. The result (refer Table 4) proves the effectiveness of using SpaBN for modeling spatio-temporal dependency among the spatially distributed meteorological variables, as accomplished by our proposed space-time prediction model.

Table 3. Comparative study of *Precipitation rate* prediction

Prediction approaches	Loc-1				Loc-2			
	Prediction metrics				Prediction metrics			
	NRMSD	MAE	MAPE	CC	NRMSD	MAE	MAPE	CC
A-ARIMA	0.401	81.274	37.245	0.388	0.410	86.448	37.718	0.387
ANN	0.202	28.286	20.277	0.912	0.153	24.462	15.913	0.940
SBN	0.217	12.947	19.572	0.985	0.098	21.457	11.917	0.976
HBAR	0.410	92.910	81.257	0.840	0.374	88.518	71.203	0.863
ST-OK	0.260	51.856	5.175	0.797	0.259	51.869	5.346	0.807
Proposed approach	**0.063**	**11.684**	**1.602**	**0.990**	**0.038**	**06.818**	**1.449**	**0.996**

Table 4. Comparative study of computation time (considering $|L| = 6$, $R = 3$, *single* prediction day, and SBN with *spatially distributed* variables)

Prediction techniques	Standard BN (SBN)	Proposed approach
Execution time (s)	1500.254	0.068195

4   Conclusions

The objective of the present work is to address the challenge of handling complex spatio-temporal dependency among the meteorological variables during multivariate time series prediction. For that purpose, we have proposed a *space-time model* based on spatial Bayesian network (SpaBN) which is inherently capable of efficiently modeling the inter-dependency among large number of spatially distributed variables. Experimental study has been carried out in comparison with several benchmarks (ARIMA, SBN, ANN) and state-of-the-art prediction techniques (HBAR, ST-OK). Overall, the proposed space-time model has shown encouraging performance with respect to both *accuracy* and *computational cost* in meteorological time series prediction.

References

1. Cressie, N., Wikle, C.K.: Statistics for Spatio-Temporal Data. Wiley, London (2015)
2. Das, M., Ghosh, S.K.: semBnet: a semantic Bayesian network for multivariate prediction of meteorological time series data. Pattern Recogn. Lett. **93**, 192–201 (2017)
3. Das, M., Ghosh, S.K., Gupta, P., Chowdary, V., Nagaraja, R., Dadhwal, V.: FORWARD: a model for FOrecasting Reservoir WAteR Dynamics using Spatial Bayesian Network (SpaBN). IEEE Trans. Knowl. Data Eng. **29**(4), 842–855 (2017)
4. Microsoft-Research: FetchClimate (2015). http://research.microsoft.com/en-us/um/cambridge/projects/fetchclimate/app/. Accessed Jan 2016
5. Sahu, S.K., Bakar, K.S.: Hierarchical Bayesian autoregressive models for large space-time data with applications to ozone concentration modelling. Appl. Stoch. Models Bus. Ind. **28**(5), 395–415 (2012)
6. Voyant, C., Nivet, M.L., Paoli, C., Muselli, M., Notton, G.: Meteorological time series forecasting based on MLP modelling using heterogeneous transfer functions. J. Phys. Conf. Ser. **574**, 1–6 (2015). IOP Publishing

Adaptive TerraSAR-X Image Registration (AIR) Using Spatial Fisher Kernel Framework

B. Sirisha[1]([✉])[iD], Chandra Sekhar Paidimarry[2][iD],
A. S. Chandrasekhara Sastry[3][iD], and B. Sandhya[4][iD]

[1] KL University, Guntur, India
sirishavamsi@gmail.com
[2] UCE, Osmania University, Hyderabad, India
sekharpaidimarry@gmail.com
[3] KL University, Guntur, India
ascssastry@gmail.com
[4] MVSR Engineering College, Hyderabad, India
sandhyab16@gmail.com

Abstract. TerraSAR-X image registration is a forerunner for remote sensing application like target detection, which need accurate spatial transformation between the real time sensed image and the reference off-line image. It is observed that the outcome of registration of two TerraSAR images even when acquired from the same sensor is unpredictable with all the parameters of the feature extraction, matching and transformation algorithm are fixed. Hence we have approached the problem by trying to predict if the given TerraSAR-X images that can be registered without actually registering them. The proposed adaptive image registration (AIR) approach incorporates a classifier into the standard pipeline of feature based image registration. The attributes for the classifier model are derived from fusing the spatial parameters of the feature detector with the descriptor vector in Fisher kernel framework. We have demonstrated that the proposed AIR approach saves the time of feature matching and transformation estimation for SAR images which cannot be registered.

1 Introduction

TerraSAR-X image registration is the fundamental task in real time target detection [1][2]. This application aims to detect target from a sequence of SAR images obtained from a reconnaissance platform in real time. In such scenarios, the processing time taken in finding whether the sensed images can be registered with reference image constitute an overhead. Hence we have approached the problem by predetermining the given TerraSAR images that can be registered without actually registering them. This has been achieved by fusing the spatial parameters of the feature detector with the descriptor vector in Fisher vector framework [3][4]. The standard pipeline of feature based image registration consists of four important stages [5–7]. They are feature detection, feature description, feature

© Springer International Publishing AG 2017
B.U. Shankar et al. (Eds.): PReMI 2017, LNCS 10597, pp. 623–629, 2017.
https://doi.org/10.1007/978-3-319-69900-4_79

matching and transformation estimation. In the proposed adaptive TerraSAR image registration (AIR) features are extracted and described in first stage. However before proceeding to the feature matching and transformation estimation, we feed the features to a prediction model which predicts if the images can be registered or not. Our contribution is twofold: (1) Incorporate knowledge into the standard feature based image registration pipeline by building a prediction model which can be used for real time registration of TerraSAR-X images. (2) Incorporate spatial information for prediction model under the Fisher kernel framework, where Gaussian mixture model fuses the spatial information (XY-location and Scale of detected feature) with feature descriptor during the learning of local features. Automatic prediction of TerraSAR-X image registration is a recent development in remote sensing and the literature is limited. The paper is organized as follows: Methodology of the proposed image registration approach is illustrated in Sects. 2, 3 reports the experimental results and in Sect. 4 the conclusion of the paper is presented.

2   Methodology of Adaptive TerraSAR-X Image Registration Approach(AIR)

The proposed approach can be divided into four main stages, (i) Local invariant feature extraction (ii) Prediction model using Fisher Kernel framework (iii) Feature correspondence (iv) Transformation Estimation

Stage 1- Local Invariant Feature Extraction

Let I_r represent off-line reference image and I_{si} represent sequence of real time sensed TerraSAR-X images obtained from a reconnaissance platform, where $i \in 1, 2, ...n$. In the first stage, local affine invariant feature points are detected from given input TerraSAR image pairs using Hessian Affine detector [8][9]. Each detected feature point is characterized by a seven element vector consisting of XY-locations, scale-λ and 4 values of affine transformation matrix $a_{11}, a_{12}, a_{21}, a_{22}$. The detected feature points are described using the recent SIFT [10] modification-RootSIFT [11].

Stage 2-Prediction Model using Fisher Kernel Framework

Fisher vector built using descriptor and detector parameters closely represents these differences in both radiometric and spatial domains [12],[13]. Hence the distance between such vectors has been used as attributes for prediction model.

The features extracted from stage 1 are fed to prediction model. The prediction model has two phases 1. Spatial Fisher vector encoding 2. Classifier.

In this paper, the Fisher vector encoding aggregates feature detector and descriptor vectors into high dimensional vector representation unlike standard FV [3]. Figure 1 shows the spatial Fisher vector encoding framework to obtain the TerraSAR image representation. The Visual word dictionary is generated by learning GMM obtained from local feature detector and descriptor. Let $\{L_i^{r,s} = L_1^{r,s}, L_2^{r,s}....L_n^{r,s}\}, \{S_i^{r,s} = S_1^{r,s}, S_2^{r,s}....S_n^{r,s}\}$ and $\{D_i^{r,s} = D_1^{r,s}, D_2^{r,s}....D_n^{r,s}\}$ be the

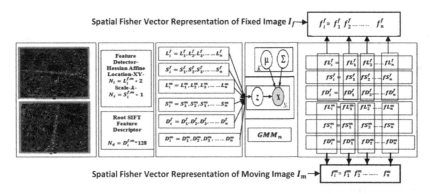

Fig. 1. Proposed spatial fisher vector encoding framework for the representation of TerraSAR-X imagery.

location-XY, scale and descriptors of reference and sensed SAR image. The probability density function of local detector and descriptor is

$$p(L_i^{r,s}, S_i^{r,s}, D_i^{r,s}|\lambda) = \sum_{i=1}^{N} w_i p_i(L_i^{r,s}, S_i^{r,s}, D_i^{r,s}|\lambda) \tag{1}$$

where $\lambda = \{w_i, \mu_i, \sum_i\}$, i={1, 2, ...N} N=Number of Gaussian components, w_i = relative frequency, μ_i = mean, $\sum_i$= mean variation of a visual word. The diagonal covariance matrix $\sum_k = diag\sigma_k^2$. GMM are trained with $\sum_k$ diagonal covariance matrix and reflect on the derivatives of Gaussian mean and Gaussian variance. The soft-assignment $\gamma_t(i)$ of given detector,descriptor to cluster i is

$$\gamma_t(i) = \frac{w_i p_i((L_i^{r,s}, S_i^{r,s}, D_i^{r,s})}{\sum_{j=1}^{k}} w_j p_j((L_i^{r,s}, S_i^{r,s}, D_i^{r,s}) \tag{2}$$

The Fisher vector representation captures the first and second order difference among the features to each GMM clusters.

$$G_{\mu,i}^d = \frac{1}{T\sqrt{wi}} \sum_{t=1}^{T} \gamma_t(\mu, i) \frac{(L_i^{r,s}, S_i^{r,s}, D_i^{r,s}) - \mu_i^d}{\sigma_i^d} \tag{3}$$

$$G_{\sigma,i}^d = \frac{1}{T\sqrt{2wi}} \sum_{t=1}^{T} \gamma_t(\mu, i) \frac{(L_i^{r,s}, S_i^{r,s}, D_i^{r,s}) - \mu_i^{2d}}{\sigma_i^{2d}} - 1 \tag{4}$$

The final gradient vector G is obtained by concatenation of $G_{\sigma,i}^d$ and $G_{\mu,i}^d$. The dimensionality of the spatial Fisher vector is 2Kd, where k is the number of Gaussian components in Gaussian mixture model, d is the dimensionality of the concatenated feature detector and descriptor vector. The classification performance of spatial fisher vector is further improved by power and L2 normalization. Finally, the distance between two SAR images I_f and I_m obtained by computing the Euclidean distance between the representations.

$$d(I_f, I_m) = \| SFV_f - SFV_m \| \tag{5}$$

This distance forms the attribute for classifier which has been trained and validated. If the classifier predicts that images cannot be aligned, subsequent image is taken for registering with reference image or else it proceeds to feature matching and transformation estimation stage. Feature descriptors of sets D_f and D_m are matched using a threshold on nearest neighbour ratio of distances. (X,Y) locations of matched descriptors are fed to RANSAC which estimates the transformation matrix H, in addition to finding inlier among the matches. The sensed image I_{si} can be transformed using H-matrix to the coordinate system of reference image I_r.

3   Experiment Results

In this section, we report experimental results of proposed AIR framework on 540 training images and 54 test images. Performance and robustness of the framework is assessed by two evaluations (1) Time analysis of proposed AIR framework. (2) Qualitative assessment of prediction model using Fisher kernel framework.

3.1   Time Analysis of Proposed AIR Framework

This sub-section reports time analysis of proposed AIR framework when executed on 2.19 Ghz/3 MB cache $IntelCore^{TM}$ i7, 8 GB RAM, x64 bit. The Fig. 2 (a) shows time taken for each stage of AIR framework. The analysis is done by comparing the processing time taken for below two scenarios. (1) If image pair is predicted to be "registered" then it proceeds to feature matching and transformation estimation stage. (2) If image pair is predicted to be "not registered" then subsequent image is taken for registration. This saves the effort and time in finding feature correspondences and homography estimation. It is observed from the Fig. 2 (b) that AIR framework takes 8 additional time units if the SAR image pair gets registered and saves 21.5 time units if image pairs could not be registered. Out of 594 synthetic TerraSAR image pairs fed to AIR framework, 220 images are predicted to be registered and 374 are not registered. It is clear that we save 8041 time units using proposed approach.

3.2   Qualitative Assessment of Prediction Model Using Fisher Kernel Framework

The possibility to register SAR image pair mainly depends on the kind and amount of deformation between the images. Since image registration aims to find a spatial transformation between the images. The spatial information present in key point locations has been exploited by using it in Fisher kernel model along with the descriptor vector. The effectiveness of the spatial fisher vector representation is tested and analyzed with three classification algorithms,viz., Naive Bayes, SVM [11] and J48 using 540 training images with tenfold cross validation. The performance of the model is evaluated and compared with Bag of

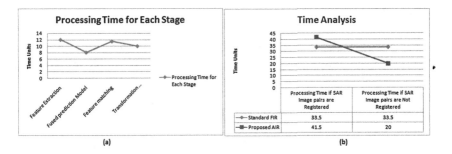

(a)   (b)

Fig. 2. Figure(a) Processing time for each stage of AIR.(b)Time analysis of FIR and AIR framework, when SAR images are subjected to registered and not registered cases.

Visual Words (BoW) [14], VLAD [15] and standard Fisher vector image representations in terms of accuracy, precision, recall, F measure and ROC area on 540 SAR images across deformations. Table 1 shows the performance when a classifier trained on 10 datasets (D1 to D10-540 SAR images) and tested on dataset 11(D11-54 SAR images). The experimental results reported in table 1 establishes that the BoW, VLAD, standard Fisher vector model falls short of its expected performance when used for predetermining possibility of image registration. The accuracy of proposed spatial Fisher vector is 90.8142%. Hence it is evident from table 1 that, accuracy of the prediction framework increases only when the spatial information extracted from feature detector is considered along with descriptor information. It is noted that feature detector location parameter (XY) plays a significant role in improving the classification accuracy irrespective to the type of classifier.

Table 1. Prediction model results on 540 training images (D1 TO D10) and 54 (D11) test images using 10 fold cross validation.

	Attributes	Accuracy	TP rate	FP rate	Precision	Recall	Fmeasure	ROC area
J48	Bag of Visual Words	73.3942	0.734	0.317	0.763	0.733	0.715	0.756
	VLAD	62.9542	0.629	0.409	0.625	0.628	0.616	0.618
	Standard FisherVector	87.0542	0.87	0.143	0.871	0.869	0.869	0.888
	Proposed FisherVector	**90.2042**	**0.889**	**0.123**	**0.888**	**0.899**	**0.898**	**0.918**
SVM	Bag of Visual Words	73.2042	0.732	0.32	0.761	0.731	0.712	0.705
	VLAD	70.8742	0.609	0.538	0.603	0.608	0.689	0.684
	Standard FisherVector	87.0542	0.87	0.137	0.869	0.869	0.869	0.866
	Proposed FisherVector	**90.8242**	**0.899**	**0.112**	**0.928**	**0.918**	**0.898**	**0.918**
Nave Bayes	Bag of Visual Words	73.3942	0.734	0.317	0.763	0.733	0.715	0.76
	VLAD	62.9542	0.629	0.409	0.625	0.628	0.616	0.617
	Standard FisherVector	88.3842	0.884	0.123	0.883	0.883	0.883	0.926
	Proposed FisherVector	**89.9242**	**0.879**	**0.134**	**0.868**	**0.897**	**0.888**	**0.898**
	54 Test Images (D11)							
SVM	Bag of Visual Words	73.2042	0.732	0.32	0.761	0.731	0.712	0.705
	VLAD	61.5742	0.576	0.378	0.625	0.634	0.544	0.66
	Standard FisherVector	84.2442	0.842	0.16	0.841	0.841	0.848	0.84
	Proposed FisherVector	**90.8142**	**0.899**	**0.12**	**0.902**	**0.902**	**0.901**	**0.909**

4   Conclusion

Look-angle varied TerraSAR image registration is a challenging task as slight shift in look-angle alters the geometric and photometric characteristics of the images. The proposed framework can predetermine if the given TerraSAR image pairs can be accurately registered. The asset of this framework is that, the attributes required for prediction model are computed from the features extracted as part of registration pipeline using spatial Fisher vector framework. It is established that detector parameters when fused with the descriptor in Fisher vector framework improves prediction accuracy. While registering two TerraSAR images without prior knowledge of deformation, the fused detector, descriptor parameters in the scrim of spatial Fisher vector framework, is productive in predicting registration outcome.

References

1. Kim, S., Song, W.-J., Kim, S.-H.: Robust ground target detection by SAR and IR sensor fusion using adaboost-based feature selection. In: Sensors (2016)
2. El-Darymli, K., Peter, M., Desmond, C.M.: Target detection in synthetic aperture radar imagery: a state-of-the-art survey. IJRS **7**(1), 071598 (2013)
3. Perronnin, F., Sánchez, J., Mensink, T.: Improving the fisher kernel for large-scale image classification. In: Daniilidis, K., Maragos, P., Paragios, N. (eds.) ECCV 2010. LNCS, vol. 6314, pp. 143–156. Springer, Heidelberg (2010). doi:10.1007/978-3-642-15561-1_11
4. Perronnin, F., Dance, C.: Fisher kernels on visual vocabularies for image categorization. In: CVPR, p. 18 (2007)
5. Zitova, B., Flusser, J.: Image registration methods: a surveyIn. Image Vis. Comput. **21**(11), 977–1000 (2003)
6. Zhou, D., Zeng, L., Liang, J., Zhang, K.: Improved method for SAR image registration based on scale invariant feature transform. IET Radar Sonar Navig. **11**(4), 4 (2017)
7. Fan, J., Wu, Y., Li, M., Liang, W., Zhang, Q.: SAR image registration using multiscale image patch features with sparse representation. Appl. Earth Observations Remote Sens. **10**(4), 1483–1493 (2017)
8. Mikolajczyk, K., Schmid, C.: Scale and affine invariant interest point detectors. IJCV **60**(1), 63–86 (2004)
9. Mikolajczyk, K., Tuytelaars, T., Schmid, C., et al.: A comparison of affine region detectors. Int. J. Comput. Vis. **65**, 43 (2005)
10. Lowe, D.: Distinctive image features from scale-invariant keypoints. IJCV **60**(2), 91–110 (2004)
11. Arandjelovic, R., Zisserman, A.: Three things everyone should know to im-prove object retrieval. In: CVPR (2012)
12. van Gemert, J.C., Geusebroek, J.-M., Veenman, C.J., Smeulders, A.W.M.: Kernel codebooks for scene categorization. In: Forsyth, D., Torr, P., Zisserman, A. (eds.) ECCV 2008. LNCS, vol. 5304, pp. 696–709. Springer, Heidelberg (2008). doi:10.1007/978-3-540-88690-7_52
13. Bombrun, L., Beaulieu, J.-M.: Fisher distribution for texture modeling of polarimetric SAR data. IEEE Geosci. Remote Sens. Lett. **5**(3), 512–516 (2008)

14. Zhang, Y., Zhu, C., Bres, S., Chen, L.: Encoding local binary descriptors by bag-of-features with hamming distance for visual object categorization. In: Serdyukov, P., Braslavski, P., Kuznetsov, S.O., Kamps, J., Rüger, S., Agichtein, E., Segalovich, I., Yilmaz, E. (eds.) ECIR 2013. LNCS, vol. 7814, pp. 630–641. Springer, Heidelberg (2013). doi:10.1007/978-3-642-36973-5_53
15. Arandjelovic, R., Zisserman, A.: All about VLAD. In: CVPR 2013, pp. 1578–1585 (2013)

Applications of Pattern Recognition and Machine Intelligence

Hierarchical Ranking of Cricket Teams Incorporating Player Composition

Abhinav Agarwalla$^{(\boxtimes)}$ ⓘ, Madhav Mantri ⓘ, and Vishal Singh ⓘ

Indian Institute of Technology, Kharagpur, India
{abhinavagarwalla,madhavmantri,vishalsingh13}@iitkgp.ac.in

Abstract. We analyze the performance of international ODI cricket teams through a hierarchical ranking scheme. Players are represented as the nodes of a graph with batsmen as authorities, and bowlers as hubs. Low level player ratings determined using weighted HITS algorithm, are fed into a higher level Elo rating system to rank teams. Strike rate, economy rate, number of boundaries, etc. determine the edge weights for player graph. Match characteristics like margin of victory, winning style and player rankings determine the K-factor in Elo ratings. We show that player composition along with match characteristics is also an important aspect of team ranking, which has not explored previously. We report significant improvements in predicting match outcomes against other ranking schemes.

Keywords: Cricket team rankings · Player ratings · Weighted HITS · Elo rating · Hierarchical ranking

1 Introduction

Cricket is a team sport in which a team of 11 players play against an opponent team. The team scoring more runs is declared as the winner. As with any sport being played for more than 30 years, cricket has a vast collection of open access historical match data comprising of match outcomes and player performances. However, rigorous analysis of the factors affecting team rankings and their correlation with player performance are very scarce. Such a study can aid selection committees in identifying players' strengths and weaknesses against a particular team, and selecting a high performing balanced team.

We address the problem of ranking cricket teams in One Day International (ODI) format of the game. A challenge in cricket team ranking is that it is often impossible for all the pairs of teams to compete against each other. Then, the set of opponents depends on players in each team such that ranking teams by simply counting the number of wins and losses is inappropriate. Thus, along with the past winning characteristics of the teams, team composition and individual player performance should also be incorporated in computing the team rankings.

A. Agarwalla and M. Mantri—Equal contribution.

© Springer International Publishing AG 2017
B.U. Shankar et al. (Eds.): PReMI 2017, LNCS 10597, pp. 633–638, 2017.
https://doi.org/10.1007/978-3-319-69900-4_80

Fig. 1. Hierarchical ranking model for cricket teams

Our aim is not only to find a preference function or a binary response prediction but the complete set of team rankings. We use a hierarchical ranking approach, as depicted in Fig. 1. First, players are ranked using HITS [1]. Then, player rankings along with match characteristics are utilised to calculate team ranking using Elo ratings [2]. We essentially combine network based and pair-wise rankings in a hierarchical fashion, which has not been explored earlier.

2   Related Work

There have been many studies to rank players as well as teams in football, basketball, tennis, etc., which is well summarized in Daniel *et al.* [3]. They compared 8 different methods tested on 4 datasets for baseball, football and basketball.

Anthony *et al.* [4], Fainmesser *et al.* [5] and Anjela *et al.* [6] discussed rank aggregation, and storing two ranks inside a single node. [7] utilised temporal information in data using a dynamic network based ranking method.

For ranking cricket teams, ICC follows a set of pre-defined rules [8]. It assigns higher weights to recent matches which has not been captured in existing work. On the other hand, it has a number of drawbacks too: 1. They do not account for venue of match, and time of the day which greatly influences the pitch type, batting and bowling conditions. 2. Margin of victory is unaccounted for. 3. Importance of the match is unaccounted for. 4. Team composition for a particular match is ignored. 5. No additional point is awarded for winning a series.

Recent approaches account for these pitfalls. Daud and Muhammad [9] devised T-index for analysing team performance which is based on h-index computation. T-index is motivated by the need to account for margin of victory. They also explored graphical methods such as PageRank [10] along with its weighted and unified variants. They use 60-20-20 for weighing final result, runs and wickets without any proper justification for the numbers.

Our main contribution is a novel hierarchical approach for ranking cricket teams, which efficiently captures team performance using player ratings and match characteristics. We also modify Elo rating scheme to incorporate margin of victory and winning style. Our approach explicitly models the batting and bowling strength of the teams.

3   Rating Methodology

3.1   Player Ranking Using HITS

Hyperlink-Induced Topic Search (HITS) [1] is a link analysis algorithm, which was initially introduced to rank web pages. It models web as hubs and authorities, which are nodes with multiple outgoing and incoming links respectively. It assigns an authority and a hub score to every node. A higher authority score occurs if the page is referred by pages with high hub scores and vice-versa. We extend the algorithm by modelling players as nodes, and directed edges from bowlers to batsmen. Each player p has an authority score a_p, and a hub score h_p, which represent the batting and bowling strength respectively. A player with a higher a_p number is a better batsman, and player with a higher h_p number a better bowler. $B(p)$ and $F(p)$ denote the set of players who bowled to, and were bowled by player p, respectively. The scores are computed iteratively until convergence.

We weight every edge from one player p to player q in a weighted HITS setting [11] as given by Eq. 1. We model edge weights(w) as a weighted combination of number of games played($G_{i,j}$), the total runs scores($R_{i,j}$), number of sixes($S_{i,j}$), fours($F_{i,j}$), dots($D_{i,j}$), and the total number of balls played($B_{i,j}$) between players i and j as given in Eq. 2.

$$a_p = \sum_{q \in B(p)} w_{a_q} * h_q \quad and \quad h_p = \sum_{q \in F(p)} w_{h_q} * a_q \tag{1}$$

$$w = \alpha_1 G_{i,j} + \alpha_2 \frac{R_{i,j}}{B_{i,j}} + \alpha_3 \frac{D_{i,j}}{B_{i,j}} + \alpha_4 S_{i,j} + \alpha_5 F_{i,j} \tag{2}$$

Let A be the weighted adjacency matrix of the player graph, and u and v denote the hub and authority score vectors.

$$v = \begin{bmatrix} a_1 \ a_2 \ \dots \ a_n \end{bmatrix}^T \quad and \quad u = \begin{bmatrix} h_1 \ h_2 \ \dots \ h_n \end{bmatrix}^T \tag{3}$$

Then the two update operations can be represented in matrix form as:

$$v = A^t.u \quad and \quad u = A^t.v \tag{4}$$

3.2   Team Ranking Using Modified Elo Rating

Elo rating [2] method is a widely used method for rating players in 2-player games like chess and Go. In Elo rating scheme, competing teams either give or take points from another team depending on whether it looses, or wins respectively. Point difference is also limited by the strength of competing teams. A strong team would gain little on winning from a weak team, but loose many points on loosing from that team. Elo rating scheme is given by Eqs. 5 and 6. $r_{a,new}$ and $r_{a,old}$ denote new and old ratings respectively. α is set to 1 if Team A wins against Team B, 0.5 in case of a draw and 0 otherwise. s_A calculates the probability of Team A winning against Team B.

$$r_{A,new} = r_{A,old} + k(\alpha - s_A) \tag{5}$$

$$s_A = \frac{1}{1 + c^{\frac{r_{B,old} - r_{A,old}}{d}}}, s_B = 1 - s_A \tag{6}$$

Parameters c, d are set to default values 10 and 400 as they only change the rating scale. The maximum point difference after a match is limited by k, which controls the volatility of the ratings. Changes in ratings should be in modest increments, but at the same time, not too modest that it takes a season for a declining teams rating to reflect its form. k can be taken as a function of ratings, as frequently done in chess. We represent k as a function of margin of victory, total runs scored, wickets taken, innings played and player ratings to appropriately model the game of cricket.

$$k = (1 + \delta_{bat})^{\lambda_{bat}} (1 + \delta_{bowl})^{\lambda_{bowl}} * \begin{cases} k_{o,r}(1 + \delta_r)^{\lambda_r} & \text{run margin} \\ k_{o,w}(1 + \delta_w)^{\lambda_w} & \text{wicket margin} \end{cases} \quad (7)$$

$$\delta_{bat} = \sum_{i \in players} (a_A(i) - a_B(i)), \qquad \delta_{bowl} = \sum_{i \in players} (h_A(i) - h_B(i)) \quad (8)$$

In cricket, a team can either win by wickets or by runs. Addressing this issue, δ_r and δ_w denote the margin of victory over runs and wickets respectively. δ_{bat} and δ_{bowl} accumulates the difference in the batting and bowling ratings of both the teams. These correspond to the authority and hubs scores obtained from the player graph. A sub-graph of the top batsmen and bowlers is depicted in Fig. 2a. The authority scores increase with the brightness of the node. $k_{o,r}$, $k_{o,w}$, λ_r and λ_p are scaling parameters for run and wicket margin.

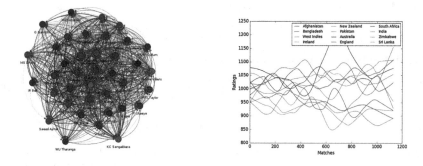

Fig. 2. (a) Player graph for top players (b) Modified Elo Rankings

4   Implementation and Results

We crawl ball by ball match data[1] for international ODI cricket matches during 2005-2017. Our data comprises of 1312 matches, 12 teams, 1385 players with 776 batsman and 609 bowlers. We divide our data into training, validation and test set consisting of 656, 328 and 328 matches respectively. The match statistics includes: venue, date, teams competing, toss results, playing-11 for both teams, match results, batsman and bowler for each ball. The data was preprocessed to

---

[1] http://cricsheet.org.

make it suitable for our algorithm. For computing player ranks, weighted directed graphs are constructed using adjacency matrices. These are updated after every match either by adding new edges or updating existing weights. To evaluate our ranking, we measure their match outcome prediction capacity. If team A has higher ratings than team B before the match, then it would win the match. We employ a rolling validation approach, and report prediction accuracy and log-loss in Table 1. All the hyper-parameters, namely $\{\lambda_{bat}, \lambda_{bowl}, \lambda_r, \lambda_w, k_{o,r}, k_{o,w}\}$ for Elo and $\{\alpha_1 .. \alpha_5\}$ for HITS, are optimised using Bayesian optimisation [12]. $W1$ and $W2$ correspond to uniform weighting, and weights obtained from Bayesian optimisation respectively.

Even though we do not utilise the match characteristics like venue, time of match, playing-11, etc. which are known before the next match, predictive accuracy is high. On using only the match characteristics data and ignoring the player performance, we observe that simple ranking schemes like Elo-method with optimal parameters give better results than network based methods like PageRank and Weighted PageRank. We also observe that incorporating the player performance data hierarchically further improves ranking accuracy. However, different weighing functions in HITS for player ranking give similar results. The obtained rankings are stable, as visualized in Fig. 2b. A closer look reveals the rise of Australian cricket team around 2010, and the recent rise of Indian cricket team, which correlates with the actual ODI performance.

Table 1. Test set accuracies of weighting function used

S.No	Model	Accuracy(%)	Log-Loss
1	PageRank	57.24	0.692
2	Weighted PageRank	67.73	0.685
3	Elo (without HITS)	96.8	0.166
4	Elo + HITS (W_1)	97.17	0.140
5	Elo + HITS (W_2)	**97.52**	**0.086**

5   Conclusion

The acquisition of large amount of player and game data is providing researchers with an unprecedented amount of information to resolve difficult ranking problems. With these large quantities of data comes the increasing challenge regarding the best methods of analysis. Focusing specifically on the network based algorithms, we suggest that traditional non-hierarchical methods are inadequate for these highly heterogeneous data sets specially in team sports, and that researchers employ more sophisticated ranking algorithms in their analysis. If we are to best extract the information present in these data sets, a sound understanding of basics of the sport combined with modern analytical techniques is necessary.

We observe that simple ranking algorithms like Elo rating method perform better than graph-based algorithms like PageRank and it's variants due to their inability to use player level data. We proposed a novel hierarchical approach to incorporate player data in team ranking using weighted HITS algorithm. Weighted HITS enabled us to analyse the batting and bowling strengths of the players separately. On testing several versions of the algorithms proposed, we observe that adding more information like team composition, player ratings and winning style in a hierarchical fashion results in improvement in terms of accuracy and stability.

Fitting arbitrary weighing functions and learning a model for edge weights, can be used for better approximation of the winning probability. This motivates the need for more sophisticated approaches for modelling weighting functions which is left to future work.

References

1. Kleinberg, J.M.: Authoritative sources in a hyperlinked environment. J. ACM **46**(5), 604–632 (1999)
2. Elo, A.E.: The Rating of Chessplayers, Past and Present. Arco Publisher, New York (1978)
3. Barrow, D., et al.: Ranking rankings: an empirical comparison of the predictive power of sports ranking methods. J. Quant. Anal. Sports **9**(2), 187–202 (2013)
4. Constantinou, A.C., Fenton, N.E., Neil, M.: Pi-football: a bayesian network model for forecasting association football match outcomes. Knowl. Based Syst. **36**, 322–339 (2012)
5. Fainmesser, I., Fershtman, C., Gandal, N.: A consistent weighted ranking scheme with an application to NCAA college football rankings. J. Sports Econ. **10**, 582–600 (2009)
6. Govan, A.Y., Langville, A.N., Meyer, C.D.: Offense-defense approach to ranking team sports. J. Quant. Anal. Sports **5**(1), 1151 (2009)
7. Motegi, S., Masuda, N.: A network-based dynamical ranking system for competitive sports. arXiv preprint arXiv:1203.2228 (2012)
8. http://www.icc-cricket.com/player-rankings/about
9. Daud, A., Muhammad, F.: Ranking cricket teams through runs and wickets. In: Yoshida, T., Kou, G., Skowron, A., Cao, J., Hacid, H., Zhong, N. (eds.) AMT 2013. LNCS, vol. 8210, pp. 156–165. Springer, Cham (2013). doi:10.1007/978-3-319-02750-0_16
10. Page, L., et al.: The PageRank citation ranking: bringing order to the web (1999)
11. Zhang, X., Yu, H., Zhang, C., Liu, X.: An Improved Weighted HITS Algorithm based on Similarity and Popularity Second International Multisymposium on Computer and Computational Sciences, pp. 477–480. IEEE 2007 (2007)
12. Snoek, J., Larochelle, H., Adams, R.P.: Practical bayesian optimization of machine learning algorithms. Neural Inf. Proces. Syst. **25**, 2960–2968 (2012)

Smart Water Management: An Ontology-Driven Context-Aware IoT Application

Deepti Goel[1]([⊠])[ID], Santanu Chaudhury[1][ID], and Hiranmay Ghosh[2][ID]

[1] Department of Electrical Engineering, IIT Delhi, New Delhi 110016, India
deeptigoyal2003@gmail.com, schaudhury@gmail.com
[2] TCS Innovation Labs, Mysuru, India
hiranmay@ieee.org

Abstract. This paper presents a context-aware ontology driven app-roach to water resource management in smart cities for providing adequate water supply to the citizens. The appropriate management of water requires exploitation of efficient action plan to review the prevailing causes of water shortage in a geospatial environment. This involves analysis of historical and real-time water specific information captured through heterogeneous sensors. Since the gathered contextual data is available in different formats so interoperability across diverse data requires converting it into a common perceivable RDF format. As the perceptual model of the Smart Water domain comprises of observable media properties of the concepts so to achieve context-aware data fusion we have employed multimedia ontology based semantic mapping. The multimedia ontology encoded in Multimedia Web Ontology Language (MOWL) forms the core of our IoT based smart water application. It supports Dynamic Bayesian Network based probabilistic reasoning to predict the changing situations in a real-time irregular environment patterns. Ultimately, the paper presents a context-aware approach to deal with uncertainties in water resource in the face of environment variability and offer timely conveyance to water authorities by circulating warnings via text-messages or emails. To illustrate the usability of the presented approach we have utilized the online available sample water data-sets.

1 Introduction

Water is a vital natural resource which drives our ecosystem but rise in population growth and urbanization has put a limit to the water supply and even led to water crisis. In these conditions, successful management of water resources requires deploying IoT technologies and utilizing efficient planning methodologies to predict causes responsible for shortage of water in a smart city. This will provide an accurate knowledge of the available water resources to meet the competing demands. The knowledge about the water domain constitutes of water quantity, it's quality etc. which is time-consuming and expensive to analyze using existing approaches. Moreover, the present water management system such as ICT lacks inter-operability standards and results in low monitoring efficacy. Thus, use of IoT technologies [2] such as smart water meters, soil sensors

© Springer International Publishing AG 2017
B.U. Shankar et al. (Eds.): PReMI 2017, LNCS 10597, pp. 639–646, 2017.
https://doi.org/10.1007/978-3-319-69900-4_81

to estimate moisture or chemical substance in the ground area etc. offers significant tracking capabilities to manage the issues generated as a consequence of lack of available water resources [1]. The data captured by the assortment of devices are of different media formats so to enable integration and for conceptual inter-operability a formal semantic representation is required. The author in [4] proposed semantic based knowledge management system for water flow and quality modeling. The work in [5] presents a concept which combines actors, hydro logic concepts and relationships among them to offer a unified approach to manage water related issues. The authors in [8] presented a concept of linked water data to create an integrated graph of information required for managing water effectively. These systems failed to reason with uncertainties involved in multimedia observations which impedes the desired vision. So, a multimedia ontology encoded in MOWL [3] would be useful for flexible media data representation. MOWL allows to represent the data with semantic properties and supports Dynamic Bayesian Networks (DBN) [7] as a probabilistic reasoning model that captures the dependencies among variables and utilizes context developed over time [6]. In smart water scenario the level of uncertainty originate from various knowledge perspectives such as unpredictable climate variation, water contamination, water pH etc. which involves ambiguities. To understand the environment and water availability over a range of temporal scales the pre-requisite context information is obtained through intelligent devices. The proposed framework utilizes this information to achieve context-aware semantic mapping so as to support data fusion and automatic interpretation of the context. Further, DBN based reasoning capabilities of MOWL helps to analyze the source of water and predict the uncertain environmental situation responsible for water shortage in the specific context. The predictability of these situations in real-time will help to provide guidance to the local water authorities about lower water supply under which management can be performed.

2   Multimedia Ontology in Smart Water Domain

In an IoT environment, use of semantic web technologies provides a common platform for knowledge access and interchange by minimizing the semantic heterogeneity that exists between various devices. The existing semantic approaches such as OWL supports conceptual modelling but fails to interpret the perceptual world due to the semantic gap that exists between the perceptual media features and the real world. The perceptual modelling comprises of observable media properties of the concepts which are useful for concept recognition or semantic interpretation of multimedia documents. So, MOWL [3] can be used as an alternate ontology representation language which associate different media features in different type of media format and at different levels of abstraction with the concepts. MOWL assumes causal model of world and supports probabilistic association of media properties with the domain concepts. MOWL based knowledge representation graph is composed of the following parameters:

(i) $\{C, M_p, M_e\}$ where, C is the set of concepts, M_p and M_e are the set of media patterns and media examples respectively; (ii) relation $\{R_p, R_h\}$ which organizes concepts and properties in a hierarchical structure, where R_p specifies the propagation of media properties between a concept and its related concepts while R_h represents the set of hierarchy among the concepts.

In smart water domain, knowledge representation in MOWL consists of water-specific concepts, with its expected media properties to deal with inherent uncertainties in observation of media patterns by setting Conditional Probability Tables (CPT's). The sensory inputs such as water-pH reading, water flow reading etc. forms the basis of context which are modeled as media patterns in the ontology. The snippet ontology using MOWL constructs shown in Fig. 1 specifies event and device ontology. Event ontology incorporates set of activities such as river-level, ground water-level etc. at a given location and time while device ontology describes the devices which are capable of monitoring objects. In figure, ellipse nodes represent domain concepts while rectangular nodes represent their observable media properties which are linked through edges. The concept is recognized on the basis of gathered evidences as a result of detection of expected media patterns. The vision to build context-aware services by aggregating knowledge from IoT devices is achieved by using DBN.

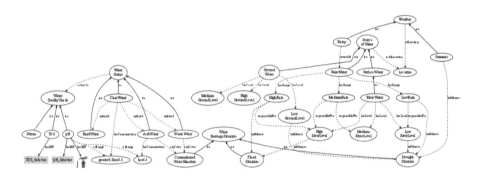

Fig. 1. Snippet ontology in smart water application

2.1   Dynamic Context-Aware Situation Modelling

Figure 2 depicts a MOWL based DBN model for context-aware situation tracking in real-time. It consists of sensor information, context state and situation state at time interval say t_1 and t_2. The situations at time slice t1 to t2 are linked through transition links (red color). The reasoning process derives a sub-graph Observation Model (OM), at each time step for concept recognition which contains the situation hierarchy and other concepts related to situation, thus enabling the modelling of dynamic situation. Here, the belief at each level is computed by considering current evidences along with prior inferred situations. The state transitions at different time stamps (say t_1 to t_2) allows to deal with changing situations in the dynamic environment. The DBN formulation on the sequence of S states and E sensor observations is as:

$P(S, E) = \prod_{t=1}^{T-1} P(S_t|S_{t-1}) \prod_{t=0}^{T-1} P(E_t|S_t) \, P(S_0)$; where $P(S_0)$ specifies likelihood of initial state, $P(S_t|S_{t-1})$ describes temporal state transitions and $P(E_t|S_t)$ specifies probability distribution for sensor observations.

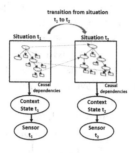

Fig. 2. DBN based situation evolution (Color figure online)

3 Ontology Based Smart Water Architecture

The management of water resource is an uncertain and dynamically complex problem. An ontology-driven smart water framework in context-aware perspective requires pre-requisite information about the change in climate, environment conditions, water quality etc. to understand the water availability over a range of temporal scales. The multimedia ontology based architecture as shown in Fig. 3 consists of the following main elements:

- **Data-acquisition Layer:** This layer is responsible for monitoring and acquiring data from multiple sources using IoT devices. The sensors and environment indicators such as smart water meters, climate sensors, water-level sensors etc. helps to sense the information of the water quality, its surroundings and communicates the collected data over a network (such as 3G, Wi-Fi etc.) for analysis. The transferred data is of different formats so to produce accurate and complete information, this low-level context information is converted into a higher-level context using a common understandable RDF format discussed in next phase.
- **Context-aware Service Layer:** The middle-tier operates in a bi-directional mode which integrates disparate sensor data to establish a common understanding of context by employing semantic web technologies. This context data serves as key source of information for inferencing and predicting dynamic situations. We have chosen MOWL for knowledge representation in smart water domain. It allows for semantic interpretation of media documents and deals with uncertainties involved in the media manifestations. MOWL uses DBN based probabilistic reasoning to track situations in a dynamic world which is passed on to the next phase depending on which appropriate recommendations are given.

- **Application Layer:** This phase ensures clear and accurate presentation, visualization of resulting information to the users. As the proof-of-concept in the Smart Water application, the derived knowledge from the previous layer is utilized to give appropriate recommendations or warnings to the water authorities to take suitable actions in water deficit areas. The warnings can be disseminated through via e-mail, text messages thus, offering optimum water supply to the users.

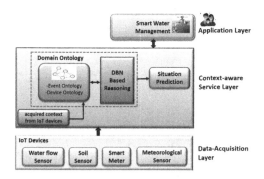

Fig. 3. Smart water architecture

4   Problem Formulation

The outdated water-infrastructure, situations such as drought, flood etc. caused due to randomly occurring climate and monsoon patterns, etc. has led to the emergence of water crisis in urban areas. Therefore, proper water management is required to overcome the imbalances caused by shortage of water. The real-time scenario which addresses the need for proper water management and planning is for example, the two consecutive droughts in Latur Maharashtra, 2016 caused acute water scarcity in the Marathwada region. The absence of timely guidance about the monsoon failure and thus, a lack of management to deal water crisis resulted in death of several farmers. So as a solution to address these shortfalls, we have come up with MOWL based inferential reasoning process in IoT domain. This allows to consider the historical data or past actions along with real-time data to assess the situation responsible for water scarcity and provide timely assistance to water authorities to take immediate actions.

4.1   Theoretical Analysis

This section allows to observe water-specific parameters collected from the distributed sensors so as to provide essential information about the quality of water and take effective decisions based on it. We referred to water quality data available on the site[1] (Avalon Peninsula) and collected samples of Faridabad city

---

[1] http://www.mae.gov.nl.ca/wrmd/ADRS/v6/Graphs_List.asp.

for analysis and assessment of the situation causing shortage of water. The water specific attributes pertaining to the individual datasets are mapped to the ontology concepts leading to updated posterior probabilities in the network. The associated semantics (such as perceiving different water-concentrations and indicators to classify water as clear, hard or acidic) and the dynamic reasoning process helped to infer the real-time situation. For instance, in the former data set the context state *ClearWater* at very time step lead to *NormalWaterSituation* with the probability value of 0.78 while in latter the context state *HardWater* pointed to *ContaminatedWaterSituation* with probability 0.74.

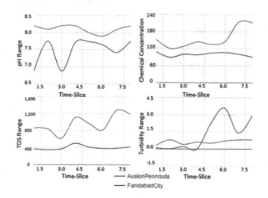

Fig. 4. Plot of few water parameters

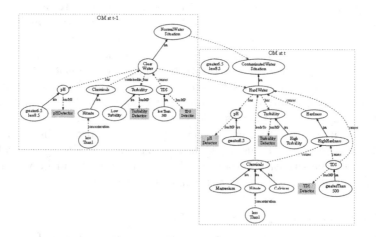

Fig. 5. MOWL based situation tracking

As there was not much variation among the pH values and other water concentrations so at every time stamp the same situations got recognized in both the scenarios. To demonstrate the real time state transitions and dynamicity of the framework for example: *clear water getting contaminated due to exposure to chemical concentrations* we combined few samples from both of the datasets to form a new relevant dataset. Some of the parameters corresponding to the dataset are plotted as shown in Fig. 4. The transition from *ClearWater* to *HardWater* is represented through transition links in the ontology. The use of transition links in the MOWL support setting of prior conditional probabilities for switching between dynamic situations. DBN depicted in Fig. 5 extrapolate results at time step *t-1* and *t* to track the current situation responsible for water crisis. To illustrate the process, let the prior probability of ClearWater and HardWater based on the transition links be P(ClearWater | HighTDS, HighChemicalConcentration, HighTurbidity) = 0.15, P(HardWater | ClearWater, HighTDS, HighChemicalConcentration, HighTurbidity) = 0.95. Following DBN based inferencing scheme, the updated posterior probability obtained for states P(ClearWater) = 0.34 and P(HardWater) = 0.76 which leads to P(NormalWaterSituation) = 0.26 and P(ContaminatedWaterSituation) = 0.68, and contributes to higher possibility of *ContaminatedWaterSituation* over *NormalWaterSituation*. The use of standard Bayesian Network approach would not have been sufficient enough to capture these dynamic transitions. Figure 6 plots the probability estimates for *ContaminatedWaterSituation* and *NormalWaterSituation*. The results shows the abrupt rise in ContaminatedWaterSituation after three time slices due to the presence of evidences affecting water quality based on which alerts can be given to water authorities to take corrective actions for hygienic water-supply, which shows efficacy of our approach.

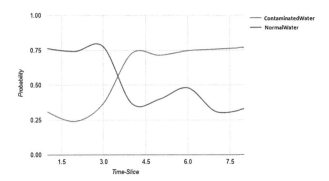

Fig. 6. Probability variation between NormalWaterSituation and ContaminatedWaterSituation

5   Conclusion

We have presented a novel semantic based context-aware framework which can dynamically acquire a range of water-specific information in an IoT environment.

This information constitutes context required for understanding the causal relationships among the concepts and to predict changing situations. The envisioned smart water architecture utilizes MOWL to enable integration and semantic interpretation of complex sensory data. MOWL inferencing with DBN helps to tackle the uncertainties involved in water domain such as change in climate which highly impacts the water service. The proposed approach would assist urban water authorities to grapple with shortfalls causing chronic water crisis under which water management is possible.

References

1. Robles, T., Alcarria, R., Martín, D., Morales, A., Navarro, M., Calero, R., Iglesias, S., López, M.: An internet of things-based model for smart water management. In: 2014 28th International Conference on Advanced Information Networking and Applications Workshops (WAINA), pp. 821–826. IEEE (2014)
2. Xia, F., Yang, L.T., Wang, L., Vinel, A.: Internet of things. Int. J. Commun. Syst. **25**(9), 1101 (2012)
3. Chaudhury, S., Mallik, A., Ghosh, H.: Multimedia Ontology: Representation and Applications. CRC Press, Boca Raton (2015)
4. Chau, K.W.: An ontology-based knowledge management system for flow and water quality modeling. Adv. Eng. Softw. **38**, 172–181 (2007)
5. Muste, M., Mocanu, M.: Interjurisdictional collaboration in water resource management. In: 2016 IEEE International Conference on Automation, Quality and Testing, Robotics (AQTR), pp. 1–6. IEEE (2016)
6. Mallik, A., Tripathi, A., Kumar, R., Chaudhury, S., Sinha, K.: Ontology based context aware situation tracking. In: 2015 IEEE 2nd World Forum on Internet of Things (WF-IoT), pp. 687–692. IEEE (2015)
7. Mihajlovic, V., Petkovic, M.: Dynamic Bayesian networks: a state of the art. University of Twente, Centre for Telematics and Information Technology (2001)
8. Curry, E., Degeler, V., Clifford, E., Coakley, D., Costa, A., Van Andel, S.-J., van de Giesen, N., Kouroupetroglou, C.: Linked water data for water information management (2014)

Structured Prediction of Music Mood with Twin Gaussian Processes

Santosh Chapaneri[(⊠)] and Deepak Jayaswal

St. Francis Institute of Technology, University of Mumbai, Mumbai, India
{santoshchapaneri,djjayaswal}@sfitengg.org

Abstract. Music mood is one of the most frequently used descriptors when people search for music, but due to its subjective nature, it is difficult to accurately estimate mood. In this work, we propose a structured prediction framework to model the valence and arousal dimensions of mood jointly without requiring multiple regressors. A confidence-interval based estimated consensus from crowdsourced annotations is first learned along with reliabilities of various annotators to serve as the ground truth and is shown to perform better than using the average annotation values. A variational Bayesian approach is used to learn the Gaussian mixture model representation for acoustic features. Using an efficient implementation of Twin Gaussian process for structured regression, the proposed work achieves an improvement in R^2 of 9.3% for arousal and 18.2% for valence relative to state-of-the-art techniques.

Keywords: Music mood · Structured prediction · Crowdsourced annotations

1 Introduction

Mood as a music descriptor is frequently used as a social tag and can be used for organizing large music collection on various smart devices thus requiring modern user interfaces for intuitive music selection and automatic playlist generation. However, the perception of music mood is difficult to quantify due to its subjective nature. Dimensional responses across valence and arousal (VA) are preferred over categorical labels to correspond to the internal human representations as well as to effectively cover all possible mood states [1,2]. It is worthwhile to note that these two dimensions are not completely uncorrelated [3], hence a structured prediction framework [4] is needed to computationally model the affective content of music mood.

1.1 Related Work

The task of music mood estimation is an active research topic [5–8] due to its predominant difficulty in accurately characterizing valence and a comprehensive review of this task is presented in [9]. Music mood being a highly subjective phenomena, multiple annotations per each music clip are required through

© Springer International Publishing AG 2017
B.U. Shankar et al. (Eds.): PReMI 2017, LNCS 10597, pp. 647–654, 2017.
https://doi.org/10.1007/978-3-319-69900-4_82

crowdsourcing to capture the variability of responses. An often over-looked (and less reliable) assumption in most supervised learning techniques for music mood estimation is that the average VA value of multiple annotator responses serves as the ground truth. This leads to the problem of truth discovery analysis for finding the estimated consensus among various annotators [5,10,11]. For feature representation, an appropriate prototype is needed for modeling the acoustic features to avoid the curse of dimensionality [7]. The commonly used regression models such as Support Vector Regression (SVR), Adaboost.RT, and Gaussian Process Regression (GPR) do not handle multi-variate responses, thus 2 different models need to be trained for VA responses. GPR [12] has been shown to outperform SVR for music emotion recognition task [13] due to its capability of hyper-parameter learning and also providing uncertainties in output prediction resulting in soft decision which is suitable for music mood data. Recently, structured regression was performed for computer vision tasks (human pose estimation) [4,14] using Twin Gaussian process (TGP) to predict multi-variate output effectively.

The **contributions** of this work are two-fold: first, we develop an algorithm for determining the estimated consensus of VA values from crowdsourced annotations by tackling the long-tail phenomena; second, we use variational Bayesian inference to compute acoustic posterior features and apply them for structured prediction of music mood using TGP at linear computational cost with a *single* regression model.

2   Proposed Methodology

2.1   Crowdsourced Annotations and Estimated Consensus

We use the AMG1608 dataset [15] that contains crowdsourced annotations of 1608 songs annotated by 665 users, along valence and arousal (VA) dimensions with values in the range $[-1,1]$. The distribution of all annotations of this dataset is shown in Fig. 1(a), where we observe that the dataset comprises of music clips with mood that cover the complete range with more annotated clips in the 1st quadrant. Since there is no gold standard response available for each music clip, we must estimate it from the available crowdsourced data. A trivial approach is to compute average values along valence and arousal dimensions, however, this assumes that all annotators are equally reliable which may not be true in practice. Extending the work of learning from crowdsourced data [16] for single-dimension target regression case, we derive a maximum-likelihood solution to determine the two-dimensional estimated consensus as well as the reliability (variance) of each annotator.

Consider the dataset $\mathcal{D} = \{\mathbf{y}_i^1, \mathbf{y}_i^2, \ldots, \mathbf{y}_i^R\}_{i=1}^N$ containing two-dimensional VA responses of N music clips by maximum R annotators. Assume a Gaussian distribution model $\mathcal{N}(\mathbf{y}_i^j | \mathbf{y}_i, \alpha^j)$ with α^j as variance of the jth annotator, $\mathbf{y}_i$ as the unknown VA ground truth, and $\mathbf{y}_i^j$ as the response of jth annotator for i^{th} music clip. The parameters to be estimated are $\theta = \{\alpha, \mathbf{y}\}$ with the likelihood

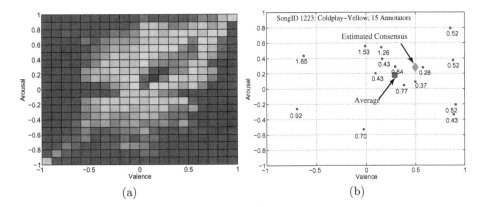

Fig. 1. (a) Annotation distribution of AMG1608 dataset, (b) annotations for a sample clip (*artist*: Coldplay − *song*: Yellow) of AMG1608 with variances of 15 annotators, average and estimated consensus values (Color figure online)

given by Eq. (1) assuming all clips are annotated independently by R annotators. In general, since not all instances will be annotated by each annotator, we define $\mathcal{T}_i$ as the set of annotators providing response for i^{th} clip and $\mathcal{T}_j$ as the set of response provided clips by the jth annotator. Obtaining the gradients of log-likelihood with respect to the parameters results in the maximum likelihood solution given by Eq. (2). This is equivalent to the EM (Expectation-Maximization) algorithm where the E-step determines annotator reliabilities (variances $\hat{\alpha}^j$) and the M-step determines the estimated consensus $\hat{\mathbf{y}}_i$; these two steps are iterated till convergence (e.g. delta change $< 10^{-6}$). The procedure is initialized with $\hat{\mathbf{y}}_i$ as the average of available annotations for i^{th} music clip.

$$P(\mathcal{D}|\boldsymbol{\theta}) = \prod_{i=1}^{N}\prod_{j=1}^{R} \frac{1}{\sqrt{2\pi\alpha^j}} \exp\left[\frac{-1}{2\alpha^j}\|\mathbf{y}_i^j - \mathbf{y}_i\|_2^2\right] \tag{1}$$

$$\hat{\alpha}^j = \frac{1}{|\mathcal{T}_j|}\sum_{i\in\mathcal{T}_j}\|\mathbf{y}_i^j - \hat{\mathbf{y}}_i\|_2^2, \quad \hat{\mathbf{y}}_i = \frac{\sum_{j\in\mathcal{T}_i}\mathbf{y}_i^j/\hat{\alpha}^j}{\sum_{j\in\mathcal{T}_i}1/\hat{\alpha}^j} \tag{2}$$

Since the AMG1608 dataset has the (commonly occurring) long-tail problem, the solution of Eq. (2) will be over-optimistic since very few annotators (36 out of 665) provided response to more than 200 music clips and most of the clips were annotated by few users. To handle this problem, we consider the $(1-\beta)$ confidence interval (CI) of annotator reliability where β is the significance value (e.g. 5%). Since the sum of squares of Gaussian random variables follows a Chi-square distribution, we obtain the $(1-\beta)$ confidence interval given by Eq. (3).

$$\frac{1}{\alpha^j}\sum_{i\in\mathcal{T}_j}\|\mathbf{y}_i^j - \hat{\mathbf{y}}_i\|_2^2 = \frac{|\mathcal{T}_j|\hat{\alpha}^j}{\alpha^j} \sim \chi^2(|\mathcal{T}_j|); \quad CI_{1-\beta} = \left\{\frac{|\mathcal{T}_j|\hat{\alpha}^j}{\chi^2_{(1-\frac{\beta}{2},|\mathcal{T}_j|)}}, \frac{|\mathcal{T}_j|\hat{\alpha}^j}{\chi^2_{(\frac{\beta}{2},|\mathcal{T}_j|)}}\right\} \tag{3}$$

$$\hat{\alpha}^j = \frac{1}{\chi^2_{(\frac{\beta}{2},|\mathcal{T}_j|)}} \sum_{i \in \mathcal{T}_j} \|\mathbf{y}_i^j - \hat{\mathbf{y}}_i\|_2^2, \quad \hat{\mathbf{y}}_i = wMedian\left(\mathbf{y}_i^j, \frac{1}{\hat{\alpha}^j}\right)_{j \in \mathcal{T}_i} \quad (4)$$

From Table 1, we observe that annotator ID 542 and ID 647 obtained similar variance $\hat{\alpha}^j$ with Eq. (2), whereas the upper bound (UB) of confidence interval provides a realistic solution. Also, since outliers may exist in the annotated data, instead of removing these outliers with techniques such as minimum covariance determinant (MCD), we propose to use weighted median which is less sensitive to outliers compared to weighted mean. The resulting equations for estimated consensus are given by Eq. (4), which are iterated till convergence. An example of the estimated consensus for a sample clip of AMG1608 is shown in Fig. 1(b) where we observe that annotators having high variance (less reliability) are given less importance for estimating the consensus, whereas the average value gets biased due to few outliers. To further improve the estimated consensus, dependence on input acoustic features needs to be considered; we leave this for future work.

Table 1. Confidence intervals of estimated annotator reliabilities for AMG1608

AnnotatorID	#Annotations	Variance (2)	95% Conf. Int. (3)
159	924	0.4150	(0.3664, 0,4270)
664	240	0.3879	(0.3143, 0,4247)
216	48	0.3724	(0.2774, 0,5462)
542	**12**	**0.4985**	**(0.2709, 1.0901)**
647	**2**	**0.4981**	**(0.1903, 11.1160)**

2.2 Bayesian Acoustic GMM Feature Representation

For each music clip in the dataset, we compute standard acoustic features across four categories: dynamics (root-mean-square energy), spectral (centroid, spread, skewness, kurtosis, entropy, flatness, 85% roll-off, 95% roll-off, brightness, roughness, irregularity), timbral (zero-crossing rate, flux, 13-dimensional MFCCs, delta MFCCs, delta-delta MFCCs) and tonal (key clarity, musical mode, harmonic change likelihood, 12-bin chroma vector, chroma peak, chroma centroid), resulting in 70-dimensional feature vector per frame of 50 msec duration with 50% overlap [7]. Each feature dimension is normalized to zero mean and unit standard deviation. Block-level features are used to capture temporal characteristics across frames where each block comprises of 16 consecutive frames with overlap of 12 frames. The block-level feature vector $\mathbf{r}_t$ consists of mean and standard deviation of frame-based feature vectors [8]. To represent the block-level features as a fixed dimensional vector, [13] computes the mean and standard deviation across all frames and stacks these into a single vector. For an effective prototypical representation, we adopt the EM-GMM clustering approach of [7] resulting in AGMM (Acoustic Gaussian Mixture Model) posterior probabilities x_{nk} given by Eq. (5), where the universal background model (UBM) parameters $\{\pi_k, \mu_k, \Sigma_k\}$ indicate the weight, mean and covariance of kth latent audio topic (or mixture), and $\mathbf{x}_n$ is the $1 \times K$ acoustic posterior probability feature vector of song s_n consisting of F_n blocks. Using EM algorithm [17], the UBM model is trained with randomly selected 25% block-level feature vectors across the entire dataset (spanning whole range of VA space) resulting in $215,000$ vectors.

$$p(\mathbf{r}_t) = \sum_{k=1}^{K} \pi_k \mathcal{N}\left(\mathbf{r}_t | \mu_k, \Sigma_k\right) ; \ x_{nk} = \frac{1}{F_n} \sum_{t=1}^{F_n} \left(\frac{\pi_k \mathcal{N}\left(\mathbf{r}_t | \mu_k, \Sigma_k\right)}{\sum_{h=1}^{K} \pi_h \mathcal{N}\left(\mathbf{r}_t | \mu_h, \Sigma_h\right)} \right) \quad (5)$$

The most crucial problem of AGMM is determining the exact number of latent audio topics K that can explain the given data. In [7], various values of K (16, 32, 64, 128, 256, 512) were used to determine the regression performance. However, this is ad-hoc as it could lead to over-fitting of data. To determine the optimal number of mixtures, we resort to variational Bayesian inference framework [17] resulting in Bayesian Acoustic GMM (BAGMM) posterior probability feature representation for each music clip. With the Bayesian treatment, all parameters of AGMM are given priors: the weight is assigned Dirichlet prior and mean and covariance are assigned Gaussian-Wishart prior. We refer the reader to [17] (Chap. 10) for detailed formulation of variational posteriors and variational EM algorithm. The algorithm is initialized with α_0 (hyper-parameter of Dirichlet prior) as 0.001, $\mathbf{m}_0$ (hyper-parameter of Gaussian prior) as k-means centroid of training data (to speed up the convergence), and $\mathbf{W}_0$ (hyper-parameter of Wishart prior) as $10\mathbf{I}$ to avoid mixtures getting trapped in local maximum (here, $\mathbf{I}$ is the identity matrix). The expected value of mixing weights in the posterior distribution of BAGMM is given by Eq. (6) with N_k as the responsibility of kth mixture, where we observe that for uninformative priors $(\alpha_0 \to \infty)$, the expected value converges to a small value of ξ $(0 < \xi < 1/K)$.

$$E[\pi_k] = \frac{\alpha_k + N_k}{K\alpha_0 + \sum_{j=1}^{K} N_j} = \frac{\alpha_0 + 2N_k}{K\alpha_0 + N} \approx \frac{\alpha_0/N}{K\alpha_0/N + 1} = \frac{1}{K + N/\alpha_0} \quad (6)$$

BAGMM determines the optimal number of latent audio topics without using cross-validation ($K_{opt} = 117$ in this work), solves the problem of singularity [17] that occurs in AGMM, and prevents over-fitting of data. Each music clip is thus represented as $1 \times K_{opt}$ acoustic posterior probability feature vector $\mathbf{x}_n$, with the corresponding estimated consensus $\hat{\mathbf{y}}_n$ (cf. Sect. 2.1), denoted as $\mathbf{y}_n$ hereafter.

2.3 Structured Prediction

The conventional regression approach of building independently two different regressors does not consider any correlation that may exist in the multi-variate response. From the estimated consensus of AMG1608 dataset, we find that the correlation coefficient between valence and arousal is 0.312, which should be accounted for during training of the regression model. We follow the work of [4] that introduced Twin Gaussian Processes (TGP) with Kullback-Leibler (KL) divergence measure for structured prediction to model not only the input but also the output covariance for effective regression performance. A generalized version of TGP was proposed in [14] with Sharma-Mittal (SM) divergence measure and was shown to perform better than KLTGP for structured prediction. However, both KLTGP and SMTGP suffer from high computational complexity since they need to solve a non-linear optimization problem requiring L-BFGS solver. An efficient approach termed as direct TGP (dTGP) was proposed in [18] that require only $O(N)$ computations compared to $O(N^2)$ of KLTGP and SMTGP.

$$l'_{\mathbf{y}} = \min\left((1 + \lambda_y)\mathbf{1}, \max\left(\mathbf{0}, \hat{\mu} K_Y u_{\mathbf{x}}\right)\right); \ u_{\mathbf{x}} = K_X^{-1} K_X^{\mathbf{x}}; \ \eta = K_X - K_X^{\mathbf{x}T} u_{\mathbf{x}} \quad (7)$$

$$\hat{\mu} = \frac{-\eta + \sqrt{\eta^2 + 4u_{\mathbf{x}}^T K_Y u_{\mathbf{x}} (1 + \lambda_y)}}{2u_{\mathbf{x}}^T K_Y u_{\mathbf{x}}}; \ \hat{\gamma}_m = \frac{l'_{\mathbf{y},m}}{\sum_{m=1}^{M} l'_{\mathbf{y},m}}; \ \mathbf{y}' = \sum_{m=1}^{M} \hat{\gamma}_m \mathbf{y}'_m \quad (8)$$

Given N training instances of input BAGMM feature vectors $\mathbf{X} \in \mathbb{R}^{N \times K_{opt}}$ and corresponding output estimated consensus $\mathbf{Y} \in \mathbb{R}^{N \times 2}$, dTGP optimizes the value of output kernel function $l_{\mathbf{y}} = K_Y^{\mathbf{y}}$ with its solution $l'_{\mathbf{y}}$ shown in Eq. (7) obtained via simple algebra, instead of optimizing for response variable $\mathbf{y}$ directly as is done in KLTGP and SMTGP. To simplify computations, dTGP further finds M nearest neighbors for a specific test input based on $\hat{\gamma}_m$ and computes the predicted bi-variate output $\mathbf{y}'$ as the weighted sum of M nearest training instances ($M = 30$ set empirically) given by Eq. (8). The weight $\hat{\gamma}_m$ captures the input-output as well as between-output correlation for structured prediction [18]. The input and output kernel functions for Gaussian processes are given by Eq. (9) with the kernel parameters (ρ = kernel bandwidth, λ = regularization parameter) determined experimentally via a grid-search [4].

$$K_X\left(\mathbf{x}_i, \mathbf{x}_j\right) = e^{-\frac{\|\mathbf{x}_i - \mathbf{x}_j\|^2}{2\rho_x^2}} + \lambda_x \delta_{ij}; \ K_Y\left(\mathbf{y}_i, \mathbf{y}_j\right) = e^{-\frac{\|\mathbf{y}_i - \mathbf{y}_j\|^2}{2\rho_y^2}} + \lambda_y \delta_{ij} \quad (9)$$

3   Experimental Results

We perform evaluation on AMG1608 dataset with two metrics: R^2 (coefficient of determination) and $RMSE$ (root mean square error) to measure the regression performance between predicted VA values and the estimated consensus.

Table 2 shows the performance of existing state-of-the-art techniques and proposed work. For [13], conventional acoustic features aggregated with mean and standard deviation were used and GPR was used with combination of Squared Exponential and Rational Quadratic kernels [12]. For histogram density modeling (HDM) of mood annotations, the number of latent histograms was set to $K = 256$ as reported in [8]. For [6], conventional acoustic features were used with adaptive aggregation of GP regressors. For GPR [13] and Aggregate GPR [6], two independent regression models were used for valence and arousal estimation with average annotation value set as the ground truth, while HDM [8] needed fine-tuning of number of latent histograms to model each latent audio

Table 2. Performance of estimating music mood with 10-fold cross-validation

Method	R^2_{Arousal}	$RMSE_{\text{Arousal}}$	R^2_{Valence}	$RMSE_{\text{Valence}}$
GPR [13]	0.654 ± 0.058	0.247 ± 0.011	0.429 ± 0.082	0.283 ± 0.073
HDM $(G = 7)$ [8]	0.632 ± 0.045	0.258 ± 0.013	0.352 ± 0.056	0.291 ± 0.027
Aggregate GPR [6]	0.678 ± 0.095	0.203 ± 0.010	0.437 ± 0.053	0.236 ± 0.013
KLTGP [4]	0.717 ± 0.061	0.184 ± 0.015	0.502 ± 0.049	0.237 ± 0.046
SMTGP [14]	$\mathbf{0.721} \pm 0.026$	$\mathbf{0.165} \pm 0.055$	$\mathbf{0.512} \pm 0.028$	$\mathbf{0.224} \pm 0.014$
Proposed	$\mathbf{0.715} \pm 0.022$	$\mathbf{0.172} \pm 0.043$	$\mathbf{0.507} \pm 0.021$	$\mathbf{0.235} \pm 0.037$

topic as well as choice of grid size $G \times G$ to represent the VA space as a heatmap. We evaluate the structured prediction performance of TGPs using the proposed BAGMM feature representation and estimated consensus set as ground truth with a single regression model. Though SMTGP performs slightly better than KLTGP, it incurs quadratic computational complexity due to inversion of kernel matrices during optimization. The performance of proposed work with dTGP is similar to KLTGP but at a linear computational cost. All values were calculated with 10 different combinations of training and test data and the means and standard deviations of these values are reported to measure the performance (10-fold cross-validation). Overall, we observe an improvement in R^2 of 9.3% for arousal and 18.2% for valence relative to GPR [13].

4   Conclusion

A structured prediction framework is presented in this work for affective modeling of music mood using TGPs and is shown to perform better than independently learning different regressors for valence and arousal dimensions. An EM-type algorithm is proposed to determine the confidence-interval based estimated consensus to serve as the ground truth for regression. Using Bayesian inference, acoustic features are represented with BAGMM posterior probabilities where the optimal number of Gaussian mixtures are determined automatically from the training data and the drawback of singularity and over-fitting of conventional GMM is simultaneously avoided. The proposed framework achieves improvement in music mood prediction with direct TGP implementation that achieves optimization with simple algebra and avoids the use of non-linear quadratic optimization of KLTGP and SMTGP. The future work includes deriving estimated consensus by considering dependence of response on input acoustic features and solving the problem of covariate shift [18] across various music mood datasets.

Acknowledgments. The authors thank Yi-Hsuan Yang for sharing the music clips of AMG1608 dataset and Mohamed Elhoseiny for sharing SMTGP implementation via personal communication.

References

1. Hu, X.: Music and mood: Where theory and reality meet. In: Proceedings of the 5th iConference, Chicago, USA (2010)
2. Brinker, B., Dinther, R., Skowronek, J.: Expressed music mood classification compared with valence and arousal ratings. EURASIP J. Audio, Speech Music Process. **24**, 1–14 (2012)
3. Kumar, N., Guha, T., Huang, C., Vaz, C., Narayanan, S.: Novel affective features for multiscale prediction of emotion in music. In: Proceedings of the 18th IEEE International Workshop on Multimedia Signal Processing (MMSP), Montreal, Canada (2016)
4. Bo, L., Sminchisescu, C.: Twin Gaussian processes for structured prediction. Springer Int. J. Comput. Vis. **87**(28), 1–25 (2010)
5. Chin, Y., Wang, J., Wang, J., Yang, Y.: Predicting the probability density function of music emotion using emotion space mapping. IEEE Trans. Affect. Comput. **PP**(99), 1–10 (2016)
6. Fukayama, S., Goto, M.: Music emotion recognition with adaptive aggregation of Gaussian process regressors. In: Proceedings of the 41st IEEE International Conference Acoustics, Speech and Signal Processing (ICASSP), Shanghai, China (2016)
7. Wang, J., Yang, Y., Wang, H., Jeng, S.: Modeling the affective content of music with a Gaussian mixture model. IEEE Trans. Affect. Comput. **6**(1), 56–68 (2015)
8. Wang, J., Wang, H., Lanckriet, G.: A histogram density modeling approach to music emotion recognition. In: Proceedings of the 40th IEEE International Conference on Acoustics, Speech and Signal Processing (ICASSP), Brisbane, Australia (2015)
9. Yang, Y., Chen, H.: Machine recognition of music emotion: a review. ACM Trans. Intell. Syst. Technol. **3**(3), 1–30 (2012)
10. Wan, M., Chen, X., Kaplan, L., Han, J., Gao, J., Zhao, B.: From truth discovery to trustworthy opinion discovery: An uncertainty-aware quantitative modeling approach. In: Proceedings of the 22nd ACM SIGKDD International Conference on Knowledge Discovery and Data Mining, San Francisco, California (2016)
11. Ramakrishna, A., Gupta, R., Grossman, R., Narayanan, S.: An expectation maximization approach to joint modeling of multidimensional ratings derived from multiple annotators. In: INTERSPEECH, San Francisco, USA (2016)
12. Rasmussen, C., Williams, C.: Gaussian Processes for Machine Learning. MIT Press, Cambridge (2006)
13. Markov, K., Matsui, T.: Music genre and emotion recognition using Gaussian processes. IEEE Access **2**, 688–697 (2014)
14. Elhoseiny, M., Elgammal, A.: Generalized twin Gaussian processes using Sharma-Mittal divergence. Springer J. Mach. Learn. **100**(2), 399–424 (2015)
15. Chen, Y., Yang, Y., Wang, J., Chen, H.: The AMG1608 dataset for music emotion recognition. In: Proceedings of the 40th IEEE International Conference on Acoustics, Speech and Signal Processing (ICASSP), Brisbane, Australia (2015)
16. Raykar, V., Yu, S., Zhao, L., Valadez, G., Florin, C., Bogoni, L., Moy, L.: Learning from crowds. J. Mach. Learn. Res. **11**, 1297–1322 (2010)
17. Bishop, C.: Pattern Recognition and Machine Learning. Springer, New York (2006)
18. Yamada, M., Sigal, L., Chang, Y.: Domain adaptation for structured regression. Int. J. Comput. Vis. **109**(2), 126–145 (2014)

Differentiating Pen Inks in Handwritten Bank Cheques Using Multi-layer Perceptron

Prabhat Dansena[1](✉)(iD), Soumen Bag[1](✉)(iD), and Rajarshi Pal[2](iD)

[1] Department of Computer Science and Engineering, Indian Institute of Technology
(Indian School of Mines), Dhanbad, Jharkhand, India
p.dansena23@gmail.com, bagsoumen@gmail.com
[2] Institute for Development and Research in Banking Technology, Hyderabad, India
iamrajarshi@gmail.com

Abstract. In handwritten Bank cheques, addition of new words using similar color pen can cause huge loss. Hence, it is important to differentiate pen ink used in these types of documents. In this work, we propose a non-destructive pen ink differentiation method using statistical features of ink and multi-layer perceptron (MLP) classifier. Large sample of blue and black pen ink is acquired from 112 Bank cheque leaves, written by nine different volunteers using fourteen different blue and black pens. Handwritten words are extracted from scanned cheque images manually. Pen ink pixels are identified using K-means binarization. Fifteen statistical features from each color handwritten words are extracted and are used to formulate the problem as a binary classification problem. MLP classifier is used to train the model for differentiating pen ink in handwritten Bank cheques. The proposed method performs efficiently on both known and unknown pen samples with an average accuracy of 94.6% and 93.5% respectively. We have compared the proposed method with other existing method to show its efficiency.

Keywords: Bank cheques · Handwritten forensics · Ink analysis · $K-$means clustering · MLP · Statistical features

1 Introduction

Forensics in handwritten Bank cheques from the perspective of differentiating pen ink have great importance to the judicial system. In handwritten Bank cheque forensics, it is often important to establish a relation between the pen inks. It helps to identify whether a single pen has been used to write the Bank cheque or multiple pens. Numerous possibilities of fraud exist in handwritten Bank cheques. In this work, we focus only on pen ink differentiation in Bank cheques. Possibilities of fraud in any Bank cheque and its consequences helps to understand the importance of the work.

Example of new words addition in Bank cheque using a different pen is depicted in Fig. 1 which is elaborated as follows. The cheque was initially issued

© Springer International Publishing AG 2017
B.U. Shankar et al. (Eds.): PReMI 2017, LNCS 10597, pp. 655–663, 2017.
https://doi.org/10.1007/978-3-319-69900-4_83

to Mr. Ravi Kumar Singh, amounting to Seventy thousand only. Later, forger appended new words in pay name and amount section as marked by red circles in Fig. 1. This difference in pen ink can not be always perceived by naked eye. This type of case helps us to understand the possibility of addition of new words in handwritten Bank cheques. A number of handwritten document frauds are possible in bill, business agreement, educational documents, etc. This motivates us to differentiate pen ink in Bank cheques.

Fig. 1. Addition of handwritten words (marked by red circles) in a Bank cheque image. (Color figure online)

Pen ink analysis techniques can be categorized in two major pathways: destructive and non-destructive techniques. Merrill and Bartick [1] have used infrared spectrum to differentiate pen ink. Taylor [2] has proposed a method to analyze intersecting lines using stereo microscope, distilled water, and wax lift techniques. Taylor [3] has also proposed TLC plate analysis method using solvent and micro-dispenser for pen ink classification. The second category of technique includes non-destructive techniques, which include modern chromatographic, image processing, and pattern recognition techniques. Khan *et al.* [4] have used spectral response and K-means clustering algorithm for pen ink difference identification. Khan *et al.* [5] have also used Principal Component Analysis for spectral response feature reduction. Then K-means clustering has been done to differentiate pen ink. Dasari and Bhagvati [6] have proposed statistical features of ink pixels from HSV color channel and distance measure based classification is performed. Kumar *et al.* [7,8] have shared statistical features as gray-level co-occurrence (GLCM), geometric, and legendre moments from YC_bC_r and opponent color models. In these methods, nearest neighbor and Support Vector Machine with feature selection have been used as classifiers to differentiate pen ink. Gorai *et al.* [9] have extracted twelve feature images from color input image and corresponding gray version using local binary pattern and Gabor filters. In this method, histograms of pen ink pixels from feature images are calculated and histogram matching has been performed to identify the ink mismatch.

It is observed that most of the works in the area of non-destructive ink analysis ranges from hyper-spectral and microscopic imaging to chromatographic technique. This requires high configuration hardwares those are too costly as well as rarely available in market. In this paper, we have proposed a method that is capable of differentiating pen ink using simple standard scanning devices. Such devices are easily available and at the same time cost effective. In this method, pen ink samples are extracted manually from scanned Bank cheque leaves. K−means binarization has been used to identify ink pixels from each color channel of word images. Statistical features of ink pixels are extracted from each channel. Extracted feature set is used to train the MLP classifier for pen ink difference identification.

The rest of the paper is organized as follows. Section 2 discusses the proposed methodology for pen ink differentiation in handwritten Bank cheques. Experimental results and relevant discussion are presented in Sect. 3. The concluding remarks are given in Sect. 4.

2   Proposed Model

In this proposed method, pair of words have been analyzed to detect whether they have been written by same pen or not. Pen ink differentiation problem is formulated into a binary classification problem where two different pens are used to write on a particular Bank cheque. If two different pens are used to write word-pairs in a same Bank cheque, then it is labeled as class-I; otherwise it is labeled as class-II. The system architecture of the proposed method is depicted in Fig. 2.

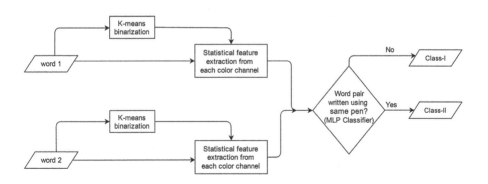

Fig. 2. System architecture of the proposed method.

2.1 K-means Algorithm Based Foreground Pixel Identification

Pen ink pixels (PI) identification is an important task in handwritten Bank cheque for differentiating pen ink. We have used K-means algorithm to binarize the word images for this purpose. Basic idea behind K-means is to minimize the objective function (i.e., inter cluster Euclidean distance), where K is an user defined parameter. In our experiment, we have chosen $K = 2$ to identify PI as foreground pixels. Color handwritten word image extracted from Fig. 1 is taken as input (Fig. 3a) and corresponding gray image is obtained. Gray version of input is used to identify the PI in color handwritten word image. K-means binarization partitions n gray values into K clusters, which separates the foreground from the background. This binarization method is used to identify PI as foreground pixels as depicted in Fig. 3b. This method works well for ink pixels identification because foreground and background intensity profiles are not overlapping in handwritten word images.

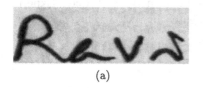
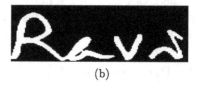

(a)   (b)

Fig. 3. K-means image binarization: (a) Color input image; (b) Binarized output image.

2.2   Extraction of Statistical Features from Ink Pixels

Once coordinates of ink pixels (i, j) are identified using K-means binarization, following five statistical features are extracted from each color channel of ink pixels.

(a) Mean:- The Mean ($\bar{m}$) for ink pixels is defined by

$$\bar{m} = \frac{m_{xy}}{N}, \text{ where} \tag{1}$$

$$m_{xy} = \sum_{j=0}^{y} \sum_{i=0}^{x} w_k(i,j) \mid (i,j)\epsilon PI \tag{2}$$

$$N = \sum_{j=0}^{y} \sum_{i=0}^{x} 1 \mid (i,j)\epsilon PI \tag{3}$$

(b) Variance:- The Variance (Var) for ink pixels is defined by

$$Var = \frac{1}{N-1} \sum_{j=0}^{y} \sum_{i=0}^{x} [w_k(i,j) - \bar{m}]^2 \mid (i,j)\epsilon PI \tag{4}$$

(c) Skewness:- The Skewness ($Skew$) for ink pixels is defined by

$$Skew = \frac{1}{N} \sum_{j=0}^{y} \sum_{i=0}^{x} \left[\frac{w_k(i,j) - \bar{m}}{\sqrt{Var}} \right]^3 \mid (i,j)\epsilon PI \tag{5}$$

(d) Kurtosis:- The Kurtosis $(Kurt)$ for ink pixels is defined by

$$Kurt = \left\{ \tfrac{1}{N} \sum_{j=0}^{y} \sum_{i=0}^{x} \left[\tfrac{w_k(i,j) - \bar{m}}{\sqrt{Var}} \right]^4 - 3 \right\} \mid (i,j) \epsilon PI \qquad (6)$$

(e) Mean Absolute Deviation:- The Mean Absolute Deviation (MAD) for ink pixels is defined by

$$MAD = \tfrac{1}{N} \sum_{j=0}^{y} \sum_{i=0}^{x} |w_k(i,j) - \bar{m}| \mid (i,j) \epsilon PI \qquad (7)$$

Where N is total number of foreground pixels, defined by the Eq. 3. Foreground pixels of handwritten word $(w(i,j))$ is defined by PI using K-means binarization. Handwritten word from each color channel R, G, and B are denoted by $w_k(i,j)$, where $k = \{R, G, B\}$ and (i,j) is coordinates of ink pixels.

2.3   Differentiation of Pen Ink Using MLP Classifier

MLP classifier is used for differentiating pen inks. MLP architecture with input layer, output layer, and one hidden layer with seventeen computational nodes is considered for our experimental purpose. Sigmoid activation function is used in our MLP architecture. Features from two words under consideration are fed into the MLP network to identify whether same pen has been used or not. This MLP architecture is trained with 5000 iterations at learning rate $\alpha = 0.2$. Post training MLP architecture is used for classification of known and unknown pen samples.

3   Experimental Results and Discussion

3.1   Data Set Acquisition

Data is extracted from the IDRBT Cheque Image Dataset [10] with diverse texture and ink color. Total 112 cheque leaves from four different Indian Banks are used as source document. In order to simulate the pen ink difference in cheque leaves, seven blue and seven black pens are used. To avoid biasness due to writing, nine different volunteers have taken active participation to prepare data set. A total of $14 \times 9 = 126$ pen−volunteer combinations (fourteen pens and nine volunteers) are used for pen ink data generation. In practical scenario, similar color pens are used for addition of new words in source document. Each cheque is written by two volunteers using two different pens (either blue or black). Hence, data set is created with $2 \times 7_{C_2} = 42$ possible combinations of blue and black pens. All the cheque leaves are scanned in normal scanner at 300 dpi resolution. Handwritten words from each scanned cheque are cropped manually and grouped based on pen used to write the words.

Table 1. Proposed method accuracy for known and unknown pen.

S.N	Pen Combination kept out	Known Pen Accuracy(%)	Unknown Pen Accuracy(%)
1	$P_1 P_2$	93.34	93.85
2	$P_1 P_3$	95.37	93.07
3	$P_1 P_4$	94.02	93.52
4	$P_1 P_5$	94.86	93.65
5	$P_1 P_6$	94.42	94.13
6	$P_1 P_7$	94.80	93.10
7	$P_2 P_3$	95.68	93.29
8	$P_2 P_4$	93.96	93.54
9	$P_2 P_5$	95.33	93.46
10	$P_2 P_6$	95.39	92.95
11	$P_2 P_7$	95.57	93.63
12	$P_3 P_4$	95.50	92.49
13	$P_3 P_5$	96.11	93.10
14	$P_3 P_6$	95.77	93.74
15	$P_3 P_7$	96.75	92.83
16	$P_4 P_5$	94.86	93.56
17	$P_4 P_6$	94.96	92.71
18	$P_4 P_7$	95.19	93.25
19	$P_5 P_6$	96.94	92.69
20	$P_5 P_7$	96.01	92.22
21	$P_6 P_7$	94.89	93.09
22	$P_8 P_9$	94.53	93.61
23	$P_8 P_{10}$	93.81	94.40
24	$P_8 P_{11}$	92.90	93.91
25	$P_8 P_{12}$	94.32	94.11
26	$P_8 P_{13}$	93.57	93.68
27	$P_8 P_{14}$	93.32	94.41
28	$P_9 P_{10}$	94.80	93.73
29	$P_9 P_{11}$	94.42	92.72
30	$P_9 P_{12}$	95.66	93.25
31	$P_9 P_{13}$	93.48	93.74
32	$P_9 P_{14}$	94.13	94.39
33	$P_{10} P_{11}$	94.12	93.13
34	$P_{10} P_{12}$	94.47	93.97
35	$P_{10} P_{13}$	94.58	93.83
36	$P_{10} P_{14}$	93.65	93.23
37	$P_{11} P_{12}$	94.47	94.23
38	$P_{11} P_{13}$	93.39	93.46
39	$P_{11} P_{14}$	92.62	93.32
40	$P_{12} P_{13}$	94.25	93.52
41	$P_{12} P_{14}$	95.20	93.95
42	$P_{13} P_{14}$	91.86	94.58
Average Accuracy	-	**94.60**	**93.50**

3.2   Experimental Set-up

In each cheque, two pens P_i and P_j are used for writing m and n number of different words respectively. Set W_{p_i} and W_{p_j} contains words written by P_i and

P_j respectively, where $W_{P_i} = \{m_1, m_2, \ldots, m_m\}$ and $W_{P_j} = \{n_1, n_2, \ldots, n_n\}$. The word pairs written by different and same pens are considered in case-I and case-II respectively.

Case-I: Two different pens are used to write the word pairs. The Cartesian product of $W_{P_i} \times W_{P_j} + W_{P_j} \times W_{P_i}$ includes the total number of word-pairs written using different pens, where $W_{P_i} \times W_{P_j} = \{(m_i, n_j) \mid m_i \in W_{P_i} \wedge n_j \in W_{P_j}\}$ and $W_{P_j} \times W_{P_i} = \{(n_j, m_i) \mid n_j \in W_{P_j} \wedge m_i \in W_{P_i}\}$. Thus, total number of word-pairs for class-I will be $2 \times (m \times n)$.

Case-II: Same pen is used to write the word pairs. The Cartesian product of $W_{P_i} \times W_{P_i} + W_{P_j} \times W_{P_j}$ includes the total number of word-pairs written using same pen, where $W_{P_i} \times W_{P_i} = \{(m_i, m_i) \mid m_i \in W_{P_i}\}$ and $W_{P_j} \times W_{P_j} = \{(n_j, n_j) \mid n_j \in W_{P_j}\}$. Thus, total number of word-pairs for class-II will be $\{(m \times m)\text{-}m\} + \{(n \times n)\text{-}n\}$, after excluding the pairs of word with itself. For each cheque, total instances of class-I and class-II are calculated and stored. The number of word pairs for case-I and case-II in Fig. 1 can be calculated as follows. Set of words written using pens P_1 and P_2 are $W_{P_1} = \{\text{J, Two, lakh}\}$ and $W_{P_2} = \{\text{Ravi, Kumar, Singh, Seventy, thousand}\}$ respectively. The total number of word pairs for case-I are $(3 \times 5) + (5 \times 3) = 30$. The number of word pairs belongs to the case-II are $(\{3 \times 3\} - 3) + \{(5 \times 5) - 5\} = 26$. Thus, total instances including class-I (30) and class-II (26) are $30 + 26 = 56$.

To simulate pen ink difference identification, seven blue and seven black pens are used on Bank cheques. Each instance has thirty features and a class value. For each instance, $2 \times 15 = 30$ features are extracted from each handwritten word pair under consideration. The whole data set is divided into three subsets, namely training, validation, and test set using leave-k-out method. $K = 2$ is used to keep two unknown pen samples out for testing and performance evaluation of MLP classifier. Keeping two pens out, total possibilities are $2 \times 7_{C_2} = 42$ for both blue and black pen samples. Remaining data set after excluding the test subset is partitioned into ten approximately equal parts. One of ten data parts is kept as validation set remaining partitions are used as training set. The process of selecting validation set is repeated ten times, with each one of the ten data parts exactly once. Training set is used to train the MLP model inter and intra class difference. Validation is performed to check MLP classifier performance on known pen ink samples. Model testing is performed on the test set to check the performance of the MLP model on unknown pen ink samples.

3.3 Experimental Results and Comparison

We evaluate the performance of the binary classification problem for differentiating pen ink in handwritten Bank cheque. Both blue and black pen average accuracy of MLP classifier is presented in Table 1 for known and unknown pen samples, where P_1–P_7 and P_8–P_{14} are black and blue pens respectively. To show the efficiency of the proposed work, result analysis is performed using leave 2 pen out method. The average accuracy on both blue and black pen of MLP classifier is 94.60% and 93.50% for known and unknown pen samples respectively.

Table 2. Comparison in between proposed and existing method.

Method	Black Pen Accuracy(%)	Blue Pen Accuracy(%)	Average Accuracy(%)
Gorai *et al.* [9]	54.71	54.8	54.76
Proposed method	**93.77**	**93.23**	**93.50**

We have compared our result with Gorai *et al.* [9], which introduced technique for ink analysis and difference identification using simple scanning devices. Moreover, this method [9] did not take biasness due to writer into consideration. Our proposed method has taken this issue into consideration and provides better results than the previous one. A comparative analysis of proposed method with method in [9] is presented in Table 2.

4   Conclusion

In this paper, we have proposed pen ink difference identification method in handwritten Bank cheques. Differentiation of pen ink problem is formulated as a binary classification problem. Thirty features for each instance of word pair are extracted. These extracted features are used to train the MLP classifier on known pen ink pixels. Performance of MLP classifier is evaluated on both known and unknown pen ink pixels. Result analysis and comparison shows the superiority of the proposes method over the existing method on both black and blue pen samples.

Acknowledgment. A part of this work is sponsored by the project "Design and Implementation of Multiple Strategies to Identify Handwritten Forgery Activities in Legal Documents" (No. ECR/2016/001251, Dt.16.03.2017), SERB, Govt. of India.

References

1. Merrill, R.A., Bartick, E.G.: Analysis of ball pen inks by diffuse reflectance infrared spectrometry. J. Forensic Sci. **29**(1), 92–98 (1992)
2. Taylor, L.R.: Intersecting lines as a means of fraud detection. J. Forensic Sci. **37**(2), 528–541 (1984)
3. Taylor, L.R.: Developments in the analysis of writing inks on questioned documents. J. Forensic Sci. **37**(2), 612–619 (1992)
4. Khan, Z., Shafait, F., Mian, A.: Hyperspectral imaging for ink mismatch detection. In: Proceedings of the International Conference on Document Analysis and Recognition, pp. 877–881 (2013)
5. Khan, Z., Shafait, F., Mian, A.: Automatic ink mismatch detection for forensic document analysis. Pattern Recogn. **48**(11), 3615–3626 (2015)
6. Dasari, H., Bhagvati, C.: Identification of non-black inks using HSV color spaces. In: Proceedings of the International Conference on Document Analysis and Recognition, pp. 486–490 (2007)

7. Kumar, R., Pal, N.R., Sharma, J.D., Chanda, B.: A novel approach for detection of alteration in ball pen writings. In: Proceedings of International Conference on Pattern Recognition and Machine Intelligence, pp. 400–405 (2009)

8. Kumar, R., Pal, N.R., Sharma, J.D., Chanda, B.: Forensic detection of fraudulent alteration in ball-point pen strokes. IEEE Trans. Inf. Forensics Secur. **7**(2), 809–820 (2012)

9. Gorai, A., Pal, R., Gupta, P.: Document fraud detection by ink analysis using texture features and histogram matching. In: International Joint Conference on Neural Networks, pp. 4512–4517 (2016)

10. IDRBT Cheque Image Dataset: http://www.idrbt.ac.in/icid.html

Analysis of Causal Interactions and Predictive Modelling of Financial Markets Using Econometric Methods, Maximal Overlap Discrete Wavelet Transformation and Machine Learning: A Study in Asian Context

Indranil Ghosh[1](✉) ⓘ, Manas K. Sanyal[2] ⓘ, and R.K. Jana[3] ⓘ

[1] Department of Operations Management, Calcutta Business School, Kolkata, India
fri.indra@gmail.com
[2] Department of Business Administration, University of Kalyani, Kalyani, India
manas_sanyal@klyuniv.ac.in
[3] Indian Institute of Management Raipur, Raipur 492015, CG, India
rkjana1@gmail.com

Abstract. Proper understanding of dynamics of equity markets in long run and short run is extremely critical for investors, speculators and arbitrageurs. It is essential to delve into causal interrelationships among different financial markets in order to assess the impact of ongoing inter country trades and forecast future movements. In this paper, initially effort has been made to comprehend the nature of temporal movements and interactions among four Asian stock indices namely, Bombay Stock Exchange (BSE), Taiwan Stock Exchange (TWSE), Jakarta Stock Exchange (JSX) and Korea Composite Stock Price Exchange (KOSPI) through conventional Econometric and Statistical methods. Subsequently a granular forecasting model comprising Maximal Overlap Discrete Wavelet Transformation (MODWT) and Support Vector Regression (SVR) has been utilized to predict the future prices of the respective indices in univariate framework.

1 Introduction

Financial markets representing developed and emerging economies largely influence intraday trading, portfolio construction and rebalancing, volatility trading in options markets, resource allocation, etc. [1–3]. Market is said to be inefficient if it is governed by distinct pattern consists of trend and periodic components thus enabling investors to wreak mayhem. Due to globalization, ease of investing in financial assets of other countries, trades, penetration of foreign institutional investors (FII) etc. shocks and volatility transmit from one country to other. So apart from evaluating individual markets to test random walk hypothesis and judging statistical properties, it is essential to study the interrelationships of different markets as well. The key endeavors of this research work are to present an integrated framework to critically extract the key characteristics of temporal behavior financial markets, to assess their causal interactions and to develop predictive model for forecasting future figures. Four Asian financial markets, Bombay Stock Exchange

© Springer International Publishing AG 2017
B.U. Shankar et al. (Eds.): PReMI 2017, LNCS 10597, pp. 664–672, 2017.
https://doi.org/10.1007/978-3-319-69900-4_84

(BSE), Taiwan Stock Exchange (TWSE), Jakarta Stock Exchange (JSX) and Korea Composite Stock Price Exchange (KOSPI) have been considered in this study. To critically examine the nexus among four indices, Pearson's correlation coefficient and cross correlation function (CCF) for checking correlations at different lags have been calculated to carry out systematic test of association. Granger causality (GC) analysis has been performed to decode the causal interactions. Next, maximal overlap discrete wavelet transformation (MODWT) is applied to decompose the stock indices into linear (detail part) and nonlinear (approximation part) components to deal with nonlinearity and presence of other erratic features in financial time series. Then support vector regression (SVR), a kernel based advanced machine learning algorithm, has been applied on decomposed components to discover the inherent patterns and make predictions. Final forecast is obtained by aggregating the obtained forecasts from individual components. As it has been well argued that the global financial markets often exhibit high volatility due to various macroeconomic and other events [4, 5]. Hence traditional forecasting models viz. autoregressive moving average (ARMA), autoregressive integrated moving average (ARIMA), autoregressive conditional heteroscedasticity (ARCH), autoregressive distributed lag (ARDL) models, etc. fail to yield good forecasts. That is why MODWT-SVR based approach has been considered in this study for predictive modelling as MODWT assists in identifying the significant nonlinear components in time series and accordingly the parameters of SVR can be well tuned to capture the pattern.

Rest of the article is planned as follows. Section 2 briefly discusses the relevant literature. Overview of the data and empirical findings are presented in Sect. 3. Causality analysis through statistical and econometric tools are narrated in Sect. 4. Section 5 elucidates the MODWT and SVR in details. Results of applied predictive modelling are highlighted and discussed in Sect. 6. Finally we conclude the paper in Sect. 7 mentioning the future research scopes.

2 Related Work

Due to its attached importance in overall economic development of a country, financial market has garnered lot of attention among academicians and practitioners worldwide. Liu and Morley [6] showed the supremacy of performance of generalized autoregressive conditional heteroscedasticity (GARCH) models in predicting the historical volatility of Hang Seng index over traditional historical average method. Sharma and Vipul [7] made a comparative research utilizing GARCH and exponential GARCH (EGARCH) models to predict conditional variance of sixteen international stock indices for a period of about fourteen years. Priyadarshini and Babu [8] utilized conventional rescaled range (R/S) analysis to estimate Hurst exponent and fractal dimensional index to investigate whether Indian stock market and mutual funds follows random walk or fractional Brownian motion. Findings strongly suggested that they followed Fractional Brownian Motion. Yin et al. [9] studied fractal nature of Chinese gold market applied both single fractal model and multi fractal detrended fluctuation analysis (MFDFA) model and identified the key responsible factors for multi fractal characteristics of the said market. Sun et al. [10] applied partition function based multifractal analysis to analyze the multifractal nature of Hang Seng Index (HSI) data for individual trading days for the timespan of January 3, 1994 to May 28, 1997. Lahmiri [11] used DWT and back propagation neural network (BPNN) that outperformed traditional ARMA model for predictive modelling of S&P 500 price index and closing prices of six different stocks during February 28, 2011 to March 11, 2011. Ramsey and Zhang [12] adopted wavelet decomposition to comprehend and model the foreign exchange rate dynamics. Study made by Gencay et al. [13] showed the effectiveness of Wavelet filtering to deal with nonstationary and time varying features of time series. Ben Ammou and Ben Mabrouk [14] carried out wavelet analysis to assess the nexus between stock returns and systematic risk in the capital asset pricing model. Jothimani et al. [15] proposed a novel framework combining MODWT and state-of-the-arts machine learning models namely, artificial neural network (ANN) and SVR to carry out predictive modelling exercise on NIFTY Index during September 2007 to July 2015.

3   Data and Empirical Results

We have collected the daily closing prices of BSE, TWSE, JSX and KOSPI during April 20, 2010 to April 20, 2017 from Yahoo Finance data repository for analysis. Before proceeding with the causal association analysis and predictive modelling some key statistical properties have been estimated to get deeper insights about the nature of temporal movements of the considered indices as shown in Table 1.

Table 1. Key properties of BSE, TWSE, JSX and KOSPI

Measures	BSE	TWSE	JSX	KOSPI
Mean	22152.91	8417.477	4451.828	1964.747
Median	20425.02	8435.329	4499.108	1978.13
Maximum	29974.24	9973.084	5680.239	2228.96
Minimum	15175.08	6633.306	2514.044	1560.83
Std. dev.	4349.962	749.9225	688.5594	103.7268
Skewness	0.246451	−0.06122	−0.41591	−0.67622
Kurtosis	1.487282	2.100136	2.426667	3.894359
Jarque-Bera	182.7786***	59.45067***	72.72089***	189.8351***
Shapiro-Wilk test	0.8911***	0.9811***	0.9676***	0.9691***
ADF test	−0.73805#	−1.97070#	−1.66328#	−3.79419**
PP test	−0.68139#	−1.80331#	−1.62591#	−3.72562**
ARCH LM test	3594.340***	3.606*	14.821***	0.007#
Hurst exponent	0.8820	0.8857	0.8775	0.8837

***Significant at 1% level of significance, **Significant at 5% level of significance, *Significant at 10% level of significance, #Not Significant.

Jarque-Bera and Shapiro-Wilk test statistic reveal that none of the indices adhere to normal distribution. Augmented-Dickey-Fuller (ADF) and Philips-Peron (PP) tests confirm that except KOSPI, other three induces are not stationary. ARCH-Lagrange multiplier (LM) test suggests the presence of conditional heteroscedasticity in BSE, TWSE and JSX. As the estimated values of Hurst Exponent for all four indices are well above 0.5, inferences can be drawn that the indices are governed by biased random walk or fractional Brownian motion.

4 Test of Associations and Causal Interactions

To identify and determine the impact of nexus among the four stock indices Pearson's correlation and GC tests have been performed to execute systematic check of association and causality. Results of bivariate pointwise correlation to measure association are tabulated below (Table 2).

Table 2. Pearson's correlation test

Pairs	Correlation coefficient	Significance
BSE and TWSE	0.794	**
BSE and JSX	0.790	**
BSE and KOSPI	0.459	**
TWSE and JSX	0.634	**
TWSE and KOSPI	0.670	**
JSX and KOSPI	0.515	**

**Significant at 5% level.

Table 3. Results of lag selection

Lag	LR	FPE	AIC	SC	HQ
1	27976.56	2.11E + 14	44.33592	44.40000*	44.35964*
2	36.58604	2.11E + 14	44.3331	44.44844	44.3758
3	43.16432	2.09E + 14	44.32633	44.49292	44.38801
4	46.60691	2.07E + 14	44.31744	44.53529	44.3981
5	48.84663	2.05E + 14	44.30716	44.57626	44.40679
6	64.95924	2.01E + 14	44.28716	44.60753	44.40577
7	101.9001	1.93E + 14	44.24493	44.61655	44.38252
8	74.11622	1.88E + 14*	44.21924*	44.64213	44.37581
9	28.07441	1.88E + 14	44.22119	44.69533	44.39673
10	29.60939*	1.89E + 14	44.22216	44.74757	44.41669
11	13.10434	1.91E + 14	44.23309	44.80975	44.44659
12	18.61316	1.92E + 14	44.24065	44.86857	44.47313

*Indicates lag order selected by the criterion, LR: sequential modified LR test statistic (each test at 5% level), FPE: Final prediction error, AIC: Akaike information criterion, SC: Schwarz information criterion, HQ: Hannan-Quinn information criterion.

It is quite evident that significant high positive associations exist between BSE-TWSE, BSE-JSX, TWSE-JSX and TWSE-KOSPI pairs. However mere study of association cannot provide insights related to existing causal influence among each other. To examine causal interactions, GC test in pair wise manner has been conducted. It is well known that outcome of GC test is highly sensitive to the lag order of the variables which also termed as structural instability. To overcome this problem, lag order selection criteria in vector auto regression (VAR) framework is utilized to find appropriate leg length. Table 3 portrays the results.

Minimum AIC value corresponds to lag order of 8. Hence GC test has been performed keeping lag order of 8. Table 4 narrates the findings of causality analysis.

Table 4. Findings of causality analysis

Null hypothesis	F-Statistic	Probability
TWSE does not Granger Cause BSE	3.16377	0.0015
BSE does not Granger Cause TWSE	5.30035	0.0000
JSX does not Granger Cause BSE	1.43128	0.1784
BSE does not Granger Cause JSX	1.7662	0.0793
KOSPI does not Granger Cause BSE	6.02818	0.0000
BSE does not Granger Cause KOSPI	1.08244	0.3724
JSX does not Granger Cause TWSE	3.83517	0.0002
TWSE does not Granger Cause JSX	2.11015	0.0320
KOSPI does not Granger Cause TWSE	23.5388	0.0000
TWSE does not Granger Cause KOSPI	1.43937	0.1751
KOSPI does not Granger Cause JSX	1.41008	0.1872
JSX does not Granger Cause KOSPI	3.12493	0.0016

It can be observed that there exists a bidirectional causal interaction between the pairs TWSE-BSE and JSX-BSE at 5% level of significance. KOSPI is found to have significant unidirectional causal influence on BSE. Similarly TWSE is significantly influenced by KOSPI. Only JSX is observed to possess significant causal influence over KOSPI.

5   Methodology for Predictive Modelling

5.1   Maximal Overlap Discrete Wavelet Transform (MODWT)

It is a novel filtering technique that segregates a time series observations into coefficients related to variation over a set of scales while preserving orthogonality to carry out multiresolution analysis. Basically it decomposes any time series data into a nonlinear (approximation) component and a series of linear components (details). In the wavelet analysis, the original function is translated and dilated onto father and mother wavelets at different scales. The mother wavelets account for the details part having unit energy and zero mean while the father wavelet defines the approximations part with mean value of one. There are several advantages of MODWT over DWT for decomposition of time series. First of all, unlike DWT, MODWT does not require the dataset to be dyadic. Secondly it is also invariant to circular shift.

5.2 Support Vector Regression

It is a kernel based machine learning model which has been widely used in various predictive modelling problems. Originated by Vapnik [16], it performs regression tasks [17, 18] to analyze the nonlinear patterns by projecting the original data set into high dimensional feature space and finding linear separation boundary in high dimensional space via quadratic optimization process. The input data $x_i \in R^p$ is first mapped onto a high dimensional feature space using a nonlinear mapping function $\phi(x)$ and then a linear model is constructed in this space with a weight w and bias b given by Eq. 1.

$$f(x) = w^T \phi(x) + b \tag{1}$$

6 Results and Analysis

In this research, 'haar' wavelets are used for six levels of decomposition in MODWT framework for individual stock indices. The following figures graphically illustrate the MODWT decomposition of BSE, TWSE, JSX and KOSPI (Figs. 1, 2, 3 and 4).

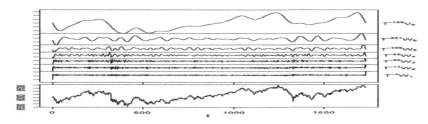

Fig. 1. Wavelets of BSE index

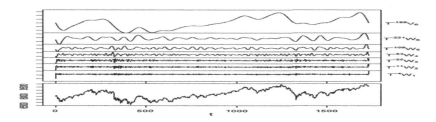

Fig. 2. Wavelets of TWSE

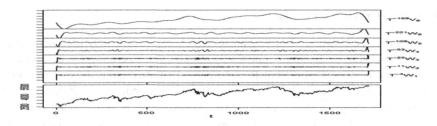

Fig. 3. Wavelets of JSX

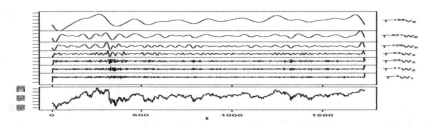

Fig. 4. Wavelets of KOSPI

To evaluate the performance of predictive modelling, three quantitative measures namely, Nash Schutcliffe Coefficients (NSE), Index of Agreement (IA) and Theil Inequality (TI) are computed. The value of NSE range between $-\infty$ to 1. Essentially closer the value of NSE to 1, better is the predictive performance. The range of IA lies between 0 (no fit) and 1 (perfect fit). TI value should be close to 0 for good prediction while a value close to 1 implies no prediction at all. Parameters of the SVR algorithm have been varied to perform ten experimental trials. Average values of the performance measures have been reported here. Table 5 summarizes the predictive performance of univariate MODWT-SVR framework considering one day lagged, two days lagged, three days lagged and four days lagged values as predictors.

Table 5. Predictive performance of MODWT-SVR

Index	Performance evaluator (training dataset)		
	NSE	IA	TI
BSE	0.9924	0.999	0.0059
TWSE	0.9947	0.9994	0.0052
JSX	0.9931	0.9982	0.0063
KOSPI	0.9886	0.9976	0.0087
Index	Performance evaluator (test dataset)		
	NSE	IA	TI
BSE	0.9904	0.9975	0.0077
TWSE	0.9911	0.9972	0.0087
JSX	0.9894	0.9954	0.0096
KOSPI	0.9835	0.9939	0.0113

As the values of NSE and IA are very close to 1 and TI values are substantially low for MODWT-SVR framework on both train and test data set, it is evident that the future prices of BSE, TWSE, JSX and KOSPI can be predicted with high degree of precision.

7   Conclusion and Future Scope

In this paper, an integrated research framework is presented to study the temporal dynamics, causal interrelationships and to perform predictive modelling in financial markets of selected countries in Asia. The MODWT-SVR based univariate framework can effectively be applied to predict future movements. Causality analysis assists heavily to understand nature of influence of one stock market to another which eventually can lead into proper construction of portfolios. Long run co-movements of the stock indices can be analyzed using Johansen's co-integration test. Also other advanced Machine Learning algorithms such as random forest (RF), multiple adaptive regression splines (MARS), elastic net (EN), adaptive boosting (AdaBoost), etc. can be utilized in conjugation with MODWT for forecasting performance and comparative performance study can be made.

References

1. Cajueiro, D.O., Tabak, B.M.: Evidence of long-range dependence in Asian equity markets: the role of liquidity and market restrictions. Phys. A Stat. Mech. Appl. **342**, 656–664 (2004)
2. Fallahpour, S., Zadeh, M.H., Lakvan, E.N.: Use of clustering approach for portfolio management. Int. SAMANM J. Finan. Account. **2**, 115–136 (2014)
3. Guhathakurta, K.: Investigating the nonlinear dynamics of emerging and developed stock markets. J. Eng. Sci. Technol. Rev. **8**, 65–71 (2015)
4. Wang, J., Ma, J.-H.: Gold markets price analysis and application studies based on complexity theories. Complex Syst. Complex. Sci. **5**, 54–59 (2011)
5. Srinivasan, P.: Modelling and forecasting time-varying conditional volatility of Indian stock market. IUP J. Finan. Risk Manag. **12**, 49–64 (2015)
6. Liu, W., Morley, B.: Volatility forecasting in the Hang Seng index using the GARCH approach. Asia-Pacific Finan. Market **16**, 51–63 (2009)
7. Sharma, P., Vipul: Forecasting stock market volatility using realized GARCH model: international evidence. Q. Rev. Econ. Finan. **59**, 222–230 (2016)
8. Priyadarshini, E., Chandra Babu, A.: Fractal analysis of Indian financial markets: an empirical approach. Asia-Pacific J. Manag. Res. Innov. **8**, 271–281 (2012)
9. Yin, K., Zhang, H., Zhang, W., Wei, Q.: Fractal analysis of gold market in China. Rom. J. Econ. Forecast. **16**, 144–163 (2013)
10. Sun, X., Chen, H.P., Yuan, Y.Z., Wu, Z.Q.: Predictability of multifractal analysis of Hang Seng stock index in Hong Kong. Phys. A Stat. Mech. Appl. **301**, 473–482 (2001)
11. Lahmiri, S.: Wavelet low- and high-frequency components as features for predicting stock prices with backpropagation neural networks. J. King Saud Univ. Comput. Inf. Sci. **26**, 218–227 (2014)
12. Ramsey, J.B., Zhang, Z.: The analysis of Foreign exchange data using waveform dictionaries. J. Empirical Finan. **4**, 341–372 (1997)

13. Gençay, R., Selçuk, F., Whitcher, B.: Multiscale systematic risk. J. Int. Money Finan. **24**, 55–70 (2005)
14. Abounoori, E., Elmi, Z., Nademi, Y.: Forecasting Tehran stock exchange volatility; Markov switching GARCH approach. Phys. A Stat. Mech. Appl. **445**, 264–282 (2016)
15. Jothimoni, D., Shankar, R., Yadac, S.S.: Discrete wavelet transformation-based prediction of stock index: a study on national stock exchange fifty index. J. Finan. Manag. Anal. **28**, 35–49 (2015)
16. Vapnik, V.: The Nature of Statistical Learning Theory. Springer, New York (1995)
17. Aich, U., Banerjee, S.: Modeling of EDM responses by support vector machine regression with parameters selected by particle swarm optimization. Appl. Math. Model. **38**, 2800–2818 (2014)
18. Markovic, N., Milinkovic, S., Tikhonov, K.S., Schonfeld, P.: Analyzing passenger train arrival delays with support vector regression. Transp. Res. Part C **56**, 251–262 (2015)

Opinion Mining Using Support Vector Machine with Web Based Diverse Data

Mir Shahriar Sabuj[1]([✉])[iD], Zakia Afrin[2][iD], and K. M. Azharul Hasan[1][iD]

[1] Department of Computer Science and Engineering,
Khulna University of Engineering and Technology, Khulna, Bangladesh
shahriar052@gmail.com, azhasan@gmail.com
[2] Department of Computer Science and Engineering,
Northern University Bangladesh, Dhaka, Bangladesh
zakia_afrin@outlook.com

Abstract. Opinions of other people always carry a very important source of information that has a major impact on the entire decision making process. With the emerging availability and popularity of online reviews, opinions, feedback and suggestions, people now actively employ these views for better decision making. Opinion mining is a natural language processing and information extraction task that aims to examine people's opinions, sentiments, emotions and attitudes about a product. This paper presents an opinion classifier based on Support Vector Machines (SVM) algorithm that can be used to analyze data for classifying opinions. We design a classifier to determine opinion from Bangla text data. We evaluate the performance and analyze comparative results.

Keywords: Machine learning · Supervised learning · Opinion mining · Support vector machine · Sentiment detection · Opinion strength · Text classification

1 Introduction

The opinion of others has a great impact on most of us while we make a decision. With the availability of World Wide Web, now we can easily understand the people's opinion about anything that we want to know. The awareness of web made it possible to get the opinions or experiences of the people who are completely unknown to us. This paper focuses on classifying opinions from text with Web based Diverse Data. It is a challenging task to perform opinion mining from Bangla data as the corpus is very small in size. The Internet has turned into a well-situated medium for people to express their feelings, emotions, attitude and opinions. Automatic opinion mining is a very useful for applications such as news reviews, blog reviews, stock market reviews, movie reviews, travel advice, social issue discussions, consumer complaints, etc. Opinion mining becomes a great interest to the social networking media such as Facebook, Twitter, Instagram, Google+ as well. Using the mined opinion, they can detect some unanticipated

© Springer International Publishing AG 2017
B.U. Shankar et al. (Eds.): PReMI 2017, LNCS 10597, pp. 673–678, 2017.
https://doi.org/10.1007/978-3-319-69900-4_85

posts, shares and comments. But these involve analyzing many languages. This work is done by resource generation which implies building the annotated dataset form Internet. The dataset we used are in English from the web specially from both Amazon product reviews and twitter. We translate these to generate Bangla corpus which are used in this research. We use Support Vector Machine (SVM) for classification task. SVM is not necessarily better than other machine learning methods, but it performs at the state-of-the-art level and has much current theoretical and empirical appeal. Related experimental results show that SVM is subject to attain significantly higher accuracy than traditional mining schemes. We also propose a method to assume polarity strength of an opinion. We label the polarity of each opinion as weak, steady and strong. The accuracy of our classifier for Bangla data shows that our generated Bangla corpus works fine to classify an unknown Bangla opinion with promising accuracy.

2 Related Works

Opinion mining from Bangla text is still in exploratory stage. Some researches have been conducted on sentiment detection, opinion mining and polarity classification of Bangla sentences. Contextual valency is used to detect sentiment from Bangla text. This work uses SentiWordNet for predefined polarity of each words [1]. Another work on sentiment analyzer that constructs phrase patterns and measures sentiment orientation using prior patterns [2]. Opinions or sentiments can be expressed as emotions or feelings, or as opinions, ideas or judgments colored by emotions [3]. Opinion mining deals with the computational treatment of opinion or sentiment in text [4]. Some supervised learning methods to classify Bangla text based on these ideas have been proposed in this decade. A classifier is designed to determine the opinion expressed in both English and Bangla using Naive Bayes. Here strength of each opinion polarity is assumed by probability [5]. The SVM classification algorithm outperforms the others and good results can be achieved using unigrams as features with presence or absence binary values rather than term frequency, unlike what usually happens in topic-based categorization [6]. A hybrid system is proposed to classify overall opinion polarity from less privileged Bangla language that works with linguistic syntactic features [7]. A hybrid approach of Support Vector Machine and Particle Swarm Optimization is used to mine opinion of movie reviews that was effective to increase the accuracy [8].

3 Resource Acquisition

Most opinion mining research efforts in the last decade deal with English text and little work with Bangla text. As Bangla is a less computational ruling language, it is a leading task to build-up a Bangla corpus. The construction of large corpus for Bangla language has historically been a difficult task. Although Bangla text from blogs, newspapers, Twitter, Facebook and many other online sources are available nowadays, it remains crucial to collect a usable set of text, carefully balanced in opinion. Our Bangla corpus is generated from two well-used English datasets. We used Amazon's watches online reviews [9] with 8,000 opinions for each positive and negative polarity. We ignored neutral reviews with rating 3. Each review is of very high polarity contains up to 10,000 characters. We also used a corpus of already classified tweets in terms of sentiment. This corpus is based on Twitter Sentiment Corpus collected from Sentiment140 [10]. The Twitter Sentiment Analysis Dataset contains 6,00,000 classified tweets. All these tweets are classified by emotion. For example, tweets with emoticon ':)' and ':(' are classified as positive and negative respectively.

We originate our Bangla corpus from these English datasets using Google Translator in two different ways [5]. A tool is used to translate every single opinion at a time. This may not bear the accurate meaning, but contains enough information with polarity. Another method is dictionary based translation. A dictionary is designed with all of the words from English dataset and each opinion is converted to Bangla word by word. This method also removes noise from Bangla data.

Table 1. Effects of negation (BANGLA)

এই হাত ঘড়িটা যথেষ্ট ভাল নয়	না_এই, না_হাত, না_ঘড়িটা, না_যথেষ্ট, না_ভাল, নয়
আমি এই ঘড়ি কিনতে হবে না	না_আমি, না_এই, না_ঘড়ি, না_কিনতে, না_হবে, না
এই পণ্য পার্শ্ব প্রতিক্রিয়া করে নি	না_এই, না_পণ্য, না_পার্শ্ব, না_প্রতিক্রিয়া, না_করে, নি

Negation plays an influential role in natural language. It inverses the polarity of a sentence. In Bangla, negation is marked by some specific words (e.g., না, নি, নয়). As most of the generated sentences contain only 'না', 'নি' and 'নয়', we consider these three as negation words for Bangla data. In some cases, generated Bangla sentence contains no negation word, though it should. As detecting the influence of negation in Bangla text is problematic, we consider every word in a sentence is compromised and a new feature না_x is created as shown in Table 1. The scope of negation cannot be properly modeled with this representation.

4 Methodology

A support vector machine (SVM) is a supervised learning technique used for both regression and classification based on the concept of decision planes. In mathematical term, SVM constructs separating hyperplane in high-dimensional vector spaces. Suppose, Data points are viewed as $(\boldsymbol{x}, y)$ tuples where x_j is the feature values and y is the class. If we consider multi dimensional feature space, we can define the hyperplane as

$$\boldsymbol{b}.\boldsymbol{x} + b_0 = 0 \tag{1}$$

This can be defined as following formula:

$$f(\boldsymbol{x}^*) = \boldsymbol{b}.\boldsymbol{x}^* + b_0 \tag{2}$$

We have to find $\boldsymbol{b}$ and b_0 so that we find maximal margin hyperplane.

To maximize margin, each data point must be on the correct side of the hyperplane and at least a distance M from it. We need to relax this requirement to allows some observations to be on the incorrect side of the margin which is called soft margin. So new parameter ϵ and C are introduced to allow violation. Maximize margin M such that:

$$\sum_{j=1}^{p} b_j^{\,2} = 1 \tag{3}$$

and

$$y_i(\boldsymbol{b}.\boldsymbol{x} + b_0) \geq M(1 - \epsilon_i), \forall_i = 1, ..., n \tag{4}$$

where,

$$\epsilon_i \geq 0, \sum_{i=1}^{n} \epsilon_i \leq C$$

Parameter C collectively controls how much the individual ϵ_i can be modified to violate the margin. We used this classifier in our experiment.

We have implemented our experiments using scikit-learn [11] tools designed for data mining and data analysis. As text data is not suitable for SVM, we extracted features from raw data in a numerical format. We have used Tfidf Vectorizer that converts a collection of text documents to a matrix of token counts and then transforms it to a normalized representation. We have applied Truncated SVD to perform linear dimensionality reduction using randomized feature selection to keep fixed dimensional vector space. We have used LinearSVC as our classifier which is implemented in terms of liblinear.

5   Experimental Results

In order to test our system, we used inverse-document-frequency for vectorization and selected 2000 features using randomized feature selection. This customized classifier is used in our experiment. 16,000 identical reviews for both Bangla and English from the watch review corpus described in Sect. 3 have been used. Of them, 13,000 reviews are used for training and 3,000 for testing. We have found 86.8% accuracy for Bangla when we consider the negation. And when we ignore negation the accuracy decreases to 85.5%. This is a clear improvement over the 85.0% that results when Nave Bayes is applied for Bangla [5]. Table 2 shows the accuracy of our dataset for both Bangla and English. In Twitter dataset, there are total 6,00,000 data. From these data, 5,99,500 data are selected as training dataset and 500 as testing dataset. We get accuracy 82.0% for SVM and 78.8%

Table 2. Accuracy comparison

Dataset		Without negation	With negation
Amazon Watches(EN)	Training	98.5%	98.9%
	Testing	89.2%	87.8%
Amazon Watches(BN)	Training	96.8%	98.0%
	Testing	85.5%	86.8%
Tweeter (EN)	Training	84.8%	86.0%
	Testing	82.0%	82.2%
Tweeter (BN)	Training	75.6%	77.1%
	Testing	77.3%	76.9%

for Nave Bayes when we ignore negation. Then by considering negation, accuracy for SVM increases to 82.2% but for Nave Bayes accuracy decreases to 77.6%. For similar Bangla corpus, SVM performs better without negation and gives accuracy 77.3%.

We classify each polarity with weak, steady and strong label. The confidence score of a classified data point is used to label the polarity. For example, if a data point is classified as negative and confidence score is poor, we assumed this data as weak negative. From our experiment we see that confidence score of all data point forms a normal distribution. We divide this score range to label our classified polarity. Table 3 shows the ranges to label positive and negative polarity. We divide the range $[\mu - 3.0\alpha, \mu + 3.0\alpha]$ into 6 portions where μ is the mean and α is the standard deviation. As score vector forms a normal distribution, 99.9% of the variance retains within this range. To verify the above decisions, we collect some reviews from different individuals about their own watches or products. Each review is then marked as positive or negative according to their opinion in Bangla. We translate these reviews to corresponding English with same meaning and sentiment. Finally, we use these reviews to test our classifier. We observe that our classifier for Bangla which is trained with translated data can identify actual polarity of our collected reviews.

Table 3. Confidence score range to label polarity

Polarity	Label	Range
Positive	Week	$(0, \mu + 0.75\alpha]$
	Steady	$(\mu + 0.75\alpha, \mu + 1.75\alpha]$
	Strong	$(\mu + 1.75\alpha, \mu + 3.0\alpha]$
Negative	Week	$[\mu - 0.75\alpha, 0)$
	Steady	$[\mu - 1.75\alpha, \mu - 0.75\alpha)$
	Strong	$[\mu - 3.0\alpha, \mu - 1.75\alpha)$

6   Conclusion

We developed a classifier to identify the polarity of both Bangla and English text data. We proposed a method to assume the strength of classified polarity based on SVM. For Bangla, we generated dataset using translation method. We removed noise from data to make them suitable for classification. We applied support vector machine as supervised learning method and got satisfactory results. We observed that classification using SVM for Bangla outperforms Naive Bayes as well. Reviews from individuals are also used to check accuracy of our classifier and found accurate outcome.

References

1. Hasan, K.M.A., Rahman, M., Badiuzzaman: Sentiment detection from bangla text using contextual valency analysis. In: 2014 17th International Conference on Computer and Information Technology (ICCIT), pp. 292–295, December 2014
2. Hasan, K.M.A., Islam, M.S., Mashrur-E-Elahi, G.M., Izhar, M.N.: Technical Challenges and Design Issues in Bangla Language Processing, first edn. Information Science Reference - Imprint of: IGI Publishing (2013)
3. Boiy, E., Hens, P., Deschacht, K., Moens, M.F.: Automatic sentiment analysis in on-line text. In: Chan, L., Martens, B. (eds.) ELPUB, pp. 349–360 (2007)
4. Pang, B., Lee, L.: Opinion mining and sentiment analysis. Found. Trends Inf. Retr. 2(12), 1–135 (2008)
5. Hasan, K.M.A., Sabuj, M.S., Afrin, Z.: Opinion mining using naive bayes. In: 2015 IEEE International WIE Conference on Electrical and Computer Engineering (WIECON-ECE), pp. 511–514, December 2015
6. Pang, B., Lee, L., Vaithyanathan, S.: Thumbs up? sentiment classification using machine learning techniques. In: Proceedings of EMNLP, pp. 79–86 (2002)
7. Das, A., Bandyopadhyay, S.: Opinion-polarity identification in Bengali (2010)
8. Basari, A.S.H., Hussin, B., Ananta, I.G.P., Zeniarja, J.: Opinion mining of movie review using hybrid method of support vector machine and particle swarm optimization. Procedia Eng. 53, 453–462 (2013)
9. McAuley, J.J., Targett, C., Shi, Q., van den Hengel, A.: Image-based recommendations on styles and substitutes. In: Baeza-Yates, R.A., Lalmas, M., Moffat, A., Ribeiro-Neto, B.A. (eds.) SIGIR, pp. 43–52. ACM (2015)
10. Twitter data from sentiment 140. http://twittersentiment.appspot.com
11. Python plugin for classifier. http://scikit-learn.org

Harnessing Online News for Sarcasm Detection in Hindi Tweets

Santosh Kumar Bharti$^{(\boxtimes)}$ ⓘ, Korra Sathya Babu ⓘ, and Sanjay Kumar Jena ⓘ

Department of Computer Science and Engineering,
National Institute of Technology, Rourkela, Odisha, India
sbharti1984@gmail.com

Abstract. Detection of sarcasm in Indian languages is one of the most challenging tasks of Natural Language Processing (NLP) because Indian languages are ambiguous in nature and rich in morphology. Though Hindi is the fourth popular language in the world, sarcasm detection in it remains unexplored. One of the reasons is the lack of annotated resources. In the absence of sufficient resources, processing the NLP tasks such as POS tagging, sentiment analysis, text mining, sarcasm detection, *etc.*, becomes tough for researchers. Here, we proposed a framework for sarcasm detection in Hindi tweets using online news. In this article, the online news is considered as the context of a given tweet during the detection of sarcasm. The proposed framework attains an accuracy of 79.4%.

Keywords: Hindi tweets · NLP · Online news · Sarcasm · Sentiment

1 Introduction

With 490 million speakers [1] across the world, Hindi stands fourth in popularity after Mandarin, Spanish, and English [2]. In social media such as Twitter, Facebook, WhatsApp, *etc.*, most of the Indians now prefer Hindi for communication, and this generates large volumes of data. The manual process of mining the sentiments from these large data is a tedious job for individuals as well as organizations. Therefore, an automated system is required to identify the sentiment automatically from Hindi text.

Sentiment analysis is a task which identifies the orientation of a text towards a specific target such as products, individuals, organizations, *etc.* With the presence of sarcasm, the prediction of sentiment in text often goes wrong in the analysis. Sarcasm often conveys negative meaning using positive or intensified positive words. For example, "I love waiting forever for the doctor". In the first look, the sentence conveys positive sentiment; but, it is sarcastic. Due to this, most of the existing sentiment analyzers fail to detect real sentiment.

Recently, many sarcasm detectors were developed by researchers for text scripted in English [3–9]. But, there is only one reported work available for detection of sarcasm in Hindi scripted text [10]. The existing work [10] does

© Springer International Publishing AG 2017
B.U. Shankar et al. (Eds.): PReMI 2017, LNCS 10597, pp. 679–686, 2017.
https://doi.org/10.1007/978-3-319-69900-4_86

not consider the natural Hindi tweets[1] for the experiment. Their training and testing set consists of Hindi tweets translated from English scripted tweets. In this article, we proposed a framework for sarcasm detection in natural Hindi tweets using online Hindi news as the context. A sample of natural Hindi sarcastic tweets is shown in Fig. 1.

1. काले धन पे पेनल्टी 200% से घटा के 10% कर दी? काला धन वालों के सामने मोदी जी ने घुटने टेक दिए?- @ArvindKejriwal

2. दो दिन बाद शाहरुख खान अपना 51वां जन्मदिन मनाने वाले हैं, लेकिन उनकी हीरोइन की उम्र लगातार कम होती जा रही है

3. @Rajrrsingh #सुना_है! #iphone7 टिम कुक के टकले पे रख के चार्ज किया जायेगा!

4. आज सुबह मुझे स्वच्छता भारत अभियान सड़क पर बिखरा हुआ मिला! #swachbharat #Hindi #clean #mock #sarcasm

5. #JioOffer का आधा से ज्यादा डेटा तो लोग सिर्फ़ ट्विटर पे अरविन्द केजरीवाल को ट्रोल करने में इस्तेमाल करते है.

Fig. 1. A sample of Hindi sarcastic tweets.

Tweets and news are very similar in nature as both describes current happenings in their way. The news gives us the authenticated knowledge about real-time happenings across the world. Similarly, users' from worldwide shares their feeling on current happening through tweets. It may or may not be authentic. It depends on the individual user and their likes and dislikes. If a user likes any current happenings, then they will share positive feeling on that happenings. If they do not like, then they may share either direct negative or sarcastic feeling. In this approach, news has been utilized as the context of the given tweet to predict the authenticity of the tweet with the truth. If a given tweet follows the orientation of the related news, then is be considered as a simple tweet, and the obtained sentiment is correct. If the tweet does not follow the orientation of the related news, then the tweet is classified as sarcastic, and the obtained sentiment is opposite.

The rest of the paper is organized as follows: Sect. 2 describes related work. The proposed scheme is discussed in Sect. 3. Analysis of the results are given in Sect. 4 and conclusion of the article is drawn in Sect. 5.

2   Related Work

Sarcasm detection in resource rich language like English is well explored [3–9]. In the context of Indian languages, it is yet to be explored. The main reason is the unavailability of benchmark resources for training and testing.

---

[1] A natural Hindi tweet is a tweet that is available on Twitter in natural Hindi language unlike translated from English to Hindi.

Desai and Dave [10] proposed a Support Vector Machine (SVM) based sarcasm detector for Hindi sentences. They used Hindi tweets as the dataset for training and testing using SVM classifier. In the absence of annotated datasets for training and testing, they converted English tweets into Hindi. Therefore, they focused on a similar set of features like emoticons and punctuation marks for sarcasm detection in English text. These methods are not applied directly for the natural Hindi sarcastic tweets as shown in Fig. 1.

3   Proposed Scheme

This section describes the proposed framework for sarcasm detection in Hindi tweets as shown in Fig. 2. Here, online news is used as a context which authenticates the given tweets with actual happenings. Here, we assume that online news is correct and authenticated.

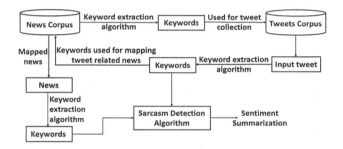

Fig. 2. Proposed framework for sarcasm detection in Hindi tweets.

For every news in the authenticated news corpus, keywords are extracted using Algorithm 1. These keywords are used to obtain the possible tweets. Further, for prediction of a sarcastic tweet, it takes a tweet as an input and extracts the important keywords using Algorithm 1. Then, the extracted keywords are used to map the related authenticated news in news corpus. Finally, it fed both the sets of keywords (input tweet and related news) to sarcasm detection algorithm to classify the tweet is sarcastic or not.

3.1   News Collection

After browsing several online news sources, we have collected a total of around 5000 one liner Hindi news manually on recent topics from top rated news sources as mentioned in Fig. 3. The collected news belongs to different categories such as sports, movies, business, politics, *etc.* In the preprocessing, redundant news are eliminated. News related to murder, rape, bomb blast, *etc.* were discarded. We believe that sarcastic tweets will not be floated on serious topics. It was thus eliminated. After preprocessing, the news corpus consists of a total of 2000 authenticated unique news.

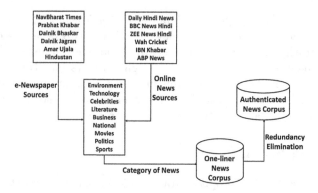

Fig. 3. Procedure for news collection.

3.2   Keyword Extraction

This section describes the procedure of keyword extraction from sentences as shown in Algorithm 1.

Algorithm 1. Keywords_Extraction_Algorithm

Data: *dataset* := Corpus of authenticated news (**C**)
Result: *classification* := ⟨*Set of Keywords*⟩ for every news in the corpus
Notation: *ADJ*: Adjective, *V*: Verb, *ADV*: Adverb, *NN*: Noun, *NS*: News sentence,
C: Corpus, *T*: Tag, *K*: Keyword, *NTS*: News-wise tagged set, *NKS*: News-wise set of
keywords, *LoK*: List of Keywords.
Initialization : $NKS = \{ \phi \}$, $LoK = \{ \phi \}$
while *NS in* **C** do
$\quad$ NTS = find_POS_tag (NS)
$\quad$ while T *in NTS* do
$\quad\quad$ if $(T == (ADJ||V||ADV||NN))$ then
$\quad\quad\quad$ $K \leftarrow$ Keyword[T]
$\quad\quad$ end
$\quad\quad$ ⟨NKS⟩ $\leftarrow NKS \cup K$
$\quad$ end
$\quad$ $LoK \leftarrow LoK \cup$ ⟨NKS⟩
end

Algorithm 1 takes authenticated news corpus (**C**) as an input and find Part-of-Speech (POS) tag information for every news in the corpus. For every news, the tags noun (NN), verb (V), adjective (ADJ) and adverb (ADV) are extracted from the tagged set, and the corresponding tokens are extracted as ⟨*Set of Keywords*⟩ for that news.

POS Tagging. To identify the POS tag information in Hindi sentences, we have developed a Hidden Markov Model (HMM) based POS tagger. It uses Indian

Language (IL) standard tagset which consists of 24 tags [11]. For example, the POS tag information of Hindi sentence क्या आपका नाम राम है? is क्या - WQ | आपका - PRP | नाम - NN | राम - NNP | है - VAUX | ? - SYM |. The Hindi POS tagger tool is available on URL: http://www.taghindi.herokuapp.com.

3.3 Tweets Collection

To get the news related tweets, we used extracted ⟨*Set of keywords*⟩ for every news from news corpus to collect the possible tweets from Twitter as shown in Fig. 4. On deploying all the sets of keywords from 2000 unique news, a total of around 5000 Hindi tweets is collected. A sample set of news and related tweets are released on URL: https://github.com/rkp768/hindi-pos-tagger/tree/master/News%20and%20tweets.

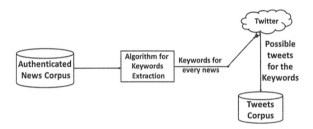

Fig. 4. Procedure of tweets collection.

3.4 Sarcasm Detection

In this section, an algorithm is proposed to classify the tweet as sarcastic or not in the context of online news information. The procedure of identifying sarcastic tweet is given in Algorithm 2.

The Algorithm 2 takes both the sets of keywords (one for input tweet and other for related news) as the input. Then, it compares both the sets of keywords. If both the sets contain similar keywords, it means the orientation of the news and tweet are same. Therefore, the tweet is authentic and not sarcastic. If both sets do not contain similar keywords, then it calculates the number of positive and negative keywords in both news and tweet using a predefined list of Hindi words with polarity value. The list of Hindi SentiWordNet is available on URL: https://github.com/smadha/SarcasmDetector/blob/master/Hindi%20SentiWordNet/HSWN_WN.txt. Further, it compares the count of positive and negative keywords. If the news contains more positive keywords than an input tweet, it indicates the user intentionally negate the temporal fact (news). In this case, the orientation of the news is positive, and the orientation of the tweet is negative. Due to this contradiction, given input tweet is classified as sarcastic. Similarly, in the case of more negative keywords in the news than input tweet, given tweet is classified as sarcastic. For rest of the cases, tweets are not sarcastic.

Algorithm 2. Sarcasm_Detection_using_Online_News

Data: $dataset := \langle Set\ of\ Keywords \rangle$ for both input tweet and corresponding related news.

Result: $classification :=$ Input tweet is sarcastic or not.

Notation: $\langle SoK \rangle_n$: Set of Keywords for news, $\langle SoK \rangle_t$: Set of Keywords for input tweet, $(PKC)_n$: positive keywords in news, $(PKC)_t$: positive keywords in input tweet, $(NKC)_n$: negative keywords in news, $(NKC)_t$: negative keywords in input tweet

if $(\langle SoK \rangle_n == \langle SoK \rangle_t)$ **then**
| Tweet is not sarcastic.
end
else
| $(PKC)_n =$ Count_postive_keywords($\langle SoK \rangle_n$)
| $(NKC)_n =$ Count_negative_keywords($\langle SoK \rangle_n$)
| $(PKC)_t =$ Count_postive_keywords($\langle SoK \rangle_t$)
| $(NKC)_t =$ Count_negative_keywords($\langle SoK \rangle_t$)
end
if $(PKC)_n > (PKC)_t$ **then**
| Tweet is sarcastic.
end
else if $(NKC)_n > (NKC)_t$ **then**
| Tweet is sarcastic.
end
else
| Tweet is not sarcastic.
end

---

4 Results and Discussion

This section describes the experimental results of the proposed approach to identify sarcasm in Hindi tweets. To test the performance, four experimental parameters have been used namely, *Precision, Recall, F1-measure* and *Accuracy*. A set of 500 random tweets from collected Hindi tweets corpus is used as a testing set to experiment. To annotate the testing set as sarcastic or not, three annotators are used, and the results of annotators are used as ground truth while testing. A confusion matrix for identifying sarcasm in 500 tweets are given in Table 1. Using the confusion matrix given in Table 1, the values of precision, recall, F1-measure and accuracy attained by the proposed approach for identifying sarcasm in Hindi tweets are given in Table 2.

Table 1. Confusion matrix for sarcasm detection in Hindi tweets.

Proposed approach	No. of tweets	T_p	T_n	F_p	F_n
Identifying sarcasm	500	137	260	51	56

Table 2. *Precision*, *Recall*, *F1-measure* and *Accuracy* attained by proposed approach

Proposed approach	*Precision*	*Recall*	*F1-measure*	*Accuracy*(%)
Identifying sarcasm	0.736	0.717	0.726	79.4

While identifying sarcasm in Hindi tweets concerning news context, we consider the comparison of ⟨*Set of Keywords*⟩ for both input tweet and corresponding related news. We assume all the news have neutral sentiments whereas tweets contain either positive, negative or neutral sentiment. Therefore, instead of sentiment comparison, we preferred the comparison of individual keywords and its orientation. If both news and tweets describe same orientation, then the tweet is non-sarcastic. If the orientation of news and tweet are not same, it means the user is trying to negate this temporal fact intentionally. Hence, the given input tweet is sarcastic.

Limitations. The proposed framework has the following limitations:

1. In this research, news time-stamp is not available. Hence, while mapping a tweet to a unique related news, we are fully dependent on keywords, which does not give full assurance that the news and tweet belong to the same time-stamp.
2. If few keywords are matched for news and tweet, but both belong to different time-stamp. In such situation prediction of sarcasm may or may not be correct.

5 Conclusion and Future Direction

In the absence of sufficient annotated dataset for training and testing, one can not apply traditional methods for sarcasm detection in Hindi tweets that are used in examples. Therefore, this article proposes a novel framework for sarcasm detection in Hindi tweets using the online news as context. As news usually carry neutral sentiment, we used the important keywords for both input tweet and its related news to decide the tweet is sarcastic or not concerning the related news. The proposed approach attains 79.4% accuracy.

In future, we will resolve the current limitation of the article. The framework will be updated with time-stamp verification while mapping a tweet to the news.

References

1. Parkvall, M.: Varldens 100 storsta sprak 2007. The Worlds 100 (2007)
2. World Language and Culture: Top 30 Languages by Number of Native Speakers (2005). http://www.vistawide.com/languages/top_30_languages.htm

3. Liebrecht, C., Kunneman, F., van den Bosch, A.: The perfect solution for detecting sarcasm in tweets# not. In: proceedings of the Association for Computational Linguistics, pp. 29–37 (2013)
4. Gonzalez-Ibanez, R., Muresan, S., Wacholder, N.: Identifying sarcasm in twitter: a closer look. In: Proceedings of the 49th Annual Meeting of the Association for Computational Linguistics: Human Language Technologies: Short Papers (2), pp. 581–586 (2011)
5. Joshi, A., Sharma, V., Bhattacharyya, P.: Harnessing context incongruity for sarcasm detection. ACL **2**, 757–762 (2015)
6. Riloff, E., Qadir, A., Surve, P., De Silva, L., Gilbert, N., Huang, R.: Sarcasm as contrast between a positive sentiment and negative situation. In: Proceedings of the Empirical Methods in Natural Language Processing, pp. 704–714 (2013)
7. Bharti, S., Sathya Babu, K., Jena, S.: Parsing-based sarcasm sentiment recognition in twitter data. In: International Conference on Advances in Social Networks Analysis and Mining (ASONAM), pp. 1373–1380. IEEE/ACM (2015)
8. Bharti, S.K., Vachha, B., Pradhan, R.K., Babu, K.S., Jena, S.K.: Sarcastic sentiment detection in tweets streamed in real time: a big data approach. Digit. Commun. Netw. **2**(3), 108–121 (2016)
9. Bharti, S.K., Pradhan, R., Babu, K.S., Jena, S.K.: Sarcasm analysis on twitter data using machine learning approaches. In: Missaoui, R., Abdessalem, T., Latapy, M. (eds.) Trends in Social Network Analysis. LNSN, pp. 51–76. Springer, Cham (2017). doi:10.1007/978-3-319-53420-6_3
10. Desai, N., Dave, A.D.: Sarcasm detection in Hindi sentences using support vector machine. Int. J. **4**(7), 8–15 (2016)
11. Bharati, A., Sangal, R., Sharma, D., Bai, L.: AnnCorra: annotating corpora guidelines for pos and chunk annotation for Indian languages. LTRC-TR31 (2006)

Concept-Based Approach for Research Paper Recommendation

Ritu Sharma$^{(\boxtimes)}$ⒾD, Dinesh GopalaniⒾD, and Yogesh MeenaⒾD

Malaviya National Institute of Technology, Jaipur, India
ritu.sharma3@hotmail.com, {dgopalani.cse,ymeena.cse}@mnit.ac.in
http://www.mnit.ac.in

Abstract. Research Paper Recommender Systems are developed to deal with the increasing amount of published information over web and provide recommendations for research articles based on the user preferences. Researchers invest their huge time in literature search to carry out the research work. To provide ease in building literature and finding useful research articles in less time, a novel concept-based recommendation approach is proposed that represents research article in terms of its concept or semantics, used to recommend conceptually related papers (based on the higher relevance of concepts) to researchers. This paper provides a brief overview of popular algorithms and previous systems developed to solve the problem of information explosion. Then, discuss the proposed approach with implementation details and a comparative analysis is presented between the proposed approach and baseline method.

Keywords: Research paper recommendation · Recommender system · Distributed representation · Concept-based approach · Semantics · Paragraph vector

1 Introduction

Due to the increasing number of articles, researchers find it difficult to search for the suitable paper. Recommender systems were developed to solve the problem of information overload and provide suggestions to choose appropriate article from a large set of available articles. Research paper recommender system finds relevant papers based on the users current requirements which can be gathered explicitly or implicitly through ratings, user profile, and text reviews.

Renown algorithms for paper recommendation are content-based filtering, collaborative filtering, co-occurrence based approaches and citation-based algorithms [1]. Content-based approaches works on the document text to find similarity between articles. For this purpose, most commonly used technique is bag-of-words (BOW) model. As this model works on word-matching principle, it do not consider the natural language ambiguities like synonym, polysemy, homonym etc. To overcome the drawbacks of existing approaches, we introduce a novel approach for recommendation which captures the semantic meaning of documents

© Springer International Publishing AG 2017
B.U. Shankar et al. (Eds.): PReMI 2017, LNCS 10597, pp. 687–692, 2017.
https://doi.org/10.1007/978-3-319-69900-4_87

via distributed representation and is used to recommend conceptually relevant papers. This paper organizes as follows: Sect. 2 presents a short survey on previous recommendation system, its approaches and their shortcomings. Section 3 discusses the proposed recommendation approach in detail. Section 4 examines the training parameter, evaluation scheme and implementation results. Finally, Sect. 5 concludes this work with future directions. In this paper, we will use the terms research paper, article and document interchangeably.

2   Related Work

The very first initiative in this field was the development of CiteSeer autonomous indexing system [6,8] which helps in developing the background knowledge by providing research articles that cites a given paper and it also displays the context of citation. Open archives were developed to offer storage and sharing of information along with recommendation services [9]. Various literature managements tools were developed like Papits [15], an academic literature suite, Docear [2,3] to facilitate writing, sharing, retrieving, classifying, annotating and recommending research articles.

Most of the research paper recommender systems use content-based approaches based on key-phrase searching [7,10,13] and document content analysis [14]. Most commonly used technique for natural language processing is Bag-of-Words model and its variants like Term Frequency-Inverse Document Frequency (TF-IDF), bag-of-n-grams etc. The basic model represents text as set of words and forms a matrix where each column represents a unique term from vocabulary and row represents the document vectors. These vectors are the sequence of 0s and 1s, 0 indicates the absence of words and 1 is used to show that the word is present in the document. Other variants this is widely used approach due to its simplicity but it has some limitations as it is completely based on the syntactic representation of the document, it is unable to capture word order and context. However, word order is considered by bag-of-n-grams in short context but strives against the curse of dimensionality. Both algorithms have little knowledge about the word semantics.

To bridge this gap, distributed representations came into existence which was first used by Bengio et al. for statistical language modeling [4]. These neural nets are used to learn a vector representation for each term, called word embedding. Later, concept of deep learning is applied to neural networks for developing deep architectures that outperform state-of-the-art in several applications [5].

3   Proposed Approach

This approach is based on the idea of representing every document in terms of its concept or semantics by constructing distributed representation in high dimensional space. This unique representation is used to find articles in accordance with the user requirements. The whole process of recommendation is bifurcated into two stages as vector generation for candidate papers and recommendation algorithm.

3.1   Vector Generation for Candidate Papers

To visualize documents (candidate papers) in high dimensional space where similar documents sharing related concepts appear in the same area of space, we employed an unsupervised algorithm called Paragraph Vector [12] which extend the methods for learning the word vectors and term 'paragraph' is used to refer text of variable length which is research document in our case. In this framework, every column of matrix D represents a unique vector for every document. Similarly, every word is mapped to a unique vector represented by a column in matrix W. Paragraph vectors are asked to predict the next word given a set of contexts, sampled from a sliding window that runs over a document. Stochastic gradient descent is used to train word vectors and paragraph vectors. At every step of training, fixed-length context is drawn from a random paragraph to figure out the gradient error and is used to update the model parameters. At the time of prediction, an inference step is performed to calculate vector for an unseen paragraph. Total words present in all papers forms the training vocabulary V which is used to train the given model.

More formally, consider a set of words $w_1, w_2, w_3.....w_{|V|}$, the paragraph vector aims to maximize the below mentioned average log probability [12]

$$\frac{1}{|V|} \sum_{v=i}^{|V|-i} logp(w_v|w_{v-i}, ..., w_{v+i}). \tag{1}$$

The model is trained for prediction tasks which is carried out using multi-class classifier. So, we have given equation [12]

$$p(w_v|w_{v-i}, ..., w_{v+i}) = \frac{e^{y_{w_v}}}{\sum_j e^{y_j}}. \tag{2}$$

Here, y_j is un-normalized log probability for output word j which can be evaluated using following equation [12]

$$y = a + Kh(w_{v-i}, ..., w_{v+i}; V). \tag{3}$$

where a, K denotes the softmax parameters and h is constructed using matrix D and concatenation of word vectors from W. When the training converges, every document is represented by a unique n-dimension vector that captures the semantic meaning of the document and these vectors are stored in database.

3.2   Recommendation Algorithm

Now, every research article is mapped to a unique n-dimension vector which is used to find research papers that interests to the target user. Preferences of researcher are recorded by collecting papers of their interest which are then transformed to n-dimension vector using the aforementioned algorithm. Later, a similarity measure is applied to derive likeness between the concepts of input paper and the candidate papers. For this, we have used the cosine similarity as follows

$$S(I, C) = \frac{\sum_{j=1}^{n} I_j C_j}{\sqrt{\sum_{j=1}^{n} I_j{}^2} \sqrt{\sum_{j=1}^{n} C_j{}^2}}. \tag{4}$$

where, I_j and C_j denotes the distributed representation for input paper and candidate paper respectively. Here, C_j belongs to C and C denotes the set of candidate papers. $S(I, C)$ varies between -1 and 1. Value tending towards positive one shows higher relevance in concepts and is negative for distinct concepts. Based on the higher similarity, N-most relevant research papers are fetched and given as recommendation.

4   Results and Discussion

We have developed a set of candidate research papers for recommendation. These are available online in PDF format, transformed to text format for further processing. Vector generation module which is based on unsupervised algorithm, distributed-memory paragraph vector [12] takes text document as input.

We have prepared our own dataset by downloading research articles freely available over internet which are categorized into six specialized fields of computer Science. To train the model for generating feature vector, we have set the value of certain parameters and default value is used for the rest. Size of feature vector is set equal to 300 i.e. each document is represented by a unique vector of size 300. Initial learning rate is set to 0.025 which is nearly drop to 0 with a step size of 0.002. Minimum count parameter is kept equal to 5 which ignores all words with frequency less than 5 and context window size as 10 which denotes the number of words taken into account to predict the next word.

To evaluate the proposed algorithm, Normalized Discounted Cumulative Gain (NDCG) [11] is used which measures accuracy of the recommendation algorithm by assigning more weight to top-ranked documents and considers two relevance levels (relevant and irrelevant) through different gain values.

$$DCG(r) = \begin{cases} G(1) & \text{if } r = 1, \\ DCG(r-1) + \frac{G(r)}{log(r)} & \text{otherwise} \end{cases}$$

where, r specifies the document position in recommendation list. Here, binary notion denotes relevance level (0 and 1), depending on whether recommended articles are relevant or not. G(r) is equal to 1 if research document is relevant to the user and is 0 for irrelevant papers.

After the realization of proposed approach and to validate the results, we used a set of 30 users for evaluation. For every user, 10-most relevant articles were retrieved and *NDCG@10* is calculated. This measure was averaged over the entire set of users to determine the overall accuracy of our recommendation algorithm. We have also implemented the baseline model of content-based technique (BOW model) for the same set of data and results were compared with the proposed approach. Figure 1 shows the normalized discounted cumulative gain value

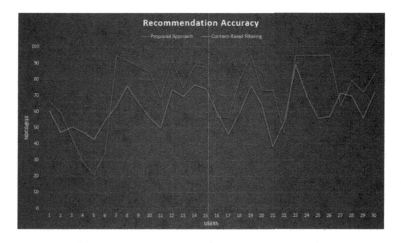

Fig. 1. Recommendation accuracy evaluated with $NDCG@10$

for all 30 users. These values are averaged over all the users and it is noted that our approach outperforms the baseline method. We have achieved recommendation accuracy ($NDGC@10$) of 61.38% for content-based filtering and 74.09% is recorded for the concept-based approach. Content-based algorithm achieved higher accuracy for papers where the same terminologies were used to represent similar concepts and in some cases, it is found that low similarity was predicted for related papers because authors have used different terms for indicating similar ideas. On the other hand, proposed method performs well and is able to recommend related documents to most of the users.

5   Conclusion and Future Work

Researchers have to spend a lot of time in searching for research papers of their interest. Content-based filtering is one of the most popular and widely used algorithms for research paper recommendation which is based on syntactic representation of document, so it is unable to capture word ordering and semantics. To overcome this limitation, we have proposed a novel concept-based approach that recommends research articles based on their semantic relatedness. Recommendation process is divided into two phases, first is vector generation which assigns a unique vector to every document and other is recommendation algorithm which make use of these vectors to recommend useful research articles. In future, this algorithm can be tested for finding the optimal value of parameters. Secondly, distributed representation of words can be combined to determine a unique vector for candidate documents which is further utilize to recommend papers, one can also compare it with the proposed algorithm.

References

1. Beel, J., Gipp, B., Langer, S., Breitinger, C.: Research-paper recommender systems: a literature survey. Int. J. Digit. Libr. **17**(4), 305–338 (2016)
2. Beel, J., Gipp, B., Langer, S., Genzmehr, M.: Docear: an academic literature suite for searching, organizing and creating academic literature. In: Proceedings of the 11th Annual International ACM/IEEE Joint Conference on Digital Libraries, pp. 465–466. ACM (2011)
3. Beel, J., Langer, S., Genzmehr, M., Nürnberger, A.: Introducing Docear's research paper recommender system. In: Proceedings of the 13th ACM/IEEE-CS Joint Conference on Digital Libraries, pp. 459–460. ACM (2013)
4. Bengio, Y., Ducharme, R., Vincent, P., Jauvin, C.: A neural probabilistic language model. J. Mach. Learn. Res. **3**, 1137–1155 (2003)
5. Bengio, Y., et al.: Learning deep architectures for AI. Found. Trends® Mach. Learn. **2**(1), 1–127 (2009)
6. Bollacker, K.D., Lawrence, S., Giles, C.L.: Citeseer: an autonomous web agent for automatic retrieval and identification of interesting publications. In: Proceedings of the Second International Conference on Autonomous Agents, pp. 116–123. ACM (1998)
7. Ferrara, F., Pudota, N., Tasso, C.: A keyphrase-based paper recommender system. In: Agosti, M., Esposito, F., Meghini, C., Orio, N. (eds.) IRCDL 2011. CCIS, vol. 249, pp. 14–25. Springer, Heidelberg (2011). doi:10.1007/978-3-642-27302-5_2
8. Giles, C.L., Bollacker, K.D., Lawrence, S.: Citeseer: an automatic citation indexing system. In: Proceedings of the Third ACM Conference on Digital Libraries, pp. 89–98. ACM (1998)
9. Gross, T.: Cyclades: a distributed system for virtual community support based on open archives. In: Eleventh Euromicro Conference on Parallel, Distributed and Network-Based Processing, 2003. Proceedings, pp. 484–491. IEEE (2003)
10. Hong, K., Jeon, H., Jeon, C.: Userprofile-based personalized research paper recommendation system. In: 2012 8th International Conference on Computing and Networking Technology (ICCNT), pp. 134–138. IEEE (2012)
11. Järvelin, K., Kekäläinen, J.: IR evaluation methods for retrieving highly relevant documents. In: Proceedings of the 23rd Annual International ACM SIGIR Conference on Research and Development in Information Retrieval, pp. 41–48. ACM (2000)
12. Le, Q.V., Mikolov, T.: Distributed representations of sentences and documents. In: ICML, vol. 14, pp. 1188–1196 (2014)
13. Le Anh, V., Hoang Hai, V., Tran, H.N., Jung, J.J.: SciRecSys: a recommendation system for scientific publication by discovering keyword relationships. In: Hwang, D., Jung, J.J., Nguyen, N.T. (eds.) ICCCI 2014. LNCS, vol. 8733, pp. 72–82. Springer, Cham (2014). doi:10.1007/978-3-319-11289-3_8
14. Philip, S., Shola, P., Ovye, A.: Application of content-based approach in research paper recommendation system for a digital library. Int. J. Adv. Comput. Sci. Appl. **5**(10), 37–40 (2014)
15. Watanabe, S., Ito, T., Ozono, T., Shintani, T.: A paper recommendation mechanism for the research support system papits. In: International Workshop on Data Engineering Issues in E-Commerce, 2005, Proceedings, pp. 71–80. IEEE (2005)

Author Index

Printed in the United States
By Bookmasters